A CLOUD ACROSS THE PACIFIC

A Cloud Across the Pacific

Essays on the Clash between Chinese and Western Political Theories Today

by

Thomas A. Metzger

The Chinese University Press

*A Cloud Across the Pacific: Essays on the Clash
between Chinese and Western Political Theories Today*
   By Thomas A. Metzger

© **The Chinese University of Hong Kong**, 2005

ISBN 962–996–122–9

THE CHINESE UNIVERSITY PRESS
The Chinese University of Hong Kong
SHA TIN, N.T., HONG KONG
Fax: +852 2603 6692
     +852 2603 7355
E-mail: cup@cuhk.edu.hk
Web-site: www.chineseupress.com

Printed in Hong Kong

For Jessica Rachel Metzger

~

General Table of Contents

Detailed Table of Contents

List of Tables

Bibliographical Data about Previously Published Parts of This Book

Ch. I.   Nearly all of it is previously unpublished, but much of sections 6 and 7 was incorporated in Thomas A. Metzger, "T'ang Chün-i and the Chinese Response to the Great Modern Western Epistemological Revolution," in Liu Shu-hsien, ed., *Chung-kuo wen-hua-te chien-t'ao yü ch'ien-chan* (Chinese Culture and its Prospects; River Edge, N.J.: Global Publishing Co., Inc., 2001), pp. 565–621. Reprinted with permission of the latter publisher.

Ch. III.   This is a revised version of Thomas A. Metzger, "Hong Kong's Oswald Spengler: H.K.H. Woo (Hu Kuo-heng) and Chinese Resistance to Convergence with the West," in *American Journal of Chinese Studies*, 4:1 (April 1997), pp. 1–49 plus a short, previously unpublished section at the end about my subsequent exchanges with Mr. Woo. Reprinted with permission of the latter journal.

Ch. IV.   Along with a previously unpublished "Postscript," this chapter is largely a reprinting of "'Transcending the West': Mao's Vision of Socialism and the Legitimization of Teng Hsiao-p'ing's Modernization Program," by Thomas A. Metzger. Reprinted with permission of the publisher, Hoover Institution Press. Copyright 1986 by the Board of Trustees of the Leland Stanford Junior University.

Ch. VII. This revises an article I published in *The Journal of Asian Studies*, 52, no. 4 (November 1993), pp. 937–948. Reprinted with permission of the Association for Asian Studies.

Ch. XI.   This is a revised version of my article in *Philosophy Now*, no. 26 (April/May 2000), pp. 30–32, a journal which leaves the copyright with the author.

Ch. XII. This is an expanded version of my "China's Current Ideological Marketplace and the Problem of 'Morally Critical Consciousness,'" in Huang Ko-wu, ed., *Ssu-hsiang, cheng-ch'üan yü she-hui li-liang* (Thought, Political Power, and Social Forces; the volume on "history" of *Ti-san-chieh kuo-chi han-hsueh hui-i lun-wen-chi* [Articles Collected from the Third International Conference on Sinology], which collection was edited by Li I-yuan. The publication of this volume on history was in 2002 by the Academia Sinica's Institute of Modern History. Reprinted with permission of the Institute.

Ch. XIV. A shortened version of this was published as "Collision Course?" in *Hoover Digest*, 2004, no. 3, pp. 111–117. This journal leaves the copyright with the author.

Foreword

This book is an expanded version of the 1994 Ch'ien Mu Lecture in History and Culture, which I had the honor of giving at New Asia College, The Chinese University of Hong Kong, as a series of four lectures called "Contemporary China's Political Agenda and the Problem of Political Rationality" (March 25, 28, 30 and April 18). This topic grew out of my interest in the rich contemporary spectrum of Chinese political thought and its historical lines of continuity and discontinuity with the Chinese tradition. That there was more continuity than most scholars recognized had been suggested by my 1977 book *Escape from Predicament*, while the notion of a contemporary intellectual spectrum went back to a 1972 lecture I had given at the Department of Oriental Studies, Princeton University, "Two Ways of Thought in Contemporary China: Yin Hai-kuang and Mao Tse-tung."

At the lecture, the distinguished sociologist Marion J. Levy Jr. had remarked that the thought of a little-known liberal philosopher in Taipei like Yin could not be compared to an ideology like Mao's followed by a huge society. I had replied that, although Mao's way of thinking was much more prominent at that time than Yin's, both were part of that complex, evolving spectrum of outlooks making up contemporary Chinese culture. Moreover, originally peripheral intellectual ideas can within some years turn into a mainstream way of thinking affecting the political development of a society. Indeed, within two decades after that lecture, the liberalism Yin epitomized had became a major Chinese ideological trend; Yin (1919–1969) had become famous throughout the Chinese intellectual world; and many scholars, albeit erroneously, had concluded that Maoism was no longer taken seriously in China. Similarly, another ideological trend obscure in 1972, modern Confucian humanism, also became a major one by 1990.

It is counterintuitive to think of a culture as not only a rather static system of customs but also a dynamic, amorphous complex of ideas or "conversation" (Robert N. Bellah) that can change much within a decade or two. Nevertheless, it was empirically accurate thus to characterize Chinese culture even in the 1970s, when John K. Fairbank said that Maoism had replaced Confucianism as China's "historical orthodoxy," and it is empirically accurate to do so today.[1] The mix of ideas making up China's ideological future cannot be exactly known today, but it will have grown out of the intellectual spectrum depicted to a considerable extent in this book.

Yet as I continued this simply empirical, historiographical effort to describe contemporary Chinese thought, I could not but succumb to the familiar principle that the study of a historical people ends up as a kind of dialogue between those people and the student of their history. A historical body of thought must be described as an empirical object, but, as an instance of "critical consciousness" (*p'i-p'an i-shih*), it "intentionally" addresses objective issues about which the person describing it also has opinions. In the 1970s, I had focused on the continuity between modern and premodern China's intellectual problematique and tried to refute the interpretations of the Confucian tradition as stagnative and authoritarian, which both Chinese iconoclasm and the Weberian theory of modernization had put forward. I had tried to show that China's modern dynamism was rooted in this tradition. During the 1980s and early 1990s, however, starting to react critically to Chinese arguments, I was struck by another aspect of this modern Chinese dynamism, arguing that it entailed a kind of utopianism at odds with the functional requirements of modernization. This criticism of mine was based on an ideological mix common in American intellectual circles and including pragmatism, Weberianism, and Reinhold Niebuhr's kind of pessimism about political life. In the 1990s, I started paying attention to the Western and Chinese criticisms of this Western mix, not just to Chinese utopianism. Thus I ended up seeing epistemic failure on both sides of the Pacific and wondering about how to define the criteria with which such a failure can be conceptualized.

True, defining these criteria requires philosophical training, and a competent philosopher, I would say, has studied Aristotle in the Greek and Hegel in the German, along with understanding *Principia Mathematica*. Lacking such accomplishments, I have been reduced to exploiting my English and Chinese to examine the clash today between two contemporary concepts of political rationality. If my analysis of this clash turns out to be faulty, I still hope it sheds light on contemporary Chinese political thought and helps undermine epistemic smugness on both sides of the Pacific — the zealous belief, reminiscent of the American missionary movement of the nineteenth century, that one's ideas about how to improve political life are correct for all societies and should be accepted and acted on by everyone everywhere.

The thesis which my book as a whole tries to support is that the emergence of a peaceful, stable, constructive relation between China and the West, particularly the U.S., is in doubt today not so much because of any specific clash of national interests but because of a conflict between tradition-rooted assumptions about how to deal with political disagreements in a rational, morally acceptable way; that, to understand the cause for this failure to find a shared framework of morality and rationality, one has to discard vague, reductionistic ideas about diverging cultural or value systems and instead base one's methodology on a textually specific concept of "discourse"; that the divergence between the mainstream contemporary discourses of China and the West is most conveniently understood by noting the way much of the Western discourse arose out of an epistemological revolution which modern Chinese intellectuals variously but unanimously rejected; and that, to alleviate this disagreement and devise a shared understanding of rationality, intellectually conscientious people on both sides of the Pacific, beginning with those in their respective ivory towers, must critically revise their patterns of thinking by uncovering and reassessing their most familiar assumptions about the nature of morality, rationality, and politics.

My book thus entails a controversial but still widely used concept of historical causation: the intellectualistic theory that the ivory tower often, after a time lag, influences widely shared definitions of common sense and so can gradually change political behavior. My methodological focus, however, is on a concept of discourse incorporating the idea of critical reflexivity (it was especially S.N. Eisenstadt who brought out the importance of reflexivity as an aspect of culturally shared orientations).

I thus began this study by trying only to offer empirically sound, comprehensive descriptions of different historical patterns of thought. Eventually, however, I realized that such descriptive efforts cannot but be logically based on some picture of the universal nature of human thought, and that I had a distinctly Western picture of it coming out of the epistemological revolution mentioned above. For me, human thought in terms of its universal nature was neither a creation of some divine cosmic power nor a Kantian or Neo-Confucian vehicle of rational awareness directly oriented toward the pursuit of universal truths. It rather was a paradoxical combination of alogical, historically bestowed premises with a reflexivity not only facilitating but also commanding the uncovering and critical assessment of these premises in the light of ideas that can be defended as universally true.

Obeying this command to pursue critical awareness, not simply focusing on the concrete specifics of political disagreement, is, I believe, the only way to avoid that clash between civilizations discussed by Samuel P. Huntington. Put in another way, what I recommend is actually a process already being pursued by the continuously crystallizing international intellectual community. Part of this actual and hopeful if still highly uncertain international conversation, my book is an effort to advertise my opinion about what are the key premises that should be uncovered and how they should be criticized.

As I see it, then, my study has been partly successful in pursuing a goal that necessarily has two aspects: describing the leading political theories in China and the liberal West today as accurately, comprehensively, and lucidly as possible, and figuring out the shared agenda implied by these many disparate trains of thought. The most basic questions on this agenda are: What is political theory? What are the main topics political theory should address? What are the criteria with which to evaluate a political theory as rational or not?

In some unavoidable way, disparate thoughts about political life bring up a certain single standard, whether the word for it is "reason" or *li-hsing*. The two aspects of my project thus end up reaffirming Hegel's seminal insight that, while human affairs do involve this principle of rationality, its meaning appears only in the form of a historically unfolding multiplicity of perspectives. What Hegel overlooked is that this multiplicity goes well beyond the conceptualizations of political rationality to which Western modernity committed itself.

My two earlier books largely reflected the well-established agendas and methodologies of my brilliant teachers when I was a graduate student, especially Robert N. Bellah, John K. Fairbank, Kwang-Ching Liu, Benjamin I. Schwartz, and Lien-sheng Yang. This book, however, is more my own concoction, an attempt to combine the study of intellectual history with discussion of the philosophical issues to which I was introduced by my father, the philosopher Arnold Metzger, and by my mother, Ilse Metzger, and which I have been mulling over ever since. The research method I used to put together the above thesis has something in common with the currently fashionable emphasis on "dialogical understanding." Since January 1981, when at a meeting chaired by Ma Ying-chou at Harvard I first tried the patience of a Chinese audience by lecturing in Chinese, I have struggled to grasp the questions Chinese intellectuals address and to find out how they address them by not only reading and listening but also giving my opinions about these questions and learning from the Chinese criticisms of my opinions. That is, I learned about Chinese intellectual life by both trying to influence it and being influenced by it. Today still going down this bumpy dialogical road, I have given a great many lectures and published some twenty articles in Taiwan, Hong Kong, and Mainland China, seen *Escape from Predicament* published, republished, and retranslated in Mainland China, and served as visiting professor at National Taiwan Normal University, The Chinese University of Hong Kong, East China Normal University in Shanghai, Wuhan University, and Peking University as well as the Chinese Academy of Social Sciences in Beijing. In the fall of 2001 I joined Professor Li Qiang of Peking University to give a course on "The Evolution of Political Ideas in Modern China" sponsored by this university's Departments of History and of Political Science; gave a day-long seminar at the Chinese Academy of Social Sciences on "The Nature of Political Theory and its Philosophical Dimension"; participated in Dr. Huang Ko-wu's (Max K.W. Huang's) two-months' seminar at Tsinghua University on the beginnings of modern political thought in China; and was honored by being appointed "Adviser to the Department of History, Tsinghua University."

This book, then, is an effort to articulate what I think I have learned from these two decades of dialogue in a way that can make sense to the Western intellectual public. Because chapter I tries to bring together all the points in this book, it is unavoidably complicated. Readers may find it convenient to begin with one of the subsequent chapters. But I do not apologize for giving the impression that the relation between Chinese and Western political thought today is complicated, because it is. The Wade-Giles system of romanization has been used throughout except in a few cases.

In writing this book, I have become indebted to a number of individuals and organizations. Apart from my limitless debt to my parents, my greatest debt is to Suzanne Kay Roten, my wife in 1972–1995, since, like *Escape from Predicament*, this book grew out of our years together. Nor can I forget Suzanne White Metzger, my wife in 1959–1972. Part of my debt to her is owed because she taught me how to organize a piece of academic writing. I am also deeply indebted to the Hoover Institution on War, Revolution and Peace at Stanford University, which has supported my work since 1990. One can only be humbly grateful for the opportunity to try to pursue scholarship at an institution as superb as Hoover. Thus I owe a great deal to two men who have done so much to make Hoover flourish, Dr. W. Glen Campbell, the director until 1989, and his successor Dr. John Raisian. Naturally I am deeply grateful to everyone — friends and critics included — who made possible the above pilgrimage to the Chinese intellectual world. I am especially grateful to New Asia College, a part of The Chinese University of Hong Kong, for inviting me to give the Ch'ien Mu Lecture; to the CUHK-Taiwan Exchange Programme for appointing me Distinguished Visiting Professor in 1994 when I was giving these lectures; and to the Department of Philosophy at CUHK for inviting me to join its faculty when I had this Exchange Programme appointment. My time with this department was one of the most valuable and enjoyable experiences I ever had. A most important relation for me has been that with Huang Ko-wu (Max K. W. Huang), who has closely worked with me for some twenty years since our days together at National Taiwan Normal University. If our continuing dialogue has been as fruitful for him as for me, he has been lucky indeed. Nor can I overlook my enormous debt to Professor Lee Kuo-chi and all my colleagues at National Taiwan Normal University when I had the privilege of teaching there in 1982–1983 and 1984–1985. The intellectual opportunities for me during those two marvelous years were immeasurable, and I hope I managed to take advantage of some of them. My many visits to

Mainland China reaped a harvest of many conversations with extraordinarily gifted scholars, especially those with Professor Liu Kuei-sheng of Tsinghua University and Peking University, Professor Li Qiang of Peking University, Professor Zheng Jia-dong of the Chinese Academy of Social Sciences, Professor Gao Rui-quan of East China Normal University, Professor Xiao Gong-qin of Shanghai Normal University, Professor Guo Qi-yong of Wuhan University, and Professor Huang Shao-hua of Lanchow University. I am greatly indebted to all of them. John Dunn's extraordinary mix of original, bold insight and felicitous wording has made a deep impression on me in recent years, and I hope I have not appropriated too many of his thoughts and terms without attribution. I am also especially indebted to my Hoover colleague Robert J. Myers for many invaluable conversations and insights into how this manuscript could be strengthened. Alex Inkeles's unforgiving skepticism and devotion to quantitative study almost made me forget how grateful I am for the innumerable opportunities I have had over the past decade of our colleagueship to learn from this brilliant scholar. Another brilliant scholar, Chang Hao, my friendship with whom began in 1959, eventually did take a look at this manuscript and, predictably, made some excellent critical suggestions. Ms. Elsie Wu of Stanford University repeatedly enlightened me when I could not be sure what a Chinese passage was driving at.

I am deeply grateful to Ms. Esther Tsang and Ms. Olivia Wong at The Chinese University Press for all their insightful editorial assistance, as well as to Dr. Steven K. Luk, Director of the Press, and Mr. Fung Yat Kong, Manager of the Editorial Division, for steering this project through to completion. Ms. Tsang did most of the work on this Augean task, and one could not imagine a more meticulous and perspicacious editor. I have long been an admirer of the prose and pictures of Chi-teng-sheng. Two of his oils and three of his pastels hang in my home, but another picture of his struck me as evoking that littoral sense of hope and uncertainty which the current dialogue between China and the West aroused in me. I am most grateful to him for allowing the Press to put this magnificent painting of his on the cover of my book. He painted it on the east coast of Taiwan at Hualien in 1994. The felicitous translation of "A Cloud Across the Pacific" was suggested by Ms. Esther Su (Li Ch'un-ling).

When I think of the scholars whose suggestions directly helped me in the writing of this book, I also remember Peter J. Boettke, Linda Chao, Chin Yao-chi (Ambrose Y.C. King), Fung Ping Kuen (Feng Ping-ch'üan), Philip J. Ivanhoe, Lee Shui Chuen, Li Hon Lam, Kwang-Ching Liu, Liu Shu Hsien, Ted V. McAllister, Katharina Mommsen, Ramon H. Myers, Diana Richards, Shun Kwong-loi, Paul H. Tai, and Piers J. Turner. I am most grateful to each of them. I am also grateful to Adrienne Bronfeld, Karen Walag, Phyllis Villec, Lisa Huynh, and Heather Campbell for meticulously typing this manuscript. Ms. Campbell electronically transferred these essays from the Hoover Institution to The Chinese University Press, an operation more complicated though not necessarily more risky than writing them. The bottom line of my gratitude goes to my wife, Kao Chiu-fen, whose presence reminds me every day how lucky I have been that my life has been so intertwined with the western, Confucian side of the Pacific. My life, however, has also been intertwined with that of Jessica Rachel Metzger, my daughter, whose spirit is part of me, and to whom this book is lovingly dedicated.

Hoover Institution, Stanford, 2002

Endnote

1.   John K. Fairbank, ed., *The Cambridge History of China*, vol. 10, *Late Ch'ing, 1800–1911*, part I (Cambridge: Cambridge University Press, 1978), p. 2.

Discourse #1 and Discourse #2: The Search for Political Rationality in China and the West Today and the Concept of Discourse

1. An Overview of This Book's Agenda

This essay collection deals with a variety of contemporary Chinese and Western ways of pursuing political theory in the sense of normative ideas about how to improve a society and revise its culture: the thought of two representatives of modern Confucian humanism, the great philosopher T'ang Chün-i (1909–1978) and Henry K.H. Woo (Hu Kuo-heng) (b. 1946), an economist and culture critic living in Hong Kong today; the Maoist thought around 1990 of Kao Li-k'o (b. 1952), who teaches at the University of Chekiang in Hangchow, as well as his somewhat post-Maoist outlook in the late 1990s; the assessment of Western liberalism set forth in 1998 by Li Qiang, associate professor of political science at Peking University (he became a full professor in 2001); the liberalism articulated in the 1980s on the eve of Taiwan's democratization by Yang Kuo-shu, a professor of psychology at National Taiwan University who became associate director of the Academia Sinica in Taipei (1996–2000); the rather Weberian theory of modernization developed by Chin Yao-chi (Ambrose Y.C. King) (b. 1935), vice-chancellor of The Chinese University of Hong Kong in 2002–2004, possibly the scholar in the Chinese intellectual world with the deepest understanding of Western sociology; the political theory of Friedrich A. Hayek (1899–1992), some of whose famous anti-Marxist writings have been translated into Chinese and are now being widely read and respected in China; that of John Dunn (b. 1940) of the University of

Cambridge, whose widely admired work on Western political theory leans toward Marx's criticism of Western democracy and capitalism; that of Harvard University's John Rawls (1921–2002), who is widely regarded as having made the greatest contribution in the twentieth century to the philosophy of liberalism; and that of Stanford University's Richard Rorty (b. 1931), whose postmodern version of American liberalism has become a focus of global philosophical discussion today.

It would be hard to prove that each of these two sets of thinkers, the Chinese and the Western, represents any intellectual mainstream in its civilization. Yet in seeing each set as exhibiting orientations widely shared in its civilization, I can adduce much evidence, especially on the Chinese side. Thus I hope these essays will shed light on the confrontation today between Chinese and Western political theories, the nature of political theory in general, and even perhaps the nature of correct or rational political theory.

This confrontation today casts a deep shadow over the prospects for world peace in the next century. The crisis in U.S.-China relations arising in May and June of 1999 shows how dangerous remain the tensions between these two nations. In the U.S., there were angry charges that Chinese spies had stolen the technological secrets basic to U.S. military primacy in the Pacific. Throughout the Chinese world, not just in China, there were angry charges that the bombing of the Chinese embassy in Belgrade by the U.S. had been intentional. On both sides of the Pacific, this anger quickly became combined with the continuing feeling that the other nation grossly violates the norms of decent political conduct — the American view that the Chinese regime is out of accord with the universal norm of democracy, and the Chinese view that the U.S. is an imperialistic power believing it alone among nations has the right to deploy its military might all around the world, hold itself up as a political model all other nations should imitate, and annually grade their efforts to imitate it. The two peoples, moreover, do not reason about political life in the same way. Thus viewing each other as irrational and immoral to a large extent, they cannot easily deal with their more concrete differences in a calm and pragmatic way.

Deep-seated and dangerous, this mutual perception of irrationality and immorality is the subject of this book. This mutual perception can be seen as constituting the boundary between two different cultures. One may say two groups are culturally different when they perceive each other as not only holding to one or another nonsensical view (the way "pro-life" and "pro-choice" Americans regard each other) but as also talking nonsense about the basic structure of human or political life. Even if "American" or "Chinese culture" denotes a vast entity that actually exists, however, there is no empirically sound way to describe such an entity embodied in the lives of millions over centuries or to show how such an entity is related to the pattern of political reasoning found in a particular set of texts. The more empirical way to proceed is to refer only to these texts themselves, regarding them as constituting one cultural strand and leaving open the question of relations between this strand and the rest of the society.

To understand the conflict between two culturally divergent patterns of political reasoning, however, two sets of problems should be distinguished. The first is a matter of social science, focusing on exactly specifying which individuals and groups in a society share a particular pattern of political reasoning, and on exactly determining the causative impact of any such pattern on particular political decisions and developments. The quest for such exactitude, which may or may not be chimerical, is outside my discussion, although I make a good case, I think, that a certain mode of political rationality has been dominant in the Anglo-Saxon world for some time and present conclusive evidence that a contradictory way of reasoning about political life has been typical of the more educated strata in China, including the political elite, during the twentieth century.

The second set of issues is a matter of intellectual history and philosophy. It is at the center of this book. From this standpoint, to understand the clash between ways of reasoning about political life, one has not only to describe them but also to ponder the philosophical question of what to do about this clash, of how to find a critical perspective which both sides of the Pacific can share, and with which they might mitigate this clash.

To pursue these issues, however, one must first deal with unfortunately complex methodological questions about the nature of political reasoning and the best way to describe it. Ultimately, this methodological problem leads to that of what a "discourse" is. This

methodological journey, however, is best begun by asking how to
define "political theory."

2. What is Political Theory?

I would contrast political science with political theory, political
philosophy, or political thought by defining the latter three as
consisting of ideas not only describing political life but also
evaluating it and recommending how to improve it. (So far as
"ideology" goes, any way of thinking is an ideology to the extent that
it consists of ideas used by a historical group to justify certain
interests.) Political theory asks how the political life of a society or
international community should be criticized. In Aristotle's terms,
political theory is a "practical science," which seeks "not knowledge
[per se] but the betterment of action," in contrast with the
"theoretical sciences" purely seeking knowledge about how things
actually are. This identification of political theory with normative
political ideas is in accord with the ways in which scholars like John
Dunn and David Held use the term.[1]

I would go a bit further, however, and say that political theory
aims to find the reasonable way to make descriptive, causal,
predictive, evaluative, and recommendatory statements about
political life, as well as epistemological ones (such as this sentence
about how to define "political theory"). To put it in still another way,
a political theory seeks to define (a) the goal of political life, (b) the
nature of political knowledge or rationality, (c) agency as the means
available to pursue this goal, and (d) all the other aspects of the given
world relevant to this pursuit, whether the historical world and its
ontological, cosmological underpinnings, including the universal
nature of society and the individual, or contemporary cultural,
political, etc. trends frustrating or facilitating this pursuit.

At the heart of a political theory, in my view, always should be an
understanding of what is wrong with the world, what the causes of
this mess are, and who can do what to clean it up. It is true that
political philosophy, as illustrated by the Leo Strauss school, has
tended to ignore these subjects and instead to argue about how to
conceptualize "the good society" and the principles with which to
distinguish good from bad. I would advance the empirical
generalization, however, that it is not possible to think about how

practically to improve political life without discussing the given world, not only the way political life should be, because ideas about goals, means, the rest of the given world, and the distinction between sense and nonsense are logically interdependent, especially to the extent that these ideas are "because" statements. (For instance, many say Chinese should democratize China *because* democracy is the best form of government and should do so gradually *because* sudden revolutions have usually failed. So basic to political theory, the idea of "because" often includes the idea of a "cause," but it is broader than the latter idea, especially in that it refers not only to posited causal relations between phenomena but also to the logical relations between principles and praxis.)

True, it is bold thus to generalize about the universal nature of political theory. For many years, however, I have been studying politically relevant texts, especially Chinese ones, continuously trying both to determine what topic every utterance pertained to and to take into account current scholarship regarding the universal aspects of political life. I began with the common idea that all moral-political thought conceptualizes the self, the group, and the cosmos (I subsumed history under the self and the group). T'ang Chün-i's writings stand out in this regard.[2] I also focused on the distinction between one's goal and one's perception of the given world. Probably this distinction was suggested especially by Talcott Parsons' theory of action[3] and W.I. Thomas's elegant idea of "the definition of the situation."[4] Inductive study of Chu Hsi's (1130–1200) writings, however, made me realize that many if not most of his utterances referred to given human conditions, both deplorable and promising, rather than to the topics most scholars had found interesting, that is, his ethical goals, their ontological underpinnings, and his recommendations about how to pursue these goals. I then realized that philosophical references to the given world were not just references to facts or usual human frailties but ways of imagining or defining the setting of human life; that these acts of imagination varied culturally; and that students of intellectual history had largely neglected analysis of them.[5] A bit later, the writings of Richard H. Popkin and Alasdair MacIntyre made me see that the conceptualization of knowledge is also culturally variable; crucial to the formation of political ideas; and typically overlooked by political and social scientists, including Parsons, whose classic book on the theory of action presupposes that the nature of knowledge is universal and self-evident.[6] Charles E. Lindblom, however, did brilliantly analyze how different definitions of knowledge have differently influenced political action (see below).[7] I thus concluded that clustering political utterances around the above four categories was the best way to describe a political theory as accurately, lucidly, and comprehensively as possible.[8] This conclusion, however, is no more than a "conjecture" (Popper). It can be falsified by finding a political utterance that cannot be logically subsumed under one or more of these four categories.

At the same time, whatever such definitional problems regarding "political theory" or "political life," my methodology is built on a common Western claim that the universally right way to think about thinking is to regard it as a paradoxical mix of opaqueness and transparency, that is, a paradoxical mix of historically-conveyed beliefs the truth of which cannot be demonstrated and reflexive, discursive ideas intentionally designed to serve as true, accurate propositions about objective reality. This claim has grown out of the arguments summed up below as the Great Modern Western Epistemological Revolution (GMWER). As Richard J. Bernstein lucidly explained, these arguments showed that it was empirically inaccurate to deny the opaqueness in human thought, and it was illogical to prelude all transparency.[9] Thus recognizing the opaqueness at the root of my methodology, I can see that my definition of "political theory" as a way of thinking practically about political life reflects the American pragmatism I grew up with, including John Dewey's ideas about "intelligent" action. Yet my definition also seems to accord with "common sense," a universal category in the opinion of Leo Strauss and some other thinkers.

Moreover, if one can hold that people discussing how to improve political life necessarily conceptualize political goals, the nature of political knowledge, means (i.e. agency), and the rest of the given world, these conceptualizations typically develop as a set of complex, nuanced ideas referring to many logically related questions, not just as a simple formula. This complexity stems from not only the complexity of political life but also the nature of political argumentation and the need to demonstrate the wrongness of contrary ideas. To use Hayek's term, a political theory is to some extent the same as a political "tradition," a set of substantial texts that probably have to be conveyed in written form.

Thus a political theory cannot be equated with a simple formula. Take the "liberal" ideas developed by intellectuals like Yen Fu (1854–1921), T'an Ssu-t'ung (1865–1898), Liang Ch'i-ch'ao (1873–1929), leaders of the May Fourth generation like Hu Shih (1891–1962), their successors like Yin Hai-kuang (1919–1969), and his successors, like Yang Kuo-shu. Some would sum up this liberalism as just a call for freedom, equality, and democracy. Others might say these liberals sought China's democratization believing that, according to universally valid principles successfully followed by modern Western nations, a democratic government is one promoting the development of a society in which individuals enjoy equality under the law and freely exercise the ability to "reason" in order to pursue "morality."[10]

Even this statement, however, only outlines these liberals' goals. It says nothing about their conceptualizations of reason, knowledge, and morality, on which their idea of their goal depended; about the means available in their eyes for the pursuit of their goal; and about the variety of historical circumstances they perceived as impeding or facilitating this pursuit. To describe these liberals' political theory then, one has to seek out the texts expressing their ideas about all such subjects.

Offering an empirical generalization, moreover, one can note that, while a political theory revolves around a series of "because" statements about goals, means, the rest of the given world, and the idea of knowledge, these statements are always based on socially shared premises that seem indisputable to a historical we-group (e.g. "our" "racism is bad") (see below). Even more, it seems empirically clear that people as a rule tend to distill from all these indisputables a generic idea of indisputability and so use generic labels such as *yu tao-li* (makes sense) and *hu-shuo pa-tao* (nonsense) to classify an indefinite number of utterances about goals, means, the rest of the given world, and the nature of knowledge. This rhetorical use of "reason" as such a generic label can be distinguished from the philosophic question of the meaning of "reason," "truth," and "knowledge" in some universal, algorismic sense. Recognizing this social, rhetorical use of generic labels to denote what seems indisputable about the world, one can say that political theories amount to disparate definitions of political rationality. For instance, when I told a learned visitor from Taiwan that, for us Americans, it is irrational to expect a government to be uninfluenced by selfish interest groups, he replied that this American willingness to accommodate political immorality appeared to him as irrational.

It is important to see that, inter- and even intra-culturally, people thus disagree about what is indisputably true regarding not only goals but also means, the rest of the given world, the nature of knowledge, and that of "evidence." In other words, contrary to the rational choice school, the calculus of instrumental rationality is not culture-free. Most important are culturally diverging views about what can rationally be said about historical causation and the question of evidence. For instance, in discussions of the causes for Taiwan's extraordinary economic success, many highly intelligent Mainland academics believe the "evidence" shows that the major cause was the gold brought over by the Kuomintang from the Mainland, but economists in the West emphasize other factors much more. Similarly, there is no single algorismic way of dealing with questions such as: What caused China to lose its international centrality? What actions in the future can cause the recovery of this centrality? Should China today put primacy on the development of the market economy or on democratization? Nor is there one for distinguishing between unimportant facts and evidence regarding the causes of other major historical events (does the encircling of Asia with U.S. military forces stretching from Korea to the Persian Gulf and Germany constitute evidence that the U.S. is seeking to dominate the international world in order to pursue its selfish interests?). The lack of an algorismic way to understand historical causation is well illustrated by the ongoing scholarly controversy about the causative impact of intellectual discussions on the course of societal development (see below). To understand political arguments, then, one cannot make a sharp distinction between culturally determined goals and a universally recognized, algorismic, rational way of assessing "evidence" about historical causes and deciding on the instrumental means to pursue these goals. Instead, one has to take into account culturally clashing definitions of political rationality as a seamlessly circular process of thinking about goals, means, the rest of the given world, and the definition of knowledge.[11] In other words, if one asks how a historical group defined "knowledge," one has to adduce all the ideas they regarded as "justified true beliefs," and these will always (so far as I have observed) logically weave together ideas about not only the nature of knowledge per se but also the goals of life, the means to reach them, and the rest of the given world.

To note these clashes between culturally different concepts of political rationality, however, is not to lapse into relativism and say that there is no way to adjudicate these disagreements. True, all "indisputables" are culturally relative (for Nazis it was indisputable that racism is good), and probably the idea of a universally rational political theory transcending cultural differences and accepted by everybody is a chimera. But the simple fact that political theories rest on "indisputables" makes relativism equally chimerical.

In other words, people in fact seem unable to conclude that all political theories are equally good (see below). To say they do is inaccurate. To say they should, chimerical. I thus presume to suggest that the problem of finding dependable standards with which to evaluate normative ideas — a problem that has obsessed modern philosophy in the West — does not exist. Such standards are not unavailable, they are unavoidable. Leo Strauss's fear that they were being made unavailable by modern "relativism" and "historicism" was simply unjustified.[12] One might say he and many others were caught in a kind of epistemic panic caused by the GMWER combined with their legitimate fear that the standards they cherished and regarded as indisputable were being replaced in the modern West by standards they regarded as either Philistine or barbaric.

I mostly share their cultural preferences but feel our cause was not helped by hyperbolically invoking the illusion of a "relativism" that precluded all beliefs and values. The problem with the Philistine or the barbarian is precisely that she deeply believes in her values and denounces ours. Strauss, like Popper, conflated a generic issue with a specific one. Strauss identified rejection of the values he cherished with the rejection of values in general. Popper identified the wrongness of a certain kind of historicism with the wrongness of historicism in general, even though his own political thought was historicist (see below).

Inveighing against this illusion of relativism, thinkers like Strauss fruitlessly and needlessly sought to reconstruct objective standards with which to evaluate normative options instead of worrying about the truly major and difficult problem — how to describe these options as historical traditions defining the goal of political life, means, the rest of the given world, and the nature of knowledge.

Why is description so important? Anyone is free creatively to imagine an utterly new political theory. But the complexity of what has to be produced has seemed to limit the range of inventiveness. People seem to be largely restricted to choosing among already produced historical theories, especially if they wish to advertise their ideas and see them widely adopted. It follows, I think, that intelligently choosing between these complex historical products requires first describing them as accurately, lucidly, and compre-hensively as possible. This is very difficult. As just mentioned, I presume to suggest that the problem of how to evaluate political theories is much simpler than that of describing them (see below).

To be sure, the idea that people should derive political theory from historical texts instead of abstractly creating it is far from new. The question, however, is that of what kinds of ideas one should look for in the historical texts. For instance, Leo Strauss and Eric Voegelin, in their search for normative political theory, greatly emphasized the analysis of historical texts. Yet instead of discussing ideas dealing with all four of the issues above, they were interested in little but the goal of political life and its epistemological or ontological basis — the principles basic to a normative order. These topics indeed constituted the subject-matter of "the works of the great philosophers," study of which Strauss saw as the key to the understanding of political life. As Strauss said, "The theologic-political problem has remained *the* theme of my studies."

More broadly, especially as I studied Leo Strauss's and Joseph Cropsey's *History of Political Philosophy*, the political theories of John Dunn and John Rawls, and Pierre Manent's *An Intellectual History of Liberalism*,[13] I slowly became aware of the great extent to which the definition of "political theory" or "political philosophy" became a still unsolved problem. Chapter X, on Rawls, argues that the very nature of political rationality partly hinges on how one answers "the initial questions" about this discipline, such as what its purpose is, what topics it should treat. But these "initial questions" have become largely open and unresolved, their meaning transformed in the West during recent centuries.

Following in the footsteps of Leo Strauss, Manent's brilliant book underlines how, building on Machiavelli's thought, Hobbes, Locke, and Rousseau turned political philosophy from a theological and rational discussion of the moral ends that the polity should embody into an attempt to derive the principle of popular sovereignty from the nature of an object that actually was metaphysical even though regarded at the time as factual: the identical condition of all human individuals when they lived free, equal, motivated only by natural impulses, and outside the presence of any political authority ("the state of nature"). Manent also touches on how, after Rousseau, political norms came to be derived less from this metaphysical object and more from another one, the teleological direction of history.

Even after these huge intellectual transformations, however, intellectuals were still innocent of the above distinction between political science and political philosophy, which today seems obvious. Indeed Marxism (not to mention the modern Chinese ideological mainstream) entirely preserved the belief precluding this distinction, the belief, namely, that all descriptive, causal, predictive, evaluative, and recommendatory propositions about political life can be correctly established by scientifically or rationally analyzing the physical and human worlds. This belief was only gradually challenged by the GMWER, discussed below. It was this intellectual revolution, not discussed by Manent, that not only gave Western liberalism its contemporary form but also turned political philosophy or political theory into a discipline in search of a definition.

Whether or not it cast doubt on the possibility of scientifically or objectively establishing descriptive, causal, and predictive propositions about political life, the GMWER at the very least left normative propositions, the very stuff of political philosophy or political theory, drifting in a cloud of uncertainty. Thus arose the "epistemological" problem of how to relieve this uncertainty. The complexity of this problem was then illuminated by the GMWER's post-Kantian, largely German insights into how reflexive efforts to devise objectively true propositions are often blurred in together with cultural and discourse patterns merely produced by one segment of human history. Such, then, was the ontological object — human thought as it really is whenever it occurs — that replaced the two metaphysical objects above.

These German insights stimulated the rise of ethical skepticism and cultural relativism, but these trends were eventually assessed as not only absurd but also illogical or chimerical (it seems impossible to find any person actually able to regard everything as equally good or bad). The epistemology of political theory then came down to a search for the way to base propositions about moral-political praxis in what Richard J. Bernstein called "the middle ground" between "objectivism and relativism."

As discussed below, however, this search has remained controversial, and no consensus has arisen about how to answer "the initial questions" about the nature of political theory. These questions not only include the by-now classic issue of how to reduce the arbitrariness of any normative propositions but also entail a whole reworking of the agenda political theory should address, as discussed especially in chapter X — the relevance of goals besides political justice to the improvement of political life (such as economic prosperity, national security, and the proper education of the citizenry); the role of culture as not only popular norms but also modes of thought shaping the very agenda of political theory; the propagation of political theory as part of the causative structure of history; the problem of whether or how to adjust priorities depending on historical circumstances, including the differences between modern Western democracies and other societies; the appropriate degree of optimism in the assessment of political practicability; and so on (see especially chapter X, section 2).

Eventually, political theory may come to be seen as a discipline not only weighing culturally formed perspectives on issues such as these but also combining these perspectives with two kinds of knowledge: the as-yet-unfalsified propositions which, according to Popper, exclusively deserve to be regarded as objective knowledge; and certain other ideas which may or may not deserve such respect. For instance, the extent to which human reflexivity can describe the objective nature of human thought or establish the normative value of language, knowledge, logic, and freedom is still in doubt. Unfortunately not fully discussed in chapter II, the most challenging views on this question, in my opinion, are those of T'ang Chün-i.

Contemporary Chinese political theories, therefore, not only constitute a distinctive way of thinking about how to improve political life. Even if largely innocent of the important epistemological considerations developed by the GMWER, they may indeed include insights contemporary Western theories have neglected. Therefore I do not agree with those who say that, because contemporary Chinese political thought is insufficiently rigorous, it should not be dignified with the term "political theory." By my definition of the term, political thought does not have to meet any standard of rigor in order to be regarded as "political theory." The question of rigor arises only when one evaluates a political theory as successful or not. My purpose is to construct a methodology with which to take a fresh look at some of the most basic differences among political theories today and at the problem of figuring out which political ideas make more sense than others. Whether the Western theories make more sense than the Chinese is not a question one should prejudge. Insofar as my essays do arrive at an evaluative position, it is that contemporary Western as well as Chinese political theories are deeply flawed, leaving the global community with normative guidelines more confused than they have to be.

Moreover, like many influenced by the GMWER, I do not see the possibility today of devising a fully successful political theory, only the promise of a knowledgeable, thoughtful debate about how to improve the political discourse of one's own society or group, or that of a foreign group interested in the opinions of foreigners. In other words, it is epistemically practicable to describe some prominent historical discourses, including the discourse of one's own we-group, compare them to each other, list the standards of evaluation that one regards as reasonable or indisputable, criticize, revise, and then apply these standards to the described discourses, logically recommend how to revise these discourses in order to improve them, and then advertise these recommendations in publications, lectures, and conversations. Such advertising can be very effective, since it can snowball, changing discourses that eventually influence policy. Reinhard Bendix's *Kings or People* and much other work supports this view of historical causation, although changing discourses are only one kind of causative variable. Again, one can never guarantee that a particular discourse change will be beneficial. The belief that useful recommendations can be devised, however, is either a hope integral to the universal human condition or a premise basic to my particular we-group's rules of successful thinking (see below).

After all, cultures are not closed envelopes. This is shown by the simple experience of thinking about one's own beliefs and arguing with people formed by a culture different from one's own. This book is based on the premise that thinking about how to improve political life cannot be just the product of either a closed cultural system or of reason as a uniform cognitive faculty with which all persons try to apprehend and reflect on objective realities or universal principles. Insisting that both dimensions are paradoxically combined in everyone's thinking, I take issue with two groups — the Western scholars fascinated just with culture, and the many Western and Chinese intellectuals who today still largely ignore how reflexivity is shaped by disparate cultural patterns.

This paradoxical combination of reflexivity with cultural patterns in turn seems to serve quite remarkably as an ontological truth coinciding with J.S. Mill's emphasis on the priority of intellectual freedom as the normative basis of political life. It seems intuitively clear that this universally, ontologically given tension between culture and reflexivity implies an imperative maximally to uncover the culturally-bequeathed premises influencing one's thought and critically to compare them with other premises. This imperative is just another way of recognizing the inherent goodness of an existing process (*pace* David Hume): knowledge. And this imperative in turn implies a whole slew of institutional norms, notably those pertaining to freedom and education. Thus the GMWER's post-Humean, post-Kantian discovery of the great role played by history-bequeathed linguistic symbols in the way people reason about moral praxis reopened the question of how "ought" may be derived from "is."

Better to show how I propose to diverge from much current writing on political theory, I may adduce a conference volume published in Hong Kong in 2001, *Cheng-chih li-lun tsai Chung-kuo* (Political Theory in China). It is made up of articles by established scholars from Hong Kong, China, and Taiwan who all have a professional grasp of Western political theory. Its introduction agrees with my definition of "political theory" as a normative approach to political life: "Facing the twentieth century, what kind of political theory does China need? As China, Hong Kong, and Taiwan meet the dawn of a new era of political, economic, and cultural development, what kind of theory offers them the most appropriate guidance?" It also agrees with me that no theory available today to Chinese — it lists "Marxism," "Liberalism," and "Confucian thought" — offers them "a long-range, systematic view with which to guide the direction of development."[14]

But what is lacking? The focus of these scholars is on the need for more constructive, cumulative efforts to develop a coherent theory;

for further elucidation of the nature of the basic liberal principles (human rights, freedom, equality, and democracy), along with a better understanding of the nature of civil society, of modern political authority, and of the modern state, as well as a grasp of how Confucian doctrines might or might not remedy the excesses of Western liberalism; for analysis of the relations between a market economy, the ideal of equality, and the question of the democratic internal organization of business enterprises; and for more specification of the institutional patterns needed to optimize development. From this standpoint, the agenda of Chinese political theory easily resonates with that of Western political theory.

In my view, however, this widespread Chinese perspective inadvertently conceals the divergence between these two agendas, the incongruence between mainstream Chinese and Western premises shaping reasoning about political life, and the challenge this incongruence poses for those seeking to harmonize U.S.-Chinese relations. Moreover, this Chinese perspective fails to uncover the extent to which political theory in China and the West has failed, not to mention exploring the epistemological basis for charging that any native or culturally different political theory has failed.

3. The Clash between Chinese and Western Political Theories

In 1966, when I finished my graduate studies at Harvard University in Chinese history and went to Taipei to learn how to speak Chinese, I took it for granted that the fully intelligent development of political theory had occurred only in the West. After all, Max Weber had announced that only the West had fully pursued the rationalization of human life, and Talcott Parsons had pictured U.S. society as exemplifying the highest stage so far of social evolution.[15] Editing their magistral essay collection *History of Political Philosophy* in 1963, Leo Strauss and Joseph Cropsey took for granted that this history included only Western philosophers. Later, when Quentin Skinner published his classic *The Foundations of Modern Political Thought*, he similarly could not imagine that any modern political theory arising outside the West should be taken seriously.[16]

I naturally had the same outlook in 1966. Regarding the Kuomintang regime in Taiwan as a corrupt dictatorship presiding over a

noisomely backward economy, hearing frightening tales about the
totalitarianism on the Mainland, reading famous books by Hsiao
Kung-ch'üan and T'ao Hsi-sheng on how Chinese scholars down
through the centuries had grappled with the problem of autocracy, and
regarding modern Chinese political thought as a series of unsuccessful
efforts to grasp the liberalism of the West, I could not imagine that any
Chinese political theories had any importance except as cultural
artifacts. Moreover, this Western ethnocentrism which I took for
granted was corroborated by the only Chinese outlook then enjoying
international respect, that widespread Chinese iconoclasm going
back at least to the May Fourth Movement at the end of World War I.

One representative of this movement was a thinker famous
today throughout the Chinese world, Yin Hai-kuang (1919–1969).
When I met him in Taipei in 1967, he was a professor of philosophy
at National Taiwan University whose defiant liberalism had led
the Kuomintang to relieve him of his teaching duties. His
driving concern was to master Western social science and political
theory in order to diagnose a pathological Chinese tradition
blocking democratization and epitomized by the dictatorship
oppressing him. His house on Wen-chou Street was filled with books
in English conveying these Western disciplines. I do not remember
ever seeing a book in Chinese in his house, except for a complete set
of the collected writings of President Chiang Kai-shek, which he was
happy to get rid of by giving it to me as a going-away present in 1968.

He also, however, gave me a copy of his main work, *Chung-kuo
wen-hua-te chan-wang* (Chinese Culture and its Prospects).[17] Reading
it in about 1970 gave me a new view of Chinese political theory. I
began to see Chinese political thought not as a cultural artifact but as
an effort as sincere and intelligent as any other to make sense out of
one part of the world's political life. In the next years, I looked at
more and more contemporary Chinese political writings from this
standpoint, including the works of other Taiwan liberals, of Hong
Kong philosophers believing modernization should be based on the
principles of Confucius, of scholars believing in the doctrine of Sun
Yat-sen, of astute Chinese Marxists like Li Tse-hou, and of the
current, often brilliant generation of intellectuals in China, Hong
Kong, Taiwan, and elsewhere seeking to go beyond the four main
Chinese ideologies of the twentieth century (Sunism, Chinese
Marxism, Chinese liberalism, and modern Confucian humanism).

This Chinese intellectual world has been filled with doctrines disagreeing with one another about whether knowledge consists only of science or also of humanistic ideas, whether knowledge comes only from the West or also from Chinese sources, whether China's democracy should accord with the British liberal model or Rousseau's theory of the general will, whether China should reform gradually or requires a revolution, and so on. These contradictory doctrines, however, have also shared many basic ideas. First, they have shared many ideals seemingly identical with popular ones in the West, such as "freedom," "equality," "democracy," "modernization," "social justice," and "self-realization." Second, they have shared many ideas largely at odds with those I had grown up to think of as rational. I became increasingly aware of an antinomy between these standards of mine and many of the contemporary Chinese views I encountered. Each side had a series of beliefs about the goal of political life, the means to reach it, other aspects of the given world, and the nature of knowledge, and each regarded its beliefs as indisputably reasonable. I eventually called the Chinese views "discourse #1," using "discourse #2" to label that prominent Anglo-American way of academic thinking I had come to identify with rationality itself.[18] These two discourses are further analyzed below, but the key contrasts between them can be summed up thus:

Table 1: An Outline of the Premises of Discourses #1 and #2

Discourse #1	Discourse #2
It is indisputably reasonable to say that:	It is indisputably reasonable to say that:
1. The world order is drastically abnormal because China has been marginalized.	1. The West is the world's model civilization, and the U.S. is the world's greatest nation. The world order largely and properly reflects this fact.
2. China's domestic problems stem largely from the selfishness and insincerity of its citizens. This is an intolerable situation that could be rectified if the right kind of culture were propagated.	2. Insincerity and selfishness are normal human frailties. No matter what the culture, these frailties will always infect human life, particularly political life.

Table 1 (Cont'd)

Discourse #1	Discourse #2
3. Knowledge is available with which to arrive at a rational solution for all major political problems, and the moral-intellectual virtuosi sincerely trying to obtain this knowledge can be publicly identified.	3. The available knowledge about political problems is often inadequate, and there is no completely reliable way to identify the persons best able to deal with these problems.
4. The relations between the state, cultural and technical elites, and the rest of the citizenry can be rectified as moral-intellectual virtuosi work with a corrigible state to influence society in a top-down way.	4. There are no moral-intellectual virtuosi and the state is incorrigibly inclined toward expansion of its own power. The citizens, who are all fallible, should interact as freely as possible in a bottom-up way, forming a civil society with which to monitor the incorrigible state.
5. Top-down control is correlated to what Isaiah Berlin called "positive freedom" and to "thick" parameters for the three marketplaces (economic, intellectual, political). In these three marketplaces, freedom is limited not only by respect for law and for scientific knowledge but also by a full philosophy of life or doctrine. Created by intellectuals, this doctrine is used to form an educational system realizing "positive freedom" by producing citizens with an "inner" dedication to virtue and so propagating a culture largely free of insincerity and selfishness. Thus, promoting "positive freedom" is a public responsibility to a large extent. Society should be like a household predictably governed by a wise and compassionate patriarch or a	5. Bottom-up control is correlated to "negative freedom" and "thin" parameters for the three marketplaces. The parameters consist of respect for law, for scientific knowledge, and for some minimal, very general moral principles. The educational system should produce citizens both respecting these thin parameters and using their freedom in the three marketplaces as creatively as possible. The knowledge is not available with which produce a philosophy of life serving as the public guidelines of an educational system focused on "positive freedom." Thus the pursuit of positive freedom should be left to private, individual impulses as much as possible. Society should be controlled by the innumerable, unpredictable

Table 1 (Cont'd)

Discourse #1	Discourse #2
school run by excellent teachers. Society is a kind of *Gemeinschaft* according with Hayek's "tribal" morality.[19]	impulses of individuals freely interacting in the three marketplaces. Each impulse should be subject as much as possible only to the moral or intellectual imagination and judgment of the individual herself. Society is a kind of *Gesellschaft* based on Hayek's "end-independent rules."

Looking for the key differences between these two ways of defining what is an indisputably reasonable way of discussing political life, one cannot overlook drastically different perceptions of the international world. The Chinese sense of a global order that is upside down contrasts with the Western feeling that the global order is essentially the way it should be. This contrast already implies a serious clash between Western and Chinese concepts of political rationality.

Another serious contrast is that between the idea of "thick parameters" limiting individual freedom and "thin" parameters. This contrast overlaps Isaiah Berlin's useful distinction between "positive freedom" and "negative freedom." To be sure, east and west, left and right, just about everyone agrees that, just as a society based purely on individual autonomy, negative freedom, and diversity is impracticable if not undesirable, so is one based purely on heteronomy, positive freedom, and conformity. The issue is that of tilting in which direction.

Confusion on these points, however, arises because of the modern liberal insistence, east and west, on regarding the maximization of autonomy as an absolute good and heteronomy as a somehow abnormal or undesirable condition that should necessarily be minimized. This notion could be labeled "the Lutheran bias," but it has flourished also in modern Chinese intellectual circles, where no one I know of has doubted that, ideally, all "constraints limiting the autonomous self" (*shu-fu*) should be eliminated. This simplistic view overlooks that, as virtually all scholars agree, the self to a large extent is the product of a process of socialization and education based on socially shared, heteronomously imposed linguistic and cultural orientations.

Besides this clash and the one regarding the global order, one has to note that between Chinese utopianism and the Western perception of history as a permanent moral limbo. The Chinese belief in ridding history of selfishness is in obvious contrast with the Aristotelian and Augustinian idea that selfishness is the normal, ineradicable condition of all actual human societies. As David Hume said, "All plans of government that suppose great reformation in the manners of mankind are plainly imaginary."[20]

Chinese utopianism, however, differs from the Platonic idea of a perfect state imagined by someone realizing it is impracticable. This concept is missing in the history of Chinese political thought.[21] What is basic to this history is a concept of political perfection put forward by Chinese believing it is practicable but regarded as impracticable by anyone agreeing with Hume's remark above. Discourses #1 and #2, then, differently determine political practicability, or, perhaps more precisely, differently define the therapeutically desirable way to think about political practicability. To improve their society, should citizens believe in the practicability of the highest political ideals or recognize that failing to realize them is the normal human condition?

A fourth basic contrast, however, lies in how discourses #1 and #2 conceptualize authority and knowledge. This is a problem Charles E. Lindblom shed much light on in his *Politics and Markets*.[22] Many would equate "top-down control" with heteronomy and authoritarianism, "bottom-up control," with autonomy and freedom. This view is roughly tenable, but only so long as one distinguishes between (a) the belief in blind, unconditional compliance with the commands of persons occupying socially established positions of authority, such as parents, teachers, and government officials, and (b) the belief that one should autonomously search in one's own conscience for the universally true principles of life (the *tao*) and then completely obey anyone who knows what these principles are. Only the latter kind of political authoritarianism can be found in discourse #1. This kind of "authoritarianism" legitimizes defiance of conventionally established political leaders as easily as it does respect for them. Thus the modern Chinese discourse #1 above has been as basic to the thinking of Chinese liberals defying Kuomintang and Communist rule as it has been to the Kuomintang (Sunist) and Chinese Marxist ideologies. To be sure, the former kind of authoritarianism (blind respect for whoever is in power) has often been a part of Chinese social practice, modern and premodern, just as it has been basic to the many patterns of dictatorship, patriarchy, and sexism in Western history. In both modern and premodern China, however, the main publicly promulgated political theories or ideologies have been "authoritarian" only in the latter sense.

This latter kind of "authoritarianism," then, turns on the question of the nature of knowledge, the problem of epistemology as the ideas with which to distinguish between sense and nonsense (*yu tao-li, mei-yu tao-li*). Is the kind of knowledge needed fully and perfectly to organize society available? Or, to put the matter more modestly, *to what extent* should people such as children, students, and ordinary citizens believe that there are people who have more knowledge than they about how they should think and live, and whose authority over them should therefore be respected?

4. Epistemological Optimism and Epistemological Pessimism

This brings up the distinction between epistemological optimism, characteristic of discourse #1, and epistemological pessimism, characteristic of discourse #2. These terms were used by Karl R. Popper by 1960 to describe two mistaken ways of thinking: the optimistic belief that "truth is manifest ... that truth, if put before us naked, is always recognizable as truth," and the pessimistic "disbelief ... in man's power to discern the truth" (Popper recommended "critical rationalism" as that correct viewpoint which should replace both these mistaken views).

When, some twenty-five years later, I used these terms, I had not yet read Popper and used them in a way different from his. Instead of using them philosophically to identify wrong ways of thinking, I used them in a purely descriptive way, which, as it turned out, was similar to Lindblom's approach. My idea was simply to distinguish between the sense of the indisputably obvious (e.g. "Obviously racism is bad, obviously I am mortal") and the sense of doubt (e.g. "I know nothing except that I know nothing, all ideas except the one expressed by this sentence are conjectures open to doubt and require some sort of verification"). The importance of doubting has been highlighted by philosophers east and west (Chu Hsi [1130–1200] also valued *i* [doubt]).[23] As John Dunn has noted, however, "credulity" is also an indispensable part of intellectual life.[24]

The pessimistic sense of doubt can also be seen as an intellectual focus on exactly investigating the boundary between the known and the unknown and a willingness to accept the unknowability or opaqueness of much of the world. This pessimism is classically illustrated by Karl Popper's denial that "all men are mortal" is a verified law of nature,[25] or by existentialism's idea that a person is "thrown" into existence, unable to fathom the ultimate meaning of life or the ultimate sources of her beliefs. Conversely, the sense of the obvious makes it silly for me to claim that I could possibly be immortal, and it is often linked to a belief in the epistemic transparency of the world (the idea that the "reason" for anything can be known, that all "because" questions can be answered).

Thus used descriptively, "epistemological optimism" and "epistemological pessimism" refer not in Popper's way to wrong theories but to two unavoidable, normal outlooks mixed together in some way to define the nature of knowledge. After all, even extreme skepticism is still based on the epistemologically optimistic belief that the universal wrongness of absolutistic thinking can be objectively demonstrated. The questions I pursued, therefore, are: How have these two attitudes been historically mixed together? What mix is the most reasonable? How can the criterion of reasonableness be established?

This viewpoint logically implies that the Chinese mix, despite its extravagant degree of optimism, is not self-evidently wrong. Before criticizing it, one has to describe it and the way its representatives have consciously defended it and rejected objections to it. This suggestion seems obvious, but it goes against the grain of virtually all modern thought to suggest that the right mix of epistemological optimism and pessimism is still an important, open question. Modern Chinese thought, with few if any exceptions, has assumed this question was settled, and so has much Western thought. For instance, Popper, Hayek, and Strauss all emphasized the complementary ills of excessive epistemological optimism and epistemological pessimism. Popper used these terms themselves and especially warned against the epistemological optimism of what he called "historicism" (e.g. Hegelianism).[26] Hayek rejected both ethical relativism and "the fatal conceit" of socialists optimistically claiming they had the knowledge with which to reorganize society. As for Strauss, he warned against both the epistemologically pessimistic relativism which he called "historicism," and the epistemologically optimistic dogmas, like Marxism, which Popper called "historicism."[27] None of these three scholars, however, suggested that the right mix of epistemological optimism and pessimism might be an open question. This was because, with the possible exception of Strauss, they all assumed that the nature of knowing was known, not an unsolved mystery. Even Strauss, after all, assumed without further ado that conceptualizations of knowledge contradicting the Western philosophic tradition were beyond the pale of serious discussion. From this Western standpoint, the extremely optimistic epistemology of discourse #1 is simply absurd.

Maybe so, but why? If some Western form of epistemological pessimism had emerged as a fully coherent theory, and if epistemological optimism had been abandoned by all sincere and perspicacious Chinese, the epistemological backwardness of the modern Chinese intellectual mainstream would be hard to deny. Such is not the case, however. The rejection of epistemological pessimism by perspicacious Chinese has been common and is illustrated by two essays in this book. Conversely, Popper's difficulties illustrate the failure in the West clearly to specify the boundary between the knowable and the unknowable. Popper perpetuated the Western tradition criticized by Eric Voegelin as a search for apodictic ideas, thus reducing knowledge to as-yet-unfalsified conjectures ("world 3") and viewing normative ideas as mere "mental states" ("world 2"). He then contradicted himself by also identifying knowledge with the *absolute* principles of logic and of experimental falsification, and by treating certain normative ideas (e.g. the value of the "open society," the wrongness of the "worship of power") as somehow privileged "mental states" amounting to absolutes. He then further contradicted himself by rooting these privileged mental states in a historical struggle between "the open society and its enemies" while simultaneously denouncing such rooting of norms in history as "historicism." Equally obvious are the contradictions Hume fell into when he tried to put ideas about unobserved activity outside the pale of knowledge, or the problems Hayek encountered when trying to derive political norms from science and the allegedly universal goals of human beings.[28]

All in all, to define the scope of knowledge one has to determine what can be known or not known about not only the given, phenomenal world (the realm of *Zweckrationalität*) but also the goals of life and human praxis (*Wertrationalität*). It makes no sense to me to reject Chinese views about these issues without first carefully describing them and establishing reasons for rejecting them. Moreover, even if China's epistemological optimism can be refuted, it persists as an important historical trend. It has been historically important especially in being logically integral to the idea of top-down control in discourse #1, that is, the concept of moral-intellectual virtuosi and that of a corrigible political center susceptible to control by such virtuosi.

According to the Chinese intellectual mainstream since Confucius, this sort of control was justified only to the extent that those actually in power had the overriding objective knowledge with which to make clear the parameters of behavior. For instance, in the basic Confucian book *Hsun-tzu* (third century B.C.; *Li-lun-p'ien*), these parameters were called *tu liang fen chieh* (standards of measurement, boundaries, and principles establishing one's proper station in life). According to *Hsun-tzu*, if these were not applied to put limits on what people "seek," "conflicts" and "chaos" would ensue. But who could apply them properly? For *Hsun-tzu*, only those who "knew the True Way" (*chih tao*), i.e. those whose "minds" were free of bias (*ta ch'ing-ming, hsu-i erh ching*) (*Chieh-pi-p'ien*). Hsun-tzu's optimism about the ability of people to know the one right way to organize life was integral to his ideas about how to organize it.[29]

Over the centuries in China, this view was never seriously challenged. When at the turn of the century the Western term "freedom" entered China and appealed to so many Chinese, Yen Fu and Liang Ch'i-ch'ao promptly combined it with the idea of "boundaries" (*chieh*) between one person's field of properly "free" action and another person's.[30] Moreover, in their thought, just as in *Hsun-tzu*'s, these "boundaries" were identified not with any currently existing set of laws or even with the laws enacted by elected but fallible officials but only with universally rational principles turned into law.

This conceptualization has never been challenged in China, so

far as I know. It persists even in Taiwan today. Thus the Taipei liberal
Yang Kuo-shu, on the one hand, called for these parameters:

> [In a] free, democratic ... open, pluralistic society ... the articles of the
> law are sufficiently clear and detailed to regulate every level of everyone's
> life. As the idea of the rule of law deeply penetrates society, just about
> every individual seeking self-realization will have a sense of his or her
> proper social place, of the proper standards and principles of conduct,
> what was popularly known in China as 'knowing the rules of moral
> propriety and understanding one's station in life.' ... The rule of law will
> prevent individualism from going astray and turning into the creed of
> selfishness.

On the other hand, the parameters Yang had in mind were based
on "reason," not on any unreasonable political tradition. He was not
referring to the actual parameters of freedom in Taiwan in 1980. He
perceived these as a system of martial law imposed by a dictatorial
group violating the rational principles known to him and his fellow
"intellectuals."[31]

Besides different conceptions of the given international world,
therefore, discourse #1 and discourse #2 clash especially in that the
former correlates epistemological optimism with thick parameters of
individual freedom, while discourse #2 correlates epistemological
pessimism with thin parameters of individual freedom. Emphasizing
thick parameters, the Chinese emphasize education transforming
the "inner" lives of citizens as the foundation of the state and as the
basis for the free pursuit of utility in the "outer" world of political and
economic institutions. In other words, free competition in the three
marketplaces can succeed only if most of the competitors have first
been educated to *k'o-chi* (transcend egotism), or, as Kao Li-k'o puts it,
to pursue *ko-t'i-chih-li* (profits accruing to an individual or group)
without lapsing into *li-chi-chu-i* (putting one's own profits above all
other considerations).[32] This Chinese view is a little similar to
Hayek's emphasis on the "ethos" of a society but shifts the emphasis
toward a much more communitarian, unambiguously moral spirit
and an education explicitly emphasizing spiritual transformation and
objective ethical principles. Western liberal theory shies away from
this emphasis, focusing instead on rationalizing the "outer," institutional world of utility. In Gilbert Ryle's terms, discourse #2 focuses on
"the machine," discourse #1, on "the ghost in the machine."[33]

According to discourse #1, then, the knowledge with which spiritually to transform the citizenry is available; the corrigible state can be expected eventually to respect the moral-intellectual virtuosi with this knowledge; and propagation of this knowledge through education can produce the thick moral parameters that will prevent the freedom of the three marketplaces from turning into license. According to discourse #2, however, maximizing this freedom even at the risk of its turning into license is the only hopeful way to try to improve society, because the knowledge needed to transform human nature and create thick parameters is unavailable, not to mention the Jacobinic dangers in trying to solder any such knowledge onto an incorrigible political center. The two discourses, as already noted, also disagree with regard to the issue of utopianism and that of international centrality. If one hesitates to call these discourses two clashing modes of "political rationality," one at least can accurately say that they are two contradictory sets of beliefs about what it is indisputably reasonable to say about the goals and means of political life.

True, not all scholars view the current interaction between Chinese and Western political ideas as the kind of clash I have described. Instead of seeing divergent discourses each with its own definition of the indisputably rational way to think about how to improve political life, many Western scholars picture a rational, Western-based political theory that should and maybe gradually will replace all opposing ideas. This outlook is at least implied by Alex Inkeles's work on the "convergence" between modernizing and modern societies and especially by the currently prominent political science literature on the spread of democracy throughout much of the world. As illustrated by Larry Diamond's recent book on the latter subject, scholars with this perspective, reflecting the influence of the GMWER, avoid trying to prove that their kind of political theory is "rational," but they present it as making more sense than any other political theory. To do this, Diamond adduces a number of political goals as in accord with his own "normative perspective," confident that he shares the latter with many readers. These political goals, indeed widely endorsed, include "civil liberties," the promotion of the "civil society," lack of violence arbitrarily inflicted by the government, not to mention genocide; government responsive to the preferences and interests of the citizens; peaceful ways of resolving ethnic and other conflicts between citizens; the promotion of "citizen competence" and "human development," along with the reduction of crime and other kinds of social degradation; economic development minimizing the ills of growth and sensitive to the needs of the poor; progress in dealing with ecological and demographic trends affecting global well-being; national security, peace; and all other goals that people can collectively aspire to.

Grounding the goodness of these goals in his own normative assumptions, Diamond then adduces empirical evidence that the most effective way to approximate realization of these goals is to institutionalize the "liberal," "constitutional" kind of democratic governance, which also includes a "political culture" emphasizing "pragmatism," "moderation," "trust," and "tolerance." Conversely, empirical evidence shows that other kinds of governance, such as the various kinds of authoritarianism, have, to a large extent, been less successful in approximating realization of these goals. Hence any political theory refusing to "push democracy forward in the coming decades," such as a theory endorsing the "'Singaporean'" model, is implicitly depicted as irrational. With this view of the global juxtaposition of rational with irrational political theory, Diamond recommends that "international actors," governmental and private, seek to promote democratic development around the world, although acting prudently with a "long-term" perspective, aware that history is a complex, uncertain mix of "setbacks" and "increments of progress."[34]

It is not easy to take issue with such an argument that the world today is graced by the presence of a single political theory with which all reasonable people of goodwill should agree, and which has in fact been widely accepted. After all, despite the protests of Clifford Geertz, the idea of a universal human nature implying universal goals, such as material well-being, is still very much alive in scholarly circles, as illustrated by my essay below on Hayek, not to mention the medical and psychological literature. There is indeed much "convergence" between different cultures and even Great Traditions. As Diamond emphasizes, the merging of ideas has been furthered still more by the modernization of communication between societies. Thus, as noted below, there is considerable overlap between discourse #1 and discourse #2, especially with regard to goals. The divergence between these two discourses is far from total.

Nevertheless, political theories diverging from Diamond's above cannot be regarded as necessarily less rational or tenable than his, except to the extent that one shares his zealous belief in the validity of his own way of mixing normative assumptions, various kinds of definitions, ways of obtaining evidence, and judgments about what is an objective way to generalize about a particular political situation. This zealous belief or faith of his does not necessarily override other political theories because: (a) as he himself emphasizes, it is not based on ideas accurately describing any objective, global, necessary direction of historical development (Diamond rejects the notion of such a direction as "teleology"); (b) it admittedly rests on the normative assumptions of just one set of historical actors, not on canons of rationality all historical groups necessarily respect; and (c) not all sincere, intelligent persons share his views, as illustrated by at least three essays in this book.

In accord with discourse #2, his views are to a large extent out of accord with those based on discourse #1. People identifying the latter with rationality have many ideas opposed to his, such as ideas about: the meaning of "rationality"; that of "freedom," of the normative mix of "positive" and "negative" freedom, of autonomy and heteronomy; the meaning of "human development"; the hierarchy of priority with which all the various goals Diamond adduces should be pursued; questions of historical causation affecting the discussion of current policy recommendations; the much-disputed issue of whether the empirical evidence does indeed demonstrate that the Western liberal democracies have been the political structures most successful in pursuing the goals that should be pursued; and the crucial problem of taking into account the particular circumstances of a particular society like China, of judging how best to "get from here to there."

On the Chinese side, not a few people call themselves "liberal" and agree with Western liberals that the only effective way to improve Chinese political life is to institute democracy. They then depict this "rational" Western approach as in conflict with "irrational," "backward," or "feudal" orientations in China, the strength of which they tend to emphasize much more than optimistic Western liberals do. Their view thus partly coincides with my emphasis on continuity with the past and on the clash between Chinese and Western political thought.[35] Chinese seemingly welcoming Western liberalism, however, do not necessarily have the same political future in mind as Western liberals have. As shown by chapters V and VI below, they recommend Western liberalism on the grounds not that it consists of plausible assumptions and has been successful in helping people improve their political lives, but that it is a basically definitive theory, that its implementation in the West has greatly reduced the impact of selfishness and irrationality on public life, and that its implementation in China would have similar results.

Expressed in 1998, the outlook of Chao T'ing-yang, a member of the Chinese Academy of Social Sciences, illustrates still another widespread Chinese position today. For him, there is no significant clash between Chinese and Western political theory, because Chinese thought has already been largely though deplorably Westernized. Any divergence between the two is not an actuality but a desirable possibility, because this Western mode of thinking is not appropriate for China, except for the "technical" knowledge it entails. Chao, in other words, wants China to pursue a political theory different from the Western one, calling for a "new wisdom" with which Chinese can create a "new culture" leaving behind the current failings of both Western and Chinese thought and ways of living.[36] In my eyes, however, his perception of an already Westernized Chinese intellectual world is inaccurate, and his rejection of Western political theory illustrates the very clash between Chinese and Western political theories which I am trying to describe (Chao's outlook is analyzed on pp. 58–61 below).

The illusion of a current convergence between Chinese and Western political theories has thus been variously created by zealous Westerners confident that their entirely appropriate sense of political rationality should and indeed may spread throughout the world; by Chinese seemingly agreeing with them but actually — I would argue — projecting their own epistemic and moral vision onto this tide of Western rationality; or by Chinese loosely deploring some alleged hegemony of undesirable Western ideas already inflicted on their country. This illusion, then, consists of a variety of partly contradictory ideas, conspicuously absent from which is any *Chinese* view that *desirable* Western ideas have already come to dominate Chinese society or are likely to (see chapter X, section 11).

Despite this illusion of current convergence, however, many observers have perceived continuing divergence between leading

Chinese and Western forms of political thought. Apart from his polemical tone, the famous journalist William Safire was accurate when he saw a confrontation between two concepts of the good society. He attacked Chinese who "deride as 'decadent' the Western ideal of individual liberty," and he saw an

> ideo-economic struggle going on in today's world. On one side are governments that put "order" above all and offer an under-the-table partnership to managers who like arranged outcomes and a docile work force.... On the other side — our side — are free enterprisers creating wealth. By combining the profit motive with political freedom, and by using state power to protect individual rights, we reward the work ethic with the merit system.[37]

His point indeed is part of a major Western tendency today defining China as a growing menace to Western civilization, a huge, increasingly powerful, increasingly nationalistic nation wedded to a collectivistic, authoritarian concept of society.[38] Conversely, the eminent Hong Kong sociologist Chin Yao-chi (Ambrose Y.C. King) has described Western "liberal democracy" as putting primacy on "ego-centered individuals.... undermining community." He argues that, with its "Confucian culture," China should seek to build a "democratic," "capitalistic," and "modern" society lacking "Western liberalism."[39] His view indeed is quite continuous with the mainstream Chinese reactions to Western culture going back at least to Yen Fu at the turn of the century. As Huang Ko-wu (Max K.W. Huang) has shown, Yen Fu pursued a vision of freedom and democracy while resisting J.S. Mill's epistemological pessimism and emphasis on negative freedom. With few exceptions if any, the public political discourse in twentieth-century China has rejected and continues to reject "the three marketplaces" to the extent that these subject society to the free, frighteningly unpredictable interactions between morally and intellectually ungraded individual impulses.[40] As Henry K.H. Woo put it, such a society is "out of control" (*shih-k'ung*).[41] Thus, it is easy to see why so many Chinese were attracted to Maoism as a system precluding the three marketplaces, and why post-Mao thinkers today continue trying to impose thick parameters on the three marketplaces.

Some might argue that this clash between two kinds of political theories is of interest only to intellectual historians, because such theorizing in the ivory tower little influences either the political development of societies or international relations. The latter, many would say, depend on the strategic considerations of leaders, the former, on trends directly affecting mass behavior, whether economic patterns, the broad cultural trends adduced by Samuel P. Huntington, or the kinds of globally converging technological, organizational, and psychological tendencies analyzed by Alex Inkeles. The causative influence of ideas in history, however, is a controversial subject, and a long list of excellent scholars have emphasized this influence, ranging from F.A. Hayek, Karl R. Popper, Max Weber, S.N. Eisenstadt, Robert N. Bellah, Reinhard Bendix, and James Q. Wilson to Alasdair MacIntyre and Leo Strauss. As Isaiah Berlin put it, "It is only a very vulgar historical materialism that denies the power of ideas, and says that ideals are mere material interests in disguise."[42]

To the extent that influential circles in China and the U.S. view the other nation as pursuing a nonsensical, immoral political theory, the international lines of communication will be clogged up with Safire-like polemics, constructive political efforts to resolve the conflicts between these two nations will falter, and these enervating, dangerous disagreements will continue and deepen. Therefore, an effort is needed to reflect on the nature of these political theories and to promote some degree of international consensus about the extent to which either of these sets of theories should be empathetically understood or revised. My own agenda should be obvious: I hope that as scholars analyze the differences between Chinese and Western political theories, they will focus more on different conceptions of knowledge than of authority, and that, as intellectual circles on both sides of the Pacific reflect on the problem of defining political knowledge, they will all become more open to ideas they previously regarded as bizarre. I agree with "conservative" thinkers like Leo Strauss and Eric Voegelin who, as Ted V. McAllister put it, believe that the "most important" political question today is "What constitutes knowledge?"[43] We cannot, however, consider only Western answers to this question. The Chinese answers may or may not be mistaken, but we cannot object to them without explaining why they are mistaken.

5. The Question of Thin Parameters in Modern Western Political Thought

The clash between Chinese and Western political theories today, then, cannot be understood without analyzing the relation in modern Western political thought between ideas about the parameters of freedom and ideas about the nature of knowledge. It is precisely the Western conceptualization of this key relation that has been rejected by the modern Chinese intellectual mainstream. In the West too, however, serious doubts about how to conceptualize this crucial relation have remained common.

Scholars like Leo Strauss seem to agree that, beginning with thinkers like Niccolo Machiavelli (1469–1527), Francis Bacon (1561–1626), Thomas Hobbes (1588–1679), Rene Descartes (1596–1650), Benedict Spinoza (1632–1677), John Locke (1632–1704), and Jean-Jacques Rousseau (1712–1778), European ideas about "the betterment of action" underwent a basic shift away from the pursuit of "inner" virtue or religious ideals and toward a greater emphasis on "outer," tangible, concrete benefits, whether Machiavelli's idea of political success, Bacon's or Descartes' quest for technological progress and material well-being, or that emphasis on freedom, equality, and government by consent of the governed developed by thinkers like Spinoza, Locke, and Rousseau.[44] This Western quest for the materialization of freedom and prosperity led via Rousseau and Hegel to the utopianism of Karl Marx, but it also became intertwined with the rise in the West of a new kind of society, one combining the structure of the sovereign nation, modernization, capitalism, an unprecedented degree of interconnections with other societies, and liberal, Millsian democracy (a political structure including a "civil society" in the sense of "civility" as a norm both inside and outside the state as well as social-political space and organizations outside the state, checking it).[45] Especially after 1991, when the Soviet Union disintegrated, many came to view this five-fold combination as the structure of the normative modern society.

At the heart of this combination is a paradigm that can be extracted most conveniently from the complementary writings of Friedrich A. Hayek and Karl R. Popper: the idea of a society not just tolerating but founded on the "three marketplaces," the free economic, intellectual, and political marketplaces. That is, both thinkers emphasized the need to maximize the individual's freedom, Hayek, most obviously in the economic sphere, Popper, most obviously with regard to the intellectual and political aspects of the "open society." Admiring each other, they both contrasted the humaneness and economic efficiency of a society based on this multifaceted freedom with the oppressiveness and economic inefficiency of a government falsely claiming to have knowledge and moral insight sufficient to plan and control the economic, intellectual, and political activities of its citizens. In other words, both rejected the Rousseauistic goal of putting society under the explicit guidance of a ruling moral intelligence and instead accepted moral and epistemic dissonance as the very medium, not just the price of freedom and prosperity. To put it in still other terms, the Hayek-Popper (or Millsian) approach, fearing Jacobinic consequences, rejected the Rousseauistic idea of an enlightened "general will" fusing together political power, knowledge, morality, and individual freedom. Instead of hoping for such a fusion as a way to realize what Isaiah Berlin criticized as "positive freedom," this Millsian approach cast doubt on all knowledge claims — even scientific ones, in Popper's eyes — and sought as much as possible to broaden and protect the scope of that "negative freedom" which Berlin celebrated.

In light of this model, the goal of prosperity increasingly became a technical problem for economists rather than an issue in political theory. Millsian political theory instead focused on the complex problem of protecting and extending the freedom of the individual. Whether of the right or the left, Millsian political theorists have continued to argue about what the proper scope of the state should be (even for Hayek, it still had to be large), how to increase the accountability of the state to the governed, how to reduce tendencies outside the state undermining freedom and equality (such as racism, sexism, and economic exploitation), or how to deal with international circumstances reducing the ability of one country's citizens to pursue freedom, equality, and prosperity.

Yet if Western political theory today pursuing human "betterment" concentrates on securing the freedom and equality of individuals competing in the three marketplaces, it is still concerned with a second problem, one which indeed is a traditional Western one, but which became more prominent in recent years as more social critics became alarmed by recent Western social trends, such as urban degradation in the U.S.: the problem of defining and institutionalizing the parameters of freedom. In other words, even in the liberty-focused Hayek-Popper model, autonomy is still complemented by heteronomy, liberty with authority and some degree of conformity. The peculiarity of the Hayek-Popper model, the reason for its divergence from contemporary Chinese thought, lies in its effort to minimize, not to eliminate conformity.

In this model, conformity is considered mainly under two basically uncontroversial headings, respect for law and for science. Hayek and Popper both admired J.S. Mill. Perhaps the classic justification for law as a boundary of freedom is J.S. Mill's concept of "self-protection," though Hayek's derivation of law from the need for economic efficiency also is central. As for respect for science, it became an essentially unchallenged premise summed up by Popper's view that progress depends on the growth of scientific knowledge.[46]

Yet in Western political theory today, even in the Hayek-Popper model, the idea has remained important that freedom should be bounded also by non-legal, non-scientific parameters. As shown by the essay on him in this book, Hayek saw the desirable society as made up of three elements: free markets based on law; a variety of important state functions; and a traditional ethical "ethos" of a certain type precluding allegedly mistaken normative views (Hayek attacked Freudianism). Popper similarly took for granted a "liberal tradition" founded on Christian and Socratic ideals. Other ways of discussing freedom's non-legal, non-scientific parameters have included Alex Inkeles's work on the normative "modern" or "democratic" personality;[47] the views of political scientists like James Q. Wilson discussing the dependence of democracy on the "character" or "virtues" of its citizens;[48] Robert N. Bellah's call for a new, anti-Lockean moral language;[49] Amitai Etzioni's "communitarianism";[50] widespread discussion of "civility" as the central norm of the civil society; and the emphasis of Francis Fukuyama on building up "social capital."[51]

These prominent discussions, however, did not always fully confront the problem of non-legal, non-scientific parameters. As Claus Offe and Ulrich K. Preuss indicate, when scholars describe citizens only in terms of civility and virtue, they picture them as just docilely following wise leaders. They fail to identify another quality citizens in a democracy should have, the intellectual ability actively to evaluate policies. Thus Offe and Preuss note the need for "political rationality." They discuss how to improve "the empirical will of citizens" by injecting "civic spirit, virtue and insight" into them, thus developing "their moral and rational capabilities," encouraging them to have "enlightened, principled and refined preferences," nurturing their "'civilized'" commitment to the "'common good,'" and so complementing the state's legal structure with "the principled action of conscientious citizens."

Yet whether the non-legal, non-scientific parameters of freedom are viewed only as a matter of morality or also as a matter of political rationality, Western theorists have often felt that Western theory has failed to show how these parameters can be defined and implemented. Offe and Preuss, for instance, indicate that Western thinkers for a long time mistakenly thought that organizational changes would make citizens moral and rational. Rousseau said that the moral-intellectual level of citizens would be raised if they controlled their own government; Marx said it would be if they controlled their own economy; and Locke thought it would be if they were empowered to take responsibility for their own private affairs. In other words, despite their great differences, all three pursued the modern goal of giving freedom to every individual in the sense of control over her concrete destiny, believing that such control was practically feasible in the context of modern social-political life, and that loss of this control was the main cause of immorality and intellectual confusion. As the chimerical nature of this peculiar belief became clearer, however, thinkers like Max Weber and Carl Schmitt gloomily concluded that the masses could not become virtuous and rational, and that the only remaining hope was to put representative government largely into the hands of a relatively rational elite.[52]

Challenging this gloomy view, Offe and Preuss suggested a third approach, really a return to that pervasive emphasis in the history of Western political philosophy on education, an emphasis going back to that Greek ideal of *paideia* discussed by Werner Jaeger.[53] Offe and Preuss argued that promoting the rationality and morality of citizens depends on the "process of learning" used by citizens to cultivate their moral and rational capabilities, and so they called for "more refined, more deliberative and more reflective formation of the motives and demands that enter the process of mass participation."[54]

As *paideia*, the shaping of motives and demands entails the formation of the inner life, of the family, and of manners, the issues of socialization and education, the whole question of a society's social-cultural-spiritual foundations, of what Max Weber called

Wertrationalität (the rationality of ends) and Isaiah Berlin called "positive freedom." Thus Offe and Preuss suggested that by means of *paideia* a society can form the non-legal, non-scientific parameters of freedom. Of course this vision of *paideia* had something in common with the traditional Confucian emphasis on *chiao* (teaching) as the basis of *cheng* (government).

Yet this approach to the formation of these parameters also ran into difficulties. To be sure, anthropologists, psychologists, and others have shed much light on the *actual paideia* structures of many different societies, the ways in which language, culture, and society in fact pervasively shape the thoughts and characters of individuals, necessarily limiting their freedom. As already mentioned, standard theorists like George Mead have convincingly argued that the ego is socially constructed, and that therefore the ideal of pure moral and intellectual autonomy — the Lutheran or Kantian bias, as it were — can be no more than an ideal.[55] The issue of *paideia*, however, is a normative one. Since these actual processes of socialization and education are inherently susceptible to criticism and revision, how should they be criticized and revised? What should be the content of education? What kind of people with what kind of worldview should control education?

Ultimately, then, *paideia* as a normative issue only seems to be a matter of abstruse intellectual debates, whether over the nature of virtue or the modern value of Confucian tradition. Actually, this issue is at the heart of perhaps the most serious political struggle in any society, the struggle to control education and thus heteronomously determine the character of one's society.

Recent Western political theory has been unable to adjudicate the conflicting claims about how to construct *paideia* and thus form freedom's non-legal, non-scientific parameters. For instance, Robert Nozick's utilitarian, libertarian approach seemingly eliminates the problem of specifying non-legal, non-scientific parameters by assuming that freedom should be bounded by nothing but respect for law and science. For many, however, this way of legitimizing the depravity of a Timothy Leary is intolerable.[56] Scholars with a communitarian bent have emphasized the need for virtue, but they have disagreed about the content of virtue. For instance, Robert N. Bellah holds that virtue lies in rejecting "Lockean individualism," while Christopher Lasch says it lies in reviving

Lockean individualism.[57] Conservative ideologues and religious figures simply bewail the mores of the day, insisting that the universal validity of the traditional virtues is self-evident.[58] Then there are the political scientists and historians who just empirically study the way that nineteenth-century liberals like J.S. Mill took for granted the validity of the Biblical and Aristotelian virtues, recommend that liberals today do likewise, but cannot explain why their recommendation makes more sense than libertarian or Freudian recommendations to the contrary. True, Lawrence Kohlberg's psychological derivation of moral norms is suggestive, but its empirical basis is a subject of debate, and, despite his protests, the Kantian ideal of moral autonomy he posits lacks specific moral content.[59] Alex Inkeles sees a globally converging psychological pattern, the formation of "modern personality" traits in all societies that industrialize, and he suggests this spreading psychological pattern itself shapes modes of thought, the normative content of education, and so the social-political ideals people will pursue. Yet even if in the distant future the whole world comes to affirm such a vision of modernity, and converging psychological trends obviate disputes about the content of *paideia*, these disputes continue today, both within the West and internationally.

6. The Great Modern Western Epistemological Revolution (GMWER)

There has, then, been much difficulty in the contemporary West in arriving at some consensus about how to form the non-legal, non-scientific (i.e. moral) parameters of freedom, in contrast with the considerable degree of Western consensus about the need to limit freedom by institutionalizing respect for law and for scientific knowledge. (For instance, science in recent years established that tobacco products injure health, and then laws were passed in the U.S. restricting the freedom to buy, advertise, and sell them.)

This lack of consensus in the West about how to define the non-legal, non-scientific kinds of parameters of freedom entails a linkage taken for granted here in the West and largely missing in contemporary Chinese intellectual circles: the link between the question of the objectivity of moral values and that of their unchangingness. As illustrated below by the thought of the young

Beijing intellectual Chao T'ing-yang, there is no link of this sort for many if not all Chinese persons thinking about culture and values. In their circles, one may or may not agree that morality consists of objective principles based on reason. Either way, the unchanging, substantive content of good and bad remains so obvious that it does not even appear as a question worth discussing.

To be sure, even in the West, many would agree with this view. Since all kinds of things, such as racism, are indisputably bad, how can one say that the nature of badness is anything but an obvious, absolute, unchangeable aspect of the human situation? Yet for an Alasdair MacIntyre or a Leo Strauss, the modern Western failure philosophically to demonstrate the objectivity of moral principles has destabilized ideas about the nature of good and bad. In their eyes, the decline of a belief in the objectivity of values, appearing as the rising influence of "skepticism" and "relativism," has caused the modern West to plunge into "crisis." As MacIntyre says, it has opened the gates to "barbarism."[60] From this standpoint, once values demonstrably lack an objective basis, people will feel free to redefine goodness. They may decide racism or indulgence in escapist drugs is good. Dostoyevski had one of his characters say that, if there is no God, anything is permitted. MacIntyre and Strauss in effect added: "Anything is permitted if there is no God or any objective ethical principles replacing Him."

Whether morality is objective and whether its content is fixed, therefore, are two distinct questions the relation between which can be variously viewed. The contrast between prominent Chinese and Western views about this relation probably reflects a still more basic contrast, one regarding the conceptualization of badness. In the mainstream Western philosophical tradition, the evils that proper philosophizing and proper governance should help people avoid are not the unavoidable manifestations of human sinfulness but gross lapses into barbarism. These horrifying lapses can be avoided if people can discover that morality consists of objective, universal principles, not just of subjective beliefs that some people happen to favor. From the standpoint of most if not all modern Chinese thought, however, sinfulness is eradicable. Thus the main evil to worry about is not gross barbarism but the prevalence of the usual human frailties, especially selfishness. These can be largely eliminated if thinkers can demonstrate not the objectivity of values but the oneness of all forms of understanding and all aspects of human life ("linkage" — see below).

Again, behind this contrast between conceptualizations of evil and of the ideas needed to overcome it lie contrasting definitions of human nature — the dark Western notion of a perpetually sinful being quite capable of conspiring with the Devil, and the sunny Confucian notion of a being who would be morally perfect but for the persistence of some removable shortcomings (despite their differences, Confucius's two major interpreters in classical times, Mencius and Hsun-tzu, shared this view, which has remained central to Chinese thought down to the present). Indeed, this sunny view of universal human nature was integral to the concept of "culture" (*wen-hua*) which Chinese intellectuals imported by about 1920. According to widespread views, people would not be selfish if "bad" "cultural" tendencies could be corrected.[61]

The causal link seen by thinkers like MacIntyre and Strauss, therefore, is not a universally recognized fact. Indeed, the Western failure to solve the problem of the objectivity of values has not *necessarily* been a chief cause for the eruptions of "barbarism" that have disfigured Western culture in modern times. First, although the intellectualistic "trickle down" theory of historical causation is not without merit, these eruptions had many causes, not just the rise of philosophical "relativism." Second, "relativism" anyway is a chimera — either an impracticable epistemological recommendation or an inaccurate way of describing how people actually think, not to mention its being inherently illogical. As Ted V. McAllister notes, Leo Strauss believed that "the true crisis of modernity, then, is the inability to affirm or believe in anything or any goal or ideal."[62] Yet Hitler and the many who courageously sacrificed their lives for his cause at Stalingrad and elsewhere deeply believed in it. As argued below, it seems to be an empirical fact that any discourse is based on premises that are indisputable in the eyes of a particular we-group, whether "our" premise that "racism is bad" or Hitler's opposite premise. Third, modern Western culture is made up of competing discourses. MacIntyre to the contrary, Nietzschean relativism does not necessarily epitomize Western modernity. The Pope is not an epiphenomenon. Fourth, whether modern life is in "crisis" or is only perceived by some circles to be in crisis remains debatable. To say that relativism has caused a crisis comes close to saying that a non-existent idea has brought about a non-existent situation. On the contrary, one could more accurately argue that modernization has reduced human suffering and disorder while arousing the feeling in some ideological circles that suffering and disorder have increased. In premodern times, the end of a dynasty like the Yuan (1279–1368) or the Ming (1368–1644) entailed catastrophic civil war reducing China's population by perhaps 10 to 20 percent, while during the allegedly horrendous twentieth century, China's population increased by 100 to 200 percent.[63] Modernization is an extremely popular phenomenon around the world, which would hardly be the case if it worsened the quality of life. Indeed, Leo Strauss's own thought utterly fails to reconcile his sense of crisis with his strong appreciation of the amenities of modernization, of liberal democracy, and of the special virtues of the United States, which he viewed as the one modern nation not founded on Machiavellian principles.

To be sure, one can grant that the rise of what Strauss called "positivism," "radical historicism," and " relativism" made it hard for elites to agree on how to conceptualize the philosophical and normative content of education and how to "thicken" the non-legal, non-scientific parameters of freedom. Yet, according to thinkers like Berlin, Hayek, and Popper, thinning out these parameters by emphasizing "negative freedom" is precisely the best way to pursue freedom, prosperity, and morality. Thus the debate continues between modern people longing for *Gemeinschaft* and those enthusiastic about the *Gesellschaft*, Bill Gates world of capitalism, democracy, and modern technology.

There is much controversy, therefore, about whether modern Western philosophical arguments about the nature of moral understanding have had important effects on the West's societal development, and whether these effects, important or not, have been good or bad. There does, however, seem to be an important intellectual connection between the Western liberal concept of a society minimizing the parameters of individual freedom (the Millsian, Hayek-Popper model); the unresolved Western controversy about how to define freedom's non-legal, non-scientific parameters; and some four centuries of philosophical discussion in the West creating widespread doubt there that the content of morality can be derived from either a sacred canon or the rational search for objective knowledge.

It is striking that this major epistemological development accompanied industrialization, democratization, and modernization in the West but has not occurred in the Chinese world as the latter industrialized, modernized, and, in part, democratized. This Western development was based on what I have tried to call "epistemological pessimism," the belief that all knowledge claims are open to doubt and so can be established only by making and assessing them in a maximally cautious and precise way. Richard H. Popkin has traced this skepticism back to its Greek roots and shown how prevalent it was in European intellectual circles by the sixteenth century. Alasdair MacIntyre has described how it was used in subsequent centuries to undermine claims that morality is based on reason.[64] This latter process can be called the Great Modern Western Epistemological Revolution (GMWER). It produced what was above called "discourse #2."

At the root of the GMWER was Plato's worry about how to distinguish between knowledge and opinion, that is, between knowledge as true, objective statements about things, conditions, or principles and opinions as merely subjective, arbitrary ideas. This distinction has usually been linked to a stratification of universal mental faculties. "Reason" (*li-hsing*) has been usually used to label the "highest," most prestigious, most authoritative mental faculty, through which "knowledge" was produced, while some less prestigious faculty, such as "emotion," has usually been linked to arbitrary, subjective ideas. Hayek, for instance, held that there were three kinds of universal mental faculties: "reason," "instincts," and the ability to create different languages and cultures.[65] Recommending policies based on "science," he regarded reason as the most authoritative faculty and so implied that people were morally obligated to accept his view as authoritative to the extent he had successfully followed reason. Arguments produced by this highest faculty should override any competitive notions the way heliocentrism overrides geocentrism.

From the standpoint of maximum epistemological optimism, objective truths are available about: (1) observable events, logic, and the principles of experimentation used to falsify predictions about events (Popper's "world 3");[66] (2) the "inner" structure of consciousness allegedly shared by all human beings and analyzed by philosophers like Hume, Kant, and Edmund Husserl; (3) some universal human characteristics with plausibly normative implications, such as the nature of reasoning as an inherently valuable activity that should be educationally promoted, the idea of the public good as necessarily implied by the social nature of human beings, or plausibly universal human desires (such as the desire for health, other aspects of material well-being, and freedom); (4) specific normative questions, such as the question of whether China should promptly democratize, of whether reparations should be paid to the descendants of U.S. slaves, of whether abortion should be legalized, or of whether a popular, capable president should be impeached if he has committed perjury with regard to his sexual behavior; (5) the way in which all these different kinds of rational truths form a logically unified system or body of knowledge (*t'i-hsi*); and (6) the unity of all realities and principles as the objects of knowledge and in terms of their ultimate, ontological nature.

From the standpoint of maximum epistemological pessimism, there are only subjective ideas about all these issues. As the GMWER progressed, the idea that there could be knowledge beyond point #3 was increasingly challenged. Point #4 has turned out to be the chief hurdle. Without the intervention of a historically specific intellectual trend or cultural, soteriological tradition, it is hard to see how consensus around point #3 can be translated into a consensus regarding more specific normative issues. After all, one may agree with Kant that one should always act according to a principle which one believes everyone should follow, but what does that principle say to Mozart about whether he should risk his life by jumping into a raging river to save a drowning child? Virtually any act can be passionately described by the interested person as an act that everyone should carry out.[67] Moreover, it is one thing for me to agree with John Rawls that the good society is so organized that I would want to live in it before knowing what my social position in it would be, but it is entirely another matter for me to figure out how such a good society should balance the often conflicting goals of freedom, justice, national security, political stability, economic well-being, and respect for the cultural inheritance. How can I decide these issues without calling on a historically particular hierarchy of values? As the essay on T'ang Chün-i shows, navigating the path from #3 to #4 without abandoning the quest for objective knowledge may be best seen as a probably inconclusive but still crucial educational undertaking. Yet epistemological optimists like T'ang have been confident that knowledge is available regarding all six issues above.

It was the GMWER that focused attention on the hurdle at point #4, increasingly revealing the epistemic opaqueness of basic beliefs and so the limits of knowledge. The origins of the GMWER cannot be separated from that transformation of European political theory mentioned above, the movement "away from the pursuit of 'inner' virtue or religious ideas and toward a greater emphasis on 'outer,' tangible, concrete benefits." Paradoxically, the quest for these concrete benefits was at first intertwined with great epistemological optimism, the belief that increasing knowledge could solve all the most important human problems. Eric Voegelin has interpreted the whole of "modernity" as stemming from a "gnostic ... belief in the power of knowledge to transform reality, to create earthly perfection." He traced this trend back to Joachim of Flora in the twelfth century, long before the era of science, industrialization, and modernization.[68] Then came the long era stretching from Machiavelli through Marx and Hayek, when thinkers argued about how rationally to obtain knowledge about norms, trying out one controversial method after another of grounding norms: in the paradigmatic aspects of Roman history (Machiavelli); in universal human egotism (Hobbes); in the universal origin of the state (Hobbes, Locke, Rousseau); in universal laws of history (often regarded as "dialectical"); in universal psychological needs, such as that desire for largely material felicity adduced by Jeremy Bentham; in universal epistemic conditions, like J.S. Mill's fallibility; in a universal "method of intelligence" used to pursue "marvelous possibilities in industry and commerce" (John Dewey); in the seemingly universal contours of consciousness introspectively accessible to the subject of experience (Kant); in the nature of communication (Jürgen Habermas); in "the ontologically ultimate organization of the material world, the biological world, the biosphere, the structure of the brain, and the structure of knowledge, as we know them" (Henry K.H. Woo); and so on.[69] Below, "discourse #3" is used to label this vast problematique centering on the problem of how rationally to obtain objective knowledge about norms.

What all the versions of discourse #3 have in common is the assumption that the objective reality which people can know by using their most authoritative mental faculty, usually called "reason," consists of not only specific observed facts but also Platonic entities, that is, general patterns represented by particular facts or symbols, such as morally neutral ideas like numbers, temporally and spatially huge entities like universal human nature, and universal moral imperatives.

If we ask why this search for objective ideas about norms was eventually challenged by epistemological pessimism, it is difficult even to list the many influences at work. Richard H. Popkin adduced the Renaissance's rediscovery of "the ancient skeptical texts, which then became basic to the theological battles of the Reformation. By the late fifteenth and sixteenth centuries, traditional knowledge claims were discredited also by Erasmus's (1466–1536) ridicule, the beginnings of modern science, the Voyages of Discovery, esoteric movements involving magic and the Cabala, and the new interest in Greek and Roman civilization."[70] Nor can one overlook the British nominalism epitomized by William of Ockham (c. 1285–1349), who pursued "a radical empiricism in which the evidential base of all knowledge is direct experience of individual things and particular events," this leading to "an extreme economy of ontological commitment in which abstract or intensional extralinguistic entities are systematically eliminated by a logical analysis of language."[71]

More broadly, Eric Voegelin linked what I call epistemological pessimism to the "gnostic" identification of knowledge with totally precise ideas. Once the knowledge available to reasoning people was redefined as a completely efficacious way to control and optimize human life, the quest for knowledge became a sacred matter of the highest importance, and great care had to be taken to prevent its becoming contaminated by dubious ideas. Thus Voegelin described the new search for the "certainty" of "apodictic knowledge": "Because knowledge played so central a role in this [modern] process .... of human-directed transformation .... moderns had to make especially sharp epistemological judgments. Only that about which they could be certain would they call knowledge."[72]

This quest for "sharp epistemological judgments" widely coincided with what Thomas Reid (1710–1796), Hume's astute critic, attacked as the "theory of ideas," the claim that people do not directly perceive objective reality, they have only ideas or sense impressions any relation of which to any objective reality has to be rigorously questioned.

The search for apodictic knowledge against this epistemologically pessimistic background then led to a two-front attack on the problem of evaluating knowledge claims. On the one hand, a series of momentous theories reduced the scope of objective knowledge. Descartes excluded from it the whole rich variety of ideas that were not "clear and distinct"; David Hume excluded from it all ideas about unobserved experience, claiming that knowledge about the unobserved could not be derived from knowledge of the observed (all the while explaining how all human beings, observed or not, form the concept of cause-and-effect); Hume also excluded all normative propositions derived from facts; Immanuel Kant (1724–1804) excluded ontological ideas; and Max Weber (1864–1920) reinforced Hume's point that knowledge of facts must be distinguished from mere "value judgments."

As my discussion in chapter VIII of John Dunn's thought illustrates, moreover, the search for "clear and distinct" ideas about causes and consequences greatly altered the conceptualization of history. In the nineteenth century, faith in the scientific study of history often included the belief that the causes for past events and the developments caused by decisions in the present could be definitely known, and that both kinds of causes were governed by the same historical laws. Even apart from the theories of Marx or Herbert Spencer, one can cite J.S. Mill's belief, inspired by Comte's faith in the scientific study of history, that scholars using certain methods of "deduction," albeit fallibly, could ascertain both kinds of causes. After Karl Popper exploded the idea of historical laws, however, it became usual in Western academic circles to distinguish between these two kinds of causes and emphasize uncertainty with regard to both the sorting out of historical causes and the consequences of present actions in the unpredictable future.

On the other hand, a series of arguments suggested that even "clear and distinct" factual ideas about observed experience were largely if not entirely subjective, not to mention norms. These arguments constituted a strikingly German contribution to intellectual history and originated with Kant's discovery that the objective world at least partly exists as an object constituted by the human act of interpretation. To analyze this act of interpretation, various Germans fathered the modern ideas of history, culture, and discourse. The "historicism" denounced by Leo Strauss is usually traced back to the thesis of Georg Wilhelm Friedrich Hegel (1770–1831) that history is not just a series of events but a series of events shaping disparate, historically limited ways of perceiving events (except for Hegel's own idea to this effect). The similar thesis of cultural relativism can be traced back to a friend of Kant's, Johann Gottfried Herder (1744–1803), the father of the modern concept of culture. The idea of reasoning as a historical, culturally shaped "discourse" also has strikingly German roots in the work of thinkers like Edmund Husserl (1859–1938) (see below). Similarly, it was Germans like Marx and Freud who led the attempt to reduce the meaning of ideas not to historically limited mental activity but to universal human impulses, such as ego's desire to dominate others. From this standpoint, instead of being possibly true propositions about objective reality, all ideas were attempts to hide or justify such impulses — again, all ideas except the idea to this effect. Elegantly analyzed by Robert K. Merton, the sociology of knowledge drew eclectically from all the above viewpoints.[73] Moreover, ideas intentionally referring to objective reality could be viewed not only as ways of rationalizing universal egoistic impulses or as references meaningful only in a limited historical or cultural environment but also as utterances expressing one individual's idiosyncratic preferences. C.L. Stevenson's philosophy illustrates this approach.[74] At the same time, skepticism about the possibility of normative knowledge was reinforced by the continuing failure to resolve the controversies among all those who continued insisting that norms could be rationally grounded in one or another universal condition.

All in all, then, the GMWER seems to have been fueled especially by (1) a British streak of nominalism and skepticism reflecting a deep feeling that godliness depends on humble recognition of the moral and cognitive shortcomings of human nature; (2) a paradoxically contrary idea, that obsession with precise thinking generated by what Voegelin saw as a search for apodictic ideas with which to master the world; (3) a largely German, ultimately romantic and aesthetic talent for exploring the extent to which subjective ideas constitute the objects of knowledge; and (4) a radical ideal of individual autonomy and freedom fathered by another German, Martin Luther. These four trends permeated much of the public discussions accompanying industrialization, modernization, and democratization in Europe and had an "elective affinity" (Weber) with the social individualism integral to this capitalistic, bourgeois development.

As the GMWER unfolded, however, the boundary between merely subjective opinion and truth about objective reality remained a central and tantalizing issue. However evocative might be the suggestions that thought is merely the subjective product of disparate historical circumstances, it has not been possible completely to refute the idea that thought also includes awareness of objective truth. After all, even apart from the nature of science, the GMWER's arguments themselves depended entirely on the possibility of making objectively true statements. Moreover, it has been impossible so far to produce a clear, elegant, comprehensive specification of the boundary between objectively true ideas and merely subjective ones. Scholars have simply been left with a paradox — abundant evidence indicating both that rationality invariably takes the form of a historically particular discourse, and that human thought continuously refers with great success to objective reality, which indeed includes this very paradox.

Ultimately, therefore, the GMWER revealed a so-far unresolved problem — does the subjective side of thought outweigh the objective, or vice versa? — and in an arbitrary, intuitive, vague, but highly suggestive way alleged that the subjective side should generally be given the benefit of the doubt. In other words, sympathizing with this allegation, many Western intellectuals "turned the corner," so to speak, putting the burden of proof on those claiming to state objective truths. In this way, the realm of ideas honored as knowledge could be kept as pure as possible. Rather than the dogmatic, illogical "relativism" or "historicism" Leo Strauss saw himself resisting, the GMWER really produced a logically viable intellectual style overlying an actually unsolved problem. As such, it reflected the "gnostic" determination to create a sacred sphere of knowledge uncontaminated with untrue ideas, and it meshed with the distinctive development of individualism in the West since the nineteenth century, which included a desire to thin down and minimize the parameters of individual freedom.[75]

The epistemological allegation produced by the GMWER can be better understood by taking into account what seems to be a basic empirical fact. As discussed elsewhere in this chapter, virtually all public discussion entails ideas regarded as indisputable by a we-

group, such as "our" idea that "racism is bad." Such ideas can be
called "clichés," ideas the veridicality of which is so obvious to anyone
participating in the discourse that they appear as uninteresting
platitudes. They form the premises of the discourse. Gadamer called
these premises "prejudices," while John Dunn and others refer to
"rock-bottom" principles. Hayek similarly referred to culturally
formed "schemata of thought" regarded by a population as "self-
evident truths."[76] I use terms such as "absolutistic rules of successful
thinking" (*ssu-hsiang kuei-chü*) (ROST) or "indisputables," i.e., ideas
trite and indisputable in the eyes of the agents of the discourse.

The idea of "indisputables" can be better appreciated by using a
distinction found in John Dunn's writings, that between the ideas of
people in the third person and thinking in the first person. Ideas
other people regard as indisputable can easily appear as disputable to
me, but the ideas I regard as indisputable, such as "racism is bad,"
exhibit the full meaning of indisputability. It is clear, however, that
this full meaning of indisputability is basic to other people's thinking
too, not only my own. Therefore antinomies are formed by the ideas
different people or cultures express about what is indisputably
reasonable, such as the contradiction between discourses #1 and #2.

The GMWER did not eliminate the empirical prevalence of
indisputables. In fact, then, indisputable principles are not
unobtainable. On the contrary, they are unavoidable. Consequently,
whether "racism is bad" can be established as an algorismically
universal principle is not necessarily important, because this
principle is anyway indisputable to the person who believes in it.
Isaiah Berlin expressed this point precisely:

> To realize the relative validity of one's convictions ... and yet stand for them
> unflinchingly ... is what distinguishes a civilized man from a barbarian ...
> Principles are not less sacred because their duration cannot be guaranteed.
> Indeed, the very desire for guarantees that our values are eternal and
> secure in some objective heaven is perhaps only a craving for the certainties
> of childhood or the absolute values of our primitive past.[77]

This approach cannot overcome the apparently absolute and
universal principle that all human thought is to a large extent
permeated with ideas that are indisputable only for a limited group
of people with a particular historical context. Historical relativism in
this sense, however, is not the same as believing that all norms are

equally valid. In other words, this approach of Berlin's obviates the danger of relativism as Strauss defined it. Again, Berlin disappoints those hoping that philosophy can end human conflict by finding the one absolutely true doctrine everyone will affirm, but this hope was dubiously based on the notion not only that such a doctrine is available but also that, if it were discovered, bad people would accept it.

What the GMWER thus produced was not a relativistic way of thinking but one that lowered the epistemic status of indisputables, or at least that of normative indisputables, such as "racism is bad." Instead of identifying such indisputable norms with knowledge produced by reason as the highest, most prestigious mental faculty, Westerners like Berlin attached to these indisputable norms a note of paradox and tentativeness by granting that they might be products of some less prestigious mental faculty, such as the ability to produce disparate cultural patterns or personal idiosyncrasy. As already mentioned, this epistemic demotion led to a kind of epistemic panic including dire warnings of a kind of epistemic "slippery slope." Nietzsche, and Leo Strauss following him, sought to avoid some abyss of relativism apparently implied by such an identification of norms with disparate human impulses. Their solution was to view these impulses as exemplifying the creativity of the human will, and then to view this creativity as a "life-giving" process with an ultimately divine source.[78]

Berlin, however, instead of trying to avoid the abyss of relativism by giving the will a more exalted status than that of reason, suggested that relativism, far from being an abyss, may be a chimera. However banal it may be to root one's moral faith in the platitudes people daily use, the simple fact that people base their lives on ideas they regard as indisputable cannot be reconciled with any urgent warning to avoid the danger of relativism.

It must be remembered, however, that the GMWER constituted only one cultural strand in the West. Even apart from major persisting religious trends and that epistemological optimism seemingly typical of the grass roots everywhere, what has been called "discourse #3" persisted. Thus the GMWER did not seriously affect Locke, the American Founding Fathers at the end of the eighteenth century, or even J.S. Mill (1806–1873), who all still believed in indisputable, objective moral principles revealed by "reason." For

Mill, as for Goethe, the synthesis of *Zweckrationalität* (instrumental rationality) and *Wertrationalität* (the rationality of moral ends) persisted untroubled. Nietzsche was outside the envelope of Mill's intellectual life. Thus Mill did not notice the contradiction in his "On Liberty" between two of his own ideas, that the fallibility of the human mind made every proposition suspect, and that the Greek philosophers, Christianity, science, German humanism, etc. had produced the accumulation of "uncontestable" "truths" on which "civilization" and "progress" depended, and which thus served as the non-scientific, non-legal parameters of *paideia* and freedom.[79]

As the influence of the GMWER spread, however, this central contradiction unnoticed by Mill became a glaring one. Hayek and Popper built on Mill's perspective, like him taking for granted the universal validity of the European Great Tradition as the context of reason and freedom. In their era, however, unlike Mill's, references to this Great Tradition appeared as a *deus ex machina*, an arbitrary claim that the normative society was based on not only Popper's "critical rationalism" but also a privileged cultural tradition. As in all cases of basic cultural change, what had been a "perception" or indisputable premise had turned into a controversial claim.

7. The Chinese Response to the GMWER

Certainly the GMWER has been a socially visible phenomenon. Besides the prominent protests against it mounted by thinkers like Eric Voegelin, Leo Strauss, and Alasdair MacIntyre, one can cite the 1998 encyclical of Pope John Paul II. It focused on the role of Nietzsche in bringing about a "'crisis of confidence in the power of reason.'"[80] It has become a platitude in the West to see a causal link between a set of "relativistic" ideas and a set of disturbing societal tendencies. From this standpoint, once the idea of knowledge was limited to empirically verifiable propositions, it was not possible to know "the essential nature of man" or any "binding principles" regarding the ends of life, good and bad, or human rights. People were stripped of all beliefs except those leaving "man as the ground of himself," i.e. with no guide but subjective impulse. This philosophical outcome then undermined not only traditional ethics but also the German humanistic ideals that inspired J.S. Mill; turned society into a commercialized cultural desert of boredom, vulgarity, banality, and conformity; and led to narcissism, drug abuse, and still more horrifying extremes of moral degeneration.[81] In other words, the GMWER destroyed the non-legal, non-scientific parameters of individual freedom.

In modern Chinese intellectual circles also, the GMWER created controversy, but the controversy was limited and included few if any views accepting the GMWER's epistemologically pessimistic conclusions. The vast majority of the Chinese, including many intellectuals, remained simply unaware of or unresponsive to the GMWER. These included the founders of modern Chinese political thought, Yen Fu and Liang Ch'i-ch'ao, as Huang Ko-Wu (Max K.W. Huang) has vividly shown. By the end of World War I, Liang saw a cultural crisis in the West, but he blamed it on philosophies exalting science and precluding free will, not on any skepticism precluding the objectivity of norms.[82] According to Kao Li-k'o's recent study, even before Liang Ch'i-ch'ao did, Tu Ya-ch'üan (1873–1933), a prominent writer and editor, drew attention to "the crisis of Western civilization." In his eyes too, however, the crisis lay in the failure to realize the known, objective goals of humanity ("the flourishing of morality and the economy"), not in any belief that such objective norms are unknowable, not to mention any conclusive finding to that effect.[83] Similarly, the widespread, epistemologically optimistic scientism studied by D.W.Y. Kwok simply brushed the GMWER aside. As Yang Kuo-jung has shown, Chinese thinkers endorsing logical positivism did not agree with Popper that there is a "dualism" between "is" and "ought" and instead reformulated positivism to derive "ought" from "is."[84] Moreover, it is hard to find any sense of being challenged by the GMWER in the writings of modern humanists like Ch'ien Mu (1895–1990) or Yü Ying-shih (b. 1930).

Real awareness of the GMWER apparently began only with Wang Kuo-wei (1877–1927), a brilliant scholar whose life ended in suicide. A student of Kant, Schopenhauer, and Nietzsche, he held that "the theories which can be loved cannot be regarded as true, and the theories which can be regarded as true cannot be loved."[85]

Wang's acceptance of the GMWER's conclusions, however, was unusual. Most of the Chinese writing responding to the GMWER has precisely sought to prove that, despite its claims, "the theories that can be loved" can be regarded as true. From this standpoint, the GMWER represented major mistakes which had plunged the West into a cultural-societal crisis, and which Chinese thinkers could correct. Besides T'ang Chün-i and Henry K.H. Woo, discussed in this book, Chinese thinkers seeking to correct the mistakes of the GMWER include Mou Tsung-san (1909–1995), Chin Yueh-lin (1895–1984), and Li Tse-hou (b. 1930). T'ang Chün-i's magnificent textbook, *Che-hsueh kai-lun* (An Introduction to Philosophy), was first published in 1961 and addressed just about all the points raised by the GMWER in an extremely systematic and insightful way. Indeed his way of refuting it deserves the most serious consideration and may open up new philosophical vistas, as I shall try to show in a forthcoming article. Mou Tsung-san's keen awareness of the GMWER and his determination to refute its conclusions are also important, given his astuteness as a philosopher and historian of ideas. In his *Chih-te chih-chueh yü Chung-kuo che-hsueh* (Chinese Philosophy and the Intuitive Understanding of Ultimate Reality; 1969), he noted that "Kant himself said that we cannot have an intuitive understanding of the nature of what things ultimately are in themselves." Mou went on: if we accept Kant's definition of this allegedly impossible intuitive understanding, and if we agree with him that such understanding is impossible, then not only is

> all of Chinese philosophy impossible but also all of Kant's own moral philosophy. This we cannot accept. The possibility of this kind of ultimate understanding can be established only by relying on the Chinese philosophical tradition. The West lacks such a tradition. Therefore even Kant with all his wisdom was unable to see that this kind of intuitive grasp of the nature of ultimate reality is actually possible.[86]

Earlier, in a 1960 book, Mou faced discourse #2 head on. He praised Hegel and denounced what he saw as "generally the attitude of intellectuals today in the Free World .... who dismiss 'reason' as a metaphysical term and dismiss 'man's universal nature' as an empty abstraction ... just lapsing into phenomenalism and nominalism, just paying attention to given facts."[87]

The confidence (and anger) with which Mou refuted Western skepticism and logical positivism is reflected in the book written by Li Jui-ch'üan (Lee Shui Chuen), one of his students, about the thought of David Hume. To be sure, Li recognizes the prominence of the GMWER and Hume's central role in it: "Some modern scholars, especially English-American practitioners of logical positivism and analytical philosophy, deeply respect Hume, focusing on his view regarding the problem of cause-and-effect and his distinction between 'is' and 'ought.' They call the former 'Hume's problem' and the latter 'Hume's law.'"

Li, however, does not see this trend as a serious challenge. Instead, he refers to the allegedly common impression that Hume with his "skepticism" and his "theory that ultimate reality is unknowable" (*pu-k'o-chih-lun*) "precisely demonstrated that empiricism is a dead-end street" (*ssu-hu-t'ung*). Hoping to save Hume from having this miserable reputation, Li argues that "at the center" of Hume's philosophy is not his unsuccessful epistemology, which so much current Western philosophy mistakenly appropriated, but his "philosophy of ethics," which Western scholars have largely overlooked, except for Norman Kemp Smith. Focusing on Hume's concept of a "moral sentiment," Li argues that it meshed with, though it was less incisive than, the Confucian philosophy of ethics. It is significant that Li's erudite book was published prominently in Taipei in a series edited by two famous scholars, Wei Cheng-t'ung and Fu Wei-hsun.[88]

Chinese scholars seeing the GMWER as a philosophical "dead end" often conflated this philosophical crisis with that dark Chinese picture, going back at least to World War I, of an imperialistic, capitalistic, dehumanizing West based on instrumental reason in the service of egoistic interests. Even or especially today, this dark picture is still accepted as fact in some of the most sophisticated, Westernized Hong Kong scholarly circles (not to mention Henry K.H. Woo's dark outlook).

In Chinese eyes, however, the trouble with the GMWER was not that it undermined the objectivity of moral principles and so exposed humanity to the danger of barbarism but that it broke apart that unity of human understanding needed to create an ideal society ("linkage"). For instance, in 1997 Ch'en Hsiao-lung, a student of the late famous philosopher Feng Ch'i (1915–1995) and an associate professor of philosophy at Northwest Normal University in Lanchou, published a book on Chin Yueh-lin. Ch'en depicted Lin as addressing an originally Western development that "every modern philosopher must face," the break-up of "the original unity of the quest for a logical understanding of things with the quest for wisdom about ultimate matters." The former

increasingly developed in opposition to the latter, becoming a negation
of the quest for philosophical wisdom about ultimate matters.... To a
significant extent the development of modern Western philosophy can
be seen as a process of increasing separation, opposition, and conflict
between originally unified aspects of existence — the quest for logical
understanding and that for wisdom about ultimate matters. Thus the
problem of the relation between these two became not only an urgent
philosophical question confronted by modern Western philosophy but
also the issue most characteristic of the era as a whole.

Moreover, this "split" (*ko-lieh*) between "scientific rationality" and
"humanism" led to an "excessive inflation" of the former's role in the
thinking of people and so "brought about" "an increasingly severe
degeneration of moral values."[89]

In modern China, however, despite the pessimism of Wang Kuo-
wei, the philosophical mainstream remained unconvinced that the
GMWER's break-up of the "original unity" of ratiocinative and moral
understanding was final. On the contrary, the Western idea it was
final was either brushed aside or regarded as a mistake awaiting
correction by Chinese thinkers.

As Ch'en Hsiao-lung explains, Chin Yueh-lin, who was influenced
by positivism, tried to bridge this gap between science and humanism
by making three basic points. First, in a way reminiscent of Thomas
Reid's "common sense" criticism of his contemporary David Hume,
Chin identified modern Western epistemological pessimism with the
allegedly mistaken premise that human knowledge of the world is
restricted to understanding of the objects appearing in the
consciousness of a thinking subject (*wei-chu fang-shih*). From this
standpoint, truth can be found only by critically examining the
contents of human consciousness, especially sense impressions and
ideas — precisely the signature concept of the GMWER. Chin argued
that "what is given in experience" (*so-yü*) directly coincides with the
real objective world in itself. Thus the "split" between consciousness
and the rest of the world was overcome. Second, with a bow to logical
positivism, Chin emphasized a clear distinction between
ratiocinative, scientific inquiry into the nature of this objective world
and the "metaphysical" "understanding of ultimate matters" (*yuan-
hsueh*). Third, he derived the unity of these two modes of
understanding from the metaphysical one.

Ch'en Hsiao-lung then joined this discussion about how to

overcome the "split" created by the GMWER. Ch'en appreciated Chin's effort but pointed out it had failed, and that the "split" between the two modes of learning thus remained. On the one hand, Ch'en said, the Neo-Confucian metaphysical ideas Chin used to reintegrate ratiocinative with metaphysical understanding were "notions without any foundation" (*hsu-kou*). On the other, it

> must be pointed out here that study of the ultimate unity of things and the discursive analysis of observable things or events inherently presuppose each other and are dialectically one. This kind of unity actually is the concrete manifestation of the dialectical method as applying to both the objective world and that of the human subject. Thus the distinction or contrast between these two modes of thinking is relative, not absolute. Absolutizing this merely relative contrast [as Chin does] creates an uncrossable boundary (*hung-kou*) between the perspective of the subject and the world as object, between ultimate reality and phenomena. Like Hume and Kant, one falls into the fallacious theory that ultimate reality is unknowable (*pu-k'o-chih-lun*).

Thus, Chin sought to "solve the question raised by Hume and Kant" (can a single model of rational knowing answer all factual, normative, and other questions?), but "because this distinction of his splits up the dialectical unity of subject-oriented and object-oriented thought, of ultimate reality and phenomena, and of the study of the ultimate unity of things and discursive knowledge, he could not attain the goal he had set for himself." Indeed, in making this distinction, far from refuting Hume and Kant, Chin had unfortunately been influenced by Hume's view that "'ought' cannot be derived from 'is'" and by Kant's distinction between "'what is it?'" and "'what should be done?'"[90]

In this epistemologically optimistic Chinese context, therefore, the epistemological pessimism of the GMWER was rejected. In many Western eyes, the GMWER had correctly discovered what Popper called an "irreducible dualism ... of facts and standards,"[91] not to mention putting ontological issues outside the boundary of knowledge. In many Chinese eyes, however, the GMWER had not discovered any such thing. Instead, it had revealed a problem which could be solved by Chinese philosophers, whether or not any of them had as yet solved it, that of unifying two modes of understanding currently "split apart." Without unifying them, Ch'en held, it would be impossible to "turn into a unified philosophy all valued ideas in the older and newer philosophies of China and the West" (*hui-t'ung Chung-Hsi*), thus accomplish "the modern transformation of traditional Chinese philosophy," answer the question of "Where should China go?" and so give guidance to the "revolution" needed to turn China from a "traditional" into a "modern society."[92]

Ch'en thus spoke of Immanuel Kant's fallacious "theory that basic aspects of reality are unknowable," just as Li Tse-hou, in his impressive critique of Kant's critiques, wrote that the Marxist philosophy of "praxis" can "turn all that is supposedly unknowable into the knowable."[93]

As already indicated, this philosophical struggle to elucidate the oneness of human understanding and the world has been basic not only to thinkers influenced by Chinese Marxism, such as Chin, Li, and Ch'en, but also to the New Confucian school. Given that this struggle is part of such a broadly shared philosophical agenda in modern China, there is no doubt that this quest for "linkage" was inherited from Neo-Confucianism. This is obvious in the case of New Confucians like T'ang Chün-i (see chapter II). Yet even Li Tse-hou, in his Marxist writings during the Cultural Revolution, explicitly saw a convergence between his views and the "linkage" ideal in Neo-Confucianism:

> If someone objects that, in the structure of the subject as depicted in epistemology and ethics, rationality still persists as a series of abstract, one-sided, fragmentary ideas about outer objects, then one can agree that only in the aesthetic understanding of humanized nature can one find a true, inner, concrete, total interpenetration and unification of society and freedom, reason and feeling, history and concrete reality, humankind and the individual.... This kind of unity is the highest unity, and it also is the human realm China's traditional philosophers referred to as "the oneness of heaven and man."[94]

Achieving this "unity," Li suggested, human "praxis" (*shih-chien*) could avoid the two equally mistaken trends arising out of Kant's epistemological pessimism: the overly "hot" schools, like humanism and existentialism, focusing just on the subject, and the overly "cold" schools, like positivism, centering just on the individual's fragmentary sensory experience and her animalistic side. A correct understanding of praxis, moreover, would also reaffirm Kant's vision of the subject and so eliminate Hegel's and Marx's insensitivity to the individual's quest for freedom and happiness. Thus correcting many Western philosophical mistakes, intellectuals could successfully guide societal processes, which Li, adjusting Marxist materialism, came to see as a process of *chi-tien* (transformation resembling the way chemical precipitates are produced and accumulate) arising out of the ultimately "rational" interaction between society's two "ontological bases" (*pen-t'i*), the materialistic one and the one made up of "culture" and "mentality." Thus aiming for linkage as they transformed China, intellectuals guiding the political center would put their emphasis on "Western learning" supplemented by Chinese learning (*Hsi-hsueh wei t'i, Chung-hsueh wei yung*). In Li's eyes, however, this would be a purified Western learning stripped by Chinese intellectuals of the major philosophical mistakes made by Westerners.[95]

Li's immensely confident way of correcting Western intellectual trends indeed reminds one of Joseph R. Levenson's seminal discovery of the modern Chinese determination to demonstrate the intellectual parity of east and west and Chang Hao's brilliant criticism of Levenson, his point that this Chinese quest for parity sprang not so much from emotion as from what Chinese intellectuals believed to be true. To be sure, what some of them believed was true was that, in learning from the West, they were similar to the traditional scholars seeking to grasp the ultimate wisdom put by the ancient sages into the classics. Many modern Chinese, however, ranging from Liang Ch'i-ch'ao to Chin Yueh-lin, Mou Tsung-san, T'ang Chün-i, Sun Yat-sen, Mao Tse-tung, Li Tse-hou, and innumerable others, had a very different epistemic paradigm in mind: ultimate wisdom could emerge only as Chinese corrected Western mistakes, because the West had produced only a limited number of new, crucial insights, not an authoritative canon solving the most basic philosophical problems and so providing the indispensable guidelines for China's successful modernization.

Yet while some Chinese thinkers thus viewed the GMWER as incorrectly pointing to a "split" between modes of understanding, others have instead used the concept of "paradox" or "irony" (*pei-lun*) to claim that the GMWER's epistemological pessimism is the very key to the "wisdom" with which to dissolve relativism and moral dissonance. Dr. Hans-Georg Möller has seen such irony in the mid-twentieth-century writings of Fung Yu-lan, Hsiung Shih-li, and Mou Tsung-san, noting how their preoccupation with T'ien-t'ai and other Buddhist schools supported this perspective.[96] Today, some avant-garde Beijing circles fluently referring to Nietzsche and Wittgenstein accept the GMWER's "split" between moral-cultural norms and the Popperian quest for scientific knowledge. They explicitly grant that norms cannot be rationally derived from universal principles and are no more than the beliefs subjectively "created" by a particular historical group. As already indicated, however, in Chinese circles, such a denial that moral principles are objective seldom if ever leads to the fear that the content of normative thinking is variable to any dangerous extent. Modern Chinese thinkers have thus proved themselves able not only to depict the GMWER as a mistake but also to accept its chief propositions and then reinterpret them to make them compatible with the premises of the modern Chinese intellectual mainstream, discourse #1.

A good example is an extremely reflexive though loosely crafted article, "The Chinese Opportunity for a Revival of Wisdom," written by Chao T'ing-yang, a philosopher who is attached to the Chinese Academy of Social Science in Beijing, and who is admired today in self-styled avant-garde Beijing circles. His article is part of *Hsueh-wen Chung-kuo* (China Today in Intellectual Perspective), a prominent collection of essays written by eight rising young scholars at leading Beijing institutions and published in 1998 in Kiangsi.

Chao both deplores what he views as the Westernization of Chinese thought and regards Western philosophy as indispensable for revealing the problems philosophy must address. He uses the GMWER to conclude that all existing philosophies or forms of social science today east and west are inadequate, whether those criticized by Wittgenstein for claiming to refer to objective realities independent of subjective beliefs or Wittgenstein's own view that the task of philosophy is just to debunk such references by describing the linguistic forms people have developed.

Consciously trapped in a paradox, then, Chao's analysis thus begins by combining dependence on the critical insights of the GMWER with a total determination to free Chinese thought from subordination to Western philosophical categories, not to mention from the Western implication that Chinese philosophy is invalid. To end this epistemic hegemony, to solve the problems Wittgenstein failed to solve, and so to give China the independent philosophy its national development requires, Chao calls for "a new wisdom":

What I here discuss is a possible way for philosophy to develop. Even though I believe this is the best idea available about how philosophy should develop, I do not know that it is.

According to this idea, we should shift our philosophical awareness, our very mode of thinking, away from the old focus on the idea of knowledge, replacing it with a focus on what is created by human thoughts and actions. That is, we should realize that a culture as a whole, or any of its parts, is just a product of human actions. The basis of a culture, in other words, is not some fixed value or some truth that has already been developed or has not yet been discovered but still is somehow "inherently set forth over there." Instead, the basis of a culture consists of acts of human will or imagination which have caused us to turn the forms of human existence into certain problems and to pursue solutions for these problems.... Simply speaking, such human acts shape history; truths and values emerge out of history; and then new creative responses shape still more history.[97]

Agreeing with the GMWER, therefore, Chao rejects the idea that discursive, rational reflection can reveal objective normative principles:

Of course, we can criticize or explain the nature of some particular cultural facts, because we can think up all kinds of principles, but explanations always end up with principles for which there is no further explanation. Where then are the reasons for these principles? Philosophy has always believed that these reasons can be found through reflection, but how can we know that reflection has anything rational about it? This is the problem that cannot be solved, as already discussed. Reflection is blind, it is a matter of arbitrary hypotheses ...

Given this "blindness" of the quest for knowledge, Chao opts for a "philosophy" that instead celebrates the purely human will to live, to "create," to "solve problems": "wisdom and the power to create are the same." Chao's celebration of the creative will has a Nietzschean ring, but it simultaneously reflects the recurring theme of "praxis" (*shih-chien*) in modern Chinese thought, the rejection of Western philosophies putting the analysis of given facts or the description of language above the task of ethically and "rationally" transforming the world.

Yet if what people should look to is not the rational quest for universal principles but "historically particular creative moments of human imagination and action" (*ch'uang-i*), how can they avoid relativism? Chao is fully aware of this problem: "... it is hard to deny that we still need some principles with which to criticize the various ideas people create."[98]

Dealing with this issue, Chao leaves Isaiah Berlin's path. Instead, he adduces various concepts the universal, meta-historical validity of which he takes for granted (just as he treats "culture" as an ontological given rather than a historical idea used to interpret what is ontologically given). In other words, he falls back on the epistemologically optimistic assumptions that such principles exist and that the human mind can know them. Logically or not, the epistemic opaqueness he noted when emphasizing the dependence of thought on culture fades away beneath the bright glare of obvious universal truths. First, he notes that "truths regarding nature and pure forms," unlike those "regarding life and culture," are "almost pre-fixed." That is, science for him, unlike for Richard J. Bernstein, is still an objective, Popperian system. Second, with regard to those truths "regarding life and culture," he refers approvingly to a variety of partial insights made available by history, east and west, such as some of Wittgenstein's ideas, some of "China's traditional philosophy," and some of Mao's thought, including Mao's idea that China needs "a new way of thinking, a new culture."[99] Thus Chao optimistically presupposes both that, despite the drastic lack of any sacred canon or successful philosophy, history has produced bits of wisdom, and that people have the cognitive resources to pull them together. Third, he takes it as obvious that, whatever the cultural differences, there is no significant disagreement between people about what is "good" and what is "bad." As is virtually always the case in China, the descriptive, anthropological idea of disparate cultures is brushed aside, and philosophical debates remain irrelevant to the unchanging, obvious, universal content of morality. Says Chao: "People sometimes misunderstand the differences between cultures. Actually, in terms of 'substance' or 'content,' the things wanted or approved by the human race are basically the same. Except for some special taboos, it's almost impossible to say that something defined as good by one culture is defined as bad by another."[100] Fourth, Chao takes it for granted that various goals are good, such as the goal of constructing a culture that is "independent," "significant," "strong," and "leading." Similarly, he obviously affirms the ideals of freedom and equality as the Chinese intellectual mainstream has defined them as well as the need for "new" Chinese cultural forms consistent with the "creative act" through which Chinese culture was historically formed.

Given this abundance of overriding criteria with which to "criticize ideas," Chao is confident that intellectuals will be able to tell which ideas are "profound" and "basic enough" to meet the "needs" of the Chinese people in this new "era" of their history, to coincide with the original historical act forming their culture, and to display what he calls "universal value," that is, a value shaping public life "and significant not merely with regard to the private activities of individuals."[101]

In this way, then, Chao ends up paying his respects to the GMWER while filtering out its epistemological pessimism and reaffirming the modern Chinese mainstream vision of an enlightened elite who, in a top-down way, grasp an overriding set of normative principles, thus give the world a "new wisdom," and then use it to transform China's culture and society. Conversely, expressing disdain for "the arguments of the academic marketplace,"[102] Chao, as basically as a Henry K.H. Woo or a T'ang Chün-i, rejects the convergence of China's modernization with the prevalent Western liberal mix of capitalism and democracy as a system governed ultimately by the unpredictable marketplace of individual preferences rather than the "wisdom" of the enlightened elite. Again applying his basic distinction between universal scientific truths and normative understanding, Chao says: "We must introduce all the different kinds of specialized, technical ideas supplied by the humanistic and social sciences of the West but not necessarily the values these disciplines promote."[103] Thus Chao's analysis come to a climax with one of the many contradictions littering the path of modern Chinese epistemological optimism: all cultures define good and bad in essentially the same way, but Chinese should adopt "values" different from those of the West.

Chao's way of reinterpreting the GMWER to filter out its epistemological pessimism is similar to that of Ts'ui I-ming, associate professor of philosophy at East China Normal University, who in 1998 published an article on Kant, "The Boundaries of Knowledge and the Wisdom Seeking the Oneness of Reality." Ts'ui's article, like Chao's, does not meet Western academic standards (e.g. he uses only Chinese translations of Kant and ignores previous work on his problem, such as Mou Tsung-san's and Li Tse-hou's). Yet it is a piece of subtle, systematic philosophizing. Like Li Tse-hou and all other Chinese thinkers I am aware of, Ts'ui vindicates epistemological optimism. Like Li, he holds that "linkage" (knowing how all aspects of existence form a unified whole) is possible. Unlike Li, however, Ts'ui sees Kant's philosophy as correctly showing how this knowledge is possible, rather than incorrectly denying it is possible.

In other words, for Ts'ui, Kant, appearances to the contrary, did not lapse into epistemological pessimism by formulating a "theory that one cannot know the nature of ultimate reality" (*pu-k'o-chih-lun*). Actually, Ts'ui holds, Kant conceptualized "linkage" (*t'ung*) by showing how "reason" not only is the basis of both factual and normative knowledge but also reveals "the unity of man and the world." Thus Kant indicated a way out of the human "predicament," the fact that "man's nature is such that he seeks to grasp absolute, unconditional existence but actually lives amidst limiting conditions."

Kant, Ts'ui recognizes, seems to preclude any way out of this predicament, because he posits "an uncrossable boundary between phenomena and things-in-themselves." As Ts'ui sees it, however, Kant erected this boundary to refute the way Descartes and conventional theology had sought knowledge of the whole. The more important effect of his philosophy, even if not intended in a completely conscious way, was to "reveal the paradox inherent in the limits of knowledge and so to transcend this very paradox."

I cannot here describe step by step Ts'ui's thought-provoking arguments that Kant "turned the problem of the unity of man and the world into the problem of the unity of reason," and so into that of the "unity of man himself" as "the subject" of experience. My point here is just to adduce one more current Chinese way of rejecting the GMWER's epistemological pessimism, its "theory that knowledge of the nature of ultimate reality is not possible" (*pu-k'o-chih-lun*).[104]

This Chinese epistemological optimism is so deeply-rooted that it is evident even in the writings of young Chinese scholars today whose training has been in the current Anglo-American tradition of academic philosophy. As discussed in chapter X below, this point is illustrated by the way John Rawls's "political liberalism" was critiqued in 2001 by Hsu Han, an assistant professor of philosophy at Chung-cheng University in Taiwan. An article published that same year in Beijing by Hsu Hsiang-tung illustrates still another epistemologically optimistic way of rejecting the ethical skepticism promoted by the

GMWER.[105] Working to obtain a Ph.D. in philosophy at Columbia University, he has no inclination to vindicate any metaphysical grasp of ontological reality. Instead, he is worried that philosophical failures to refute ethical relativism undermine the universalism of human rights, which China too should respect. Rejecting such "relativism," his erudite, thoughtful article is focused on the discussions developed by contemporary British and American academic philosophers such as Alasdair MacIntyre, Bernard Williams, John Rawls, Amartya Sen, Martha Nussbaum, and Barbara Herman.

Unlike many Chinese scholars, therefore, Hsu accepts the fundamental GMWER finding that critical reasoning about ethics, if not all reasoning, is blurred in together with actually questionable assumptions uncritically regarded as indisputable by one historical segment of humanity (a "tradition" or "culture") and not necessarily regarded as such by any other segment. Thus Hsu's problem, like MacIntyre's, is how both to recognize this apparently objective fact about the nature of critical thinking and to vindicate the "objectivity" and "universal" validity of moral principles by refuting the moral relativism implied by this apparent fact. He addresses this problem by using the current Western academic discussions revolving around Aristotle's "practical reason" and Kant's idea of a universal moral imperative implied by reason.

All these discussions try in a cautious and nuanced way to establish some "middle ground" between relativism and objective truth (see below, section 11). They often start by noting that the human mind, however entangled in a particular culture, must have some ability to make true statements about the objective nature of the universal human condition. Otherwise, the proposition that all critical reasoning is entangled in a particular culture could not be true. Moreover, the idea of universal norms applying to all cultures is logically implied when members of different cultures compare each other's cultures and argue about which cultural pattern is better. The tension between this universalistic horizon and any culturally given set of norms is similarly illustrated by what Hsu sees as another objective fact, "the shattering of values in modern society."[106]

Given this hint of a universalistic horizon, Western philosophers have probed in at least two directions. On the one hand, they have tried to distinguish as precisely as possible between this horizon and ideas misleadingly projected into it by a particular cultural tradition.

On the other hand, they have sought to outline a limbo where the separation between cultural bias and universal norm is a struggle that can never be completed. Hsu wants to offer as optimistic as possible a view of this limbo, if not to dispel it altogether. His goal is "mainly to reveal how [MacIntyre's] 'transcendence' of relativism is not thorough enough."[107]

Like MacIntyre, he starts with the premise that humans inherently are "social" beings. Living in a group creates the possibility of conceptualizing a totally "good life." Hsu also draws on Rawls's idea that one can devise "an appropriately constructed view of society that everyone can accept."[108] For Hsu, moreover, the ideal of a "good life" implies that all people are individuals equally able as "moral subjects" freely to decide to act with self-respect and compassion for others. Only in this way can people be truly "human." From this understanding one can derive rules of conduct that can be applied in a "sensitive," "correct," "appropriate" way to culturally different circumstances. Thus to apply them, however, one has to develop "habits" needed to form "virtues" and "correct moral judgments." One also has to achieve "reflective equilibrium" by "thinking profoundly" about how to combine seemingly universal imperatives with the norms of the concretely given historical situation. Politically in modern times, as Hsu sees it, the universalistic rules thus grasped logically imply human rights and obligations, the national right of self-determination, a principle of legitimate governance based on some notion of a social contract, and so on. Hsu grants that the extent to which such political ideals can be practically implemented is limited by the national need for "unity" and "stability." This practical need, however, does not itself amount to a principle of morality, he holds, and so it cannot be rationally adduced to preclude efforts increasingly to implement morality. Hsu's optimistic conclusion:

> Using inferences derived from the theories of the relevant [cultural] background, we can determine which principles best match judgments based on a process of profound reflection, the latter in turn beginning with a certain narrow reflective equilibrium. If these culturally derived influences support these principles, the latter in turn will exert pressure on and so lead to revision of the above judgments originally reached through profound reflection. Eventually, these judgments, principles, and culturally derived influences will support each other. Thus in a broad

sense they will reach equilibrium, and so these principles and judgments can be rather effectively defended.[109]

Apart from Hsu's optimistic approach to this Western philosophical problematique, I would add that the latter, in my view, does correctly identify the universal nature of human thinking as paradoxically poised between culturally inherited premises and a reflective ability to refer to objective reality and universal issues. This widely recognized paradox indeed is the ontological starting point for my concept of discourse discussed below.

According to my concept, however, the objective facts that one can directly grasp and reason about without the intervention of a particular interpretative framework provided by one's own historically-rooted discourse are very limited. Indeed, there may be none except for the linguistic content of this discourse itself, including its absolutistic rules of successful thinking (see below). I would say that even the very concept above of discourse as a paradoxical ontological starting point is a way of interpreting my ontological setting, as opposed to the full ontological reality of the linguistic symbols I directly apprehend and use. As I see it, therefore, one cannot state as an objective fact that human beings are "social beings" (*pace* George Mead), or that there has been a "shattering of values in modern society." (Similarly, one cannot regard "culture" as an ontological given.) These are merely interpretative, controversial ideas based on a historically particular set of rules of successful thinking, including the sociologistical perspective. Similarly, such rules, not some algorismic rationality, are the basis for Hsu's distinction between moral political demands and some amoral view that the need for political stability limits the extent to which certain moral principles can be implemented. According to my rules of successful thinking, a program to implement certain moral ideals does not necessarily carry more moral weight than the goal of political stability, because both affect the happiness and well-being of others, the citizenry. From my standpoint, then, "profound reflection" to develop moral standards in a critical way means trying to uncover the rules of successful thinking basic to one's reasoning and critically comparing them to other rules (e.g. comparing discourse #1 to discourse #2, as discussed below). This differs from Hsu's way of treating some historical interpretations of what is ontologically given as perceived facts and applying to them unexamined rules of successful thinking labeled "rationality." Behind every use of "reason," "knowledge," "morality," or "culture" or of terms like "thinking profoundly," "reflective equilibrium," or "appropriate" lies a historically particular set of rules of successful thinking regarded as indisputable by the we-group involved, and these have to be unpacked if one is to pursue critical moral awareness (see sections 8, 11, and 13 below and chapter VIII, section 6).

It is convenient here to put into further context this distinction between my notion about how to pursue critical awareness and that developed by Hsu. Both come out of the GMWER, as do Richard J. Bernstein's emphasis on dialogue, John Rawls's concept of "the reasonable," and John Dunn's way of extracting overriding principles from historicism (see section 11). All of these efforts struggle with the ontologically ultimate paradox of a human mind both limited by the linguistic symbols peculiar to only one segment of humanity and able to refer to objective reality and universal issues. Therefore they all preclude metaphysical efforts to realize critical awareness by ignoring the historicity of human thought and assuming that human reflexivity (or even "intuition" or "dialectical reasoning") can directly grasp the ultimate, ontological nature of the cosmos as the objective source of the rules of morality, history, and physical nature. This metaphysical approach has constituted the Chinese philosophical mainstream in the twentieth century, as Yü Chen-hua has shown.

This is not, however, to preclude all philosophical efforts to refute Hume and derive morality from objective, factual conditions of human existence common to all cultures and historical periods. Discussed in chapter IX, Hayek's scientistic effort in this direction is not successful, according to my rules of successful thinking, but T'ang Chün-i's suggestions strike me as profound, though he simultaneously veers off in the above metaphysical direction. His reasoning in this context, however, is only partly touched on in chapter II.

Li Qiang's 1998 book on liberalism, discussed in chapter V below, illustrates still another Chinese response to the GMWER. He displays considerable understanding of the GMWER combined with an effort to evade its epistemological pessimism. His approach also picks up on the currently fashionable term "irony" or "paradox." He makes use of it to show how Humean epistemological pessimism is actually an extraordinarily effective way to vindicate absolute moral values and instill them in people. In a most incisive way, Li emphasizes the moral implications of two values that indeed escaped the relativization of the GMWER and were strongly institutionalized in Western liberal democracies, equality and individual moral-intellectual autonomy. In Li's eyes, the institutionalization of these two values meant that Westerners to a large extent became individuals filled with a deep respect for each other's dignity and autonomy. In other words, they realized the Confucian golden rule in practice (*chi yü li erh li jen*). For Li, therefore, the Hayek-Popper model of Western liberalism is only seemingly based on a morally-neutral legal structure, because this structure, more than any philosophy could, powerfully implements the universal basis of all forms of substantive morality and so reduces the amount of selfishness in history.

8. Controversies about How to Describe Political Theories: Political Theories as Criticizable Discourses

Yet despite his accepting much of the Hayek-Popper model, it is far from clear that Li has fully thought through the question of transferring this model to China, or that, if he has, he represents a growing intellectual trend. All in all, the GMWER helped create a major, distinctive kind of Western political theory clashing with the contemporary Chinese intellectual mainstream, notably by defining the good society as one using only thin parameters to limit the free interplay of individual preferences in the three marketplaces. But how should people think about this clash?

Theoretically, one could simply contemplate it as a factual aspect of the global intellectual situation. In fact, however, it consists of polemical exchanges that aggravate dangerous international tensions. Can these tensions be assuaged? Are people on both sides of the Pacific reflexive and open enough critically to seek out some common ground? Li Qiang notes that Western liberalism was an evolving tradition repeatedly reviving itself by incorporating the ideas of its critics. Why should not the clash between Chinese and Western political theories lead to similar dialogical processes of internal criticism and cultural revision? In this case, however, the ideas that need to be debated are not simple concrete proposals, such as Marx's of a progressive income tax, but epistemological, soteriological perspectives that form the contours of a civilization.

To criticize such contours while standing outside the envelope of one's own intellectual tradition seems impossible. Thus my way of describing and critiquing the clash between discourse #1 and discourse #2 is itself rooted in discourse #2. I necessarily begin in an epistemologically optimistic way by expressing my basically unshakable assumptions regarding the ontologically ultimate nature of the paradoxical universal human condition: human life is opaque to a large extent, but reflection leading to truth is possible, including the truth that all political thought has to conceptualize the four aspects of political life noted above. Moreover, pursuing this process of reflection, one affirms what J.S. Mill called "the dignity of man as a thinking being," an ideal founded in the West on the image of Socrates and resonating with the common modern Chinese intellectual ideal of *tzu-chueh* (becoming as aware as possible of all the aspects of one's own life situation). This ideal implies that, to understand a political theory in a balanced, unprejudiced way, two steps are needed: describing it as accurately, comprehensively, and lucidly as possible, so as to avoid misunderstanding it, and identifying and critically debating the criteria of successful thinking with which to evaluate it. In other words, one has to be thoroughly empirical and inductive in ascertaining what the ideas are which make up a historical body of thought about political life, and one has to be as thoughtful and open as possible when arguing about how to evaluate them.

As mentioned in section 2 above, my view of political theory is not a mainstream view, and this includes my strongly differentiating the problem of describing the ideas making up a political text from that of evaluating them. One can, for instance, describe the contributions made by thinkers from Hobbes through Hegel to the evolution of the Western idea of the civil society, but it is quite another thing to state that "Hegel's theory ... shows the underlying dilemmas of modern ethical life." This implies that there is an identical condition experienced by various historical societies east and west ("modern ethical life"), and that Hegel's statements about this metaphysical object are true. Whether it is useful to posit the existence of such a metaphysical object and whether one can verify Hegel's statements about it are all questions that require careful consideration on their own, and that have to be distinguished from the task of describing what Hegel said and meant.

One would think that controversies about the evaluation of ideas would be particularly hard to resolve. After all, as just discussed, the GMWER highlighted the difficulty or impossibility of finding objective normative standards. Conversely, in a positivistic era exalting the importance of empirical data, it should be easy to agree on the need for a thoroughly empirical, inductive approach to the description of historical ideas such as political theories.

Strangely enough, however, the question of how to describe political theories is extremely complex and controversial, while the problem of evaluating them, as I have already presumed to suggest, is actually a non-problem, since indisputable, absolutistic standards of evaluation are not unavailable, they are unavoidable (though they still need to be uncovered and critically discussed).

In seeking to describe a political theory comprehensively, I assume, as already argued, that an actual political theory which influences behavior consists of a complex variety of logically interdependent "because" considerations about how to improve political life, not just of a few prominent ideas. To describe such a theory, one first has to identify it as a delimited, specific object that can be empirically observed. Only then can one hope to minimize the projection of subjective stereotypes into this object, arrive at some cumulative set of falsifiable propositions about it, and so achieve some emic, empathetic understanding (*Verstehen*) of the way other people have felt and thought about their political lives. Probably such understanding is possible, moreover, only if this delimited object is a long written text or series of texts. According to my experience, worldviews, whether platitudinous or original, are so complicated that understanding them is impossible without leisurely analysis, and only their availability in written form permits such leisurely study. One cannot, therefore, describe Chinese political theory as some aspect of "Chinese culture," that is, an essentially identical way of thinking typical of untold millions of Chinese over thousands of years. Such a culture might or might not exist, but it cannot be observed. What can be observed are specific written texts, specific social scenes, and the inventoried responses of individuals to an opinion survey. To be sure, a text can only constitute one or more cultural strands, and the representativeness of any such strand is a further empirical issue (see below).

Then there is the problem of spotting every important utterance in the text or set of texts, whether a single word, a sentence, or a series of sentences forming a single idea. This criterion of importance is especially controversial. It requires a decision about the whole structure formed by all the "because" ideas in the text. An idea is important if it is logically indispensable to maintain that structure, the way that a stone pillar is indispensable to the structure of a building. Probably an utterance is indispensable in this sense whenever it is much repeated or when it is logically needed to link together much-repeated utterances.

Yet this definition of "indispensability" will hardly settle all controversy. When, for instance, I tried to describe all the clichés common to all the main Neo-Confucian texts (*Sung-Ming li-hsueh*), I noted a pair of much-repeated terms brushed aside in most modern discussions of Neo-Confucianism, *wei-fa* (not yet issued) and *i-fa* (already issued). This culturally distinctive way of conceptualizing the human condition depicted the "feelings" in the human mind as constantly moving out of a state of absolute moral purity ("not yet issued") and into a realm of concrete experience fraught with the danger of moral pollution ("already issued"). One of my colleagues said these terms were not "important" for one of the leading Neo-Confucians, Wang Yang-ming (1472–1529), about whom he had written an excellent book.

I replied that these terms were used some seventeen times in the main Wang Yang-ming text, that they appeared in this text as an uncontroversial way of describing the universal functioning of the human mind, and that the mental process they depicted was logically integral to the whole structure of reality articulated in this text.[110]

My colleague never agreed with me. His disagreement precisely illustrates how controversial an issue the description of ideas is. As I see it, my desire to describe a body of thought as a whole clashed with his intention to pull out those ideas in a text that shed light on certain issues important to him. Along with many other scholars (see below), this scholar rejected the idea of first describing a set of ideas comprehensively and only then arguing about what the currently significant issues are, and about whether this particular set of ideas shed any light on them.

What is clear, however, is that if a scholar wants to pursue the goal of description, she has to maximize her "openness" to historical voices by maximally replacing her judgments with a certain "ignorance" or innocence, recovering a kind of original wonder at the variety of ways in which words can constitute the world, much as Robert Redfield tried to observe a "little community" by promiscuously or even "stupidly" shifting his attention from one detail to another; much as Leo Strauss tried simply to "listen" to historical conversations; and much as Martin Heidegger tried to bypass the conventions of European philosophy in order to recover the "original experience of the mystery and wonder of existence."[111] It is necessary to notice the much-repeated utterances making up the premises of a discourse, rather than using twentieth-century categories to prejudge the discourse as being of a certain type. This kind of prejudgment is illustrated by the way some philosophers today analyze Confucian texts only by first assuming that these texts represent a primarily "practical" approach to life. Such a word is loaded with modern connotations. Whatever the "practical" ideas of Confucians, these were in the context of their highly distinctive way of perceiving the given world as the *setting* of their practical efforts. Whether their ideas were utopian and highly impracticable is still another issue one should not prejudge.

Moreover, in the case of utterances that are very general in meaning, such as the modern Chinese words *min-chu* (democracy) and *tzu-yu* (freedom), the connotations of the utterance have to be unpacked. This is especially important when the Chinese word is presented by the Chinese as the translation of a foreign word but then is filled by them with meanings drawn from their own tradition.[112] Yet deciding what utterances can be regarded as forming a cluster of connotations is often a highly controversial matter. Can utterances from spatially or temporally separated passages be lifted out of these passages and put into one cluster of meanings? If they cannot be, unpacking the meanings conveyed by an utterance may be impossible.

Ultimately the question is how to decide what the context of any idea is. Asking what *jen* (caring as much for others as for oneself) meant in *The Analects of Confucius,* is one permitted to use as the context of this term only those passages in which this particular word occurs, or can one cluster together all the utterances expressing Confucius's vision of the ideal personality, such as *te* (virtue), *chung-shu* (sincerity and empathy), *chi yü li erh li jen* (seek to realize for others what you seek to realize for yourself), or the emphasis on avoiding *yuan* (resentment)?

In other words, to what extent can an outside observer shift around passages in the text in order to define the context of an utterance? To what extent can she decide questions of context by setting up modern analytical categories such as "the ideal personality" and then clustering together all utterances she finds logically pertinent to such a category? To what extent are any such categories arbitrarily made up?

That is, as one unavoidably divides up the utterances making up a political theory into a series of topics, is there any universal list of topics addressed by all political theories and so serving as a kind of common denominator of political theories?

Trying to find such a common denominator, most scholars cautiously use only very general ideas, such as "the concept of man," "basic philosophical commitments," or "way of seeing the world." I think, however, that some "middle-range" concepts are available to define the universal agenda of political theories. Thus, as already discussed, I use four categories (the goal of political life, the means to reach it, other aspects of the given world, and the nature of knowledge) (see section 2 above).

The need to describe ideas comprehensively, however, led me also to take note of the insight of scholars like Robert N. Bellah and Benjamin I. Schwartz that historical ideas appear not only as rather static belief structures but also as ongoing "arguments" or "problematiques." I thus suggested in *Escape from Predicament* that, whether pertaining to goals, means, the rest of the given world, or the nature of knowledge, all utterances appeared either as controversial if not idiosyncratic "claims" energetically defended in the text or as uncontroversial "perceptions" requiring no defense, that is, clichés. The latter, indeed, were precisely those ideas discussed above that are regarded by a group as indisputably obvious, including the group's shared agenda of unresolved issues.[113]

This analytical approach has much in common with Leo Strauss's point about "the persistence through historical change of the same fundamental problems, not any particular solution to them."[114] There do seem to be topics of discussion common to all political philosophy. Strauss, however, excessively wary of cultural relativism, proposed to infer what these topics were from study of the "great"

Western thinkers, instead of listing the most basic aspects of political life (goals, means, the rest of the given world, and the idea of knowledge), describing how culturally different intellectual traditions have conceptualized them, and then addressing the philosophical problem of how to evaluate these disparate conceptualizations. For instance, as McAllister put it, he held that the "permanent problems concern the irremovable tensions between politics and philosophy, between practical matters and theory, between is and ought," instead of comparing the Western concept of knowledge, out of which this tension had arisen, with Chinese concepts of knowledge, which preclude such tension. In other words, Strauss equated Western epistemological pessimism and indeed certain Western goals as well (such as the Greek ideals of "the noble, the excellent, the good") with the inherent nature of the universal human situation, instead of asking how to evaluate culturally different conceptualizations of this situation.[115] As already mentioned, asking how to evaluate culturally different concepts is hardly to lapse into cultural relativism, since no one can avoid an evaluation based on premises indisputable to her. The only question is whether she will just arbitrarily and uncritically use the premises she grew up on or identify them and then critically assess them in the light of alternative premises.

Thus seeking a way to describe political theories accurately, comprehensively, and lucidly, I realized that the framework I had come to use coincided with an idea that has become increasingly fashionable, that of a "discourse." The history of the idea of discourse has not yet been fully worked out. Like the modern concepts of history and culture, its roots are German.[116] It goes back at least to the turn of the century, when the GMWER was underway. Skepticism and empiricism were eroding the widespread nineteenth-century faith in progress based on scientific laws of history or social evolution. Increasingly prevalent was what Heidegger attacked as the "subjectivity" of modern life, the tendency to define values as purely human products and so risk the danger, as Heidegger saw it, of "historicism and relativism."[117] One way out of this danger was behaviorism, which appeared as a methodology seemingly putting the study of human existence on a completely scientific footing. As Richard J. Bernstein has shown, however, scholars like Max Weber, Edmund Husserl, Alfred Schutz, Ludwig Wittgenstein, Jürgen

Habermas, Isaiah Berlin, Peter Winch, and Wilfrid Sellars resisted behaviorism. Generally speaking, their efforts led to a picture of human beings as "self-interpreting," inherently "social" creatures using language to form an "intersubjective," "meaningful" "everyday life world" inherently susceptible to "criticism." This picture of an "intersubjective world" could then easily be combined with a naturalistic, sociologistical view of human beings as biological, symbol-making creatures forming communities. It also meshed with increasing interest in the problem of language. That is, it was increasingly combined with an interest in describing a particular "life world" as a kind of verbalized structure. As Berlin put it in 1962, "the first step to understanding of men is the bringing to consciousness of the model or models that dominate and penetrate their thought and action." Besides "model" and "discourse," terms like "paradigm" and "grammar" appeared.[118] As used by gifted scholars like Kenneth Burke, Quentin Skinner, and J.G.A. Pocock, this way of describing ideas was particularly innovative and valuable in revealing how the meaning of a body of thought turned on not only the doctrine it explicitly emphasized but also many other verbalized notions forming the doctrine's context and regarded in their day as too ordinary to serve as the subject matter of any serious analysis. Scholars digging up such notions and showing how they affected the meanings of key ideas such as "nature" or "democracy" showed how the idea of discourse could be empirically and profitably used. Their approach was very different from the loose use of "discourse" to refer in a vague, stereotypical way to some body of ideas allegedly typical of one society or another, as illustrated by how one Chinese intellectual in the 1990s spoke of another's "strong identification with the mainstream discourse and ideology of the West."[119]

To be sure, as noted especially by S.N. Eisenstadt, any culturally inherited paradigm or grammar can be or even necessarily is combined with reflexivity, that open-ended ability to be critical, imaginative, and oriented to objective reality as one uncovers and considers revising inherited premises. How else could the GMWER have occurred or that revolution in male-female relations sparked by the writings of Simone de Beauvoir? The discussion in section 7 above of Li Qiang's, Ts'ui I-ming's, Chao T'ing-yang's, and Hsu Hsiang-tung's reactions to the GMWER illustrates how the cogency of an argument carries over from one cultural setting to another. Even if any of these scholars tried to change the meaning of the GMWER's arguments, he still was intellectually "pushed" by these arguments into reformulating his own views. Indeed, Ts'ui I-ming's idea of "paradox" amounts to not only an effort to make clear what Kant allegedly failed to see fully but also some acceptance of Kant's argument about the scope of knowledge. Linkage was still possible, Ts'ui insisted, but only on Kant's terms.

Moreover, far from moving along the prefixed tracks of a closed, clearly structured symbol system, thinking is often unclear, convoluted, or intentionally paradoxical. It is even unclear that either an individual himself or someone who knows him intimately can on demand produce a clear inventory of all the verbalized beliefs motivating him, not to mention unverbalized ones. After all, this inventory includes many clichés, as opposed to those ideas that make up a viewpoint or doctrine consciously pursued by an individual in the face of objections, and that therefore are at the forefront of her consciousness. Having the goal of overriding these objections, an individual seldom also has the goal of comprehensively describing all of his or her own thoughts, including the many clichés of the day. Only someone else who has this goal can succeed in describing them. A discourse is not manifest, it has to be uncovered.

Thinking in a vacillating way without clearly understanding all of one's own beliefs is typical especially of people participating in more than one discourse. Thus the boundaries between discourses are inherently amorphous, as noted below. Nevertheless, widely shared, habitual, logically interrelated utterances are still basic to the "life worlds" occupied by large groups.

Each of these verbalized life worlds, it should be added, has been that of a we-group. This point was implied by Charles Peirce's idea of truth as something affirmed by a community.[120] Ideas are believed in by "us." For instance, John Dunn has written: "If we are most of us nationalists in some measure now, we are certainly not necessarily insensitive to claims of supra-national human solidarities and we are still more certainly most of us not at all like Nazis."[121] Or take a typical philosophical remark: "The purpose of moral philosophy is to identify principles by which we can tell right from wrong."

Who are "we"? The term is typically used to denote humanity as a whole throughout history as a kind of existence invariably exposed to and able to become aware of certain unchanging aspects of human life. Thus Hume and Kant assumed that certain structures each perceived in his own mind were necessarily present in every human being's mind: "Our experience tell us ..." This assumption, however, refers to a metaphysical object, since the structure of all human minds can be neither empirically observed nor inferred from logic. It is open to doubt, however, that there are such metaphysical objects whose nature can be described. What is empirically verifiable is that many if not all discourses depend on this concept of "we" to make publicly meaningful points. What "we" at the very least refers to, then, is the idea of an idealized and amorphous community with which ego identifies. A good example of this paradigm is the common Chinese reference to "we intellectuals" (*wo-men chih-shih fen-tzu*) as an epistemically privileged community.

Such epistemic communities, however, are not entirely amorphous. Each is necessarily identified with an epistemically privileged historical development, if not a geographical location as well. This idea of an epistemic community, in other words, imposes on global history a certain system of stratification according to which humankind is divided up into the more and the less enlightened. For instance, my we-group to a large extent identifies itself with the GMWER, which Chinese we-groups, to a large extent at least, have regarded as unenlightened. A large population regarded as "a society" or "a culture" typically consists of a number of such we-groups. The discourse of each partly overlaps, partly conflicts with the discourses of the other we-groups, and the degree of overall integration varies greatly from society to society. Unless one can demonstrate a high degree of such integration or show that a population possesses only one discourse, one cannot precisely describe "a culture." That is, one can precisely describe only particular discourses, as this book tries to do (as well as other kinds of empirically determinate objects).

Finally, it should be noted that the idea of a we-group's discourse coincides with what John Dunn calls thinking in the first person and so raises the question of "emic" understanding, to use the anthropological term. "Etic" categories, such as "goal" and "given world," unavoidably intrude into any understanding of a third person's discourse, but the effort to approximate emic understanding lies at the very heart of the description of discourses.

A discourse, then, is a discussion carried on by a we-group

agreeing that certain ideas are indisputable, sharing a sense of what the indisputably unresolved issues are, and arguing about how to address this agenda. Addressing such an agenda, a political theory is a claim about how to improve the political life of such a group. Thus it is a series of logically interdependent "because" utterances defining the goal of political life, the means to reach it, other aspects of the given world, and the nature of knowledge, or, more precisely, addressing those questions left unresolved by the shared beliefs of the group about these four seemingly universal topics. The discourse of the group consists of these shared beliefs plus all the controversial claims spawned by them. At bottom, a discourse is a paradoxical combination of culturally inherited premises with a reflexivity oriented to objective reality and universal issues. To describe a discourse, then, one has to strive for the kind of astuteness with which Leo Strauss read a text, but this astuteness has to be used to spot not only the intent of a particular "great" thinker but also the ordinary, platitudinous utterances everyone in the discourse uses to denote what she regards as the obvious nature of the goal of life, the means to reach it, the rest of the given world, and knowledge.

This idea of discourse overlaps that concept of culture recently revived by scholars like Daniel Jonah Goldhagen, Francis Fukuyama, Thomas Sowell, Samuel P. Huntington, and David S. Landes.[122] They have all revived the old objections to rational choice theory by adducing vast amounts of empirical data to illustrate the persistence of prevalent, alogical, culturally-rooted premises and habits underpinning political and economic behavior. Alex Inkeles has similarly helped revive the idea of "national character" as a socially inherited pattern of values.[123]

My idea of "discourse," however, leans toward Robert N. Bellah's idea of culture as an ongoing "argument" rather than as a more static set of mass beliefs.[124] Moreover, applied to describe a set of "arguments" about goals, means, the rest of the given world, and the nature of knowledge, the image or the idea of a discourse makes clearer what people often mean by "rationality" as an indisputable way of thinking about praxis and its phenomenal setting.

I am not qualified to discuss the many philosophical theories about how "logic," "rationality," "knowledge," and "truth" should be defined, such as the well-known definition of "knowledge" as "justified true belief" or Alfred Tarski's definition of "truth," which

Popper embraced. There is no need here to debate whether any of these concepts can be defined in a transcultural, algorismic way. My point here is only the empirical one that, according to my observation, the discourse of any we-group is based on ideas regarded as indisputable by that we-group, and that we-groups loosely use generic labels like "reasonable," "truth," and "knowledge" to lump together all the kinds of thinking based on these indisputables and to reject all the kinds that are not.

Contrary to the rational choice school, these generic labels cover many instrumental calculations, not only goals. True, logic and natural science clearly constitute a universally rational algorism vital to instrumental calculations. The latter, however, also include ideas about historical causation in the past and the future; these ideas are logically integral to the pursuit of human goals; and they too take the form of knowledge in the eyes of the historical groups following them. Like goals, therefore, ideas about means and evidence are culturally influenced, varying from one discourse to the next. This is illustrated below by the contrast between discourse #1 and discourse #2. True, the idea of "discourse" still implies the existence of a universally identical reflexivity oriented to objective reality and universal issues. This reflexivity, however, does not amount to access to a cleanly distinctive, universally correct way to think about truth, morality, political goals, and evidence about means, because it is paradoxically intertwined with culturally acquired premises.

Again, if "rationality" thus should be seen as a criterion formed by a culturally shaped discourse, this may imply cultural relativism as the theory that preference for a particular discourse cannot be based on a universal, unchanging, algorismic standard. It does not, however, imply cultural relativism as the theory that such a preference is arbitrary. A preference for, say, a discourse favoring equality and freedom cannot be arbitrary if, like Isaiah Berlin, one perceives these principles as indisputably preferable to competitive ones.

Relativism, therefore, does not exist as a problem impeding the search for indisputable standards with which to evaluate historical discourses after describing them. To repeat, such standards are not unavailable but rather unavoidably present in the discourse of virtually anyone participating in a discourse. From this simple point, moreover, one can infer the definition of a correct political theory: part of a discourse, it is a set of ideas that elucidate the nature of political goals, of means, of the rest of the given world, and of knowledge and elucidate them in a way according with the epistemic standards or rules of successful thinking regarded as indisputable by the we-group evaluating this theory. (This methodology is applied below.)

Yet even if relativistic theories cannot lessen the sense of indisputability with which people view the ideas they use to evaluate political ideas and situations, many scholars use relativistic views to argue that there can be no objective description of ideas, only subjective interpretations shaped by the historical conditions responsible for the mentality of the interpreter. Thus once again the relativism allegedly produced by the GMWER threatens to invalidate the methodology used in this book: describing a political theory and then evaluating it.

To be sure, the boundary between texts as objective facts and subjectively formed indisputables used to interpret them tends to be blurred. For instance, as already noted, in arguing that political theories should be described as objective facts, I have had to define a political theory as a certain kind of empirical object, and this definition turned out to reflect my own culturally inherited, pragmatic ideas about how to think intelligently about political life.

Yet, going back to the paradox above, facts and ideas can be objectively described. The evidence is overwhelming. John K. Fairbank's *The Great Chinese Revolution, 1800–1985*, published in 1987, is based on a mainstream American academic culture vastly different from the Maoist and post-Mao Chinese intellectual conditions that influenced the thinking of Chin Kuan-t'ao and Liu Ch'ing-feng when they wrote *K'ai-fang-chung-te pien-ch'ien: Tsai lun Chung-kuo she-hui ch'ao wen-ting chieh-kou* (China's Transformation in the Course of Becoming Open to the Cosmopolitan World: Another Analysis of Chinese Society's Ultra-stable Structure; 1993). To a large extent, however, both books report the same familiar facts about the Opium War and the rest of modern Chinese history. When scholars are not liars, they repeat each other, indeed ad nauseam, when discussing the same objective reality, even when their cultural, intellectual, and political backgrounds and interests are vastly different.[125]

Or take the case of Li Tse-hou. Born in central China, he was nineteen years old when the Communists took power in 1949, was subsequently educated at Peking University, and developed as an intensely Marxist scholar whose enthusiastic endorsement of Mao's basic vision persisted at least through the middle 1980s. In the 1970s, he used Chinese translations of Immanuel Kant's writings to write and publish a famous critique of Kant's philosophy.[126] Hardly the same background and political interests as those of W.H. Walsh, a professor of logic and metaphysics at the University of Edinburgh, who wrote the lucid section on Kant's philosophy in the *Encyclopedia of Philosophy*, published in 1967, just before the Cultural Revolution dispatched Li to endure for four years the harsh regime of a "school for cadres." Yet to find significant differences between their descriptions of Kant's complex philosophy would be extremely difficult, as I discovered after closely studying both descriptions. This magnificent accessibility of objective reality to human observation thus paradoxically complements the way that human beings make sense out of objective reality only by using culturally disparate ideas they have inherited and regard as indisputable.

If then a discourse illustrated by specific historical texts can be objectively described, major questions still remain regarding the social distribution of such a discourse and its causative effects on economic-political development. These questions I can answer only impressionistically. Already mentioned are the many famous scholars, ranging from Reinhard Bendix to Isaiah Berlin, believing that the way influential individuals reason about political life can in the long run greatly change economic-political development: the intellectualistic "trickle down theory" of historical causation. So far as goes the extent to which, say, the Chinese population today accepts the beliefs basic to discourse #1, I depend on extensive but hardly exhaustive immersion in the primary materials and on the nature of the textual evidence.[127] Crucial is the idea of a cliché. It is reasonable to assume that a set of clichés amounts to orientations widely shared within a population group. Utterances would not be clichés if they were not treated as such by large numbers of people. Like the epistemological "we," clichés reflect the existence of an actually constituted community. This is especially so if the same cliché appears in a great variety of texts, not only contemporaneous ones attacking each other but also texts stretching far back into the history of this population. Good examples are the clichés constituting epistemological optimism in China, the peculiarly optimistic Chinese concept of political practicability, and the ideal of "linkage" discussed in section 7 above.

A major point here is that the fact that an utterance is a cliché is often obvious from its context. For instance, when T'ang Chün-i rejected the way contemporary Western culture "confusedly mixed together the sacred and the evil aspects of life" (*shen-mo hun-tsa*), he could be confident that virtually all his readers would agree with his point, instead of objecting, as St. Augustine would have, that human history unavoidably is a mix of these two. In other words, T'ang's utopian idea that a society without evil could practicably be established aroused little criticism in China, as was the case also with innumerable other such utopian Chinese utterances. Had his point about overcoming *shen-mo hun-tsa* seemed dubious to many Chinese readers, T'ang Chün-i, a writer constantly seeking to address the doubts felt by his readers, would not have tried to make it without further explanation.[128]

Whether an idea expressed by one member of a society is a cliché can also be determined by noting how other members react to it. When I showed them my article on Yang Kuo-shu's liberalism, some other Taiwan intellectuals criticized me for paying so much attention to essays that merely repeated what everyone already took for granted. When I showed my article on Li Qiang to another Mainland intellectual, he similarly criticized me for paying so much attention to a "kindergarten-level" book that merely reviewed the "ABCs" of liberalism. There is little doubt, therefore, that the very similar orientations toward liberal democracy found in the writings of Yang and Li were respectively widespread in Taiwan during the 1980s and in China during the late 1990s. (To be sure, such Chinese reactions to Chinese writings also reflect the deeply-rooted tendency of Chinese intellectuals to disparage one another's work [*wen-jen hsiang ch'ing*].)

The durability of a cliché as part of a historical discourse can also be inferred when the cliché remains unchallenged in the writing of an agent of the discourse greatly exposed to a contrary discourse. For instance, even after the astute philosopher Fung Yu-lan spent four years (1919–1923) at Columbia University obtaining his Ph.D. under John Dewey, he still took "epistemological optimism" for granted, writing his book on the nature of universal moral norms (*Hsin-li-hsueh*) in the late 1930s without even bothering to refute then-prevalent Western doubts that there can be knowledge of objective, universal moral norms.[129] Admitting these universal moral norms were purely "formal," Fung still regarded them as distinguishing clearly between good and bad. For him, modern philosophy had refuted the Confucian idea that someone fully understanding cosmic and moral reality necessarily had the power to make the concrete world morally perfect, but it had cast no doubt at all on the traditional assumption that the distinction between good and bad is based on universal, objective principles. Time and again in the twentieth century, Fung, T'ang Chün-i, and other Chinese philosophers fully aware of Humean skepticism brushed it aside to reaffirm the knowability of universal, objective moral principles. While this skepticism was becoming influential in Western philosophical circles, the New Realism of philosophers like Ralph Barton Perry and William P. Montague was being enthusiastically greeted by philosophers like T'ang and Fung. Obviously, Chinese unaware of Humean skepticism — certainly more than 90 percent of the population — took the objectivity of moral principles still more for granted. Thus the intellectual careers of a few astute Chinese intellectuals studying in American universities can reveal much about broadly shared cultural patterns back home. Such points are basic to my claim in this book that I describe widely shared Chinese orientations.

Precisely how widely, however, is an open empirical question. Readers will probably agree I describe cultural strands, but just how these are interwoven with other cultural strands is a question this book does not strongly address. True, it could be partly addressed by quantitative opinion surveys. Such surveys, however, cannot adequately reveal the contents of the discourses constituting a society. In other words, as scholars try to grasp the values animating a society, statistical approaches and textual studies complement each other. Indeed, one could speak of a Heisenberg effect: the more precisely one understands an orientation, the less precisely can one understand its social distribution, and vice versa.

After all, Weberian sociology teaches that, because different patterns in a society are not necessarily congruent with one another, an intellectual trend, even if important, is not necessarily similar to the values animating everyday life in the society as a whole. Many Western scholars, therefore, would resist the typically Mainland view of Ch'en Hsiao-lung, who, quoting his eminent teacher Feng Ch'i, suggests that "the history of philosophy can be seen as an unfolding dialectical intellectual movement rooted in the social practice of humankind and revolving mainly around the problem of the relation between thought and existence."[130] Yet some degree of "elective affinity" between intellectual patterns and mass values seems plausible. Confronting the widespread Western tendency to accept a breach between humanistic and scientific learning, Ch'en Hsiao-lung takes it for granted that the central goal of philosophy today, east and west, is to overcome this breach and unify these two. Would it not be surprising if American philosophers today in their highly individualistic and capitalistic society were as concerned as Ch'en Hsiao-lung with devising a philosophical system unifying all the branches of learning?

Nor, despite Popper's objections, can one overlook a certain cosmic trend toward regularity allowing one inductively to make generalizations based on a limited sampling of the data. Astronomers having discovered twenty-two planets outside our solar system by April 1999, some then immediately inferred that "there could be at least a billion full-fledged solar systems around sunlike stars in the Milky Way galaxy." In the spring of 2000, scientists for the first time found the remains of one heart of a dinosaur, concluded this particular animal was warm-blooded, and inferred that therefore all dinosaurs were warm-blooded. Indeed, without such regularity in nature, how could interviews with 3000 Americans reveal public opinion trends in a society of 250 million persons? Similarly, when innumerable Chinese texts I have seen, modern and premodern, Marxist and non-Marxist, express the belief that propagation of the right kind of thinking can rid history of selfishness, then it is certain that this belief has been and continues to be a major aspect of Chinese political thought, even though I certainly have not read every major Chinese political statement ever made.

If, then, people internationally and nationally should deal with clashes between their political theories by working together as dispassionately as possible to describe and then evaluate these theories, the above discussion shows that such a project cannot rise above a sea of controversies. Even if the problem of evaluation is not a problem, as I claim, the controversies regarding the seemingly simple procedure of empirically describing ideas as parts of one or more discourses are formidable. No doubt it is at least partly because of these controversies that just about all the relevant disciplinary approaches have avoided this procedure.

For instance, philosophers are more interested in abstractly making recommendations about how people should think (e.g. use only "clear and distinct ideas," avoid "objectivism," pursue "falsifiable conjectures") than in describing how people actually think. I have not found in any philosophical work the idea that, in order to make practicable recommendations about how to think, one should first describe and compare actual ways of thinking the practicability of which has been historically demonstrated and only then ask how to choose between or revise any of them. How can epistemologists recommend that people apply a few abstract rules of successful thinking without first finding out whether these rules can be practicably used?

Needless to add, describing actual ways of thought is especially uninteresting for philosophers propounding the one philosophical recommendation or doctrine they regard as correct. So far as go studies of the history of philosophy, they have been less concerned with comprehensively describing all the ideas making up a text than in highlighting the doctrine explicitly emphasized in the text, in establishing a typology of philosophies, or in selecting out ancient notions appealing by modern standards, such as "liberal" ones. Leo Strauss's formidable scholarship sought to reveal the trains of reasoning pursued by "great" Western thinkers, but, as already mentioned, he eschewed analysis of culturally inherited vocabularies. Proposing to describe and reflect on historical ideas about the main aspects of political life, Strauss and his students looked only at those ideas put forward by certain learned persons in the West, not at culturally shared assumptions about these matters. Thus he failed to offer a way of reflecting on the broad range of ideas, east and west, about these matters. Benjamin I. Schwartz was more interested than Strauss in culturally shared assumptions, but instead of pursuing the kind of systematically comprehensive description of important utterances discussed above, he studied Chinese ideas largely to assess other Western interpretations of them, such as those of Joseph Needham, Herbert Fingarette, A.C. Graham, and Chad Hansen.[131] Popular today among some philosophers working on China is textual study pulling together all passages in a text containing the same word, instead of establishing the context of an idea by analytically setting up a category (such as "conceptualization of the given world") and then clustering around it all utterances pertinent to it. Students of intellectual history usually discuss historical ideas by summing them up selectively while focusing on biographical context, or by searching through hard-to-use primary sources to find scattered references to ideas previously regarded as unexpressed during the era in question. Then there are the reductionists like Chin Kuan-t'ao who ignore arguments in the texts, seeking instead to grasp a culture's "deep structure." Similar to the reductionists are sociologists like Samuel P. Huntington, who believe they can sum up the nature of a complex cultural tradition by offering a few generalizations about it. Still another genre is that created by Westerners selectively discussing Chinese ideas by reading Western books about them, such as F.S.C. Northrop in his *The Meeting of East and West.*[132]

Given all these clashing notions about how to describe ideas, I suspect that the description of ideas, a major part of human reflexivity, is inherently a hermeneutic project vulnerable to the most basic vicissitudes and uncertainties of human life. This idea that any methodology of description is inherently mired in these uncertainties is simultaneously a typical product of the GMWER and a seemingly accurate ontological proposition about the universal human condition. Thus the idea of a political theory as part of a discourse cannot cancel this kind of primordial epistemic uncertainty as a universal ontological given discovered during the course of the GMWER.

Even so, there do seem to be two true, empirically sound, indeed universally valid ontological principles — the factual existence of humankind as we-groups forming discourses based on historical, culturally inherited ideas appearing to them as indisputable, and the accessibility to human observation of objective reality, including the factual reality of those historical ideas that are regarded as indisputable by a we-group. On this basis, the description and evaluation of political theories as parts of discourses seem to be feasible. At least, I can think of no other way to extend my own reflexivity and look for some relatively unbiased methodology with which to evaluate the Chinese and Western political theories currently clashing with each other.

9. Six Discourses

Given, then, this conception of a criticizable discourse, how can one distinguish one discourse from another? It is true that, ex hypothesi, the agents of one discourse regard another discourse as nonsense, but nonsense is also the form that any intra-cultural argument (e.g. "pro-life" vs. "pro-choice") has in the eyes of those who reject it. At what point does the intra-cultural perception of nonsense turn into an inter-cultural one signifying the presence of a different discourse? This is purely a matter of judgment, though I would suggest that, in the intra-cultural perception of nonsense, disagreements tend to center on the question of means rather than that of epistemology, goals, historical patterns of causation, and so ways of assessing "evidence." The latter topics are basic to the differences among the six discourses outlined below. In general, the shift from one discourse to another can be compared to what Thomas Kuhn called a shift from one paradigm to another.

One boundary scholars tend to agree on is that between what the Straussians call "classical" or "ancient political philosophy" (discourse #4) and "modern political philosophy" (discourse #3). As already mentioned, this boundary began to emerge around 1500, when the political goal in Europe was increasingly conceptualized in a more mundane way emphasizing practical political success, prosperity, freedom, and equality, rather than aiming to realize the morally or religiously best regime in the face of varying practical conditions. Plato and Aristotle had not objected to heteronomy imposed by the wise. After about 1500, a far more critical attitude toward heteronomy gradually crystallized. Besides this shift in goals, people developed new conceptualizations of the universal principle justifying these new goals, especially as "scientific" reasoning came to be seen by many as the only correct kind of reasoning. In the classical world of Plato, Aristotle, St. Augustine, or St. Thomas Aquinas, non-scientific reasoning referred to nature, to the universal nature of man and society, or to God in order to set forth the principles of the ethically proper regime. After medieval times, people instead sought to derive normative knowledge from various aspects of "experience" or "history," as discussed above.

Few will disagree that this modern, post-1500 way of discussing goals and their universal rationale (discourse #3) differed from the classical Greco-Roman and Christian discourse stretching from Plato through at least Richard Hooker (1553–1600) and Hugo Grotius (1583–1645) (discourse #4). Scholars may also agree that another, vastly different discourse (discourse #5) was exemplified by medieval Islamic and Jewish thought. The epistemological optimism of these two traditions was much stronger. More broadly, this discourse, overlapping Christian fundamentalism, was based on a total belief in Biblical Revelation as the perfect source of all significant truths. As Ralph Lerner notes, medieval Muslim and Jewish political philosophers, such as Alfarabi (ca. 870–950) and Moses Maimonides (1135–1204), differed from medieval Christian ones in having "to justify their philosophical activity before the tribunal of the revealed law." Moreover, both Alfarabi and Maimonides envisaged the best regime as one led by a supreme ruler obeying God, exercising total power over his society, and ruthlessly using war to enlarge God's dominion. In this Islamic and Jewish discourse, the epistemologically optimistic belief in a sacred canon precluded the horizon of epistemological pessimism discovered by Greek thought. Impervious to epistemological pessimism and Western liberalism, the fiery religious fanaticism that we still see in the Middle East is logically consistent with the strangely revered doctrines of Alfarabi and Maimonides.[133]

If these three discourses, #3, #4, and #5, can be distinguished from one another, the later evolution of discourse #3 is more debatable. Certainly there has been great continuity in the Western pursuit of mundane political goals (political success, prosperity, freedom, equality), that dynamic Faustian-Promethean spirit discussed by Benjamin Schwartz.[134] But what about the GMWER? As already discussed, Leo Strauss described this development as the rise of "late modern doctrines that denied the possibility of rational knowledge of the universal validity of any purpose or principle," namely, "the fact-value disjunction, relativism, and historicism" (the latter not in Popper's sense but as the opposite belief that "all human thought and action are essentially dependent on historical situations, the sequence of which proves to have no rational goal or meaning").

For Strauss, this epistemological development amounted to "the present crisis of the West and of modernity." He then tried to overcome this "crisis" by looking into "classical political philosophy .... to recover .... the deepest premises of modern political philosophy."[135] As already indicated, though, leaving aside the problem of evaluating the GMWER, one can instead simply note that the GMWER produced a new discourse, discourse #2.

It was this GMWER that created the major chasm between much current Western political theory (discourse #2) and current Chinese political theory (discourse #1). Diverging from the West's discourse #2, modern China's discourse #1 had much in common with the West's discourse #3. This is evident from John Dunn's elegant outline of the Western revolutionary tradition:

> Modern conceptions of revolution assemble precariously together a variety of distinct ideas: the destruction of old and putatively obsolete political, social and economic orders; the purposeful political creation of new political, social and economic orders which are proclaimed by their architects to be decisively superior to their predecessors; a view of modern world history which renders the collapse of the old regimes and the emergence of the new regimes evidently desirable, causally unsurprising and perhaps even causally ineluctable; the existential value and causal importance of human lives lived in the endeavor to speed the collapse of the old and the reconstruction of the new.[136]

As modern Chinese thinkers surveyed the Western intellectual scene, they were easily attracted to this modern Western vision of revolution (part of discourse #3). Yet their image of it cannot be separated from their traditional modes of thought (discourse #6). Modern scholarship has now to some extent shifted over to a greater emphasis than was common in the 1970s on the continuity between modern and premodern Chinese thought. Evidence regarding this continuity is scattered throughout this volume. I would especially emphasize the continuity of a Chinese epistemological scene free of epistemological pessimism, the utopian belief in the political practicability of greatly reducing the role of selfishness in political-economic life, and the belief that societal transformation can be accomplished by intellectual virtuosi as super-citizens working with a corrigible political center.[137] All these ideas were central equally to the modern Chinese discourse #1 and the Confucian discourse #6; motivated Chinese as they embraced and reformulated the post-Renaissance Western discourse #3; and clashed with the contemporary Western liberal tradition represented by discourse #2.

10. Discourse #1 and Discourse #2

The two tables below depicting discourses #1 and #2 list only the *premises* shared by the persons carrying on the particular discourse, which, as already explained, consists also of the conflicting ideological claims advanced to answer the questions implied or raised by these premises. The extent to which these listed premises accord with any actual segment of history is a further question. Both lists can be seen as "ideal types" in Weber's sense, since they select ideas out of a historical verbal "soup" and then etically put them into a verbal sequence different from this "soup." The list of discourse #1 premises, however, is a much more empirical, inductive, emic pattern than the usual Weberian "ideal type." It is based on extensive study of Chinese primary materials making up the four leading Chinese ideologies of the twentieth century (Chinese Marxism, Sunism, modern Confucian humanism, and Chinese liberalism) as well as the primary and secondary literature pertaining to the genesis of these four at the turn of the century and much of the recent Chinese writing, which partly seeks to go beyond these four.[138] Thus each discourse #1 premise both was a historically concrete, widely shared orientation and is a proposition part of my analytical device, even if my phrasing is not always identical with the original wording. For instance, in discourse #1, the idea of China as a "*Gemeinschaft* eliminating insincerity, selfishness" etc. is both a premise listed as part of my analytical presentation and a goal fully affirmed by historical people as they participated in this discourse, even if they did not use the term *Gemeinschaft*. Moreover, if it is correct or plausible to say that in *all* social discussion about public issues, the key topics are the goal of public action, the means, the rest of the given cosmic, historical, and practical world, and the nature of knowledge, then my discourse #1 scheme is a rather comprehensive description of the way in which members of the Chinese ideological mainstream in the twentieth century conceptualized public issues.

My analysis of discourse #2, however, is not the outcome of such systematic inductive study. To use an epistemological idea popular with Chinese scholars, the list of premises making up the basis of discourse #2 was "arrived at by drawing together much data and coming to a conclusion about the whole nature of the matter at hand" (*tsung-chieh-ch'u-lai-te*). As a product of the GMWER, discourse

#2 mixes many of the clichés of logical positivism, ethical skepticism, pragmatism, and that pessimism about human nature so eloquently expressed by Reinhold Niebuhr. To a considerable extent, my analysis of it is based on my own impressions as a native informant who has been part of the U.S. academic scene for some four decades and has spent many years trying to spot differences between his beliefs and the Chinese ones he encountered. I admit that the ideas of major Western figures, such as Karl R. Popper and F.A. Hayek, who exemplify crucial aspects of discourse #2, also include ideas outside of it, particularly remnants of the epistemological optimism basic to discourse #3. My impression is that the current U.S. academic mainstream tends to consist of an eclectic, incompletely analyzed mix of discourse #3 and discourse #2, not just of discourse #2. As already mentioned, the very idea of a discourse refers to an unclearly bounded pattern of communication and the human tendency to mix ideas together in fluctuating, partly illogical ways. Nevertheless, many Western, especially U.S. academics will see in discourse #2 a mirror reflection of their own analytical perspective. Alex Inkeles's or Samuel P. Huntington's widely respected writings, I would claim, to a large extent illustrate discourse #2.

As just mentioned, a discourse consists not only of premises shared by people who regard them as true or uncontroversial and platitudinous. It consists also of the questions that are implied by these necessarily vague premises, and that these people agree are the significant questions worth arguing about. Central to the agenda of unanswered questions implied by discourse #1 was the question of the extent to which a "total system of thought answering all key questions about human life" (*t'i-hsi*) has already been formed, and so that of the extent to which intellectual-moral dissonance should be tolerated. This question overlaps that of the extent to which pluralism should be legitimized. In the history of Maoism and Sunism, for instance, it was often asserted that one or more "great" (*wei-ta*) thinkers had already largely established a definitive *t'i-hsi*. Modern Chinese intellectuals, however, often leaned toward the idea that the formation of such a *t'i-hsi* was still an unrealized goal, and that Chinese society was in a long, currently ongoing transitional

Table 2: The Premises of Discourse #1 and Discourse #2[139]

A. Political Goal: The Problem of Utopianism

Discourse #1 and discourse #2 share: the search for national security, economic prosperity, equality and freedom (democracy), and modernization, and both ask whether modernization means mainly putting primacy on adaptation and instrumental rationality or whether it centers on trying to combine the latter with sacred-moral values, a "moral language."

Their conceptualizations of the goal differ as follows:

#1.	#2.
1. Utopian vision of China as a *Gemeinschaft* eliminating insincerity, selfishness, constraints improperly limiting individual freedom, exploitation, alienation, and confusing ideological contradictions and so becoming the world's model civilization. Ridding history of moral and epistemic dissonance.	1. Pragmatic, "piecemeal" progress perpetuating Western civilization as the world's model civilization.
2. Transformative change as indicated by Ernst Troeltsch's idea of a "sect" and Ch'ien Mu's idea of action purely based on the classics.	2. Accommodative change as indicated by Troeltsch's idea of "the church" and Ch'ien Mu's idea of "historical learning."
3. The principles of political practicability derived from faith in the goodness and rationality of universal human nature.	3. The principle of political practicability derived from a posteriori knowledge about political history.
4. The Rousseauistic concept of democracy as moral, rational government by the governed.	4. The Millsian concept of democracy as institutions seeking to maximize the freedom of the individual and the practical accountability of government to the governed.

Table 2 (Cont'd)

5. The fusion of political power, knowledge, morality, and individual freedom, and so the rejection or top-down control of "the three marketplaces." A "top-down," hierarchical vision of society as led by a morally and intellectually enlightened elite controlling a corrigible political center.

5. Putting primacy on individual freedom and accepting "the three marketplaces." A "bottom-up" vision of society as basically guided by the morally and intellectually unsupervised and ungraded preferences of the majority. Fallible citizens with incomplete knowledge monitoring an incorrigible political center.

6. Emphasizing *paideia* and so seeking some degree of conformity in both the "inner" and "outer" aspects of social life, i.e. emphasizing the non-legal, non-scientific parameters of freedom, i.e. thick parameters, i.e. Isaiah Berlin's "positive freedom."

6. Minimizing conformity, maximally restricting heteronomy to "outer" circumstances and respect for science, i.e. thin parameters, "negative freedom."

7. Rejecting Taiwan and Hong Kong as models of Chinese modernization.

7. Viewing Taiwan and Hong Kong as models of practicable Chinese modernization.

8. Using transformative criteria to criticize the current situation.

8. Using accommodative criteria to criticize it.

Table 2 (Cont'd)

B. Epistemology: The Problem of Epistemological Optimism

#1.   #2.

Leaning toward epistemological optimism   *Leaning toward epistemological pessimism*

1. In claiming a statement is true and
   wanting to avoid "arbitrary" (*tu-tuan*)
   or "baseless" (*hsu-kou*) claims, one
   can depend on not only logic and
   empirical evidence but also ideas
   such as "rational intuition,"
   "dialectical reasoning," "the understanding of the virtue inherent in
   one's own nature," and "feelings
   stemming from the ultimate nature
   of the cosmos."

1. Without depending on logic and
   empirical evidence, it is impossible
   to show that any statement is not
   only indisputable (e.g. "racism
   is bad") but also universally true.

2. Objectivism, reason as an algorismic
   code (based on or illustrated by the
   writings of, say, Marx, Karl Popper,
   Weber, or the analytical philosophers)
   that can be promulgated as the basis
   of public life. "Subjective" ideas do
   not close off access to objective
   knowledge.

2. Relativism or some version of the
   "middle ground" between
   relativism and objectivism as
   discussed by Richard J. Bernstein.

3. Can know what alter feels and tell
   whether he or she is sincere.

3. Alter's feelings fully known only to
   alter.

4. Induction reliable because cosmic
   and historical regularities exist.

4. Induction cannot even demonstrate that "all men are mortal."

5. The ultimate nature of reality as
   an ontological, historical, cultural,
   and normative whole can be known.
   Can know essences. Can grasp a
   whole that is implied by and is more
   than the observed parts.

5. One must precisely define the
   boundary between the knowable
   and the unknowable. Cannot
   know essences. Cannot grasp
   any unobserved whole.

Table 2 (Cont'd)

6. "Ought" grounded in "is," "was," or "about to be" (whether in the cosmos, in science, in history, in universal conditions of human existence); the goal of life has determinate, specific features (e.g. "modernization").

6. "Ought" cannot be grounded except in human decisions, and human goals are not determinate ends that one should necessarily prefer over other possible ends.

7. The six kinds of statements (descriptive, causal, predictive, evaluative, recommendatory, and epistemological) can be logically integrated by inferring them from some overarching concept such as Marx's "laws of history" or Chu Hsi's *ta-t'ou-nao-ch'u.* Cause as a category in the analysis of phenomena is the same thing as cause as a category in the analysis of praxis.

7. The six kinds of statements must be carefully disaggregated without any a priori assumptions about their logical interrelations. Only then can one determine the extent to which any statement is justified and is not "arbitrary" (*tu-tuan*) or "baseless" (*hsu-kou*). Causal connections in the analysis of phenomena are different from those in the analysis of praxis.

8. Thus a grand theory of human existence can be established (*t'i-hsi*), logically integrating all valid ideas "past and present, east and west" (*ku-chin Chung-wai*), and including the correct, exact guidelines for revising Chinese culture. Cultural crisis stems from the failure to understand the ontological basis of existence.

8. No *t'i-hsi* is possible. Even the descriptive or causal under-standing of history is often inaccessible or controversial, not to mention the difficulties entailed by predictions, evaluations, and recommenda-tions. Knowledge about history is mostly descriptive and Weberian, and historical discourse replaces universal theory. Cultural crisis is due to a mistaken epistemology.

9. Understanding this *t'i-hsi* produces a faith (*hsin-hsin*), a spirit of determination to pursue ideals without compromise. Discursive thought and moral feeling form a single mental process or epistemic mode.

9. Faith is a matter of impulse or moral imagination, all of which are distinctly different from the purely discursive use of reason and essentially "subjective," i.e. based on historically limited cultural, linguistic, psychological, biographical, etc. circumstances.

Table 2 (Cont'd)

10. The world has an epistemic center producing "classics" for which scholars in the epistemic periphery can write the "commentaries."	10. No necessary epistemic center but West in fact is the epistemic center. (This, at the expense of contradiction, reflects epistemological optimism.)
11. *T'i-hsi* can be summed up in a single slogan such as "Western learning for the fundamental principles, Chinese learning for the application of the principles" (Li Tse-hou).	11. Cumulative, fragmented understanding.

Table 2 (Cont'd)

C. Conceptualization of the Given World, Especially History: Causal Analysis and the Problem of Teleology or Historicism (in Popper's Sense)

1. *The given world as a negation of the goal.* Because I and II have different goals, including different ideas about the hierarchy of the global order, their descriptions of the actual, given conditions today negating the goal differ considerably. Most important, according to discourse I, one's own society is in an intolerable predicament both because insincerity, selfishness, and intellectual confusion pervade it, and because it has lost the central international position it should have. Conversely, according to discourse II, one's own society is a largely satisfactory one. To the extent that it suffers from insincerity, selfishness, and intellectual confusion, these are normal human frailties, and it enjoys the central international position it should have. Despite this contrast, however, there is considerable consensus about the nature of the ills today afflicting humankind, whether those afflicting it generally, such as poverty, insufficient equality and freedom, social, psychological, and ethical deficiencies, ethnic and international conflicts threatening to turn violent, and ecological misbehavior; those seen as especially characteristic of modern nations, such as urban degradation and anomie; or those associated with many non-Western nations, especially lack of modernization.

2. *The analysis of the given historical causes for such ills and the historically given means available to overcome these ills.* In this regard there also are major contrasts between #1 and #2. Therefore there are major contrasts between #1 and #2 with regard to how data are "rationally" presented as "evidence" for the existence of the key conditions causing the above ills, and with regard to the nature of the hopeful conditions on which agents of progress might depend. Thus culturally varying discourses influence the content of instrumental rationality as well as that of goals.

2a. Universal human nature and causal analysis.

#1.	#2.
Universal human frailties are not the main causes for the behaviors preventing the realization of goals. Correctable cultural patterns are the main cause.	The main cause for these unfortunate behaviors lies in universal human frailties. (This contradicts epistemological pessimism, which precludes knowledge of universal human nature.)

Table 2 (Cont'd)

2b. Nationalism or ethnocentrism and causal analysis.

#1.	#2.
China as victim of Western oppression and a temporarily crippled superman, backward today but able to surpass the West.	The West as the world's best vehicle of rationalization, innovation, modernization, and democratization. (This usually unspoken premise of much Western academic thinking has been articulated especially by Max Weber and S.N. Eisenstadt.)

2c. Reification and causal analysis.

This is the question of the relationship between the factual or ontological units making up history and epistemic, purely mental, often controversial devices, such as historical sagas or Weber's "ideal types." To what extent is the general, not only the particular, an ontological unit? Are there huge historical facts, patterns that remain largely identical over many years consistently influencing the behavior of many millions of people, such as "the feudal system" or "the Confucian ideology" posited by many Chinese thinkers? There are such "huge facts," such as languages, but discourse #2 often regards references to such huge facts as purely epistemic, partly misleading heuristic devices.

2d. Determinateness and causal analysis.

#1.	#2.
Causal patterns knowable, whether or not prediction possible.	Often not clear.
"Systems" or "structures" are formed by the various kinds of activities, e.g. economic, ideological, cultural.	Much historical life not systemic. For instance, unpredictable leadership decisions often crucial.
A system has a center or a causally dominant part, such as a central value, and the system is rather homogeneous, often susceptible to simple description (e.g. "The West puts primacy on reason").	Any systemic patterns often combine different premises or trends.

Table 2 (Cont'd)

A society is an "organic whole," a system with clear causal relations between all its parts.	A society is not a system but a mix of patterns, episodes, and personalities.
Its changes take the form of dominant trends (*ch'ao-liu*) and a clear sequence of stages.	Changes caused by combinations of trends, and stages, if any, overlap.
These changes follow laws.	There are few if any laws of change.

3. *History and teleology*

#1.   #2.

History indicates the moral mission everyone should affirm.	Morality cannot be grounded in history. Historical facts have no meaning apart from interpretation of them, and interpretations vary indefinitely.
China today is in a predicament, but the history of one or another civilization includes a stage during which people have been, will be, or already are much smarter and more moral than they are in China today.	People in all historical periods have been and will continue to be afflicted by selfishness and cognitive failings.
A society or a culture should be described by distinguishing between the bad features out of accord with history's moral goal and the good ones in accord with it.	The goal of description is not to make this distinction but to be as comprehensive and precise as possible.

Table 2 (Cont'd)

D. The Means Available to Pursue the Goal (Agency): The Problem of Revolution or Transformation

1. *How socially visible and objectively identifiable is the social distribution of morality and political wisdom?*

#1.	#2.
Very visible.	Not very.

2. *How are they geographically distributed?*

#1.	#2.
Partly in China, partly in West.	Concentrated in West (this point contradicts the previous one).

3. *Is political wisdom concentrated in certain social strata or broadly scattered?*

#1.	#2.
Concentrated, whether in a political party or in intellectual circles. "The people" just follow or reject the wisdom of the moral-intellectual virtuosi.	Broadly scattered throughout the state, intellectual circles, and "the people." There are no such virtuosi.

4. *Can the state be the prime agent of progress? Is it corrigible? Can it be morally and epistemically competent?*

#1.	#2.
Yes (*te-chih, jen-cheng, nei-sheng wai-wang*).	No. Hope lies mainly in the civil society outside the state.

Table 2 (Cont'd)

5. *How should the agents of progress revise their culture?*

#1.	#2.
By using a *t'i-hsi* or at least an intellectually profound understanding to enact the needed changes and by transforming society morally. Transformation, however, can include a long period of transition during which moral-intellectual dissonance should be tolerated.	As some Chinese scholars too have noted, cultural revision is based on a mix of motivations that cannot be analyzed and controlled by any *t'i-hsi*, on "psychological bargaining" at all levels of society, a mix of disparate, largely crescive trends, but susceptible partly to the advertising of various values by various elites.

6. *What is the relation between cultural revision and economic-political development?*

#1.	#2.
Everything depends on cultural revision, the transformation of values, the finding of the right spiritual mode.	These two issues should not be conflated. Revision of institutions should be differentiated from cultural transformation and carried out in a piecemeal way.

7. *Does history offer clear instruction about how to effect economic-political progress in China?*

#1.	#2.
Only in broad terms. Something can be learned from the West and perhaps from Chinese history, but the transformation of China and the world depends on a new creative Chinese intellectual synthesis.	Yes. Capitalism is the key to the alleviation of poverty, even though it needs to be regulated in some ways, and Millsian democracy is needed to prevent tyranny. Both Hong Kong and Taiwan have demonstrated how capitalism can be institutionalized in the Chinese context, and Taiwan has demonstrated how Millsian democracy can be.

Table 2 (Cont'd)

8. *How effective can the agents of progress be? how effective is good political theory?*

#1.	#2.
Very. History can be guided. The means are available to transform and perfect China.	Hard to say. History may be unguidable. Means are available only to pursue piecemeal progress.

period during which the prevalence of competing incorrect theories was unavoidable and proper. This idea, common in Taiwan by the 1970s and the Mainland by the 1990s, thus legitimized considerable pluralism by referring not in J.S. Mill's fashion to the universal epistemic fragility of the human mind but to a transitional period of doctrinal uncertainty caused by historical difficulties that would eventually be overcome. T'ang Chün-i's thought illustrates this viewpoint.

A second key question was that of which doctrine or combination of doctrines or philosophies should be selected out of the variety of new and old, Chinese and foreign ideas to answer epistemological, ontological, cosmological, and historical questions. The range of possibilities here from Dewey and Marx to Chu Hsi, Wang Yang-ming, Kant, Hegel, Habermas, Weber, Wittfogel, Eisenstadt, and Aristotle is beyond the possibility of summation.

In the 1920s, arguments about these questions, as illustrated again by T'ang Chün-i's thought, often centered on the ontological issue of materialism versus idealism, which overlapped the epistemological one of science versus metaphysical or intuitive understanding, which in turn overlapped the historical question of whether the West was the sole source of proper intellectual method, or whether the humanistic, intuitive, metaphysical ideas found in the Chinese tradition also amounted to a kind of knowledge China needed in order to modernize, which in turn overlapped the question of which Western tradition, if any, should be given the most respect — the one endorsing or the one denouncing the liberal mix of capitalism and democracy. As intellectuals formed the concept of the "new culture" China should have, how should they mix together old and new, Chinese and foreign ideas? This question is still a burning one in Mainland intellectual circles, which in the 1990s debated the question of how to "synthesize" that "intuitive" understanding of "the nature of Man" developed by the Chinese tradition with "analysis" as that Western attempt to maximize verbal, conceptual, and logical clarity. As discussed in section 7 above, there is a virtually unbroken modern Chinese consensus rejecting the GMWER's claim that such a "synthesis" is impossible and insisting that how to conceptualize this "synthesis" or "linkage" is a question on which the fate of China and the world hangs. This assumption was one of the uncontroversial premises of discourse #1, but Chinese intellectuals have not so far settled their controversies about how to answer the questions raised by this assumption.

A third key question is that of which persons constitute the "enlightened" group (*hsien-chih hsien-chueh*) qualified to serve as the agents of Chinese progress. The controversies in this regard are obvious, as are those about the correct organizational forms and policies that the government of China should effect. Should it act violently and transformatively or moderately and accommodatively?

Given this agenda implied by the premises of discourse #1, many competing Chinese viewpoints arose as different combinations of answers to the questions on it. For instance, a widespread kind of Chinese Marxism arose holding that a largely definitive system of thought was already available; that it had been produced by Marx, Engels, Lenin, Stalin, and Mao; that the knowledge China today needed stemmed from the West and some current Chinese thought, not the Confucian tradition; that this correct theory was being implemented by the Chinese Communist Party; that it called for socialism rather than the liberal mix of democracy and capitalism; and that some violence would be needed to accomplish the transformation for which it aimed. Within the Chinese intellectual world, each of these propositions was controversial. For instance, the radicalism they constituted was prominently challenged on the Mainland by the 1980s; but the liberal, humanistic, and Sunist voices rejecting it had been alive all along.

All in all, then, Chinese intellectuals today still disagree on what the correct answers are to questions such as those above, and writers on Chinese intellectual history have often successfully described their debates, explaining how one or another debated position was developed by, say, Mao or Hu Shih. The premises of discourse #1 largely shared by all the participants in this huge historical debate, however, also are important. They are important not only for those scholars who want to understand the picture of the world treated as uncontroversial knowledge by many in China during the twentieth century but also for those Chinese intellectuals seeking to maximize their "self-awareness" (*tzu-chueh*) and "critical consciousness" (*p'i-p'an i-shih*) by uncovering and critically assessing their own historically shaped premises.

11. Evaluating Discourses: Looking for the "Middle Ground"

As already argued, the big problem in criticizing a political theory and the discourse of which it is part lies in accurately, lucidly, and comprehensively describing them so as to avoid criticizing ideas one has misunderstood. The description of ideas is so difficult because the methodology of description is such a controversial issue, because the problem of real or perceived misunderstanding is existentially integral to the very nature of discourse, and because ideas, like so much of the world, are often complicated. Thus there cannot be a complete consensus that discourse #1 and discourse #2 each accurately denotes a widespread pattern of political communication.

As opposed to describing them, however, the problem of evaluating them as making sense or not is not a real problem, despite the fashionable Western philosophical view that it is impossible to base evaluative propositions on anything except arbitrary preference. To be sure, as discussed in section 7 above, one can distinguish between various current philosophical approaches to the problem of how to avoid relativism in determining the norms with which to evaluate ideas and actions — some objectivistic approaches, and some taking into account the historicity of human thought, including my concept of discourse. Moreover, in my view, such approaches have left plenty of room for further debate. In this section, however, I try to show that, however this debate turns out, the plain empirical facts about discourse themselves include a secure basis for the evaluation of ideas (chapter VIII further develops this argument).

As already argued, if one can agree that a good political theory, including the discourse it is based on, should *successfully* discuss four topics (the goal of political life, the means to reach it, other aspects of the given world, and the epistemological standards used to determine which ideas about these three subjects count as knowledge), the definition of "successfully" also is clear. A discussion is successful or "rational" when it accords with the premises that a historical we-group evaluating the discussion regard as indisputable. More precisely, the idea of such an evaluation is not a definition but an observation about how in fact evaluations are unavoidably carried out.

This concept of "indisputables," meshing with the thought of Isaiah Berlin, has already been discussed. A few more comments about its philosophical provenance are needed, however, to distinguish it more clearly from the other approaches recognizing the historicity of thinking.

The suggestion that ideas about truth, knowledge, and rationality can be largely grounded in the particular beliefs which a historical we-group regards as indisputable goes back to not only the idea of discourse but also the recent and widespread search by Western philosophers for a "middle ground" between "objectivism," which refers to the discourse #3 idea that there is a single, "rational," universally and objectively correct way to think, and "relativism," the discourse #2 denial that there is such an algorism. The perception of this dichotomy between relativism and objectivism was thus a valuable product of the GMWER.

Richard J. Bernstein's study illuminated the nature of this search for a "middle ground," which he saw formed by the "hermeneutic" tradition associated especially with Hans-Georg Gadamer and Jürgen Habermas. As Bernstein put it, one could avoid pursuing both the chimera of objectivism and the abyss of relativism by recognizing how people of good will could through ongoing discussion create lines of consensus.[140] If objectivism likens the evaluation of ideas to a seminar in which the authoritative, overriding word of the professor settles all arguments, and relativism, to a seminar in which no view can override any other, then the hermeneutic approach likens it to a seminar in which the flow of argument shifts around the table and can lead to some overriding of some views, but whose views will prevail is not clear in advance. This model of global argument indeed seems to fit the historical facts better than the other two, and it is also normatively appealing in our era of egalitarianism.

Also seeking such a "middle ground," John Dunn tries to make clear how any evaluation of an idea can override the evaluation of this idea by the person whose idea it is.[141] Extremely attentive to the historical context of this person, Dunn argues that any overriding or "rational" standard by which a historical agent can be judged must be a reason to act making sense to that specific person given her historically limited motivations and frame of understanding.[142] Thus, the obligations of a historical agent are neither reduced in a relativistic way to her "impulses" nor based on some "superhuman cognitive vantage point," such as that posited by objectivism.[143]

In other words, Dunn tries to specify that limited extent to which an historical agent can be held responsible for following overriding norms going beyond her historically given impulses. On the one hand, much weight must be put on these impulses: "What historical agents have good reason to do depends, inter alia, on what, within a scheme of beliefs which is truly theirs, they have good reason to judge efficacious." On the other hand, as this very formulation presupposes, there are universal, overriding standards of judgment and, especially, "plausibility" that one should use when passing judgment on any historical actor. Another example: "The view that men have political duties which hold *whatever* the consequences of observing them is not plausible."[144] Many of these overriding principles center on a virtue cherished by Dunn as universally important, prudence. Imposing on a historical agent duties that she is causally unable to carry out is to commit a "central error," falling into "the political vice of imprudence.... To presume on eliciting a level of mutual charity and energy higher than will in practice be available and to issue injunctions, on the basis of [this] presumption, which will impose, if they are followed, real costs on those so enjoined is an error in practical reason."[145] Similarly, "to be irrationally sanguine ... cannot plausibly be excused even by the contingency of subsequent success." Phrased like the others to apply to all people throughout history, this principle overrides utopian views such as Maoism.

Dunn also refers to an overriding "standard of intrinsic human value," which also holds for any historical agent. This includes "'rock-bottom duties,'" such as the duty "to feed the starving, when well and safely able to do so." Any "theory of value" that does not recognize these duties is "intrinsically discreditable" as "an unsound theory of what is of value for human beings."[146] Thus Dunn even implies a concept of universal human nature. In other writing (unpublished), moreover, he follows a worldwide consensus defining the criteria of national success and failure, which for him include "democracy" as an epistemically privileged ideal created by the Athenians and now accepted across the globe. This ideal, in turn, is integral to what he calls "modern politics," a condition today crosscutting many cultural and historical disparities. Whether or not ideas can transcend historically specific content, a good bit of this content for Dunn is uniform, however disparate historical and cultural circumstances might be. (This point is made still more clearly in the Dunn writings chapter VIII discusses.)

To understand Dunn's view of the "middle ground" between objectivism and relativism, however, one has to appreciate still better the great extent to which his thinking relies on universally applicable or overriding standards of judgment and other concepts. Besides his "standard of intrinsic human value" and universal norms like "prudence," Dunn makes many overriding statements about the nature of the human world throughout the historical past, present, and future and then logically uses these to make overriding recommendations about how to think coherently about historical activity.

For instance, exemplifying discourse #2, he holds to a view of history as a far less knowable, structured, teleological, and controllable process than has been perceived by many other thinkers. He also makes many other statements applying to "any" historical case:

> Surprise is intrinsic to human history.... In any actual society the causal theories of what is at stake in politics which are held will vary drastically in scope and density between individuals.... But there are no simple and stable and trustworthy recipes for how to judge human properties and potentialities correctly.... In any historical society the political responsibilities of its members differ greatly because their powers (what they are capable of bringing about) and their understanding of what is politically at stake will differ very greatly.... Duties which it *must* be irrational for historical agents to deny are few and far between in politics.[147]

Dunn then logically uses his distinctive picture of the overall nature of human history to make overriding recommendations about how to think properly. Distinguishing between more "coherent" kinds of thinking and "blatantly intellectually inconsequential," "ludicrous," or "superstitious" kinds,[148] Dunn does not take the relativistic view that all definitions of what is ludicrous are equally acceptable. When he calls a view "ludicrous," he means it is objectively ludicrous, even if I think it's profound. For instance, coherence, he holds, can be found *only* by pursuing the "middle ground." While relativism and objectivism both bite the dust, he refutes utilitarianism in particular (a form of objectivism) and rejects all views that the "scope and limits of political duty are ... securely given by conventional categories of law and public authority" (still another form of objectivism).

But how does Dunn ground (justify the use of) all these overriding ideas about moral or political norms, about the nature of the human world throughout history, and about the nature of coherent thinking? In his cultural milieu, he lacks the discourse #3 option, grounding these veridical ideas in "reason" as a universal capacity to think logically and morally. On the other hand, he shies away from the discourse #2 option of grounding these ideas in specific experience, presumably because such a tactic smacks of the nihilistic arbitrariness of relativism. Dunn's famous work on John Locke, let us not forget, is not only admirable but also filled with admiration for this deeply religious, discourse #3 philosopher. For Dunn, it seems, the denunciation of evil requires a bar of judgment more awesome and conclusive than whatever force of public opinion can be generated by one population group among others. *Vox populi* can't make it without *vox dei*. Hinting that human experience does have a kind of transcendent if ineffable moral dimension, Dunn is uneasy with the idea of history as the ground of all meaning.

He thus refuses to view the evaluation of a historical set of ideas as just a historically specific act of understanding or epistemic competition whereby a historically specific we-group, using their rules of successful thinking, argues with another, whether vicariously or not, and discovers whether or not agreement is possible. True, given Dunn's own emphasis on the historicity of ideas, it is hard to see how there can be any ahistorical, algorismic evaluation of what historical actors have said or done. How can one think of the evaluation of ideas as an ahistorical appraisal or judgment based on abstract, general principles applying to all historical actors and carried out by no one in particular for the benefit of anyone who might be interested? Yet Dunn is unable to reject this ahistorical perspective.

On the one hand, he repeatedly tries to ground morality in some concept of "reason," "human nature," or even "the state of nature" (see chapter VIII). On the other hand, although insisting that any historical agent should be judged on the basis of the reasoning historically grasped by that person, Dunn refuses to ground this overriding idea and his other overriding concepts in the thinking of a historical we-group. Similarly, he discusses the problem of evaluating historical actors without conceptualizing a historically particular agent of evaluation. He is also ahistorical in dealing with the question of who or what is being evaluated, and with that of the nature of the evaluation. What he discusses, then, are the universal principles of evaluation to be used by any historical actor when evaluating any other historical actor and arriving at a universally valid judgment. Thus, of all the concepts making up his methodology, only one refers to historically particular experience: the principle of judging historical individuals mainly in the light of the "beliefs" they themselves had. This very principle of judgment, however, and all his other methodological concepts are presented by Dunn as the intellectual products not of a specific historical group but of a kind of anonymous mind able to determine what is "plausible" or "intrinsically discreditable" with regard to all of human history. He asks how is it "epistemically appropriate to conceive of and to judge political and social actuality and possibility"? How can we construct "a theory of rational political duty ... devised principally for the appraisal of actual historical agents"?[149]

To be sure, his theory in this regard probably accords with my own rules of successful thinking. I also would not blame Confucius for failing to lead a movement against sexism, since in his historical context, there was no "good reason" to lead one. In evaluating Confucius, however, I want to know not only whether he is blameless but also whether I should affirm any of his views. A theory of evaluation, in other words, has to tell me how, in this world of clashing cultures and philosophies, I should go about figuring out what is nonsense and what makes sense. If one's quest for "the middle ground" between objectivism and relativism remains so ahistorical, how can it yield the substantive standards of judgment needed to figure this out?

My use of "indisputables" thus resembles Bernstein's and Dunn's quest for a "middle ground" in that I too see the evaluation of ideas as based not on a universal algorism but on the ideas of historical agents, and in that I too try nevertheless to view these historical evaluations as something more than arbitrary, subjective preferences.

Seeking this non-subjective quality, however, Bernstein relies on some undefinable sense of enlightenment arising out of argument, and Dunn somewhat peremptorily announces that there are universally overriding, "rational" standards with which "a theory of rational duty" can be established. My point, meshing with Isaiah Berlin's, is to minimize the controversy about what ideas if any constitute such standards governing all human history. This can be done by simply citing the empirically undeniable existence of evaluative standards that are indisputable in the eyes of the historical we-group evaluating what people have said and done. More precisely, by describing how people in fact unavoidably use ideas indisputable to them to evaluate other ideas, one obviates the whole debate about how to avoid basing the evaluation of ideas on either merely arbitrary, subjective notions or the ability of some anonymous mind to figure out the principles of plausibility applying to all human history. As a member of a we-group identifying the rules of successful thinking we regard as indisputable, I not only can evaluate ideas in a way we regard as indisputable but also will do so anyhow. What, then, are our rules of successful thinking?

Table 3: Those Rules of Successful Thinking about Political Theory Regarded by My We-group as Platitudinous and Indisputable

A. Rules Regarding Epistemology

1. *Tzu-chueh* (maximizing critical awareness of the nature of one's life) is necessary. This includes having ideas (such as this idea of discourse and the four topics of political theory) about the best way to describe and evaluate ideas and so about the universal nature of human existence (e.g. the thesis of its partly

Table 3 (Cont'd)

sociologistical nature implied by the idea of discourse). Critical
awareness includes seeking maximum precision in distinguishing
between arbitrary assertions and ideas that are necessarily correct
or somehow indisputable. It also implies "truth in advertising" in
the sense of maximally avoiding public presentation of an
arbitrary assertion as a necessary truth.

2.   It is necessary to pursue discursive, propositional thinking,
     expressing one's ideas to others by using a historically established
     language, following its rules with regard to grammar and style,
     and organizing one's statements so that others can understand
     them as easily as possible.

3.   Logical consistency is necessary, including consistency between
     one's recommendations about how to think and one's actual
     ways of using ideas. Socrates' denunciation of misology is
     absolutely irrefutable. (Popper, I argue, recommends rejecting
     historicism while actually establishing a historicist connection
     between his ideals and the moral meaning of European history.)

4.   The epistemic autonomy of the individual is a necessary idea
     requiring minimum dependence on publicly disseminated
     doctrines that the individual has not herself critically assessed,
     whether a sacred canon, a conventional culture, an allegedly
     authoritative philosophy endorsed by the state, an academically
     established methodology, or some widely accepted definition of
     the contemporaneous world. There can be no perfect epistemic
     autonomy, but my premise tips the balance away from epistemic
     heteronomy, toward which Chinese thought partly inadvertently
     leans.

5.   To be clear, it is necessary to disaggregate clusters of meaning,
     reducing them to "clear and distinct ideas." The key distinctions
     among types of ideas are those between descriptive, causative,
     predictive, evaluative, recommendatory, and epistemological
     propositions. Virtually all Chinese political theory is at odds
     with this distinctly Western view. More broadly, except for its
     illogical relativism, the Great Modern Western Epistemological

Table 3 (Cont'd)

Revolution, based on epistemological pessimism, contributed greatly to the precious search for clarity.

6. As Popper and the positivists agree, descriptive, causal, or predictive statements make sense only to the extent that they accord with logic and empirical evidence. Generally speaking, all the statements of this kind that can be quantified make up "science."

7. It is important to see, however, that the "empirical given" (*tang-hsia ch'eng-hsien*; *so-yü*) includes not only Kant's "sensory manifold," secondary reports about it, and those "inner" contours of the mind self-consciously perceived by the mind (e.g. Kant's realm of categories), but also all the empirically observed linguistic and other symbolic activities of human beings, including discourses. For instance, the characteristics of discourses listed in this chapter are empirical givens. Praxis as a process carried out by a human agent acting in the first person by translating an inner goal into an outer fact is also an empirical given. Not all empirically given data can be scientifically analyzed, and any arbitrary reduction of one empirical given to another is unsound. This applies especially to the reduction of praxis in the first person to the observed behaviors of third persons.

8. Contrary to the Humean tradition prevalent in the U.S. academy, what is empirically given does not necessarily consist only of observable, quantifiable data free of any necessary normative implication. First, directly unobservable wholes or essences also are given. For instance, it is a given fact not only that Michael Jordan scored 52 points in a basketball game on Tuesday and 48 points in one on Thursday but also that he has existed continuously over a period of time as an extraordinarily able basketball player. This ability existed also on Wednesday, when he did not exhibit it by playing in a game. In Chinese terms, this ability is part of his "essence" (*t'i*) over time, which he "applied" (*yung*) on Tuesday and Thursday. Second, as an example of an existing process that is inherently valuable and should be cultivated, one can bring up the question of truth, the mental

Table 3 (Cont'd)

activities supposedly revealing it, and the problem of logic. If truth has value, and if logic should be seen as revealing truth, the logical mental activities revealing truth are inherently valuable and should be cultivated. Therefore, education is inherently good. If truth and logic have no value, Hume's idea that "ought" cannot be derived from "is" has no value even if true. Because it is hard to see that Hume believed his philosophy had no value, his attempt to disconnect value and fact clearly contradicted his own beliefs.

9. Epistemic practicability is crucial when making recommendations about how to think. In other words, epistemology should not boil down to chimerical recommendations such as "depend only on clear and distinct ideas." It should offer recommendations that can be implemented as a way of discussing factual and normative issues, i.e. a living discourse. Therefore a recommendation to discard a discourse characteristic common to all actual historical discourses is probably impracticable. At the very least, a person making such a recommendation should be able herself to demonstrate its practicability. For instance, if Popper recommends discarding historicism and epistemological optimism, his own discourse should be free of them.

10. Epistemic practicability, like the political practicability discussed below, brings up the epistemic question of how to know whether goals are practicable. How does one know that historicism cannot be discarded in the designing of political goals? How does one know that a polity basically lacking selfish interests is an impracticable goal? My premise is that the practicability of an idea should be determined largely but not wholly on the basis of a posteriori knowledge of history. This premise is in direct conflict with modern Chinese utopianism.

B. Rules Regarding Goals

11. "Unenlightened selfishness" (the world should be organized to maximize Thomas Metzger's pleasure) is untenable as a publicly articulated goal. All public political discourses emphasize the good of a group. Thus libertarianism, ethical relativism, and

Table 3 (Cont'd)

utilitarianism are all untenable except when adulterated with some concept of an absolute ethical commitment to the public good. When Yang Chu recommended "acting purely to satisfy one's own desires," he was talking about what everyone should do, not asking that everyone act only to satisfy Yang Chu's desires.

12. Equality is a necessary norm and takes various forms, such as the golden rule; the idea of "being neither arrogant nor overly humble" when arguing with others (*pu-k'ang pu-pei*); and the principle in *Mo-tzu* that "one should not criticize others for affirming an idea one affirms, and one should not ask of others that they affirm an idea one does not affirm" (*yu chu chi pu fei chu jen, wu chu chi pu ch'iu chu jen*). Popper violated this latter principle of equality when he retained historicism while asking others to reject it.

13. Freedom (i.e. "negative freedom," to use Isaiah Berlin's term) also is essential for human well-being.

14. Politics should be seen as a matter of pursuing often conflicting goals, especially government maximizing freedom and equality; prosperity as modern economic growth minus the ills of growth (such as excessive economic inequality and ecological damage); national security; pursuit of global benefits essential to all nations; and civilizational values (i.e. the non-legal, non-scientific parameters of freedom). The idea of political progress, therefore, emphasizes material well-being but cannot be reduced to purely instrumental considerations. It instead refers to a combination of what Weber called "the rationality of means" and "the rationality of ends," not just freedom but also the parameters of the three marketplaces, not just autonomy but also *paideia* as a heteronomous process inculcating in credulous children a rationality of ends and thus enhancing the social capital of a society.

15. Political goals should be based on the pessimistic idea that the perfect society cannot be realized. Selfishness and intellectual confusion will continue to shape history for the foreseeable future. Political progress is from one imperfect condition to

Table 3 (Cont'd)

---

another, not a process ending what T'ang Chün-i called "the conflation of the sacred with the demonic" (*shen-mo hun-tsa*). Progress is thus a matter of prudent judgment, not utopianism.

C. Rules about the Given World

16. I have not thought these through except to note agreement with discourse #2's largely Weberian premises about the given world. Especially important is the indeterminateness of history, its form as a mix of regularities and irregularities (Hayek) and so as a combination of repeated patterns, unique episodes, and unique personalities. I accept Popper's argument about the human inability to predict the human future with the confidence of scientists predicting physical events and add that, in a multicausal world, it seems impossible definitively to weight the historical causes for important events and so make definitive recommendations about how to pursue goals, not to mention the problem of assuming that the causal principles which governed the past will govern the future. Nevertheless, the causal importance of selfishness and intellectual confusion seems to be an established law of history and is certainly recognized as such in discourse #2. Admittedly, the ability to know this law is hard to reconcile with Hume's and Popper's epistemological pessimism.

D. Rules about Agency

17. Effective agency is correlated to a teleological interpretation of history. This point stems from both the indeterminateness of history and the principle of epistemic practicability. The former objectively gives much leeway to the agent of action selecting an account of historical causation, making predictions, making recommendations, and acting. How should this leeway be used? As Kant suggested, commitment to the goal of life implies commitment to use the means needed to realize it. These means include a spirit of determination and hope, and, as Kant noted, this spirit seems inseparable from interpreting the past and predicting the future in as hopeful a way as is logically compatible with the empirical understanding of history. At the same time, as illustrated by Popper's own view of history as a struggle between

Table 3 (Cont'd)

"the open society and its enemies," any first-person discussion of political goals grounds them in a morally meaningful, teleological, historicist picture of history.

18. If, moreover, a political theory is to be propagated as a way of influencing popular behavior, a large part of the population involved must be able to understand it. Thus it has to incorporate much of the discourse familiar to these people, i.e. traditional, popular ways of thinking that have accumulated over the centuries. In other words, an advertised political theory cannot become widely accepted by a group of citizens unless it accords with their most deeply felt beliefs. Clearly, along with the principle of epistemic practicability, this need to accommodate tradition puts into doubt some leading Western criticisms of Chinese political theory.

19. The forms of agency are various, including popular, "crescive" trends as well as changes "enacted" either quickly and directly by the political center or in a slower, more indirect way by prominent, relatively educated groups outside the political center able to advertise their beliefs throughout much of society. The idea that such groups ("intellectuals") necessarily can control the course of history has been disapproved by history, but not the idea that they are often highly influential in the long run.

By thus publishing this list of nineteen rules of successful thinking (ROST) that we regard as indisputable, my we-group is precisely trying to act as an agent of improvement, entering the competition between advertised definitions of political rationality, and so trying to influence the evolving "critical consciousness" (*p'i-p'an i-shih*) of influential strata on both sides of the Pacific.

12. The Seesaw Effect

Our advertisement is an aggressive one, implying that two currently prevalent political discourses, #1 and #2, are irrational, suffering from epistemological smugness and failure. Although the agents of each discourse confidently see themselves as effectively struggling toward the conceptualization of a wholly rational or indisputable political theory, both groups are caught on a seesaw, able to pursue some rational dimensions of political theory only at the cost of neglecting other ones.

To be sure, the failures of political theories are not due only to this seesaw effect. For one thing, history indicates that, no matter how brilliant, any person trying to discuss coherently the four topics of political theory will carelessly violate various canons of effective thinking recognized by intellectual circles around the world, whatever the nature of their discourses, such as the need to avoid contradiction, one-sidedness, and neglect of relevant issues. There also is the difficulty of reconciling norms universally applying to all political situations with nationalism or some other way of identifying oneself with only one particular segment of humanity. This involves the problem of triage, whereby every political theory, whether openly or not, decides that some kinds of human suffering are more important than some others. Both discourse #1 and discourse #2 have failed to resolve this problem, and this failure causes much of the current tension between China and the West today. According to discourse #1, it is rational to view China's lack of international centrality as a painfully abnormal condition to be rectified, but this condition is a quite normal one from the standpoint of discourse #2. Other problems distinct from the seesaw issue include the controversies about how to pursue empiricism and the description of ideas, discussed above.

The seesaw issue stems from a dichotomy on which my we-group focuses (point #14), and which is so basic to thought east and west that one suspects it reflects the universal human situation. In the West, we speak of the tension between "the rationality of ends" and "instrumental rationality" (as Max Weber put it) or between "value" and "history," "freedom" and "necessity," "faith" and "reason," or *Gemeinschaft* and *Gesellschaft*. In Chinese history, many terms, going back to the sayings of Confucius in the fifth century B.C., have similarly distinguished between a kind of "inner," ineffable focus on ultimate values and some form of discursive reason, the most famous being the pair *tao* (the True Way all should follow) and *ch'i* (instrumentalities) in the *Classic of Changes*.

According to my we-group's nineteen premises, there is a successful and an unsuccessful approach to each of these two poles. The idea of a seesaw refers to the way that a promising approach to one pole seems to have a kind of perverse affinity to an unsuccessful approach to the other. If the Chinese and Western discourses discussed in this book are typical, no historical discourse has escaped this perverse affinity. In other words, one has to distinguish between the general, abstract ideal of a political theory which cogently addresses both poles as it conceptualizes the goal of political life, means, the rest of the given world, and epistemology, on the one hand, and, on the other, the actually available historical discourses which deal specifically and usefully with these four topics, which influence political action, and which seem trapped in this pattern of perverse affinities. (As discussed in chapter X, this notion of a seesaw effect has points in common with a basic criticism of Western liberalism set forth most famously by Carl Schmitt but going back to at least Benjamin Constant and François Guizot.)

Table 3 outlines the nature of this ideal political theory implied by our nineteen premises as well as the two kinds of perverse affinity in which discourses #1 and #2 are respectively trapped.

Two kinds of affinity have never been realized by any historical discourse I am aware of: the ideal link-up, AB, and the worst possible case, XY. History instead seems to have confined itself to the seesaw alternatives of AY and BX. At least, discourse #1 well illustrates AY, while discourse #2 illustrates BX equally well. We thus view the clash between Chinese and Western political theories as a clash between historical discourses that are both flawed but in different ways. The picture of this painful clash in turn implies a model of the normative political theory, AB, which intellectuals in both arenas could aim to construct and advertise.

To be sure, this approach is not entirely novel. Going back at least to Cheng Kuan-ying (1842–1923), many Chinese intellectuals have held that, in the search for an ideal political theory doing justice to both the question of the *tao* (the True Way) and that of *ch'i* (instrumentalities), China has neglected the latter, the West, the former.[150] This point indeed has almost turned into an iron law for modern Chinese philosophers, who have often made it since the last years of the Ch'ing dynasty by contrasting knowledge about the "inner" basis of "praxis" (*shih-chien*) with knowledge about the "phenomena" of the "outer" world. So close to Weber's between "the rationality of ends" and "instrumental rationality," this Chinese distinction seems to accord with the universal structure of human

Table 3: The Seesaw Effect

		Promising Approaches	*Unsuccessful Approaches*
Ideas mostly revolving around the rationality of ends	**Epistemology and the general nature of history as part of given world**	A. Does not "turn the corner." Knowledge of truths about objective reality available.	X. "Turns the corner" toward relativism and skepticism.
		Hegelian truths. History is partly transparent, exhibiting regularities, stages, progress, values.	No Hegelian truths. History opaque, unpredictable, lacks regularities, exhibits no stages, progress, values.
	Agency	"Convex" focus on praxis as resolute effort to shape future. Education as heteronomous public effort to influence inner life, realize positive freedom. Marketplaces have thick parameters. Diversity and pluralism justified as transitional historical stage.	Agency "concave," adjusts to observed trends. Education centers on knowledge about phenomena. Maximally thin parameters for the three marketplaces. Diversity justified on grounds of universal epistemic frailty.
Ideas mostly revolving around discursive or instrumental rationality	**Epistemological issues pertaining to the physical, historical, and practical aspects of the given world**	B. Disaggregating the six kinds of propositions in order to focus on boundary between knowable and unknowable.	Y. Voluntarism, often combined with ontological idealism. Deducing the six kinds of propositions from a central concept to build grand theory.
		Weberian empiricism, including a focus on culture, discourse, and emic understanding. Naturalistic ontology.	Sociological reductionism. Cultural differences little affect how people reason. Emic understanding brushed aside.
	Goals	Political theory as inconclusive guidelines with which prudently to pursue piecemeal progress in the moral limbo of a particular society.	Political theory as a conclusive system with which to transform political life and realize a society without moral dissonance.
		Emphasizing the negative freedom of citizens in the three marketplaces and resisting tyranny.	Utopian vision of three marketplaces directly based on positive freedom.

life. My table just tries to make clearer how actual political theories have invariably failed to do justice to both parts of this structure. The heart of the problem, as my we-group sees it, is how to combine an emphasis on hopeful, resolute political action with one on accuracy in depicting facts and caution in defining the scope of knowledge.

Probably most readers, east and west, will understand why my we-group regards the ideas under B as rational. There will be more controversy about our conclusion that the ideas under A are rational. According to them, a political theory successfully pursues the rationality of ends when it explicitly affirms considerable epistemological optimism, refusing to "turn the corner" by going down the road of relativism and skepticism. Instead, it explicitly recognizes the possibility of knowing truths about objective reality, including the basic Platonic-Hegelian truths about history. By Platonic-Hegelian truths I mean history's relative transparency, the central role of regularities, essences, and wholes in its constitution, and the way it exhibits stages, progress, and values.

Why my we-group defies the GMWER and refuses to "turn the corner" is explained especially in my essays on T'ang Chün-i and John Dunn. All in all, we (1) insist on the primordial paradox of human thought as a combination of historically disparate assumptions with a reflexive ability to make true statements about objective reality, and so we reject the inclination to reduce thought to merely arbitrary, subjective notions; (2) reject as illogical any relativistic suggestion that an idea has meaning only in the context of one limited segment of human history; (3) note that "the Platonic-Hegelian truths" are categories that no known discourse has been able to discard; (4) therefore reject any political theory that does not openly, directly and fully incorporate them into the apparatus of knowledge; (5) note that, in all known discourses, the conceptualiza-tion of indisputable goals is logically based on these "truths"; (6) call for a "convex" conceptualization of praxis and *paideia* as first-person efforts to turn these ideals into empirical fact; and (7) accept the sociological thesis that the advertisement of relativistic theories rejecting these points 1 through 6 has indeed helped cause all the civilizational problems that have been repeatedly blamed on the GMWER (see above).

If, then, this is the promising approach to the rationality of ends in the eyes of my we-group, it is an outlook that seems to have a perverse affinity to an irrational way of dealing with instrumental issues. No discourse I know of, certainly not discourse #1, has combined it with a promising approach to instrumental issues by affirming a naturalistic ontology (Popper's world 1, "the physical world"); by using a properly pessimistic epistemology that cautiously distinguishes between descriptive, causal, predictive, evaluative, recommendatory, and epistemological propositions; by analyzing institutions, cultures, and discourses in a spirit of Weberian empiricism and pursuing emic understanding (*Verstehen*); by avoiding utopianism; by viewing political theory as inconclusive guidelines with which prudently to pursue piecemeal progress in the moral limbo of a particular historical environment; and by effectively pursuing prosperity and resisting tyranny, emphasizing the negative freedom of citizens competing in the three marketplaces.

Instead of being combined with this discourse #2 approach to the more instrumental issues, with which my we-group agrees, the promising approach above to the rationality of ends seems to have a perverse affinity with an unsuccessful way of dealing with the instrumental side of political life, that is, an affinity for ontological idealism and voluntarism; for the pursuit of grand, "dialectical" theories, like Maoism, which claim to deduce the six kinds of propositions from a central idea like "contradiction"; for the innocent view that normative reasoning is little affected by cultural differences; for the equally innocent paradigm of political theory as a conclusive philosophical system transforming political life to realize a society without moral dissonance; and for the utopian goal of three morally harmonious marketplaces directly based on "positive freedom."

Conversely, people with that promising approach to instrumental issues just outlined seem unable to integrate it with a promising approach to the rationality of ends. Instead, they "turn the corner" to go down the road of relativism and skepticism; illogically deny that people are able to know objective reality; thus brush aside the "Platonic-Hegelian truths"; and so try to picture history as an opaque, unpredictable process made up essentially of juxtaposed events and exhibiting few if any regularities, not to mention stages, signs of progress, or values. Moreover, agency from this standpoint is a passive process, "concavely" responding to observed trends; education revolves around the analysis of observed phenomena, not praxis; and diversity and pluralism are justified on the grounds that there is no knowledge of objective norms, instead of justifying them by defining the historical present as a transitional stage during which pluralism is appropriate.

In other words, if "political rationality" is a generic term denoting all the political ideas that a we-group regards as indisputable and as apprehended by the most authoritative mental faculty, "reason," the current clash between Chinese and Western political theories entails at least three different competitive ways of viewing "reason" and the global distribution of sense and nonsense. From the standpoint of discourse #1, only AY is rational, and the Western leaning toward BX is either unimportant, pathological, or a "paradoxical" way of expressing AY. From the standpoint of discourse #2, BX is essentially rational, while AY is a naive, backward, irrational way to think. According to the premises (AB) that my we-group regard as indisputable, however, both AY and BX are irrational.

Yet, in reflecting on these premises, my we-group recognizes that any success it might have in combining A and B depends on the idea of a paradoxical relation in all human discourse between culturally disparate premises and the ability to think reflexively about objective reality. Close to the Marxist idea of "contradiction" and "dialectical" relationships, or to the current Chinese notions about "paradox," this idea of a paradox does not strike us as a particularly sturdy one on which to base our worldview. In the spirit of the GMWER, however, we suspect that no sturdier basis is available at present for the pursuit of political theory. Being able to entertain the ideal of a completely transparent, paradox-free ontological situation is like being able to conceive of eternal life: being able to think of the situation does not guarantee that one will ever be in that situation. Given that mismatch spotted by William of Ockham between what could be known about human life and what people are capable of understanding, there is nothing paradoxical about the apparent fact that all we can ultimately grasp is a paradox.

13. A Cloud Across the Pacific: The Persisting Clash between Two Partly Irrational Discourses

a. The Quest for a Transcultural Critical Perspective

The essays in this book, therefore, seek to describe and evaluate clashing Chinese and Western political theories so as to attenuate the differences between them. Finding a shared critical perspective transcending this intellectual clash is an urgent need, because, so long as this clash persists, the international discussions needed to resolve concrete political issues will falter, and the current tendency toward mutual alienation will persist. Trying to resolve this clash, however, is an unavoidably complex if not convoluted process. As usual, it is easy for humankind to fall into misunderstanding, difficult to devise a lucid analysis that all parties can accept. This will disconcert many readers, especially the many political scientists who are willing to accept abstruseness in economics and natural science but feel explanations about history and culture should be simple. My project has shown once again that the historical-cultural circumstances impeding the rational pursuit of human interests are so convoluted that only a complex analysis can even begin to make clear what they are.

I began by trying to find a common denominator between Western and Chinese political theories: an acceptable definition of what a political theory is as something to be described and evaluated. This effort, however, required my addressing an epistemological question: what is the basis for any human ability to make credible if not true and overriding statements about this question?

Delving into this epistemological problem, I have, like so many in recent centuries east and west, looked in "experience," not a sacred canon, for an ontological starting point, necessarily presuming, like all other empiricists, that the basic categories I have encountered are somehow common to all human experience, and seizing on the empirical observation that people repeatedly if not invariably base their thinking on ideas they regard as indisputable, such as "our" "racism is bad." I then combined this empirical observation with other plausible versions of empiricism: conventional naturalistic, sociologistical views along with some recent, partly "hermeneutic" trends growing out of the GMWER (especially relying on Richard J. Bernstein, John Dunn, and Isaiah Berlin). The result was the idea of premises or "rules of successful thinking" (ROST) that are largely indisputable for a particular historical we-group. I thus hoped to avoid both the modern illusion that evaluations of ideas are necessarily arbitrary and any rash endorsement of selected ideas as universally true.

According to the ideas "we" regard as indisputable, people seek to improve their political lives by discussing them, not only by acting. The final goal of such discussion, however, is action — the improvement of governmental and citizen behaviors. Therefore I agree with the focus of Chinese thought on "praxis" (*shih-chien*) and sympathize with the ideal of *chih-hsing ho-i* (the unity of action and knowledge). The causative path from theory to action, however, has to be spelled out.

I see the pursuit of political theory as presupposing a central premise about historical causation that Reinhard Bendix summed up as "intellectual mobilization": ideas created in the intellectuals' ivory tower can be advertised by means of publications, conversations, etc. and thus, slowly infiltrating the mass media and the processes of legislation, adjudication, education, socialization, and so on, eventually change a society's definition of knowledge and common sense. This change then eventually influences decision-making by political and economic leaders, because they almost invariably find it advantageous to pursue interests according with the prevalent canons of common sense.

This intellectualistic theory of historical causation, which Lin Yü-sheng identified as basic to Chinese thought, modern and premodern, has actually been basic also to Western political philosophy from Spinoza and Hobbes through Leo Strauss. The GMWER, however, suggested a new way of viewing the political ideas being propagated to rectify political behavior. They had been seen "objectivistically" as conveying eternal truths all people would affirm no matter what their cultural milieu. They now could instead or also be seen as an advertisement, an effort to present a convincing analysis of the goals of political life; of the means to reach them; of the causative processes of human history, along with other aspects of the given world; and of epistemology as the criteria with which to distinguish sense from nonsense when discussing all the latter topics. Such discussion invariably takes the form of a group discourse made up of the premises regarded as "rational" or indisputable by that group, including a shared agenda of unresolved questions, as well as controversial claims advanced by one or more persons within that group to address this agenda, if not also claims reflexively challenging the premises themselves. A political theory is a set of controversial claims advertised in the context of such a discourse.

Admittedly, the premises my we-group regard as indisputable thus can negate themselves, since they include the possibility of casting doubt on even our original epistemological stance. We depicted ourselves in an empirical, naturalistic way as a social group with a shared, historically-shaped language and set of beliefs, not, say, as children of God or Kantian beings oriented exclusively to universal principles of reason. This act of self-definition, however, is just another belief or perspective that could be challenged. Thus it unavoidably is a historical product born out of the GMWER, a distinctly Western way of offering an objectively accurate description of the nature of all human mental life.

Ultimately, therefore, my methodology awkwardly rests not just on empiricism but also on an apparent fact that this empiricism reveals: human thinking as a paradoxical combination of culturally disparate assumptions and the reflexivity with which rationally to seek truth, knowledge, and a critical understanding of objective reality, including the relations between thought, natural phenomena, and history. My viewpoint thus has much in common with the preoccupation of thinkers like Husserl with the relation between history and reason. It also is close to Karl R. Popper's way of distinguishing between world 1, "the world of physical objects," world 2, that of "mental states," and world 3, that of the "objective contents of thought." My argument, however, in line with the post-Popperian "hermeneutic" trends discussed by Richard J. Bernstein, is that the relation between worlds 2 and 3 is tighter and more "paradoxical" than Popper suggested. Trying to identify my view regarding the ultimate nature of that form of existence in which I find myself "thrown," as the existentialists have nicely put it, I do end up awkwardly straddling two widespread intellectual traditions: the discursive, empirical effort to identify ontological reality with logically discussed physical objects or events and the unavoidably "mystical" sense that reality as an object of discussion is ultimately a matter of paradox, contradiction, or so-called "dialectical" relationships that are not susceptible to the dictates of verbal clarity.

Whatever its ontological nature, then, a political theory is a series of controversial claims, but the meaning of a claim is not conveyed by the claim alone. It is inseparable from the context of the claim, the particular discourse or mix of discourses of which the claim is an integral part. There is, after all, no meaning without context. My dependence on the idea of discourse and my quarrel with much of the scholarship on Chinese intellectual history and on intellectual history and philosophy more generally stem from my emphasis on the need empirically to grasp the context of an idea. (My emphasis on the context side of history, rather than historical episodes and biographies, began with my publications in the 1970s.)

These methodological considerations led to an idea that, I think, is new. In the effort to choose among available political theories in order to find the best guidelines with which to improve political life, how to evaluate political theories in an indisputable way is not the most serious problem. The GMWER suggested it was, because, according to the seemingly ineluctable logic of the GMWER, such evaluations appear to be just arbitrary, subjective value judgments. Therefore, thinkers like Husserl, Heidegger, Leo Strauss, and Alasdair MacIntyre poured their energies into overcoming this "crisis" of "relativism." The GMWER, however, could only ignore, it could not alter the empirical fact that, in human discourses, evaluative standards regarded as indisputable are not unavailable but unavoidable, such as the nineteen basic platitudes of my particular we-group listed above.

To be sure, as just discussed, once such premises are uncovered, they become objects of reflexivity and so can be philosophically debated and revised. As uncovered premises are compared with those from another discourse, what was a platitude can turn into an intriguing problem. Ultimately, as I argue especially in chapters VIII and X, political rationality at least largely lies in identifying clashing rules of successful thinking, debating them, and then choosing between them. Any such revision of premises, however, will in turn rest on other premises regarded as indisputable. Therefore, although it is important to ask, as T'ang Chün-i does, whether any premises escape relativism and are part of a universal algorism, the very unavoidability of indisputable criteria with which to judge among clashing premises turns the task of uncovering, describing, and comparing alternative premises into the key intellectual exercise needed to reduce misunderstanding, as opposed to the traditional epistemological goal of anchoring these ultimate criteria in some sort of ontological or universal reality.

Moreover, given the unavoidability of these ultimate criteria of successful thinking (as discussed in section 11 above), the definition of a successful political theory is obvious: a successful political theory discusses the four topics a political theory should discuss (goal, means, other aspects of the given world, epistemology) and does so in a way according with those rules of successful thinking regarded as indisputable by the we-group evaluating that theory, such as the nineteen platitudes above.

Thus, the pursuit of political theory centers on the task of describing different discourses so as to learn more about the variety of ideas different groups can regard as indisputable and to become able to obtain a comparative and critical perspective on the way each defines the four above aspects of political life. This approach not only replaces the chimerical quest for the ontological foundations of indisputables with a feasible empirical task but also offers a way out of Straussian ethnocentrism.

Again, this definition of a correct political theory is relativistic. There is no way to escape the fact that, ultimately, political rationality is dependent on a historically limited perspective. For instance, a racist political theory will appear to be indisputable to a Nazi audience. Relativism in this sense is unacceptable to those who believe political rationality can and must be anchored in absolute, algorismic principles.[151] I suspect, though, that, even if there are such absolute principles, they are always too general and formal to give substantive normative guidance, especially in the case of conflicting political goals. Thus historicist relativism — paradoxically enough — seems to be a universal condition. This unavoidable condition, however, by no means interferes with the accessibility of indisputable principles and strong beliefs, as Isaiah Berlin pointed out. The nihilistic idea that all political beliefs are equally acceptable may or may not be logical and psychologically practicable (conceivably, there could be a totally wishy-washy person agreeing with every view, including absolutism). In the actual historical world of competing political theories, however, such nihilism is seldom if ever found. Instead of fearing this chimera, we need to fear powerful beliefs that are misguided, i.e. out of accord with the values indisputable for us.

The urgent problem, then, is not that of finding criteria with which to define what a good political theory is. What is difficult is finding an available, practically specific and useful political theory in accord with this obvious definition. Originating a whole new political theory seems to be infeasible, because the production of a political theory in all its complexity seems to require a cumulative process taking generations. What is feasible is advertising criticisms so as gradually to revise inherited discourses. But these cannot be effectively criticized without first describing them.

The methodology of description, however, is highly controversial, as I have tried to show in some detail. Calling for an empirical, inductive effort to describe historical paths of political reasoning as accurately, lucidly, and comprehensively as possible, my essays in this book in an unavoidably inadequate way plunge into a most difficult task. My point is that undertaking this entirely empirical, historiographical task of description is not just a historiographical task. Description is precisely the chief function of political theory or political philosophy. Conversely, because the epistemological problem of how to evaluate historical paths of political reasoning is not urgent, addressing this still prominent issue should not be the chief task of scholars pursuing political theory.

b. The Key Question of Knowledge about Political Norms

Applying the critical perspective just discussed, I concluded that discourse #1 and discourse #2, those discourses most saliently involved in the current clash between Chinese and Western political theories, are both to a large extent irrational. Both fail to accord with the rules of successful thinking my we-group regards as indisputable (see section 11), but they fail in drastically different ways and so clash with each other. Trying to advertise our rules of successful thinking by using them to criticize discourses #1 and #2 is the only way I can think of to seek a new critical perspective with which mitigation of the clash between these two concepts of political rationality might be feasible.

This critical perspective centers on the thesis that these two discourses both badly failed to deal with the question of knowledge about political norms. Political rationality in our eyes presupposes the GMWER's refutation of at least the boldest metaphysical claim, the epistemologically optimistic claim still basic to discourse #1 that the human mind can use means like "intuition" or "dialectical reasoning" to obtain knowledge of that one, ineffable ultimate reality which is the existing source of the principles governing the natural world, history, and ethical life; can come to know how all these principles form a unified conceptual system; and can even become one with this ultimate reality, working with it to dispel all evil in the world.

Besides rejecting this metaphysical claim, my we-group's rules of successful thinking accord with the GMWER or with parts of it in two major ways. First, we largely accept the epistemological demotion of normative ideas from the status of true propositions or knowledge to that of ideas to which the standard of truth is not applicable. More precisely, we accept this demotion at least in the case of specific answers to policy questions. Such specific answers can be developed only by privileging a particular historical discourse, but we remain open to the possibility that the most general norms, such as the golden rule, have some objective basis.

Second, we accept the GMWER's insight that, even if natural science has a strongly objective basis, the conceptualization of not only political goals but also of the causative patterns of history and of the nature of evidence about them is inseparable from ideas peculiar to a particular discourse and so cannot be regarded as just based on objective knowledge. In other words, the human world of historical events, everyday life, and moral-political praxis (*Lebenswelt*) cannot be directly known as a set of objectively existing, causatively connected processes. What can be known is the discourse with which a particular we-group has depicted these processes.

Advertising my we-group's rules of successful thinking, I thus hope to persuade readers to prefer them over much of China's discourse #1. Acording to my scheme, discourse #1 has to be revised if the ideological conflict between the Chinese and the Western intellectual worlds is to be reduced, but revision of Western political theories is also needed, as chapters VIII, IX, X, XI, and XIII argue.

As argued in chapter XIII, however, the GMWER yielded two tracks for the rational revision of Western political theories, one building on and one challenging the GMWER. On the one hand, as best illustrated by chapter X on Rawls, I criticize some of these theories for insufficiently incorporating the insights of the GMWER, especially its post-Kantian insights into the ways in which culture and reflexivity are intertwined. On the other hand, I argue that the GMWER exaggerated the extent of human fallibility. That is, it failed to explore the limits of fallibility, the extent to which general moral-political norms can be based on objective knowledge, not only on the "indisputables" of a discourse or some other version of that "middle ground" between "relativism" and "objectivism" so effectively depicted by Richard J. Bernstein.

This is the question on which contemporary Chinese philosophy, notably T'ang Chün-i's writings, may shed light. The concept of political rationality my we-group hopes eventually to grasp would combine this light with the insights of the GMWER, thus defining political rationality as a combination of knowledge (normative as well as factual) with the indisputables of a particular historical discourse.

To find this light, which I am only beginning to assess, one can begin by questioning Popper's classic claim that the idea of knowledge can apply only to propositions which logical empirical experimentation can falsify. This claim makes sense only if Popper knew what the meaning of this word "knowledge" is. Without knowing what knowledge is, how could Popper have held that mere states of mind are not forms of knowledge, while so-far-unfalsified propositions are? Yet this knowledge he had about what knowledge is lies outside the scope of what he said knowledge is, namely, propositions that can be experimentally falsified. Popper himself viewed knowledge as made up of more than such propositions.

Moreover, although Popper disagreed with many philosophers about what ideas should be regarded as forms of knowledge, all philosophers I have encountered agree that the universal nature and scope of knowledge can be known. In other words, for them, knowledge can increase or decrease but the nature of knowledge does not change, as relativists would be the first to agree when they claim either that knowledge is unobtainable or that its scope is limited. Even more, knowledge, it seems, has to include some ontological concept, that is, some idea believed to be true about what ultimately, objectively is so. For instance, however uncertain we may be regarding the availability of ontological knowledge about either the natural or the historical worlds, my we-group cannot avoid regarding the paradoxical combination of reflexivity with historically-bequeathed linguistic symbols as something ultimately and objectively existing precisely as it appears to exist (see chapter VIII, section 6) and as actually forming an unlimited number of discourses exhibiting an identical formal structure (see section 2 above on the six kinds of statements and the four universal topics addressed by all discourses). The chapters below on Dunn and Rawls, not to mention the one on Hayek, show how even astute Western thinkers deeply influenced by empiricism cannot construct a political theory without depending on some concept of the true universal nature of human nature or of the actual way that human thought whenever and wherever it occurs is related to the rest of reality. Needless to add, China's epistemological optimists depend on such a concept at least as much. If, then, people cannot avoid believing they have some knowledge about the universal nature of knowledge, human nature, and other aspects of what ultimately exists, can one say that such knowledge is necessarily free of normative, moral, and teleological implications? My suspicion is that the GMWER botched this question in the very course of arriving at its profound insights, finding no way to articulate the latter without neglecting the former.

If thought is indeed a paradoxical combination of reflexivity with historically-bequeathed linguistic symbols, it seems impossible to deny that this combination implies an imperative maximally to develop this reflexivity, the Socratic demand to examine one's life, to pursue knowledge, to uncover and critically assess these inherited beliefs, to decide which to retain, which to discard (*ch'ü-she*). This imperative, *pace* David Hume, implies that knowledge as an existing process is inherently good and should be pursued. If it should be pursued, moreover, much of J.S. Mill's liberalism can be justified as based on knowledge (the need for education, freedom, etc.).

The imperative maximally to develop reflexivity, moreover, itself implies an emphasis on freedom and autonomy, the determination freely to construct one's own self by excluding from its makeup any ideas which one has not critically assessed. This notion of radical inner autonomy, strikingly enough, resonates with not only the Lutheran tradition but also the prevalent modern Chinese ideal of *tzu-chueh* (full critical awareness of all aspects of one's existence), of freedom from all *shu-fu* (constraints wrongly imposed on the self). Even more, as illustrated by the title of Karl Popper's *The Open Society and Its Enemies*, it seems to be impossible to regard these epistemological, ontological, and moral ideas as true without inferring from them a teleological historical struggle between those pursuing and those blocking the expression and implementation of these principles, a struggle equating these principles with "enlightenment." Finally, one cannot just ignore philosophers like

T'ang Chün-i who have not been impressed by the GMWER's assertion that morality is a purely human process none of the content of which can be derived from that cosmos of which this human process is actually a part.

The extent to which political rationality can be based on knowledge, therefore, is still an open question. To whatever extent it can be, however, political theory has to address many key questions to which answers are available only in "the middle ground." The most challenging of these questions is: what are the questions that should be raised in "the middle ground"? So far as I can see, this challenge has not been strongly met by any version of either discourse #1 or discourse #2. I have tried to address it in chapters VIII and X and especially XIII. One can perhaps divide these questions into two groups.

First, there are the "initial questions," such as those dealing with the kinds of ultimate premises just discussed, with the articulation of one's rules of successful thinking, with the purpose of political theory, and with the historical roots of one's own agenda and categories — all the questions that have to be asked if political theory is to be based on a maximally critical perspective rather than conventional ideas.

Second, our concept of political rationality demands avoidance of "the seesaw effect," and this cannot be avoided without addressing a good number of much-debated questions. John Dunn has done much to reveal these questions, although I mostly disagree with his answers to them. They include: What is the standard of clarity and precision that a political theory should meet? What is the ratiocinative exercise (e.g. Rawls's construction of "the original position") through which political ideas can best be clarified? How knowable or opaque are the causative processes of history? What are these processes? How should the goals and means of political life be conceptualized? Given the persistence of political conditions drastically at odds with goals, how should one assess the practicability of proposals to realize goals? What does the historical record say about such practicability? Is progress practicable? Has it occurred?

As my we-group sees it, then, the extent to which political rationality can be based on knowledge, not just on the rules of successful thinking we regard as indisputable, is a still challenging question. To whatever extent we speak from knowledge, however, we believe political rationality requires avoiding the seesaw effect, and that avoiding it depends on how one answers the questions just adduced. Such is the new perspective with which we hope to soften the clash between contemporary Chinese and Western political theories.

c. More on the Irrationality of the Two Clashing Discourses

Thus trying to redefine the nature of a rational political theory, my effort must be shocking. This is because it is severely at odds with the outlooks of two intellectual-cultural camps regarding each other as partly irrational, each serenely reigning in its own civilization, each utterly comfortable with its own conventional definition of political rationality (AY and BX), each intertwined with deeply-rooted political interests, especially those of academic groups whose power, prestige, wealth, and psychological equilibrium depend on the credibility of their thoroughly institutionalized disciplinary commitments. As I see it, both groups fail to avoid "the seesaw effect" as well as common intellectual shortcomings, like lapsing into contradiction, while also failing to provide sufficiently specific guidelines of development useful for all the major kinds of societies east and west. Moreover, the methodologies favored by each group for the study of ideas are all at odds with "our" belief in focusing on the crucial empirical problem of describing as accurately, lucidly, and comprehensively as possible the ways in which people actually think about political life.

On the Western side, rational choice theory illustrates some of the problems afflicting discourse #2. Most disconcerting is its frequent claim, quite irreconcilable with empiricism, that one can know what the interests or goals of a group are without inductively seeking an understanding of this group's desires. Even when holding that goals are defined in culturally disparate ways, moreover, the rational choice school wrongly assumes that there is one globally algorismic way to reason about means and identify "evidence." Popper similarly drew too clean a boundary between "world 2" as "beliefs" or "states of mind" and "world 3" as discursive, falsifiable propositions. He overlooked how falsifiable political recommendations are logically based on causative statements about history, not just about physical nature. Partly because questions of historical causation are inherently difficult if not impossible to answer in an exact, definitive way, the answers to them often stem from culturally disparate ways of perceiving history and defining the given world. This is illustrated vividly by the contrast between discourse #1 and discourse #2 described in table 2.

In other words, Popper's epistemology is interwoven with his picture of world history in *The Open Society and Its Enemies* and in *The Poverty of Historicism*, but in fact his "critical rationalism" has not settled the endless disputes about what the patterns of historical causation have been and how to identify the data that should serve as "evidence" regarding their nature. Like Marxism, utilitarian approaches like Popper's unfortunately always presuppose the availability of an algorismic way of understanding which data constitute reliable evidence regarding historical causes and the means for attaining policy objectives. This misunderstanding also mars Hayek's scientism.

I also venture to criticize Leo Strauss for emphasizing two logically linked ideas: the illusion that cultural relativism is preventing people from having any firm normative beliefs, and the refusal to delve into the culturally disparate, socially shared discourses forming the contexts of political reasoning. These problems, however, stemmed from a still more basic outlook of his.

Strauss, like John Dunn and unlike Hayek, rejected any effort to understand political life by depending on any allegedly scientific methodology, whether Marxism, Weberian social science, or the derivation of normative principles from disciplines like biology and anthropology. Largely accepting the GMWER, however, Strauss, much more than Dunn, retained the epistemological optimism challenged by the GMWER. He believed not only that the Jewish vision of God could not be abandoned but also that Greek philosophers had grasped absolute political principles in a "natural" way unadulterated by culturally disparate modes of thought. He thus depicted the history of Western political philosophy by contrasting this "natural" Greek understanding of the universal nature of political life with a subsequent evolution of misunderstandings from Machiavelli and Hobbes through Weber. By equating the study of political theory with examination of this gradual corruption of political reasoning in the West, Strauss not only neglected the cultural contexts of *all* political thought, whether Greek or Korean, but also failed systematically to raise two questions logically implied by the very idea of a political theory or philosophy: that of which questions a political theory should deal with, and that of which criteria should be used to evaluate any answers to these questions. As with Popper, the emotional crisis of World War II let Strauss feel that the humanistic mission which political theory should pursue was so obvious that these two issues need not be directly addressed. Instead, he looked in Western historical texts for reasoning either vindicating this humanistic mission or misunderstanding if not betraying it.

I do believe that his vision of this mission was badly ethnocentric, especially in failing to take the problem of knowledge out of its Western cultural context. Like Popper, who viewed the "dualism" of facts and values as indisputable, Strauss, who deeply admired Nietzsche, failed to achieve critical distance from the GMWER, and so did not respond to the various culturally divergent definitions of knowledge with any Socratic sense of wonder and suspended judgment, with any need to reopen the most basic questions about how to determine which ideas should count as knowledge, or with any fear of being misled by that ethnocentric belief in Western "rationality" which Weber had so eloquently expressed. Although Strauss is an important critic of the GMWER and its "relativistic" "historicism," he criticized it in terms of a privileged Greek outlook allegedly transcending cultural bias, instead of systematically confronting the epistemological questions it raised. I believe that one has to step outside the envelope of the GMWER in order to realize a relatively critical perspective on the key problem of what knowledge is, and that pondering the Chinese criticisms of the GMWER may be the best way to do this. Unlike Popper, however, Strauss did emphasize the description of ideas, believing that the pursuit of political theory is primarily an effort to trace out the meaning of political rationality by describing the ways in which historical cases of political reasoning succeeded or failed to convey that meaning.

While Strauss wanted to vindicate some of the epistemological optimism of discourse #3, John Dunn's thought still more clearly illustrates the dilemma of discourse #2. Dunn, more inclined than Strauss toward the epistemological pessimism fostered by the GMWER, avoids the epistemologically optimistic enthusiasm with which Strauss privileged the Jewish and Greek visions of the eternal "whole" to which human life supposedly belongs. Instead of these absolutistic visions, Dunn can only depend on a peremptory manner with which to affirm the basic humanistic ideals of "western political theory" and so try to avoid ethical relativism. Basing his normative principles just on this peremptory manner, Dunn not only lacks any epistemological basis for a coherent theory of progress but also tries to present a bleak view of human nature, "politics," and history as a process without either progress in the past or hope for the future. His thought thus epitomizes discourse #2's tendency to combine an emphasis on empirical accuracy and caution in defining the scope of knowledge with lack of a hopeful, resolute way to conceptualize political praxis — the very opposite of discourse #1.

Like Dunn's, John Rawls's formidable work on the problems of political theory is indispensable for anyone trying to figure out what these problems are. From my point of view, Rawls sought to reconstruct the epistemological foundation of political theory by straddling discourses #2 and #3, instead of building on discourse #2. On the one hand, he basically accepted the GMWER's epistemological demotion of normative concepts, mostly agreeing that moral principles could not be true ideas about some objective order of things. On the other hand, he brushed aside the GMWER's post-Kantian insight into the impact of culturally disparate perspectives on the formation of ideas regarded as constituting objective knowledge. By ignoring this impact, Rawls could try to recover the Enlightenment's belief in the use of "reason" to define political norms. Moreover, unlike Dunn, Rawls shared the Enlightenment's optimistic if not utopian view of history and political practicability.

In Rawls's case, then, the "seesaw effect" could conceivably have turned into one combining a hopeful conceptualization of progress with a lack of caution in examining the nature of knowledge. Nevertheless, as chapter X argues, his theory exemplified discourse #2 in not only accepting the GMWER's epistemological demotion of normative ideas but also lacking a coherent conceptualization of resolute action to improve political life. This lack may well have been due to his liberal determination to regard equality, freedom, and justice as supreme political goals overriding all others. Yet it also reflected the epistemological inhibitions basic to discourse #2. Unlike Hayek, Rawls was very conscious of the GMWER's objections to the inferring of normative considerations from rationally devised principles. Like Jürgen Habermas, I would say, Rawls thought these objections could be overcome by demonstrating reason's inherent affinity with the most universalistic norms: openness, freedom, and equality. He remained doubtful, however, that there could be such an affinity in the case of substantive norms like progress, which entailed some degree of closure to the world of infinite possibilities, a determinate commitment to act this way and not that.

For Rawls, therefore, squeezing a commitment to the ideal of justice out of reason, not just to openness and freedom, was already a precarious enterprise. After all, even this inference had to be filled out with principles derived not from reason but from a historical tradition, "the public political culture of a democratic society." How then could Rawls's already precarious conceptualization of "the reasonable" have been enlarged to include a coherent idea of progress, not only justice?

In other words, Rawls distinguished between values that could be derived by reflecting on the nature of reason or of "the public political culture of a democratic society" and goals that could be determined only through the unpredictable votes of free and equal citizens. Openness, freedom, and justice belonged to the former category, progress, to the latter.

This epistemological stance, however, left Rawls's liberalism open to Carl Schmitt's criticism that liberalism and parliamentary democracy reduce politics to ineffectual discussion (see chapter X). In other words, it left the concept of resolute action to improve political life unintegrated with rationally acceptable premises of political discussion.

The dilemma of discourse #2 and of the GMWER is still more exposed in the philosophy of the erudite, world-renowned philosopher Richard Rorty. Like Strauss, Hayek, Dunn, and Rawls, Rorty reveres the Enlightenment ideals of freedom and equality. He does not, however, join these thinkers in their struggle to avoid relativism by proving that these ideals of the Enlightenment can somehow be based on "reason" or knowledge as true propositions about what is objectively so. On the contrary, inspired by Ludwig Wittgenstein, John Dewey, and Martin Heidegger, Rorty claims that this very struggle against relativism is the problem, not the solution. For him, the authoritarian subversion of these Enlightenment ideals stems precisely from the way Western culture crystallized around the unfortunate suggestion of Socrates, Plato, and Aristotle that human beings need the authoritative idea of an objective reality which their ideas should mirror. The idea of such a reality, Rorty seeks to show, is irrelevant to human needs. Therefore, instead of organizing intellectual life and society around it, people should organize them around William James's pragmatic goal of believing whatever "it is better for us to believe." Rorty tries to show that such pragmatism leads neither to anarchy nor to a social order based on nothing but the conventional beliefs history has thrust one's way. It just means discarding the Socratic myth that there is any objective truth distinguishable from the rhetoric of the day, and so discarding the illusion that people can shape their history by basing their actions on standards transcending the historical-cultural parameters within which they find themselves.

In thus adducing the parameters of "what society lets us say," however, Rorty relies on simplistic though fashionable sociologistic ideas about "culture," "society," and "history" that are hard to reconcile with the empirical study of human life. To the extent that culture consists of not just customs but also "conversations" or "discourses" including "because" statements, socially imposed parameters empirically appear as indeterminate and criticizable. In empirical fact, therefore, social-political life exhibits not a dichotomy between determinate historical parameters and the chimera of standards transcending them but living discourses in which shared, historically bequeathed beliefs evolve inseparable from ideas criticizing them in the name of objective reality and universal truth. To put it in terms of that holistic theory of meaning which Rorty follows, the meaning of these historical beliefs lies in the relations not only between them but also between them and the critical views competing with them. Indeed this holistic point is illustrated throughout my book by textual evidence about how people in fact publicly discuss the improvement of political life and the revision of inherited cultural patterns.

Given this empirical nature of politically relevant discourses, Rorty's recommendation to eschew belief in objective reality and universal truth is not practicable. True, he holds his philosophy demonstrates it is practicable, that such a belief can be replaced by an "ironical" outlook on any assertion about truth and reality. As I argue in chapter XIII, however, this claim is contradicted by his own verbal behavior. Indeed, nothing better illustrates the tension between historicity and critical reflexivity than his own drastically iconoclastic criticism of the Western philosophical tradition.

Consciously caught in this contradiction, he has to rest not on his thesis of "irony" but on a claim that, in the quest for freedom and equality, poetry trumps respect for logic. Even more, his political philosophy so drastically separates this quest for freedom from any Burkean respect for tradition and the problem of political practicability that it can be called "utopian."

Strangely enough, therefore, what Rorty took from James's pragmatism was not any emphasis on that practicability most people associate with "pragmatism." Oscillating between a radically individualistic emphasis on "self-creation" and a sociologistic reification of the linguistically unified group, Rorty tried to turn pragmatism into a Promethean, poetic, utopian search for a world in which people are free and equal because they need to follow nothing but their own ideas about what "is better for us."

In his hands, then, GMWER doubts about the scope of knowledge turned into a rejection of the very idea of epistemology as an unnatural attempt to limit freedom by demanding subservience to myth (i.e. the standards of objective reality and universal truth Socrates mistakenly adduced to criticize what people said). Rorty's truly brilliant work, then, comes down to this argument: it is impossible to show that these Socratic standards are not mythical when one takes seriously the insights of the GMWER about the influence of culture and language on reflexivity.

As chapter XIII discusses, however, Rorty's attempt to show this has been widely disputed. My own view is that showing this is difficult, not impossible. Moreover, while Rorty assures people that rejecting these standards as mythical is "what it is better for us to believe," my hunch is that pragmatic, practical action to do what is "better for us" depends precisely on the vindication of these standards as the basis for collective, resolute, hopeful, trustful, and prudent action to minimize the forces threatening our well-being. Such action indeed is "better for us." As I see it, if one rejects rather than vindicates these standards, one cannot avoid the seesaw effect and that dilemma of liberal passivity which Carl Schmitt discussed. Moreover, if one rejects these standards, how can the individual's freedom be realized as critical control over the content of her own desires?

Like Rawls's philosophy, Rorty's helps readers confront what seems to be the key question raised by the GMWER: What is the normative relation between critical reflexivity and one's cultural-linguistic heritage? Should the latter be regarded as the starting point or the object of the former? Regarding it as the object, I see the uncovering and the critical, comparative discussion of inherited premises as the proper exercise of critical reflexivity and so resist Rawls's and Rorty's tendency to turn critical reflexivity into the handmaiden of culture.

My concern throughout has been with maximally reconstituting the link between political rationality or knowledge and hopeful moral-political praxis. As I see it, overcoming the seesaw effect means philosophically reconstituting this link and on this basis reshaping the educational foundation of society (*paideia*). According to this concept of political rationality, which I am trying to advertise, citizens educated to seek freedom through the pursuit of critical reflexivity would be inclined seriously to explore all the issues pertaining to the improvement of political life. Thus they would debate the "initial questions" and the more specific questions listed above in section b.

From this standpoint, the purpose of philosophy is the improvement of political life through education. This purpose was certainly that of classical political theory east and west during what S.N. Eisenstadt called "the axial age," and in modern times this focus remained central to the intellectual mainstream in China. In the modern West, however, this perspective was increasingly challenged as the ideals of liberalism became combined with the epistemological pessimism of the GMWER as well as a widespread "bourgeois," "individualistic" desire to minimize the parameters limiting individual freedom.

This modern Western criticism of that classical vision which Leo Strauss so admired was indeed dubious in many ways, raising questions that have troubled Strauss and so many other critics to this day. It also, however, entailed a new insight into the nature of freedom. From this standpoint, freedom lies in more than the beneficent "outer" circumstances of political and economic development emphasized since the Renaissance. Freedom also is "inner" or "Lutheran," so to speak; "inner" freedom lies in the ability critically to select one's beliefs and thus autonomously to determine the makeup of one's own self; this ability depends on distinguishing between passively imbibed and critically selected beliefs; and distinguishing between these depends on successfully analyzing the historical, cultural, and biographical context of one's own reflexivity (not just its social class context, as Marxists would have it). To use Rorty's terms, the idea of freedom necessarily bridges the public and private spheres.

Leo Strauss was certainly aware of this new insight into the nature of freedom. Yet he failed to acknowledge that the Greek concept of political philosophy he exalted was entirely innocent of this post-Kantian insight. By the same token, he erred in brushing aside the social scientists' discovery of culture. He brusquely reduced their insights to a relativistic assault on the value of reflexivity. They actually had discovered a new dimension in the quest for autonomy as critical control over one's own makeup.

Therefore Strauss overlooked the challenge posed by the GMWER's new insight into the nature of freedom. Given this new insight into the impact of culture and language on the exercise of critical reflexivity, the liberal, Enlightenment ideal of freedom required not only liberal institutions and scientific control over nature but also critical control over the premises or "rules of successful thinking" on which people depend to reason about reality. How then could critical scrutiny of these premises be logically integrated with the classical concept of collective, resolute, trustful, hopeful, prudent action to improve political life? In other words, how can this latter concept be rediscovered without lapsing into the myths or misunderstandings of an excessively optimistic epistemology? How can the classical or even primordial concept of effective political action be combined with the GMWER's post-Kantian insight into the nature of freedom? Entangled with the problems we call "epistemological," this question, I argue, is the puzzle in the face of which political theories east and west today founder, failing to avoid the seesaw effect.

All in all, then, Rorty sees the human quest for well-being as undermined by a philosophical aberration whereby the Greeks induced Westerners for more than two thousand years to go against their "natural" inclinations by imagining that accord with a somehow objective standard was the key to human well-being. As chapter XIII notes, however, this allegedly unnatural idea has been a common one east and west. What I see as an aberration is the outlook epitomized by Rorty's admittedly brilliant philosophic effort. Human well-being, I believe, was furthered precisely by the GMWER's initial steps in pursuing that objective standard raised up by the Greeks, that is, by the GMWER's finding that the definition of this objective standard is a profound problem. Human well-being was endangered, however, as this finding turned into doubts that such a standard is at all available or even desirable.

As I see it, the problem with such relativistic doubts is not that they lead to anarchy. After all, history has always revolved around groups with shared beliefs about what is indisputable, not to mention the major human tendency, east and west, to embrace epistemologically optimistic dogmas or intellectual fashions. The danger in accepting Rorty's recommendation to follow Protagoras rather than Socrates lies rather in relaxing the struggle to turn shared beliefs into objects of critical scrutiny.

As I have just argued, this relaxation can be seen in the tendency of Western liberalism, exemplified by both Rawls and Rorty, to co-opt the sociologistic concept of culture, regarding whatever cultural surrounding into which one has been fortuitously thrust as the unavoidable basis rather than the object of critical reflection. By thus truncating the scope of critical reflection, liberal philosophers welcome the melding of any currently conventional, critically unexamined ideologies, whether chauvinistic or socially radical, with the ideals of freedom and equality. At that point, the liberalism intertwined with the GMWER does not sacrifice resolute political action on the altar of a scrupulous search for epistemological clarification, it instead aborts this search to license policies based on unexamined ideological impulses. The problem with Western liberal political theory then is not the miasma of indecision Carl Schmitt deplored but Erich Fromm's "escape from freedom." It is unfortunate that Karl R. Popper used the unclear term "open society" to describe the Socratic liberalism he had in mind. This term facilitated the iconoclastic attack against the Socratic spirit in the name of openness. Practically speaking, the openness of "the three marketplaces" always has to be limited by certain parameters, as argued in section 5 above. The only question is the extent to which the definition of these parameters is to rely on critical reflection or on critically unscrutinized assumptions or ideologies. With the GMWER's hugely important introduction of the idea of culture, however, the nature or even the possibility of critical reflection became a seemingly insoluble puzzle, as discussed especially in chapter XIII.

Such is the dilemma of Western liberalism. With regard to the Chinese side, the reader should easily appreciate the abundance of evidence indicating the prevalence of discourse #1 and the failure of discourse #1 to rectify "the seesaw effect." In my essays on T'ang Chün-i, Henry K.H. Woo, Kao Li-k'o, Li Qiang, Yang Kuo-shu, and Ambrose Y.C. King, this failure is repeatedly pointed out. A more subtle question is how this Chinese way of failing to avoid "the seesaw effect" has clashed with the Western way.

d. Chinese Doubts about Western Modernity

To be sure, one important aspect of this clash is obvious: conflict between the West's perception of its own global centrality and the Chinese premise that China's current more peripheral role is abnormal. The Western sense of actually being a super-civilization confronts the Chinese sense of being a temporally crippled but ultimately still more successful and admirable civilization. Apart from this antinomy, however, there is a variety of Chinese reactions to the societal and epistemological features of the West today.

In the case of T'ang Chün-i and Henry K.H. Woo, two representatives of modern Confucian humanism, the rejection of discourse #2 includes both pessimism about Western societal tendencies and a philosophically knowledgeable criticism of the GMWER, that is, the epistemological part of discourse #2. Mou Tsung-san's monumental oeuvre and Li Jui-ch'üan's (Lee Shui Chuen's) book on Hume also pursue this epistemological criticism. A similar combination of social and philosophical criticism has also been common in the Mainland's Marxist or semi-Marxist circles, as illustrated by the views of Chin Yueh-lin, Feng Ch'i, Ch'en Hsiao-lung, and Li Tse-hou, discussed above. Chapter IV on Kao Li-k'o, however, describes a Maoist rejection of Western modernity oriented more to societal than epistemological issues. Similarly, in the case of Ambrose Y.C. King, the focus is more sociological than epistemological. King admires the "rationality" of the global "modernization" movement initiated by the West. Influenced by modern Confucian humanism, however, King wants China to adopt this "rationality" along with "democracy" but without the West's "liberalism" and "individualism."

Indeed, along with these thinkers I discuss, the standard writings produced by three of modern China's four main ideological trends (Maoism, Sunism, and modern Confucian humanism) have all strongly objected to what can be broadly called the West's "liberalism" and "individualism." Thus it is clear that in China not only objections to the West's global centrality and imperialism but also impulses to diverge from the Western model of modernity are far from exceptional. They are indeed widespread and deeply-rooted, easily linking up with a continuing tendency in the popular culture to view the West as embodying "'those poisonous vapors of the capitalist class that come to China in the deceptive form of a fragrant breeze'" (*hsiang-feng tu-wu*) and to hold that "socialist China and the capitalist West cannot peacefully coexist."[152] Moreover, the criticisms of Western culture found in writings like T'ang Chün-i's are not necessarily off target, reinforcing as they do the West's internal critique by pointing to not only grave societal problems but also problems pertaining to epistemology and moral education (*paideia*). In joining Western critics to identify discourse #2 as a threat to *paideia*, modern Chinese humanists like T'ang Chün-i and Henry K.H. Woo did not demonstrably fail to understand Western modernity. Instead, they reinforced rational doubts about it. Using the framework discussed above, one can say these humanists pointed out that discourse #2 is subject to the seesaw effect, since it undermines praxis while successfully pursuing empiricism and avoiding utopianism.

This varied, deeply-rooted Chinese criticism of Western modernity is often intertwined with nationalistic hostility to the U.S. as a nation projecting its power all along the coastal regions of Asia and Europe. But it is also often intertwined with a similarly strong admiration of the U.S. and Western modernity. The combination of these feelings in one heart was illustrated by the response of Peking University students to the September 11, 2001 Arab attacks on New York and the Pentagon. Many if not the vast majority of them want nothing more than a chance to enter a U.S. university, but these same students were filled with joy by the devastation the Arab terrorists caused in the U.S. A Chinese friend of mine called them "crazy," but their happiness exemplified the Janus-faced way China's intellectual world today views the West.

China's fourth leading modern ideology, Chinese liberalism, epitomizes the pro-Western side of this Janus-faced outlook. Indeed Chinese liberalism has typically combined a Panglossian view of Western modernity with a lack of interest in if not even awareness of the philosophical questions raised by the GMWER. My essay on the representative Taipei liberal Yang Kuo-shu describes his scientistic, philosophically innocent way of celebrating the "democratic," "free," "open," "pluralistic," and "individualistic" societies of the "liberal," "modern" West. The essay on the Beijing political scientist Li Qiang describes a similarly abundant appreciation of the liberal West. To be sure, Li differs from Yang in discussing the epistemological aspects of liberalism. Li, however, is as enthusiastic as Yang about the liberal West. He rejects the criticism of Western liberalism's "relativism" and "skepticism" mounted by the Marxists and the Confucian humanists. Instead, like some other Beijing intellectuals today, he applies a sense of "paradox" to this epistemological problem, concluding that this very relativism and skepticism in the West have been the key to raising the moral level of the citizens of the liberal Western nations above that of the Chinese.

The admiration of Western liberalism shared by such learned and astute scholars in Taipei and Beijing raises a basic question. Picturing the liberal West as based on "reason" and "morality" and regarding its pathologies as insignificant relative to its successes, are they mistakenly idealizing the West as a civilization that has overcome selfishness and intellectual disarray? That is, are they resisting Western liberalism's perception of Western progress as piecemeal amelioration within the moral limbo of political life, and so actually joining their Marxist, humanistic, and Sunist compatriots in rejecting the liberal West as it really is? Or are they taking advantage of a comparative perspective we Westerners lack to congratulate us on successes we take for granted? Is it possible that the Western successes admired by Chinese liberals are somehow more important than the Western failings on which the Chinese Marxists, humanists, and Sunists have dwelled? Is it possible that Leo Strauss's qualms and John Dunn's dismay have been gratuitous? Is it possible that some Chinese liberals by reinterpreting the GMWER have vindicated Western modernity in a philosophically satisfactory way? Should Chinese confronting the spreading power of Western modernity share Henry K.H. Woo's fears about it or Li Qiang's appreciation of it?

e. The Struggle against Epistemic Smugness East and West

Quite possibly, the Chinese hopes as well as qualms about the West are justified. It would hardly be reasonable to expect any civilization to offer only hope unadulterated by worrisome tendencies. Yet even if we Westerners have built up a relatively admirable civilization, we have nothing to gain by refusing to recognize those persisting failings of ours that have aroused Chinese misgivings. It is not enough to admit that we have not lived up to our ideals. Often enough, we admit it while insisting that the basic rationale of our modernity and freedom is impeccable — that, as Francis Fukuyama said, it signifies "the end of history." This kind of epistemic smugness is as worrisome as the kind on the other side of the Pacific. Even more, brilliant as John Dunn's oeuvre is, I argue in chapter VIII that critics of this Western rationale like him have dwelled only on the contradictions between Western political practice and the traditional ideals of "western political theory," rather than finding a methodology with which to uncover and assess the premises of this "morally fastidious" Western intellectual tradition, including the GMWER. Though less bluntly than Leo Strauss, Dunn still bases political theory on a vision of a privileged Western intellectual tradition.

Uncritically privileging one or another segment of the Western philosophical tradition has gone hand in hand with assuming that Western modernity is a paradigm necessarily appropriate for all societies. Yet how can such an assumption make sense when this paradigm fails to deal cogently with not only the problems of Western modernity but also the developmental options of foreign peoples contemplating the possibility of adopting this Western paradigm? The political theories of Dunn, Rawls, and Hayek, for instance, are virtually mute with regard to this latter developmental issue in the non-Western world today. For all three of them, political theory is a matter of fine-tuning Western modernity, not of defining the norms of political life in non-modern societies. Western scholars discussing the latter issue have offered little besides applause for anyone seeming to accept one version or another of the Western paradigm. Scholars like Dunn and Strauss privileging parts of the

Western philosophical tradition and scholars like Rawls privileging conventional democratic values have thus complemented not only the celebration of Western civilization in Weber's and S.N. Eisenstadt's sociology but also the philosophically innocent way many American political scientists and leaders depict the American way of seeking "freedom" and "prosperity" as a model for the world.

To be sure, this Western refusal to discard uncritically ethnocentric paradigms of world history sometimes seems needed to meet the danger of that nihilistic cultural relativism rightly denounced by Allan Bloom.[153] This danger, however, stems only from academics with risible notions about how to describe and evaluate ideas. I trust this book has made clear that serious descriptive and critical approaches to the history of Western ideas, such as Strauss's, are a necessary complement to the in-depth study of ideas developed outside the West, and that the crosscultural comparison of ideas goes hand in hand not with relativism but with firm convictions about which ideas indisputably make sense. Shallow talk about cultural relativism is a serious problem in the U.S. academic world, but nothing illustrates this shallowness better than the way it is often illogically intertwined with a belief in the universality of liberal ideals popular today in the West. Apart from its role in degrading academic standards, then, this popular Western multiculturalism, paradoxically enough, illustrates the deep-seated Western inability to discard an ethnocentric paradigm of world history. Therefore it hinders the rise of enlightened public opinion trends in the West supporting constructive ways of designing the relationships between Western modernity and the powerful civilizational complexes outside it. But Chinese efforts to construct a rational political theory are equally in disarray.

Admittedly, this diagnosis will be accepted only by those who agree with the rules of successful thinking that constitute my we-group's concept of political rationality. My hope is that by now advertising this concept of political rationality, I can help persuade intellectual circles east and west that their inherited concepts of political rationality need revision. With such revision, new patterns of political common sense could emerge and state policies in accord with them could eventually crystallize. Such are, I believe, the causative patterns to which history is susceptible. I do not agree with John Dunn's gloomy outlook on historical possibilities.

But any such happy change in the intellectual climate will be very slow in coming. It is impeded by epistemic smugness on both sides of the Pacific. On the American side of the ocean as well as the Chinese, most intellectuals and other people zealously believe that their definition of political rationality should be accepted and eventually will be by everyone everywhere, instead of humbly equating their own stumbling efforts to pursue political rationality with the efforts of those who disagree with them. East and west, fashionable talk about cultural differences, toleration, pluralism, openness, and Habermasian dialogue has hardly dented deep-rooted biases about how to distinguish sense from nonsense. Many Western academics are quite modest and appealing in their conversations with Western colleagues but dismiss discourse #1 as obviously "bizarre." Their Chinese counterparts are innumerable. By the year 2000, some Mainland Chinese scholars had picked up the fashionable theme of "globalization" by claiming that, through reviving the true spirit of Confucianism, Taoism, and Buddhism, China could overcome the whole "cultural crisis" and "moral crisis" into which globalization, with its roots in a morally and intellectually aberrant Western culture, had plunged the world. Said the famous liberal Li Shen-chih: "As a Chinese, I believe that, in principle, the core philosophy of Chinese culture can open up the best path to resolve China's cultural crisis and that of the whole world."[154] So long as such epistemic smugness, a not so distant cousin of fanaticism, is not replaced by a new, shared sense of epistemic failure and Socratic inquiry, discourse #1 and discourse #2 will persist as clashing definitions of political rationality. The resulting mutual sense of confronting an irrational adversary will thus long continue to aggravate political communication between the U.S. and China.

Harder to resolve than concrete conflicts of interest, generated by the divergence between two old, equally proud intellectual traditions, this disagreement about the nature of political rationality indeed is the cloud across the Pacific. It well illustrates how that tendency toward the global convergence of values analyzed by Alex Inkeles is complicated by the way civilizational patterns continue to diverge from each other, as discussed by Samuel P. Huntington. The following essays, then, can be seen as an effort to uncover the epistemological basis of a major pattern of international tension today. Epistemic smugness, however, does not only aggravate disagreement among nations, it also undermines political development more broadly. In the case of economically backward nations humiliatingly stuck in the periphery of the global community, it blocks the self-criticism needed to revise the inherited culture and reorganize the society. In the case of a great nation at the center of the global community, it tends to lead to a kind of missionary fervor based on the disastrous illusion that the whole global community has now finally become almost ready to "see the light" emanating from this center, that is, to make this center's discourse the lingua franca of political rationality throughout the world.

Yet it is one thing to speak of epistemic smugness in the abstract, sighing over the continuing failure of human beings to deal with their fallibility and moral frailty. It is another to try to do something about this excessive self-confidence by analyzing the clashing trains of thought of sincere and brilliant thinkers in order to grasp the scope of this epistemic smugness, question one's own familiar premises, and so reassess the distinction between such smugness and insight into the nature of political life. The following essays are attempts to explore this distinction more effectively than it has been so far and so to pursue political rationality.

Endnotes

1. See e.g. John Dunn, *Western Political Theory in the Face of the Future* (Cambridge: Cambridge University Press, 1990), and David Held, ed., *Political Theory Today* (Stanford: Stanford University Press, 1991). For Aristotle's distinction between "theoretical sciences" and "practical science," see Leo Strauss and Joseph Cropsey, eds., *History of Political Philosophy* (Chicago: The University of Chicago Press, 1987), p. 119. The term "political life" was used by Strauss sometimes. I started to use it to denote the political activities of a society as an ongoing mix of ideas and overt acts that should be empirically described with a minimum of reductionism. "Politics" focuses too much just on overt acts, "political culture" has usually been used in a reductionist way to denote a closed system of beliefs, and "political development" usually refers to fairly long-term trends analyzed in nomothetic terms. The term "political life" was used in Linda Chao and Ramon H. Myers, *The First Chinese Democracy: Political Life in the Republic of China on Taiwan* (Baltimore: The Johns Hopkins University Press, 1998).

2. In a good deal of his writing, T'ang has referred to "four existential issues," those concerned with "the self" (*chi*), with "others" (*jen*), with

"nature" (*ti*), and with "heaven or God or spiritual beings" (*t'ien*). I presumed to subsume the last two under "cosmos." See e.g. T'ang Chün-i, *Chung-hua jen-wen yü tang-chin shih-chieh* (The Chinese Humanistic Ideal and the Contemporary World), 2 vols. (Taipei: T'ai-wan hsueh-sheng shu-chü, 1986), vol. 2, p. 424.

3. Talcott Parsons, *The Structure of Social Action* (New York: The Free Press of Glencoe, 1961), p. 44.

4. William I. Thomas, "The Four Wishes and the Definition of the Situation," in *Theories of Society*, 2 vols., ed. Talcott Parsons et al. (New York: Free Press of Glencoe, 1961), vol. 2, pp. 741–744.

5. Thomas A. Metzger, *Escape from Predicament: Neo-Confucianism and China's Evolving Political Culture* (New York: Columbia University Press, 1977), ch. 3.

6. See Richard H. Popkin's article on "Skepticism" in the *Encyclopedia of Philosophy*, 8 vols. (New York: Macmillan, 1972), vol. 7, pp. 449–461, and especially his "The Sceptical Origins of the Modern Problem of Knowledge," in *Perception and Personal Identity*, ed. Norman S. Care and Robert H. Grim (Cleveland: The Press of Case Western Reserve University, 1969), pp. 3–24, and Alasdair MacIntyre, *After Virtue* (Notre Dame: University of Notre Dame Press, 1981).

7. Charles E. Lindblom, *Politics and Markets* (New York: Basic Books, Inc., Publishers, 1977).

8. The earliest version of these four categories is in my *Escape*, pp. 5–6. This attempt to list the universal topics of political theory overlapped my effort to list the topics making up the agenda of early Chinese political thought. For the diagram I used to sum these up, see my "An Historical Perspective on Mainland China's Current Ideological Crisis," in *Proceedings of the Seventh Sino-American Conference on Mainland China (1978)* (Taipei: Institute of International Relations, 1978), pp. IV–2–1 — IV–2–17.

9. Richard J. Bernstein, *Beyond Objectivism and Relativism: Science, Hermeneutics, and Praxis* (Philadelphia: University of Pennsylvania Press, 1983).

10. This has been the Chinese liberal goal as depicted in an exceptionally thoughtful and erudite book, Hu Weixi, Gao Ruiquan, and Zhang Limin, *Shih-tzu chieh-t'ou yü t'a: Chung-kuo chin-tai tzu-yu-chu-i ssu-ch'ao yen-chiu* (The Ivory Tower at the Crossroads of Tyranny and Revolution: A Study of Modern Liberal Intellectual Trends in China; Shanghai: Shang-hai jen-min ch'u-pan-she, 1991).

11. In one account of "rational choice theory," for instance, Jon Elster grants that this theory "does not, in the standard version, tell us what our aims ought to be," but it demands that these aims "should be optimally related to the evidence available to the agent," and that "the collection of evidence itself be subject to the canons of rationality.... The processes of evidence collection and of belief formation may be distorted by motivational bias or

skewed by erroneous cognition." This formulation presupposes that the nature of "evidence" is an objective characteristic which can be correctly recognized by using "the canons of rationality," that is, an algorismicly correct way of thinking impeded only by "motivational bias" or "erroneous cognition." At least with regard to historical and political causation, however, different groups or cultures disagree about which data are "evidence" regarding the existence of which cause, and, as illustrated by discourses #1 and #2, these disagreements often stem from culturally different ways of perceiving the causative structure of the given historical world. Elster suggests that objective rational standards are available with which to resolve such disagreements, but, as I argue below, such an "objectivistic" approach seems untenable. See Jon Elster, "The Possibility of Rational Politics," in *Political Theory Today*, ed. Held, pp. 117–118. See note 42 below. In thinking about this issue, I have benefited from discussion with Professor Diana Richards of the University of Minnesota.

12. See Ted V. McAllister, *Revolt against Modernity: Leo Strauss, Eric Voegelin, and the Search for a Postliberal Order* (Lawrence: University Press of Kansas, 1995); Strauss and Cropsey, pp. 907–938.

13. Pierre Manent, *An Intellectual History of Liberalism*, trans. Rebecca Balenski (Princeton: Princeton University Press, 1994). I am much indebted to Dr. Robert J. Myers for recommending this book. The Strauss quote is from McAllister, p. 26.

14. Ch'en Tsu-wei and Liang Wen-t'ao, eds., *Cheng-chih li-lun tsai Chung-kuo* (Political Theory in China; Hong Kong: Oxford University Press, 2001), pp. 1–2. I thank Professor Li Qiang for bringing this important book to my attention.

15. For Weber's view, see his "Introduction" to "The Protestant Ethic and the Spirit of Capitalism," in which he referred to "the specific and peculiar rationalism of Western culture" and said that someone who is a "product of modern European civilization ... is bound to ask himself" why only his civilization has led to developments that "(as we like to think)" have "*universal* significance and value." This is from the version of this essay translated by Talcott Parsons and first published by Charles Scribner's Sons and Greenberg Publishers (I have this version in the form of a 1946 edition of the University of Chicago's *Social Sciences 2 Selected Readings, vol. 1*). Also see Talcott Parsons, *Societies: Evolutionary and Comparative Perspectives* (Englewood Cliffs: Prentice-Hall, Inc., 1966) and his *The System of Modern Societies* (Englewood Cliffs: Prentice-Hall, Inc., 1971).

16. Quentin Skinner, *The Foundations of Modern Political Thought*, 2 vols. (Cambridge: Cambridge University Press, 1978).

17. See note 138 below for the bibliographical reference.

18. Note 138 below also discusses the documentary evidence for the prevalence

of discourse #1 in modern Chinese intellectual circles. There can be disagreement about what China's most important ideologies in the twentieth century were. The influence of each of the four I cite has waxed and waned. In the 1970s, many would have denied Chinese liberalism and modern Confucian humanism were more than side currents. Today Sunism is on the wane in Taiwan, and it is excluded in chapter XII below from my list of leading ideologies in China today. Sun's thought, however, continues to be widely admired in the Chinese world, especially by the increasing number of scholars today promoting modern Confucian humanism. See e.g. the admiring essay on Sun's thought by the extremely astute professor of Chinese philosophy at Wuhan University, Kuo Ch'i-yung, in his *Tzu-hsuan-chi* (A Collection of Essays Chosen by the Author; Guilin: Kuang-hsi shih-fan ta-hsueh ch'u-pan-she, 1999), pp. 341–359. For the many conferences in Hawaii, Beijing, Wuhan, and Shanghai held in 2001 to honor the 135th anniversary of Sun's birth and the ninetieth of the 1911 Revolution, see *Chin-tai Chung-kuo-shih yen-chiu t'ung-hsun* 33 (March 2002): pp. 1–52. Yet however one assesses the influence of Sunism, modern Confucian humanism, Chinese Marxism, and Chinese liberalism, it would be hard to deny that premises shared by these four were part of a widespread discourse.

19. Berlin's famous and very useful distinction is between "negative freedom" as the freedom of a person from "interference" on the part of others in his or her life, and "positive freedom" as the freedom to be a "rational" person "moved by reasons, by conscious purposes, which are my own, not by causes which affect me, as it were, from outside." See Isaiah Berlin, "Two Concepts of Liberty," in his *Four Essays on Liberty* (Oxford: Oxford University Press, 1969), pp. 121–122, 131. "Positive freedom," close to what J.S. Mill called "the dignity of man as a thinking being," is the freedom to realize oneself as a rational and moral person and so, unlike the idea of negative freedom, is not easily turned into a standard with which empirically to distinguish one behavior from another. Borrowing Ferdinand Toennies' famous distinction, I have used *Gemeinschaft* to refer to the ideal of "a fundamentally rural, agricultural community bound together by kinship and kinship-like ties ... fusing together morality, knowledge, and political power and so fulfilling the true needs of every individual," and *Gesellschaft* to refer to a society in which individuals enjoying negative freedom can pursue their interests and goals by interacting with one another in an often impersonal, materialistic, morally unpredictable world that is increasingly complex, commercialized, and urbanized and is largely outside state control. The former ideal is close to what Hayek called "tribal" morality, the latter, to his "end-independent rules." For these concepts of his, see Chapter IX below. My notion above is developed in my "The Western

Concept of Civil Society in the Context of Chinese History," in *Civil Society: History and Possibilities*, ed. Sudipta Kaviraj and Sunil Khilnani (Cambridge: Cambridge University Press, 2001), pp. 204–231. On "the three market-places," see Thomas A. Metzger, "The Chinese Reconciliation of Moral-Sacred Values with Modern Pluralism: Political Discourse in the ROC, 1949–1989," in *Two Societies in Opposition: The Republic of China and the People's Republic of China after Forty Years*, ed. Ramon H. Myers (Stanford: Hoover Institution Press, 1991), pp. 3–56; Thomas A. Metzger, "Will China Democratize? Sources of Resistance," *Journal of Democracy* 9 (January 1998): pp. 18–26; and other publications, including my earliest foray in this direction, Thomas A. Metzger, "Confucian Culture and Economic Modernization: An Historical Approach," in *Conference on Confucianism and Economic Development in East Asia* (Taipei: Chung-Hua Institution for Economic Research, Conference Series, No. 13, 1989), pp. 141–195. There is nothing new in suggesting that the writings of F.A. Hayek and Karl R. Popper jointly emphasized the freedom of the economic, intellectual, and political "marketplaces." My point has been that, to varying extents, the legitimization and institutionalization of the "three marketplaces" has been difficult in China to the extent that they entailed the free, unpredictable interaction between morally and intellectually unsupervised, ungraded individual impulses precluding the ultimate control of society by a morally and intellectually enlightened political "center" (Edward Shils). This relation between Chinese culture and "the three marketplaces" overlaps that between Chinese culture and the distinction between the Rousseauistic and the Millsian versions of democracy. See Huang Ko-wu's (Max K.W. Huang's) book on Yen Fu adduced in note 138 below.

20. Cited in Strauss and Cropsey, p. 555.

21. The only possible exception I am aware of is a famous literary piece by T'ao Ch'ien (T'ao Yuan-ming) (365–427), "T'ao-hua-yuan chi" (A Record of the Spring amidst the Peach Blossoms), which tells of a harmonious, prosperous society hidden away from the normal traffic of the world and accidentally discovered by a fisherman.

22. Lindblom, *Politics and Markets*. See note 139 below.

23. Karl R. Popper, *Conjectures and Refutations: The Growth of Scientific Knowledge* (London: Routledge, 1992), pp. 6–7. On the appreciation of "doubting" on the part of late imperial China's Confucian thinkers, see my *Escape*, p. 66 and Hu Shih's essay in Charles A. Moore, ed., *The Chinese Mind* (Honolulu: University of Hawaii Press, 1967), pp. 116–117. See note 138 below for more bibliographical references regarding epistemological optimism and section 6 below, including note 66, for further discussion of the distinction between epistemological optimism and pessimism.

24. John Dunn, *Rethinking Modern Political Theory* (Cambridge: Cambridge University Press, 1985).

25. Karl R. Popper, *Objective Knowledge* (Oxford: Clarendon Press, 1994), p. 10. For the bibliography regarding my own use of "epistemological optimism and pessimism," see note 138 below.

26. Karl R. Popper, *The Poverty of Historicism* (London: Routledge, 1991), and *The Open Society and Its Enemies*, 2 vols. (Princeton: Princeton University Press, 1966).

27. On Hayek, see chapter IX below. On Strauss, see notes 12 and 114.

28. For these points about Hayek and Popper, which, I believe, are not very original, see section 13 in this chapter; chapter IX on Hayek; and notes on Popper, 81 and 129, in chapter II below. See also chapter XIII.

29. These two chapters from *Hsun-tzu* were translated by Burton Watson in *Hsun Tzu: Basic Writings* (New York: Columbia University Press, 1969), pp. 89–111, 121–138. An important work on *Hsun-tzu* is John Knoblock, *Xunzi* (Stanford: Stanford University Press, 1988).

30. See the two books respectively on these two figures by Huang Ko-wu (Max K.W. Huang) adduced in note 138 below. Also see his "In Search of Wealth, Power, and Freedom: Yan Fu and the Origins of Modern Chinese Liberalism" (Ph.D. diss., Stanford University, 2001).

31. Yang Kuo-shu, *K'ai-fang-te to-yuan she-hui*, pp. 191–192. For full bibliographical reference, see note 138 below. Also see chapter VI.

32. See chapter IV in this book.

33. See *Encyclopedia of Philosophy*, vol. 7, p. 270.

34. Larry Diamond, *Developing Democracy: Toward Consolidation* (Baltimore: The Johns Hopkins University Press, 1999), pp. 2–7, 21, 161, 167, 263, 272, 274, 276. Much of Inkeles's work on convergence is in Alex Inkeles, *One World Emerging: Convergences and Divergence in Industrial Societies* (Boulder: Westview Press, 1998). Unlike Inkeles's work, Diamond's boldly conflates "political science" and "political theory" as I have tried to define them. In other words, he tries to integrate the normative theory of liberalism classically expressed by J.S. Mill with the empirical work done by social scientists on culture and political development. In implying that Chinese political theories opposed to his are less rational than his and calling for efforts to "push" for the democratization of China, Diamond shares the zealous belief of leading Democrats and Republicans like Richard Gephardt and Newt Gingrich that it is the duty of the U.S. to bring democracy to China. With this zeal, reminiscent of the American missionary movement in the nineteenth century, Americans present themselves to Chinese as their teachers — not a constructive approach to foreign policy, I believe. On these policy issues, see Thomas A. Metzger and Ramon H. Myers, "Chinese Nationalism and American Policy," *Orbis*, 42

(winter 1998): pp. 21–36. Also see Robert J. Samuelson's astute criticism, in *Newsweek*, May 31, 1999, of the "global vision" of "America's foreign policy elite," who have "overestimated our ability to export the U.S. political model and its associated political virtues." Much the same point was made by George Will (*San Jose Mercury News*, August 17, 2003) in a brilliant column pointing out that the "neoconservatives" believing that the U.S. can institute democracy in Iraq and Afghanistan base themselves on a theory "antithetical to all that conservatism teaches about the importance of cultural inertia and historical circumstances."

35.   An insightful book emphasizing continuity is a study of post-Mao Mainland intellectual trends, Ku Hsin, *Chung-kuo ch'i-meng-te li-shih t'u-ching* (The Historical Setting of the Chinese Enlightenment; Hong Kong: Oxford University Press, 1992). Ku grew up in the Mainland intellectual milieu, and his emphasis on intellectual continuities with the tradition is now common in Mainland studies of modern Chinese thought. See, for instance, the books by Li Tse-hou and by Chin Kuan-t'ao and Liu Ch'ing-feng adduced in note 138 below. As this book by Ku illustrates, the Chinese translation of Lin Yü-sheng, *The Crisis of Chinese Consciousness: Radical Antitraditionalism in the May Fourth Era* (Madison: The University of Wisconsin Press, 1979), had a major impact on Mainland scholars, causing them to question their standard belief that May Fourth iconoclasm was based purely on universal canons of "reason." Lin's thesis that this iconoclastic outlook was also shaped by unconsciously persisting, tradition-rooted modes of thought thus strengthened the case for continuity between modern and premodern Chinese thought. This case is also made in Liu Hsiao-feng's highly insightful article in Ku Pin, et al., *Chi-tu-chiao, ju-chiao yü Chung-kuo-ko-ming ching-shen* (Christianity, Confucianism, and China's Revolutionary Spirit; Hong Kong: Han-yü chi-tu-chiao wen-hua yen-chiu-so, 1999), pp. 27–114, which argues for the Confucian roots of the revolutionary vision expressed by many modern Chinese including Mao. His approach to the problem of continuity, like that of Ku, Lin, Chin Kuan-t'ao, and Liu Ch'ing-feng, has to be distinguished from that of the New Confucians, illustrated by my essay on T'ang Chün-i in this book. True, both approaches are normative, evaluating the continuity being discussed in the light of some conceptualization of objectively desirable thinking. T'ang, however, refers to a hoped-for continuity with invaluable traditional ideals in danger of being lost, while the others refer to an actual continuity that is deplorable or at least open to criticism. The latter approach was easily accepted by many on the Mainland, since it meshed with the standard May Fourth picture of a contemporary Chinese society still struggling to get rid of "the poisons inherited from feudalism" by trying to go down a road of desirable development discontinuous with the past. A third normative

approach, however, has also become common and is illustrated by the books of Li Tse-hou adduced in note 138 below. This third approach seeks a subtle way of sorting out traditional values, discarding some while embracing others. This approach is also present in the work of Gao Rui-quan, who traces the "voluntarism" so powerful in modern Chinese thought back to Kung Tzu-chen (1792–1841). See his *T'ien-ming-te mo-lo: Chung-huo chin-tai wei-i-chih-lun ssu-ch'ao yen-chiu* (The Collapse of Fatalism and of the Normative Cosmic Order: A Study of Modern Chinese Voluntarism; Shanghai: Shang-hai jen-min ch'u-pan-she, 1991). To be sure, Kao is critical of voluntarism, and in his book he depicts the Neo-Confucian mainstream in the standard iconoclastic way as an outlook hostile to the modern ideals of freedom and equality. In his eyes, however, the Chinese impulse to affirm these ideals and overthrow the repressive system of Neo-Confucianism had traditional roots; it was not just a product of Western influence. This third approach is also illustrated by Yang Kuo-jung's solid study, *Ts'ung Yen Fu tao Chin Yueh-lin: Shih-cheng-lun yü Chung-kuo che-hsueh* (From Yen Fu to Chin Yueh-lin: Positivism and Chinese Philosophy; Beijing: Kao-teng chiao-yü ch'u-pan-she, 1996), pp. 152–153. According to Yang, "the deep-rooted influence of China's traditional philosophy" was to a large extent responsible for the persistent way that modern Chinese philosophers attracted to positivism differed from their Western counterparts by trying to combine positivism with the pursuit of metaphysical truths.

Apart from these three normative perspectives on the problem of continuity between modern and premodern Chinese thought, a more emphatically descriptive approach to this issue has also come to the fore. Actually, Liu Hsiao-feng's brilliant essay cited above also belongs in this category. At least as early as 1986, the extraordinarily learned and astute Liu Kuei-sheng, who became professor of history at Tsinghua University while also holding this position at Peking University, emphasized that late Ch'ing intellectuals grasped Western ideas like socialism only by comparing them to Chinese ideas, such as those of Mo-tzu, and by putting them into the context of Chinese concerns. Particularly telling are his suggestions about how the deep, widespread fear that the Chinese nation and civilization might be destroyed, caused by the defeat of China by Japan in 1895, provoked that radical reorientation of the intellectual world leading to the search for ancient Chinese wisdom outside the classics (*chu-tzu-hsueh*). See Liu Kuei-sheng, *Hsueh-shu wen-hua sui-pi* (Notes and Essays on Scholarship and Culture; Beijing: Chung-kuo ch'ing-nien ch'u-pan-she, 2000), pp. 46–57. Among the many Mainland scholars fully recognizing how modern Chinese thought mixed continuities and discontinuities with the tradition is Hu Wei-hsi. See his *Kuan-nien-te hsuan-tse: 20 shih-chi Chung-kuo che-hsueh yü ssu-hsiang t'ou-hsi* (Choosing Concepts: A Study of Chinese

Philosophy and Thought in the Twentieth Century; Kunming: Yun-nan jen-min ch'u-pan-she, 2002). Another example is Yao Ta-li. See his essay in *Hsueh-shuo Chung-kuo* (China Today in Scholarly Perspective; Nan-ch'ang: Chiang-hsi chiao-yü ch'u-pan-she, 1999), p. 193. An important, brilliant work emphasizing continuity in a descriptive way is Wang Fan-sen's book on the traditional roots of modern Chinese iconoclastic anti-traditionalism, *Ku-shih-pien yun-tung-te hsing-ch'i* (The Rise of the Movement Critiquing the Traditional Conceptualization of Ancient Chinese History; Taipei: Yun-ch'en wen-hua shih-yeh ku-fen yu-hsien kung-ssu, 1987). An excellent analytical survey of all the main branches of modern Chinese philosophy (especially Marxism, New Confucianism, and the Tsinghua school) in effect shows they all pursued what I have called the Neo-Confucian goal of "linkage." See Yü Chen-hua, *Hsing-shang-te chih-hui ju-ho k'o-neng?* (How is Metaphysical Wisdom Possible? Shanghai: Hua-tung shih-fan ta-hsueh ch'u-pan-she, 2000). Adduced in note 138 below, Huang Ko-wu's (Max K.W. Huang's) two books, on Liang Ch'i-ch'ao and Yen Fu respectively, along with his article "Liang Ch'i-ch'ao and Kant," have greatly strengthened the argument that a basic Confucian outlook has been central to the development of the whole twentieth-century spectrum of Chinese ideas about how to modernize China. In other words, the Confucian tradition cannot be regarded as ideas and modes of thought largely rejected to the extent that Chinese sought modernization. This latter, older interpretation emphasizing discontinuity between the Confucian tradition and Chinese modernization was developed especially by Joseph R. Levenson, Benjamin I. Schwartz, and Chang Hao and was long paralleled by similar historiographical views in Taiwan and the Mainland. It was first challenged in the 1970s by the writings of Lü Shih-ch'iang and Wang Erh-min and by my *Escape*. In his later work, Chang Hao too moved somewhat away from it.

While the discussion of continuity between modern and premodern Chinese thought thus can be roughly analyzed as pursuing four viewpoints (one being mainly descriptive, three being distinctly normative), the issue of continuity also was brought to the fore in recent decades by the successful modernization record of Japan and "the four little dragons." Looking at this record, many scholars came to mix a list of standard complaints about popular traditional Chinese culture with a list of popular norms allegedly facilitating democratization; see e.g. Thomas A. Metzger, "Continuities between Modern and Premodern China," p. 283 (for full bibliographical reference, see note 138 below). This outlook is far from uncommon on the Mainland today, as illustrated by Kao Li-k'o's view: "As is shown by the historical experience of modernization in Japan and East Asia's 'four little dragons,' the modernization of the East Asian nations by no means is a process of Westernization for which must be paid the price of discarding traditional resources." See Kao Li-k'o, *T'iao-shih-te chih-hui: Tu Ya-ch'üan ssu-hsiang yen-chiu* (The Wisdom of the Accommodative Approach: A Study of the Thought of Tu Ya-ch'üan; Hangchow: Che-chiang jen-min ch'u-pan-she, 1998), p. 51.

Since the 1970s, then, there has been a sea change in the way scholars east and west have come to view the question of continuity between modern and premodern China, whether pursuing descriptive or normative lines of thought. This hardly means discontinuities are unimportant. It simply means that the a priori primacy over continuities they once enjoyed, thanks to the May Fourth Movement, Max Weber, and Western ethnocentrism, is no longer intellectually tenable, though it is far indeed from being intellectually dead. The problem of continuity and discontinuity in modern China is now one that can be dealt with in an empirical, philosophically open way.

36.   See his article in Chao T'ing-yang et al., *Hsueh-wen Chung-kuo* (China in Intellectual Perspective; Nan-ch'ang: Chiang-hsi chiao-yü ch'u-pan-she, 1998), pp. 1–48. The sense of Chinese scholars that their intellectual world has come to be unhappily dominated by Western academic modes is common, as illustrated by Yang Kuo-shu and Wen Ch'ung-i, eds., *She-hui chi hsing-wei k'o-hsueh yen-chiu-te Chung-kuo-hua* (The Sinification of Research in the Social and Behavioral Sciences; Taipei: Chung-yang yen-chiu-yuan, Min-tsu-hsueh yen-chiu-so, 1982). This outlook was basic in the 1990s to the rise of "postmodernism" in China. See below, chapter XII.

37.   *San Francisco Chronicle*, October 23, 1996. Similarly, in ibid., March 24, 1997, the political scientist John Bunzel denounced "China's Inhumane Rights Policy," adducing "irreducible differences between those who attach primary importance to the inherent rights and self-determination of the individual and those who maintain that the individual is subordinate to the state. This is a conflict of 'discordant principles.' Compromise is not an option." If we are talking of "principles," I know of no modern Chinese ideology holding that "the individual is subordinate to the state." So far as Confucianism goes, even Hsun-tzu (mainly third century B.C.), the most "authoritarian" of the classic Confucians, said "Follow the True Way, not the ruler" in case of conflict between the two. See *Hsun-tzu*, beginning of chapter 29.

38.   See e.g. Richard Bernstein and Ross H. Munro, *The Coming Conflict with China* (New York: A.A. Knopf, 1997).

39.   Chin Yao-chi, *Chung-kuo cheng-chih yü wen-hua* (China's Culture and Forms of Governance; Hong Kong: Oxford University Press, 1997), ch. 7. See in particular pp. xiii, 155, 160, 162, 173, and see chapter VII below.

40.   Huang's book on Yen Fu is adduced in note 138 below. See also his Ph.D. dissertation adduced in note 30 above.

41. See chapter III below.

42. Berlin, p. 119. Nathan Tarcov and Thomas L. Pangle referred to Leo Strauss's "attribution of profound practical effects to profound theoretical arguments." See Strauss and Cropsey, p. 918. As I mentioned in my article on the civil society cited in note 19 above, "James Q. Wilson has largely agreed with MacIntyre in developing his thesis that 'elites' in the United States propagated a kind of 'skepticism' altering U.S culture by promoting an 'ethos of self-expression' that undermined 'the "civilizing" process.'" See James Q. Wilson, *On Character* (Washington, D.C.: AEI Press, 1991), pp. 28–29, 38. This article of mine, pp. 7–8, thus outlined some of the different approaches used by scholars to emphasize the causative impact of ideas on history, and I tried to highlight the convergence between sociologists like Bendix and Eisenstadt and philosophically-oriented scholars like Strauss and MacIntyre in this regard. The ongoing debate about the extent to which intellectual circles produce ideas affecting societal development is particularly significant with regard to the issues touched on in note 11 above regarding the shortage of knowledge about causative patterns in history. If the argument about the causative importance of ideas in history cannot be settled, ideas about the instrumental means needed to realize chosen goals can consist of objective knowledge only to a limited extent. In using the idea of an "advertisement" to define the nature of political theories and the kind of causative role they can play in the evolution of popular orientations, I was inspired by Norman Mailer, *Advertisements for Myself* (New York: Signet Books, 1959). But this idea is common in circles inspired by the GMWER (discussed in section 6). For instance, the important American Marxist culture critic Fredric Jameson remarks: "the whole point of the public sphere is that you make your own interpretation and then people take it or leave it; they find it plausible or not plausible." See Michael Hart and Kathi Weeks, eds., *The Jameson Reader* (Oxford: Blackwell Publishers Ltd., 2000), p. 157.

43. McAllister, p. 264.

44. See the essays in Strauss and Cropsey as well and as the Quentin Skinner study cited in note 16 above.

45. For a standard definition of "modernization," see Inkeles, *One World Emerging*, p. 101. By "capitalism" I basically mean the free enterprise system conceptualized by Hayek, however one might argue about the scope of state intervention. By liberal or Millsian democracy, I have in mind the definition of democracy cumulatively developed by scholars like Joseph Schumpeter, Samuel P. Huntington, Alex Inkeles, and Larry Diamond. See the discussion in Diamond, *Developing Democracy*, p. 8. He focuses not only on "regular, free, and fair" elections to determine the composition of a society's political leadership but also "nonelectoral dimensions," i.e. civil

liberty. On the idea of the civil society and the complex literature this has brought into being, see ibid., pp. 218–260 and my "The Western Concept of the Civil Society in the Context of Chinese History." On the theory of the sovereign state, see the articles by David Held and Charles R. Beitz in Held, ed., *Political Theory Today*. On the greatly increasing extent to which societies today are "interconnected," see Inkeles, *One World Emerging*, pp. 195–228.

46. I refer here to a powerful impression made on readers by Popper's thought, since he nowhere, so far as I know, entered the dangerous waters of trying to define "progress." He did speak of "the growth of scientific knowledge" (e.g. the subtitle of *Conjectures and Refutations*); he also made clear his reverence for this process, exalting the ideals of "the Open Society" and stating that "The phenomenon of human knowledge is no doubt the greatest miracle in our universe" (this actually dubious statement was made in the 1971 preface for *Objective Knowledge*); and he held that "The course of human history is strongly influenced by the growth of human knowledge" (see *The Poverty of Historicism*, p. vi).

47. See Alex Inkeles, *National Character: A Psycho-Social Perspective* (New Brunswick: Transaction Publishers, 1997), pp. 237–247 and his "A Model of the Modern Man: Theoretical and Methodological Issues," in *Social Science and the New Societies: Problems in Cross-Cultural Research and Theory Building*, ed. Nancy Hammond (East Lansing: Social Science Research Bureau, Michigan State University, 1973), pp. 59–92. See also Diamond, *Developing Democracy*, pp. 161–163.

48. Wilson, *On Character*.

49. Robert N. Bellah et al., *The Good Society* (New York: Vintage Books, 1992).

50. Amitai Etzioni, *The Spirit of Community* (New York: Crown Publishers, Inc., 1993).

51. Francis Fukuyama, *Trust: The Social Virtues and the Creation of Prosperity* (New York: Free Press, 1995).

52. Held, ed., *Political Theory Today*, pp. 160, 162–166.

53. Werner Jaeger, *Paideia: The Ideals of Greek Culture*, 3 vols. (New York: Oxford University Press, 1945, 1943, 1944). Strauss and Cropsey makes clear the pervasive emphasis on moral and other education throughout the history of Western political theory at least through the nineteenth century. The idea of *paideia* overlaps that of *Sittlichkeit* (ethics), with which Hegel was so concerned. See Charles Taylor, *Hegel and Modern Society* (Cambridge: Cambridge University Press, 1999).

54. Held, ed., *Political Theory Today*, p. 168.

55. For George H. Mead and the foundations of modern sociology as the Parsonian school saw it, see Parsons et al., eds., *Theories of Society*.

56. David Held, *Models of Democracy* (Stanford: Stanford University Press, 1987), pp. 244–247. Possibly Nozick's "libertarian" position does not even require

that society in some collective sense cultivate respect for science. At any rate, he certainly seeks to minimize the parameters of individual freedom.

57.   Christopher Lasch, *The Revolt of Elites and the Betrayal of Democracy* (New York: W.W. Norton, 1995).

58.   See e.g. William J. Bennett, ed. and commentator, *The Book of Virtues: A Treasury of Great Moral Stories* (New York: Simon and Schuster, 1993).

59.   Sohan Modgil and Celia Modgil, eds., *Lawrence Kohlberg: Consensus and Controversy* (Philadelphia: The Falmer Press, 1986). See note 67 below.

60.   MacIntyre, *After Virtue.*

61.   Metzger, *Escape*, pp. 70–77, 136–154, analyzed how the goal of a multi-faceted oneness or "linkage" was central to late imperial China's Neo-Confucianism (*Sung Ming li-hsueh*). The persistence of this goal in modern Chinese thought, discussed in section 7 below, is a major example of the continuity between modern and premodern Chinese thought, as discussed in note 35 above. With regard to the earliest Chinese use of the term *wen-hua*, I learned much from an unpublished paper by Ishikawa Yoshihiro kindly sent to me by Huang Ko-wu.

62.   McAllister, p. 33.

63.   See e.g. table for period 1393–1957 in Dwight H. Perkins, *Agricultural Development in China, 1368–1968* (Chicago: Aldine Publishing Company, 1969), p. 216. Population in 1913 was around 430 million, in 1989, 1.2 billion. The latter figure is from John K. Fairbank, *China: A New History* (Cambridge, Mass.: The Belknap Press of Harvard University Press, 1992), p. 409.

64.   See note 6 above for the Popkin and MacIntyre references. Their analyses, which inspired my outline of the GMWER, of course do not constitute a definitive, comprehensive account of modern Western intellectual trends. It is clear, however, that any account of these trends failing to deal with the skepticism MacIntyre and Popkin focused on is unbalanced. This point is illustrated by Charles Taylor's otherwise brilliant *Hegel and Modern Society.*

Taylor (ibid., p. 138) asks why Hegel's ontology — his vision of a cosmic *Geist* determining both the structure of physical nature and the course of history — came to be eclipsed by the twentieth century. Taylor's answer omits mention of the arguments developed by the GMWER to refute this ontology. Instead, he turns to a macroscopically sociologistical theory rooted in Hegel's thought.

Hegel's account of *Geist*, Taylor notes, "carries precisely this idea that our institutions and practices embody a certain view of ourselves both as individuals and social beings," and it makes clear that "alienation arises where the important ideas of man and society and their relation to nature embedded in the institutions of a given society cease to be those by which its members identify themselves" (ibid., pp. 126–127). Two important ideas of this kind, Taylor continues, arose in Hegel's day and "are still of fundamental importance in our civilization." One was "the mainstream Enlightenment view of man," a "scientific," "utilitarian" emphasis on "man as the subject of egoistic desires" (ibid., p. 1). The other was "expressivism," the "aspiration to expressive unity between man and the natural and social world on which he depends" (ibid., p. 140). Hegel's ontology, Taylor urges, should be seen as an attempt to combine these two cultural trends and thus to check the "illusions and distortions" that each of them, as Hegel clearly saw, tended to generate (ibid., p. 134).

Why, then, did Hegel's synthesis fail? Taylor partly blames Hegel's optimistic affirmation of current historical trends. As these trends provoked all the now familiar complaints about modernity, and as the horrors of totalitarianism and war took center stage, the expressivist impulse required a philosophical stance precisely opposite to Hegel's, one protesting rather than celebrating the course of history. Moreover, the "search for an underlying meaningful structure must seem arbitrary in an ever expanding and diversifying field of scientific knowledge" (ibid., pp. 137–138). Thus Taylor explains the decline of Hegel's influence with hardly a word about the epistemological arguments which had developed since at least Hume and showed that Hegel had vastly exaggerated the scope of the knowledge available to the human mind.

Taylor's thesis is one-sided if not seriously misleading, despite his lucid analysis of Hegel's train of thought. Very briefly, I would first note that Taylor's Hegelian kind of macroscopic sociology will be rejected by the many scholars preferring Max Weber's empirical and nuanced approach to the variety of causative variables affecting the course of history. Second, Taylor's exemplary description of Hegel's thought is neither simplistic nor reductionistic, but his account of the social orientations in Hegel's day is. As I have argued throughout this book, orientations widely shared in a society cannot be accurately described without selecting a limited set of them respresented by specific historical texts and then, in the manner, say, of Quentin Skinner, looking in these texts for the shared premises of the discourse illustrated by these texts. With such a vigorously empirical methodology, one can avoid stereotypes and put the conflicting theories of famous thinkers into context. Third, many will object to Taylor's reductionistic way of seeing the evolution of philosophy as largely contingent on changing social-cultural orientations rather than on arguments advanced critically in order to pursue knowledge. One can well argue about whether philosophical discourse in a society is just a handmaiden of societal trends or can itself as an exercise of critical reflexivity gradually have some influence on popular opinion. I cannot agree, however, that whether philosophical theories become influential depends only on whether they do or do not mesh with non-philosophical trends, not on whether they make sense.

Fourth, Taylor's own perspective on Hegel stems from the very GMWER that his analysis ignores. That is, Taylor agrees with the GMWER that Hegel's ontology is untenable, "a complete non-starter for us today" (ibid., p. 129). Taylor is a denizen of discourse #2, Hegel, of discourse #3 (see below). Taylor's book is precisely an effort to show that Hegel's philosophy has value when one judges it by abandoning the ideas which most concerned Hegel (his ontology). But Taylor's assumption that abandoning them makes sense did not emerge out of thin air. It emerged out of a complex epistemological trend offering reasons to abandon them. How then can this trend — the GMWER — be ignored as a cause for the decline of Hegel's influence? Both ignoring and presupposing this trend, Taylor's analytical route is nothing short of oblique. This obliqueness facilitates neither the description not the philosophical assessment of the intellectual trends integral to the formation of modern Western society.

As its title suggests, Taylor's book is a call to appreciate the value of some of Hegel's categories for the understanding of "modern society." To be sure, Taylor's dichotomy between expressivism and utilitarianism captures a major part of Hegel's outlook and is one of a series of similarly suggestive dichotomies (most notably Ferdinand Toennies' *Gemeinschaft* and *Gesellschaft*). Indeed I have argued elsewhere that the culture of Western modernity has differed from that of Chinese modernity especially in including a much more vigorous legitimization of *Gesellschaft*. As already noted, however, the value of such macro-sociologistical generalizations can easily be exaggerated. The excesses of postmodernism have once more made this obvious. Empirically adequate analysis of modern life in societies like the U.S. or China cannot be contained within the bounds of some macroscopic polarity. Robert Merton's call for "middle-range" categories cannot be so easily ignored. Lacking an adequate sociological approach to the study of "modern society," Taylor is simply not in a position to explain the relevance of Hegel's thought to such a study.

Highly general concepts, however, are needed to make explicit the presuppositions of any methodology. Hegel's thought, I agree with Taylor, is most challenging on that level. I have in mind the way Hegel and Herder discovered the changing historical-cultural-linguistic contexts of the rational quest for freedom and knowledge, and Hegel's insistence that the unity of this quest somehow survives the disparities between these contexts. This paradox that Hegel more than anyone else pointed to is indeed the overarching ontological notion toward which my own attempt to describe Chinese and Western intellectual discourses has, quite unintentionally, come to move. Hegel's vision of this paradox can be transferred from the cosmic context in which he put it into the context of linguistic symbols as these are used to form discourses embodying both culturally formed premises and the reflexivity able to turn these premises into objects of critical scrutiny — what Noam Chomsky called "the creative aspect of language use." Hegel's discovery of this paradox, a discovery that became clear to me only after reading Taylor's invaluable book, strikes me as more valuable than any Hegelian insights into societal dynamics. The methodological and other implications of this paradox, however, are a further issue, my opinions regarding which are summed up in chapter XIII.

65. See chapter IX.

66. Popper's *Objective Knowledge* includes much discussion of "the three worlds." On p. 154, he speaks of "three ontologically distinct sub-worlds," #1 being "the physical world," #2, that of "mental states," and #3, that of "ideas in the objective sense," basically, falsifiable propositions. My most systematic effort to distinguish between epistemological optimism and epistemological pessimism is in my "Tao-t'ung-te shih-chieh-hua: Lun Mou Tsung-san, Cheng Chia-tung, yü hsun-ch'iu p'i-p'an i-shih-te li-ch'eng" (Replacing the Chinese Idea of an Absolute Wisdom Uniquely Handed down in the Course of Chinese History with the Idea of a Global Search for Knowledge: A Discussion about Mou Tsung-san, Cheng Chia-tung, and the Evolving Quest for Morally Critical Consciousness), *She-hui li-lun hsueh-pao* 5 (spring 2002): pp. 79–152. Adduced in note 86 below, T'ang Chün-i's magnificent textbook on philosophy in effect addresses systematically just about all the points raised by the GMWER while strongly defending epistemological optimism. A forthcoming article of mine on this book's train of thought, therefore, should arrive at a still more precise understanding of this whole epistemological issue.

67. In a 1999 television interview, Linda Tripp, with obvious sincerity, said that, in secretly recording intimate phone conversations during which Monica Lewinsky revealed her secret affair with President Clinton, and then handing the tapes to the authorities, she was treating her friend just as everyone should treat a friend under such circumstances. (Were her daughter in Monica's situation, she said, she hoped someone would treat her as she had treated Monica, helping her escape from a situation harming her.) The "emptiness" of Kant's concept of rational moral autonomy is discussed in Taylor, *Hegel and Modern Society*, p. 77.

68. McAllister, pp. 21–22.

69. See Strauss and Cropsey for the theories of these Western thinkers. The quotation summing up Henry K.H. Woo's position is from my description of his ideas in chapter III below.

70. This outline of Popkin's view is from my article "Some Ancient Roots of

Modern Chinese Thought," the full bibliographical reference to which is in note 138 below.

71. *Encyclopedia of Philosophy*, vol. 8, p. 307.
72. McAllister, pp. 77, 120, 132.
73. Robert K. Merton, *Social Theory and Social Structure* (Glencoe: The Free Press, 1959), pp. 439–488. For J.S. Mill's concepts of deduction, see Strauss and Cropsey, pp. 785–786.
74. See MacIntyre's analysis of his thought in *After Virtue*.
75. On Western individualism, see S. Lukes, *Individualism* (Oxford: Basil Blackwell, 1973). On recent GMWER thinking about the problem of knowledge, see Chapter XIII below.
76. On Dunn's view, see section 11 below. Hayek's is discussed in chapter IX below. For H.-Georg Gadamer's thought, see Bernstein, *Beyond Objectivism and Relativism*. Professor P.J. Ivanhoe was helpful in a discussion I had with him about Gadamer.
77. Berlin, ed., *Four Essays on Liberty*, p. 172.
78. This follows McAllister, p. 143.
79. See the essay on Mill in Strauss and Cropsey and section 13 below.
80. *Newsweek*, October 26, 1998.
81. McAllister documents these charges in the case of Strauss and Voegelin.
82. See works by Huang Ko-wu adduced in note 138 below. Professor Wang Hsien-ming of Tsinghua University, however, has evidence that Yen Fu eventually did become aware of the GMWER (conversation with me in July 1999). My characterization of the Chinese responses to the GMWER has been challenged in some unpublished comments made by Chinese critics, to whom I respond in note 138 below.
83. Kao Li-k'o, *T'iao-shih-chih chih-hui*, pp. 45–46, 50.
84. See Yang Kuo-jung, *Ts'ung Yen Fu tao Chin Yueh-lin*; and D.W.Y. Kwok, *Scientism in Chinese Thought, 1900–1950* (New Haven: Yale University Press, 1965). Published in Taiwan in 1989, Li Ch'ang-ching's erudite study of John Dewey's theory of valuation again illustrates how Chinese scholars have typically not been convinced by any GMWER demonstration that normative judgments lack any objective basis. Appreciating Dewey's way of refuting this GMWER outlook, Li emphasizes that, according to anthropology, all cultures agree on the content of basic values and ethical principles, and he agrees with Dewey that reasoning about how to implement these values can be "unprejudiced." For Li, therefore, lack of moral order stems mainly from conditions like "the force of irrationality in human nature," not from the inability of "reason" to reveal objective moral principles. For Li, the ability of reason to reveal them remains intact, and the main human challenge lies in cultivating the strength of character needed to act on them. See Li Ch'ang-ching, *Tu-wei-te p'ing-chia li-lun* (John

Dewey's Theory of Valuation; Taipei: Chung-yang yen-chiu-yuan, San-min-chu-i yen-chiu-so ts'ung-k'an #23, April 1989), pp. 47, 55.

85. For a sensitive account of Wang Kuo-wei's thought, see Gao Rui-quan, *T'ien-ming-te mo-lo*, pp. 43–57.

86. See T'ang Chün-i, *Che-hsueh kai-lun* (An Introduction to Philosophy), 2 vols. (Taipei: T'ai-wan hsueh-sheng shu-chü, 1974) and Mou Tsung-san, *Chih-te chih-chueh yü Chung-kuo che-hsueh* (Chinese Philosophy and the Intuitive Understanding of Noumenal Reality; Taipei: T'ai-wan shang-wu yin-shu-kuan, 1971), introduction, pp. 2–3. An excellent study eruditely analyzes how, by the 1920s, Marxist and New Confucian philosophers, as well as the Tsinghua group, had agreed that "metaphysical wisdom" was reachable, thus rejecting the GMWER. Unlike the main Western objections to the GMWER, which have been concerned only with re-establishing the objectivity of moral principles, this Chinese consensus centered on the search for the ontological basis of morality. See Yü Chen-hua, *Hsing-shang-te chih-hui ju-ho k'o-neng?* — *Chung-kuo hsien-tai che-hsueh-te ch'en-ssu* (How is Metaphysical Wisdom Possible? — Reflections on Modern Chinese Philosophy; Shanghai: Hua-tung shih-fan ta-hsueh ch'u-pan-she, 2000). My review of this book is in *She-hui li-lun hsueh-pao* 4 (fall 2001): pp. 445–472. Yü's response to my review is in ibid. 5 (fall 2002): pp. 251–274.

87. Mou Tsung-san, *Cheng-tao yü chih-tao* (The Philosophy of Political Authority; Taipei: T'ai-wan hsueh-sheng shu-chü, 1980), p. 158. For a brilliant critique of Mou's philosophy, see Cheng Chia-tung, *Mou Tsung-san* (Taipei: Tung-ta t'u-shu kung-ssu, 2000). My critique of Cheng's book is adduced in note 66 above. I am grateful to Ms. Esther Su (Li Ch'un-ling) for recommending I study Mou Tsung-san's thought further by reading his *Chung-kuo che-hsueh shih-chiu chiang* (Nineteen Lectures on Chinese Philosophy; Taipei: T'ai-wan hsueh-sheng shu-chü, 2002), first published in 1983, a series of lectures given in 1978 at National Taiwan University and now in its eighth reprinting at least. Summing up Mou's brilliant overview of the global history of philosophy, this book makes much use of Mahayana philosophy to emphasize that the ultimate understanding of human life and the political salvation of the world require the rejection not just of the GMWER but of the whole Western philosophical tradition's refusal to move beyond logically discursive thinking to "mysticism," which, Mou suggested, is "the mode through which the true possibilities of reason can be found" (ibid., pp. 334–335).

88. Li Jui-ch'üan, *Hsiu-mo* (Hume; Taipei: Tung-ta t'u-shu ku-fen yu-hsien kung-ssu, 1993), pp. i, 121, 130, 134–135, 163–164. Li's explicit refutation of the Western *pu-k'o-chih-lun* (theory that ultimate reality is unknowable) is incompatible with the strange claim of an anonymous critic of my book that, in the modern Chinese intellectual world, it was only the Marxists who

objected to the Western theory given this Chinese name. As this section 7 shows, all three of the leading Chinese philosophical schools (New Confucian, Tsinghua, and Marxist) rejected the GMWER claim that there is no knowledge about the nature of ultimate reality and moral norms. T'ang Chün-i used this very term (*pu-k'o-chih-lun*) to describe such GMWER ideas, which he rejected. See his *Che-hsueh kai-lun*, vol. 1, pp. 95, 93, 403. Chin Yueh-lin was making much the same point when he focused much of his philosophy on refuting the GMWER's central thesis that available knowledge about what exists is only about what appears in one's consciousness (*wei-chu fang-shih*). On the latter, see books listed in note 89.

89.   Ch'en Hsiao-lung, *Chih-shih yü chih-hui: Chin Yueh-lin che-hsueh yen-chiu* (Discursive Knowledge and the Understanding of Ultimate Reality: A Study of Chin Yueh-lin's Philosophy; Beijing: Kao-teng chiao-yü ch'u-pan-she, 1997), author's preface pp. 2–3, and, in the text, pp. 3–5. For a valuable discussion of the thought of Chin Yueh-lin and Feng Ch'i, see Yang Kuo-jung, *Ts'ung Yen Fu tao Chin Yueh-lin*, pp. 115–170. Much of Feng's philosophy can be found in Feng Ch'i, *Chih-hui-te t'an-so* (The Quest for Wisdom; Shanghai: Hua-tung shih-fan ta-hsueh ch'u-pan-she, 1994), and his *Chung-kuo chin-tai che-hsueh-te ko-ming chin-ch'eng* (The Revolutionary Evolution of Modern Chinese Philosophy; Shanghai: Shang-hai jen-min ch'u-pan-she, 1989). A brilliantly lucid and highly critical analysis of Chin Yueh-lin's epistemology (especially his views about the relation between "ideas," "true propositions," and "objective reality") can be found in Hu Chün, *Chin Yueh-lin* (Taipei: Tung-ta t'u-shu kung-ssu, 1993). Dealing with Chin's attempts to refute the GMWER's *pu-k'o-chih-lun* (the theory that ultimate reality is unknowable), Hu largely agrees with the GMWER. But he ignores both the problem of the objectivity of moral norms and that of historical-cultural influences on *i-nien* (ideas). Hu's fascinating book thus illustrates another Chinese response to the GMWER: accepting many of its epistemologically technical arguments, ignoring the post-Kantian GMWER's emphasis on the cultural shaping of categories defining moral-political praxis, and not being alarmed by the GMWER's conclusion that there are no objective moral principles. Hu's *Tao yü chen* (The True Way and Truth; Beijing: Jen-min ch'u-pan-she, 2002) is a still richer version of his dialogue with Chin. Talking with me in December 2004, when I gave a lecture in Peking University's Department of Philosophy, Hu expressed a view of these epistemological issues similar to mine.

90.   Ch'en Hsiao-lung, pp. 173–177.

91.   Popper, *Open Society*, vol. 2, pp. 383–384.

92.   Ch'en Hsiao-lung, pp. 3–7.

93.   Li Tse-hou, *P'i-p'an che-hsueh-te p'i-p'an*, p. 323. For full bibliographical reference, see note 138 below.

94. Ibid., pp. 559, 579–580.

95. Li Tse-hou, *Wo-te che-hsueh t'i-kang* (An Outline of My Philosophy; Taipei: Feng-yun shih-tai ch'u-pan kung-ssu, 1990), pp. 65–66, 9, 21, 24–25, 27, 39–40, 172, 176–177, 192, 206. The telling "hot/cold" metaphor is on p. 206. The idea of Western learning as "the basis" is in Li's *Chung-kuo hsien-tai ssu-hsiang shih-lun*, pp. 397–433 (for full bibliographical reference, see note 138 below). For a valuable discussion of Li's thought, see Huang Ko-wu's (Max K.W. Huang's) article on it in *Chin-tai-shih yen-chiu-so chi-k'an* 25 (June 1996), pp. 425–460.

96. Letter to me of November 26, 1998.

97. Chao T'ing-yang et al., p. 47.

98. Ibid., pp. 43, 35, 37.

99. Ibid., pp. 46, 28, 24, 7.

100. Ibid., p. 18.

101. Ibid., pp. 5, 25, 41, 42, 44.

102. Ibid., p. 32.

103. Ibid., p. 16.

104. Ts'ui I-ming, "Jen-shih-te chieh-hsien ho ch'iu-t'ung-te chih-hui" (The Boundaries of Knowledge and the Wisdom Seeking the Oneness of Reality), *Hua-tung shih-fan ta-hsueh hsueh-pao* 6 (November 1998): pp. 11–16.

105. Hsu Hsiang-tung, "Hsiang-tui-chu-i, ch'uan-tung yü p'u-pien lun-li" (Relativism, Tradition, and Universal Ethics), *Chung-kuo hsueh-shu* 2 (fall, 2001): pp. 1–38. Still another example of a Chinese intellectual rejection of the GMWER's epistemological pessimism is an article trying to use Habermas's hermeneutic approach to show how the universal dynamics of social communication imply absolute, universal moral principles. This article is distinguished by the author's sensitive appreciation of the GMWER objections to such a derivation. See Yuen Sun Pong (Juan Hsin-pang), "Chih-shih yü shih-chien: Ju-chia hsueh-shuo, che-hsueh ch'üan-shih-hsueh chi she-hui kung-tso-chih k'o-neng ch'i-ho" (Knowledge and Moral Praxis: The Possible Convergence between Confucian Doctrine, the Philosophical Hermeneutic Approach, and Social Work), *She-hui li-lun hsueh-pao* 4 (fall 2001): pp. 259–331.

106. Hsu Hsiang-tung, p. 34.

107. Ibid., p. 15.

108. Ibid., p. 15.

109. Ibid., p. 32.

110. Metzger, *Escape*, pp. 85–108.

111. Strauss and Cropsey, pp. 890, 916.

112. This point is carefully developed in Huang Ko-wu's book on Yen Fu (see note 138 below).

113. This attempt to describe values by looking at shared points of concern

rather than agreed-on ideals influenced David D. Laitin, *Hegemony and Culture: Politics and Religious Change among the Yoruba* (Chicago: The University of Chicago Press, 1986), pp. 28–29. See also Laitin's comments on the problem of political culture in *American Political Science Review* 82 (June 1998): pp. 589–596. For the difference between my concept of discourse and much of contemporary linguistic philosophy, see chapter XIII.

114. Strauss and Cropsey, p. 916. Strauss assumed that the Greek philosophers, instead of being influenced by culturally distinctive orientations, had a "natural" understanding of "political life" and the ultimate universal ideals it should embody, and that the subsequent history of Western political thought, culminating in the absurdities of Weberian social science, was a process through which this understanding was increasingly lost. Given these convictions, he had no use for a triangular methodology dis-aggregating the questions political theory addresses, the answers historically developed to deal with them, and the problem of how to compare and evaluate these answers. Moreover, he did not use the idea of "discourse" to put these answers fully into context. See e.g. Leo Strauss, *What is Political Philosophy?* (Glencoe: The Free Press, 1959), pp. 9–55.

115. McAllister, p. 109.

116. My discussion here is based on Richard J. Bernstein, *The Restructuring of Social and Political Theory* (Philadelphia: University of Pennsylvania Press, 1976).

117. Strauss and Cropsey, pp. 897–898.

118. Bernstein, *Restructuring*, p. 57. The term "paradigm," associated especially with T.S. Kuhn, *The Structure of Scientific Revolutions* (Chicago: University of Chicago Press, 1962), was also part of this trend, but I here discuss only modes of thought regarding conscious human life, not those regarding purely physical events. In recognizing these modes, however, it is important to remember that human thought is shaped not only by them but also by the reflexive ability to refer to universal truth and objective reality, as discussed in chapter XIII. Thus I accept Steven Weinberg's criticism of Kuhn as failing to put sufficient emphasis on the objective content of natural science. See Steven Weinberg, *Facing Up: Science and Its Cultural Adversaries* (Cambridge, Mass.: Harvard University Press, 2001).

119. Apart from the Skinner volume cited in note 16 above, see e.g. Kenneth Burke, *A Grammar of Motives and a Rhetoric of Motives* (Cleveland: The World Publishing Company, Meridian Books, 1962); and J.G.A. Pocock, *The Machiavellian Moment* (Princeton: Princeton University Press, 1975). The loose use of "discourse" in the debates on postmodernism in the Chinese world during the 1990s is illustrated by the writing in Wang Hui, Yü Kuo-liang, eds., *90-nien-tai-te 'hou-hsueh' lun-cheng* (The Debate in the 1990s

about "Post-ism"; Hong Kong: The Chinese University of Hong Kong, 1998), pp. 181–182 and elsewhere. On this debate, see chapter XII.

120. See Bernstein, *Beyond Objectivism and Relativism*, p. 77.

121. Dunn, *Western Political Theory in the Face of the Future*, p. 57.

122. See e.g. Daniel Jonah Goldhagen, *Hitler's Willing Executioners* (New York: A.A. Knopf, 1996); the study by Fukuyama cited in note 51 above; David S. Landes, *The Wealth and Poverty of Nations* (New York: W.W. Norton, 1998); Samuel P. Huntington, *The Clash of Civilizations and the Remaking of World Order* (New York: Simon and Schuster, 1996); and Thomas Sowell, *Migrations and Cultures: A World View* (New York: Basic Books, 1996).

123. Inkeles, *National Character*.

124. Robert N. Bellah et al., *Habits of the Heart* (Berkeley: University of California Press, 1985), p. 303, holds that "any living tradition is a conversation, an argument in the best sense, about the meaning and value of our common life." In my view, however, whether an argument is "in the best sense" is an evaluative question best distinguished from the task of describing a discourse. Cultural patterns are not the monopoly of people of good will. I would especially agree that the best if not the only window on a culture is what Bellah calls a "conversation," which can be effectively described by analyzing the written texts it produces. Less useful to me are the descriptions — much favored by anthropologists — of overt behaviors making up ceremonies and other episodes.

125. Fairbank's book was published in 1987 as part of the Perennial Library, Harper & Row, Publishers, New York. See note 138 below for full bibliographical reference to book by Chin and Liu. As this example shows, the paradoxical merging of historically bequeathed values with the reflexive ability to refer to objective reality does not prevent some grasp of objective facts much the same for observers with extremely different cultural backgrounds. Therefore, as I see it, Professor Yuen Sun Pong's "the strong thesis of value involvement" (*ch'iang-lieh chia-chih chieh-ju-lun*) overemphasizes the extent to which values determine how people understand human life. See his "Chih-shih yü shih-chien," pp. 259–331. If one grants that, to understand human life, one needs descriptive, causal, predictive, evaluative, recommendatory, and epistemological propositions, the cultural baggage of the observer affects some of these propositions more than others. It has little basic effect on descriptive statements about the sinking of the German battleship *Bismark* by the British during World War II, but it has considerable effect on causal statements about the economic development of Taiwan under the Kuomintang. The understanding of human life is a matter of not only culturally variable categories but also objective facts. Epistemology has to put emphasis on both dimensions. At the same time, an epistemological proposition such as

that formed by the previous sentence or Popper's definition of objective knowledge seems contingent mainly on the reflexive pursuit of objective knowledge. These points have been challenged especially by scholars accepting Willard Van Orman Quine's concept of the "indeterminacy of translation" and of "ontological relativity," but these theories are controversial. I offer my objections to them in chapter XIII. After all, if historical ideas cannot be accurately described, one has to reject Rorty's thesis that Western philosophy has for centuries been dominated by the conceptualization of the mind as a "mirror of nature."

126. See note 138 below for full bibliographical reference to Li's *P'i-p'an che-hsueh-te p'i-p'an*. It is important to note that Li, no less than I, believed one can systematically distinguish between a lucid, comprehensive, empathetic description of a body of writing and a critical assessment of the ideas in it. Thus the subtitle of his book is *K'ang-te shu-p'ing* (A Description and Critique of Kant's Philosophy), and he magnificently succeeded in keeping distinct these two aspects of his study. I differ from him, however, in that he sees the object of his description as a doctrine or "train of thought" (*ssu-lu*), while I am interested in the way a doctrine fits into a discourse. Also, the criteria of successful thinking he used to evaluate Kant's philosophy are different from mine (which, far from his Marxism or his mix of Marx, Kant, and Piaget, are listed in section 11 below).

127. See note 138 below.

128. See chapter II below.

129. For full bibliographical reference, see note 138 below.

130. Ch'en Hsiao-lung, pp. 5–6.

131. Benjamin I. Schwartz, *The World of Thought in Ancient China* (Cambridge, Mass.: The Belknap Press of Harvard University Press, 1985). My review of this important book is in *The American Asian Review* 4 (summer 1986): pp. 68–116. My objections to the methodology of Wm. Theodore de Bary and Tu Wei-ming are expressed in my review of Wm. Theodore de Bary and John W. Chaffee, eds., *Neo-Confucian Education: The Formative Stage* (Berkeley: University of California Press, 1989) in *Harvard Journal of Asiatic Studies* 54 (December 1994): pp. 615–638.

132. The volume by Chin Kuan-t'ao and Liu Ch'ing-feng is adduced in note 138 below. Samuel P. Huntington's superficial, mistaken description of Confucian culture is in his generally impressive *The Third Wave: Democratization in the Late Twentieth Century* (Norman: University of Oklahoma Press, 1993). His mistake is pointed out in my "The Western Concept of the Civil Society in the Context of Chinese History," p. 24. The Northrop book was published in 1946 by The MacMillan Co. in New York. Scholars with a background in analytic philosophy have sometimes turned from general issues to the study of a historical discourse. A very interesting, valuable

example is Stephen C. Angle, *Human Rights and Chinese Thought: A Cross-Cultural Inquiry* (Cambridge: Cambridge University Press, 2002). In my view, Angle's description of the Chinese human rights "discourse" falls short especially in not covering the whole Chinese rights discourse, not putting Chinese ideas sufficiently into context, and so not making clear the major divergence between these ideas and the leading Western discussions regarding human rights. Chapter XIII offers some other reactions to the "linguistic turn" taken in U.S. philosophic circles today.

133. Again, I rely here on Strauss and Cropsey. The quotation from Ralph Lerner is taken from ibid., p. 229.

134. Benjamin I. Schwartz, *In Search of Wealth and Power: Yen Fu and the West* (Cambridge, Mass.: The Belknap Press of Harvard University Press, 1964).

135. Strauss and Cropsey, pp. 907–908, 910. See note 114 above.

136. John Dunn, *Interpreting Political Responsibility* (Cambridge: Polity Press, 1990), p. 86.

137. See note 35 above on the historiography of the problem of continuity and discontinuity between modern and premodern Chinese political thought and table 1.

138. To provide all the documentation supporting my thesis that epistemological optimism has dominated premodern and modern Chinese intellectual thought, besides the documentation in this book, I would have to adduce much of the reading in English and Chinese that I have done since the early 1960s. Here I can refer only to some of the items, primary and secondary, that have been particularly important in this regard. My *Escape from Predicament* did not focus on the problem of epistemology but still argued that the "ethos of interdependence" which modern Chinese intellectuals with otherwise conflicting outlooks had inherited from the Neo-Confucian tradition included "an epistemology emphasizing the knowability of universal moral truth as an object of cognition and reasoning" (ibid., p. 197). This book was based on a study of T'ang Chün-i's *Chung-kuo wen-hua-chih ching-shen chia-chih* (The Value of the Spirit of Chinese Culture; Taipei: Cheng-chung shu-chü, 1972), and many statements made by Chu Hsi (1130–1200) and collected by Ch'ien Mu in his *Chu-tzu hsin-hsueh-an* (A New Scholarly Record Regarding Chu Hsi), 5 vols. (Taipei: San-min shu-tien, 1971), as well as a good deal of other Chinese material, primary and secondary, regarding Neo-Confucianism and modern Chinese thought. A couple of years later, I published "Chinese Communism and the Evolution of China's Political Culture: A Preliminary Appraisal" in *The Enduring Chinese Dimension: Proceedings of the Eighth Sino-American Conference on Mainland China (1979)* (Institute of International Relations, University of South Carolina, 1979), pp. 63–75. Using Richard H. Popkin's work on skepticism in the West, I emphasized the contrast

between this skepticism and the "Chinese faith in the availability of secure moral knowledge" going back "especially to Hsun-tzu" (ibid., p. 67). This article analyzed Ku Ying, *I-ko hsiao shih-min-te hsin-sheng* (An Ordinary Citizen Speaks Out; Taipei: Chung-yang jih-pao, 1972), to illustrate the existence of this epistemic outlook in the thought of an educated member of the Taipei business world who stood outside the standard intellectual currents and sought to express the dominant viewpoint at the grass roots about Taiwan's current political development. From 1982 to 1983 and 1984 to 1985, I twice taught a course in Chinese for undergraduates at National Taiwan Normal University on pre-Ch'in political thought focusing on *Lun-yü, Mo-tzu, Meng-tzu,* and *Hsun-tzu* and in these lectures dealt much with the concept of knowledge in these books. During those years, Professor Kwang-Ching Liu sent me MacIntyre, *After Virtue,* which picked up the story of Western skepticism during the modern centuries subsequent to the period Popkin had discussed. At that time I thought of using the terms "epistemological optimism" and "epistemological pessimism" to avoid any prejudgments about what the right epistemic stance is while describing the contrast between the mainstream Chinese view and a major trend in the modern West. This work resulted in my "Some Ancient Roots of Modern Chinese Thought: This-worldliness, Epistemological Optimism, Doctrinality, and the Emergence of Reflexivity in the Eastern Chou," in *Early China,* vols. 11–12 (1985–1987), pp. 61–117, which focused on *Lun-yü* and *Mo-tzu,* analyzing the pervasive epistemological optimism in them and its close connection to the emphasis of these books on perfectly evaluating people so as to realize a society in which everyone receives the wealth and social position he or she deserves, as opposed to the Christian view that the final judgment of an individual's worth rests with God and occurs after the person dies. This article also analyzed the epistemological optimism in T'ang Chün-i, *Che-hsueh kai-lun,* vol. 2, pp. 1041–1203, the section on ethics and values. I also tried to put the traditional epistemological optimism into the context of seven other premises prevalent in Chou times and thereafter in my "Chung-kuo chin-tai ssu-hsiang-shih yen-chiu fang-fa-shang-te i-hsieh wen-t'i" (Some Methodological Issues Regarding Modern Chinese Intellectual History), in *Chin-tai Chung-kuo-shih yen-chiu t'ung-hsun* 2 (September 1986): pp. 38–52. This was reprinted in *Hsueh-shu ssu-hsiang p'ing-lun* 5 (1999): pp. 410–425.

I then published some articles which, along with those in this volume, sought to establish that the four main ideologies arising in twentieth-century China were Chinese Marxism, Sunism, Chinese liberalism, and modern Confucian humanism; to show that they all shared certain premises, including epistemological optimism; and to describe their shared agenda of unanswered questions to which they offered often conflicting answers. Regarding modern Confucian humanism, a broad category including the New Confucian school, I studied not only a good many of T'ang Chün-i's writings, as discussed elsewhere in this volume, but also Hsu Fu-kuan, *Hsueh-shu yü cheng-chih-chih chien* (Between the Realms of Scholarship and Politics; Taipei: T'ai-wan hsueh-sheng shu-chü, 1980); Hsu Fu-kuan, *Ju-chia cheng-chih ssu-hsiang yü min-chu tzu-yu jen-ch'üan* (Democracy, Freedom, Human Rights, and Confucian Political Thought), ed. Hsiao Hsin-i (Taipei: Pa-shih nien-tai ch'u-pan-she, 1979); Mou Tsung-san, *Cheng-tao yü chih-tao*; Lao Ssu-kuang, *Chung-kuo-chih lu-hsiang* (China's Direction of Development; Hong Kong: Shang-chih ch'u-pan-she, 1981); Yü Ying-shih, *Ts'ung chia-chih hsi-t'ung k'an Chung-kuo wen-hua-te hsien-tai i-i* (Modern Values and the Value System of Chinese Culture; Taipei: Shih-pao wen-hua ch'u-pan shih-yeh yu-hsien kung-ssu, 1984); Yü Ying-shih, *Hsien-tai ju-hsueh-lun* (Essays on Confucian Learning in the Modern Era; River Edge: Global Publishing Co., 1996); Yü Ying-shih, *Li-shih jen-wu yü wen-hua wei-chi* (Essays on Historical Figures in a Period of Cultural Crisis; Taipei: Tung-ta t'u-shu ku-fen yu-hsien kung-ssu, 1995); Tu Wei-ming, *Ju-hsueh ti-san-ch'i fa-chan-te ch'ien-ching wen-t'i* (Reflections on the Dawning of the Third Era in the Evolution of Confucian Learning; Taipei: Lien-ching ch'u-pan shih-yeh kung-ssu, 1989); and a good number of Fung Yu-lan's books, especially *Hsin li-hsueh* (A New Study of the Principles of Existence; Hong Kong: Chung-kuo che-hsueh yen-chiu-hui, 1972).

Regarding Sunism, I paid special attention to Ch'in Hsiao-i, ed., *Kuo-fu ch'üan-chi* (The Collected Writings and Comments of Our Nation's Father), 12 vols. (Taipei: Chin-tai Chung-kuo ch'u-pan-she, 1989); *Kuo-fu ch'üan-chi* (The Collected Writings and Comments of Our Nation's Father), 6 vols. (Taipei: Chung-kuo Kuo-min-tang chung-yang wei-yuan-hui tang-shih wei-yuan-hui, 1981); *Chiang Tsung-t'ung yen-lun hui-pien* (President Chiang K'ai-shek's Categorized Writings and Comments), 24 vols. (Taipei: Cheng-chung shu-chü, 1956); Lin Kuei-p'u, *Kuo-fu ssu-hsiang ching-i* (The Essence of the Thought of Our Nation's Father; Taipei: Cheng-chung shu-chü, 1981); Ting Ti, *Kuo-fu ssu-hsiang yen-chiu* (A Study of the Thought of Our Nation's Father; Taipei: P'a-mi-erh shu-tien, 1979); Ch'eng Chung-ying, *Chung-kuo hsien-tai-hua-te che-hsueh hsing-ssu* (Philosophical Reflections on China's Modernization; Taipei: Tung-ta t'u-shu ku-fen yu-hsien kung-ssu, 1988); and Hu Ch'iu-yuan, *I-pai-san-shih-nien-lai Chung-kuo ssu-hsiang-shih-kang* (An Outline of the History of Chinese Thought during the Last One-hundred-thirty Years; Taipei: Hsueh-shu ch'u-pan-she, 1980).

With regard to Chinese liberalism, I paid special attention to Yin Hai-kuang, *Chung-kuo wen-hua-te chan-wang* (Chinese Culture and Its Prospects), 2 vols. (Taipei: Wen-hsing shu-tien, 1966); Yin Hai-kuang, *Yin Hai-kuang hsuan-chi, ti-i-chüan, she-hui cheng-chih yen-lun* (Selected Writings of Yin Hai-

kuang, volume 1, Writings on Society and Politics; Hong Kong: Yu-lien
ch'u-pan-she yu-hsien kung-ssu, 1971) (I have not studied the "complete
collection" of writings by Yin edited by Lin Cheng-hung and published by
Kuei-kuan t'u-shu kung-ssu in eighteen volumes including one of essays by
others paying tribute to Yin); Yang Kuo-shu, *K'ai-fang-te to-yuan she-hui* (The
Open, Pluralistic Society; Taipei: Tung-ta t'u-shu ku-fen yu-hsien kung-ssu,
1985); Yang Kuo-shu, *Chung-kuo-jen-te shui-pien* (The Metamorphosis of the
Chinese People; Taipei: Kuei-kuan t'u-shu ku-fen yu-hsien kung-ssu, 1988);
Yeh Ch'i-cheng, *She-hui wen-hua ho chih-shih fen-tzu* (Society, Culture, and
Intellectuals; Taipei: Tung-ta t'u-shu yu-hsien kung-ssu, 1984); and P'eng
Ming-min, *Tzu-yu-te tzu-wei* (The Taste of Freedom), trans. Lin Mei-hui
from the English (Irvine: Taiwan Publishing Co., 1986).

   With regard to Chinese Marxism, I paid special attention to some of the
essays in Mao Tse-tung, *Mao Tse-tung hsuan-chi* (Selected Writings of Mao
Tse-tung), 4 vols. (Beijing: Jen-min ch'u-pan-she, 1967 except 1966 for vol.
3), such as his "Mao-tun-lun" (On Contradictions), "Shih-chien-lun" (On
Practice), and "Hsin min-chu-chu-i-lun" (On New Democracy); "The Little
Red Book," that is, Mao Tse-tung, *Mao chu-hsi yü-lu* (Sayings of Chairman
Mao; Beijing: Chung-kuo jen-min chieh-fang-chün tsung-cheng-chih-pu,
1967); Li Tse-hou, *P'i-pan che-hsueh-te p'i-p'an: K'ang-te shu-p'ing* (A Critique
of Critical Philosophy: A Description and Critique of Kant's Philosophy;
Taipei: Feng-yun shih-tai ch'u-pan kung-ssu, 1990); Li Tse-hou, *Chung-kuo
chin-tai ssu-hsiang-shih-lun* (Essays on the Intellectual History of Modern
China; Taipei: Feng-yun shih-tai ch'u-pan kung-ssu, 1990); Li Tse-hou,
Chung-kuo hsien-tai ssu-hsiang-shih-lun (The Intellectual History of China in
Recent Times; Taipei: Feng-yun shih-tai ch'u-pan kung-ssu, 1990); the
writings of Feng Ch'i listed in note 89 above; and Chin Kuan-t'ao and Liu
Ch'ing-feng, *K'ai-fang-chung-te pien-ch'ien: Tsai lun Chung-kuo she-hui ch'ao
wen-ting chieh-kou* (China's Transformation in the Course of Becoming
Open to the Cosmopolitan World: Another Analysis of Chinese Society's
Ultrastable Structure; Hong Kong: The Chinese University Press, 1993).
For Huang Ko-wu's (Max K.W. Huang's) critiques of the latter and of Li
Tse-hou's later thought, see respectively *Chin-tai Chung-kuo-shih yen-chiu
t'ung-hsun* 17 (March 1994): pp. 44–45 and *Chin-tai-shih yen-chiu-so chi-k'an*
25 (June 1996): pp. 425–460.

   Variously using such sources, a number of my articles started trying to
pull together those premises that were apparently common to the four
leading ideologies, and that I eventually listed in the form of "discourse
#1." In "An Historical Perspective on Mainland China's Current Ideological
Crisis," I listed nine such premises, arguing that they were rooted in Neo-
Confucianism and shared by Mao with T'ang Chün-i. I particularly
emphasized the complex ideal of "oneness" or "linkage" that T'ang's

thought shared with both Neo-Confucianism and Mao's philosophy, as well as the shared belief that a total philosophical system (*t'i-hsi*) founded on "reason" (*li-hsing*) can and should be devised fully to clarify the nature of existence and guide all human activities. In "T'ang Chün-i and the Conditions of Transformative Thinking in Contemporary China," *The American Asian Review* 3 (spring 1985): pp. 1–47, more data from T'ang's writings were presented to depict a "transformative" view of societal change that emphasized "linkage," and that T'ang shared with Mao. I argued that "If the conditions of transformative thinking in China can no longer be met, a less politically mobilized society may emerge" (ibid., p. 13).

This point in turn led to the notion that, while the premises shared by T'ang with Mao and others included a shared agenda of unresolved issues, the differences between the answers supplied by the four ideologies to these questions included the difference between primarily "transformative" and primarily "accommodative" approaches to cultural-political change. This notion was developed in my "The Chinese Reconciliation of Moral-Sacred Values with Modern Pluralism: Political Discourse in the ROC, 1949–1989," as well as my "Developmental Criteria and Indigenously Conceptualized Options: A Normative Approach to China's Modernization in Recent Times," *Issues & Studies* 23 (February 1987): pp. 19–81. Four other pieces also can be singled out as moving toward the "discourse #1" formulation by discussing the premises shared by the four ideologies and trying to trace them back to the Confucian or at least the Neo-Confucian tradition: (1) My "Continuities between Modern and Premodern China: Some Neglected Methodological and Substantive Issues," in *Ideas Across Cultures: Essays on Chinese Thought in Honor of Benjamin I. Schwartz*, ed. Paul A. Cohen and Merle Goldman (Cambridge, Mass.: Council on East Asian Studies, Harvard University, 1990), pp. 263–292; (2) my "Erh-shih shih-chi Chung-kuo chih-shih fen-tzu-te tzu-chueh wen-t'i: I-ko wai-kuo-jen-te k'an-fa" (Chinese Intellectuals in the Twentieth Century and the Problem of Self-awareness: A Foreigner's Outlook) — this can be found in Yü Ying-shih et al., *Chung-kuo li-shih chuan-hsing shih-ch'i-te chih-shih fen-tzu* (Intellectuals during Periods of Transformation in Chinese History; Taipei: Lien-ching ch'u-pan shih-yeh kung-ssu, 1992), pp. 83–138; in *Tang-tai* 73 (May 1, 1992): pp. 56–74 (part one) and ibid. 74 (June 1, 1992): pp. 62–79 (part two); and in *Hsueh-shu ssu-hsiang p'ing-lun* 3 (1998): pp. 183–229; (3) my "A Confucian Kind of Modern Thought: Secularization and the Concept of the *T'i-hsi*" (A Deductive, Comprehensive, Correct System of Political Principles), in *Chung-kuo hsien-tai-hua lun-wen-chi* (Symposium on Modernization in China), ed. Institute of Modern History, Academia Sinica (Taipei: Institute of Modern History, Academia Sinica, 1991), pp. 277–330; and (4) "The Western Concept of the Civil Society in the Context of

Chinese History." In the fall of 2001, the idea of epistemological optimism was central to both a two-month seminar taught by Huang Ko-wu (Max K.W. Huang) at Tsinghua University and a two-month course I taught at Peking University together with Professor Li Qiang. Both classes were on the history of modern Chinese thought.

The thesis that Chinese thought from Confucius down to the present has been dominated by epistemological optimism has had a mixed reception. It was not even mentioned in Hans Lenk and Gregor Paul, eds., *Epistemological Issues in Classical Chinese Philosophy* (Albany: State University of New York Press, 1993), but it was supported by Dr. Hans-Georg Möller, a sinologist at the University of Bonn, in a paper he delivered at the Sixth International Conference on Neo-Confucianism in Jinan in 1998. David N. Keightley approvingly used my *Early China* article above to link the "epistemological optimism" it had found in the thought of Confucius and Mo-tzu to other aspects of ancient China's culture. See his "Epistemology in Cultural Context: Disguise and Deception in Early China and Early Greece," in *Early China/Ancient Greece: Thinking Through Comparisons*, ed. Steven Shankman and Stephen Durrant (Albany: State University of New York Press, 2002), pp. 119–153. Huang Ko-wu in his books respectively on Yen Fu and Liang Ch'i-ch'ao found epistemological optimism to be basic to the thought of both. See his *I-ko pei fang-ch'i-te hsuan-tse: Liang Ch'i-ch'ao t'iao-shih ssu-hsiang-chih yen-chiu* (The Rejected Path: A Study of Liang Ch'i-ch'ao's Accommodative Thinking; Taipei: Institute of Modern History, Academia Sinica, 1994); his *Tzu-yu-te so-i-jan: Yen Fu tui Yueh-han Mi-erh tzu-yu ssu-hsiang-te jen-shih yü p'i-p'an* (The Raison d'être of Freedom: Yen Fu's Understanding and Critique of John Stuart Mill's Liberalism; Taipei: Yun-ch'en wen-hua shih-yeh ku-fen yu-hsien kung-ssu, 1998), republished in 2000 by Shang-hai shu-tien ch'u-pan-she; and his 2001 Ph.D. dissertation adduced in note 30. See also his "Liang Ch'i-ch'ao yü K'ang-te" (Liang Ch'i-ch'ao and Kant), *Chin-tai-shih yen-chiu-so chi-k'an* 30 (December 1998): pp. 101–147, which analyzes how Liang's epistemological optimism shaped his understanding of Kant's philosophy. The English version of this article by Huang is in Joshua A. Fogel, *The Role of Japan in Liang Qichao's Introduction of Modern Western Civilization to China* (Berkeley: Institute of East Asian Studies, University of California, 2004), pp. 125–155. Following Popper's epistemology to criticize modern Chinese "Hegelianism" as it has allegedly influenced Li Tse-hou, Ku Hsin agreed with my thesis that, as he put it, "Chinese intellectuals with few if any exceptions believe that humans have the ability to grasp moral truth and the ultimate nature of history, and that in particular those intellectuals more enlightened than others are able to find that unique path of action with which to solve humankind's social, moral, cultural, and historical problems. [Metzger] calls this 'an optimistic epistemology,' which he contrasts with the West's mainstream 'pessimistic epistemology.' As I pointed out in an article about the debate in the 1930s on the question of 'democracy versus dictatorship,' Chinese intellectuals, including liberals, have from start to finish lacked an 'awareness of darkness' with regard to reason [to borrow Chang Hao's term]. This has been a major cause for the weakness of liberal thought in China and the flourishing of utopianism and of authoritarianism in all its varied forms. 'A sense of darkness with regard to reason' refers to the limited scope of rational understanding. Educated persons with this awareness of darkness of course believe that, in the expansion of knowledge, reason plays a great role, but they realize that ignorance and uncertainty always persist." See Ku Hsin, *Hei-ko-erh-chu-i-te yu-ling yü Chung-kuo chih-shih fen-tzu* (The Dark Spirit of Hegelianism and Chinese Intellectuals; Taipei: Feng-yun shih-tai ch'u-pan ku-fen yu-hsien kung-ssu, 1994), pp. 137–138.

Ku Hsin is a scholar brought up in the Mainland intellectual milieu and using ideas about epistemology to participate in the ongoing ideological battles there rather than in a more purely descriptive way. Moreover, the GMWER was not about "ignorance and uncertainty." Saying he agreed with my views, he actually furnished another example of how contemporary Chinese thought has ignored, resisted, or misunderstood the GMWER. Another Mainland scholar has also agreed with the thesis of modern Chinese epistemological optimism, especially with regard to Huang Ko-wu's analysis of Yen Fu's work. See Gao Rui-quan, "Lo-kuan-chu-i chi ch'i wen-t'i" (Optimism and Its Problems), *T'ien-chin she-hui k'o-hsueh* 94 (May 1997): pp. 34–39, and his review of Huang Ko-wu's book on Yen Fu in *Erh-shih-i shih-chi* 52 (April 1999): pp. 81–84. Also interesting was Henry K.H. Woo's response to my review of his *Tu-kung nan-shan shou Chung-kuo* (The West in Distress — Resurrecting Confucius's Teachings for a New Cultural Vision and Synthesis; Hong Kong: The Chinese University Press, 1995). After this review (largely reprinted in this book) appeared in *American Journal of Chinese Studies* 4 (April 1997): pp. 1–49, he replied to my point that his outlook included the pervasive epistemological optimism of the modern Chinese intellectual mainstream. He said that, while my characterization of this mainstream was correct, and while he regarded himself as "an epistemological optimist," his standpoint did not stem from this mainstream and instead was based on his own epistemological argument, which he energetically defended as a valid philosophical position. My exchange with him is further described in a note appended to my article in this volume on him. See his answer to me in *American Journal of Chinese Studies* 4 (October 1997): pp. 253–263.

All in all, not a few Mainland scholars have agreed with my way of characterizing the modern Chinese ideological mainstream. For instance,

Professor Yao Ta-li of Fudan University, using the version of my position in Cohen and Goldman, eds., *Ideas Across Cultures*, incorporated much of it without qualification in his own account of this mainstream. See *Hsueh-shuo Chung-kuo*, p. 189. His article leaves the impression — valid or not, I cannot judge — that I merely articulated what was obvious all along.

Assuming that the definition of "epistemological optimism and pessimism" as given in this chapter is clear, I do maintain that there is a conclusive accumulation of evidence that epistemological optimism has dominated the Chinese intellectual mainstream from the days of Confucius until today, especially given the rich evidence of its importance in Chou Confucianism, in the Neo-Confucian tradition of late imperial China, in the thought of Yen Fu and Liang Ch'i-ch'ao, and in all four of the leading Chinese ideologies of the twentieth century, along with the fact that a good number of Marxist and humanistic Chinese scholars in the twentieth century became fully aware of that Western epistemology which I have identified with the GMWER, viewing it as different from theirs, and vindicating theirs by regarding it as wrong. Indeed the common Chinese term for this allegedly incorrect Western epistemology, *pu-k'o-chih-lun* (the theory that ultimate reality is unknowable), is similar to my "epistemological pessimism." Moreover, not a few scholars east and west have agreed that the modern Chinese intellectual mainstream has been dominated by epistemological optimism, as noted above. On the other hand, not a few Chinese scholars, apparently believing that the nature of reason is universal and self-evident, do not agree that a useful distinction can be made between epistemologically optimistic and pessimistic modes of reasoning. This view has not, so far as I know, been expressed in any publication, but it comes up in professional evaluations the authors of which are left unnamed.

In such sources, I have also found the view that epistemological optimism was not a major Chinese trend in either modern or premodern times, and that, at least in modern times, epistemological issues were fully understood in many or all Chinese intellectual circles, which admirably avoided the overemphasis on them in Western ones. According to this view, Chinese intellectuals at least from the twelfth century A.D. on, even if not engaged in the systematic study of logic and epistemology, were fully aware of the difficulties in pursuing knowledge, as illustrated by Lü Tsu-ch'ien's (1137–1181) famous "It is not easy to grasp principles clearly." This Neo-Confucian emphasis on the "elusiveness" of such knowledge, however, discussed at length in my *Escape from Predicament*, is different from the GMWER's central idea that such knowledge (knowledge about the one ultimate reality as the source of the principles governing the physical, historical, and ethical worlds) is not elusive but unobtainable. Regarding it as elusive, Chinese philosophy, modern and premodern, continued trying to obtain it, and the Chinese philosophical problematique continued revolving around the problem of why a particular philosophy had failed to obtain this supposedly obtainable knowledge (see e.g. Ch'en Hsiao-lung's critique of Chin Yueh-lin's thought in section 7 of this chapter). By contrast Western thinkers influenced by the GMWER faced the problem of how to conceptualize a moral-political order when this kind of knowledge is unobtainable, as chapters VIII and X, on Dunn and Rawls, illustrate. It is indeed mistaken to equate Lü Tsu-ch'ien's doubts with the systematic skepticism of Hume and Kant. Moreover, whatever the nature of his doubts, they failed to form a significant intellectual current, as Hu Shih lamented.

It is also incorrectly claimed that, led from the 1920s on by historians like Ku Chieh-kang, the movement critically to re-examine ancient Chinese history (*ku-shih-pien yun-tung*) exhibited the same kind of skepticism as did the GMWER. In fact, this movement marked the transition from a historiography based on a sacred canon, the Confucian classics, to one based on the use of reason to sort out empirical historical data. By contrast, the GMWER questioned the ability of reason to grasp ontological and moral truths; it took for granted that knowledge could not be based on a sacred canon. Certainly Chinese thought and values were deeply affected when, beginning with Yen Fu, "science" or "experience" replaced a sacred canon as the source of knowledge. This kind of intellectual change occurred also in the West to the extent that classical rationalism and then science challenged the authority of the Bible. The GMWER, however, effected a further challenge, one limiting the scope of the knowledge that could be scientifically or rationally derived from experience. Indeed, it even led to doubts that reason could fully control the interpretation of historical data, arguing that in this task reason had to be supplemented with categories drawn purely from a particular historical discourse or set of assumptions. Clearly, Ku Chieh-kang's thought had nothing to do with this second kind of intellectual shift. To use some contemporary Western philosophical terms, his skepticism was much less far-reaching than even Pyrrhonian skepticism, not to mention "the specifically 'Cartesian' form of skepticism which invokes the 'veil of ideas' as a justification for a skeptical attitude." See Richard Rorty, *Philosophy and the Mirror of Nature* (Princeton: Princeton University Press, 1980), p. 94 n. 8. Much the same point is made in Shao Tung-fang's recent impressive study about how Ts'ui Shu's (1740–1816) work on ascertaining the factual accuracy of texts about the ancient era of the sages was related to both the Chinese tradition of textual criticism going back to the Sung dynasty and subsequent textual criticism, including the radically critical movement led by Ku Chieh-kang. See Shao

Tung-fang, *Ts'ui Shu yü Chung-kuo hsueh-shu-shih yen-chiu* (Ts'ui Shu and the Study of Chinese Intellectual History; Beijing: Jen-min ch'u-pan-she, 1998), pp. 277–278. Professor Shao explains that Ku Chieh-kang's and Hu Shih's kind of skepticism "stopped on the level of historical fact," being only "a kind of empiricistic skepticism.... emphasizing sensory experience and ordinary common sense." It thus "was basically on the same level as Ts'ui Shu's skepticism. By contrast, the skepticism developed in Western philosophy had two aspects: it doubted the human ability to know the truth; and this doubt led to the abandoning of judgment, the thesis that what is ultimately real cannot be known (*pu-k'o-chih-lun*).... Ts'ui Shu, Hu Shih, and Ku Chieh-kang ... did not have any doubts about their own ability to obtain knowledge." Confusing these various kinds of skepticism with one another is still another way that Chinese have responded to the GMWER by either refuting, misunderstanding, or not being aware of it.

Another mistaken view is that, in the modern Chinese intellectual world, it has only been the Marxists who have been concerned with refuting the Western skeptical ideas referred to in China as *pu-k'o-chih-lun* (the theory that the nature of ultimate reality is unknowable) (see note 88 above). It is also claimed that modern Chinese intellectuals accepted all the valid ideas of the GMWER even though they remained silent about them. The study of epistemological trends, however, is not of silently held but of publicly promulgated ideas. Contradicting this high opinion of Chinese epistemological understanding there is another common Chinese criticism of my thesis: it is often held that, before the introduction of Western philosophical methods, Chinese ideas about the nature of knowledge were so crude that they should not be regarded as forming any definite epistemological standpoint. In other words, "epistemological pessimism" really refers to the rational epistemology developed in the modern West, while "epistemological optimism" refers to the crude ideas Chinese had about the nature of knowledge before becoming enlightened by Western philosophy. Arbitrarily assuming that the latter is definitive, this view aborts any open philosophical inquiry into the nature of knowledge. That Western epistemology is not necessarily definitive is precisely one of the points T'ang Chün-i so astutely made. A contrary but actually similar prejudgment is that Western epistemology has differed from the Chinese not or not only in being more rational but in overemphasizing the importance of epistemological problems. Both these views presuppose that the objective nature of knowledge and the extent to which epistemology should be emphasized are both already obvious to enlightened intellectuals in China and the West; that the concept of knowledge is not shaped by varying cultural orientations; and that therefore the latter need not be examined and critically evaluated. The evidence in this book, however, shows that the nature of knowledge is indeed a topic the understanding of which varies culturally.

To be sure, this claim of mine reflects epistemological pessimism, just as it is epistemologically optimistic to claim that the human mind can transcend cultural influences in grasping the nature of knowledge. Thus my epistemologically pessimistic view indeed rests on my claim that my view is more supported by empirical evidence and so more enlightened than the epistemologically optimistic criticisms of it. At this point I indeed am not just empirically describing historical discourses but claiming to set forth a true statement about objective reality and so to justify my empirical effort.

The reader, then, has to determine not only how strong my empirical evidence is but also to what extent the truth about objective reality is revealed by "logically consecutive reasoning" (*ssu-pien*) and empirical evidence, as opposed, say, to intuition, "tacit knowledge," or "dialectical reasoning." Admittedly, since I am a card-carrying if critical denizen of discourse #2, my "indisputable rules of successful thinking" emphasize empiricism and *ssu-pien.*

These objections in unpublished sources notwithstanding, scholars have long been aware of the shortage of "skepticism" in the Confucian intellectual tradition, and the prevalence of epistemological optimism in modern Chinese thought is being increasingly treated as a fact long obvious to everyone. What has troubled some scholars is that, if the prevalence of this trend is a fact, it raises basic questions with regard to modern Chinese thought that they have neglected so far: does this modern Chinese trend indicate that there is much more continuity between modern and premodern Chinese thought than was previously thought? Given the contrast between this modern Chinese epistemic mode and a major if not dominant modern Western trend (discourse #2), which epistemological ideas should be affirmed? This question is particularly urgent for the many Chinese intellectuals today seeking a global philosophical synthesis of all correct ideas (*hui-t'ung*). As the Confucian tradition goes through its current process of reappraisal, to what extent should its epistemology be criticized and rejected? What have been the modern Chinese criticisms of epistemological pessimism and how much of a challenge to Western thought do they constitute? To what extent will China's epistemology affect its political development?

Some of these questions are discussed in chapters XI, XII, and XIII below. Most basically, perhaps, an attempt critically to assess both China's mainstream epistemological optimism and the GMWER reveals not only problems with the GMWER that the New Confucians and Chin Yueh-lin at least partly addressed but also problems with the epistemological optimism which they inherited from the Confucian tradition, and of which they failed to become critically aware. Chinese scholars spent more than a century debating what is right and what is wrong with the Confucian tradition (the *ch'ü-she* problem) without realizing that the epistemological dimension of this tradition needs to be assessed. This oversight hardly confirms their claim that they have the unique philosophical ability to figure out what went wrong with Western philosophy. It also is a shadow lying over Tu Wei-ming's prominent claim to have critically assessed Confucian philosophy in the light of contemporary Western philosophical outlooks. Only recently have a few Chinese scholars, such as Zheng Jia-dong, Yuen Sun Pong (Juan Hsin-pang), and Yu Zhen-hua, started to address this problem. In Xiao Gong-qin, *Chih-shih fen-tzu yü kuan-nien-jen* (The True Intellectual and the Person Only Immersed in Abstract Ideas; Tianjin: T'ien-chin jen-min ch'u-pan-she, 2001), one finds an analysis of the Chinese intellectual mainstream in the twentieth century as "romantic," "radical," "utopian," and "iconoclastic." Although Hsiao praises my views, I perhaps can be permitted to say that his analysis is extraordinarily insightful and rich. His portrait of contemporary Chinese intellectuals (e.g. ibid., pp. 125–142) is nothing short of delicious, but he offers a balanced, empathetic account of their plight. Many of his insights coincide with my opinions, but his methodology excludes discussion of epistemological issues, and he touches only in passing on the traditional roots of the modern "romanticism" which he criticizes (ibid., p. 68).

　　As mentioned above, my thesis that the structure of authority in China is closely connected to a tradition-rooted, pervasive form of epistemological optimism contrasting with a much more pessimistic epistemology in Western liberal democracies meshes with Charles E. Lindblom's view regarding the contrast between the epistemology of the latter societies and that of the U.S.S.R. Although his *Politics and Markets* came out in 1977, I did not become aware of it until a decade or so later. I feel his emphasis on the epistemological basis of politics supports my thesis, but my effort, unlike his, has focused on understanding the epistemological ideas within Chinese history, the philosophical questions raised by them, especially as they were used to confront the GMWER, and their role in the evolution of Chinese "political theory."

139. A number of points should be made to help the reader understand this outline. First, as already indicated, my argument that discourse #2 is *a* major Western cultural strand meshes with Charles E. Lindblom's bolder, broader thesis about the contrast between "communism and liberal democracy." He argues that "communism"(by which he meant the U.S.S.R.'s political system) was based on the idea of an "intellectually guided society. It derives from a buoyant or optimistic view of man's

intellectual capacities." This "optimistic" idea is to some extent similar to the "epistemological optimism" of the modern Chinese intellectual mainstream. "Democracy," he says, has "a more pessimistic view of man's intellectual capacities." Here Lindblom in effect is referring to the "epistemological pessimism" of discourse #2. See Lindblom, *Politics and Markets*, p. 248. Second, for Troeltsch's distinction between "the sect" as a religious group wanting morally to purify the world and the "church" as a religious group willing largely to accommodate itself to the world as it actually is, see his essay in Parsons et al., eds., *Theories of Society*, vol. 1, pp. 664–670. Ch'ien Mu's strikingly similar distinction was between *ching-hsueh* (study devoted to purifying the world morally by directly applying to it the principles of the Confucian classics) and *shih-hsueh* (study seeking gradual improvement by taking into account changing historical conditions). Ch'ien Mu's distinction went back at least to an essay "Ching-hsueh yü shih-hsueh" he first published in the September 1952 issue of the famous liberal journal *Min-chu p'ing-lun*. See Huang Ko-wu (Max K.W. Huang), "Ch'ien Mu-te hsueh-shu ssu-hsiang yü cheng-chih chien-chieh" (Ch'ien Mu's Concept of Scholarship and His Political Perspective), *Kuo-li T'ai-wan shih-fan ta-hsueh li-shih hsueh-pao* (June 1987): pp. 393–412. Third, the terms *te-chih* (government based on virtue), *jen-cheng* (rule based on total concern with the needs of the people), and *nei-sheng wai-wang* (within, a sage, without, a true king) are ancient ones denoting the standard Confucian ideal of rule by a perfectly moral man. Fourth, for the Neo-Confucian concept of *ta-t'ou-nao-ch'u* (the concept that is the key for understanding a complex issue as a whole), see Metzger, *Escape*, pp. 66, 67, 77. For the important modern concept of *t'i-hsi* (a deductive, comprehensive, correct system of political principles), see my article on this term adduced in note 138 above. Fifth, on "the three marketplaces" and the distinction between the Millsian and the Rousseauistic conceptualizations of democracy, see note 19 above.

140. Bernstein, *Beyond Objectivism and Relativism*. It seems clear that relativism is untenable as the thesis that objectively, universally true statements cannot be made. Most basically, this thesis refutes itself to the extent that it presupposes logic and itself is presented as a true proposition describing an objectively factual state of affairs. Moreover, if relativism is a theory about how varying historical and cultural conditions alter the perception of truth, there is no way to show that such alterations preclude the reflexivity with which people can identify and transcend the cultural influences on their minds and refer to objective reality or universal truths; there is widespread, cross-cultural agreement about some of the norms of successful thinking and communication, such as respect for logic, the grammatically and stylistically proper employment of a historical language, and awareness of

relevant topics; it seems undeniable that natural science grasps objective truth, as argued in Steven Weinberg's critique of Thomas Kuhn's work; there are actions that are undeniably horrible and immoral; and, as discussed in this chapter, because any discourse is based on premises indisputable within the context of that discourse, relativism is not a viewpoint that any discourse can practicably adopt.

141. This section deals with chapter 10 of John Dunn, *Political Obligation in Its Historical Context* (Cambridge: Cambridge University Press, 1980). The "middle ground" reference is from ibid., p. 268.

142. Ibid., pp. 245, 248, 288, 253.

143. Ibid., pp. 268, 293.

144. Ibid., pp. 288–289, 283, 291.

145. Ibid., pp. 288, 261.

146. Ibid., pp. 286, 251, 291.

147. Ibid., pp. 282, 279, 261, 291, 253, 284.

148. Ibid., pp. 255, 244, 297–298.

149. Ibid., pp. 267, 281.

150. Metzger, *Escape*, p. 215.

151. Edmund Husserl faced this problem in a particularly lucid way, resisting this kind of relativism which I suggest is unavoidable. See Strauss and Cropsey, pp. 879–881.

152. Hsiao Kung-ch'in, *Chih-shih fen-tzu yü kuan-nien-jen*, pp. 120–121. Hsiao criticizes this anti-Western outlook.

153. Allan Bloom, *The Closing of the American Mind* (New York: Simon & Schuster Inc., 1987).

154. Li Shen-chih, "Ch'üan-ch'iu-hua yü Chung-kuo wen-hua (Globalization and Chinese Culture)," *Huang-Yen wen-hua yen-chiu* 13 (January 2000): pp. 1–9. The quote is from p. 8.

CHAPTER II

T'ang Chün-i's Rejection of
Western Modernity

1. Introduction

T'ang Chün-i (1909–1978) was one of modern China's most famous
and prolific philosophers. From the standpoint of my own reading
experience, there has never been a more astute, moving, or
analytically challenging thinker, whether Chinese or Western,
ancient or modern. Having a deep knowledge of the main Chinese
philosophical traditions and a considerable grasp of Western
philosophy, he was a morally serious person facing the salient issues
of his era and evoking saintly traditional ideals, while pondering the
arguments and modern tendencies impeding their realization. His
was a Buddhist-Confucian faith which he inherited from his beloved
parents and used to structure his whole philosophy to the end of his
life. Thus his writing is fairly redundant, reflecting the religious
impulse to return repeatedly to the same healing message. Yet
reading his works is an exhausting task, like climbing ever higher up
a mountain trail, because he was forever devising strikingly fresh,
brilliant, and linguistically seductive ways of rephrasing his insights in
order to relate them to different circumstances and philosophies.
The intellectual frontier along which he worked was one where
soteriological ideas directly provided by the Chinese tradition were

I am indebted to Ms. Elsie Wu and Ms. Linda L. Chao for most valuable help with
regard to a number of factual points and translation problems.

challenged or corroborated by discursive trains of thought stemming largely from Western philosophy. Trying to analyze the contents of his huge oeuvre is like trying to describe a vast lake in the mountains on the waves of which the sunlight glints in ever-changing ways.

Presuming to inject a personal note, I may mention that my father, the philosopher Arnold Metzger, was a close friend of the philosopher Ernst Bloch. With phenomenology and existentialism as part of his background, my father sometimes discussed the question of human "suffering," while Bloch is famous for his book on "hope." Neither had in mind just empirical phenomena like the suffering inflicted by war or the hope of prosperity. Both were concerned with a more general existential situation involving human finitude, historicity, and the desire to overcome these.[1] As one tries to see as a whole all the building blocks of T'ang's philosophy, one finds a human being not only analyzing the philosophical intersection of Chinese and Western culture but also expressing the suffering brought on him by his own historical "circumstances" (*chi*) and the hope that seemingly "transcends" any such "circumstances." T'ang was more than an erudite interpreter of the history of philosophy. He was both a tragic and a consoling figure in history.

Like his brilliant friends Mou Tsung-san and Hsu Fu-kuan, T'ang has been widely recognized as a "New Confucian" (*hsin-ju*) and also can be put into a broader category, modern Confucian humanism. The latter includes scholars like the late historian Ch'ien Mu who did not necessarily approve of the New Confucians' metaphysical approach based on the Neo-Confucianism of late imperial times (*Sung-Ming li-hsueh*).[2] Going back especially to Liang Ch'i-ch'ao (1873–1929), Liang Shu-ming (1893–1988), and Hsiung Shih-li (1885–1968), modern Confucian humanism was a reaction against the May Fourth Movement's iconoclastic rejection of Confucian values. From the standpoint of the Confucian humanists, Confucian and other traditional ideas were the only proper foundation of Chinese modernization. Just like all the modern Chinese ideologies, as well as the Confucian tradition with its central ideal of the morally perfect sage as king (*nei-sheng wai-wang*), modern Confucian humanism saw the good society as a hierarchy with morally and intellectually enlightened persons at the top and regarded the actual world as a perverse hierarchy with unenlightened persons at the top. Those who picture Confucian humanism as just another way of shedding light on "what it means to be human" overlook that what it demanded was not only the creation of a perfect person but also political installation of him as "king." Sharing this concept of hierarchy with all the other modern Chinese ideologies, modern Confucian humanism differed from them in holding that rectification of the current perverse hierarchy in both the domestic and the international world required putting Confucian humanists and China on top instead of scientists (Chinese or Western) and Western culture. The thought of New Confucians like T'ang connoted problems of social status and professional prestige, not only philosophy and cultural pride.

With this standpoint, the New Confucians by 1949 seemed hopelessly backward, futilely inveighing against the tide of history as China's "unfolding revolution" produced the victory of the Communists. Even in the late 1970s, a book widely admired in the West, and later in China, depicted the New Confucians as pursuing "absurd" arguments contradicting the "structural possibility" presented by history. Today, however, endorsement of Confucian values in the light of modern values has become common in Western and Chinese sinological circles, even Marxist and liberal ones previously devoted to iconoclasm.[3]

One common way in China of vindicating Confucian values, illustrated by at least some of Ch'ien Mu's and Yü Ying-shih's approach, is to regard their worthwhileness as self-evident. The close study of Chinese historical documents can then be emphasized as the single way of grasping an inherently valuable historical tradition, and brilliant command of the historical sources becomes a rhetorical device used to brush aside contrary views.

Another way of vindicating Confucian values is to seek "reasons" (*li-yu*) for affirming them instead of Western values. In other words, "reasons" are sought to determine that cultural revision, i.e. choices about "what to adopt, what to discard" (*ch'ü-she*), should be carried out one way instead of another. This requires understanding Western outlooks and explaining why certain Chinese views are or are not preferable to them, i.e. developing an international "dialogue" or "argument." This has to include the confrontation between Chinese and Western philosophies as the most accessible forms of these values, although philosophically expressed values are not the only ones. Such is the kind of vindication of the tradition that the New

Confucians sought. They called it *tzu-chueh* (full awareness of all the issues and circumstances affecting one's life).

Although it was part of the reaction against the May Fourth iconoclasm that came to the fore around 1919, this analytical quest for philosophically defensible traditional values was rooted in a seminal idea that arose during the last years of the nineteenth century. The first Chinese effort after the Opium War (1839–1842) to introduce Western ideas had called for retaining most of the currently existing institutional and intellectual heritage while combining it with some Western ideas. This outlook was forcefully expressed by the famous Chang Chih-tung (1832–1909). The contrary notion that emerged by the late 1890s was that much but not all of this existing tradition was perverse. Liang Ch'i-ch'ao (1873–1926) expressed this view by 1897 in Hunan: Western values should be combined only with a certain ancient Chinese cultural spirit that could be critically recovered by scholars in the present clearing away the perversities that had accumulated after the Ch'in unification of China in 221 B.C. and re-analyzing this ancient spirit in the light of modern principles like "freedom" and "democracy."[4]

In other words, just as Christian theologians like Paul Tillich tried to extract existential principles out of an ancient religion otherwise threatened with invalidation by science, a series of modern Chinese thinkers sought to distinguish between the obsolete ideas and the universal truths entangled with them in the historical Chinese tradition. The contemporary Confucian philosopher Lao Ssu-kuang, for instance, distinguished between "closed" and "open" ideas in the Confucian tradition.[5]

In particular, for more than two thousand years, Confucian ethics had been interwoven with a non-scientific picture of the physical cosmos (the *yin-yang* cosmology), a belief in divinely-endorsed monarchy, a perception of history as including an ancient golden age, and identification of a sacred Chinese canon as the source of all basic truths. Unless disentangled from these ideas, Confucian values could not be vindicated as worth preserving in the modern world. Even more, vindicating them in modern Chinese eyes required refutation of the powerful accusation that Confucianism was authoritarian (that it centered on *ming-chiao* [Confucian teachings justifying social hierarchy]).

In a famous 1984 book, for instance, Yü Ying-shih tried to

demonstrate the compatibility of the Confucian tradition with modern values by arguing that this tradition was an "integrated" "culture" the "center" of which was a "value system" revolving around not the authoritarian idea of *ming-chiao* (Confucian teachings justifying social hierarchy) but a certain autonomy-enhancing vision of the human-divine relation, "inner transcendence"(*nei-tsai ch'ao-yueh*). He had borrowed this idea from the New Confucians. They had developed this idea more than thirty years earlier when trying to vindicate Confucianism by discarding its cosmology and celebrating its way of depicting the moral efforts of the autonomous subject of experience (*kung-fu*).[6]

Given the widespread recognition that much of the tradition had to be discarded, any contemporary recommendation to integrate Confucian principles with modern values has had to turn on some such abstract reevaluation of the Confucian tradition in the light of modern science and the Western philosophies celebrating freedom. Such an effort is different equally from just using historical sources to describe the lives and ideas of Confucian scholars during the traditional era and just personally practicing the norms Confucius stood for. Neither of these two activities can itself logically amount to a cogent recommendation that Chinese today devoted to modernization and democracy follow rather than reject the Confucian way.

Yet Yü Ying-shih has bitterly denounced the New Confucians for thus developing a philosophical analysis of the Confucian tradition to demonstrate that it ought to be the foundation of modern Chinese life. His emphasis has not been on their particular philosophical arguments. After all, he himself repeated one of their main theses, that the Confucian tradition's idea of "inner transcendence" is at least as tenable as Judeo-Christian theology. Yü's claim is that, however "subtle and refined," philosophical discussions are irrelevant to the task of reviving Confucian values. His argument is that "Confucian values necessarily call for their own realization in daily practice and so preclude being reduced to nothing more than an academic ethical theory or religious philosophy." This Confucian principle, he holds, was implemented in premodern times: "in traditional China, the Chinese people's modes of daily life expressed the Confucian principles, and this way of life was part of the whole social structure." When this "traditional social structure disintegrated

from the twentieth century on," Confucian values became a
"wandering, disembodied soul." That is, Chinese then were able to
"engage in empty talk" about Confucian values but could seldom put
them into practice. This situation contradicted the very nature of
Confucian values as principles inherently demanding their own
realization in practice. Therefore, the New Confucians'
philosophical discussion of Confucian values in a global context has
been essentially irrelevant to the problem of understanding and
practicing these values.[7] Moreover, the turning of Confucian values
into a "wandering soul" was part of a general "crisis" of modern
Chinese culture. The Chinese in the twentieth century were left
without any clear set of values, not only having lost their Confucian
values but also being unable to understand and appropriate Western
ones.[8]

Yet almost any complex society combines actual social
interaction with abstract arguments about the past, the future, and
the nature of ultimate reality, analyzing the historical condition of
the society and recommending goals as yet unrealized. This point
applies especially to societies undergoing great revision of the
culture, such as the non-Western societies today confronting Western
models of modernization. As people in such a society discuss "what to
adopt, what to discard" (*ch'ü-she*), why should they avoid analyzing
abstract principles as yet unrealized, whether principles found in
indigenous or in foreign literatures? A good example of such an
abstract argument is precisely Yü Ying-shih's own analysis of "inner
transcendence" as a "value system" that the Chinese have inherited,
that accords with their modern ideals, and that they should use to
modernize. According to the sociologist Reinhard Bendix, moreover,
as such abstract arguments accumulate, they can turn into a process
of "intellectual mobilization" gradually altering a society's everyday
discourse and practices.[9]

If, then, competing abstract arguments are integral to the way
people challenge one another as they revise their cultures, such
arguments cannot just refer to the mundane realities of the present.
They may well seek to evoke not only the hopes of the future but also
the dreams of the past. In fact, however, this process of cultural
revision in twentieth-century China has not turned all basic
Confucian values into mere dreams or "ghosts." There is a large
literature today, including some of Yü's own writings, recognizing the

perpetuation of many Confucian values and modes of thought in China during the twentieth century.[10] Finally, whether this ongoing process of cultural revision in China should be seen as a "crisis" is still another issue. Chinese in the twentieth century endured much change and suffering, but so did many other peoples. If "cultural crisis" denotes such troubles, it has been a characteristic of virtually every modern society. If, however, it denotes a kind of intellectual or spiritual "disorientation" somehow "worse" than that typical of all modern or even all human life, it is far from self-evident that twentieth-century China was afflicted by a "cultural crisis" (see below). On the contrary, the life of T'ang Chün-i and many other Chinese in this period can be seen as remarkably free of any such disorientation.

The philosophy of the New Confucians, then, is an example of the way partly abstract arguments arise as people address the problem of cultural revision. To be sure, T'ang Chün-i did not achieve what chapter I above defined as "epistemic success." His thought exemplified the "seesaw" effect. On the one hand, he avoided the fallacy of relativism; conceptualized praxis as a resolute "inner" effort to implement ideals rather than a passive response to empirical trends; and emphasized the parameters of freedom. On the other hand, he failed to analyze the "outer" conditions threatening individual freedom; failed to pursue an empirical understanding of the given world; lapsed into utopianism; and even failed to appreciate morally imperfect progress with regard to the material well-being and political organization of vast populations — the values of prosperity and political freedom.

What is unusual about T'ang is the thoughtfulness and intellectual honesty with which he insisted on this particular seesaw effect rather than the opposite one, vindicating discourse #1.[11] His outlook challenges Westerners unable to imagine a rational rejection of discourse #2 and shows that the rationality of their discourse is not necessarily obvious to people with a Chinese cultural background. The clash between two modes of rationality (lists of indisputables) becomes apparent only when a perspicacious person familiar with both modes consciously rejects one of them. Most basically, T'ang's thought suggests that the scope of reason and knowledge is still debatable. Yes, the "fallibility" J.S. Mill emphasized is a huge obstacle limiting the development of knowledge, but just how huge? Given the epistemic resources people have, to what extent is this obstacle superable? T'ang finds that the gloomy Western philosophies in this regard are unconvincing, if not ideological, illogical, and insincere, and his argument stems from neither ignorance nor insincerity.

Confronting T'ang's output of some 300 articles and twenty books, I started to study his thought more than twenty-five years ago by reading his classic *Chung-kuo wen-hua-chih ching-shen chia-chih* (The Value of the Spirit of Chinese Culture), which had first been published almost twenty years before, in 1953. (In 1976, it was in its ninth edition.) This reading experience was my most important since Arthur O. Lovejoy's *The Great Chain of Being.*[12] The latter had given me a manageable way of thinking about the history of ideas, while the former lucidly used Western philosophical concepts familiar to me to explain how Confucian thinkers had conceptualized moral autonomy and its cosmic context of "unending creation" (*sheng-sheng pu-i*). The richness of his analysis and textual evidence refuted the then prevalent view of the Confucian tradition as the authoritarian antithesis of the modern celebration of individual freedom and creativity. I then realized that the New Confucians had not "absurdly" resisted the May Fourth Movement's "rational" demand for Westernization but instead had complemented the May Fourth Movement's iconoclasm by formulating an alternative, equally plausible approach to the problem of Chinese modernization. This view is platitudinous today, but it raised eyebrows in 1977, when I published *Escape from Predicament.*

Besides the latter's chapter on T'ang, which pleased him, I published two articles on his thought and a short piece describing the premises it shared with Maoism — again, an almost platitudinous point today but a shocking one in 1978, or in 1983, when I regrettably outraged a scholarly audience at Tung-hai University in Taiwan by discussing such premises as a shared cultural pattern that the New Confucians took for granted.[13]

All those efforts to discuss T'ang's thought, however, were tentative, since I had not read enough to figure out just what his points of emphasis were. In 1997, however, I finally turned to his last book, *Sheng-ming ts'un-tsai yü hsin-ling ching-chieh.* This had been written during the last decade of his life. He had checked the proofs for the first time in late 1976, just before being operated on for lung cancer.[14] It was published in September 1977, about four months before his death. Its title can be rather literally translated as "Human Existence and the Dimensions of the Mind," but I suggest translating it as "Human Existence and the Nine Worlds," thinking of "worlds" as Karl R. Popper brilliantly used the term when he wrote about "world 1," "world 2," and "world 3." Popper had suggested there were "three ontologically distinct sub-worlds": "world 1" is "the physical world," "world 2" is that of "mental states," and "world 3" is that of "ideas in the objective sense," e.g. theories one critically evaluates.[15] T'ang's unapologetically metaphysical and idealistic book offers nine such "sub-worlds." He does not even recognize Popper's world 1, since he is an idealist for whom the ultimate elements of existence are what Buddhists call *hsiang* (objects of consciousness), not the physical things or forces posited by modern naturalism. He then equates Popper's treasured world 3 of scientific inquiry with the three lowest "worlds" of the mind and divides Popper's less favored world 2 of mere "beliefs" into six worlds, including a sublime metaphysical world Popper precluded. While Popper had posited the full reality of physical objects, T'ang was intent on proving that these objects were no more real and objective than those "worlds" accessible only to human reflexivity and beyond the possibility of empirical, experimental falsification.

For many years I avoided this book, fearful that with its frankly metaphysical rejection of empiricism, T'ang had put aside both his critical sense and his fruitful focus on the interpretation of historical texts. When I happened to glance at it, however, I found a highly critical, intellectually concentrated effort to sum up the shared categories of human thought that for about forty years he had been trying to infer from the history of philosophy in China and the West. Best of all, the last part of the book — "Epilogue: The Problems of the Contemporary Era, the Formation of This Book's Intellectual Background, and the Meaning of Its Philosophical Teaching" — was an effort to sum up all his main philosophical points and explain how in the course of his life he had arrived at them. It was a kind of intellectual last testament. I then realized that the philosophical stance in this book was close to the outlook he had formed four decades earlier, by the time he was thirty, and that there even was a deep continuity between his outlook then and the convictions he had formed by 1926, when he entered Peking University as a boy of seventeen. What emerged was a stunning combination of the deep convictions he had held continuously since his teens with a philosophical investigation carried out over half a century. True, looking back at his life in 1976, he saw an unfolding logic no doubt more coherent than the sequence of his thoughts was when he had them.[16] Nevertheless, I am confident that I finally can offer a reliable account of the basic mix of faith and reasoning with which T'ang rejected the most fundamental premises of Western modernity.

To describe and put it into perspective, I shall first offer an intellectual biography based largely on T'ang's reminiscences; then describe the beliefs he summed up in his last book; then explore the question of his epistemic failure or success; and, finally, discuss the main continuities and discontinuities between his thought and the Neo-Confucian tradition before the modern era. I should add that each of my translations of his statements is intended to convey his own meaning exactly, not my interpretation of it. To do this in English, however, I had to allow myself a little freedom of expression.

2. Biographical Outline

a. A Teenager's Worldview

T'ang's life (1909–1978) began on the eve of the 1911 Revolution, after the Ch'ing empire had already been undermined by domestic rebellions, by Western and Japanese imperialism, and by the realization in many circles that much of the traditional institutional and intellectual heritage had to be redesigned along Western lines. From his earliest years, he was intellectually confronted with powerfully dissonant realities: the global centrality of the West, the hegemony of science, the high prestige of scientists, the need to derive philosophical principles from "experience" rather than a sacred canon, and a hideous political turmoil culminating in the 1949 victory of the Communists and his exile in a Western colony, Hong Kong. Yet from his earliest years on, he forcefully reduced these agonizing realities to the ephemeral manifestations of a historical process ultimately based on Buddhist and Confucian principles that utterly confirmed the absolute value of everything he had cherished since his youth. So far as his life goes, if Chinese civilization before the upheavals of the nineteenth and twentieth centuries included an unquestioned core of values, these upheavals notwithstanding, this core remained unquestioned.

Certainly he felt China to be in a crisis — the victory of the "demonic" over the "sacred," as he put it later — but, instead of being "disoriented" by this crisis, he confronted it with moral-philosophical convictions as unwavering as any that I at least have ever found in history.[17] As I argued in 1977,

> Not self-doubt and the relaxation of worldly commitment, but a powerful belief that one's moral ideals are fully valid has been a common response of Chinese intellectuals to our turbulent century.... the Chinese have traditionally regarded humiliating and convulsive disasters as a normal part of their history and indeed as serving to define the moral-political missions to be undertaken by succeeding generations.[18]

A good deal of T'ang's most creative work was done precisely during one of modern China's most agonizing episodes, the horrendous Japanese invasion of China (1937–1945), which forced him to flee to Szechwan from his alma mater in Nanking, Nanking National Central University.

T'ang was born on January 17, 1909 in I-pin district, an important center of commerce in Szechwan near the Yunnan border at the confluence of the Min River, the Chin-sha River, and the Yangtze. His home was about one hundred yards from the bank of the Chin-sha. Exiled in Hong Kong forty years later, he spoke with longing of "again from the door of my home seeing the mountains to the south and hearing the sound of the river flowing east." The endless, life-giving flow of a stream (*liu*) was an ancient ontological image in Chinese thought associated with the Taoist and Buddhist advice to avoid trying to *chih-cho* (artificially cling to and keep static the inherently moving). This concept came to be at the heart of T'ang's philosophy, and he alluded to this in later years, noting that he had repeatedly resided near rivers: "There is a kind of destined affinity (*yuan*) between me and rivers."[19]

In his mind as he grew up, love of his home and its physical setting, of his mother and father, and of the whole Chinese cultural tradition conveyed to him by them formed a single feeling that in turn meshed with the sense of material comfort provided by his landlord family. Conversely, feelings of alienation from the traditional society were never produced in him by either a tense relation with a father imposing traditional learning on him or scenes of mass suffering.[20] His was a Hakka (*K'o-chia*) family from Kwangtung. By about 1800, one of T'ang's ancestors had moved from Kwangtung to Szechwan, made some money in the production of sugar, bought land, and settled in I-pin. His family came to own perhaps one hundred acres. T'ang's grandfather was the first scholar it produced. T'ang's father, T'ang Ti-feng, obtained the lowest degree (*sheng-yuan*) in the traditional examination system. He was a teacher who wrote a book about *Mencius* and studied in Nanking with the famous Buddhist thinker Ou-yang Ching-wu (1871–1943). The latter thought highly of both him and T'ang's mother.

T'ang's family moved from I-pin to the major Szechwan city of Ch'eng-tu when he was about four, perhaps 1913. Before T'ang entered primary school in 1920, at the age of eleven, he was taught by his father, who made him memorize explanations in the ancient dictionary *Shuo-wen*: "I dreaded this task."[21] Szechwan was steeped in history, and his father took him to visit many of the historical sites, such as those associated with the great poets Tu Fu (712–770) and Su Tung-p'o (1036–1101). His father had him bow before images of famous historical figures. T'ang later remembered these experiences vividly, grateful that his father had nurtured in him deep feelings of attachment to China's past. T'ang also had glowing memories of all the festival days and the other traditional forms of social intercourse. He remembered warm relations between his family and their tenants.[22] As a little boy in Ch'eng-tu, he noticed that the principal of the school where his father taught would bow to his father when handing him his letter of appointment, thus showing respect for the grave responsibilities of a teacher. T'ang was treated the same way in 1929 when he taught in Ch'eng-tu at Szechwan University. By 1932, however, when he taught high school in Ch'eng-tu, the principal would just shake his hand. T'ang regretted this change. He associated this act of bowing not with an authoritarian hierarchy but with a feeling of mutual respect based on shared ideals.[23]

In T'ang's family, these ideals included encouragement of independent, philosophically critical reflection. At the age of fifteen, disagreeing with his father's interpretation of Mencius, T'ang stood his ground without fear of offending him. When he was sixteen and influenced by May Fourth iconoclasm, he refused to kneel during ceremonies at the family grave site. His father's way of nurturing his intellectual imagination is illustrated by a conversation between them when T'ang was seven or eight.[24] His father told him of a scientific prediction that one day the sun's light and heat would die out and suggested that, on that very day, there would perhaps be left on earth just one man and his dog. The little boy was fascinated by this image. A few days later, after a rainstorm, the sun came out and dried out his family's courtyard, causing the dirt there to crack open a bit. T'ang then feared that the planet was about to break up. Forty years later, in Hong Kong, he mused:

> I think that was the start of my whole outlook on philosophy and human nature. Why would a person want to think about the destruction of the world? This really entails the whole problem of the dignity of human nature, its mysterious tendency toward transcendence, the difference between humans and other animals. Can this interest in some remote time when the world will end be explained in terms of the desire to survive, sexual desire, the desire for power, or life as responses to stimuli? Of course not, because all such impulses presuppose the world's existence. When one is concerned about the end of the world, the world in which these desires occur is no longer a matter of concern. But how can it not be a matter of concern? Later I was able to understand this: the human form of existence includes concerns transcending the material world. Of course, all this I did not know [when I feared as a little boy that the earth was about to come to an end].[25]

From the start, then, T'ang was interested more in the general human situation than the situation faced by China in the twentieth century. This philosophical spirit was further stimulated when T'ang, age eleven, started going to school and found himself in a class reading the Taoist masterpiece *Chuang-tzu*.[26] The next year, 1921, the family moved to Chungking, where T'ang's father had found another teaching post. The following years in Chungking, before T'ang in 1926 entered Peking University, were a time when the teenager became aware of the intellectual turmoil and philosophical debates then spreading throughout much of urban China. In other words, it was during his high school years that, though still mainly immersed in the traditional literature, he became familiar with the new intellectual discourse that the generation of K'ang Yu-wei and Liang Ch'i-ch'ao had crystallized. In 1922, at the age of thirteen, when he still did not know what the word "philosophy" meant, his father told him he had a "philosophical" bent. The May Fourth Movement was just then moving into Chungking, including speakers favoring the Communists. Kuomintang activities also were underway there. In 1923, the nationally famous debate about metaphysics and science erupted. The fourteen-year-old lad read just about every article it produced.[27]

These new trends made an impact on him. When he was sixteen and went back to his I-pin home for the first time, he was uninterested in his ancestral roots. That was the first time he visited the family grave site. When he went there, he refused to kneel, influenced by an article criticizing this custom. Despite his grandmother's urging, he had no interest in reading the family genealogy.[28]

On the other hand, he was not only unconvinced by the new iconoclastic, scientistic philosophies but also critical of the anti-scientistic positions, including Liang Shu-ming's famous book, *Eastern and Western Cultures*.[29] With some schoolmates, especially Yu Hung-ju, T'ang looked down on all the intellectual tides of the day; studied mainly books from the Chinese tradition, such as the great work on Sung and Yuan intellectual history partly written by Huang Tsung-hsi in the seventeenth century (*Sung-Yuan hsueh-an*); aimed to "integrate the thought of the present and the past, of China and the West"; and had the ultimate goal of becoming a "sage." For these male teenagers, "all the desires of the ear and the eyes were evil, and the physical body was the basest thing." A few years later, as a college student in Beijing, T'ang similarly viewed the physical body of a person as a "constraint" (*shu-fu*) from which "the mind," in its quest for "self-awareness," sought to "extricate itself."[30]

Even at the age of fifteen, he was already preoccupied with what was becoming the central philosophical problem for many in his generation: integrating modern science with the spiritual and ontological principles revealed by Buddhism and Neo-Confucianism. On the one hand, he was interested in theories about human nature. Disagreeing with his father's view of Mencius, he wrote a long essay arguing (correctly) that both Mencius and Hsun-tzu believed human nature had both good and bad aspects. He also tried to reduce a magazine's psychological discussion of human faculties to "the quest for oneness through full awareness of the nature of reality" (*tzu-chueh-te ch'iu-t'ung*). On the other hand, turning from the given nature of things to the question of ideals, he pondered "the question of what the ultimate goal of human life is. I concluded that, while man seeks happiness, happiness and the elimination of suffering are possible only if all desires are completely eliminated. Therefore Buddhism's elimination of desire is the supreme goal. After the self is forgotten, one can benefit others, and so morality is realized." This Buddhist ideal, in turn linked by T'ang with that of Confucius, was a common one in twentieth-century China. A famous version of it was Chang Ping-lin's (1868–1936) idea of "the five kinds of non-differentiation" (*wu-wu*).

Along with this traditional moral totalism and asceticism, the teenager also began to refute materialism and naturalism by using a formula that remained basic throughout his life and led him eventually to Kant:

> The mind is able to be aware of itself, but the things of which it is aware do not necessarily have this ability. These two [the mind and what it is aware of] must be different in their ultimate nature. I understood this point about the mind's ability to be aware of itself by the time I was fifteen and to the end of my life did not change this view.... The mind's self-awareness definitely cannot be wholly identified with or reduced to the body or thing of which it is aware.

This view in turn reflected T'ang's still earlier fascination with the grammatical distinction between subject and object.[31]

Also during these high school years, T'ang's thought about human awareness included an inclination toward Buddhist idealism (*wei-shih-lun*). This reflected his relation with a father who had studied under Ou-yang Ching-wu. When T'ang was fourteen, he saw the river near his Chungking house rise during a rainfall and cover over a stone. "Does the stone exist when I cannot see it?" he asked himself. He concluded it did not. (He did not, however, ask whether his father and mother existed when unobserved by him.) The next year he read an article arguing in favor of Buddhist idealism and agreed with it. About a year later, in 1925, he traveled with some of his family to Nanking and received instruction about Buddhism from his father's teacher, the famous Ou-yang Ching-wu. While his son struggled to make sense out of all these colliding intellectual perspectives, T'ang Ti-feng remained close to him. When T'ang was fourteen and told his father he had been moved by the "passage about Mencius leaving Ch'i," "My father recited it by heart. I started weeping, unable to stop."[32]

At the age of seventeen, T'ang entered Peking University with a largely inherited outlook that he never abandoned: China had a civilization of limitless value and occupied a or the central place in human history; this value stemmed from a vision of total, saintly morality expressed by Buddhism, Confucianism, and Taoism; this moral ideal was based on the nature of cosmic reality as a "flowing process" violated by any intellectual or moral act treating it as a static entity onto which one could "hold" (*chih-cho*); this ultimate reality had itself to be a form of moral awareness, not morally dumb matter, since if it were the latter, becoming one with it as the goal of moral effort would make no sense; differing human "cultures" had arisen trying successfully or unsuccessfully to grasp the nature of the cosmos and infer from it the right way to organize society; one of these cultures, the Western, challenged the centrality of China and, with its science-centered philosophies, created dangerous misunderstandings about the nature of reality and morality; therefore "reasons" (*li-yu*) would have to be found to prove to others in a science-driven world that they should adopt the proper understanding of existence and morality.

For T'ang, these arguments about the "reasons" for this or that revolved around the problem of what ultimately exists and how it is related to human ideals — ontology: "In general, the chief philosophical problems I was concerned with when I went to Peking University were those regarding the relation between mind and material objects."[33] In other words, a central issue on the agenda for his generation of Chinese intellectuals was how to negotiate the dispute between materialist and idealist positions on the nature of what ultimately exists. With their epistemological optimism, T'ang's generation took for granted that this question could be answered, instead of setting aside this ontological issue to focus on the Popperian quest for falsifiable "conjectures" about the factual world and on the epistemological issue of whether knowledge of universally overriding moral principles is possible.

Even more, T'ang was always sure that discursive discussion of the ontological issue could be reinforced by identifying certain subjective "feelings" (*ch'ing*) stemming from the ultimate reality of the cosmos as a kind of moral awareness. Lacking epistemological pessimism, he never worried that what he felt might be no more than what Arthur O. Lovejoy called a "pathos," that is, a type of feeling stemming from cultural or psychological rather than cosmic conditions. In T'ang's defense, let it be noted that my ability to think and feel is a biological, cosmically given faculty. I may be responsible for what I think but not for my ability to think. Moreover, there is no proof that all altruistic, moral feelings in me stem not from this cosmic faculty and are exclusively the product of the culture I internalized or of my own mental initiatives. On the contrary, moral feeling is connected to love, which seems connected to the erotic impulse, a biological trait. At any rate, whether or not T'ang was justified in his belief that he could reliably identify cosmically-grounded pathos, this belief was always unchallenged in his eyes.

This Mencian "feeling" uniting him with all humanity was something T'ang experienced not infrequently as a powerful emotion evoking the universe of Chinese poetry. For instance, T'ang remembered that when, as a lad of seventeen in 1926, he went off to college, soon to enter Peking University,

> [my] father came with me to the ship and spent the night on it with me. At dawn, we heard the sound of the ship's engine, and my father had to return to shore. The emotion I felt on parting from him suddenly made me think of how, from the past until today, this same emotion had been felt by numberless fathers and sons, brothers, husbands and wives. This moved me greatly.

Another memory from that year was similar:

> I went once to an outdoor showing at the university of a movie about the life of Sun Yat-sen. The sky was filled with stars. I thought about how, in this vast cosmos, the actions of dedicated men like Sun Yat-sen are like specks of grain in the ocean. Yet they give their last ounce of energy for the nation. Why? As I both looked up at the heavens and thought of humanity, an unstoppable feeling of moral empathy welled up in me. It seemed to be without limit, filling up the cosmos and giving me the sense of being suspended between heaven and earth.[34]

Again, the Mencian pathos evoked by this experience should not be overlooked. In his twenties, T'ang repeatedly sought through "quiet sitting" to "see" that "brightly spiritual mind" (*ling-ming*) he regarded as the foundation of the cosmos (see below).

b. T'ang as a Young Philosopher

During the period 1926–1937, T'ang turned from a college freshman of seventeen into a philosopher of twenty-eight confident he had solved the ontological problem. As he put it in 1977, "Such was the intellectual framework I had formed by the age of twenty-seven or twenty-eight, and to this day I have been unable to go beyond it."[35] From his first days at Peking University in 1926, he was not distracted by arguments comparing the "cultures" into which humankind was divided. He listened to the lectures of Hu Shih, Liang Shu-ming, and Liang Ch'i-ch'ao and rapidly dismissed as "totally wrong" Hu Shih's celebration of Western culture. Conversely, he sympathized with the more tradition-oriented views of the two Liangs.[36] In his eyes, however, comparing the cultures into which humankind was divided required first understanding the nature of humankind, and this question in turn depended on a still more basic one: what is the nature of reality (the ontological issue, as one may phrase it)?

In dealing with this question, T'ang throughout insisted on at least three overlapping points that epitomized not only the epistemological optimism of the inherited intellectual tradition but also its insistence on an anthropocentric cosmic order. First, he refused to accept any principle or condition of existence as simply given or "accidental." There had to be a transparent reason for any principle — its *so-i-jan* (raison d'être), as Neo-Confucianism had put it. For instance, admitting that he lacked training in mathematics and logic, he nevertheless studied the famous writings of Bertrand Russell and Alfred North Whitehead on the principles of mathematics. As he put it in later years,

> They start by establishing some primary concepts, basic propositions, principles of inference but never give the reason why a principle must be the way it is. This left me very dissatisfied.... I think that when people seek knowledge or progress in thinking rationally, the basic principle is that whenever one says something is so-and-so, one ought also to explain why it is not so-and-so. Only then can one satisfy the demands of reason.[37]

(Admittedly, he neglected to ask what the reason was for *this* "basic principle.")

Second, this search for the ultimate "reason" overlapped the idea that this reason must stem from some kind of existing entity. In this context, T'ang's writings lack any reference to "reification" or "misplaced concreteness" as intellectual dangers. Referring in his later years to his early study of Western logic, T'ang noted: "My question with regard to these most basic concepts and propositions was: where ultimately did these things come from? Can they be reduced to some one irreducible something? I then thought of a 'Logos' as the source of these things."[38] (T'ang used the English version of this Greek word as well as phonetically used Chinese logographs.) For T'ang, morality had to be indisputable, and only something fully existing could have this quality of universality or indisputability.

Third, T'ang's Buddhist-Confucian ideal of human dignity and total morality beyond all selfishness demanded a concept of existence endowing his own awareness with access to the very top of the ontological hierarchy. For instance, he could not bear any evolutionary theory according to which future beings would grasp truths outside the envelope of his own awareness. Reminiscent of the *t'ai-chi* (supreme ultimate) concept in Neo-Confucianism, the term *tsui-kao* (highest) was central to his hierarchical and entirely traditional vision of human dignity. Whitehead's theory of a creative cosmic process of evolution "putting thinking human beings at the highest level of natural evolution was able to ensure the dignity of man," he thought. But when other thinkers suggested that "the cosmos in the future could through evolution produce a being still higher than thinking beings today," "a being related to man today the way man today is related to the general run of animals," T'ang objected. If such a theory put forward today by human beings is a true account of the overall possibilities of evolution, he argued, these human beings must be able to conceptualize the nature of human existence as a whole. If they were unable to do so, they would be unable to think of the possibility that evolution may produce beings with a mentality beyond what they can understand. The very suggestion that evolution may do so refutes itself. Thus it is certain that the "highest" kind of consciousness possible is possessed by humans as they are today.

T'ang thus conflated the point that any kind of relativism contradicts itself with the idea that, as beings able to grasp universal principles, humans were "at the highest level" of existence — *wan-wu-chih ling* (the finest spiritual beings among the ten thousand things).

This conflation remained fundamental to the solution T'ang devised for the ontological problem. He was always driven by the belief that human reflexivity could grasp the ultimate rationale of the cosmos, that this rationale existed as a spiritual cosmic force, not just as a human conjecture, and that, through their reflexivity, human beings could identity themselves with this "highest" cosmic level of existence. Thus he argued that

> although the natural world could produce a form of existence higher than we humans, the very fact that we are able to think of the idea of all possible forms of existence shows that this mind we have occupies a position above all the forms of existence of which it can think or have knowledge. From this standpoint above or outside the whole temporal process (*li-ch'eng*) of natural creation, this mind can think about the nature of this whole process.

Moreover, it could think of itself thinking about this process and so on *ad infinitum*:

> This mind's thinking about this whole natural process is also a process, and this latter mental process is also something the mind can think about, and so on. Therefore one must affirm the existence of a thinking subject (*hsin-ling chu-t'i*) able to transcend any notion of any processes. Otherwise, all knowledge and philosophies pertaining to any processes are impossible. All processes involve evolution and change, but the conscious subject thinking about evolution and change must itself be without evolution or change, because if it too were subject to change, then it could not establish any theory about change.[39]

That is, because the idea that there can be no unchangeably true idea refutes itself, the human mind cannot be in a process of change with no access to absolute truth. So basic to him, these ideas celebrating reflexivity and indeed harking back to much Buddhist philosophy had germinated in his high school days.

Basically armed with this concept of reasoning already when he went to college, T'ang did not specialize in any one school of Western philosophy. He saw himself as "choosing between" (*chüeh-tse*) different philosophical positions:

> This process of choosing per se had no inherent value, but, subjectively speaking, it was a way of battling with myself, a history of how I gradually and bloodily fought my way out of my own preconceptions.... I hope that my young friends, those who seek learning, can learn from my story that, when we look for ideas we can believe in, we must compare what we believe with what others believe in order to figure out the strengths and shortcomings of every view.... all my intellectual changes and progress

came drop by drop as I struggled with my own beliefs. Therefore, my mistaken beliefs never returned after I definitely understood they were mistaken.[40]

Notable here was the combination of a critical spirit with great epistemological optimism. T'ang did not view himself as trapped in human fallibility. As discussed below, T'ang like J.S. Mill weighed both human intellectual frailty and the human capacity to think correctly, but he weighed them in a distinctive way.

It is striking that T'ang focused his energies on this "bloody" intellectual struggle while his nation was in political turmoil, indeed, in the eyes of many Chinese, on the verge of "extinction." In 1927, as Chiang Kai-shek's Northern Expedition was trying to reunify the country, T'ang moved from Peking University to the Department of Philosophy at Nanking Central University, where teachers like Fang Tung-mei and T'ang Hsi-yü could help him find his way through recent Western philosophical writings. Already in 1926 at Peking University, he and his close high school friend Yu Hung-ju, who also was a student there, had sympathized with the "social ideals of communism," as T'ang later put it. Indeed, T'ang retained this sympathy even after 1949, when the Communist victory forced him to flee to Hong Kong. T'ang, however, could not join the Communists because he had concluded that their philosophical foundation, materialism, was mistaken. He thought of joining the Nationalist Party (Kuomintang). Disgusted by the struggle in it between rightist and leftist factions for control of student groups, however, he took a stereotypical path of Chinese intellectuals: the scholar "disgusted with politics." Yu Hung-ju, however, joined the Communists. He laughed at T'ang's suggestion that the Communists should discard their philosophy of materialism. When T'ang suggested to Yu that they remain friends even if they differed politically, Yu replied: "People on the battlefield cannot shake hands." But after the Kuomintang on April 12, 1927 started its bloody purge of Communists, Yu saved himself by hiding in T'ang's home in Nanking. Yu then was close to suicide, suffering from both the loss of friends executed by the Kuomintang forces and a failed romance. Five years after the purge, in 1932, T'ang saw his old friend again in Chungking. They visited their old haunts of high school days and stopped in a tea house to talk. There, Yu suddenly announced: "I have been in the Communists' youth corps, I've been in the Communist Party, I've been in the Kuomintang, I've lived as a Confucian scholar and a Taoist, and I've studied Buddhist and Western books. Now I want to establish a philosophy of life for the Chinese people, and I want you to help me." T'ang was both moved and saddened by this "somewhat laughable" performance. Their paths diverged after this, but around 1936 T'ang suddenly received a letter from him. Yu had turned to Buddhism but was already dying from tuberculosis. He asked that, after he died, T'ang in his memory read from the *Diamond Sutra* for half a month, "because [he wrote] only I had understood his life." T'ang shortly heard from Yu's wife that Yu, still not thirty, was dead. T'ang read from the sutra as requested. His grief was deep: "This event filled me with sadness as I thought of the numberless young Chinese who had died in the course of political struggles. I then understood the tragedies resulting from the conflicts between old and new cultures, Chinese and Western culture, as well as the many deep mysteries of the heart these tragedies entailed."[41]

Five years before, in 1931, T'ang's father had died.[42] It was only then, when he was 22, that T'ang, "filled with feelings beyond my control, understood the need to kneel during ceremonies at the family grave site," leaving behind the iconoclastic rejection of this custom that had earlier influenced him. As he later wrote:

> Thereafter, whenever I went back home, I would always visit the family grave site, burning incense at dawn and at dusk before the ancestral tablets and the tablet honoring heaven, earth, the ruler, one's relatives, and one's teachers. At the same time, I understood that human moral awareness itself, our limitless feeling of moral compassion, it all comes out of this idea of "conducting the funeral of your parents meticulously and not neglecting the rituals honoring remote ancestors" [, which Tseng-tzu, Confucius's disciple, put forward]. It was this insight that led me to hate the Communists for destroying the relation with parents and ancestors.[43]

A kind of melancholy was becoming a basic part of T'ang's life, and it can be seen in the photographs of his face in later years. It was reinforced during his long years of exile in Hong Kong, where he had to endure the rejection of his philosophy by a world largely given over to either Marxism or utilitarianism and had to engage in bitter struggles over the intellectual direction of The Chinese University of Hong Kong.

When his mother died in 1964, T'ang stayed in a Buddhist temple for ten days, "my grief seeming to spread out throughout all the realms of existence."[44] He wanted never to do any scholarly writing again.[45] A decade or so earlier, noting how all his writings and activities in Hong Kong had failed to give him any relief from the suffering in his heart, he wrote:

> I think that what a person really wants is to return from where he came. As for me, I often think that if I just could now really go back to the graves of my dead friends, my father, my ancestors, or to the places where the tablets of my ancestors are, and there burn some incense, and if I could stand before the front door of my home, again seeing the mountains in the south, again hearing the sound of the river moving east, then I could be content.[46]

This sadness, however, never turned into an ultimate melancholy. In an essay full of admiration for Heidegger, T'ang criticized his thought as "tending to lead people down the path of dark, overly metaphysical thoughts far removed from real human concerns."[47] T'ang always found within this melancholy a still more basic feeling, "a true sense of moral concern" (*chen-ch'eng ts'e-ta*), which for him always stemmed from an ultimately cosmic moral impulse or entity (*hsin-ling chu-t'i, jen-t'i,* etc.)[48] Indeed, T'ang's thought, especially during the horrendous 1940s, was typically filled with what has been called "a kind of Panglossian optimism."[49] What T'ang was persistently looking for, as he put it at the end of his life, was not necessarily a successful transformation of society but a spirituality so intense that with it one could either "save the world" or have the "great bravery needed to endure its annihilation." By "saving" it, he meant totally ending the power of the "demonic," ending the historical condition of a world in which "the sacred and the demonic are confusedly mixed together" (*shen-mo hun-tsa*).[50]

It is clear that this stance of his was far from alien to the radical, transformative, utopian vision which originally inspired Mao and was utterly alien to that Western vision of partial, material progress in a morally imperfect world so magnificently summed up in Jeremy Bentham's mundane words, "the greatest happiness for the greatest number." Even if one disagrees with T'ang's stance, however, one can ponder his suggestion that the key philosophical problem is not, as Popper thought, finding the principles that most directly encourage the search for scientific knowledge and technological progress but finding the spiritual stance that best promotes both the rationality of the given world and that of agency, as discussed in chapter I.

Looking for that outlook during the tumultuous decade following the unification of China in 1927 and consolidating it precisely during the horrendous years of the Japanese invasion and the Chinese civil war (1937–1949), T'ang, as already mentioned, saw it as revolving precisely around the ontological problems contemporaneous Western thought was increasingly placing outside the boundaries of the knowable. T'ang already in his teens had rejected the idea that material objects constitute the only kind of ultimate reality, and that awareness is just the activity of one material object, the brain. His point, which he found again later in Kant, was that the subject of awareness cannot be the same as any sensory object of awareness, such as a brain. T'ang also was tempted by idealism, the theory that all existence is merely an aspect of human awareness. But he had also rejected that theory when he was less than twenty. Sympathetic from the start to the Neo-Confucian idea of a cosmic moral impulse both manifest within an individual's mind and responsible for the reality of material objects, T'ang rejected any idealism boiling down to "the theory that nothing exists but me."

In his first college years, therefore, having rejected both such idealism and materialism, T'ang was left with an ontological "dualism," as he put it later, since he insisted on not only the reality of material objects but also awareness of these objects as a second, irreducible reality.[51] Such a dualism, however, could never satisfy a mind like his rooted in a Buddhist-Confucian faith with its focus on "linkage," the oneness of all the facets of existence.[52] He was wrestling with this problem in 1927 when he left Peking University to study in the Department of Philosophy at Nanking Central University. There he listened to lectures from one of the great founders of the modern New Confucian movement, Hsiung Shih-li, whose largely Confucian way of overcoming dualism and solving the above "linkage" problem was certainly not without its appeal for T'ang. T'ang, however, "could not grasp his meaning." Thinking at the time that philosophical problems could be solved only "by means of science,"[53] T'ang was groping his way toward a methodology that Hsiung lacked and that in T'ang's eyes might be persuasive for modern audiences insisting on "science," "experience" (*ching-yen*), or "what is given in experience" (*tang-hsia ch'eng-hsien*) (*so-yü*) as the gate to all knowledge.

In other words, like Hsiung, T'ang was aiming for the final "linkage" (*kuan-t'ung*): the Neo-Confucian goal of oneness between self, group, and cosmos; of the dissolution of all "false opinion" (*wang-chih*); of understanding how all insights of "value" are consistent with each other (*hui-t'ung*); and of the oneness of ideals with all actualities.[54] The validity of this goal was obvious in the world of the sacred canons of Buddhism and Confucianism. But how could it be discussed in modern terms as a necessary, universal implication of "experience"?

As T'ang later put it, the "True Way" (*tao*) can be made clear only if one "begins with how people are used to explaining things to each other in ordinary conversation and then gradually ascends to a grasp of that sacred realm beyond what can be imagined, though unable fully to fathom the meaning of this ultimate realm."[55] This methodology was reminiscent of both Kant's deduction of the categories and some Buddhist philosophy. As illustrated by the famous Consciousness-Only school of Hsuan-tsang (596–664),[56] the Buddhist tradition included a view of consciousness as a series of levels descending from this highest realm down to the level of ordinary experience. What T'ang with his modern respect for "science" and "experience" was searching for was a way to start at the bottom of this ontological ladder (science) and climb up it. His philosophy, then, far from being impressed by the Humean breach between "is" and "ought," would totally reject this breach by "teaching" (*chiao*) people why the mundane facts of the empirical, scientific world they were fixated on necessarily required their affirmation of this highest, indeed bluntly "metaphysical" "world" that was the "source" of morality. In this way he hoped he could successfully not only grasp the truth but also propagate it in this modern world (*tzu-chueh ch'iu chueh-t'a* [find enlightenment for himself and then seek to enlighten others]).[57] Such propagation, from his intellectualistic standpoint, was the sole means available to cause the international as well as the domestic community to turn from a "demonic" into a "sacred" hierarchy.

Looking for a way to turn the scientific understanding of "experience" into the bottom rung of an ontological ladder, getting no help from Hsiung Shih-li, and dissatisfied with his own "dualism," T'ang was deeply impressed by William James's famous essay "Does Consciousness Exist?" It struck him as both restoring the oneness of reality and according with the modern predilection for arguments based strictly on concrete experience. James had suggested that the breach between consciousness and the objects of consciousness was false, because both were merely phases of "experience": an object was just an earlier experience turned into an object as a person remembered it in the context of a later experience.

This argument so impressed T'ang that he started to veer toward "logical positivism," as he later put it. He started believing that there were only two secure sources of knowledge, "the law of identity [logic] and the relations between sense experiences." He sought to use these two "to explain all that exists in the cosmos and all the different kinds of customs and mental activities of humankind. The application of these two principles was limited to experience. The idea of any ultimate reality or existence transcending experience was out of the question."

Yet this standpoint too was in conflict with T'ang's youthful vision, since it amounted to the central fallacy of "holding" or "clinging" (*chih-cho*), what T'ang later described as "sinking into the mistake of clinging to factual reality."[58] With his focus on the rationality of praxis or agency (*kung-fu*), T'ang throughout his life attacked this mistake: it undermined the nature of moral action as pursuit of ideals transforming factual reality. From his standpoint, logical positivism, Marxism, and the Ch'ing textual studies movement, were equally guilty of "clinging to" instead of transforming facts (*hsien-ni yü shih-jan-che chih chih-ch'ih*).

In Nanking Central University in 1927, T'ang started to find a way out of his ontological dilemma when he encountered the New Realism of philosophers like Ralph Barton Perry, G.E. Moore, William P. Montague, and Edward G. Spaulding. By this time, T'ang no doubt was making progress with his English, the only foreign language he ever learned, I believe. As shown by the rich bibliographical references to works in English in his two-volume textbook on philosophy (*Che-hsueh kai-lun*, first published in 1961), T'ang became able to deal with this language, though the many misspellings in his publications show that penetrating the mysteries of a foreign language was not one of his passions.

Reading these philosophers, T'ang again made use of a foreign philosophy to pursue his own purposes. New Realism in the West was a reaction against the doctrines holding that perceived objects had no existence independent of the subject perceiving them. Accepting the New Realist arguments to the contrary, T'ang had found a way to reject both William James and logical positivism. Even more, having thus generously filled the universe with objects existing independent of any particular person's experience, T'ang could begin to see a way "scientifically" to demonstrate the "existence" of the high ideals to which he had been unceasingly committed:

> At that time I encountered the New Realism of the British and Americans, reading books by Moore, Perry, Montague, and Spaulding. With them, I did not need to stop with the ideas of empiricism and phenomenalism. New Realism enabled me to believe in latently existing universals (*kung-hsiang*) which could be but had not yet been experienced. My happiness was unlimited when I could believe that the cosmos included latently existing universals with the possibility of fully existing, including numberless values expressing the true, the good, and the beautiful.[59]

Grasping this cosmos filled with not only concrete experiences but also other levels of "existence," T'ang in the next years used Kant, Fichte, Hegel, Rudolph Hermann Lotze, Friedrich Paulsen, Josiah Royce, and others to conceptualize it in a way corroborating his original youthful convictions rooted in Buddhism and Neo-Confucianism. If one looks at the way T'ang in 1977 summed up this philosophical path he took in his twenties,[60] one can see that, with his immense, tradition-rooted epistemological optimism, he sought to corroborate these convictions by deriving from "experience" an idealist ontology with "reasons" demonstrating that: (1) the saintly moral ideals which he wished the world would follow are universally valid norms somehow stemming from something as real as any concrete experience; (2) this something is an ontological hierarchy at the top of which is a kind of cosmic, "flowing" general awareness and "feeling" (*ch'ing*) both coinciding with "reason" (*li-hsing*) and putting "morality" above all else; (3) human beings can through human reasoning, their boundless reflexivity, and their "feeling" grasp this ultimate nature of "reason" and "morality" and identify themselves with "the highest" rung of the ontological ladder; (4) since the cosmos is governed by "reason" (*li-hsing*), and "reason" is a human faculty, the cosmos has a definite structure making sense to the human mind, despite the contemporary theories that its organization is open to a bewildering variety of possibilities, such as the theory that space could have more than three dimensions; (5) thus there are "reasons" (*li-yu*) for all the cosmos's definite aspects, i.e. the being-thus-and-thus of things is not "accidental" or something just to be noted without knowing why there is not a different arrangement — this point applies to the rules of logic, the categories identified by Kant (quantity, quality, relation, etc.), the structure of space and time, the major empirical distinctions between animate and inanimate things, plants and animals, etc., and the need for the mind to exist in a physical body; (6) thus one can grasp the reason for the congruence between the logical reasoning people do and the laws of nature; (7) another "reason" one can grasp is the reason why that moral awareness at the foundation of the cosmos, which inherently includes the option of disassociating itself from concrete experience, chooses to involve itself in it, thus effecting the "congruence" above.

For T'ang with his Buddhist background and even his thought as a little boy about the end of the world, this option was a basic issue:

> But for me, the central problem was why I as an individual [participating in this cosmically ultimate awareness] must accept this world made up of nature, society, and history. Since I have a mind that can transcend any particular idea and is able to form the idea of all that can possibly exist, and since this mind can then discard this latter idea and so reject this world, there must be, based on the very nature of this mind or on the rationality inherent in it, an incontrovertible reason why this mind accepts the world. This reason would make clear why this mind can proceed forth and accept this world or reject the world, returning back into itself. My feelings about life before I was thirty in fact at times led me to think of my mind as located at the edge of this world. There were times when I wanted to become an immortal in the Taoist sense. Practicing the "quiet sitting" [of the Neo-Confucian tradition], I would experience something like the enlightenment referred to in Western mysticism. I felt that my mind had seemingly retreated from the world, and that I could see in my mind a limitless spiritual clarity. Thus I could enter eternity and transcend life and death. The reason why I must live and exist in this world must lie in the very nature of this limitless spiritual clarity or of the rationality inherent in it. Most people live in this world, fully accepting it — generally speaking, scientists and philosophers accept the world and on this basis

try to understand it. But as for me, from the start I had a certain feeling about life that my relation with this world was such that I could either adhere to it or remove myself from it. The spiritually clear mind in me (*ling-ming*) was at the edge of the world, able either to enter or depart from it. Thus there must be a reason for my entering and accepting it.

T'ang then conflated this question of a spiritual ability to transcend the empirical world with that central problem of congruence Einstein once referred to as an insoluble mystery, the congruence between the laws actually followed by predictable physical events and the trains of logical thought followed by the human mind to predict events: "Moreover, there must be a certain congruence (*hsiang-ying-ho*) between the very nature of my mind or the rationality (*li-hsing*) inherent in it, on the one hand, and, on the other, the major types of existing things in this world we can decide to accept, that is, the fixed, existing laws according to which things and events are thus-and-so."[61] T'ang wanted to see this congruence as the result of the "necessary" decision on the part of the cosmic mind to involve and reveal itself in the painful empirical world.

Looking for a philosophy definitively demonstrating the truth of the above points, T'ang could not be content with the cautiously phrased claims of New Realism or even with Kant's idealism. He appreciated Kant's idea of a "unifying consciousness transcending [the given sensory manifold]" and providing the "categories" turning raw sense data into a world human beings can understand. For T'ang, Kant had thus correctly referred to a consciousness "occupying an unshakable position above the natural world." Moreover, Kant had recognized "the ability of reason abstractly to construct transcendent objects," complementing New Realism's implication that transcendent universals exist, and Kant had splendidly insisted that "the moral imperative was higher in its significance than empirical reality."[62]

With his epistemological optimism, however, T'ang had no use at all for Kant's epistemologically pessimistic view that discursive reasoning cannot prove many of the above points T'ang insisted on demonstrating. Kant has been widely admired in the West for showing that the ultimate nature of reality (noumena) lies outside the bounds of the knowable, but T'ang could not accept this emphasis of Kant's on the decisive boundary between empirically verifiable, discursively established ideas and ideas based only on faith or human will. Similarly, he could not accept Kant's idea that one could only describe the universal categories basic to experience, not give the "reason why" these categories are as they are:

> Kant says that people in using inner and outer sense perception to know the world must depend on the ideas of time and three-dimensional space, but he gives no reason why this is so or why space has three dimensions. I was not satisfied with the notion that space's having three dimensions was purely a matter of accident.... [Similarly,] I saw that Russell and Whitehead in their study of the principles of mathematics start out by setting forth certain primary concepts, basic propositions, and principles of inference, but they wholly fail to offer a reason why they had to set them forth in this way. This made me very dissatisfied.[63]

T'ang went on to explain why "among Western philosophers I most appreciated Fichte and Hegel."[64] To a large extent, he felt, they showed a way to demonstrate the seven points above, showing how to expand the scope of discursive reasoning so as to break down the boundary Kant had drawn between the knowable and the unknowable. The valuable discursive point T'ang found in their work was criticism of Kant's way of "critiquing" the conditions of knowledge, their way of reversing the direction of Kant's critique. Kant had restricted himself to drawing inferences from the nature of experience, T'ang felt. What T'ang admired in Fichte and Hegel was their decision to begin their analysis not with sensory experience as a given but with the consciousness implied by experience:

> What I came to think later was that people know the world through experience, then reflect philosophically on the nature of their knowledge of experience, coming to understand that there is a unifying consciousness transcending any given experience. This is Kant's philosophy, and indeed this is a necessary philosophical path. But Kant's whole philosophy is a matter of critiquing the knowledge of experience in order to grasp what this knowledge implies, namely, *a priori* conditions determining the scope of experience as well as the establishment of a moral and aesthetic world. But in thus directly accepting the given knowledge of experience and then critiquing it, there is no real critique. Kant discovers there are space and time and then speaks of space and time; he discovers there are twelve categories and then speaks of twelve categories; he himself sees that all these are related to each other and so entail a unifying process, but he never explains why this process of interrelation is necessary. This is not

so good as the way Fichte directly begins with the transcendent self [implied by experience] to infer the necessity of its facing what is not itself, namely nature and society, thus explaining why the self exists in nature and in society. Nor is Kant's approach as good as the way Hegel derives all the categories from pure thought, using absolute reason as his starting point, then noting its necessarily objectifying itself in the form of nature, and then using this relation between nature and absolute reason to analyze the world of spirit, not only the subjective aspects of spirit such as desire and reason but also its objective aspects, namely moral law, art, religion, and philosophy.

T'ang reasoned that, just as the idea of self necessarily implied something that is not the self, so the idea of "irrationality" necessarily

presupposed a rational foundation. This foundation is a *li-t'i* (principle of reason as an ultimate reality) or "Logos".... This is a principle of reason as a three-dimensional ultimate reality, and it ultimately rests on a mind that is spiritual but empty of any specific impressions or appearances (*hsu-ling wu-hsiang-chih hsin*). The principle of reason as an ultimate reality underlying the nature of this "Logos" is this spiritually alive awareness beyond any specifics. This ultimate reality as reason clearly is congruent with three-dimensional space and with the basic distinctions between the different types of existing things in nature (such as those between inanimate, animate, plant, and animal existence), as well as with the basic fixed laws of the universe, such as gravity, and the various directions of the spiritual life of human beings [as I have analyzed them in this book].

T'ang also felt he had an answer to the question of how this cosmically universal principle of reason or "Logos" could have existed before the natural evolution of species produced a human being with a mind able to understand it:

Thus if this mind is not itself in a state of evolution, one cannot say either that it was suddenly created after natural evolution reached a certain stage or that nature at first consisted only of material things. One ought to say: even when the natural world consisted only of material things, this mind itself already existed. At that point, however, it lay hidden, it was not manifest. Thus when one considers the way that there was a natural evolution from merely material things to animate things and then to animals and finally to human beings with minds, one ought to say that, through this process, the mind, at first latent, gradually became manifest. Since this mind today is fully manifest as a transcendent subject able to have the idea of all that can possibly exist as a totality, and since it therefore occupies a position above all that can possibly exist, it can in the future only further realize what it already is. One cannot say it itself will further evolve and turn into something different from and transcending itself. To be sure, this mind can itself transcend whatever manifest form it has acquired, manifesting itself as more than it was. But this transcendence of itself cannot cause it not to be itself. Its ability to transcend itself is just a faculty internal to itself. This was a train of reasoning I developed myself as I reflected on the philosophical implications of the theory of evolution. Only then did I start reading books in the tradition of Kant, Fichte, Hegel, Bradley, and Paulsen.[65]

T'ang thus used these thinkers to corroborate his own most fundamental convictions rooted in the saintly ideal of Neo-Confucianism and its primary concept of *hsu-ling ming-chueh* (intelligent awareness in its pure, naturally given, cosmically individual form, empty of any consciously specific concepts or sensations) as the basis of the cosmos, as well as the overlapping Buddhist concept of Brahma.[66] This philosophical path, which he arrived at by his late twenties and never basically deviated from, overlapped precisely the Hegelian path rejected by much of the contemporary Western world. As W.H. Walsh amusingly wrote in the entry on Kant in *The Encyclopedia of Philosophy*, Kant at the end of his life was tempted to take a similar path: "It is perhaps fortunate for Kant's reputation that he was not able to get his final philosophical thoughts into publishable form."[67] Even though aware, as already mentioned, that empirical experience was the touchstone of modern life and of plausible modern philosophical explanation, T'ang's determination to avoid "sinking into the mistake of clinging to factual reality," along with his belief that moral belief must be anchored in the transparent rationality of the ultimate ground of existence, led him to climb up without reservations into the realm of metaphysics, even to the point of insisting on the congruence between the structure of the spiritual inner life and the three dimensions of physical space, not to mention his inclination to seek out the path of Taoist mysticism.

His thought thus abundantly illustrates how thoroughly an influential contemporary Chinese student of Western philosophy could dismiss out of hand the premises widely regarded in the West as the indispensable basis of an intelligent life — discourse #2. The issue that challenges Western agents of discourse #2, such as me, is:

how could an intelligent, erudite, intellectually honest person familiar with discourse #2 reject it?

A major reason is soteriological, the strength of the utterly traditional religious faith T'ang obtained from his parents and cultural environment in Szechwan. His unqualified discursive defense of this faith, however, is what illustrates its ability to persist as a way to make sense out of the Chinese confrontation with modernity. First of all, T'ang — somewhat like Leo Strauss — could question the tendency to make human agency subservient to scientific knowledge of the past instead of recognizing fully the ability of human agents to imagine and create new goals, impose them on the factual world, and cause it to change in accord with these goals. T'ang was opposing any definition of knowledge "sinking into the mistake of clinging to factual reality." His provocative point was that, if the idea of knowledge of what exists is reduced to such factual knowledge, then the power of the actual world, where "the sacred was defiled by being blurredly mixed in with the demonic" (*shen-mo hun-tsa*), would be unchallenged. If one focuses on pursuing the knowledge of facts violating ideals and gives facts a higher ontological status than ideals, a determined, socially unified effort to implement ideals cannot materialize, T'ang held. Action displacing known factual tendencies, action defying empirical reality, could be based only on knowledge, and knowledge could consist only of true ideas, those accurately corresponding with what "exists."

Looking for a way to depict universally binding goals, moreover, T'ang at least managed to refute the main argument that such depiction is impossible, relativism. By "relativism" I refer to the belief that, because all human ideas arise out of a particular person's or group's particular desires, history, cultural setting, language, or psychology, they lack meaning and so any truth content apart from the context of that one particular part of humanity, and therefore they cannot serve as truths universally overriding all contradictory ideas arising in the course of human history as a whole. This idea refutes itself, since, if it is true, it applies to all human ideas and so is universal in significance. Thus, as already discussed, T'ang held that, if the human mind cannot conceptualize human experience as a whole, it cannot know that all human ideas are merely relative to particular historical or evolutionary circumstances. He also held that any notion of historical change could apply only to empirically observed objects, and that such an object always implies a thinking subject that cannot be reduced to an observed object (such as the brain as a biological phenomenon) and so is not subject to biological or historical change. T'ang could also have adduced a point emphasized by his older contemporary Fung Yu-lan in his powerful *Hsin-li-hsueh* (A New Study of the Nature of Universal Principles). First published in Kunming in 1938, this great book appeared just as T'ang's own maturation as a philosopher occurred — at the very moment China was descending into the agony of the Japanese invasion. T'ang obviously rejected Fung's neglect of the question of the moral subject of experience and his treatment of ideals (*li*) as purely "formal" objects empty of any power to realize themselves concretely. Yet at least Fung emphasized that ideas denoting a universal set of infinitely numerous particular instances were an unavoidable part of linguistic communication, as illustrated by the universal idea of "boy" when I say "Jim is a boy."

Moreover, even apart from the role of universal categories in ordinary language, modern Western philosophies have proved unable to dispense with concepts of universal truth. David Hume made the famous point that knowledge about what has not been observed cannot be derived from knowledge about what has been observed. Yet he derived knowledge about how all human beings form the idea of a cause from nothing more than observation of his own mind. Thus he called his book *A Treatise of Human Nature*, not *A Treatise about Those Human Activities Observed by David Hume*. Similarly, many modern writers, such as F.A. Hayek, have had much to say about universal human nature, not to mention the vast, prestigious medical and psychological literature on this subject. Even if one still insists that there is no universal human nature as an observable entity, or that there are no universal norms applying to all persons no matter what their culture, empirically observed human discourse patterns, as I argue in chapter I, seem necessarily to include ideas denoting universal human nature and indisputable norms everyone should respect. Even more, good will toward others seems to be a norm basic to all human social life, not a norm peculiar to a particular culture. All public discourses seem to embrace the goal of pursuing the good of a group, as opposed to just the speaker's selfish desires. One can publicly argue that everyone should pursue only her selfish interests, not that no one should except me. Even Yang Chu, the ancient Chinese egotist, did not claim that others should respond to his egotism by serving him. When Yang Chu said he would not pluck one hair out of his head to help others, he was participating in a public discourse and arguing everyone should act this way. Hitler did not advocate racist genocide by arguing that its purpose was purely to enrich him. Like all persons participating in public discourse, he said that his ideas would benefit his group and even humanity as a whole.

If, then, unselfish devotion to the public good is a norm universally integral to all public discourse, one might say that the public good is a purely formal or very general concept susceptible to an indefinite historical variety of interpretations. This could not be a significant argument for T'ang's generation, however, since for it, just as for J.S. Mill's (and Hayek's), the basic inherited list of vices and virtues was utterly uncontroversial as a universal normative program, not to mention T'ang's affirmation of the highly spiritual, saintly ideas of Buddhism and Confucianism. The Western Freudian or libertarian revolt against traditional ascetic morality and self-abnegation was not a meaningful option for T'ang, who found abhorrent any notion of morality as a marketplace of alternative, equally valid lifestyles (see below), just as he regarded any kind of oppressive nationalism, mass violence, or deliberate corruption of public health as obviously abominable. In other words, T'ang's thought bluntly challenges the widespread but purely Western notion that there can be no substantive, specific, objective definition of the universal public good. Very simply, can anyone deny that pursuit of the public good requires action to prevent epidemics?

Convinced that the human mind has this access to ideas applying to all human life, T'ang never treated the term "subjective" (*chu-kuan*) as describing a mental condition — whether historically, culturally, linguistically, or psychologically shaped — threatening to block off this access. In his writing, "subjective" refers merely to ideas or feelings arising within the mind of a person, in contrast to what this person perceives as occurring outside herself.[68] The historicism that alarmed Leo Strauss was for T'ang a chimera hardly worth noticing.

To be sure, even if one grants that relativism is impossible because human thought in fact depends on rather specific, universally valid categories, one could still cautiously regard these categories as irremovable aspects of language or discourse, instead of asserting that they denote an existing cosmic structure generating not only a "feeling of moral concern" in me but also the laws of the physical universe. What was the "train of thought" (*ssu-lu*) convincing T'ang that he could climb up into the realm of metaphysics?

I would sum it up thus: T'ang regarded as definitive Kant's thesis that sensory experience implies a context of unchanging ideas like time and space which are needed to put disparate sense data into relation with each other; which thus serve as a "unifying" framework of experience; which are "presupposed" by any awareness of sense data rather than thought up by particular persons independently reflecting on the nature of sense data; and which thus are somehow provided by the very nature of human consciousness rather than through the intellectual achievements of individuals. Therefore, for T'ang, as for Fichte and Hegel, sensory experience implied the idea of a conscious self as a kind of *general* subject of experience, "the mind as subject" (*hsin-ling chu-t'i*), not only as a specific, flesh-and-blood individual. The individual in his or her mind could become aware of that general subject of experience which made possible his or her individual awareness and experiences.

This line of thought indeed coincided with the idea T'ang had embraced as a teenager, that the subject aware of a perceived object could not itself be described as a perceived object, i.e. a specific individual like me existing in time and space. Moreover, as already noted, T'ang lacked Kant's scruples about the possibility of reifying this general subject of experience. One could discursively prove, Kant held, that sensory experience implied a priori categories but not that these categories were provided by a general self which "existed" just as did an empirically observed object. T'ang, however, as already noted, always believed that anything that was so-and-so, any *hsiang* (appearance), to use the Buddhist term, must have an ontological address, an "existing" "source" or "ultimate reality" (*t'i*) from which it stemmed. For T'ang, therefore, this general self had to "exist," just as Fichte and Hegel had suggested. Moreover, because it existed, one could describe it directly, not just cautiously discuss those aspects of it implied by sensory experience. The rejection of this Kantian caution is precisely one of the hallmarks of epistemological optimism as I have tried to define it.

Regarding the features of this universal, cosmic self, T'ang concluded: (1) discovered when human beings analyzed human consciousness as the context of experience, it had to be a form of "mind" or consciousness similar to human consciousness; (2) being basic to all the specific aspects of experience and consciousness, it must itself be more general than any of these specific aspects of experience, i.e. it must be a pure consciousness empty of all specific perceptions or appearances; (3) thus "transcending" all specifics, it obviously coincided with that unlimited reflexivity of the mind on which T'ang since his youth had put so much emphasis; (4) revealed through discursive reasoning, just as are the scientific laws of the cosmos, it must itself be a form of rationality and must be the ultimate source ("Logos") of the rationally knowable structure of the cosmos, including time and three-dimensional space; (5) it could not be a coincidence that the "realms" or "worlds" (*ching-chieh*) encountered by the human mind seemed similarly to be based on the distinctions between "inner" and "outer," "higher" and "lower," and "earlier" and "later" (see below) — clearly, the structure of the mind and of the physical cosmos studied by science both bore the stamp of the same ultimate reality, a general self based on reason in its most general sense; (6) even more, the "feeling" (*ch'ing*) an individual can experience merging himself or herself with all of humanity and the cosmos must emanate from that very same general self; and (7) inherently unselfish (given the very nature of unspecific existence), this feeling emerging in the context of specific material entities necessarily appeared as a sense of self-abnegation and "moral concern," i.e. concern about the well-being of all those other than the self.

The most distinctive point about this train of thought, however, has yet to be mentioned. After all, from a religious point of view T'ang's ideas were hardly remarkable. They merely pointed to a divine being serving simultaneously as a model of morality and the creator of the physical universe, hardly a novel thought for any Christian or Jew. Indeed T'ang repeatedly recognized that his views to a large extent coincided with "religious" ones. What set him apart from discourse #2 was his refusal to make any fundamental distinction between "reason" (*li-hsing*) and "faith" (*hsin-yang*), his insistence on using discursive reason to prove the "existence" of that whole cosmic structure in which he had "faith." Not for him was Wang Kuo-wei's (1877–1927) belief in an unbridgeable gap between "the ideas that are true" and "the ideas that can be loved."

Nor was T'ang's allegedly "rational" argument about the nature of the cosmos *necessarily* irrational. Possibly one can imagine a chaotic universe consisting of nothing but unpredictable accidents. In point of fact, however, the universe appears as a structure made up of immensely complex physical and biological forms following logically decipherable principles. There is something wonderfully intriguing about the now fashionable idea that this appearance of structure is just a product of the way human beings think and so does not depend on the existence of cosmic structure independent of human thought. Rejecting this bold suggestion, however, is not necessarily irrational. Similarly, the idea that cosmic structure grew out of nothing but an accidental event is not obviously a brilliant insight that necessarily commands affirmation. No one has ever observed a structure arising out of an accident, such as a goblet formed without the intervention of an artisan out of the splinters created by the accidental shattering of a piece of glass. All in all, then, just as some empiricists today regard the idea of a cosmic "Logos" as preposterous, so T'ang could not take seriously the idea of a structure arising out of nothing but accident and chaos without the intervention of a guiding spirit. Indeed, since observation can verify neither idea, both are equally metaphysical. Having accepted this "metaphysical" idea of a "Logos," T'ang logically regarded existence as an issue that could be explored metaphysically, not only empirically, and he thus proceeded down a philosophical path largely rejected today in the Western academic world.

c. T'ang's Last Four Decades: Consolidating and Propagating His Philosophy

Having put together this metaphysical ontology by 1937, T'ang escaped the horrors of the Japanese invasion by moving in 1937 from Nanking to Ch'eng-tu, where he taught at Hua-hsi University. In 1940 he became assistant professor at Nanking Central University, which had moved to Chungking, the wartime capital of the Republic of China's Kuomintang government. In 1944 he was promoted there to professor.

It is significant that he stayed in Kuomintang-dominated Chungking instead of joining the faculty of the Consolidated University in Kunming, the intellectual center of wartime China.

Presumably, this reflected the tension between his metaphysical approach and the more positivistic trends influential in Kunming. Yet these years were extremely fruitful ones for him. He met Mou Tsung-san, whose thought about logic reinforced his own metaphysical bent, and he saw much of his old teachers Hsiung Shih-li, Ou-yang Ching-wu, and Liang Shu-ming.[69] The New Confucian movement was crystallizing, and the number of his publications was impressive. In the period 1937–1945, he published four books and laid the foundation for one of his masterpieces, *Chung-kuo wen-hua-chih ching-shen chia-chih* (The Value of the Spirit of Chinese Culture), which was finished in Hong Kong in 1951. He also published some twenty articles.[70]

In 1946, after the defeat of Japan, he went back to Nanking, continuing on in the faculty of Nanking Central University. In 1946–1949, while the civil war was raging, he published nine articles. In 1949, he accepted a teaching post in Canton and then fled to Hong Kong as the Communists took over the mainland. The next year, with the great Ch'ien Mu and others, he founded New Asia College, which became a part of The Chinese University of Hong Kong when the latter was established in 1963.

Thus began T'ang's long institutional struggle to use an educational base to propagate a proper understanding of Chinese humanism as the key way to resolve "the political crisis faced today by the world." As he put it in 1951 and 1952, T'ang hoped "to complement other new forms of learning in the world" and so to create "a truly new China, a truly new Asia, a truly new world."

With a spirit of defiance hardly unlike Mao's in Yenan, T'ang viewed himself and his colleagues as carrying out a kind of David-Goliath struggle. They saw themselves representing the true moral logic of a world currently dominated by the "hated" Communists ruling China, by the "utilitarian" spirit of the West, which also was prevalent in their place of exile, and by a Kuomintang regime in Taiwan only remotely reflecting their ideals. In 1949–1966, T'ang published some forty-seven articles in *Min-chu p'ing-lun* (Critical Discussions from the Standpoint of Democracy), a Hong Kong journal serving as one of the major Chinese liberal voices at odds with the Taipei regime. Hostility to the New Confucians' metaphysical approach was also apparent in the intellectual center of Taiwan, the Academia Sinica in Nankang, which had largely allied itself with the kind of Anglo-American empiricism and May Fourth iconoclasm represented by Hu Shih. Even as late as the 1960s and 1970s, moreover, most Western China scholars had either not heard of the New Confucians or regarded them as deluded followers of an obsolete tradition. In 1976, Harvard University Press published *The Limits of Change*, an essay collection that included a few articles on the New Confucians but located them in that penumbra of "conservative alternatives" accompanying China's "unfolding revolution," to use the Fairbankian term.

Facing overwhelming odds, however, is precisely the situation defined by the Confucian tradition as the normal fate of the person pursuing the *tao*, who "does it even while thinking he knows it cannot be done" (*chih ch'i pu k'o erh wei chih*). T'ang admitted to moments when his "life and spirit tended to fall apart," but his basic faith persisted. Again, he was enormously productive. During the period 1949–1977, he published fifteen books. A number of these were multi-volume studies, including his superb historical studies *Chung-kuo che-hsueh yuan-lun* (Essays on the Foundations of Chinese Philosophy; 1966, 1968, 1973, 1975), and his brilliant survey and critique of philosophies around the world, *Che-hsueh kai-lun* (An Outline of Philosophy; 1961). Many of these books were republished more than once. He also published some 250 articles and shorter pieces. In 1958 came the New Confucians' famous manifesto, "Respectfully Addressing the Scholars of the World on behalf of Chinese Culture," signed by T'ang, Mou Tsung-san, Hsu Fu-kuan, and Carsun Chang. In his famous 1966 book bringing Western modernization theory into Chinese discussions of Chinese cultural change, the sociologist Chin Yao-chi (Ambrose Y.C. King) incorporated some of the New Confucians' perspective on the value of the Confucian tradition.[71] By the late 1970s, the New Confucians' had won some respect in Western academic circles due to the efforts of a few prominent scholars like Wm. Theodore de Bary and Tu Wei-ming. The New Confucians' philosophical goals remained suspect, but the creative and erudite way they had analyzed the history of Chinese thought impressed Western scholars. T'ang was invited to a number of international conferences. A major volume of essays put out in 1975 by Columbia University Press, *The Unfolding of New-Confucianism*, was dedicated to him.

Moreover, the increasingly successful modernization of Taiwan as a society encouraging the perpetuation of traditional ways affected attitudes around the world toward Confucianism. The old claim that Confucianism was incompatible with modernization apparently had been refuted by history. Many came to see the New Confucians as prescient. From the 1980s on, a good deal of the Chinese Marxist and liberal literature softened its criticism of the traditional culture, as illustrated by the thought of Li Tse-hou and Yang Kuo-shu. A wide variety of Chinese books came to regard the modern affirmation of Confucian values as an easily defensible position, as illustrated by the essay in this volume on the thought of the Hong Kong economist Hu Kuo-heng (H.K.H. Woo).

None of these developments, however, gave T'ang relief from the feeling that he was living in a largely "demonic" world. He remained utterly unimpressed by the Western idea of piecemeal material and organizational progress in a partially immoral world. Rising living standards for the masses in Hong Kong and Taiwan impressed him as little as had the same phenomenon in the case of the West. Just as the transformation of Chu Hsi's thought after 1200 into a revered orthodoxy failed to put a dent in the predicament Chu Hsi had addressed, so the increasing influence of the New Confucians in the contemporary Chinese world, however striking, failed to mitigate the global predicament as they perceived it. As early as 1958, five years before New Asia College became part of The Chinese University of Hong Kong (CUHK), T'ang worried that its students were becoming crassly career-oriented rather than dedicated to "the revival of Chinese culture." By 1968, five years after the founding of CUHK, T'ang worried that it was merely becoming a copy of the University of Hong Kong, emphasizing specialized training instead of the humanistic vision he regarded as crucial for China and the world. An essay in 1972 deplored the "cosmopolitanism" and "Hong Kong-ism" he saw threatening CUHK. The seriousness of the crisis he perceived is clear when one remembers that, in his thought, the university was the prime institutional agency of political improvement, just as the party was in Mao's thought, and that, for him as for Mao, institutional efficacy depended on the successful transmission of correct doctrine. In a 1973 newspaper interview, he lamented "the general corruption of society today": "the widespread greed, lust, opportunism, and desire to get ahead by depending on luck rather than real effort — all these are quite sufficient to destroy real human relations and moral feeling."

In 1976, he was operated on for lung cancer. He died on February 2, 1978, at the age of sixty-nine. Since then, many scholars, mostly Chinese, have remained even more eager to express their respect for him as a thinker and a person, as illustrated by the volume of commemorative essays put out a year after his death and the four-volume collection of essays on his thought put out in 1991.[72] In 2003, the Center for Chinese Studies at the University of Michigan, Ann Arbor, initiated a lecture series named after him.

3. From Ontology to Epistemology: T'ang's Philosophical Development from 1938 to 1978

a. Redefining the Epistemological Problem

As just discussed, T'ang by the age of twenty-eight had pondered the nature of existence and arrived at an understanding of it the correctness of which he never doubted during his remaining four decades. As he said, having thought through his errors, he never made them again (see above). (One is reminded of K'ang Yu-wei's statement that, after the age of thirty, he never again had to revise any of his basic ideas.) But this feeling of pride, power, and elation quickly raised a major question for him: "If this truth about the cosmos and human life is universal and eternal, something everyone can see, how could it have been unknown until I came along? This made no sense."

T'ang quickly drew the logical conclusion: inherently manifest throughout the cosmos, this truth had been widely known by others who had understood it just as deeply as he had. In particular "everyone" must have experienced the elation that comes with realizing that, in terms of the inherent structure of reflexivity, "one's thought transcends all that has been known and thought throughout history." In other words, the sense of uniquely transcending all objectifiable experience was both valid and easily misunderstood, since it was integral to the existence of all sentient beings but appeared as the unique property of the individual thinking subject. As T'ang walked one day in Nanking alongside Hsuan-wu Lake (presumably in 1936), he further reasoned that, since full awareness of the nature of the cosmos was the highest form of spiritual life, that is, the achievement of sagehood or Buddhahood, everyone must be able to become a sage, a Buddha; and that, if this truth simultaneously is a cosmic truth, it must be a truth on which not only human beings but also all other living beings rely to exist. Therefore, if human beings are able to see this truth, why should other sentient beings be unable to become aware of this truth?... I concluded that the failure of human and other sentient beings to become aware of this truth and become sages and Buddhas must be due to obstacles that could all be removed. In the end, all sentient beings could become sages and Buddhas.

This insight into the public ordinariness or universal nature of even the most privately grasped truths defined T'ang's intellectual challenges during his last four decades in two ways. First, it gave him a systematic methodology for the study of intellectual history as well as current philosophical discussion:

I then changed my intellectual direction, thinking that what I had regarded as truths newly discovered by me must have been long ago discovered by others, or even discussed by them, or at least implied by them. Thus I should focus on looking for the points of convergence between what I knew and thought and what philosophers of the past and present had said. Once I grasped this, I repeatedly discovered that what I had regarded as a newly discovered idea had in fact been discovered earlier by others.... Thereafter in reading books and having discussions with others, I mostly sought to find out what was correct about the views I encountered — an approach different indeed from my focus in the past in finding out what was wrong about them.[73]

This viewpoint not only arose out of his reflections in his twenties but also harked back to his essay written when he was fifteen about how the seemingly disparate views of Mencius and Hsun-tzu actually coincided. Still more basically, it was rooted in the traditional quest for "linkage," including pursuit of the common Chinese ideal, embraced by T'ang, of a harmonious world without basic disagreement. A proper analysis of the history of ideas would show how, "in all cases, ideas that seem to be different and contradict each other can coincide and form a single truth without conflicting with each other (*hui erh t'ung chih*)."[74]

Second, carrying epistemological optimism to an extreme point, T'ang concluded that, given the basis of human thought in the rationality of the cosmos itself, the ideas arising in human minds must usually be true or rational. This extreme version of epistemological optimism can be best grasped by going back to T'ang's flirtation in his college years with logical positivism, when he rejected ideas about "a transcendent ultimate reality" in favor of those "limited to experience," that is, those based on "the laws of identity" (logic) and "sensory observations." Instead of adhering to this epistemologically pessimistic view that ideas of the former kind cannot be true because — as Popper would put it — they cannot be falsified by sensory observations or logical reasoning, T'ang optimistically decided they would be untrue only if they contradicted logic or sensory observation.

For instance, in his eyes, the partly Hegelian ontological position he ended up with in his twenties did not contradict logic or sensory observation. Therefore it had to be valid, even though it metaphysically referred to "a transcendent ultimate reality" and so could not be falsified by logical reasoning or sensory experience. In other words, in a completely confident way, T'ang utterly rejected the epistemological heart of discourse #2, the central modern Western idea, going back not just to Hume and Locke but to Francis Bacon and Galileo, that the most reliable ideas, the ones most worthy of being regarded as knowledge, were those verified by logically ordered sense observations. To restrict the idea of knowledge to those ideas, T'ang believed, was a disastrous mistake, because, by thus "clinging to factual reality," one undermined the transformative potential of praxis and agency. In T'ang's eyes, no kind of knowledge was more important than the kind based not on sense observations but on "reason" and its inseparable companion, "feeling stemming from a cosmic source transcending sensory experience" (*ch'ao-yueh-te kan-ch'ing*) — the experience, so to speak, of being a morally-aware subject of experience. Only this kind of knowledge could enable people to realize the potential of praxis.

As already mentioned, the New Confucians had appropriated the Neo-Confucian premise that concrete human "feeling" (*ch'ing*) includes not only ephemeral or culturally fashionable emotions felt by one person or group but also morally significant sensation emanating from the ultimate nature of the cosmos as a whole — T'ang usually called it *ts'e-ta-chih ch'ing* (the anxious sense of moral concern). Understanding of this point, T'ang repeatedly asserted, was the all-important, unique contribution that Chinese philosophy had made to the world:

This anxious sense of moral concern is what Confucian scholars regarded as the point where feelings link up with the ultimate nature of humanity. Their teaching about the link between heaven and humanity refers to this. Western rationalism and idealism cannot match this insight. What Western rationalism and idealism view as reason does not allow one to think in a way which directly follows along with this anxious sense of moral concern, which makes the continuity between reason and feeling the ultimate conclusion reached by one's thought, and which thus fills one with that strong moral feeling of confidence needed to accomplish great things.

While the modern celebration of "reason" led many in the West strictly to restrict the idea of knowledge to ideas based on logically ordered sense impressions, T'ang confidently restricted it to "what is demanded by rational thought and by the feelings stemming from universal human nature."[75]

Drawing on this two-fold primordial source of knowledge, T'ang outlined the huge scope of true ideas:

… I held that, relying on a feeling in me stemming from a cosmic source transcending sensory experience, I could arrive at a variety of full insights with this transcendent basis. Among these was that all statements in the world expressing philosophically different principles can be established as valid when put into a certain context, except for words put together in a meaningless way, words contradicting each other, and words about experienced facts obviously out of accord with these facts.

In thus referring to a way of grasping the value of almost any proposition by understanding its context, T'ang turned to the Buddhist tradition he had imbibed from his father and mother, referring to the Buddhist notion that contradictory teachings are necessary gradually to reveal a single truth. This was the Buddhist idea of *p'an-chiao*, which, going back at least to the T'ien-t'ai (sixth century) and Hua-yen (seventh century) schools, sought to resolve contradictions between all the various Hinayana and Mahayana sutras by holding that all the sutras had emerged from different lectures given by the Buddha under different circumstances as he adjusted his one actually consistent teaching to the varying intellectual capacities of his different audiences.[76] As T'ang put it, applying this Buddhist principle to the wealth of philosophies east and west:

If one takes into account differences in the levels or categories to which ideas belong, follows a clear sequence in addressing the questions of students, and shows how a view addressed a particular set of circumstances, one can benefit from any philosophy. Even more, one can see how every philosophy is of the highest excellence. Understanding this, I could appreciate the Buddhist teaching regarding the way the Buddha's wisdom was divided into different views set forth at different times to accommodate different kinds of audiences (*p'an-chiao*), the idea that every sutra is of the highest excellence, that words which seem to be different and to contradict each other really coincide to form one truth and do not conflict with each other.[77]

T'ang then proceeded to illustrate this point by publishing a number of major studies analyzing philosophies east and west.[78]

Viewing rationality as cosmically ubiquitous also led T'ang to another problem. If all existence stemmed from an ultimate cosmic rationality that was ubiquitously manifest, why was nearly all of humankind under the sway of either grossly false doctrines, such as the Mainland's Maoism, or less "hateful" but still "demonic" trends such as that scientism, fixation on specialized technical education, and crass careerism which T'ang perceived after 1949 as dominating education in Hong Kong? Perhaps still more troubling for T'ang was the seeming impossibility for people, however astute and sincere, fully to understand each other and agree on the truth — the ultimately insoluble problem Chinese philosophy had always promised to solve, that of *ko-ho* (the state of being separated from others because of misunderstanding and lack of empathy). T'ang sorrowfully recalled his wartime days in Szechwan, where he had frequently discussed philosophical problems with Hsiung Shih-li and Ou-yang Ching-wu. They were thinkers conversant with the same heritage of Buddhism and Neo-Confucianism, and T'ang regarded them both as brilliant and sincere, but they were unable to see how their views coincided:

> To the end, they remained unable to understand each other and find agreement, leaving one with the feeling that each would continue on his solitary way even after death. From this time on, I came to understand that tragedy is part and parcel of the quest for wisdom, that there is no escape from this tragedy for any philosopher, east and west. However genuine might be the insight he finds in the deepest recesses of his own soul [putting it into words to convey it to another person cannot but lead

to misunderstanding]. This dilemma greatly troubled me. I could not find a way out of it.[79]

Given T'ang's belief that he could and should grasp the "reason" for everything, how could he explain this central feature of the cosmos: the seeming contradiction between the existence of misunderstanding and the ubiquitously manifest rationality of the cosmos? How could ubiquitous rationality coexist with irrationality? To be sure, this problem would not have arisen for him had he, like Hayek, adopted a naturalistic view that the quest for truth is carried out by a biological brain that is fallible and influenced by "instincts" as well as "reason." It was T'ang's metaphysical insistence on turning "rationality" into a ubiquitously manifest cosmic property that created this mysterious contradiction for him. As already indicated, he took this metaphysical path not only because he could not accept the idea of accident as the origin of cosmic structure but also because he could not accept naturalism as a way of "passively" "clinging to factual reality" and accepting evil as normal.

T'ang tried to resolve this contradiction. On the one hand, he recognized the obvious breach between the way things concretely exist and existence as the property of ideals (*chen-shih ts'un-tsai*). For T'ang, there of course was an obvious breach between ideals and concretely existing facts, such as persons "foolishly clinging to doctrine and illusion" (*wang-chih*): "This feeling of an opposition between what ought to be and what actually is is a feeling from which people can never escape. If they could, there would be no ideals at all, the affairs of human life would cease, and the cosmos would be destroyed."

On the other hand, he held, it was important to understand that existence itself was a seamless continuum made up of ideals as well as concrete facts. T'ang made two points in this regard. First, he emphasized what was for him an amazing property of ideals: the fact that they were inherently susceptible to being turned into existing facts. Going back to the Confucian preoccupation with the transla- tion of "knowledge" into "action," the wonder of this metamorphosis was always at the center of T'ang's philosophical fascination with praxis. If ideals could be turned by action (*kung-fu*) into existing facts, they must be somehow "connected" (*lien*) to the processes of "existence." Second, T'ang believed ideals implied the goal of their *total* realization. For instance, the idea of a world free of racism would necessarily be at odds with the reality of a society free of racism only to a large extent. Therefore, he inferred from this "connection" to "existence" the idea of the world as a "truly existing reality" (*chen-shih ts'un-tsai*) totally free of any evil. This explicitly "metaphysical" view, he held, must be "alternated" and so "united" with the complementary metaphysical view that this "truly existing reality of ideals" "regulates the actual world" but is distinct from it.[80]

Given T'ang's unabashedly metaphysical approach, it is not surprising that he devised this metaphysical answer to the problem of how a cosmically ubiquitous rationality could coexist with human misunderstanding. From the standpoint of his confrontation with Western thought, however, it is important that his concern with this problem led to a challenging version of epistemological optimism. As illustrated by many examples in this book, epistemological optimism has often consisted just of naive assertions that the human mind can fully understand all the major aspects of human life. T'ang, however, was concerned with the problem of the obstacles to understanding. Thus epistemological optimism in his philosophy led to a distinctively optimistic and plausible way of weighing epistemic obstacles against the sources of knowledge.

In other words, is there any leeway in weighing the extent to which epistemic obstacles are superable and to which reason, feeling, and intuition should be distrusted? Should epistemic resources or epistemic obstacles be viewed as primary? That is, should reasoning be seen as trapped within the "subjective" limitations of the intellect or should the analysis of fallibility be viewed as knowledge produced by reason? Does fallibility have limits or is it an insurmountable condition casting doubt on any proposition? Should the propensity of human beings to disagree be regarded as primary or their remarkable propensity to affirm the same ideas? Are all truths relative, that is, applicable only to a part of the human experience? Suffering from fallibility, is the human mind like a normal person trying to find her way in a strange city on a dark night or like a blind person forced to cross an impassable mine field? T'ang tried to develop the former view.

b. The Relation between Fallibility and the Resources of Reason

The pessimistic epistemology basic to discourse #2 both emphasizes epistemic obstacles and minimizes epistemic resources. It reduces the status of useful ideas about reality from that of certain truths to that of mere "conjectures" that can be falsified and "beliefs" that can be neither falsified nor verified. For Popper, "induction" cannot even prove that I shall die one day. I could be immortal. There is no verified law of nature according to which I shall die. I can only "conjecture" that people are all mortal and then rely on that "conjecture" so long as it has not been "falsified."[81] In T'ang's view, however, obstacles impeding the grasp of universal truths can be fully appreciated without seeing them as insuperable. Conversely, superable obstacles have to be considered from the standpoint of a less suspicious view of reason and feeling as the sources of knowledge.

To put it still otherwise, T'ang in effect raised the question of how to characterize what chapter I described as a certain kind of idea seemingly used by all people, namely, premises regarded as indisputable by all those carrying on a shared discourse. Given the seeming fact that it is impossible to banish these "indisputables" from one's discourse by calling on the idea that all truth is relative, how should one characterize them? T'ang was not satisfied to view indisputable premises in any of the modern Western ways. To be sure, he did not quibble with the basing of science on respect for logic, mathematics, and empirical observation, whether or not he was satisfied with any of the explanations for the sources of this respect. But what about indisputable premises of a normative sort? T'ang did not accept the identification of them by a John Milton with absolute Biblical truth; the various rationalistic or scientistic efforts to deduce them from empirical conditions (such as historical or psychological ones, or the aspects of communication analyzed by Habermas); the various appeals to sheer "faith" independent of discursive reasoning; John Stuart Mill's decision simply to accept a contradiction between the "uncontested ... truths" of European civilization and human "fallibility" as the cause for the ultimate unreliability of all discursive reasoning;[82] the view of indisputable normative premises taken by Karl Popper, who treated the Socratic and Christian ideals as simply obvious to any decent person; John Dunn's similarly peremptory way of dismissing ethical relativism as obviously absurd; Gadamer's reduction of indisputables to mere "prejudices"; or my similar reduction of them to language, i.e. the irremovable features of any empirically known discourse.

These alternatives can be considered in the context of Hayek's view of universal human nature as a threefold mix of "instinct," "reason," and the ability to create a great variety of languages and cultures (one might add, as a fourth feature, the tendency toward individual idiosyncrasy). Given this apparently universal mix, and given a widespread human inclination, east and west, to certify and advertise ideas by declaring that they are based on "reason," people can in an epistemologically optimistic way celebrate the ideas they regard as indisputable by claiming they are revealed by "reason," or, in an epistemologically pessimistic way, denigrate them by viewing them as merely spawned by instinct, culture, or individual idiosyncrasy. Denigrating them, viewing them as somewhat tentative, can be seen as the intellectual basis for loosening the parameters of freedom; celebrating them, for tightening these parameters. In effect, T'ang sought to identify the indisputables with "reason" in order to restore the "rationality" of praxis, agency, and *paideia* and thus firm up the parameters of freedom. To put it more generally, given the widespread human tendency to stratify the components of the mind, T'ang celebrated the indisputables as based on the mind's most elite component, calling it "reason." He believed, however, that by drawing on the Confucian tradition, he could offer a truer concept of reason than any other.

To be sure, trying to raise the epistemic status of the indisputables from that of beliefs peculiar to a particular individual or group to that of "rational" principles universally and objectively overriding all competitive ideas, T'ang was not necessarily successful. He faltered especially in conflating a possibly universal human tendency to see a "contrast between ideals and the actual world" with the saintly Confucian-Buddhist ideals he had been raised to think of as the only ideals worthy of the name, just as Christians today regard the Bible's ethical ideals as indisputable. Instead of saying only that these ideals of unqualified self-abnegation and compassion (*jen-i, ai, wu-ssu,* etc.) were indisputably absolute for a particular historical tradition or for his we-group, T'ang said they stemmed from *hsing-ch'ing* (the feelings emanating from the ultimate, universal nature of all human beings). He also asserted that seeing a "contrast between ideals and the actual world" was a matter of "reason," not a matter of making a value judgment.

Yet whether or not he succeeded in justifying these jumps in his argument, was T'ang able to show that, despite the obstacles impeding the grasp of universal truth, the highest, most prestigious mental faculty — reason — is able not only to produce science but also to grasp universally overriding normative principles that should be the basis of praxis and *paideia*? He thus inquired into reason's ability to understand: its own nature; existence as a mix of facts and ideals; the way to evaluate philosophies and cultures; praxis (agency); and the sources and limits of fallibility.

c. The Nature of Reason and the Objects of Consciousness

His argument depended on his conceptualization of reason. His views have already been outlined. He had in mind a blend of capabilities or intuitions that were interdependent. There is no way, I suspect, of listing them comprehensively, but the following were central: the ability to "think" (*ssu*) logically about all the "elements of existence" (T'ang liked the Buddhist term "the realm of dharmas" [*fa-chieh*]) and so to infer from them the "principles" (*i-li*) of existence; unbounded reflexivity; the intuition that understanding dharmas has to begin with *tang-hsia ch'eng-hsien* (what is immediately given in experience) and "the way people in their everyday discussions understand each other";[83] awareness that reason necessarily includes the positing of "ideals"; awareness that ideals are inseparable from "the anxious feeling of moral concern"; the ability to distinguish this moral feeling from other emotions; the ability to grasp that ideals inherently call for their own concrete, total realization; and awareness of the ability to reason (*pace* David Hume) as an inherently valuable fact. The very nature of reason, at least for T'ang, implies that *tzu-chueh* (full awareness of all the circumstances affecting one's life and thought) is inherently desirable, valuable, and good and so should be maximally pursued. Indeed this very premise was integral, paradoxically enough, to Hume's own brilliant effort to disentangle "is" from "ought."

In thinking about dharmas or *hsiang* (an overlapping, standard Buddhist term meaning "an object of consciousness" or "the specific or determinate appearance of something"), people became aware that these were various. "Appearances" included *shih-jan hsiang* (appearances of actual things), *tang-jan hsiang* (ideas appearing as principles one should act on), and *ch'un-hsiang* (appearances of things pure and abstract) or *ch'ao-yueh-hsiang* (appearances transcending material objects), such as numbers. All these "appearances" were found "within human life as it is directly given to us in our experience."[84]

T'ang also referred to *nei-tsai hsiang* (appearances of something within the mind of an individual), but whether "appearances" included "the mind as the ultimate subject of awareness" (*hsin-ling chu-t'i*), along with "reason" and its unbounded, "transcendent" reflexivity, is not clear to me. Presumably, the "transcendent" basis of the cosmos in T'ang's eyes "transcended" all determinate "appearances." Whether or not it did, however, he rejected any ultimate dualism, insisting that all existence formed a seamless continuum.

"Appearances of actual things" included the natural cosmos, the group, and the self. T'ang sometimes used the list *t'ien, ti, jen, chi* (the realm of the divine, the physical cosmos, other people, and the self).[85] The latter two made up *jen-lei* (humankind), in turn made up "societies" with "economies," "politics," "cultures," etc. These different social formations existed in historical time, thus endlessly creating new *shih-tai* (historical eras) and new *chi* (sets of contingencies or circumstances). As has been common in the modern Chinese intellectual world, T'ang assumed that the nature of these social units, their "processes" (*li-ch'eng*), and the "sets of contingencies" they formed were transparent to the human intellect. Chinese epistemological optimism invariably posits that the whole formed by specifically observed concrete particulars is not a heuristic concept but a systemic structure as real, objective, and knowable as the particulars. Whenever discussing a culture and its development, T'ang referred with confidence to one or a few features determining the nature of the whole, just as he confidently characterized the evolution of humanity as a whole, noting it increasingly manifested the rationality basic to the structure of the cosmos (see above).[86] Illustrating the nature of the "sets of circumstances" formed by history were the divergent cultural developments of China and the West, which T'ang summed up by following conventional Chinese humanistic views going back at least to Liang Shu-ming (see below). Historical causation for T'ang was largely "intellectualistic," to use Lin Yü-sheng's term: the historical development of a people was determined by the nature of the philosophies they chose to follow.

Freedom of choice between philosophies was for T'ang a supreme fact of history, though he did not explicitly conceptualize it or ask how it was compatible with the existence of "cultures."

In T'ang's eyes, reasoning about historical circumstances was demonstrably inseparable from "objective," "publicly shared," intersubjective "ideals" based on "feeling." To use an American example, one could not view racist behavior without either approving or disapproving it. "Appearances of actual things" could not be divorced from "appearances as ideas about what should be." As people observed the *chi* (sets of circumstances) presented by history, they necessarily perceived "a contrast between ideals and the actual world and then experienced a sense of moral concern stemming from their ultimate nature as human beings, making them like what is good, hate what is bad."[87] In other words, they perceived a contrast between the "sacred" and the "demonic" (*shen, mo*), and they also felt a need to realize the sacred by "addressing the circumstances" of their era (*tang-chi*). Thus ideals juxtaposed with historical circumstances turned into a moral mission, "that which this era has called on me to do" (*hu-chao, hu-huan, ming-ling*).[88]

These ideals or moral missions, T'ang held, necessarily had a public, objective nature. In opposing racism, for instance, I am not expressing a private opinion divorced from the beliefs of a community, and, in courageously standing up to oppressors, my moral character is not distinct from publicly respected models of behavior:

> ... these ideals indeed universally and actually exist outside of my subjective world and within the objective world of the mind and existing forms of life.... I know that my reason is not just a subjective reason, it is an objectively significant reason implying affirmation of the reasoning going on within the minds of other persons. My character is not just my character as I subjectively experience it. It is an objectively significant kind of human character implying affirmation of the moral character of others as they have experienced their own morality within their own minds. Thus one can see how the idea of human character inherently refers to both the self and the other, just as the idea of reason does. Just because of this double reference, the world of human character, reason, and ideals is an objective, actually existing world based on the confluence of the moral reasoning going on in the minds of different individuals.[89]

To be sure, as already indicated, T'ang here was conflating a

variety of ideas: the idea of logical thinking; the social, public nature
of language and discourse as symbolic media integrating ego and
alter; the apparently universal tendency for groups to perceive
history as a saga depicting a struggle between good and evil; and his
claim that only some sagas are "rational." That is, anti-racist goals
stem from the ultimate, universal nature of human beings, but the
fervently pursued racist goals of the Nazis, say, did not. In T'ang's
intellectual world, however, there was no need to fend off the
argument of a Ronald Dworkin that there is no rational way to grade
the expressed goals of human beings.

The view he was interested in refuting was the denial that "ideals"
"exist" and are inherently filled with a "dynamic power necessarily
tending toward their realization."

To be sure, one might say this point was crucial for him because
of therapeutic considerations. Praxis or agency as the "effort" (*kung-
fu*) needed to overcome evil depended, in T'ang's eyes, on removing
"doubts" (*i*) that evil could be overcome and so developing a "mind
filled with faith and confidence" (*hsin-hsin*).

T'ang, however, believed that these doubts could be removed
only by knowledge that ideals were not just objects of "contemplation" (*kuan-chao*) empty of the power to realize themselves.[90]
Especially because of his lack of interest in morally imperfect human
efforts to pursue partially successful reforms, he believed that people
could not resolutely act unless they had faith in the practical
possibility of the world's total moral transformation. A morally mixed
world blurring together good and evil (*shen-mo hun-tsa*) was not
acceptable for T'ang as a normal historical condition:

> I have above fully revealed the starting point and ultimate conclusion of
> this book. It is rooted in the feelings that stem from the ultimate nature
> of human beings as found in human life and directly given to us in our
> experience. Human nature is reason revealed in practice. As people
> rationally react to the various dimensions of experience, they necessarily
> have rational feelings of liking and disliking. With these feelings come
> ideals, as well as the belief that these ideals should and necessarily will
> be realized. Thus people come to have minds filled with this belief.
> When ideals are developed to the utmost, the world is saved. All people
> become sages and not one of them fails to achieve salvation as the Buddha
> did.[91]

d. The Rational Analysis of Existence

Once again, then, the key problem was ontological. Doubts about the practicability of morally transforming the world could not be removed by the explanation that psychologically effective action required removal of these doubts. They could be removed only by knowledge that evil could be overcome because ideals exist and inherently tend toward their full realization. Therefore praxis — effective moral action — required a further application of reason to clarify the extent to which the various dharmas or *hsiang* (appearances of something) existed. While the Clinton campaign in 1994 had the slogan "It's the economy, stupid!" T'ang's slogan, as always, was "It's the ontological problem, stupid!"

As already discussed, T'ang by the age of twenty-eight or so had with the help of German metaphysics solved this ontological problem to his own satisfaction. But he still had to propagate this solution, especially by overcoming the prevalent modern arguments taking *shih-jan hsiang* (things appearing as actual) more seriously than *ying-jan hsiang* (appearances as ideas about what should be), claiming that only the former "existed"; that the latter inherently were no more than objects of "contemplation"; and that deviation of the former from the latter — evil — was a normal aspect of existence. T'ang set out to refute this pessimistic way of conceptualizing existence, which was integral to discourse #2 and has been viewed by Chang Hao as indispensable for the successful functioning of democracy (*yu-an i-shih*). For T'ang, this "dark" concept of human existence precluded the optimization of praxis.

To refute it, T'ang set forth his famous scheme of the nine "worlds" (*ching-chieh*). As already indicated, he held that reason could display these as an ontological hierarchy "up" which people would necessarily climb when "thinking about existence by following its principles" (*shun-li erh ssu*), thus "corroborating their understanding of it by reflecting on the nature of their own moral lives."[92] In other words, the *i-li* (principles) that people would discover through reflection revealed an ontological order of hierarchically interrelated worlds (just as, one might recall, the popular religion revealed a supernatural bureaucratic hierarchy of spiritual beings).

Using reason to reveal this ontological hierarchy, T'ang began with some propositions that, he felt, were transparently self-evident, in contrast to those unacceptably unexplained assumptions on which, he claimed, Western philosophers like Kant and Whitehead had depended. First, he assumed that, as reason focused on those key *hsiang* (appearances) constituting "what is directly given in experience," it could somehow reduce them to three categories: "existence," "life," and "mind" (*ts'un-tsai, sheng-ming, hsin-ling*). These three were properties of "mine" or "ours" (*wu-jen*). Second, he took into account "that toward which [the mind] inclined," that is, all the *hsiang* "of which it became aware" (*kan*) or which it "observed" (*kuan*). Third, he noted that the mind's "observations" followed "three directions" (*fang-hsiang*): "horizontal observation," distinguishing between "inner" and "outer," "near" and "far," with a focus on "appearances as objects" relative to the subject of experience; "longitudinal observation," focusing on this subject and temporal sequence; and "vertical observation," which "transcended subject and object" and focused on "higher" and "lower," "deep" and "shallow."[93]

T'ang thus believed that the kinds of categories Kant had identified as the necessary, a priori context only of sensory observations were really the ontological dimensions of all existence. They were integral not only to *shih-jan-hsiang* (appearances of something actual), *nei-tsai-hsiang* (appearances of something within the mind of the self), and *ch'ao-yueh-hsiang* (appearances of something transcending sensory objects) but also to the ultimate nature of "rationality" as the "transcendent" basis of all "appearances." This view of T'ang's went back at least to 1947, when he used spatial dimensions to describe the "directions" of "spirit."[94] In using spatio-temporal terminology to analyze the universal structure of human life, T'ang saw himself as articulating an insight into the nature of the cosmic basis for congruence between the laws of nature and the human uses of reason, not just as metaphorically describing the human spirit by adducing space and time.

Even more, the very nature of the human moral struggle stemmed from the dimensional cosmic arrangement, that is, from the disruption of cosmic unity by two contrary, dimensional tendencies: the human affinity for the "lower" and the "outer," and the affinity of the "transcendent subject" for the "inner" and the "higher." This contradiction in dimensional tendencies as the ultimate cosmic cause for all the problems of human life is integral to T'ang's discussion, but he never took the unnerving step of explicitly conceptualizing it. Insisting that the cosmos inherently tends toward the full realization of its *jen-t'i* (ultimate essence as benevolence), he had no way of demonstrating that this ultimate essence somehow overrode the above dimensional contradiction. He wished to think of tragedy as superable rather than inexorable but did not assure his readers it really was superable in terms of any predictable historical future.

Yet this contradiction is obvious as one looks at how T'ang derived nine "realms" or "worlds" ("ontologically distinct sub-worlds," as Popper might have said) from these three dimensions. "Horizontal observation" distinguishing between "inner" and "outer" was the basis of the three lowest worlds: world 1, "appearances of things material" or "the world of diverse things and events"; world 2, "the world of changes of something from belonging under one category to belonging under another"; and world 3, "the world of cause and effect." Ways of thought preoccupied with these three worlds or kinds of ideas included natural and social science, naturalism, materialism, and empiricism.

"The middle three worlds" (4, 5, and 6) revolved around "longitudinal observation," the conscious subject of experience in Kant's sense and socially shared beliefs. World 4 was "the world of subjects of experience clasping each other in terms of socially shared consciousness." World 5 was "the contemplative world of purely abstract ideas." This was a world of *ch'un-hsiang* (symbols, appearances of things that are pure in that they are detachable from any specific material objects). It included linguistic, mathematical, and aesthetic symbols. World 6 was "the world of moral practice," a realm made up of ethical norms, such as filial piety.

The "last three worlds" (7, 8, and 9) "transcended subject and object." World 7 was "the world where all is under one divine being" (essentially, Judeo-Christian theology). World 8 was "the world where there is nothing existing to be attached to, neither self nor any other dharma" (the Buddhist vision). World 9 referred to the Neo-Confucian vision that has been called "linkage." In this world, one referred to the benevolence of the cosmos rather than just to freedom from selfish attachments. T'ang spoke of how "the flowing forth of heavenly virtue dissolves the distinction between subject and object, heaven and man, things and self." This was the "world of ultimate moral practice," "the world filled with the flow of heavenly virtue," also called "the world in which one fully realizes human nature by becoming one with the moral imperative implied by the cosmos itself, Heaven's mandate."[95]

In analyzing the relations among the highest worlds (7, 8, and 9), T'ang developed a distinction between Confucian and Western spirituality later used by Yü Ying-shih in a book on Chinese culture, the difference between viewing the divine as a dimension of the human and viewing it as external to the human.[96] For a good number of Chinese intellectuals, Western thought has been immature in viewing divine cosmic power as something higher than human life. For T'ang and others, only Chinese thought mastered the paradox of a divine cosmic power within "ordinary" human life (*jih-yung shih-chien*). Grasping this paradox was understanding world 9. This meant losing the sense of being powerless to overcome evil by understanding that the divine "power" (*li*) to "transform the world" (*hsuan-ch'ien chuan-k'un*) and so eliminate "the contrast between ought and is" lay in human existence itself. For T'ang, it was crucial to distinguish this Confucian understanding from "two types of religious thought" people naturally turned to to overcome their sense of powerlessness and despair. T'ang equated these two religious outlooks with worlds 7 and 8: belief in an omnipotent God who guaranteed the triumph of virtue (world 7) and the Buddhist belief that evil actually does not exist, since what appears as evil is just a result of "clinging to false doctrine and illusion" (*wang-chih*) (world 8).

For T'ang, these two "religious" insights could help one find the "faith" that evil can be overcome, but fully depending on them led to the fallacy of "yearning for what is too high and distant to be reached (*hsi-kao mu-yuan*) and so neglecting action taken in the directly present realm of affairs in order fully to realize human nature and life's moral mandate."

To avoid this fallacy, T'ang recognized, was "extremely difficult." It was difficult especially because T'ang rejected the modern humanistic idea of relying on purely human efforts in a simply concrete, empirical sense (David Riesman's "the nerve of failure"). To adopt it would merely have landed him in the middle of his favorite fallacy, "sinking down into the error of clinging to the purely factual." T'ang had entirely inherited the Neo-Confucian view that the right sort of human effort brings into play a supporting, omnipotent cosmic "force" (*tung-li*). Without "belief" (*hsin*) in the existence of this force, people could not find the "sense of absolute confidence" that evil could be overcome. And this belief, for T'ang, could not be formed just as a pure faith. It could arise only out of discursive reasoning, knowledge that this force "existed." Yet how could this knowledge be produced if one discarded — as T'ang did to a large extent discard — the Neo-Confucian premise of an organismic cosmos based on the forces of yin and yang and so somehow susceptible to being controlled through intense spiritual efforts within the individual's mind?

For T'ang, the answer lay in an elusive formula supported by his theory of the nine worlds. This depended on a Buddhist emphasis on the world as "objects of consciousness" (*hsiang*) instead of the Neo-Confucians' organismic, yin-yang cosmos of "heaven, earth, and man." T'ang's strategy was first to say that "the contrast between ought and is" was, after all, not an objective fact but a human perception. What he implied was that, since the badness in the world had, so to speak, been switched on by human consciousness, the latter could also switch it off. The way T'ang put it was to say that the universal "anxious sense of moral concern.... controlled this whole contrast" between ought and is, in the sense that this contrast presupposed this universal feeling. This moral sense, in turn, implied a "central pivot point" (*chung-shu*), that is, the prospect of a "turning around (*chuan-yun*) within my mind" as the latter, acting on its sense of moral concern, "caused that out of accord with the ideal to become unreal and that in accord with the ideal to turn from a state of seeming unreality into a state of reality." T'ang's point was that this change was not just a psychological or physical phenomenon. It "implied a heavenly pivot point able to transform the world by causing the heavenly imperative about how things should be to turn into the virtuous projects of the actual world." In other words, moral action was not a human invention but a cosmically given possibility implying unlimited efficacy. To realize this was to be so filled with faith in the power to overcome evil that any reference to evil would be irrelevant. Trying to distinguish his point from both modern humanism and traditional "religion," T'ang said it "builds on China's traditional thought, subsuming the two religious views under an expanded understanding of what is implied by the central meaning of the Chinese tradition."[97]

Thus T'ang's metaphysical theory of the nine worlds was topped off by a two-fold subtlety canceling the monopoly over existence that philosophies like empiricism had bestowed on world 1. First, as already mentioned, it was necessary to "alternate" between the belief in a seamless continuum of existence uniting ideals and mundane reality and the belief in a "contrast" between ideals and evil actualities. Second, reaching for the faith that ideals could be fully realized, one could use the religious worlds 7 and 8 to begin to conceptualize the power of ideals but could not be completely successful unless one grasped that elusive world 9 exclusively discovered by Chinese thinkers and giving the ordinary human self god-like power.

For T'ang, therefore, understanding the "existence" of ideals required a subtle understanding of the nature of the "highest" ideals (worlds 7, 8, and 9) and so of the nature of the moral project. Reason as the ubiquitously manifest structure of the cosmos revealed not only a cosmos caught in a predicament but also a strangely omnipotent human will. On the one hand, T'ang recognized the need to act in order to "link together" or "unify" (*kuan-t'ung*) "the world of ideals and that of actual events and things."[98] In other words, while the highest worlds fully existed as *hsing-shang chen-shih* (metaphysical realities), they were unable inherently to actualize themselves and really were "half actual, half empty of reality."[99] This was the irreducible cosmic shortcoming responsible for human suffering. T'ang would not admit it, but his own account revealed a certain cosmic perversity. At its very heart, the cosmos had a frustrating tendency to withdraw into the "inner" and move toward the "higher." Thus it depended for its full realization on the human mind. But the latter was a frail vessel. It naturally gravitated toward the "outer" and the "lower," habitually resisting the "heavenly" command to move "inward" and "higher." As in the case of Wang Yang-ming, this human inclination toward disaster was so powerful that it could be overcome only through metaphysical acrobatics which many people had proved themselves incapable of performing. This difficulty was only aggravated by the intellectual temptations of the modern world.

Using the categories of modern philosophy, therefore, "reason" revealed precisely the same predicament revealed in the writings of Neo-Confucian tradition, which also emphasized the complementary relation between the elusiveness of the cosmos's healing power and the fragility of the human mind needed to evoke this power. As I have long argued, Chinese thought contradicts the Western original sin doctrine only in positing the perfectibility of human beings, not in conceptualizing evil as stemming from an a priori condition of existence.[100]

On the other hand, for T'ang as well as the Neo-Confucians, this huge cosmic predicament could be overcome by the human mind. He entirely shared their paradoxical way of combining a sense of predicament with a sense of omnipotence. Reason provided the clues with which human beings could demonstrate the existence of the highest worlds, remove "doubts" to the effect that ideals were just objects of "contemplation" lacking the power to overcome evil, and so overcome the tendency of the highest worlds to withdraw into themselves instead of uniting with the lowest ones. What were these clues on the grasp of which world salvation depended?

Again take the American ideal of "overcoming racism." In T'ang's eyes, one cannot say that this ideal exists in human minds only as an object of "contemplation." This ideal, he would have pointed out, necessarily arises as people reason about racial relations. It appears in their minds as an "order" (*ming-ling*) to "act"; it implies that "knowing it is to act on it." It also implies a "feeling": "the feeling of liking what is good, hating what is bad," "the feeling of compassion" (*ts'e-yin-chih ch'ing*), "the anxious feeling of moral concern" (*ts'e-ta-chih ch'ing*), "a mind anxious to do what is right" (*fen-fei-chih hsin*).

This feeling that racism is bad, moreover, is not something that just starts and stops spasmodically. People experience it as something going on continuously and indefinitely. T'ang said moral feeling stems from an "inexhaustible source." In the way that ideals implied their own realization, therefore, they "extended outward [from their metaphysical essence] like the eaves of a house." Moreover, in that "source" which their "unceasingness" implied, T'ang saw that ultimate basis of the cosmos he had philosophically discovered with the help of Fichte and Hegel, *li-t'i* (reason in terms of its ultimate nature, the Logos), *jen-t'i* (the ultimate basis of benevolence), or *pen-hsin* (the mind in terms of its ultimate nature). Hence the imperative nature of ideals stemmed from the divine nature of the cosmos, "heaven."

This divine aspect, as already mentioned, was for T'ang a "central pivot point" impinging on human life and so making possible the transformation of reality, the wondrous metamorphosis through action of ideals into facts.

For T'ang, then, the change from a racist society into one without racism was a metamorphosis that, just like any natural event, could not occur unless the structure of the cosmos allowed for such an occurrence. To the extent that the cosmos thus came equipped with the heartening possibility of this metamorphosis, then, ideals included a "dynamic power" (*tung-li*) inclining them toward their own realization:

> People can by reflecting on their moral lives know that this metaphysical power uniting heaven and humanity, this actual entity, this moral mandate actually exists. Then, knowing it exists, we can rationally command ourselves to cause existing actions and thoughts out of accord with ideals to stop existing, and to cause so-far unrealized actions and thoughts according with ideals to come into full existence.[101]

For T'ang, moreover, this metamorphosis of ideals into actualities, once believed in, was a socially contagious, unstoppable process: "As this hope goes forth, it can transcend current actualities, which cannot impede it." A virtuous circle thus emerged. Actions based on faith produced "great enterprises, flourishing with virtue," and these enterprises and the faith leading to them then "corroborated each other."[102] For instance, examples of inter-racial harmony would corroborate the idea that this ideal can be realized. The power of commercial or political advertising, T'ang might have said, illustrates this kind of circular causation. Moral action typically comes in the form of social escalation, a spreading group enthusiasm, so to speak.

While thus regarding the realization of ideals as a process based on a cosmic impulse inherently more powerful than all the world's forces of evil, T'ang, as already noted, also viewed ideals as implying their *maximum* realization. This horizon of saintly perfection was necessarily implied by ideals: "According to the feelings that stem from the universal nature of humanity, one must hope that all persons will become sages, that all sentient beings will achieve salvation as the Buddha did; one cannot bear that one person will fail to become a sage, that one living being will fail to achieve salvation."[103] Finally, it should be noted again that T'ang's phenomenology of moral action defined "ideals" not as any fervently pursued goals but as certain particular ideals, those of the Confucian-Buddhist tradition. Racist Nazis or fervent followers of Mao also zealously pursued their goals, but T'ang held that "reason" could distinguish between their evil goals and "ideals."

Knowledge of ideals as an "existing" "dynamic power" could thus be built up by distinguishing universally moral "feeling" from false enthusiasms; reasoning out subtle distinctions between different ways of conceptualizing the divine and its relation to mundane reality; recognizing the role of the divine in the formation of moral feeling and action; and so grasping the existing structure of the interaction between a cosmos and a human will simultaneously veering toward and away from each other. In T'ang's eyes, moral action depended on understanding that ideals exist, and understanding they exist required obviously controversial metaphysical acrobatics. T'ang, then, did not offer an easy way to pursue morality and develop praxis. In his eyes, however, such an easy way was simply unavailable. He could have added that there also is no easy way to pursue science or art. In effect, he was saying that *paideia* depends on making students understand that the moral project is so difficult because it depends on human action evoking a divine impulse to transform mundane experience.

e. The Rational Evaluation of Historical Philosophies and Cultures

While reason thus illuminated the nature of the cosmos as nine equally existing worlds ever tending toward the full unification (*kuan-t'ung*) of ideals and actualities, it also served as a standard with which to identify mistaken ways of thinking, *wang-chih* (clinging to illusion and false doctrine). T'ang had to deal with these, even though, as already mentioned, he held that the idea of such intellectual dissonance must be balanced against knowledge that ideals and facts form a seamless continuum of existence. As already noted, T'ang offered as a comprehensive list of intellectual failings "words put together in a meaningless way, words contradicting each other, and words about but obviously out of accord with experienced facts."[104] An example of "meaningless" words would be some of the arguments about "why a totally good and rational God created a world including irrationality," or the similar Hua-yen and T'ien-t'ai arguments about "why living things with the Buddha nature in them could fall into misunderstanding." If people "reasoned about these problems following only one line of reasoning, they would necessarily end up in a state of circular reasoning, unable in the end to grasp the problem.... [and] playing with words in an overly metaphysical, specious way outside the pale of reasonable discussion (*hsi-lun*)."[105] T'ang felt that he had somewhat solved this problem of evil, and that, in so doing, he had "cut through some of the tangled-up difficulties (*ko-t'eng*) preventing understanding of these philosophical principles (*i-li*)."[106]

This list of three kinds of "tangles" or mistakes, however, does not clearly cover the most serious mistake: failing to grasp relations among the nine ontological worlds and instead collapsing all of reality into one or some of them. The contradictions among the world's philosophies had largely arisen as this generic mistake was made in different ways.

The main one was "sinking down into the error of clinging to the purely factual" (the lower five worlds), as illustrated by scientism, positivism, materialism, naturalism, utilitarianism, etc. T'ang saw this as passively accepting the actual world with all its badness. In this context, he summed up the tension between the rationality of the given world and the rationality of praxis:

> When people just use reason in an analytical way [failing to exploit its synthetic side], they can only passively accept the things of experience or nature, the language or knowledge that has already been produced. Confronting and analyzing them, they arrive at their understanding. Such is scientific knowledge, generally speaking. In this case, the things of experience and nature that people accept are there first and then are followed by the analyzing and understanding of them. Reason in this sense just accords with how the things of experience appear, it accords with already produced knowledge, it accords with the original meanings of words, applying to these [objects] the rational ability to understand. This kind of reason is of the yin or earth type, not of the yang or heaven type. Willingly occupying the lower position, this kind of reason "starts with what heaven has already produced and accepts it.".... [On the other hand,] synthetic reason ... unceasingly transcends what it receives. It gradually turns from the path of yin, of the earth, into that of yang, of heaven.... Because this reason ascends ever higher, it transcends the limits previously formed, the limits of the things known about. That is, it can

base itself on its original normative understanding of things, thus synthetically forming its ideals regarding these things and seeing that these ideals indeed are at a level higher than these known things.[107]

Escaping the pull "downward" to the lower worlds, however, was only one basic problem. The other was properly finding one's way through the highest worlds. People often stopped with world 7 or 8, failing to grasp the elusive subtleties of world 9, to which T'ang devoted so much discussion.

True, despite these mistakes, human history had evolved toward the full manifestation of the rationality of the cosmos. Because of them, however, the evolution had been rocky. Barely mentioning the West's imperialism in China, T'ang heaped criticism on Western religions as well as Western modernity. True, the West's "classical society and culture" had "turned upward and inward." Yet it had been unable to proceed beyond world 5, "the contemplative world of purely abstract ideas." Christianity, in turn, had failed to grasp worlds 8 and 9. More ominously, "the basic direction" of "the modern society and culture" was "outward and downward" and had been set mainly by "the transformation of Western culture." This disaster went back to the original shift during the Renaissance toward a more "outer," mundane definition of human betterment as based on material well-being and on freedom in the "outer" world of utility and concrete institutions. In a fairly knowledgeable way, T'ang outlined this shift since the Renaissance toward the celebration of the beauty of nature and the human body; the application of mathematics to physical events; occupational differentiation to increase efficiency; and the resulting "modern concept of freedom" and of "the independence of the individual" in freely choosing among different occupations.

This development "cannot be regarded as without some value for the spirit of humanity," T'ang said, since "in the beginning it emerged out of a widespread rational consciousness emphasizing respect for every individual and for every occupation and profession." The modern emphasis on bringing affluence out of the aristocratic mansions into the villages, however, did not impress T'ang. What was important for him was that this pursuit of material well-being, freedom, and instrumental rationality had created "a great crisis for the culture of humankind and the whole human world."

This was a crisis of contention and of estrangement from sacred values — in other words, the degeneration of society into an economic, intellectual, and political marketplace of free, contending human impulses uncontrolled by overarching moral, religious, and philosophical standards. A more direct way of rejecting the Hayek-Popper model of the free, prosperous society would be hard to imagine.

As T'ang saw it, individuals with purely "utilitarian" (*kung-li-hsing*) goals freely pursuing their professions became "closed off within their occupational affairs," their lives becoming increasingly "narrow." The result was a "deepening of the way all sorts of individuals and occupations were divided off from one another and faced one another as adversaries (*fen-li tui-chih*)." Specialization and factionalization even fragmented the fields of religion, ethics, and philosophy, and, "given the pervasiveness of modern individualism, almost every individual has his own religion, his own philosophy, his own view of ethics."

Thus depicting and rejecting the economic and intellectual marketplaces integral to Western modernity, T'ang also criticized the modern democratic processes dealing with "all these conflicts and contradictions created by the way society is split up into contending individuals and occupations." In this situation, he said, "those able to be political and social leaders are just persons who themselves lack any character, ideals, or independence and can deal with these conflicts and fissures by devising some temporary adjustments."[108] (So much for politics as "the art of the possible"!)

At the same time, the Renaissance shift toward the "lower" and the "outer" eventually led to societies not only filled with a spirit of aggressive contention but also alienated from the sacred: "The modern world can be truly called an age in which the sacred is defiled by being blurred in together with the demonic (*shen-mo hun-tsa*)."

T'ang had in mind all the ways in which "utilitarian" considerations took precedence over all others. As already noted, T'ang had grave doubts about that very preoccupation with material well-being around which modernization has proudly revolved. In modern societies, he held, the "political focus" of the characterless leaders

> is entirely on those matters in accord with the shared needs of the majority in a society or nation, those policies that can elicit the support of the

people. These needs are just about always the ones based on biological, instinctual appetites, those economic and military policies needed to protect the material existence of society. Thus political decisions are determined by economic and military needs, and the fate of all of humanity's scholarship and culture is necessarily controlled by economic and military needs. Scholarship and culture either become means to meet these needs or are treated as dispensable.

More generally still, given the "pervasiveness of the utilitarian consciousness, the religious, ethical, and philosophical work and occupation of every individual tend to become a way to satisfy that person's quest for profits and fame.... in a modern society, the value of all sacred things can be turned upside down, just as though being made use of for the purposes of demons."

"This pervasiveness of utilitarianism in all human hearts," moreover, led to not only such evil manipulation of sacred values but also a widespread "skepticism, anxiety, indifference, and fearfulness" with regard to "sacred matters." This situation, T'ang said, had not been fully understood by Hegel and Marx. True, they had understood how sacred values are typically misused just to rationalize class interests or personal ambition. Yet the "full depth of this decline," T'ang said, had been grasped only by "the psychology of the unconsciousness, Kierkegaard, Nietzsche, and existentialist philosophy."[109]

What T'ang saw in such modern Western critiques of Western modernity, therefore, was not an effort to arrive at a more authentic understanding of human life, or to slough off dogmatic philosophies based on a naive view of God or reason, or to reveal the epistemic obstacles limiting reason and impeding access to any knowledge of universal moral principles or laws of history. What he praised was an objective description of a civilizational decline caused by an entirely avoidable failure to grasp entirely accessible, universal truths about the nature of reason and history. As always, he actively appropriated Western critiques to pursue his own conceptualization of knowledge and the world rather than just trying to describe Western intellectual history accurately.

Reason also revealed the modern plight of Chinese culture. Originally, China had avoided the disaster of the Renaissance and modernization. After all, only Confucian learning had grasped world 9. Moreover,

One may say that, of all the world's societies, it was China through the Ming period [1368–1644] that came closest to the standard of a society based on humanistic ideals. The position of merchants all along was below that of scholars, farmers, and artisans, and, although the rulers typically tried to use scholarship and culture for their own selfish purposes, they still could not but respect them. The great decline of Chinese culture, one should say, began when the Manchu tribe came to power. It destroyed something vital to Chinese culture, the people's sense of constituting a nation, and then it just emphasized the preservation and ordering of historical documents instead of seeking the social realization of those humanistic ideals integral to China's historical tradition.[110]

Thus T'ang, echoing the old tensions between Neo-Confucian metaphysics (*Sung-Ming li-hsueh*) and the prominent "textual studies" (*k'ao-cheng*) movement under the Manchus, saw the latter as largely taking the same path of "passively" empirical, specialized scholarship that the modern West had taken, forsaking the metaphysical outlook needed actively to confront and transform the given empirical world.[111] In China, however, unlike the West, specialization was restricted to the world of books instead of having an effect on society. Thus China failed to keep up with the West's societal development. True, when the West invaded China and the empire was shaken by the Taiping Rebellion, some late nineteenth-century officials were able "somewhat to manifest the spirit of the traditional Chinese scholar" (Tseng Kuo-fan, Tso Tsung-t'ang, Li Hung-chang, Hu Lin-i). Yet "matters became worse daily":

> Although this spirit of the scholars repeatedly appeared, it also repeatedly collapsed. From then until now, China's destiny as a whole has been no more than a series of changes based on following Western political, economic, religious, cultural, and scholarly trends. So the Western way of blurring together the sacred and the demonic has to a large extent appeared also in China during the last century. During the last twenty years, the West's Marxism conquered China, and China's Communist Party came to power. At first it expressed the desire of the Chinese people, with their five-thousand-year-old culture, to stand up proudly before the world. There was, one must say, something sacred about this. The Communists, however, felt only skepticism, indifference, and fear with regard to the eternally valuable aspects of both the Chinese and the Western cultural traditions. Thus they pursued a kind of instinctual, fanatical, arrogant nationalism, closing China off from the rest of the world, treating the latter as an enemy. This precisely was a collectivistic

way of blurring together the sacred and the demonic. Although not the same as the Western individualistic way of blurring these together, these two versions of estrangement from the sacred are equally unable to lead humankind toward a spiritual realm that is sublime, great, long-lasting, and sacred.

In both cases,

> specialized knowledge and techniques pertaining to nature and society tend to become no more than the tools of greed and ambition, whether individualistic or collectivistic. More and more, people today just instinctively seek survival, satisfaction of the desire to reproduce themselves. This will cause an endless population increase with the result that humanity will eventually become sick of its own existence, and people will want to destroy each other.[112]

Yet this global crisis also was part of a hopeful process of historical evolution. T'ang saw biological and social evolution as a process that already had splendidly produced a human mind able to make "manifest" the cosmic "Logos" that at first was only "latent." Even more, history was currently leaving behind a stage when "morality was limited to the moral outlook of a particular people, class, profession, or occupation. Such an outlook is indeed a closed morality, one just emphasizing certain ethical items or rules of conduct — a closed morality indeed." History was entering a stage when morality would be based on "an open mind" allowing people with "all kinds of moralities" to "understand and appreciate" one another. Similarly, a new "philosophical theory will necessarily appear" making clear the "shared essence" of all moral and religious thought and "explaining why this religious morality and philosophical wisdom should control all intellectual and technological activities."[113]

f. The Rational Analysis of Praxis and the Problem of Pluralism

While reason revealed both a historical crisis and the necessary advent of a better historical stage, it also made clear the uphill mission that humanists like T'ang now had to undertake in order to save the world from demonic forces and establish a moral hierarchy in the organization of humanity:

> Today the only hope lies in having true religious, moral, and philosophical wisdom control all specialized knowledge and techniques, causing all

the individuals making up society's contending classes, occupations, and professions more or less to acquire the understanding that comes from true religious faith, effective moral upbringing, and philosophical wisdom.[114]

T'ang's thought, however, was not restricted to a simply Manichaean, transformative, utopian view rejecting the accommodation of viewpoints and activities out of accord with his own ideals. Along with his celebration of an "open mind," his philosophy exemplified a distinctive way of accommodating pluralism and the freedom of the three marketplaces.

His argument presupposes that *paideia* ultimately centers on a certain perspective, a spiritual stance. What had to be refuted, he held, was a passive acceptance, not to mention an active endorsement, of "greed and ambition." *Paideia* had to produce an elite able to emphasize the universal validity of reason, the saintly vision of the public good inseparable from it, the total moral transformation of society, the decisive containment of "greed and ambition," and so the development of human beings with the character needed to pursue this transformation.

That accomplished, however, this elite had to be aware that this transformation will require "an endless series of developments" during which different "sets of circumstances" will require different responses (*tang-chi*), the pursuit of truth will continuously evolve in new ways, and doctrinal conflicts cannot be avoided.[115] In dealing with these conflicts, then, T'ang sought to avoid trying to "repel" wrong views while still "criticizing" them.[116]

Paideia, as he saw it, would produce individuals able to deal "benevolently" (*jen*) with the entropy of the three marketplaces without accepting it as normal. Apart from dealing with the entropy of the economic and political marketplaces, such persons would respect the value of ultimately wrong philosophies. T'ang had in mind the contradictions among philosophies narrowly clustering themselves around one or a few "worlds," such as "objectivism," "realism," "materialism," "naturalism," the various moral philosophies and religions, and so on. Since each of these shed light on an aspect of existence, each had to be respected as one indispensable part of a total philosophical sequence that could not be mastered by just jumping over the lower worlds into the higher.

Moreover, the philosophical grasp of this total sequence, dissolving contradictions, required "an endless series of developments." Still more, T'ang emphasized that even his own synthesis of the nine worlds could not be regarded as "the end of philosophy," if I may adapt Francis Fukuyama's phrase. T'ang said: "If outside my philosophy there were no philosophy, then my philosophy would destroy the world's philosophies and thus violate the principle of *jen* (regarding with love the world outside oneself)." While the necessary goal of philosophy was to show how all philosophical insights "are consistent with each other" (*t'ung*), the "merging" of philosophies was still in the future. Consequently,

> if I say all philosophies can be merged together, this also allows for a period of time during which [they have not merged, and] people will say they necessarily cannot be unified.... because people's ideals differ and are greater or narrower, higher or lower, the metaphysical realities they perceive are different and are greater or narrower, higher or lower.

Even more, despite his fixation on "philosophy" as the vehicle of world transformation, T'ang could — with the help of Buddhism — see beyond his own philosophical preoccupations:

> Those who philosophize must understand that philosophy is just a way to benefit living beings by using verbalized learning, to bring forth the right teachings and save the world, a matter of seeking to realize virtue by emulating worthy and perfect persons. But those who cultivate other kinds of learning and other teachings, they too can benefit living beings and save the world.[117]

T'ang's philosophy, therefore, reminds us that Chinese thought includes a way of accommodating if not celebrating pluralism. After all, going back at least to the writings of Hsun-tzu (third century B.C.), the idea of "heterodox doctrine" (*hsieh-shuo*) has been combined with that of a variety of doctrines each illuminating one "corner" (*ch'ü*) of the truth. Similarly, the Buddhist *p'an-chiao* doctrine to which T'ang appealed legitimized the play of contradictory views.

The difference between this kind of legitimization and that offered by the Hayek-Popper model of the "open society" is a subtle one, especially since the latter too combines pluralism with a list of indisputable logical and ethical principles. The chief difference seems to lies in the way tolerance is justified. In neither case is it justified by appealing to any version of the illogical thesis of relativism, whether ethical skepticism or the "historicism" Leo Strauss attacked, although such illogical theories are often enough loosely combined with some form of libertarianism or utilitarianism. In the case of the Hayek-Popper model, I would say, tolerance is justified especially through that epistemic downgrading of indisputables accomplished by the Great Modern Western Epistemological Revolution, the idea, summed up by Isaiah Berlin, that many ideas indisputable for a we-group are not deducible from reason. Epistemic self-confidence is thus tempered by a note of tentativeness. Moreover, there is a way of relishing the fruitfulness of contradictions and disagreements as the soil needed to nurture creativity and innovation. This feeling is quite different from T'ang's view that such conflicts may be endurable but ultimately violate the very nature of existence.[118]

In T'ang's case, there is a deep, obviously traditional longing for agreement and harmony alien to the Millsian, liberal tradition Hayek and Popper exemplified. For T'ang, the justification of tolerance hangs not on the epistemic downgrading of indisputables but on the idea that the realization of harmony requires a long, complex transitional historical period during which the rise of contradictory doctrines is unavoidable and indeed necessary. Thus intellectual and moral dissonance is endured as the price of progress instead of prized as the essence of a vital society encouraging individual spontaneity.

Presumably this conceptualization of tolerance makes it easier for educational leaders to impose some intellectual and moral parameters on *paideia*. Most important, T'ang roots tolerance in a temporary condition, while Hayek-Popper roots it in a perpetual epistemic condition.

g. The Rational Analysis of the Sources of Fallibility

Besides identifying its own nature, the forms of existence, the types of intellectual mistakes, the shortcomings of cultures, the promise of history, and the nature of successful agency, reason shed light on the causes for the difficulties of humankind. As already mentioned, T'ang in effect depicted a cosmically ultimate contradiction between a divine rationality tending "inward" and "upward" and a human rationality tending "downward" and "outward." Rather than directly confronting this cruel contradiction, however, T'ang spoke of "the deepest secret of the cosmos." By this he meant that, "whether consciously or not," philosophers filling the world with contradictory doctrines were actually helping people "deal with different and contradictory historical circumstances" and thus indirectly and gradually revealing the overarching philosophical truths of humanity. He then described himself as "not intending to reveal this secret but having no choice but to leak it out."[119]

Unwilling to lament or even recognize the dimensional contradiction built into the cosmos, T'ang also was unwilling to blame the cosmos for being so complex as to confuse the human agent responsible for understanding it. He did, however, recognize that this complexity was a necessary cause of intellectual confusion:

> If one asks why our human quest for knowledge necessarily leads to a variety of misunderstandings, it lies in the fact that, as our mental activity seeks truth, we confront such a variety of realms of existence or worlds. If there were just one kind of mental activity which could not be further subdivided into a number of kinds, this mental activity and its world would be unique and absolute [in their lack of relation to anything else]. There would then be no possibility of confusing this world with any other, and so no possibility of misunderstanding.

A maze was created by the variety of mental activities pertaining to the nine worlds and the many ways in which different kinds of mental activities can be connected to one another: "This variety is as great and confusing as can be" (*chih-fan*).[120]

Conversely, T'ang implied, the human mind by its very nature was constitutionally incapable of easily mastering this complexity. Even though T'ang referred repeatedly to the ideal of "the sage or superior person" (*sheng-hsien jen-wu*) who had perfect understanding and implied that this perfection was attainable, he had to admit that, at least in his case, the cosmos had left the task of understanding it in the hands of highly imperfect beings. Referring to his own "minuscule ability" as a thinker (*chüan-ti-chih li*), T'ang was not only being conventionally modest but also expressing awareness of this constitutional incapability.[121] Even apart from this mix of constitutional and personal weakness, T'ang viewed the ultimate truths he was reaching for as beyond the possibility of verbal clarification (*pu-k'o ssu-i*). Although convinced that "in understanding the principles of the world, there are no contradictions or mis-understandings that cannot be resolved," he granted that he had so far "tried but failed" to demonstrate this, and that his own "discussions had not disposed of all misunderstandings."[122]

Moreover, appreciating Heidegger's notion that human beings are "thrown" into existence,[123] T'ang was deeply aware that the starting point of his own intellectual endeavors was a tangle of unique accidental biographical circumstances and impulses the ultimate nature of which could not become transparent to him:

> Ultimately, what the current era calls on us to do is a matter of how we understand its distinctive nature. Because the events and changes making it up are so many and so complex, no one can fully understand them, and people may well disagree about what the distinctive character of the era is and what moral mission it has assigned them.[124]

Still more, T'ang's consciousness of how thought depends on individual historical circumstances (*chi*) included awareness that the construction of an analytical approach such as his own system with its "the three directions and the nine worlds" was itself an idiosyncratic act. Refusing to regard his philosophy as a kind of terminal truth, he avoided claiming that his categories necessarily override other ways of categorizing the aspects of human life or the types of propositions: "But this book of mine is something I made myself. What is in it naturally are my discussions of the views I myself have, and these cannot but partly differ from the views discussed by others." Remembering how he had as a youth come to equate happiness with "the elimination of desire," T'ang noted that "it is hard to explain how I arrived at this view. But really it was because youths have such strong desires. When desires are strongest, the desire to eliminate them appears."[125] I would not call this explanation profound, but his comment reflects some awareness that the origin of one's own intellectual direction may be unknowable.

4. Conclusion

a. The Limits of Fallibility: Not Turning the Corner

As discussed in chapter I, the Great Modern Western Epistemological Revolution weighed the ability to establish objective truths and normative principles against the tendency to base norms and other ideas on subjective preferences and images, and it "turned the corner." That is, leaning to skepticism, relativism, and "historicism," it left the impression that the content of norms and other ideas was more subjective than objective. T'ang's thought reminds us that whether or not to turn this corner is no more than a matter of choice and judgment. Given the nature of human thought, one can emphasize subjectivity and fallibility, but one can also highlight the limits of fallibility even while confronting the obstacles to the apprehension of any objective reality.

T'ang was very aware of the asymmetry between the immense complexity of human life and the limited human ability to understand complex matters. He also thought much about the deep effects of *chi* (particular sets of concrete circumstances) on how people think about what knowledge is — the historical, cultural, linguistic, psychological, or biographical circumstances into which a particular person has been "thrown." He was also quite clear about the personal intellectual shortcomings of persons like him pursuing the disciplines, such as philosophy, available to understand human life better. And he could make lists of the types of mistakes such persons made, especially illogical statements and statements contradicted by sensory observation.

Nevertheless, he noted the illogicality of any claim that all human ideas are "arbitrary," "baseless," or meaningful only for a historically limited segment of humanity. Thus human thought not only entailed fallibility but also presupposed that fallibility is limited. While the sociology of knowledge implied that "circumstances" relativized all knowledge,[126] T'ang regarded "circumstances" as challenges to be met by individuals rationally oriented to universal truths.

The epistemological optimism that prevented him from "turning the corner" in the direction of relativism and skepticism is epitomized by the following passage:

> ... coming to the question of how I came to write this book, it has been a matter of using every bit of my minuscule ability to respond to the call of this era. As I see myself, I certainly am not a sage or person of superior ability with regard to matters of religion and morality. Moreover, during the last thirty years, my life and spirit often faltered as I tried to make my way in today's academic world, surrounded by vulgarities and trying to avoid the dust and dirt of mortal existence. But that is not how heaven

made me. In philosophizing, I always went back to the questions genuinely raised by my own life, and indeed these questions to a large extent did not stem just from the purely personal impressions or desires of a single individual.[127]

After all, as already mentioned, T'ang was confident he had revealed "the secret" of the cosmos.

In other words, all the "circumstances" (*chi*) impeding human understanding notwithstanding, T'ang had no doubt he could objectively understand a great deal: that "what is immediately given in experience" (*tang-hsia*), not a sacred canon, is the starting point of knowledge; that "reason" as an ability to grasp "principles" (*i-li*) appears as part of "what is given"; that reason can reveal the nature of "existence" as a variety of *hsiang* (objects of consciousness) forming a number of *ching-chieh* (worlds); that these worlds include "ideals," the subtle relations among the three highest worlds, and the nature of the "circumstances" making up the three lowest worlds, including the differences between "cultures," such as Chinese and Western culture; that reason also reveals itself as an invaluable process of unbounded reflexivity the human agent of which can identify herself with the "highest" of these worlds, thus gazing out at existence as a whole *sub specie aeternitatis*; that he or she can thus grasp how the highest world is a kind of cosmic "Logos" not only effecting congruence between human reasoning and the laws of nature but also producing in every individual a "feeling" of concern for the well-being of all living things; that this concern takes the form of substantive moral principles calling for a saintly, "sacred" transcendence of all selfishness; that there is a "contrast" between these moral principles and the "circumstances" of the historical world, since this world has been progressing only in a faltering way, given the profusion of "misunderstandings" and the cultural "crises" produced by them; that the ultimate causes for this faltering can be known, including the human tendency to "cling to" the lower worlds, along with the asymmetry between the maze of the nine worlds and the limited capabilities of the average human intellect; that nevertheless ideals inherently tend toward their own, total realization; that all these "principles" or "truths" (*i-li*) take the form of ideas ubiquitously manifest in all human thinking yet repeatedly misunderstood because of the above conditions impeding understanding; that "philosophical" efforts can eventually eliminate these misunderstandings; and that eliminating them will morally transform all concrete human life, ending the existence of "demonic" tendencies.

T'ang thus was sure he himself had grasped accessible universal truths and so had been able to "enlighten" himself. His intellectual weaknesses, he felt, had merely limited his ability to "try to enlighten others" (*tzu-chueh ch'iu chueh-t'a*).[128] Intellectual frailty was defined more as impeding intellectual communication than preventing anyone from arduously achieving "a full awareness of the key conditions affecting his or her life" (*tzu-chueh*). Instead of the prominent contemporary American emphasis on the sociality of thinking, T'ang contrasted the individual's ability to become enlightened with the resistance in society to the propagation of enlightenment.

This way of conceptualizing fallibility was basic to T'ang's attitude toward society. On the one hand, he was convinced he had serious access to the knowledge that should be propagated to serve as the parameters of freedom and the basis of *paideia*. On the other hand, T'ang did not propose suppressing all ideas out of accord with these parameters. In his mind, the need to grasp and propagate absolute truths as the parameters of freedom could and should be combined with tolerance. He held that one should respond to seemingly wrong views by following three indisputable principles: that the need for self-criticism is inseparable from the human mind's most prestigious faculty, its ability rationally to find indisputable universal truths; that one of these truths is that the historical evolution of ideas, because of constantly shifting "circumstances," inherently consists of clashing doctrines; and that another of these truths is that one should act "benevolently" and in an "open" way toward people whatever their views. Thus T'ang preached an absolutism that simultaneously accommodated the intellectual marketplace as well as the economic if not the political marketplaces. This kind of tolerance and pluralism, to be sure, precluded the absolutization of individual freedom and idiosyncrasy. Precluding it, however, T'ang was less interested in limiting the scope of diversity than in cultivating the overarching, shared intentions with which an enlightened elite publicly guiding society should deal with diversity.

b. T'ang and the Seesaw Effect

T'ang's philosophy, with its immense epistemological optimism, its teleological picture of history, its vision of philosophers as the agents of progress, and its utopian quest for a free society under the control of moral wisdom, perfectly illustrates discourse #1. It also illustrates the "seesaw effect" discussed in chapter I above (the AY pattern).

In other words, if one comes to the question of evaluating T'ang's knowledge claims, if one accepts the methodology of evaluation I discussed in chapter I, and if one then shares the nineteen platitudinous "rules of successful thinking" that my we-group regards as indisputable, one will accept some of T'ang's knowledge claims and have doubts about some others.

What is doubtful to us centers on his ontological idealism; his belief that one can combine knowledge about phenomena and about praxis to form a single logically unified philosophy (*t'i-hsi*); his sociological reductionism; his inadequate understanding of how culture shapes thinking; his utopian belief in the practical possibility of taking selfishness and misunderstanding out of history to form a free society under the control of moral wisdom; his consequent, really deplorable failure to appreciate pragmatic, imperfect, incremental economic and political progress in the moral limbo of history; and his general bias in favor of the "inner" at the expense of the "outer."

More particularly, one may note that his idealistic rejection of naturalism presupposes that human evil and misunderstanding are the only disruptive force in the cosmos, that the cosmos otherwise facilitates the realization of human goals. This kind of hopeful anthropocentrism so basic to Neo-Confucianism became untenable after modern cosmology showed that the human race and most other species might well be destroyed by a collision with one of the innumerable pieces of cosmic debris frequently crossing the earth's path around the sun. True, T'ang since boyhood had understood that a remote cosmic event could end life on earth. The new idea of such a likely collision, however, still more vividly demonstrates the objective cosmic existence of "outer" things rudely unrelated to the human struggle between good and evil as well as the unpleasantly enormous importance of the scientists able to understand these physical forces and perhaps even prevent them from blowing up humanity.

Along with his rejection of naturalism, many of T'ang's epistemologically optimistic views are not easily tenable, such as his rejection of epistemology as a cautious attempt to define the boundary between the knowable and the unknowable; his assumption, reminiscent of St. Anselm's proof of God's existence, that human reflexivity by itself without empirical evidence can reveal "worlds" that "exist"; his claim that the cosmos itself embodies the goodness that is the goal of human life; his claim to have understood why there is congruence between human reasoning and the principles seemingly followed by rationally predictable physical events; his gratuitous if not impious insistence that human consciousness occupies the "highest" rung of the ontological ladder; his idea that mental life is inherently and universally organized according to three "directions"; and the confidence with which he distinguished between "feelings" stemming from a cosmic source and "feelings" shaped by historically particular soteriological circumstances. He did not ask how, apart from such circumstances, there could be any substantive definition of the public good. All in all, the disaggregation of descriptive, causal, predictive, evaluative, recommendatory, and epistemological ideas is the road to clarity for my we-group but not for T'ang's.

Despite such doubtful aspects of T'ang's thought, however, my we-group accepts his most basic claims about the human ability to use reason to obtain knowledge about the universal conditions of praxis and *paideia*. First, we agree with T'ang that reasoning consists of thoughts denoting a variety of objects according with a variety of conceptualizations or principles; that these objects include "what is given in sensory experience"; that the conceptualization of "what is given" includes a variety of categories such as humankind, history, and cultural differences; that history appears as both implying and violating ideals;[129] that ideals imply the obligation resolutely to pursue them and arouse feelings of moral determination distinguishable from merely selfish desires; and that the pursuit of ideals is inherently difficult and leads to a tragic mix of success and failure.

Second, revealing the inherent goodness of an ideal realm distinguished from egotistic impulse, reason also reveals not only the limitlessness or indeterminateness of reflexivity but also the inherent, necessary goodness of reflexivity as an aspect of human life and so the inherent goodness of education (as Socrates said, contradicting Hume's theory but not his scholarly practice, "The unexamined life is worthless"). Third, reason reveals the individual person as the subject or the agent of this inherently valuable reflexivity and so recognizes the value and dignity of the individual person ("the dignity of man as a thinking being," as J.S. Mill put it). Moreover, reason reveals that this dignity is equally possessed by all persons, because the reflexivity which implies this dignity appears as a potentiality enjoyed by all human beings. Thus reason may imply even the "universal brotherhood of man" (*ssu-hai chih nei chieh hsiung-ti*) and all the familiar humane civilizational values on which so many philosophers, east and west, ancient and contemporary, have dilated.

Fourth, reason reveals that, as objects within the life of this agent of reflexivity, ideals inherently demand of this agent that she resolutely pursue them, turning them into palpable facts. In other words, praxis is a "convex" process of reshaping the world by turning imagined ideals into facts, instead of "concavely" obtaining information about facts and then just prudently adjusting actions to accord with them. Praxis can well be interpreted as requiring prudence, but the obligation to pursue ideals resolutely cannot be interpreted as necessarily precluding vigorous, enthusiastic, even violent actions to overcome obstacles.

Fifth, just as reflexivity appears as a shared human characteristic, so reason reveals that the moral subject of action is an individual who is part of a community. Ideals imply the joining of ego and alter in shared, escalating social movements enthusiastically pursuing ideals. Reason also reveals that community action to realize ideals occurs in the context of a historical process perpetually in a period of transition. Hence the need to accommodate pluralism.

All these points about the universal nature of praxis were strongly made by T'ang, and my we-group agrees with him. Because T'ang's thought combines these points, tenable in "our" eyes, with the ones above, which "we" regard as doubtful, T'ang's thought exhibits the "seesaw" effect AY discussed in chapter I.

Perhaps the key problem lies in T'ang's claim that the universal principles of praxis above imply a particular, substantive definition of morality. True, we grant that these principles have some substantive, though very general implications. As argued in chapter I, however, the GMWER effectively cast doubt on the possibility of making the jump from the formal principles of praxis to a substantive, practically useful hierarchy of values.

T'ang believed that the above formal, universal principles of praxis necessarily implied his own Buddhist-Confucian vision of saintliness as a concrete moral program. I think it clear, however, that these formal, universal principles of praxis could also be plausibly integrated with a great variety of value systems, even, perhaps, with Hitlerism. So far as I can see, these formal, universal principles of praxis cannot be turned into a substantive, specific, useful moral program or hierarchy of values without the intervention of a historically particular cultural or soteriological tradition. By overlooking the need for this historical intervention, T'ang cut short the process of reasoning about moral experience and so fell into the dilemma of the seesaw effect.

This hardly means, however, that the light T'ang cast on the universal principles of praxis is unneeded. What I infer from his thought is that these universal principles imply the need to join together a historically particular soteriological tradition with an understanding of these principles. His argument, as I see it, was about *paideia*, the educational forms a society needs to shape a moral, responsible citizenry. Education, he argued in effect, may depend on what Hayek called a historically particular "tradition," but it also depends on grasping the universal conditions of praxis. With this argument, which my we-group accepts, T'ang rejected the Western liberal thesis that freedom is enhanced when all pronouncements about the universal conditions of praxis are treated with skepticism. If they are, T'ang implied, the centuries of labor through which traditions were formed will have been in vain. An exaggerated emphasis on human fallibility stunts the ability to think about the relation between egotistic desires and the knowledge claims accumulated over the course of history. T'ang thus brilliantly brought out the need to ponder the limits of human fallibility and sinfulness instead of exaggerating the scope of human fallibility and feeling engulfed and disoriented by the tragedies of history.

One might add that, in effect rejecting Popper's rejection of "historicism," T'ang linked praxis and the conceptualization of history in a way partly similar to Kant's. T'ang's main point was that resolute moral action requires "a mind believing that morality will be fully realized" (*hsin-hsin*), and so he tried to prove that moral ideals "exist" full of a "dynamic power" tending toward their full realization.

True, Kant, unlike T'ang, did not try rationally to demonstrate the existence of such a power. Holding that moral action requires belief in historical or natural tendencies facilitating it, Kant sought to build this belief on just a hopeful interpretation of history, not a proof that history necessarily tends toward progress. Nevertheless, he, like T'ang, suggested that the understanding of history cannot be divorced from the intellectual requirements of praxis, and that effective praxis requires a picture of history and the cosmos as somehow supporting the efforts of people to pursue their moral goals.[130] If, for instance, the idea of a cosmic structure based on sheer accident were as metaphysical and immune to experimental falsification as that of a cosmos governed by a "Logos," and if the latter idea were therapeutically more useful than the former, T'ang was not far from Kant in suggesting that the therapeutically useful metaphysical point should be preferred to the therapeutically useless or harmful one.

c. Continuities and Discontinuities with the Tradition

The prevalence of discourse #1 also raises the question of its genesis, of its continuity or discontinuity with the Chinese tradition and Western thought. There has long been a debate pertaining to this question, and scholarly opinion since the middle 1970s has increasingly emphasized the continuity of modern Chinese thought with the Chinese tradition and its discontinuity with the West, instead of vice versa.[131] Moreover, even if the genealogy of iconoclasm is debatable, the genealogy of T'ang's philosophy is unmistakable. From an emic standpoint (i.e. T'ang's own), his ideas were rooted in the Neo-Confucian and Buddhist traditions, especially the thought of Wang Yang-ming. This is clear too when one looks at his ideas from an etic standpoint (the best analytical perspective an observer of his thought is able to devise). T'ang's thought was what he thought it to be, a way of using basic Neo-Confucian beliefs to deal with some new issues.

To be sure, discontinuities with the Neo-Confucian discourse were important. The generation of K'ang Yu-wei, Liang Ch'i-ch'ao, and Yen Fu changed the political discourse. The pivotal change was a new sense of impending doom. For those whose voices mattered politically, it had become necessary not just to change policies but to *chiu-wang* (act to save their nation and civilization from destruction).

This "definition of the situation" was not just a matter of simply describing objective facts. As Wang Erh-min's research has shown, it was a collective act of imagination whereby the politically articulate minority concluded that a series of recent political crises amounted to an almost unprecedented turn in the course of global history (*pien-chü*), leaving China exposed to forces out of its control and opening it up to the possibility of a kind of ultimate destruction. Liu Kuei-sheng has discussed how China's defeat in 1895 at the hands of Japan intensified the sense of impending doom, and how it was this feeling that motivated intellectuals to radicalize their search in both Chinese history and the modern West for new categories and theories with which to "save China."

This new definition of the present was also accompanied by an intellectual return to the classical problem of the political center. The preoccupation of the late imperial "statecraft" tradition (*ching-shih*) with small-scale, local reform was largely replaced by discussion about how the central government and its nation-wide institutions should be changed.

The public discourse was then further altered as intellectuals, beginning especially with Yen Fu, changed the epistemology of this discussion. This point has been made especially well in the book by Hu Wei-xi, Gao Rui-quan, and Zhang Li-min. Enthusiastic about the Western tradition of empiricism and positivism, Yen Fu emphasized that knowledge about policy should be derived not from the classics but from theory based on fact.[132] He then embraced Western evolutionary theory, according to which China's current crisis had been caused by China's failure to progress quickly enough, and democracy was integral to the most advanced stage of evolution. Moreover, the Western idea of "culture" was adopted in the early twentieth century, helping Chinese picture the global parade of societies in different stages of evolution.

Scholars have not yet adequately analyzed this vast change in China's public discourse (the origin of "discourse #1"). It is doubtful, however, that this change can be pictured as an event shattering the traditional worldview (*chieh-t'i*) and leaving Chinese confused and anxious, floundering in a sea of clashing ideas. This still prevalent interpretative paradigm should be replaced by one taking into account the persistence of major, deeply-rooted orientations. So far as T'ang was concerned, this change in discourse left intact

Confucian and Buddhist beliefs to which he was intensely committed
throughout his life.

Certainly these beliefs included that much-discussed range of
everyday ethics grounded in Confucian teachings, such as the
emphasis on family cohesion, frugality and savings, hard work,
respect for authority, and respect for education. Clearly, widespread
Chinese respect for these traditional ethical principles and the
distinctive emotional logic of Chinese social life were little affected by
the modern Chinese shift away from the authoritarian and
ceremonial extremes of the *san-kang* tradition and the restructuring
of educational curricula in the direction of science. T'ang took all
these traditional values for granted.

The core Neo-Confucian ideas that preoccupied or influenced
him were the belief in the global centrality of China; the utopian,
saintly goal of "linkage" (the oneness of self, group, and cosmos, the
convergence of all doctrines in the world following the dissolution of
"misunderstandings," and so the oneness of ideals and mundane
reality, including the elimination of selfishness and insincerity); the
correlated goal of a global hierarchy headed by Chinese moral-
intellectual virtuosi understanding linkage; the belief that this goal
can be realized by "my mind" (*wu-hsin*), if I can perfectly develop the
"feelings" with which I am cosmically endowed; hence the
precedence of praxis (*kung-fu*) over empirical analysis of the given
world; the idea that the constitution of ultimate reality, whether the
cosmos or a historical process following cosmic principles, exists as a
latent but ultimately decisive moral "power" (*tung-li*) on which praxis
can depend to end all evil; the idealistic view of the Lu-Wang
tradition (Lu Chiu-yuan [1139–1192], Wang Yang-ming) that the
ultimate reality of the cosmos is a function of praxis rather than
some naturalistic, morally dumb mix of particles or forces;[133] the
frustrating ontological combination of a cosmic power only elusively
tending toward human ideals with the intellectually and morally
fragile nature of the human minds charged with the pursuit of these
ideals (to cite the basic Neo-Confucian idea taken from the ancient
script version of the *Book of History*, "The human mind is ever in a
state of danger, while the mind of the *tao* is almost imperceptible in
its subtlety");[134] and so the central self-image of the scholar as a
person struggling with his frailities while trying to rectify a
contemporary era caught in a "predicament" or a "crisis."

In Tang's mind, these fully Neo-Confucian ideas brought forth centuries ago were hardly "ghosts" of the past that he was vainly trying to resuscitate. They were the beliefs constituting who he was, the ideas defining his life mission as he faced the ordeals of the twentieth century. In his mind, these ideas were the undiscardable "inner" part of a heritage also including dispensable, fungible ideas about how to picture the "outer" world: physical nature, history, social forms, and the historical texts from which wisdom could be derived. In T'ang's case, at least, this "inner" part of the heritage could readily be combined with the new discourse — science, the vocabulary of "social evolution" and "cultures," and the bibliographical basis of the latter two — taken from the West to depict the "outer" world and to explain how to achieve instrumental mastery over it.

Whether this distinction in the minds of many modern Chinese intellectuals between the indispensable and the fungible aspects of the Confucian tradition was an invention of theirs or a distinction integral to the "inner logic" of this tradition itself can be debated. Yet it is clear that the Confucian tradition, with the help of classical Taoism, had for centuries posited two linked distinctions: that between primary (e.g. *ta-t'ou-nao-ch'u*) and secondary norms, and that between ancient, very general moral ideals and later misinterpretations of them. As Wang Fan-sen discussed, trying to remove the latter in order to grasp the true wisdom of the sages had long become the central paradigm of Confucian scholarship. Similarly, the commonly used ontological dyads (*pen-mo, t'i-yung,* etc.) amounted to a distinction between ultimate reality and the mundane, ephemeral manifestations of it. As important, Buddhist philosophy, widely revered in modern and late imperial China, furnished basic concepts with which to distinguish between highly generalized moral-ontological principles and any concretely particular formulations characterizing the "outer" world, including the ritual order. These abstract but well-established Buddhist notions were central to T'ang's philosophical ability to separate out his moral project from any particular traditional beliefs about the nature of institutions, history, knowledge, and the cosmos. Most basic were the Buddhist idea of reality as *hsiang* (objects of consciousness) and that concerning the ultimate convergence of seemingly contradictory doctrines (*p'an-chiao*). Moreover, the old discussion about how to design *hsueh-shu* (learning) had accustomed Chinese intellectuals to the problem of weighing controversial ideas about the sources of knowledge, such as those about *li-hsueh* (the study of principle) and *shih-hsueh* (substantial learning), not to mention the Neo-Confucian principle putting personal insight above the authority of any classic.

One may, therefore, argue about whether or not the Neo-Confucian tradition itself distinguished between absolute truths and more tentative, fungible ideas that could be conveniently revised, and whether the former were precisely the ones above listed as T'ang's core Neo-Confucian beliefs. What is a fact is that T'ang exhibited no distress or confusion in combining these beliefs with a variety of ideas arising out of China's modern contact with the West. One is reminded of the ease with which Chinese thinkers assimilated Buddhist ideas from the fourth century A.D. on without disrupting the inheritance of basic Confucian ideals. For instance, affirming the Western idea of democracy, he simply merged this goal together with the traditional one of a "great harmony" (*t'ai-ho*) based on "linkage," the ideal of a society as a hierarchy "controlled" by intellectual virtuosi committed to this goal. For more than two thousand years, Confucians had believed that this hierarchy could be best controlled by a single moral virtuoso: the "king" fully realizing his moral obligations as the "son of heaven." The 1911 Revolution canceled this traditional mechanism of moral control, but T'ang never lamented this cancellation. On the contrary, he clearly was enthusiastic about the way this cancellation had shifted the responsibility for this control onto the shoulders of "philosophers."

Nor did his thought indicate any regret about ending the exclusive epistemic position of the Thirteen Classics. This position had anyway for some centuries been complemented by the idea of "the three teachings" (Confucianism, Buddhism, Taoism) and the search for "convergence" (*hui-t'ung*) among these three. For T'ang at least, there was no detectable pain caused by having to shift this quest for convergence to the study of all the world's philosophies "ancient and modern, Chinese and foreign." Basing this search on the familiar Buddhist doctrine that all true doctrines converge even if seeming to contradict each other (*p'an-chiao*), T'ang felt he was moving from a more "closed" to a more "open" era in the human struggle to end the "contrast" between ideals and actualities. Despite his strong criticism of the West and his deep admiration for the "humanistic" quality of premodern China, he relished rather than was disoriented by the cross-cultural philosophical challenges of his era and welcomed the challenge of deriving all truths from "experience." This is especially evident from his magnificent textbook, *Che-hsueh kai-lun* (An Introduction to Philosophy).

Similarly, any replacement of Confucianism's organismic cosmology with science did not trouble T'ang, because he could use Buddhism to define all phenomena as *hsiang* (objects of consciousness) and then derive this consciousness, just as Neo-Confucianism had, from an indivisible cosmic mind (*tao-hsin, hsu-ling ming-chueh*). This cosmic mind with its *tung-li* (dynamic power) in turn supported his moral efforts just as the traditional organismic cosmos had, while science and the threateningly presumptuous specialists who did it were neatly tucked into the "lowest" levels of reality.

If T'ang, though still idealizing the Chinese past, did give up the idea of a golden age of antiquity (*san-tai*), he was able to retain the still more basic Confucian point, that history is a teleological struggle between "sacred" and "demonic" elements (*t'ien-li* and *jen-yü*), and that the outcome of this struggle depends on the efforts of moral-intellectual virtuosi facing the contemporary crisis.

To be sure, cancellation of the ancient belief in an ancient, golden age altered the agenda of Chinese thought. One of T'ang Chün-i's most basic premises was that, in order to realize ideals, people must act feeling confident that full realization of them is practicable. Moreover, in his view, this feeling of confidence can stem only from *knowledge* that the full realization of ideals is practicable. People with the ancient belief in a golden age assumed they had this knowledge. Similarly, during the early decades of the twentieth century, many intellectuals believed that the "global tide of history" ensured realization of the highest ideals. As Ch'ien Mu noted, they continued believing history included an era of total moral success, merely changing the temporal if not geographical identity of that era.

In his later years, however, T'ang lacked not only the traditional belief in a past golden age but also the belief that a morally successful society had materialized in New York or Moscow, as well as any optimism about the immediate future of a world dominated by Western utilitarianism.

With the promise of history thus put into doubt, how could the practicability of the highest political ideals be demonstrated? This indeed was a difficult and quite new question. Since history did not guarantee steady progress and was often disastrous, how could absolute morality as a *political* condition be realized? As discussed above, T'ang in his last years was preoccupied especially by this problem.

Yet even in the traditional period, faith in history had not been untroubled, being intertwined with a "sense of predicament." Confucians had been habitually troubled by the gap between "knowledge" and the "actions" implied by "knowledge." True, the agenda of modern Chinese thought was altered when the ancient belief in the practicability of the highest political ideals was combined with a new view of historical potentiality much more pessimistic than the Confucian view. In this new situation, Buddhist pessimism about "this world" was not enough, because T'ang could not discard the Confucian goal of political salvation. Nor could he redefine political salvation as a morally imperfect condition. Therefore, political hope could come only from the kind of metaphysical acrobatics T'ang performed to refute the view of a Fung Yu-lan that the reality of ideals was only "formal." In rising to this philosophical challenge, however, T'ang exhibited a spirit of resolution and self-confidence, not one of despair and bewilderment.

Neither did the philosophical challenge posed by modern science dismay him. True, aiming to prevent the epistemic hegemony of modern science, T'ang avoided the classical Confucian celebration of the "outer," material aspects of nature and human existence. One does not find in T'ang's thought the "cathedral pathos" with which Hsun-tzu viewed the grand "outer" structure of "heaven and earth" (e.g. in *T'ien-lun-p'ien*). Awkwardly enough, T'ang refused to celebrate what had become the actually wondrous domain of the scientists. Yet he still exhibited his usual philosophical serenity as he subsumed this "outer" grandeur and scientific phenomena under the Buddhist concept of "objects of consciousness."

More striking, perhaps, in T'ang's thought, the state lost its Confucian centrality. T'ang once compared the state to the policeman at the entrance to a theatre, who "does not create and realize the aesthetic qualities of the theatre performance."[135] As just mentioned, he did not lament the cancellation of the monarchy and had no inclination to conceptualize the state as anything but an instrument of the moral wisdom provided by "philosophers" or "intellectuals." If political leaders today ignored this wisdom, their successors would heed it after intellectuals, "through their work and thought, literature, and art, had given the edifice of Chinese government a reliable foundation," as Hu Shih put it around 1922.

Common in modern China, moreover, this approach had solid Confucian roots. Already since the classics *Ta-hsueh* and *Chung-yung*, produced by about 200 B.C., not to mention the Neo-Confucianism that began to emerge by the eleventh century, the agent of world transformation was often identified not as the king but as *wu-hsin* (my mind), that is, whoever could become a sage. The subject of the *kung-fu* (efficacious moral efforts) at the center of Neo-Confucian thought was anyone who "set his goal" (*li-chih*) on the achievement of sagehood. Apart from some ambiguity introduced especially by Wang Yang-ming, immense efficacy was ascribed to any sage, not just to the king who turned himself into a sage.[136] Moreover, the idea of horizontal moral and intellectual influence emanating from a scholar working outside or even shunned by the political center became basic to late imperial Chinese thought, complementing if not overshadowing the classical idea of influence flowing down vertically from the king or his prime minister (*tsai-hsiang*).[137] In putting the burden of agency on "my mind" instead of the state, therefore, T'ang was adopting an entirely familiar perspective classically summed up when Fan Chung-yen (989–1052) demanded that every scholar "resolutely make himself responsible for the well-being of the whole world."

Moreover, although playing down the role of the state, T'ang still connoted the basic Confucian emphasis on the corrigibility of the political center and so its ability fully to respect the moral-intellectual virtuosi "controlling" society, just as the policeman respected the artists performing inside the theater. T'ang's friend Hsu Fu-kuan forcefully argued in the 1950s and 1960s that China's democratization would bring about "government based on virtue" (*te-chih*),[138] and T'ang with his utopianism never questioned the practicability of that ideal. T'ang thus never strayed anywhere near the discourse #2 concept of an incorrigible political center monitored not by moral virtuosi but by fallible, economically preoccupied citizens outside it organizing a civil society.[139]

Along with this solid historical continuity between late imperial Neo-Confucianism and the thought of New Confucians like T'ang, there also were continuities even with the old traditions that seemingly had been discarded. After all, during the twentieth century, the imperviousness of widespread traditional attitudes to modern arguments was reflected in the flood of intellectual complaints about China's cultural "backwardness." As noted above, after T'ang's flirtation with iconoclasm ended during his twenties, even his sophisticated, partly Hegelian views did not prevent him from "morning and evening burning incense before the ancestral tablets and the tablet honoring heaven, earth, the ruler, one's relatives, and one's teachers" whenever he visited the family grave site in Szechwan. The latter tablet with five logographs had not even been changed by his family, as many were after 1911, to read *t'ien ti kuo ch'in shih* (heaven, earth, the nation, relatives, and teachers), replacing "ruler" with "nation." As Yü Ying-shih has written, after about the thirteenth century, it became a widespread custom in China to write the five logographs for "heaven, earth, the ruler, relatives, and teachers" on either a tablet or a red piece of paper pasted to a wall in one's home. These five logographs epitomized a vision of the proper order going back to *Hsun-tzu* (third century B.C.).[140]

All in all, then, the personal suffering, political turmoil, institutional upheavals, and intellectual dissonances of the twentieth century did not disintegrate or even impair T'ang's ability to draw on the resources of his inherited cultural tradition to deal with the problems of life. To be sure, all these continuities with the traditional heritage notwithstanding, T'ang did not see himself as serenely imbibing and propagating a traditional cultural spirit. On the contrary, he saw himself living in an age of "crisis," struggling desperately to retrieve an ancient, elusive Chinese "cultural spirit" on the verge of being lost because the minds of most people east and west were currently filled with "misunderstandings" (*wang-chih*) not only stemming from the influx of foreign ideas but also introduced by the "textual studies" movement in China during the eighteenth century. Lamenting this alienation from the old cultural spirit, he was being logical insofar as he identified the successful retrieval of this spirit with its total realization in the form of a morally complete transformation of the whole world. Apart from such a sublime transformation, the mere historical continuity of Neo-Confucian beliefs and analytical modes was no consolation for him.

Many Chinese historians, however, have confused this factual problem of historical continuity with the consciousness of crisis expressed by modern Confucians. First, they have overlooked that this sense of crisis and of being alienated from an elusive ancient spirit was integral to the Neo-Confucian tradition itself, at the very core of which was the idea of a current fragile effort carried out in a corrupt society in order to retrieve elusive ancient truths almost entirely obscured by subsequent misunderstandings. Therefore, to the extent that modern Chinese feared they were disastrously losing touch with ancient values, they were not that different from their Confucian ancestors.[141] The idea of a disastrous discontinuity with a valued past was actually a form of continuity with the Confucian tradition, hard as it may be for some historians today to understand this paradoxical but factual point. Second, many historians have not recognized the above continuities. Instead, they have exaggerated the historical discontinuity between the Confucian tradition and modern Chinese thought and then used this exaggerated notion of discontinuity to identify the cause for modern China's "intellectual crisis."

In an influential article, Chang Hao argued that

> [China's] crisis of meaning…. became a widely disturbing one as new world views and new systems of value flooded into China and broke the protective canopy which the traditional *Weltanschauung* and *Lebensanschauung* — or what Susanne Langer calls the symbols of general orientation — provided to shield people from the threat of outer chaos and inner anxiety. With the traditional symbols of orientation eclipsed by the variety of conflicting new ones, the Chinese were plunged into a spiritual disorientation of a magnitude perhaps unprecedented since the influx of Buddhism in medieval times.

This "spiritual disorientation" consisted of a "fusion of … three kinds of disorientation…. the moral, the existential, and the metaphysical," and this "fusion" lay "at the root of the modern Chinese crisis of meaning." Thus the New Confucians' thought was "an attempt to overcome the spiritual disorientation felt by many sensitive souls among Chinese intellectuals."[142]

But does "spiritual disorientation" describe T'ang Chün-i's state of mind? If "disorientation" means being aware of much political and intellectual change and turmoil, suffering on account of national and personal circumstances, having existential anxieties, having doubts about the moral potentiality of history, and trying in a critical and creative way to make sense out this situation, T'ang was "disoriented." But is this what "disorientation" means? Presumably, it really means dealing with the troubles of life while lacking core convictions consistently serving as the spiritual basis for one's intellectual endeavors throughout one's life, that is, dealing with these troubles while lacking what "Suzanne Langer calls the symbols of general orientation." As just noted, T'ang had plenty of "symbols of general orientation" in the form of coherent beliefs firmly rooted in his earliest experiences. After all, discourse #1 was precisely a set of "symbols of general orientation," it stayed utterly intact, and it proved to be rationally defensible, at least in T'ang's eyes. Thus he was not at all "disoriented" so far as go the abundant biographical data presented here. In this regard, he was typical of many modern Chinese intellectuals.

To be sure, Chang Hao's article connotes the iconoclastic May Fourth judgment that, however firm the beliefs of the New Confucians were, they were somehow invalid or even "absurd" and so cannot be regarded as effective "symbols of general orientation." Whether they were rationally or philosophically invalid, however, is far from obvious, as I have just noted, and Chang did not undertake to show that they were. Apart from this issue, Chang Hao did not distinguish between two different questions: the extent to which an individual securely grasps "symbols of general orientation" as he or she copes with the difficulties of life, and the extent to which this individual views these difficulties as a "crisis" of one sort or another. If a "crisis of meaning" is defined etically as "lack of the symbols of general orientation," T'ang's thought does not at all illustrate such a crisis, although, from his own emic standpoint, he lived in an era of "crisis." Chang Hao uses Langer's etic category to define "crisis," but then, instead of logically applying this category to the data, he just echoes the emic complaint.

In other words, T'ang securely possessed "symbols of general orientation" basic to the "traditional *Weltanschauung*." "New world views and new systems of value flood[ing] into China" did not "br[eak] the protective canopy" provided by "the traditional

2. T'ang Chün-i's Rejection of Western Modernity

Weltanschauung ... to shield people from the threat of outer chaos and inner anxiety." On the contrary, T'ang dealt with this inner and outer threat precisely by depending on much the same symbolic "canopy" his parents had lived under. It was from this inheritance that he drew the criteria with which to "choose" among the bewildering, intriguing, and indeed hopeful philosophical options he confronted. After all, by the age of twenty-eight, he had gone through a period of "choice" (*chueh-tse*) to form philosophical principles the truth of which he never doubted during his remaining four decades. Moreover, this youthful period of philosophical "choosing" and "struggle" was a state of creative development, not of disorientation, being based on a proud spirit of intellectual autonomy and immense self-confidence.

T'ang's thought, then, was not a disoriented attempt to deal with a confusing situation but an effort to analyze this situation by consistently following deep Neo-Confucian beliefs about the validity of which he never had any doubt. Indeed, he can be criticized for failing critically to uncover these beliefs and consider reasons to doubt them. Entirely possessed by them, he evaluated with a spirit of supreme if not excessive self-confidence exactly those Western ideas allegedly disorienting him and then unequivocally rejected those philosophical premises of Western modernity basic to the currently salient mix of capitalism and democracy. These Western ideas existed for him only as objects of intellectual inquiry, not as a competitive framework or as ideas threatening his own psychological and soteriological equilibrium.

True, T'ang was very worried by the difficulty of retrieving the Confucian spirit. Paradoxically enough, however, as his philosophy defined the scope of reason and the parameters of freedom, it illustrated not just the persisting vitality and flexibility of this unquenchable historical spirit in modern times but also its granite-like imperviousness to some of the key rationales of Western modernity. His discourse thus complements contemporary Western critiques revealing the vulnerability of these Western rationales, but it does not offer a less objectionable way of conceptualizing human betterment. T'ang's thought, I believe, did what philosophy is supposed to do. It did not solve the problems people everywhere should be worrying about. It helped identify them and so surpassed the great amount of philosophical discussion, east and west, unconcerned with them.

Endnotes

1. On Ernst Bloch (1885–1977), see Paul Edwards, ed., *The Encyclopedia of Philosophy*, 8 vols. (New York: Macmillan Publishing Co., Inc. & The Free Press, 1967), vol. 1, pp. 321–323. One of Arnold Metzger's (1892–1974) books is *Freedom and Death*, trans. Ralph Manheim (London: Human Context Books, Chaucer Publishing Co., Ltd., 1973). See also Karola Bloch et al., eds., *Ernst Bloch — Arnold Metzger: Briefwechsel 1942–1972* (Frankfurt am Main: Suhrkamp Verlag, 1987).

2. See Yü Ying-shih, "Ch'ien Mu yü hsin-ju-chia (Ch'ien Mu and the New Confucians)," in Yü Ying-shih, *Hsien-tai ju-hsueh-lun* (Essays on Confucian Learning in the Modern Era; River Edge: Global Publishing Co. Inc., 1996), pp. 159–164. On the treatment of the New Confucians as "cultural conservatives," see Charlotte Furth, ed., *The Limits of Change* (Cambridge, Mass.: Harvard University Press, 1976), especially Chang Hao, "New Confucianism and the Intellectual Crisis of Contemporary China," ibid., pp. 276–302. For essays on the New Confucians reflecting the rising interest in them in China, see the books by Cheng Chia-tung and Kuo Ch'i-yung adduced in chapter XII, notes 8 and 43, and in chapter II, note 8, and Lo I-chün, ed., *P'ing hsin ju-chia* (Critiquing the New Confucians; Shanghai: Shang-hai jen-min ch'u-pan-she, 1989). For an example of recent Chinese work outside the Mainland on the New Confucians, see Chai Chih-ch'eng, *Tang-tai hsin-ju-hsueh shih-lun* (Historical Studies on the Learning of the Contemporary New Confucians; Taipei: Yun-ch'en wen-hua ch'u-pan, 1993). On the broader category of "modern Confucian humanism," see Thomas A. Metzger, "The Chinese Reconciliation of Moral-Sacred Values with Modern Pluralism: Political Discourse in the ROC, 1949–1989," in *Two Societies in Opposition: The Republic of China and the People's Republic of China after Forty Years*, ed. Ramon H. Myers (Stanford: Hoover Institution Press, 1991), pp. 3–56.

3. The assessment as "absurd" of the modern defense of Confucian values in the face of May Fourth conoclasm can be found in Yü-sheng Lin, *The Crisis of Chinese Consciousness: Radical Antitraditionalism in the May Fourth Era* (Madison: University of Wisconsin Press, 1979), pp. 17–18. Li Tse-hou's combination of Marxism with affirmation of certain core Confucian ideas is illustrated by his *Chung-kuo ku-tai ssu-hsiang shih-lun* (Historical Studies on Ancient Chinese Thought; Taipei: Feng-yun shih-tai ch'u-pan kung-ssu, 1990).

4. Chang P'eng-yuan, *Liang Ch'i-ch'ao yü Ch'ing-chi ko-ming* (Liang Ch'i-ch'ao

and the Revolution at the End of the Ch'ing Period; Taipei: Academia Sinica, Chin-tai-shih yen-chiu-so, 1969), pp. 49–57 and elsewhere.

5. Lao Ssu-kuang, *Chung-kuo-chih lu-hsiang* (China's Direction of Development; Hong Kong: Shang-chih ch'u-pan-she, 1981).

6. Yü Ying-shih, *Ts'ung chia-chih hsi-t'ung k'an Chung-kuo wen-hua-te hsien-tai i-i* (Modern Values and the Value System of Chinese Culture; Taipei: Shih-pao wen-hua ch'u-pan shih-yeh yu-hsien kung-ssu, 1984), pp. 6, 25–26. On the concept of "transcendence" as "inner," see T'ang Chün-i, *Chung-kuo wen-hua-chih ching-shen chia-chih* (The Value of the Spirit of Chinese Culture; Taipei: Cheng-chung shu-chü, 1972), pref., p. 2.

7. Yü Ying-shih, *Hsien-tai ju-hsueh-lun*, pref., pp. iv–viii.

8. Yü Ying-shih, *Chien Mu yü Chung-kuo wen-hua* (Ch'ien Mu and Chinese Culture; Shanghai: Shang-hai yuan-tung ch'u-pan-she, 1994), pp. 253–254. Also his *Li-shih jen-wu yü wen-hua wei-chi* (Essays on Historical Figures in a Period of Cultural Crisis; Taipei: Tung-ta t'u-shu ku-fen yu-hsien kung-ssu, 1995), preface. Cheng Chia-tung offers a similar thesis about the New Confucians in a brilliant study going far beyond Yü's polemical comments. See Cheng Chia-tung, *Mou Tsung-san* (Mou Tsung-san; Taipei: Tung-ta t'u-shu kung-ssu, 2000) and Mo-tzu-k'o (Thomas H. Metzger), "Tao-t'ung-te shih-chieh-hua: Lun Mou Tsung-san, Cheng Chia-tung, yü hsun-ch'iu p'i-p'an i-shih-te li-ch'eng" (Replacing the Chinese Idea of an Absolute Wisdom Uniquely Handed down in the Course of Chinese History with the Idea of a Global Search for Knowledge: A Discussion about Mou Tsung-san, Cheng Chia-tung, and the Evolving Quest for Morally Critical Consciousness), *She-hui li-lun hsueh-pao* 5 (Spring 2002): pp. 79–152.

9. Reinhard Bendix, *Kings or People: Power and the Mandate to Rule* (Berkeley: University of California Press, 1978).

10. See his *Ch'ien Mu yü Chung-kuo wen-hua*, pp. 253–254. For discussion of Chinese scholarship emphasizing this continuity, see Huang Ko-wu (Max K.W. Huang), "'Wu-ssu hua-yü' chih fan-hsing-te tsai-fan-hsing: Tang-tai ta-lu ssu-ch'ao yü Ku Hsin-te 'Chung-kuo ch'i-meng-te li-shih t'u-ching'" (Reflections on Reflections on 'the May Fourth Discourse': Contemporary Intellectual Trends on the Mainland and Ku Hsin's *The Historical Setting and Prospects of China's Enlightenment*), *Chin-tai Chung-kuo-shih yen-chiu t'ung-hsun* 17 (March 1994): pp. 44–45, and his review in ibid. 19 (March 1995): pp. 130–155, of Chin Kuan-t'ao and Liu Ch'ing-feng, *Kai-fang-chung-te pien-ch'ien: Tsai lun Chung-kuo she-hui ch'ao wen-ting chieh-kou* (China's Transformation in the Course of Becoming Open to the Cosmopolitan World: Another Analysis of Chinese Society's Ultrastable Structure; Hong Kong: The Chinese University Press, 1993). See also note 35 in chapter I.

11. On discourse #1 as assumptions shared by all the leading modern Chinese

ideologies and discourse #2 as a prominent set of assumptions widely shared in the contemporary West, see chapter I.

12. A possibly comprehensive list of T'ang's articles and books is in Feng Ai-ch'ün, *T'ang Chün-i hsien-sheng chi-nien-chi* (Essays and Other Writings Collected in Honor of T'ang Chün-i; Taipei: T'ai-wan hsueh-sheng shu-chü, 1979), pp. 5–28.

13. Thomas A. Metzger, *Escape from Predicament: Neo-Confucianism and China's Evolving Political Culture* (New York: Columbia University Press, 1977); his "T'ang Chün-i and the Conditions of Transformative Thinking in Contemporary China," *The American Asia Review* 3 (spring 1985): pp. 1–47; his "A Historical Perspective on Mainland China's Current Ideological Crisis," in *Proceedings of the Seventh Sino-American Conference on Mainland China (1978)* (Taipei: Institute of International Relations, 1978), pp. IV-2-1–IV-2-17; and his "The Thought of T'ang Chün-i (1909–1978): A Preliminary Response," in *T'ang Chün-i ssu-hsiang: kuo-chi hui-i lun-wen-chi* (The Thought of T'ang Chün-i: A Collection of Essays Resulting from an International Conference), 4 vols., ed. Huo T'ao-hui (Hong Kong: Fa-chu ch'u-pan-she, 1992), vol. 1, pp. 165–198.

14. T'ang Chün-i, *Sheng-ming ts'un-tsai yü hsin-ling ching-chieh* (Human Existence and the Dimensions of the Mind), 2 vols. (Taipei: T'ai-wan hsueh-sheng shu-chü, 1978). Hereafter "T'ang." See T'ang, vol. 1, pref., pp. 1–3, vol. 2, 1202. Feng Ai-ch'ün, p. 139.

15. Karl R. Popper, *Objective Knowledge* (Oxford: Clarendon Press, 1994), p. 154.

16. On T'ang's idea that his basic philosophical principles hardly changed after he was about 30, see T'ang, vol. 2, pp. 1157, 1155, and for the period of difficult struggle and "war within myself" through which he went to form these principles, see T'ang Chün-i, *Jen-wen ching-shen-chih ch'ung-chien* (The Reconstruction of the Humanistic Spirit; Hong Kong: Hsin-Ya yen-chiu-so, 1955), pp. 563, 565–566 (hereafter "*ch'ung-chien*").

17. Feng Ai-ch'ün, p. 119, gives his birth date as the 26th day of the 12th month of wu-shen, which should be January 17, 1909, but Feng gives the Western date as February 3, 1909. For Chang Hao's thesis that the New Confucians' thought arose out of the "disorientation" caused by the alleged collapse of the traditional Confucian worldview, see his article adduced in note 2 above. His thesis is discussed at the end of this chapter.

18. Metzger, *Escape*, p. 223.

19. T'ang, *ch'ung-chien*, pp. 625, 628. On the centrality in T'ang's thought of the idea of avoiding *chih-cho* because reality is a kind of "flow," see Metzger, *Escape*, pp. 32–33, and the various references to the idea of flowing or turbulent water in Neo-Confucian writings as listed under "water" in *Escape*'s Glossary and Index.

20. My biographical material comes largely from Feng Ai-ch'ün, pp. 119–139, but see also T'ang, *ch'ung-chien*, pp. 560–566, 621–628.
21. Feng Ai-ch'ün, p. 120.
22. T'ang, *ch'ung-chien*, pp. 622–623.
23. Ibid., p. 625.
24. Feng Ai-ch'ün, p. 119.
25. T'ang, *ch'ung-chien*, p. 560. My translation is a bit free.
26. Feng Ai-ch'ün, p. 624.
27. Ibid., pp. 561–562.
28. T'ang, *ch'ung-chien*, p. 624.
29. Feng Ai-ch'ün, pp. 121–122.
30. Ibid., pp. 121, 124. T'ang, *ch'ung-chien*, pp. 626, 561. T'ang, vol. 2, p. 1146.
31. T'ang, vol. 2, p. 1148. T'ang, *ch'ung-chien*, pp. 562, 579. Feng Ai-ch'ün, p. 121.
32. Feng Ai-ch'ün, p. 120. This may refer to *Meng-tzu*, sections 12–14 in book 4.
33. T'ang, vol. 2, p. 1147.
34. Feng Ai-ch'ün, p. 123.
35. T'ang, vol. 2, pp. 1155, 1157. Mou Tsung-san, in a book first published in 1983, five years after T'ang's death, in effect agreed with this statement by his friend, holding that T'ang's "thought reached its mature state by the time he was thirty," and that, because of administrative and other distractions, "there was not much progress in his understanding of scholarly problems after he was thirty." See Mou Tsung-san, *Chung-kuo che-hsueh shih-chiu chiang* (Nineteen Lectures on Chinese Philosophy; Taipei: T'ai-wan hsueh-sheng shu-chü, 2002), pp. 407–409. Mou's evaluation is further evidence that T'ang's basic outlook was formed by the age of thirty, but it also is a superficial one reflecting Mou's own controversial ideas about how to pursue philosophical "progress" and how to describe a body of thought like T'ang's. See chapter I, note 87.
36. Feng Ai-ch'ün, pp. 122–123.
37. T'ang, vol. 2, p. 1155.
38. Ibid. and T'ang, *ch'ung-chien*, p. 564. T'ang was well aware of the problem of reification. See T'ang Chün-i, *Che-hsueh kai-lun* (An Introduction to Philosophy), 2 vols. (Taipei: T'ai-wan hsueh-sheng shu-chü, 1974), vol. 1, pp. 645–651.
39. T'ang, vol. 2, pp. 1149–1150.
40. T'ang, *ch'ung-chien*, pp. 563, 565–566.
41. Ibid., pp. 626–627. For T'ang's empathetic view of Chinese who embraced Communism, see ibid., pp. 267–271.
42. Feng Ai-ch'ün, p. 124.
43. T'ang, *ch'ung-chien*, p. 624. For the passage from *Lun-yü*, I used D.C. Lau's translation.

282 A Cloud Across the Pacific

44. Feng Ai-ch'ün, p. 134, T'ang, vol. 2, p. 1144.
45. Ibid., vol. 1, pref., p. 2.
46. T'ang, ch'ung-chien, p. 628.
47. T'ang Chün-i, "Hai-te-ko-chih 'Jen-sheng ts'un-tsai hsing-hsiang lun'" (Heidegger's 'On the Possible Modes of Human Existence'), O-hu (August 1984): p. 30. Similarly, Leo Ou-fan Lee has astutely noted that modern Chinese literature, even though without the "sustained optimism" of the major Chinese ideologies of its day, generally lacked the "'consuming negative passion'" found in contemporaneous European writing expressing "profound disillusionment with the positive notions of reason and progress." See his "In Search of Modernity: Some Reflections on a New Mode of Consciousness in Twentieth-century Chinese History and Literature," in *Ideas Across Cultures: Essays on Chinese Thought in Honor of Benjamin I. Schwartz*, ed. Paul A. Cohen and Merle Goldman (Cambridge, Mass.: Council on East Asian Studies, Harvard University, 1990), pp. 124–125, 127–128, 134–135.
48. T'ang, vol. 2, p. 1145.
49. Metzger, *Escape*, ch. 2.
50. T'ang, vol. 2, pp. 1184, 1143, 1140 (this page makes especially clear the use of *shen* for *shen-sheng* [sacred]), vol. 2, p. 1139.
51. T'ang, ch'ung-chien, pp. 562–563.
52. On "linkage" as the central goal for both T'ang and Sung-Ming Confucian metaphysics, see Metzger, *Escape*, ch. 3, and Metzger, "T'ang Chün'i and the Conditions of Transformative Thinking in Contemporary China."
53. T'ang, vol. 2, pp. 1148–1149.
54. See note 52 above.
55. T'ang, vol. 2, p. 1160. The effort to derive philosophical truths from "experience" was basic to T'ang's classic *Chung-kuo wen-hua-chih ching-shen chia-chih*, completed in 1951. Its argument is outlined in *Escape*, ch. 2.
56. Wing-tsit Chan, *A Source Book in Chinese Philosophy* (Princeton: Princeton University Press, 1963), pp. 370–395.
57. T'ang, vol. 2, p. 1197.
58. Ibid., vol. 2, p. 1170.
59. T'ang, ch'ung-chien, pp. 563–564.
60. T'ang, vol. 2, pp. 1151–1155.
61. Ibid., vol. 2, pp. 1153–1154.
62. Ibid., vol. 2, pp. 1151–1152.
63. Ibid., vol. 2, pp. 1152, 1155.
64. Ibid., vol. 2, p. 1154.
65. Ibid., vol. 2, pp. 1153, 1155, 1150–1151.
66. For this Neo-Confucian concept, see Metzger, *Escape*, p. 289, entry for *hsu-ling ming-chueh*.

67. *Encyclopedia of Philosophy*, vol. 4, p. 323.

68. See e.g. T'ang, vol. 2, pp. 1169, 1171.

69. Feng Ai-ch'ün, pp. 122–127. I am grateful to Ms. Elsie Wu for finding evidence that Hua-hsi University was in Ch'eng-tu.

70. On his publications, see note 12 above, which refers to a chronologically organized list.

71. On this manifesto, see article by Chang Hao adduced in note 2 above. On Chin Yao-chi, see chapter VII.

72. This refers to the Feng Ai-ch'ün volume and the Huo T'ao-hui book referred to respectively in notes 12 and 13 above.

73. T'ang, vol. 2, pp. 1155–1156.

74. Ibid., vol. 2, p. 1159. On "linkage," see note 52 above.

75. T'ang, vol. 2, pp. 1174–1175.

76. See Kenneth K.S. Ch'en, *Buddhism in China* (Princeton: Princeton University Press, 1964), pp. 305–306. Ch'en paraphrases the meaning of *p'an-chiao* as "dividing the periods of teachings."

77. T'ang, vol. 2, p. 1159. The idea that doctrines contradicting each other can be seen as one part of the larger truth which each doctrine by itself fails to reveal and even by its narrowness obscures was put forward in *Hsun-tzu* (third century B.C.) and partly resembles the *p'an-chiao* doctrine's way of reconciling doctrinal differences. See *Hsun-tzu* chapters on "Refuting Twelve Teachers" and "Freeing the Mind from Misunderstandings."

78. See his series of volumes called *Chung-kuo che-hsueh yuan-lun* (Essays on the Foundations of Chinese Philosophy) and his *Che-hsueh kai-lun* (An Introduction to Philosophy), all produced after he moved to Hong Kong. Feng Ai-ch'ün has detailed bibliographical information.

79. T'ang, vol. 2, pp. 1158–1159.

80. Ibid., vol. 2, pp. 1188–1196, 1169, 1172, 1170.

81. Popper, *Objective Knowledge*, pp. 9–11. Insisting that "we must regard *all laws or theories as hypothetical or conjectural*, that is, as guesses" (italics in original), Popper argued that "all men are mortal" does not amount to an "'established law'" because it has been discovered that "bacteria are not bound to die," and that "living matter is not in general bound to decay and die ..." With what I would call "epistemological pessimism," Popper rejected the epistemologically optimistic "commonsense theory of knowledge," according to which "repeated observations made in the past" of events like sunrises justify the belief that such events will almost certainly occur in the future (ibid., p. 3). Popper, I would say, wanted to know what kinds of statements can be regarded as absolutely true, while T'ang was interested in what kinds of statements are generally true and are the most useful for the optimization of praxis. From the standpoint of practical social organization, the view that all people are mortal can be fully affirmed

as true, but Popper insisted it was no more than a "guess." Popper is much admired in China, and Henry K.H. Woo, whose typically Chinese epistemological optimism is described in chapter III below, has sought to equate his epistemology with Popper's: "Like Popper, I am a staunch defender of epistemological optimism in that we both believe in the existence of objective knowledge"(*American Journal of Chinese Studies* 4 [November 1997], p. 256). The looseness of this utterly misleading statement coming from a scholar of undoubted astuteness is precisely typical of epistemological optimism as an outlook inherently denying the need to be extremely careful and precise when discussing the nature of knowledge. The fact may be left aside that Popper himself used "epistemological optimism" only to denote a wrong way of thinking; see Karl R. Popper, *Conjectures and Refutations: The Growth of Scientific Knowledge* (London: Routledge, 1992), pp. 5–6. My main point is that, according to the definitions of "epistemological optimism" and "epistemological pessimism" that I have consistently used to describe a difference between "discourse #1" and "discourse #2," and which Woo was referring to, Popper's thought perfectly exemplifies epistemological pessimism, because, instead of holding that he can know the laws that physical nature follows, the ultimate nature of all existence, the ultimate nature of historical development and of the main cultures, and the objective moral norms all humankind should follow, along with the overarching principles common to all these types of knowledge, Popper held that the theories people have about observable facts are no more than "guesses," while all the other ideas they have, including normative ones, are no more than "beliefs" that cannot be called "true" because they cannot be falsified through empirical experiment. Thus he logically implied that all moral norms are equally arbitrary, and that none is universally valid and overriding. True, his assumptions seem to contradict this explicit philosophical position of his. In *The Open Society and Its Enemies* and elsewhere, he displayed his absolute belief that the norms of "the Open Society," rooted in the Socratic spirit and Christian ethics, override those of its "enemies," the totalitarians of the right and the left (see note 129 below). Furthermore, he treated as absolute and universal truths not only the principles of logic but also the idea that scientific experiment can falsify a proposition. He also posited the reality of "the physical world," rejecting idealism. These absolutistic assumptions, however, merely reflected the apparent fact that all human thought, however skeptical, has to rest on some principles regarded as indisputable by the thinker in question and so cannot avoid all epistemological optimism. These assumptions are still compatible with Popper's exemplary epistemological pessimism, which caused him to focus on precisely distinguishing between scientific knowledge and other kinds of ideas, to conclude that scientific knowledge consists only of "guesses," and to avoid any claim that reason can establish objective, universally overriding moral norms, not to mention rejecting the possibility of using reason to construct a grand philosophy logically integrating all knowledge about the factual and normative aspects of human life, the kind of *t'i-hsi* Woo and countless other Chinese intellectuals in this century have pursued. This is not to say they have been wrong, Popper, right, only to describe the contrast between them, which Woo refuses to recognize.

82. Mill's point about "doctrines" or "truths which have reached the point of being uncontested" is hard to reconcile logically with his emphasis on "fallibility" and is found in "On Liberty" as published in *The English Philosophers from Bacon to Mill*, ed. Edwin A. Burtt (New York: The Modern Library, 1939), p. 982.

83. T'ang, vol. 2, pp. 1160, 1158, 1184.

84. Ibid., vol. 2, pp. 1135, 1194.

85. This categorization is basic to his major essay on Confucius in his *Chung-kuo che-hsueh yuan-lun — yuan-tao-p'ien chüan-i* (Essays on the Foundations of Chinese Philosophy — Volume One of the Section on Investigations into the Nature of the True Way; Hong Kong: Hsin-Ya yen-chiu-so, 1976). See e.g. p. 6, where T'ang uses *wu* (things) instead of *ti* (earth). Perhaps the clearest account is in his *Chung-hua jen-wen yü tang-tai shih-chieh* (Chinese Humanism and the Contemporary World), 2 vols. (Taipei: T'ai-wan hsueh-sheng shu-chü, 1975), vol. 2, p. 424. This kind of categorizing goes back at least to Liang Shu-ming, who spoke about humankind's three great problems: the relation between man and nature, between men, and between different impulses within the self. See Hu Wei-xi, Gao Rui-quan, Zhang Li-min, *Shih-tzu chieh-t'ou yü t'a: Chung-kuo chin-tai tzu-yu-chu-i ssu-ch'ao yen-chiu* (The Ivory Tower at the Crossroads of Tyranny and Revolution: A Study of Modern Liberal Intellectual Trends in China; Shanghai: Shang-hai jen-min ch'u-pan-she, 1991), p. 209.

86. This belief that cultures are organic wholes with a central feature which can be conveniently summed up is typical of discourse #1. Apart from this chapter's discussion of the way T'ang described the cultures of China and the West, examples of his approach are given in my "T'ang Chün-i and the Conditions of Transformative Thinking in Contemporary China," pp. 29–30. The formation in China of the concept of "culture" in the twentieth century remains to be studied fully. Yen Fu did not use this term and conceptualized the elements of human life — philosophies, institutions, etc. — in a rather loose, open-ended way more similar to the methodology I incline to than to the theory that cultures are bounded systems of some sort. Yet in his way of contrasting China with the West, one indeed can see the idea that human beings organize their social lives around a single

leading principle. See Huang Ko-wu (Max K.W. Huang), *Tzu-yu-te so-i-jan: Yen Fu tui Yueh-han Mi-erh tzu-yu ssu-hsiang-te jen-shih yü p'i-p'an* (The Raison d'être of Freedom: Yen Fu's Understanding and Critique of John Stuart Mill's Liberalism; Taipei: Yun-ch'en wen-hua shih-yeh ku-fen yu-hsien kung-ssu, 1998). An unpublished article by Ishikawa Yoshihiro, a copy of which Dr. Huang kindly gave me, sensitively describes Liang Ch'i-ch'ao's major role in bringing the term *wen-hua* (culture) into Chinese circles during the early twentieth century.

87. T'ang, vol. 2, pp. 1189, 1169.
88. Ibid., vol. 2, pp. 1171, 1131.
89. Ibid., vol. 2, pp. 1168–1169, 1171. This point coincides with the prevalent use of "we" or "us" in contemporary Western philosophy as the agent of reflection and moral action, as illustrated by Richard Rorty's pragmatism. On both sides of the Pacific, however, the concept of the sociality of thinking had to be weighed against the problem of a "private language" used by a person to resist social trends around her. See section 4a below.
90. Ibid., vol. 2, pp. 1171, 1184–1185, 1165.
91. Ibid., vol. 2, p. 1184.
92. Ibid., vol. 2, pp. 1187, 1171.
93. T'ang, vol. 1, pp. 1–4.
94. T'ang, *ch'ung-chien*, pp. 91, 568–569. Metzger, "T'ang Chün-i and the Conditions of Transformative Thinking in Contemporary China," pp. 14–15. Mou Tsung-san's partly similar scheme distinguishes between a "perpendicular" way of thinking culminating in the "mystical" "wisdom of intuition," and a "horizontal" way pursuing logical and empirical ideas. See his *Chung-kuo che-hsueh shih-chiu chiang*, p. 441.
95. T'ang, vol. 1, pp. 39–46, vol. 2, p. 1186.
96. See the book by Yü adduced in note 6 above.
97. T'ang, vol. 2, pp. 1173–1176.
98. Ibid., vol. 2, p. 1187.
99. Ibid., vol. 2, pp. 1181–1182.
100. Metzger, *Escape*, p. 111.
101. T'ang, vol. 2, pp. 1171, 1172–1173.
102. Ibid., vol. 2, p. 1174.
103. Ibid., vol. 2, p. 1180.
104. Ibid., vol. 2, p. 1159.
105. Ibid., vol. 2, pp. 1179–1180. In T'ang's eyes, Heidegger's thought had erred in a similar way. See T'ang's article on Heidegger adduced in note 47 above.
106. T'ang, vol. 2, p. 1201.
107. Ibid., vol. 2, pp. 1162–1163.
108. Ibid., vol. 2, pp. 1137–1138.

109. Ibid., vol. 2, pp. 1138–1140.
110. Ibid., vol. 2, p. 1141.
111. Ibid. Also see T'ang, *ch'ung-chien*, pp. 105–115.
112. T'ang, vol. 2, p. 1142.
113. Ibid., vol. 2, pp. 1143–1144.
114. Ibid. Also see T'ang, *ch'ung-chien*, p. 338. See the discussion of T'ang's political views in Metzger, "T'ang Chün-i and the Conditions of Transformative Thinking in Contemporary China," p. 15. The views T'ang had by 1955 (and no doubt all along) about the need for the control of public opinion by leaders with true philosophical wisdom persisted throughout his life.
115. T'ang, vol. 2, pp. 1170, 1185, 1196.
116. Ibid., vol. 2, pp. 1185–1187.
117. Ibid., vol. 2, pp. 1197, 1187, 1185.
118. Ibid., vol. 2, p. 1176. Here T'ang posits: "Things contradicting or in a state of conflict with each other must necessarily destroy each other and cease to exist. They cannot be something that truly and actually exists." I also do not recall T'ang's ever using the idea of "dialectical" development to endorse the value of conflict and contradiction.
119. Ibid., vol. 2, p. 1159.
120. Ibid., vol. 1, pp. 11–14.
121. Ibid., vol. 2, p. 1144.
122. Ibid., vol. 2, pp. 1159–1160.
123. See T'ang's article on Heidegger adduced in note 47 above.
124. T'ang, vol. 2, p. 1132.
125. Ibid., vol. 2, pp. 1160, 1148.
126. Robert K. Merton, *Social Theory and Social Structure* (Glencoe: The Free Press, 1959), pp. 456–508 and especially pp. 460–461.
127. T'ang, vol. 2, p. 1144.
128. T'ang, vol. 2, p. 1197.
129. I do not think T'ang's view was refuted by Popper. See Karl R. Popper, *The Open Society and Its Enemies*, 2 vols. (Princeton: Princeton University Press, 1966), vol. 2, pp. 269, 278–280. Popper said: "*History has no meaning*" (original italicized). His point was that: "Facts as such have no meaning; they can gain it only through our decisions." Therefore "we" can find purpose and hope only in ourselves: "we must become the makers of our fate." That is, "we bear the ultimate responsibility even for the standards we choose." Conversely, it is wrong to think of these standards or goals as given by history (not to mention unscientific to infer from history any law of progress). This thesis of his requires careful evaluation. First, many would agree with his refutation of any theory that history follows "laws" just as physical events do and so is predictable just as they are. Even here, however,

Popper himself came close to the idea of a historical law of evolution when he described this book as attempting to show "that this civilization has not yet fully recovered from the shock of its birth — the transition from the tribal or 'closed society', with its submission to magical forces, to the 'open society' which sets free the critical powers of man. It attempts to show that the shock of this transition is one of the factors that have made possible the rise of those reactionary movements which have tried, and still try, to overthrow civilization and to return to tribalism" (ibid., vol. 1, p. 1). See also Karl R. Popper, *The Poverty of Historicism* (London: Routledge, 1991). Second, one can also appreciate Popper's emphasis on the ability and responsibility of people in the present autonomously to imagine and pursue their goals rather than believe in the primacy of goals actually or supposedly set in the past by others. Yet it is hard to see how goals actually or allegedly set in the past can be that clearly distinguished from goals autonomously set in the present. On the contrary, if one looks at how people actually set their goals, they virtually always do this by thinking of a responsibility thrust on them by history. It is hard to see how Popper himself differs in this regard from the historicists he attacked. This very book (*The Open Society and Its Enemies*), written during "the darkness of the present world situation" (World War II), was precisely an attempt to help dispel this "darkness" by refuting the ideas he saw as powerful historical trends currently threatening "to overthrow civilization and to return to tribalism." Like historicism, his view identified an old historical struggle between forces he defined as indisputably good and indisputably bad. This struggle presented every individual with the choice to uphold "standards of freedom, of humaneness, and of rational criticism" or to betray them, to continue or to undermine "what is perhaps the greatest of all moral and spiritual revolutions of history, a movement which began three centuries ago. It is the longing of uncounted unknown men to free themselves and their minds from the tutelage of authority and prejudice" (ibid., vol. 1, p. ix). Popper might claim that his viewpoint, unlike historicism, differentiates between the fact of such a movement and his personal evaluation of it as "perhaps the greatest of all moral and spiritual revolutions of history," but his description of the past is not purely factual and, his "perhaps" notwithstanding, absolutely precludes any judgment that overthrowing "civilization" and returning to tribalism could be a good thing. Thus the distinction between his concepts of progress and of historical destiny and the visions of these found in the historical theories he condemned lies less in epistemic form (the derivation of goals from an evaluative, interpretative, not purely factual account of history) than in substantive moral content: he saw a historical mission to fight for freedom and oppose totalitarianism where others saw a historical mission to impose socialism or a racial hegemony on the world. Most important, as illustrated by the passages quoted above, the agent of history for Popper was a kind of collective ego, a "we" ("we must become the makers of our fate," etc.). To be sure, Popper aimed for a free society maximizing the role of individual decisions. Nevertheless, like just about all political thinkers, he could not help positing a socially shared consciousness (Robert N. Bellah has spoken of "a community of memory"), and it is indeed hard to see how any coherent "we" deciding on goals can be formed without a socially shared history or saga inextricably intertwined with a shared sense of right and wrong. Thus "our" history — history told in the first person — seems necessarily to be a struggle between right and wrong. A detailed analysis of Popper's writings would reveal still more conclusively just how inextricably his version of Western history was intertwined with moral ideals he regarded as indisputable. Note, for instance, the passion with which he denounced "the idolatrous worship of power, of success": "For Christianity teaches, if anything, that worldly success is not decisive" (ibid., vol. 2, p. 272). This contradiction between Popper's own historicism and his theory condemning historicism was complemented by the contradiction between this very concept of a lesson "taught" by a historical movement and his theory of knowledge, which precludes the possibility of any knowledge (any universally valid teaching) except for "conjectures" so far unfalsified by empirical observation. That is, his theory of knowledge turns on the dichotomy between empirically falsifiable "conjectures" or "guesses" and beliefs that are neither falsifiable nor verifiable, but his discourse divides the latter category into indisputable and disputable beliefs (or teachings) and thus implies a standard of falsification other than empirical observation. See note 81 above. Given these two major contradictions in his thought, Popper's epistemology cannot be regarded as a standard with which to evaluate Chinese epistemological approaches. For an effort to use it this way, see Gregor Simon Paul, *Aspects of Confucianism* (Frankfurt am Main: Peter Lang, 1990). It should be noted that the highly absolutistic "historicism" Popper denounced is a view utterly different from the kind of relativism that Leo Strauss called "historicism" and denounced.

130. Leo Strauss and Joseph Cropsey, eds., *History of Political Philosophy* (Chicago: The University of Chicago Press, 1987), pp. 596–602.

131. On the problem of continuity, see chapter I, note 35.

132. See note 136 below and Liu Kuei-sheng, *Hsueh-shu wen-hua sui-pi* (Notes and Essays on Scholarship and Culture; Beijing: Chung-kuo ch'ing-nien ch'u-pan-she, 2000), pp. 46–57.

133. On Wang Yang-ming, see the books by Tu Wei-ming and Julia Ching or my *Escape*, pp. 146–154.

134. Metzger, *Escape*, p. 138.

135. T'ang, *ch'ung-chien*, pp. 383–384.

136. Metzger, *Escape*, pp. 77–79. For a profound discussion of how modern Chinese iconoclastic liberals similarly confronted the modern problem of translating ideals of absolute morality into political reality, see Hu Wei-xi, Gao Rui-quan, and Zhang Li-min, *Shih-tzu chieh-t'ou yü t'a*, pp. 1–77. The Hu Shih passage is quoted in ibid., p. 205.

137. See, for instance, the four-fold typology worked out regarding *ching-shih* (statecraft) thought in late imperial times by Huang Ko-wu: transformative action taken from within the political center by the emperor or the prime office or from outside it, and accommodative action taken by the political center or by officials or even gentry working just locally: Huang Ko-wu (Max K.W. Huang), "Li-hsueh yü ching-shih (Neo-Confucian Philosophy and the Statecraft Outlook)," *Chin-tai-shih yen-chiu-so chi-k'an* 16 (June 1987): pp. 39–40. The rising intellectual importance by the eighteenth century of accommodative action taken locally is reflected in Yü Ying-shih's thesis regarding a "new central theme" in Chinese political thought after the fifteenth century. See Yü Ying-shih, *Hsien-tai ju-hsueh-lun*, pp. viii, 1–59, and elsewhere.

138. Hsu Fu-kuan, *Hsueh-shu yü cheng-chih-chih chien* (Between the Realms of Scholarship and Politics; Taipei: T'ai-wan hsueh-sheng shu-chü, 1980).

139. Thomas A. Metzger, "The Western Concept of Civil Society in the Context of Chinese History," in *Civil Society: History and Possibilities*, ed. Sudipta Kaviraj and Sunil Khilnani (Cambridge: Cambridge University Press, 2001), pp. 204–231.

140. Yü Ying-shih, *Hsien-tai ju-hsueh-lun*, pp. 98–101.

141. For the importance of this traditional paradigm in modern Chinese thought, see Wang Fan-sen, *Ku-shih-pien yun-tung-te hsing-ch'i* (The Rise of the Movement to Study the Chinese Past Critically; Taipei: Yun-ch'en wen-hua shih-yeh ku-fen yu-hsien kung-ssu, 1987), and my *Escape*, chap. 3.

142. See pp. 280–283 in the article by Chang Hao adduced in note 2 above.

CHAPTER III

⬳

Hong Kong's Oswald Spengler: H.K.H. Woo (Hu Kuo-heng) and Chinese Resistance to Convergence with the West[1]

1. Convergence and Divergence

The work of Alex Inkeles and others has abundantly demonstrated the myriad ways in which modernizing and modern societies today are becoming increasingly similar with regard to not only the institutions and values instrumentally needed to pursue mass material prosperity but also various other political and cultural patterns.[2] Indeed Inkeles's theory of "convergence" was robust enough even before 1991, when Soviet Communism broke down. Earlier, Inkeles had cautiously assumed that convergence would not necessarily include the organization of the economy and the polity, since the divergence between socialism and capitalism and between authoritarianism and democracy might well persist. By 1991, however, it became apparent that, even in the case of economic-political organization, there also was an important tendency toward convergence. True, as Larry Diamond has pointed out, the "third wave" of democratization, beginning in 1974, slowed down or stopped by 1996. Yet the percentage of countries in the world governed "democratically" in the narrow sense of free elections rose from 27.5 percent in 1974 to 61.3 percent in 1995, while the percentage of countries enjoying freedom in a broader sense as well as free elections rose also, although not so impressively.[3] These facts of themselves strongly corroborate Inkeles's theory, which logically accounts for divergence as well as convergence.

Cultural divergences are easily understandable when one notes that apparently universal human needs, notably the need for material well-being, as well as the ability to think in a logical way, entail much interpretation. Thus Hayek astutely described universal human nature as having three aspects, "innate desires," "reason," and the ability to create an enormous variety of languages and "complex cultural structures" made up to a large extent of "non-rational customs." Like many biological species, *homo faber* has the ability to produce a huge variety of subspecies. Human beings in virtually all cultures tend to use reason to pursue material well-being, but culture and religion lead to great disparities when ego faces the choice between using reason to pursue her well-being and using it to pursue the well-being of others or the good of society, or between using it to pursue her immediate pleasures and using it to pursue her long-term benefits. Culture and religion, as S.N. Eisenstadt recently emphasized, also lead to great differences in how the good society is conceptualized. As important, they deeply affect how the actual, given world is perceived, that saga of suffering and glory with which every "community of memory" defines its hierarchy of goals.[4] Viewed from this perspective, China's civilization has diverged and probably will continue to diverge from Western patterns in various important ways, including linguistic, religious, social, aesthetic, and even political and economic patterns.[5]

Yet whatever the tendencies toward divergence and convergence, it is clear that the Chinese today are still free to influence these trends, tilting their civilization one way or the other. Policy-makers will do some of the steering, but so will public opinion and the intellectual trends competing to influence it. From the days of Wo-jen (d. 1871) and Chang Chih-tung (1837–1909) to those of Li Tse-hou (b. 1930) and Chin Yao-chi (Ambrose Y.C. King) (b. 1935), Chinese intellectuals have been arguing about whether to tilt toward divergence (e.g. *Chung-hsueh wei-t'i*) or convergence (e.g. *Hsi-hsueh wei-t'i*).

The demonstration effect of Western success, especially after the downfall of Soviet Communism in 1991, seemingly vindicated the Western combination of capitalism and democracy and ensured convergence. Yet the tendency toward divergence has remained extremely significant. First, it is often overlooked, especially by Westerners, that, whether in the case of political leaders like Sun Yat-sen (1866–1925) and Mao Tse-tung (1893–1976) or intellectual leaders like Liang Ch'i-ch'ao (1873–1926), T'ang Chün-i (1909–1978), and Li Tse-hou, the Chinese have typically assumed that they were fully qualified not just to learn from the West but also to evaluate Western thought and activities and lead humankind toward a new philosophy and a new, ideal civilization "transcending the West."[6] Second, while the Western combination of capitalism and democracy has indeed come to be institutionalized in Taiwan, it must be remembered that the Taiwan experience has not exhibited the full character of Chinese nationalism, not to mention the rise of Taiwanese nationalism. In Taiwan, to an important extent, elites have been motivated to outdo the Mainland by successfully imitating the West. Mainland elites, however, have considerable interest in outdoing the West, and this cannot be done without being different from it. Nationalistic Mainland elites thus have much more of a vested interest in divergence than the Taiwan elites. Third, Westerners do not like to realize that the demonstration effect of their civilization on non-Western audiences has been deeply ambiguous. In China since World War I, a dark image of the West has increasingly competed with the earlier view, epitomized by Liang Ch'i-ch'ao's earlier writings, of the West as the world's model civilization.[7] Today, the gloomy views of Jürgen Habermas about Western modernization are often regarded as uncontroversial factual statements, whether in Taipei, Hong Kong, or Shanghai. This view in turn can easily blend in with nationalistic opposition to the leading international role of the United States.[8]

Perhaps the most striking example of this Chinese tendency radically to criticize the most basic premises and values of Western modernity is H.K.H. Woo's book, which was published in 1995. He translates its recondite title, *Tu-kung nan-shan shou Chung-kuo*, as *The West in Distress — Resurrecting Confucius's Teachings for a New Cultural Vision and Synthesis*. In its radicalness, Woo's frontal assault on the Western, especially the American pursuit of freedom and prosperity, is reminiscent of Rousseau's denunciation of science and of culture critics like Erich Heller, who used the Faust legend to argue that the modern scientific transformation of the world has turned it into a place "'so sinister ... that no one could live in it.'"[9] Where the Promethean "dynamism" (*tung*) of the West has enormously appealed to Chinese since Yen Fu (1854–1921) and Liang Ch'i-ch'ao, Woo is deeply suspicious of it.

Woo's assault is significant especially because its provenance is some of China's most Westernized, sophisticated circles. It was published by a leading university press, The Chinese University Press in Hong Kong, and is based on a research grant provided by a Hong Kong fund established in 1988 to honor Milton Friedman and managed by the Hong Kong Center for Economic Research and the Institute of Economics and Finance at the University of Hong Kong. Woo is a prominent Hong Kong entrepreneur and scholar whose many books include *Cognition, Value and Price: A General Theory of Value* (Ann Arbor: The University of Michigan Press, 1992). Most striking, his sharply reasoned assault on Western modernity is informed by not only a fervent appreciation of the Confucian approach to life but also full admiration for some of the most salient qualities of the modern West, such as its love of liberty, its intellectual openness, and its analytical prowess. Woo precisely confronts the vision of the free society classically formulated by F.A. Hayek and Karl R. Popper, expresses admiration for it, but then, instead of viewing this vision as the key to overcoming humankind's pathologies, sees it as the main cultural source of these pathologies! If even a scholar of his astuteness working in the most modern part of China is so critical of Western civilization, it is likely that many less educated, more simply xenophobic Chinese living inland far away from cosmopolitan influences can easily reject Western values.

Woo's book, then, is worth careful study because it is a significant part of the contemporary Chinese spectrum of political-cultural thought; because it indicates that a part of this spectrum resists "convergence," even entailing a denial that democracy is the only legitimate form of governance, and easily blending in with nationalistic, "New Left," and postmodernist opposition to the globally central role to which the U.S. has become accustomed; and because it is useful in our own Western search for Western and non-Western critical perspectives on the modern modes of thought we most take for granted.

Preoccupied with studying exotic cultures, we Westerners seldom remember that weighing the reactions of foreigners to what we are is one of the most valuable ways we have to obtain insight into ourselves, instead of just perpetuating ourselves as natives naively equating our cultural values with universal truth. In his introduction to Benjamin I. Schwartz's 1964 classic on Yen Fu, Louis Hartz perspicaciously stated: "It is the genius of the foreign critic to bring to the surface aspects of the thought implicit in the life of the nation he studies but explicit for him because of the contrasts supplied by his own culture."[10] Woo's understanding of the West far surpasses Yen Fu's, but, like Yen, he points to the "Faustian dynamism" of the West as its most crucial feature and seeks to find the proper evaluation of this trait. Does he appropriately describe and evaluate it?

2. Discourse #1 and Discourse #2: Woo's Assumptions about the Nature of Culture and History

Woo's thought is a version of discourse #1, discussed in chapter I above. Analyzing Western thought, Woo in effect analyzes discourse #2, attacking the very ideas Popper regarded as the essence of freedom and rationality, but Woo does so without uncovering and critically evaluating the discourse #1 assumptions on which his evaluation of discourse #2 rests. The problem of culture is a good example. While the Western discourse #2 tries to restrict its description of human life to empirically if not statistically specific statements about particular episodes, trends, or personalities, Woo, like so many Chinese scholars, perceives the main units of historical activity as huge, empirically unspecific, homogenous entities, "cultures," each of which is a "system" or "structure" permeated by a single knowable "spirit," "basic nature," or "ontologically ultimate nature" (*pen-t'i*) (8) and a process following a "logic of inner development" and historical "laws" (8, 43).

Thus he refers to "cultural systems" (*wen-hua t'i-hsi*) (167, 170), to "the structure of Western culture," to the way this "structure ... goes back to a structure which takes the atomistic individual as the center" (61), to the fact that "what permeates Western culture is the emphasis on ratiocinative intelligence (*chih-hsing*)" (52), or to "the ontologically ultimate reality behind Western culture, its cultural atomism" (8).

True, Woo recognizes the role in history of "accident," which coexists with "historical laws" (43). Moreover, he recognizes the human ability to develop a critical perspective on a culture, such as the West's own "internal critique," on which his book consciously feeds (83, 215). The rise of such a critical perspective implies that human beings who are part of a "cultural system" can, paradoxically enough, still think beyond it and perhaps even act to alter it, "making decisions as to what to select, what to discard" (*ch'ü-she*) (214, 204, xvi, 201).

Woo's emphasis, however, is on the systemic aspects of history. "Chinese culture" and "Western culture" each refers to a single mind-set that has been homogeneously internalized in many millions of persons occupying a large physical space for many centuries. This mind-set or "spirit" is a huge fact that he has somehow observed, even though many scholars would accuse him of reifying some simple ideas instead of relying on empirical data to describe historical complexities in a specific way.

Yet in his defense it might be said that, if he is guilty of misplaced concreteness, the empiricists offended by his generalizations might be guilty of a misplaced emphasis on specificness and precision. After all, Aristotle said that the degree of precision should be a function of subject matter. Woo's subject matter is basically normative and therapeutic, and his manner of generalization is not necessarily unsuited to it. At this point, I want only to describe his epistemic style, not evaluate it.

With his optimistic epistemology, Woo feels not only that he can fully understand the "ontologically ultimate reality" underlying a culture, but also that he can "objectively" compare cultures to each other and "evaluate" them as "higher or lower ... excellent or bad." He is aware that cultures are hard to compare to each other, because they are "dynamic" processes the students of which "easily confuse the part for the whole" or lapse into "subjective judgments." Nevertheless, he confidently sets up "a framework for the cross-sectional comparison and evaluation of cultures" (166, 214).

In evaluating any culture, he uses "reason as the standard" (214). This broad, uncritical use of "reason" is virtually unchallenged in Chinese circles today, though Woo astutely notes how it has been challenged in the West (141). This "objective standard" according to which cultures are "excellent" or "bad" (*yu-lieh*) "is not necessarily absolutely universal," and it should not be used to "force the layout (*fang-an*) of one culture on another people," but "to some extent it allows for comparison" (214). Thus, Woo allows for Western doubts about such evaluative frameworks without being swayed by them.

The standard revealed by reason for evaluating cultures is nature in a broad sense: "the ontologically ultimate organization of the material world, the biological world, the biosphere, the structure of the brain, the structure of language, and the structure of knowledge as we know them" (8, 54). He also describes this standard as "rationally understood factors such as human nature, social organization, and the long-term evolution of humankind" (214). Again, he is aware of the criticism that "we cannot compare biological and cultural evolution" (193), but he insists on his point: "To be sure, biological and cultural evolution will follow different laws. Yet if we grant that history develops in a cumulative way, it follows that making good use of resources developed in the past and incorporating past achievements should turn out to be the law followed by both biological and cultural evolutionary progress" (195).

To be sure, even apart from the problem of inferring "ought" from "is," this formulation conflates a norm people can choose to follow or violate with an empirical account of biological facts. The difficulties in deducing human norms from nature are formidable. For instance, how could the principle of treating another human being as an end, not a means, ever be inferred from nature's food chain? Woo urges us to "incorporate past achievements," but, as noted below, there is much disagreement about which past developments should be counted as "achievements." Again, however, my interest at this point is in describing, not evaluating Woo's premises.

Woo is thus aware that the premises of discourse #1 would be challenged in Western, discourse #2 circles, which dismiss the possibility of devising the kind of grand theory he pursues. He concedes that he cannot devise a perfect system of thought, that the Confucian outlook he depends on is only "relatively unflawed," and that his own argument is partly heuristic and just a hypothesis (xxiv, 83, 168). His dependence on discourse #1 categories, however, is not based on a critical evaluation of them. Despite a touch of epistemological pessimism, his book is filled with the confidence of epistemological optimism, the sense that he has found the theoretical key to a better future for China. Above all, agency, for him, as for so many Chinese thinkers, is overwhelmingly intellectual: "The problems discussed in this book … concern not only the future of the Chinese but also that of all humankind. In this situation at this time, we cannot again bury our heads in the sand like ostriches. It is not too late. The fate of our generation and succeeding ones will be decided by how we think about these issues" (xxv).

3. The Problem with the West

What is Woo's picture of the given world? As already noted, Woo's critique of Western culture follows in a long Chinese tradition of disillusionment with the West going back at least to Liang Ch'i-ch'ao and Sun Yat-sen around World War I.[11] Today, the idea that "alienation," "dehumanization," social disintegration, and excessive freedom are basic aspects of the modern West is widely accepted as an obvious truth by many Chinese intellectuals. In Woo's case, this Chinese endorsement of what he calls the West's "internal critique" (83) has led to an impressive grasp of the relevant Western literature, as evidenced by his bibliography, which includes works by scholars such as Kenneth Arrow, Daniel Bell, Ernest Becker, Allan Bloom, James M. Buchanan, Jürgen Habermas, William Robert Catton Jr., Paul R. Erlich, Jon Elster, Paul K. Feyerabend, Michel Foucault, Gertrude Himmelfarb, Samuel P. Huntington, Paul R. Krugman, Christopher Lasch, Alasdair MacIntyre, Jerry Mander, Herbert Marcuse, Douglass North, Robert Nozick, John Rawls, Joseph A. Tainter, Alvin Tofler, Peter Douglas Ward, and Amartya Sen, not to mention older, standard figures like Adorno, Freud, Hayek, Hegel, Heidegger, Hobbes, Hume, Kant, Kierkegaard, Locke, J.S. Mill, von Mises, Piaget, Popper, Adam Smith, Spengler, Spinoza, and Max Weber.

This is not to say that Woo, like some Western critics such as Leo Strauss, simply sees the contemporary West as enveloped in a "crisis." True, Woo would reject Alex Inkeles's provocatively optimistic and strongly argued thesis that modernization should be primarily viewed as enhancing human well-being. Indeed, when Woo turns to the problem of defining "modernization," he depends on Weber, Habermas, and Heidegger to adduce five traits all of which have ominous connotations: "the reduction of nature to mathematics and science"; "mechanistic technology and specialization"; "the withdrawal of God from human consciousness and the emphasis on human subjectivity"; "the attempt to set up a global cultural model"; and "the turning of art into emotional experience" (204–205).

Nevertheless, Woo is deeply aware that the modern Western

values which have so deeply attracted so many Chinese are not a sham, they are values he himself deeply admires. He not only admires the West for bringing forth science, the market economy, industrialization, the rule of law, and democracy but also dwells on Western superiority in developing sociological, psychological, and aesthetic analysis, in generating critical self-awareness, and in promoting those virtues implied by the ratiocinative pursuit of knowledge, such as intellectual openness and the sense of individual responsibility (189–190, 83, 7, 37, 149):

> Western culture includes not a few precious elements: it can more effectively protect the individual; it can provide us with relatively reasonable material conditions of life; it can help us more clearly understand the outer world; it can help us more deeply understand the nature of art, grasp our psychological circumstances, etc. These elements can supplement and enrich the Confucian teachings that should be at the center of our lives.

He also holds that "a set of unflawed (*wan-cheng*) Western institutions including the rule of law are needed to give support" to the social order he has in mind, one based primarily on the Confucian concept of "morality" (213). Even more, while deploring how Western culture encourages "the aggressiveness of the individual and ... fierce struggle between individuals," Woo simultaneously views the above positive features (especially the market, rule of law, democracy, and the emphasis on the pursuit of knowledge) as not only "checking" this destructive individualism but also serving as "self-regulating mechanisms" that almost enable Western culture to perpetuate itself, instead of dying out as other cultures routinely have (43, 198). Thus Woo rather precisely identifies the structure hailed by Hayek and Popper as the key to freedom and progress, one maximizing the freedom of the individual by minimizing conformity, restricting it to respect for law, for scientific knowledge, and for some very minimal, vague moral principles (e.g. Hayek's "ethos").

What then can be wrong with such a brilliant civilization? Woo's argument is that, despite its brilliance, it is "out of control" (*shih-k'ung*) and "hides within itself the seeds of its own destruction" (xxiv, 54, 212, 45, 73). Destruction is probable because its "ontologically ultimate nature" (*pen-t'i*) is incompatible with that of nature itself (8).

The West thus seems caught up in "a nightmare of evolution," a "crisis of self-destruction" (182). Therefore it is no more than "a detour in human evolution," a "tiny moment" in the long span of global history (54). Conversely, Western peoples lack a civilization in accord with the natural principles of evolution, and they lack "independence and autonomy" in that they cannot control their own destiny (212). Unable to cultivate "virtuous circles," their culture cannot achieve "pliability" and "longevity" (169). Woo skillfully explains that just about all previous Chinese scholars have assumed the fundamental desirability of modernization, arguing only about whether the Chinese tradition was compatible with it, while his book questions its desirability (216–217).

Woo's criticism, as already mentioned, resembles old Western doubts about modernization as a Faustian process violating the divine or natural order. It is also distinctively Chinese, however, in focusing precisely on that feature of the modern liberal West that has with virtually no exceptions been rejected by Chinese intellectuals as unthinkable: the tendency, endorsed by Hayek and Popper, to leave society outside the control of a dominating moral intelligence, at the mercy of free, unpredictable, "chaotic," morally and intellectually ungraded individual impulses, the free choices of individuals pursuing their own individual goals in the "three marketplaces" (economic, intellectual, and political). Vigorously rejecting this Western tendency to design society as an unpredictable marketplace rather than a morally guided, unified system, Woo seeks to analyze this chaotic tendency, figure out how Chinese can keep it out of their civilization, help the West get rid of it, and simultaneously adopt the West's desirable traits.

Woo starts with a list of points overlapping those made about the U.S. by culture critics such as Christopher Lasch. While Lasch's analysis in *The Revolt of Elites and the Betrayal of Democracy* (1995) more precisely and sensitively fits the facts of U.S. history, Woo similarly covers the phenomena of urban degradation (mental illness, substance abuse, family disintegration, teenage pregnancy and chronic welfarism, crime and the breakdown of education) (xiv, 23, 21, 42) and links these with the old discussions of anomie: "atomistic individuals" whose characters have broken down and whose world is filled with anxiety, emptiness, and the sense of being overwhelmed with death are alienated from each other, dehumanized, and doomed to lives of vapid (if financially strapped) consumerism (8, 42, 32–33, 64, 49, 73, 89).

The breakdown in education, Woo notes, citing Herrnstein and Murray's *The Bell Curve* (1994), increases economic inequality, in that it reduces the access of Blacks and others to the learning needed to become part of "the cognitive elite" (34–35). The great amount of economic inequality accompanying capitalism has long been a standard Chinese theme, and Woo emphasizes it (5). He cites the unavailability of expensive medical services to many and concludes that, in this context of "evolutionary nightmare," "people devour people" as they ruthlessly compete with each other (127–129, 77). Moreover, the buildup of huge government deficits signifies the subjection of future generations to the needs of the current ones.

His discussion of political inequality in a democracy is nothing new for Western political scientists raised on the writings of Weber and Schumpeter but a breakthrough in the non-Marxist Chinese world, where liberals like Yang Kuo-shu have long pictured democracy in an obstinately naive way as a system based on "reason" and therefore free of serious political and economic inequality. Woo would reject Samuel P. Huntington's argument that "democracy is a solution to the problem of tyranny."[12] A Robert N. Bellah or John Dunn would easily agree with Woo's claim that, in countries like the U.S., the political rights of citizens are often merely "formal," and that elites, including corrupt interest groups, dominate politics (78, 101–102, 116, 120–121). As Woo sees it, "tricky politicians" (*cheng-k'o*) unscrupulously compete for votes without considering whether the demands of the electorate are compatible with the public good, while they and their innumerable lawyers also manipulate legislation and the application of the law, turning "the rule of law" into "a system where you plot against me while I try to deceive you" (124–128).

But the big problem undermining the ideal of rule by the people is not avoidable corruption. It is structural: Western modernization has been accompanied by a huge increase in highly specialized kinds of knowledge accessible only to a minority and so forming a dominating "external entity" inherently out of the control of citizens, or, more generally, of human beings as moral subjects determining their destinies (72). This point is central to Woo's overall charge that the West's focus on the pursuit of ratiocinative understanding (*chih-hsing*) at the expense of "morality" and "spirituality" (see below) has created a civilization that is "out of control." Woo also connects political inequality to that reduction of freedom often adduced by conservatives in the U.S. objecting to the expansion of state controls over the individual (94–95, 100).

Thus citing urban degradation, anomie, economic inequality, political inequality, and the reduction of freedom, Woo develops his argument that the West's "inner logic" leads it to subvert the pursuit of its own ideals. This point, he feels, applies also to its emphasis on maximizing instrumental rationality in the "conquest of nature." On the one hand, the West has created the military means to annihilate humankind, and it pursues endless economic growth to the point of not only injuring the biosphere but also threatening to exhaust the world's natural resources (4, 45, xiv, 9, 51, 47). On the other hand, efficient economic growth is impeded by the way democratic politics, bureaucracy, and other factors divert resources away from production (124).

For Woo, this self-destructive inner logic is illustrated not only by the "unpredictable" ways in which the complex variables of technological change affect the physical environment (45) but also by other paradoxical ways in which technological progress originally intended to benefit the individual has harmed the individual. Here he cites not only that huge expansion of specialized knowledge controlled by a small elite already touched on but also "the poison of television," which, especially injuring destitute Blacks, appeals to the "lowest" part of the brain, arousing animal desires and resulting in intellectual "passivity" (21, 35, 14). Even more basically, the information revolution, including the "information superhighway," centers on "visualism" and "imagism" and so "weakens the individual's sense of self" to the extent that this sense depends on "the cultivation of the ability to think critically" (36) and on "the unceasing interaction between our memory system and the theoretical structures developed by our processes of reasoning" (12–13, 24–25, 28–34).

Internationally, the West, disseminating these deleterious tendencies, "weakens or destroys ... different cultures" (xxiv) while generating increasing global inequality and competition over resources (4, 80).

All these undesirable tendencies are regarded by Woo as integrally connected to an unacceptable state of intellectual disarray. Despite its analytical prowess and strong capacity for self-criticism, the West in Woo's eyes has been unable to figure out the nature of the premises that drive it forward on its perverse course, not to mention correcting them. Besides the moral liabilities of capitalism, he claims, the West lacks a political theory justifying the political system it is committed to, democracy. He uses the work of Kenneth Arrow to argue that the democratic accumulation of individual preferences cannot per se be the basis of government, because it cannot lead to a single consistent policy choice (115). Even if it could, he goes on, individual and mass preferences are often unwise, as Plato said (123).

Woo develops this point by objecting to the honoring of preferences when they contradict the public good. As is common in the West too, he is looking for a theory that makes the freedom of the individual completely consistent with a rational understanding and pursuit of the public good. He correctly points out that this consistency is not supplied by leading Western theories such as social contract theory, utilitarianism, and the liberalism of John Rawls, since none of them can guarantee that the free exercise of individual rights will in a rationally necessary way realize the public good. As Schumpeter long ago pointed out, "the voice of the people" is not necessarily "the voice of God." In Woo's eyes, therefore, Western democratic theory leaves society at the mercy of morally ungraded individual preferences, including the "animal feelings" aroused by television, and then, claiming there is no way objectively to grade preferences, descends into the abyss of "moral relativism" (111, 85, 216) and "positivism" (143–144). Thus in his eyes democracy has not been philosophically legitimized as a system of governance necessarily better than all others.

His criticism of "moral relativism" and "positivism" accords with how Western thinkers like Leo Strauss and Alasdair MacIntyre view the Western intellectual "crisis." Where Woo completely disagrees with them is in confidently assuming that resolution of this epistemological dilemma is a quite feasible task Western theorists could handily perform were they not so confused. His assumption stems from the tradition-rooted epistemological optimism mentioned above. For him, as for any other modern Chinese thinker I'm aware of, rational understanding of the public good is obviously attainable and should be emphasized as integral to the desirable political order.

This is clear, he claims, as soon as one grasps the objectively correct definition of "reason." The concept of reason was wrongly narrowed down in the modern West to nothing more than "an excuse for rationalizing utility and individual needs" (141) or the realm of "instrumental rationality" (133). Instead,

> three relationships should appear in the form taken by reason. The first centers on the ratiocinative understanding of the actual world (is-axis); the second refers to instrumental applications and the accumulation of resources (can-axis); the third refers to values and the choice of goals (ought-axis).... The ideal situation is when it is possible fully to attend to all three aspects.... If it is impossible to do so, attention to values should probably come first. The most basic and key factor determining whether a society can exist within the context of reason is its value system. Values come first, then attention to actual circumstances and to capabilities — this is the only way for society to enter the realm of reason. (133–134)

In other words, values defining the public good are not a matter of arbitrary individual preferences, tides of political opinion, or cultural biases. Nor do they just come down to some empirically determined set of preferences broadly shared by most people throughout the world, no matter what their culture, such as a preference for survival, efficiency in adaptation, peace, justice, morals, and freedom, to use Hayek's list.[13] Instead, the nature of the public good can be determined in a "rational" way through the reasoning of enlightened persons of good will.

Nor is this rational understanding of the public good limited to vague goals, such as peace and prosperity, or to purely formal principles, such as Kant's rule that everyone should make only those decisions which he or she would want to turn into a universal law. Woo objects to the "ontologization of morality" (160) but himself looks for moral-political principles grounded in nature, and these principles, far from being merely formal, entail substantive content determining concrete choices in political reform and cultural revision. Explicitly basing himself on "reason" (214), Woo proposes to demonstrate that the public good of the Chinese people lies in emphasizing Confucius's understanding of morality and rejecting the popular Western model of capitalism, democracy, and individualism (see below).

My point here is not that Woo's theory is correct or incorrect. I just want to note that, with his epistemological optimism, he is certain that the understanding of the public good can be derived in a rationally necessary and objective way from the universally natural conditions of human life. The Western Humean circles believing that this derivation of "ought" from "is" is impossible and thus reducing the understanding of the public good to a marketplace or "middle ground" of opinions are, in Woo's eyes, mistaken. Although these Western circles proudly see themselves as having successfully discovered the previously unnoticed limitations on the logical pursuit of knowledge, he is dismayed by what he sees as their failure to understand how to exercise reason.

Woo adds that this Western intellectual disarray also stems from the fact that Western culture critics today discuss their culture's problems only in a "one-sided, piecemeal fashion, unable to find the central point and so not easily arriving at a clear, unified outlook" (216). In other words, Woo brushes aside the common Western, anti-Hegelian claim that the proper structure of knowledge is not a grand theory illuminating all aspects of human life in a systematically unified way (*t'i-hsi*). His assumption that the proper form of knowledge is a *t'i-hsi* is basic to the epistemological optimism of discourse #1. For him, it is unthinkable that learning *should* appear as what Robert Musil called "the broken form."[14]

Woo thus pulls together a list of very serious charges, analyzing the modern West as undermining pursuit of its own ideals by generating urban degradation, psychological degradation, anomie, economic inequality, political inequality, the reduction of freedom, military inventions threatening to annihilate humankind, a mindless process of economic growth injuring the biosphere as well as exhausting the globe's natural resources, contradictions between economic efficiency and political demands, global conflict, global economic inequality, and the destruction of non-Western cultures, as well as being unable intellectually to grasp the nature of these tendencies, not to mention arresting them. Woo is well aware of the optimistic arguments that all these deficiencies are just the price that must be paid for enjoying the fruits of modernization and democracy, if not problems that can be contained or solved (29, 204). After all, as already mentioned, his book is filled with enthusiasm about basic aspects of this civilization which he simultaneously views as pathological. Thus he realizes that his argument has to be carried a step further to demonstrate that the above pathologies of the modern West are somehow decisive, that they are rooted in mistaken premises integral to the very "ontological" nature of the Western "cultural system."

Much like Yen Fu a century earlier, therefore, Woo has identified a kind of "Faustian dynamism" as the modern West's basic trait.[15] Unlike Yen Fu, however, he rejects this dynamism. Also unlike Yen Fu, he tries to reveal the cultural premises that led to it. What Woo in effect seeks to do is turn the Hayek-Popper vision of the free society on its head: instead of seeing it in their terms as a goal dynamic pursuit of which will minimize humanity's pathologies, Woo wants to portray it as the central historical premise of Western culture and the main source of Western pathologies today.

To do this, Woo brushes aside scholarly Western sources. As already mentioned, Chinese intellectuals, ever since they first confronted the Western intellectual discourse during the late nineteenth century, have habitually taken for granted two ideas: that the West furnishes them with many new views only some of which are correct, and that they are completely able to establish the correct criteria with which to assess all these views and create a new intellectual system more correct than any of these Western views. Thus Woo, constructing an allegedly universal standard of normal cultural development with which the West has been grossly out of accord, does not hesitate to depend on ideas that are commonly accepted in Chinese intellectual circles but would mostly be extremely vulnerable to criticism in Western ones. These ideas epitomize the epistemological optimism of discourse #1.

Woo never in one place sums up all the ideas he packs into his "rational" standard (214) for evaluating cultures and so only implicitly indicates the logical relations among these ideas. These seven ideas are: (1) the three aspects of "reason" just discussed (understanding of actualities, of instrumentalities, and of goals); (2) "the shared ontological organization of the material world, the biological world, the biosphere, the human brain, language, and knowledge as we understand them," along with the two norms Woo infers from this whole natural structure, "balance" (*chün-heng, p'ing-heng*) (187) and "cumulative" development (195), which naturally preclude any self-destructive "inner logic"; (3) the three aspects of the human brain — "spirituality" (*ling-hsing*), "ratiocinative thinking" (*chih-hsing*), and "the animal nature" or "sentiment" (187–188, 39–42) (compare Hayek's three, "reason," "innate desires," and the ability to create "complex cultural structures"); (4) "morality" (190, 213, 174, 171, 146); (5) the distinction between "self" and "group"; (6) that between the "inner" and the "outer" aspects of human life (172, 168); and (7) that between being preoccupied with death as a basic category of existence and not being preoccupied with it (177–179).

I would interpret Woo as logically linking these seven items by implying that the brain, with its capacity for observation and ratiocination, can establish the objective existence of these seven items, including the overarching principle of "reason" and the norms of "balance" and "cumulative development," and then can apply these two norms to all these conditions of human life. Most basically for Woo, the "rational" understanding of "goals" calls for the seeking of "balance" and "cumulative" development. The "balance" Woo throughout is most concerned with is that between "spirituality," "morality," and the "inner" on one side and, on the other, the "ratiocinative" focus on pursuing the "goals" of the "self" in the "outer" world. In other words, what nature and "reason" call for is subordinating the energetic ratiocinative pursuit of each individual's own desires to his or her "inner" cultivation of "spirituality" and "morality" and so to the morally justified needs of the group. One therefore could say that while the Hayek-Popper paradigm mixes freedom and conformity by emphasizing the former, Woo shifts the ratio toward conformity. He seeks partly to replace "outer" with "inner" freedom.

This normative vision, along with the epistemological insistence that it lacks ambiguity, is, again, integral to discourse #1, differing little in substance from either the Taipei liberalism of Yang Kuo-shu in the 1980s or the Maoism of Kao Li-k'o around 1990. (See chapters IV and VI.) All three seek a mix of doctrine and character cultivation with which to put limits on egotistic desires (*k'o-chi*). What is significant is Woo's spontaneous return to this vision after his unusually penetrating, complex, and empathetic analysis of Western civilization. Woo's thought, in other words, not only explicitly exhalts the doctrine of Confucius (*k'o-chi*) (see below) but also in its most theoretical moments depends on a concept of rational under-standing much closer to Confucian rationality than to that of the positivistic Western mainstream, which Woo indeed explicitly defies.

Given his view of the *k'o-chi* ideal as called for by reason and nature, Woo argues that the West violated it by greatly over-emphasizing the ratiocinative focus on freely pursuing the goals of the self in the outer world. Never grasping the essential *k'o-chi* ideal, the West gradually undermined the "inner," "spiritual" quest for "a kind of space and time transcending ordinary life" (39) and so undermined "morality."

In claiming that the pathologically decisive, "ontological" aspect of the West has been its way of forming the self, Woo strikes a chord deep in the soul of many Chinese. Schwartz in 1964 had analyzed Yen Fu as appreciating the importance of both the individual and the group in the culture of the West but as filtering out of his thought the Western idea that each individual has "intrinsic value" as an end in himself, since for Yen ultimate value lay only in the dynamic development of the nation.[16] In fact, as Huang Ko-wu (Max K.W. Huang) has shown, in Yen's eyes, as well as those of Liang Ch'i-ch'ao, neither the individual nor the group was more important than the other. These thinkers both had a tradition-rooted, distinctively Chinese vision of a third alternative that is common in China to this day, though it strikes many Westerners as unrealistic or utopian, namely, that the group and the individual are equally important, and that there is no conflict between the two in a rationally ordered society. This concept, again, presupposes discourse #1, the epistemologically optimistic view that there is an objectively just solution for any conflict between group and individual, that this solution can be understood and propagated, and that most people will act on it after understanding it.

Woo entirely shares this view, seeking a "balance" between self and group, and so, like Yen and Liang, rejecting not the view that the individual has "intrinsic value" but the idea that Woo places at the center of Western culture, namely, that the individual is *more* important than the group. As Huang Ko-wu has shown, Schwartz's highly influential work missed this distinction between an idea in full accord with Confucian values (that the individual has intrinsic worth) and a Western idea that modern Chinese thought has generally rejected (that the individual is more important than the group).

"The structure of Western culture," Woo writes,

> originates with a structure at the center of which is the atomistic individual entity (*tan-yuan ko-t'i*). The distinctive feature of this structure is that the

ultimate value of the whole system comes from the individual entity. Social organization is designed to satisfy the needs of this individual entity, not to prolong the existence of the group. Society itself cannot be regarded as having interests more important than those of the individual. Since the value of the individual entity is the ultimate one, the starting point of any discussion must be what benefits the individual, and the world is viewed from the standpoint of the individual. (61)

This focus on the individual, Woo goes on, necessarily implies a cultural focus on "the outer" and so an "opposition between subject and object," since the individual is led to seek gratification by "developing the space he occupies and the right to control or own part of the outer world" (64, 66). Even more, yearning for not only maximum control over worldly goods but also "eternal life" (64), the individual becomes focused on the problem of death (177–179) and carries out an "externalization of the spiritual" (180). Woo's implication is that this "externalization," taking the form of a belief in a Supreme Being external to human beings, was needed in the West to conceptualize an agency able to save one from death. (Woo here implicitly builds on Yü Ying-shih's influential argument that in Western culture, the divine has been conceptualized as "external" to the human, in Chinese culture, as "internal." Yü's point in turn built on T'ang Chün-i's.)

While the focus on the individual thus led necessarily to a focus on "the outer" and death, it also led to a one-sided emphasis on the ratiocinative faculty: "One can say that the Western emphasis on reason and rationalism revolved around the idea that the individual is at the center of all values" (64). Woo argues that putting supreme value on satisfying individual needs necessarily brings to the fore material desires regarding "outer," material things, and that the control of outer things can be accomplished only through ratiocination, not through spirituality. This alliance between ratiocination and material desire undermined the third faculty of the brain, that able to cultivate spirituality and morality, Woo holds.

Moreover, while the "balance" between the brain's faculties was lost, the emphasis on ratiocination eventually violated the evolutionary principle of "cumulative," "gradualistic" development. That is, "Western individualism and openness encouraged innovation. The West's cultural emphasis on ratiocination led unceasingly to the creation of novelties satisfying the desires of the individual.

This strategy of change, aiming to restructure the environment rather than adapt to it, led the Western economy to go speedily down the path of short-term profits, satisfying present needs by borrowing on resources needed in the future" (44–45).

In Woo's eyes, then, this Western focus on the self, the outer, and ratiocination violated the natural principles of "balance" and "cumulative" development and so led to the contemporary pathologies described above. Admittedly, if one wants specific historical answers to the question of just when this Western focus emerged and just how it caused the modern pathologies, Woo's account furnishes only hints. Seeing Western culture as a systemic whole, he cannot avoid implying that, in some way, Socrates and Jesus are responsible for drug addiction in New York today. He certainly has no strong reply to those like Strauss and MacIntyre who prefer to blame such pathologies on later European intellectual trends rather than the logic of the West as a whole.

Yet one cannot say Woo's thesis necessarily lacks a shred of plausibility. He grants that the Western syndrome he is concerned with was greatly aggravated by the advent of science and industrialization, but he sees an early inclination toward it in the ancient religious "affirmation of the value of the individual"; the "yearning for eternal life"; the invention of the alphabet, which facilitated the development of abstract thinking (64–65); and the early emphasis on property rights and commerce. Thus he sees the Western focus on ratiocination as continuous throughout Western history and as responsible for not only science and industrialization, along with their unintended consequences, but also the intellectual disarray of the modern West.

This disarray was created as the relentless progress of ratiocination stripped away the "smoke screen" or "lies" needed to support the spiritual idea of a "space and time transcending ordinary life" (39–40, 53). Modern technology has been intertwined with a "ratiocinative culture which.... relies on a distinctive mode of reasoning, a highly logical language of science, a kind of outlook that rejects 'unscientific' reasoning" (204). Similarly, although positivism today has been refuted in Western philosophical circles, Woo says, it still reigns in the Western world of the humanities and the social sciences, since it accords with the ideology of "instrumental rationality constituting the deep structure of Western culture." From this positivistic viewpoint, "only evidence that can be observed is evidence." In fact, though, as Confucius saw, "the things and phenomena of the world are actually controlled by factors that cannot be seen or tangibly encountered.... moral factors" (144–146). Thus while Western culture has placed morality outside the validating framework of "reason," it has also precluded intellectually respectable reference to the invisible spiritual sources of morality. Hence the rise of "moral relativism," which, in Woo's eyes, contradicts the nature of morality. This "rationalistic," "atomistic" mind-set, "permeating the whole of Western culture, the unconscious of every Western person, her sense of morality, her concept of right and wrong" (64), thus blocks rational understanding of those "inner," "spiritual," "moral" aspects of human life that actually determine the course of events. "Reason," as Woo sees it, was undermined by "ratiocination."

Woo's thesis inherently refutes a major objection to it, much as Freudianism can dismiss any objection to it as "resistance." In Woo's eyes, the epistemologically pessimistic claim that his thesis about the West is not adequately supported by specific empirical evidence merely reflects the erroneous empiricism and positivism at the heart of the West's current intellectual disarray — its inability to grasp the cultural logic that clearly underlies a great variety of phenomena, its unwillingness to draw conclusions from mountains of evidence. To a large extent, then, Woo's analysis can succeed only to the extent that one accepts his assumptions about the nature in general of history, culture, and knowledge (discourse #1).

4. The Problem with China

As already indicated, the idea that Chinese culture was pathological from the start while Western culture was normal goes back at least to Liang Ch'i-ch'ao's famous *Hsin-min-shuo* (1902–1903) and is still influential.[17] Woo, however, argues exactly the reverse: China's pathologies, unlike the Western ones, do not stem from the systemic nature of its culture. They were secondary from the start and became grave only as a result of Western influence. The primordial source of serious pathology in the world is Western, not Chinese. This thesis is an unusual if not unique one in the history of Chinese thought after Chang Chih-tung.

Referring to the universally normative framework described above as violated by Western culture, Woo argues that the thought of Confucius was to a large extent in accord with it. "To be sure," Woo says, "the doctrine of Confucius did not directly touch on the theory of rationality. Moreover, from the standpoint of the social realities of his day, it certainly did not find a balance between the three dimensions of reason (ought, is, and can). Yet on different levels it did touch on the concept of reason and approach this ideal of balance" (134). Most important, it properly emphasized "spirituality," "morality," and the "inner" (188, 213). Woo, like many other modern Chinese writers, is particularly eloquent in explaining how Confucius sought a kind of self-realization free of any anxious dependence on outer success. Much like Admiral Jim Stockdale's Stoic philosophy, the Confucian doctrine, as Woo, justifiably I believe, celebrates it, emphasizes that "an individual can only try to do what he himself is responsible for," that he should concentrate his efforts on "those matters within the scope of what he can control," thus trying to perfect his own character (118–119).[18] Such an individual is not going to be preoccupied with maximizing his ratiocinative understanding of physical nature, his control over the outer world, and his understanding of what happens after death.

To be sure, Woo rejects only the excesses of the West, not all of its emphasis on ratiocination. Therefore he does not claim Confucius fully realized the balance between the "inner," "spiritual," "moral" side of life and the ratiocinative side. Nevertheless, Woo claims that the "practicalness" (*shih-yung*) of Confucius's thought enables it "subtly to resolve many of the contradictions in human life, to find the point of balance between different goals and ideals" (155). It is "relatively flawless. Even when mistaken, it tends toward moderation" (213). (This is similar to Li Tse-hou's view.)

This outlook, Woo says, greatly influenced Chinese civilization as a whole. Partly, he suggests, this may have been due to the lack of factors in Chinese history that could have tempted the Chinese people to stray down the pathological path of the West: China remained without an alphabet, science, and elections (xv).

The pathologies that arose, therefore, were serious but secondary. Woo admits that "The doctrine of Confucius is definitely not the same as Confucianism.... The history of Chinese culture is the history of alienation from the doctrine of Confucius" (xxiv, 173–

174). Confucius's view of ritual could easily turn into empty "formalism" and an emphasis on hierarchy. Another early problem was Mencius's over-idealization of Confucius. Then came the "ontologization of morality" with the *Doctrine of the Mean* and the *Great Learning*, followed by the devising of "metaphysical systems," increasingly leading to "dogmatism" and "ideology." There also were the problems of politicization and careerism. Hence all the decadence with which China encountered the West (121, 159–160).

Yet China, unlike the West, had started with a way of thinking fundamentally in accord with the universal norms of social evolution. Moreover, despite the later pathologies, Woo repeatedly makes clear, this "sublime, profound vision of morality" continued to inform Chinese culture to a large extent down to modern times (161, 113, 135, 168, 171–172, 149, 155, 157).

In modern times, however, Chinese culture became infected by the West, and its pathologies became so serious that they threatened to destroy its originally sound structure. After the Opium War, "Chinese culture continuously retreated," especially after a good number of intellectuals concluded that cultural revision could not be carried out by "discarding something here, putting in something there," since "a culture is rather like an organic whole" (200–201). True, this retreat was not entirely unsuccessful. Woo admits that the rise of "Asia's four little dragons caused the whole world to look at the economic performance of Confucian societies with new respect, utterly surprised that the Confucian ethical tradition, which seemingly did not support materialism, should turn out to be a factor encouraging economic development" (xiii).

Woo, however, brushes aside this Chinese success in combining Confucian ethics with certain modern forms. "I believe," he writes, that this development "can be sustained only for a short period. In the long term, these Confucian elements will be replaced by the individualistic values of modernization" (xiii). While he thus brushes aside Taiwan's success in economic modernization as ephemeral, Woo with immaculate logic utterly ignores Taiwan's successful democratization, since in his eyes it signifies nothing more than the pathologies of democracy his book dwells on (200).

In other words, celebrating Chinese culture as superior to Western culture hardly means taking a positive view of China's actual nature during the last century. Like virtually all contemporary

Chinese intellectuals, Woo has a "sense of predicament" defining China's failures during the last century as the essence of the situation, its successes, as epiphenomenal.[19] What he seeks to portray is a current global disaster. Underlying it are elusive values east and west the synthesis of which can turn disaster into a wondrous success. The West has used a mix of admirable and pathological traits to seize the center of world power and is "out of control," while China wallows in the periphery graced by a boundless potential that has almost been extinguished.

In Woo's eyes, the infection of China by the West was facilitated by the intellectual failure of Chinese to understand how revision of their culture should be carried out. Marxism per se was not the culprit. Woo's book is curiously free of any sense of outrage directed against the horrors of Maoism. He regards Marxism as erroneous but focuses his criticism on the iconclastic May Fourth Movement, which, including Marxism, started around World War I and has ever since remained at the center of the Chinese intellectuals' moral imagination. Woo charges that this movement not only undermined confidence in Confucian values and failed to grasp the dark side of modernization but also failed to understand the admirable aspects of the West. It failed to grasp how, in the Western model of modernization, the aggressive assertion of selfish interests is "checked" by a complex set of "mechanisms" — the market, the law, democracy, and the intellectual tradition — that cannot be quickly developed (198–199, 216). As a result of this Chinese mix of ignorance and destructive iconoclasm, selfishness in modern China could assert itself unchecked by either these mechanisms or the old constraints of religion and morality.

Westernizing in this way, then, the Chinese brought about "a culture muddling together Chinese and Western traits" in the worst possible way: "Why must we adopt the worst of the West, fail to adopt its relative good points? Why must we discard our own best points and just perpetuate our deficiencies?" (203). Given these deficiencies, Chinese today are "incomparably selfish and preoccupied with empty ostentation," their leaders are corrupt and incapable, and so "it is clear that the Chinese nation faces a crisis of decline and imminent destruction." Even more, nothing has yet been done to deal with this crisis. The Chinese are like a ship lost at sea, unable to turn back, uncertain of how to reach land. Oscillating between "arrogance" and

a "sense of inferiority," they are "constantly trapped in contradictions, advancing and retreating without any rational basis for their
action" (202–204, 218). The suggestion is that while all societies have
problems, China's are exceptionally grave and frightening.

Yet China is like a temporarily crippled superman. Woo like
many Chinese intellectuals believes the Chinese have the
extraordinary ability to understand and discard all the "bad" aspects
of their culture and the West and thus help all humankind realize an
ideal culture combining all cultures' "good" aspects and never before
realized in history. In other words, China has a great "power" it has
not yet learned to use:

> The still more fearful result is that what sustains the power of our nation,
> our identification with Chinese culture, has already been eroded by
> Chinese-style-Westernization to the point of being a total mess. The
> consumerism, egoism, unprincipled competition, and contempt for
> history and culture brought about by modernization have caused us to
> become numb and apathetic, caused us to forget our own culture's unique
> and excellent points and blindly to take Western standards as our own,
> Western values as our own. (203–204)

5. Saving China and the West: The Question of Agency

Facing a systemically pathological Western culture "out of control"
and a systemically sound Chinese culture in a state of disastrous
decline, Woo has the transformative goal of synthesizing the best of
China and the West to replace the current Chinese synthesis of their
worst aspects. Most important, he wants to check the currently
"unlimited expansion of 'externalization'" under the sponsorship of
Western culture, restoring humanity's "independence and autonomy" by eliminating the power of that huge "external entity" made
up of specialized knowledge resources accessible only to a small elite
using them to control popular opinion and values. "How," he asks,

> can we strengthen inner resources to check this external entity's influence
> and tendency to be out of control? To attain this goal, we lack any means
> but relying on the establishment and development of the individual's
> moral nature (with the teachings of Confucius as the basis) and spirituality
> (Buddhism) so as to enlarge the space within the individual's mind, once
> more shifting the value of life into the individual's inner world ...

To do this, Woo proposes a doctrine called "An Expanded Version of the Thought of Confucius," "synthesizing (*jung-ho*) [the wisdom of Confucius] with the best of Western and Buddhist culture" (212–214).

Such indeed has been the standard goal of modern Chinese thought, bringing together into one coherent system (*hui-t'ung*) all the truths of "the ancient world and the modern, the Chinese and the foreign." Any such synthesis, however, has always been criticized either for losing connection with the Chinese heritage or for failing to convince Chinese they should value this heritage as they eagerly seek the rewards of Westernization. Woo is painfully aware of the latter criticism. He knows he has to reverse the current outlook of most Chinese, who are attracted by Western modernity and are "filled with doubt" about the value of their own heritage (xi). He hopes he can convince them by demonstrating how pathological and dangerous is that modernity they so admire, and how Confucius's principles accord with the natural order. He is not optimistic he can succeed, in effect granting that human nature is perversely driven by material desires toward preoccupation with the outer — a tradition-rooted point close indeed to the Western idea of original sin. As he sees it, Chinese crave the very modernization and democratization that will doom them. In his cosmology, then, the natural order includes a powerful force tending to violate it, but, unlike Kant or Hegel, he does not try to account for this paradox. Ultimately, his concept of agency depends on "a cultivation of the sense of morality and of cooperation that must begin early in the life of the individual." This can be done through an education informed by the proper doctrine, and, if social, political, economic conditions are stable, he argues, "virtuous circles" can begin to appear (169).

Most important, like many other Chinese thinkers, including Sun Yat-sen, who always sought to "save China, save the world," Woo addresses his argument not just to China but to "humankind": "Theoretically speaking, the teachings of Confucius actually can rectify the shortcomings of the West's modern culture" (210, xviii).

Like the Neo-Confucian vision in late Chinese imperial times, then, this hopeful vision of world transformation is combined with a sense of predicament. Even more, Neo-Confucians at least could believe that their efforts to clear away false doctrines and morally awake humankind might be facilitated by the appearance of a "sincere" emperor, who would have enormous influence over the world. Similarly, their followers in the twentieth century, the New Confucians, saw the latent "power" of "Chinese culture" as turning into a historical "tide" that would eventually bring China into an era of morality and reason. Other Chinese had long seen democracy and modernization as such a "tide" bringing hope to China. In Woo's conception of agency, however, intellectual discussion and individual moral efforts are unsupported by either history or hope in the advent of a morally inspired political center. On the contrary, he sees Western modernization as a historical tide moving against him at least for the immediate future, before the West's eventual doom. In Woo's eyes, therefore, the forces currently available to realize humanity's goals are even more outmatched and elusive than in the Neo-Confucian worldview. The utopian character of modern Chinese optimism is epitomized by the way this optimism has evaporated in the mind of this sophisticated observer of all the recent vigorous efforts to modernize and democratize in Taiwan and China. From the utopian point of view basic to discourse #1, the achievements of China and Taiwan in recent times are utterly unimpressive. Indeed, utopianism and "the sense of predicament" are two sides of the same coin.

6. Woo's Thought in Historical Perspective

Woo's argument, therefore, falls well within the scope of that modern Chinese discourse which, labeled discourse #1, has been common to all the leading modern Chinese ideologies. Therefore it is out of accord with discourse #2, the categories regarded as veridical by the prominent if not mainstream Western intellectual circles revolving around positivism. This can be seen by contrasting Woo's conceptualization of the goal of contemporary Chinese life, of knowledge, of history, and of agency with the corresponding ideas familiar to "us" who accept discourse #2.

In thinking of our goal, for instance, "we" would think it rational for Chinese to worry mainly about how to develop China economically and politically, but Woo — like Li Tse-hou — wants to address the global human condition. We would want empirically to identify current trends affecting China, such as the trends toward convergence and divergence discussed above, and then seek practicably to accept or revise them. Woo insists on a structural transformation of two vast, complex cultures, wanting to "resurrect" values in them that are either elusive or easily perverted, synthesize these values, and then discard all other aspects of the two cultures. Woo claims his approach is "gradualistic." Actually, instead of gradualistically building on existing trends in an accommodative, Burkean way, he seeks a transformation eradicating existing Western trends that, he claims, violate the natural law of gradualistic development. For him, except for a latent spirit that has almost been extinguished, there are no values or institutions existing in China or Taiwan today worth building on. That is indeed an amazingly gloomy judgment epitomizing "the sense of predicament."

"We" would not imagine that China will turn into a society generally free of immorality and conflicting interests, but Woo without qualification endorses the Confucian goal of bringing political morality up to the highest level of personal morality (*nei-sheng wai-wang*). Without discussion, he brushes aside the mainstream Western view, from Aristotle through Max Weber, that this political goal is impracticable (171–172, 146, 113). More precisely, he seems unaware of it. He thus juxtaposes a morally disastrous present with a utopian culture synthesizing only the best of east and west, while we juxtapose the mixed record of a developing society with the hope of further imperfect development.

With regard to the conceptualization of knowledge, our positivistic discourse #2, as Woo recognizes, narrows down the concept of reason to logic and denies that logic by itself can define the public good. Woo's discourse #1, however, insists reason can define the public good, can be used to compare and evaluate different cultures, and can resolve any conflicts between self and group. We ground the public good in empirical human preferences, whether individual preferences, opinion trends, cultural biases, or goods like health and prosperity apparently preferred by almost everybody in the world. Woo's discourse #1, however, grounds norms in the universal principles of nature. His norms, therefore, are indisputable absolutes, unlike ours. Discourse #2 restricts the concrete objects of knowledge to empirically verifiable phenomena, but Woo's discourse #1 can grasp the "ontological," underlying "structure" of nature or a culture. We derive the concept of political practicability from the a posteriori study of history. Woo derives it from his "rational" understanding of underlying or elusive cultural tendencies that human beings inherently should be able to control and rearrange, even if they have never historically displayed this ability. Our discourse #2 denies that all learning can be turned into a single, systematic philosophical system (*t'i-hsi*). Woo's discourse #1 seeks to present such a system synthesizing aspects of Western culture, Buddhism, and Confucian learning.

With regard to the conceptualization of the given world, our discourse #2 posits the existence of empirically verified events and trends, what Hayek called a mix of regularities and irregularities, and many of us doubt that a vast civilization like China or the West is a "system" "permeated" by a core set of values. Woo's version of discourse #1, however, assumes that such systems exist, and that the "ontological organization" of each can be known, as discussed in section 2 above. Our discourse #2 sees history as a mix of patterns and particularities the goodness or badness of which are the subject of argument. Woo's discourse #1, however, posits a black-and-white contrast between a morally disastrous present throughout the world and a historically immanent but underlying, elusive set of objectively good attitudes. Discourse #1 has often defined these good attitudes as forming a powerful "tide" in the contemporary world (*shih-chieh-te ch'ao-liu*), but this hopeful teleological idea is omitted by Woo, as already mentioned. In his eyes, the current global "tide" of modernization and convergence is pathological.

With regard to agency, discourse #1 focuses on the intellectual identification and propagation of these historically immanent, elusive attitudes, while discourse #2 oscillates more pragmatically between intellectualistic concepts of agency and reliance on more immediately efficacious kinds of political or economic action, such as changes in the fiscal system or efforts to build up the civil society. There is a fairly close match between the modest, un-utopian goal of gradual, piecemeal progress and the concept of agency in discourse #2, but there is a drastic incongruence between the goal of world transformation and the fragile forces of progress envisaged in discourse #1.

If Woo's outlook is part of a culturally distinctive intellectual mainstream in twentieth-century China, however, it differs from a major part of this Chinese mainstream in the way it locates those underlying good cultural resources in world history that intellectuals should bring to the fore. Unlike the many Chinese who located them largely in the West, Woo follows a view going back at least to Cheng Kuan-ying (1842–1923). According to this view, human reality is divided into two realms: the "inner" realm, closely connected to "the true moral way" (*tao*), and the "outer" realm, the medium for "tools and concrete things" (*ch'i*). Like Chang Chih-tung, Cheng held that China excelled in understanding "the inner," while the West excelled in understanding the "outer." Thus in his eyes, the Chinese task in the present was to unite both these understandings and so create a society surpassing both traditional China and the contemporary West. The New Confucian school, rising after World War II, also had this standard view, and Woo follows in their footsteps. Indeed, Woo's way of contrasting Chinese with Western culture is close to that of T'ang Chün-i or Liang Shu-ming and reflects the increasing influence of the New Confucian outlook in contemporary Chinese circles.

But Woo correctly sees himself as going beyond the New Confucians in depicting the pathologies of the West, since, unlike them, he not only deplores alienation and dehumanization in the West but even questions the very values of science, democracy, and modernization. The revered New Confucian Hsu Fu-kuan had proclaimed in the 1950s that democratization would cure all the public ills with which Chinese had been afflicted throughout their history. Woo struck a new note in modern Chinese thought by tapping into a rich Western literature showing how the concrete functioning of democracy has failed to realize government by the governed. Questioning the value of the Western ability to control "the outer," Woo even rejected that Western dynamism (*tung*) admired by virtually all Chinese intellectuals since Yen Fu and Liang Ch'i-ch'ao.

Yet in rejecting the West's dynamism and its way of controlling "the outer," Woo did not entirely diverge from the views of Yen Fu, Liang, and Cheng Kuan-ying. What Woo rejected was the way in which the West was "out of control." As already mentioned, he thus rejected something that Chinese thinkers in the last century have virtually all rejected — the idea of a society outside the control of a guiding moral intelligence and at the mercy of morally and intellectually ungraded individual preferences freely competing in the economic, intellectual, and political marketplaces. In one way or another, Chinese admirers of Western dynamism had all seen it as leading to the rule of "morality" and "reason." As Schwartz wrote, Yen Fu envisioned dynamism as leading to a kind of moral equilibrium fully realizing all values. Thus the Chinese admiration of Western dynamism typically evaded endorsement of that central Western model of the free society conceptualized by Hayek and Popper. What Woo strikingly did was to make that evasion explicit, disconnecting the Chinese picture of Western dynamism from that moral equilibrium which virtually all modern Chinese thinkers have viewed as the necessary goal of political development. He demonized Western dynamism, turning the most precious ideals of Western liberalism into the sources of pathology. Thus he expressed a Chinese tendency to attenuate convergence with the West, even to the point of casting doubt on the central ideals of the widely revered May Fourth Movement, science and democracy.

True, his argument is part of an intellectual discourse that has always been different from the more practical views of the less intellectual Chinese strata. Their fascination with the "outer" values of material well-being is not about to decline. This difference perpetuates the old Chinese tension between intellectual idealists and the *hsiao-shih-min* (petty bourgeoisie) and others preoccupied with the material well-being and happiness of their families. What must be remembered, however, is that the latter strata, which typically dismiss scholarly hair-splitting as irrelevant to their concerns, have never in Chinese history formed a sovereign political center. They lack a vocabulary rising above their private interests and defining an overarching, morally justified public structure of authority. Moreover, for more than two thousand years, they have been accustomed to leaving the erection of this structure to that elite minority using such a vocabulary to express society's interests and aspirations. Therefore the intellectual discourse in which Woo is participating is still a causatively important aspect of Chinese history, just as it was when it gave birth to Maoism.

At the same time, the complex current Chinese discourse consists not only of this counterpoint between highly intellectual analyses and the culture of the small property-holders, urban and rural, seeking primarily peace and prosperity. As already indicated, the intellectual belief that current Western international dominance is just a minor historical detour feeds into the nationalistic views expressed in the 1996 bestseller *China Can Say "No!"* This book also dwells on the internal weaknesses of the U.S., the deficiencies of its culture, society, and economy. Unlike Woo's, however, it is primarily animated by feelings of outrage directed against the U.S.'s international posture as a "terroristic nation" arrogantly dispatching its military forces to all corners of the globe. From this popular nationalistic point of view, the issue is not so much how to revise Chinese culture by resisting convergence with the West as it is how to design an international alliance between China, Russia, and other countries in order to eject the U.S. from the western Pacific, destroy its world leadership role, and so wrest control from it over the world's seemingly diminishing natural resources, notably those in the Middle East. There is, then, a central geopolitical issue here outside the scope of Woo's book, the reluctance of many Chinese to accept the basic U.S. strategy inherited from the British empire, that of maintaining a maritime belt of political power stretching from east Asia to the Suez Canal and western Europe in order to contain Eurasia and ensure world peace. For many Chinese, the role of the U.S. as the leader of the "world system" is not necessarily more palatable than the British empire was. The leaders of other nations, Japan or Great Britain, say, seem content to play second fiddle to the U.S. China's leaders, however, are uneasy playing second fiddle to any other nation.

A single desire, therefore, repeatedly expressed by the common saying *hou-lai chü-shang* (the one who develops his talents later and currently still occupies an inferior position will eventually occupy the superior position), animates both Chinese nationalism and the central Chinese intellectual search for a new philosophical synthesis with which to solve the problems that defeated all Western thinkers and so to create "a new civilization" "transcending the West."

Mainstream Americans see themselves not as an empire but as "the world's greatest nation." It is a fact, at least in our eyes, that we have helped one society after another achieve prosperity and freedom, even former enemies. We thus see ourselves as embodying a new political rationality that all the world, sooner or later, is bound to accept. That is, following scholars like Hayek, Popper, Friedman, and Inkeles, many of us believe that people, whatever their culture, are in general psychologically constituted to prefer prosperity and freedom and use reason to pursue them. Since we see ourselves erecting a multicultural world system offering prosperity and freedom to all, we cannot understand how any nation can rationally refuse to join it. Indeed, the ideology of the U.S.'s global leadership role coincides with rational choice theory.

Yet even if there is such a universal algorism, to what extent can it be practically applied to resolve the inter- and intra-cultural disagreements people face? To what extent are people facing them guided by disparate ways of reasoning each shared only by a limited population? To what extent can this algorism resolve the disagreement about capitalism and democracy between Milton Friedman and the Hong Kong scholar whose research was subsidized by a fund established in Friedman's name? To what extent can it be used to prove to the authors of *China Can Say "No!"* that the world system we Americans believe in has benefited societies like Japan or Taiwan? They see the world system as designed to benefit the West at the expense of China, while H.K.H. Woo sees it as a Western culture dynamically defying the laws of nature and destroying Chinese culture.

In these Chinese minds, the rational analysis of the facts leads to conclusions contradicting those we mainstream Americans feel are rationally justified. Even more, just as the followers of Hayek and Popper think they can correct the thinking of Chinese still pursuing discourse #1, so do such Chinese, including H.K.H. Woo, believe they can help the West rectify its thinking. This historically concrete contradiction between the views of two groups each believing in its rationality is partly different from an intracultural dispute, such as that today in the U.S. regarding abortion. In the case of both intra- and intercultural disputes, the disputants see each other as irrational; the claim that people should make "rational" decisions cannot by itself resolve their dispute; and the thesis that they in fact do rationally pursue their interests is of limited use in describing or predicting their behavior. The intercultural case is distinctive, it would seem, in that there is still less agreement on the content of rationality, i.e. the rules of successful discourse defining the veridical nature of the goal of life, knowledge, the given world, and agency. To the extent that the rational pursuit of interests requires evaluations of events (e.g. Taiwan's development is good) and ideas about how they were historically caused (e.g. it was caused by Taiwan's joining the world system), the idea that people rationally pursue their interests cannot denote a kind of homogeneous action or algorism. As Hayek said, following Hume, the "opinions" of people define their "interests," and these opinions often diverge, because there is no recognized algorism for evaluating events, ascertaining their historical causes, and so devising recommendations for action in the present.

Convergence, then, is a major tendency in the world today, but so is divergence, abetted as it is by incongruent ways of reasoning as well as nationalistic passions. Nevertheless, ideas about what makes sense seem to be susceptible to argument in international as well as domestic arenas. The active intervention of reasoning people in history is needed to promote the kind of convergence that is most likely to benefit humanity. At the very least, the impulse to execute such an intervention seems integral either to universal human nature or to the kind of "axial" culture exemplified by both China and the West.

7. Woo's Response to Metzger's Criticisms

The original version of the above included criticisms of Mr. Woo's thesis omitted here. After my article was published in 1997, Mr. Woo responded to it by reaffirming both the substance of his thesis and the methodology he had used. His reaffirmation serves as further evidence that Chinese carrying on discourse #1 include not only those naively unaware of how it has been contradicted by the GMWER but also astute scholars of great intellectual integrity reaffirming discourse #1 premises while critically aware of the questions about these premises raised by the GMWER.

Woo, accepting an invitation extended by the editor of *American Journal of Chinese Studies*, published a rebuttal of my critique (*American Journal of Chinese Studies* 4 [October 1997]: pp. 253–263). A shortened version of my critique along with his rebuttal were then published in Chinese by a journal sponsored by Lanchow University (*She-hui, ching-chi, k'o-hsueh* 15 [December 1997]: pp. 10–27, 9; ibid. 16 [March 1998]: pp. 16–22). Woo and I also spent a most pleasant evening together in Hong Kong in July 1998 and exchanged a number of letters, including my attempt on November 27, 1998 to sum up his position and his critique of this attempt, which he sent off on December 11, 1998. Moreover, in late 1998, Mr. Woo kindly sent me a draft of his new book, *Tu-tiao han-chiang-hsueh* (Alone amidst Cold and Snow Fishing in the River), a sequel to the one I had reviewed. It completely reaffirms the argument in his previous book, seeking to support it with a grand theory of human history.

According to this theory, the way "Western culture" has dealt with the variety of "contradictions" inherent in the universal human condition has created ecological and other conditions that, if unchecked, will end up catastrophically in the unspecified future. The combination of these "contradictions" and the "hazards" to which they have led constitutes the heart of his thesis. Conversely, Confucius showed how these contradictions could be successfully managed, especially by cultivating a more spiritual personality less focused on the direct, "outer" pursuit of immediate self-interest. Therefore, by applying largely Confucian principles, humankind should create a "new culture" shifting the focus of people onto what benefits them in the long term.

To create this new culture, people must employ patterns of not only governance but also moral education. With regard to governance, they must gradually dismantle the capitalistic engines of unchecked economic growth, especially the current legal structure of corporations, and must minimize abuses of the legal and electoral systems. This requires maximally replacing the fortuitous outcomes of elections with knowledge-based decisions and politics with administration. These steps, combined with the emphasis on moral education, can both "protect the individual from being oppressed by society" and "protect society from being injured by the irrational activities of individuals." Woo notes that Western culture has pursued the former goal effectively but not the latter, failing especially to check the excesses of free enterprise.

This political theory fully accords with most of the categories of discourse #1. Instead of building on currently inherited cultural-political patterns in an accommodative, Burkean way, Woo seeks, albeit gradually, to enact a cultural transformation by appealing to an enlightened elite. They should propagate a doctrine — "An Expanded Version of the Teachings of Confucius" — contradicting currently prevalent cultural trends and reducing human selfishness. Human beings would thus become more morally sensitive and intellectually capable than they have been throughout history so far.

This cultural transformation is possible not only because

humanity is extremely malleable but also because intellectuals can rationally obtain the objective knowledge justifying this transformation. Dealing with "ought" as well as "is," this knowledge is about the universal nature of human nature, the essential structure of Chinese and Western culture, history's "long-term realities" or "great realities," and the nature of the Confucian norms with which people can alter these "great realities" and so avoid or at least postpone global catastrophe. Using this knowledge to reform education and governance, people will put what I call "thick parameters" on the freedoms of the economic and political marketplaces, if not the intellectual marketplace as well.

This transformation should be pursued, Woo holds, even if it seems impracticable and unpopular, but he is virtually certain that it will not be — hence the title of his book, taken from a poem that was written by Liu Tsung-yuan (A.D. 773–819), and the poignancy of which is lost in translation. Admittedly, with this pessimism, Woo diverges from discourse #1, most versions of which posit a cosmic, cultural, or historical "force" (*li-liang*) supporting the struggle of the enlightened elite to reform the world. For Woo, history supplies not only humanity's objective moral mission but also reasons for despair.

Mr. Woo does not deny his outlook at least partly resembles discourse #1, and he does not hesitate to admit it might suffer from some lapses in logic or inaccuracies. Objecting to my critique of his views, however, he holds that his degree of epistemological optimism should not be confused with any "naive" belief in the total knowability of the world. Emphasizing the difference between his "sophisticated epistemological optimism" and the "naive epistemological optimism" of "most" Chinese thought, he holds that he has not been influenced by the latter and instead has developed a rationally justified epistemology.

According to it, he holds, the extent of the world's knowability is a major issue, and knowledge can be gained only step-by-step. Nevertheless, the knowledge that can be rationally derived from the facts of human cognition and evolution includes objective knowledge with which to select norms, not only knowledge about the observable events referred to in scientific experimentation. Normative ideas can also be rationally evaluated in some other ways, especially by assessing "the epistemic opportunity cost incurred in holding a certain normative view." Woo apparently believes that such an evaluation of a normative view can be objectively carried out without depending on any alogical, purely subjective belief held by a historical individual or group.

While this "sophisticated epistemological optimism" is very different from the prevalent forms of "naive" Chinese epistemological optimism, my description of which Woo accepted, it also differs in his eyes from epistemological pessimism, a position he rejects as "flawed": "This view is incompatible with the laws of cognition and evolution, apart from the tensions and paradoxes inherent in the view."

In making these distinctions between different kinds of epistemologies, however, Woo deliberately substitutes his definition of epistemological pessimism for mine. In terms of mine, Karl Popper's reduction of objective knowledge to scientific, falsifiable "conjectures" is a classic case of epistemological pessimism. In terms of Woo's, Popper was epistemologically optimistic. Woo recognizes that, from the standpoint of Popper's cautious definition of objective knowledge, norms are based only on "beliefs," and there is no objective knowledge with which to establish them. For Woo, however, Popper did not seriously arrive at this pessimistic conclusion putting norms outside the scope of objective knowledge. Instead, optimistically and correctly affirming the possibility of objective knowledge, Popper simply failed to understand what Woo understood, that there is knowledge with which to establish "the partial objectivity of normative statements."

In all these discussions with Woo, he was at least as analytical as I, but we were unable to arrive at a meeting of the minds. Most basically, he rejected my effort to separate the task of describing ideas defining knowledge from that of evaluating these epistemological ideas. In this regard, he held to an epistemologically optimistic view that there is a readily available way to evaluate the different versions of epistemological optimism and epistemological pessimism, determining which is the most rational. Conversely, he rejected my epistemologically pessimistic view about this problem of evaluation, especially my view that epistemological optimism and pessimism are both unavoidable ingredients of all human thinking; that the proper mix of them is an unsolved problem; that resolution of it may be a matter of making a judgment rather than finding a truth; and that a useful way to resolve it is critically to compare different historical ways of mixing these two modes.

True, he granted that evaluating epistemological positions is difficult. Believing that such evaluation requires a meta-cultural, neutral, algorismic standard, however, he rejected my suggestion that such a standard might well be unavailable. Thus, he rejected my effort to devise a way of evaluating epistemologies without depending on such a standard. He held that thus to separate the task of description from that of evaluation was to try to avoid evaluation — an "escapist" position. In other words, he rejected what Richard J. Bernstein or John Dunn would call the search for a "middle ground" between "relativism" and "objectivism." We also disagreed about whether he was successful in using his optimistic concept of knowledge to develop a grand normative theory of Chinese and Western history.

All in all, our disagreement can be seen as either a clash between two historical ways of defining rationality (i.e. the indisputable) or a disagreement about who has misunderstood what. This ambiguous nature of our disagreement, I believe, reflects the very nature of human discourse as an indeterminate mix of historical premises and reflexivity (see chapter I). Recently, he graciously joined in a request that I provide a preface for a volume of his collected writings published by the Lanchow University Press. While my preface outlined our areas of agreement and disagreement, his in general terms expressed his awareness that his standpoint might be open to objections.[20]

Even though or perhaps because Woo's dark view of the West is a non-Marxist analysis corroborating much of the Chinese Marxist view of the West, the Mainland academic world has been slow to take it seriously. Some Mainland scholars brushed off Woo as a businessman supposedly without scholarly credentials. In the fall of 2001, however, Li Qiang, professor of political science at Peking University and one of the Mainland scholars most respected there for his knowledge of the Western political tradition, for the first time looked at *Tu-kung nan-shan shou Chung-kuo* and immediately ordered ten copies of this book as must reading for his graduate students.

Endnotes

1.   This chapter is a critique of H.K.H. Woo (Hu Kuo-heng), *Tu-kung nan-shan shou Chung-kuo* (The West in Distress — Resurrecting Confucius's

Teachings for a New Cultural Vision and Synthesis; Hong Kong: The Chinese University Press, 1995). All page references in the text of this chapter are to this book. All passages quoted from Woo's book are my translations from the Chinese.

2. See Alex Inkeles, *One World Emerging: Convergence and Divergence in Industrial Societies* (Boulder: Westview Press, 1998), and *National Character: A Psycho-Social Perspective* (New Brunswick: Transaction Publishers, 1997). I do not here discuss all the complex relations between the three concepts of "modernization," "Westernization," and "convergence." By "convergence" Inkeles has in mind many documented similarities between industrial societies, such as those centered on modes of production, organizational differentiation and specialization, the nature of education and stratification, and personality traits. Full convergence would include the combination of capitalism and liberal democracy. Whether convergence stems from imitation of the West or universal psychological propensities can be left as a separate question.

3. Larry Diamond, "Is the Third Wave Over?" *Journal of Democracy* 7 (July 1996): pp. 26–27. For an argument that the Chinese mainland will democratize in the next few decades, see Henry S. Rowen, "The Short March: China's Road to Democracy," *The National Interest* (fall 1996): pp. 61–70.

4. See Friedrich A. Hayek, *Law, Legislation and Liberty*, 3 vols. (Chicago: The University of Chicago Press, 1983, 1976, 1979), vol. 1, p. 11, vol. 3, pp. 153–155; S.N. Eisenstadt, "Barbarism and Modernity," *Society* 33 (May/June 1996): pp. 36–37 (Eisenstadt here criticizes rational choice theory); Robert N. Bellah et al., *Habits of the Heart* (Berkeley: University of California Press, 1985); Thomas A. Metzger, *Escape from Predicament: Neo-Confucianism and China's Evolving Political Culture* (New York: Columbia University Press, 1977) (this emphasizes perceptions of the given world, not just goals or ideals, as basic to value orientations).

5. See e.g. Yang Kuo-shu, "Will Societal Modernization Eventually Eliminate Cross-Cultural Psychological Difference?" in *The Cross Cultural Challenge to Social Psychology*, ed. Michael Bond (Newbury Park: Sage Publications, Inc., 1988), pp. 67–85.

6. See e.g. the views of Kao Li-k'o in chapter IV.

7. On Liang's earlier view of the West, see Huang Ko-wu (Max K.W. Huang), *I-ko pei fang-ch'i-te hsuan-tse: Liang Ch'i-ch'ao t'iao-shih ssu-hsiang-chih yen-chiu* (The Rejected Path: A Study of Liang Ch'i-ch'ao's Accommodative Thinking; Taipei: Institute of Modern History, Academia Sinica, 1994), ch. 5.

8. Sung Ch'iang et al., *Chung-kuo k'o-i shuo pu* (China Can Say "No!"; Beijing: Chung-Hua kung-shang lien-ho ch'u-pan-she, 1996).

9. See Erich Heller, "On Goethe's Faust," in *Goethe: A Collection of Critical Essays*, ed. Victor Lange (Englewood Cliffs: Prentice-Hall, Inc., 1968), p. 144. I am grateful for this reference to Professor Katharina Mommsen. See also Ted V. McAllister, *Revolt against Modernity: Leo Strauss, Eric Voegelin, and the Search for a Postliberal Order* (Lawrence: University Press of Kansas, 1995).

10. Benjamin I. Schwartz, *In Search of Wealth and Power: Yen Fu and the West* (Cambridge, Mass.: The Belknap Press of Harvard University Press, 1964), p. xi. On the New Left and postmodernism in China today, see chapter XII below.

11. The huge impact of World War I on the Chinese image of the West is described most effectively in Liu Kuei-sheng, ed., *Shih-tai-te ts'o-wei yü li-lun-te hsuan-tse: Hsi-fang chin-tai ssu-ch'ao yü Chung-kuo 'wu-ssu' ch'i-meng ssu-hsiang* (Shaping Political Theory during the Wrong Era: Modern Western Intellectual Trends and the Enlightenment in China during the May Fourth Period; Beijing: Ch'ing-hua ta-hsueh ch'u-pan-she, 1989), pp. 206–241. See ibid., p. 235 n. 1, for references to pre–World War I statements by Sun Yat-sen, Chang T'ai-yen, and Liang Ch'i-ch'ao about the "dark" aspects of the West (as early as 1904). Yet Kao Li-k'o says Tu Ya-ch'üan (1873–1933) was the first Chinese thinker to set forth a critical view of Western culture in reaction to the spectacle of World War I. See Kao Li-k'o, *T'iao-shih-te chih-hui: Tu Ya-ch'üan ssu-hsiang yen-chiu* (The Wisdom of the Accommodative Approach: A Study of the Thought of Tu Ya-ch'üan; Hangchow: Che-chiang jen-min ch'u-pan-she, 1998), p. 45.

12. Samuel P. Huntington, *The Third Wave: Democratization in the Late Twentieth Century* (Norman: University of Oklahoma Press, 1993), p. 263. For Yang's view, see chapter VI.

13. Hayek, vol. 1, pp. 11–12, 18, 74, vol. 3, pp. 129–130, 33, vol. 1, p. 18.

14. On "the broken form," see David S. Luft, *Robert Musil and the Crisis of European Culture, 1880–1942* (Berkeley: University of California Press, 1980).

15. On Yen Fu's thought, see Schwartz and Huang Ko-wu, *Tzu-yu-te so-i-jan: Yen Fu tui Yueh-han Mi-erh tzu-yu ssu-hsiang-te jen-shih yü p'i-p'an* (The Raison d'être of Freedom: Yen Fu's Understanding and Critique of John Stuart Mill's Liberalism; Taipei: Yun-ch'en wen-hua shih-yeh ku-fen yu-hsien kung-ssu, 1998). Also published in 2000 by Shang-hai shu-tien ch'u-pan-she.

16. Schwartz, pp. 240–241.

17. On Liang's view of the contrast between Chinese culture's pathology and the normalness of Western culture, see Huang Ko-wu, *I-ko pei fang-ch'i-te hsuan-tse*, ch. 5.

18. Jim Stockdale, *Thoughts of a Philosophical Fighter Pilot* (Stanford: Hoover Institution Press, 1995).

19. On the pervasive "sense of predicament" in contemporary Chinese thought, see Thomas A. Metzger, "The Chinese Reconciliation of Moral-Sacred Values with Modern Pluralism: Political Discourses in the ROC, 1949–1989," in *Two Societies in Opposition: The Republic of China and the People's Republic of China after Forty Years*, ed. Ramon H. Myers (Stanford: Hoover Institution Press, 1991), pp. 43–51.

20. Hu Kuo-heng, *Hu Kuo-heng wen-chi* (A Collection of Writings by Hu Kuo-heng; Lanchow: Lan-chou ta-hsueh ch'u-pan-she, 2000), pp. 5–9, 17.

⟿

CHAPTER IV

"Transcending the West": Mao's Vision of Socialism and the Legitimization of Teng Hsiao-p'ing's Modernization Program

1. The Problem of Legitimization

Almost as unpredicted and astounding as the end of the Cold War has been the success of the People's Republic of China (PRC) since the 1980s in creating a fast-growing economy animated by much free enterprise while paradoxically encased to a large extent in socialistic modes of thought and organization. So astute a scholar as Jan Prybyla said in 1990 that under "the post-Tiananmen leadership, marketization and privatization of the system are clinically dead."[1] A 1991 collection of articles on the PRC and the Republic of China on Taiwan (ROC) written by mainstream specialists was more cautious but similarly emphasized the institutional obstacles in the PRC impeding the rise of the market economy. Ramon H. Myers and I, writing the introduction for this volume, concurred with this widespread view.[2] Although our emphasis on the "systemic" contrasts between the PRC and the ROC as societies was, I believe, correct, we failed to appreciate the extent to which PRC institutions could

---

I am most grateful to Ramon H. Myers and Robert J. Myers for valuable advice about how to revise this piece. Apart from the postscript, this essay describes trends I perceived as of about 1996. Chapter XII tries to deal with the ideological situation that had evolved by 2003. By then, the picture of competing and interweaving ideological strands, including Maoist and other Marxist perspectives, had become still clearer. Yet the logic that a few years later nourished the rise of the New Left can be seen in the 1996 intellectual situation.

facilitate modern economic growth. The award for prescience in this case goes to the sociologist Ezra Vogel, whose meticulous fieldwork over many years in the Canton area enabled him to predict in 1988 that the PRC's coastal areas would come close to matching Taiwan's economic performance.[3] As recently pointed out by Myers, the PRC has indeed to a large extent succeeded in forming a "new socialist market economy" seeking growth with equity, combining free enterprise with planning, and based on a complex mix of ownership forms. Myers holds that, especially because of the PRC's decision in 1992 to restructure its 150,000 state-owned enterprises, its economy may well be able to "sustain annual growth rates of around 8 percent."[4]

But what are the ideas that have been widely used by Chinese to describe, morally justify, and so make sense out of their convoluted economic and indeed societal transformation? What, in other words, have been the ideological underpinnings of this transformation? Certainly, the idea of the "Four Modernizations" (in agriculture, industry, science and technology, and defense), first proposed in 1964 by Chou En-lai and iterated by him in 1975, has been basic to Teng Hsiao-p'ing's reforms, but so have been the Four Cardinal Principles, promulgated by Teng in 1979, according to which China must follow the socialist path, the dictatorship of the proletariat, the leadership of the Party, and the thought of Marx, Lenin, and Mao. Mao by 1981 was officially evaluated as 70 percent good, 30 percent bad, and it was officially held that his early thought in particular "could still be the guide to China's future," as John K. Fairbank put it.[5]

Apart from the official line of the Teng regime, however, does Mao's thought still command respect in China today? Do thoughtful persons still take it seriously? Does it serve as a *ssu-lu* (a train of thought, a path of reasoning) adopted by many Chinese to justify Teng's policies and build up their hopes for the future? Does it, in other words, legitimize and so stabilize the current regime, or does stability depend only on some calculus of coercion and self-interest?

Many Chinese and non-Chinese answer that indeed the regime depends on this calculus, not on any living, legitimizing belief in Mao's basic vision, and so is unlegitimized and unstable. Western public opinion generally regards Mao's thought as little more than a utopian fantasy contradicted by any rational understanding of modernization and democratization. To be sure, few in China or the

West were dismayed when Mao's regime killed a million or two landlords during the late 1940s and early 1950s in the course of a catastrophic land reform program that years later had to be junked. Even today in China, these mass killings are usually regarded as quite proper, and John K. Fairbank in 1992 blithely described them as a process meting out "rough justice."[6] But the disaster of the Great Leap Forward in 1959 and 1960, when famine killed twenty to thirty million, the atrocities of the Cultural Revolution (1966–1976), the T'ien-an-men tragedy of June 4, 1989, the cruelties of "the Chinese Gulag" revealed by Harry Wu, and the need to dismantle so much of Mao's socialist system have in the eyes of many thoroughly stripped Mao's thought and heritage of any credibility.[7] The collapse of Soviet Communism also put a bad light on Mao's thought, since Mao had repeatedly hailed Lenin and Stalin as authoritative spokesmen for the Marxism with which he identified himself. Moreover, while history, in the PRC as elsewhere, has vindicated F.A. Hayek's point that economic efficiency depends on "spontaneously" formed market relations, many intellectuals, east and west, have come to believe that "at present the modern constitutional republic stands virtually unchallenged as the sole surviving candidate for a model of legitimate political authority in the modern world," as John Dunn put it in 1993.[8] Undemocratic, accommodating the market without fully institutionalizing it, following no established model of society, the PRC appears as neither fish nor fowl (*pu-san pu-ssu*). In this light, how could Maoism be anything more than a propaganda line to which people with a vested interest in the Teng regime give lip service? Indeed, if the ever-popular theory of rational choice is to be at all applicable to moral-political options, not only to simply tangible or instrumental choices, Maoism could not possibly be affirmed by any person aware of the catastrophes undeniably associated with it. (Conversely, if intelligent, well-meaning persons aware of these catastrophes have remained committed to Mao's vision, it is hard to see how any form of rational choice theory can explain why people prefer one political vision over another.)

That indeed no intelligent, well-meaning person continues to believe in Maoism was indicated when the Princeton sinologist Yü Ying-shih, who is deeply respected in Mainland, Taiwan, and Hong Kong circles, as well as throughout the Western academic world, said in 1994 that "Marxism has become a joke."[9] Similarly, at a Hoover conference (December 6–7, 1994), Professor Merle Goldman, author of a recent book on contemporary Chinese intellectuals published by Harvard University Press, said that no serious Chinese intellectual still takes Mao's thought seriously. During a discussion period, I pointed out that Li Tse-hou, one of the most respected Mainland thinkers today, had expressed deep admiration for Mao's thought and career in books published years after the Cultural Revolution, but Professor Goldman stuck by her claim, adding that she knew Li personally.[10] On December 14, 1994, when I gave a paper at Hoover's U.S. & World Affairs Seminar, an astute young Chinese political scientist raised in China, Professor Minxin Pei of Princeton, completely disagreed with my thesis that Maoism was alive and well today in the minds of many Mainland intellectuals, not to mention cadres. In 1995, a famous and astute Mainland scholar dropped by to see me during his visit to the Stanford University area. We had met in 1994 for the first time, in Beijing, and had ended up chatting for five hours. I was confident he would be candid with me. I asked him whether any serious Chinese intellectual still admired Mao. He agreed with Goldman and Pei. But what about Li Tse-hou, I insisted: "Li admires Mao and many of you admire Li." "That's not what we admire about Li," my visitor replied.

In other words, except for lip service to the Party line, including the vast recent literature explaining how Mao, despite later mistakes, still laid the foundation for Chinese modernization,[11] Chinese who think seriously about politics all reject or ignore Mao's ideas and the rest of Marxism, having one or more of a number of alternative outlooks, such as purely technocratic or pragmatic views, including the idea of "neoauthoritarianism" (Xiao Gong-qin); the modernization theories of U.S. social scientists; a simple focus on the material well-being of one's own family; the search for some blend of Confucian and modern values; the liberalism of a Fang Li-chih; the view that Maoism is just part of a pathological Chinese "deep structure"(Chin Kuan-t'ao, Liu Ch'ing-feng); the view that the current regime should be overthrown; or the kind of cutting iconoclasm if not nihilism of a Liu Hsiao-po.[12]

Yet, despite all these indications to the contrary, it is clear that, within the spectrum of current Chinese political attitudes, a fervent endorsement of Mao Tse-tung's basic political vision plays a major role. I started to suspect this in the late 1980s. When the debacle caused by Mao's policies was coming to light, I at first, like others, took for granted that it had extinguished the credibility of his ideas in Chinese circles. As meetings with Mainland intellectuals in the United States became more common, I lapsed into the habit of haranguing them on the virtues of Sun's doctrine and the Taiwan experience. So I was startled one day in a San Diego coffee shop when one of them, as though sizing me up for an insightful fellow, suddenly suggested: "Wouldn't you say Mao built on Sun's wisdom?" At a conference in Lexington, Virginia in September, 1990, another such visitor had a long talk with me lasting well into the night. What he felt was that Confucian values were profoundly important for China, and that they largely coincided with Marxism. Then in 1993 I read the historiographically outstanding essays on modern Chinese thought written by Li Tse-hou, the dominant intellectual force in China at least through the 1980s, a scholar deeply respected in Western intellectual circles as well. What Li said, still in 1986 and 1987, was that Mao had erred only in trying to develop socialism too quickly. Li reprinted these essays in 1990 in Taipei without any indication that his views had changed.

True, by 1989, Li was trying to develop what he called a kind of "Chinese post-Marxism," according to which

> the last century or more of history has without exception gloriously demonstrated that Marx's most basic concepts are completely correct, those pertaining to his philosophy of moral praxis, his historical materialism, but at the same time it has proved that his theory of revolution, his ideas about political strategy, are definitely incorrect, and the price of following the latter ideas has indeed been terrible and enormous. Yet from the standpoint of logic and the inner structure of theory, there definitely is no "necessary" connection between these two sides of his thought.[13]

Then, in 1995, together with Liu Tsai-fu, Li published *Kao-pieh ko-ming — hui-wang erh-shih shih-chi Chung-kuo* (Goodbye to Revolution: Looking Back on Twentieth-century China), which, as Huang Ko-wu (Max K.W. Huang) has argued, staked out a position seemingly much closer to Western liberalism.[14]

Just what Li thinks about Mao today, however, is still far from clear, perhaps not even to himself, and neither is it obvious what various Chinese intellectuals today think about either Mao or Li, who has been subjected to the usual attacks by Chinese intellectuals jealous of his fame and vigorously putting into practice the ancient maxim *wen-jen hsiang-ch'ing* (intellectuals make a practice of looking down on one another). Moreover, the complexity of the Chinese discourse is hard for foreigners, or indeed for anyone, to penetrate. As an example, here is the following conversation which recently took place at Hoover between me and a Mainland friend:

I: Do intellectuals in China still take Mao's thought seriously?
He: No. Definitely not.
I: What about Li Tse-hou?
He: Oh, his generation perhaps [Li was born in 1930]. Certainly Mao's philosophy still has value, "On Contradiction," "On Practice," and so on.
I: Mao's political thought?
He: No. No one takes that seriously.
I: What about his thesis about "New Democracy"?
He: Oh, there's nothing wrong with that.
I: But that's political thought.
He: Yes, but that's before 1949. All his thought up to 1949 is fine. It revolved around the idea of "New Democracy." Just about all Chinese intellectuals would agree with his ideas up to that point. It was after 1949, when he turned to socialism, that his thought became corrupted. The first four volumes of *Mao Tse-tung hsuan-chi* (The Selected Writings of Mao Tse-tung) are all fine.[15]

Thus my friend at first denied that Mao's thought was still taken seriously by Chinese but ended up largely agreeing with Li Tse-hou's way of endorsing it, as well as Kao Li-k'o's, discussed in detail below. Had our conversation ended after his first reply, I would have concluded that writers like Li Tse-hou and Kao Li-k'o, embracing so many of Mao's most basic epistemological, ontological, moral, historical, and political ideas, were either exceptions or sycophants.

To be sure, even if one can grasp the complexities of the Chinese discourse and ascertain the existence of a genuine intellectual affirmation of Maoism, a quantitative analysis of the exact social distribution of this Maoist viewpoint is not possible here. Yet a good deal can be learned from the methods I have used for more than thirty-five years: the study of China's intellectual and institutional

history combined with considerable immersion in the contemporary
Chinese discussion, oral and written, of China's history, thought, and
current situation, an immersion that included two-and-a-half years
holding visiting professorships in Taipei, Hong Kong, and Shanghai.

From December 4 through December 17, 1995, Huang Ko-wu
(Max K.W. Huang) and I visited a number of academic institutions in
Shanghai and Hangchow, especially East China Normal University
and the University of Chekiang. Huang has been my student since
1982, when I taught in Taipei, and currently is a Ph.D. candidate in
history at Stanford University and an associate research fellow at the
Institute of Modern History, Academia Sinica, Taipei. In 1995 he was
appointed visiting research fellow by East China Normal University,
while I went there as visiting professor. Discussing the history of
Chinese thought, we gave some ten lectures and agreed to try to start
a three-year program of intellectual cooperation proposed by our
colleagues at this university. In these concentrated exchanges
between colleagues (a one-hour-and-a-half lecture was followed by a
three-hour discussion with faculty about it), Huang and I repeatedly
found an intellectually firm and thoughtful commitment to Marxism,
and these conversational impressions were reinforced when I started
to read the books given to us by our Chekiang and Shanghai
colleagues, beginning with those by Kao Li-k'o and Yang Kuo-jung, as
well as the learned and lucid writings of the late Marxist philosopher
Feng Ch'i, the guiding spirit of the Department of Philosophy at East
China Normal University.

Kao was born in 1952. His book *Li-shih yü chia-chih-te chang-li —
Chung-kuo hsien-tai-hua ssu-hsiang shih-lun* (The Tension between
Historical Necessity and the Quest for Humanistic Values: An Essay
on the Intellectual History of Chinese Modernization), is a revised
version of his 1990 Ph.D. thesis at Beijing Normal University and was
published in 1992.[16] He today is on the faculty of the Department of
Philosophy and Sociology at the University of Chekiang. In Ku Hsin's
book on post-Mao intellectual trends, which is highly critical of not
only the Teng regime but also many Mainland intellectuals both
inside and outside the political center, Kao is greatly praised for
seeking a "scholarly" rather than an "ideological" understanding of
the May Fourth Movement.[17] I too see Kao as a serious scholar, not
one necessarily eager to follow the Party line.

Yang Kuo-jung was born in 1957 and, at East China Normal

University's Department of Philosophy, he was promoted to the rank of professor in an extraordinarily short period of time, in 1991. The book of his I use here was published in 1994, *Shan-te li-ch'eng: Ju-chia chia-chih hsi-t'ung-te li-shih yen-hua chi ch'i hsien-tai chuan-huan* (The Good as an Unfolding Process: The Historical Evolution and Modern Development of the Confucian Value System). Without discussing Mao's thought, this book analyzes modernity as a problem in the evolution of Confucian culture.[18]

These two books and much other contemporary Chinese thought, Maoist as well as non-Maoist, depend on certain assumptions which for many Mainland Chinese are what Hayek called "self-evident truths," historically or culturally distinctive ideas the validity of which is so obvious in these authors' circles that they are "clichés," the term I used in an earlier work on premodern Chinese thought.[19] To see the vitality of Maoism today, one has to see how Maoist ideas are logically and rhetorically successful in meeting the standards of successful thinking inherent in these Chinese clichés defining the obvious nature of human reality.

2. Some Basic Assumptions in Mainland Circles Today

The most basic cliché is that Chinese today in the process of "modernization" must center on the problem of cultural revision, "the question of what to adopt, what to discard" (*ch'ü-she*); that in this process of revision, they must choose between old and new aspects of the Chinese "tradition" (*ch'uan-t'ung, Chung, tung,* as in *ku-chin Chung-wai, tung-hsi*) and "the West"; and that they must also take into account China's goals and capabilities.

In other words, modernization is seldom if ever seen by Chinese in the more generalized way with which U.S. social scientists tend to view it, as a rational effort that people everywhere, no matter what their culture, can carry out to pursue universal goods like survival, prosperity, peace, justice, morals, and freedom (to use Hayek's list). While Chinese also often affirmed such goals, they were painfully preoccupied with the problem of how their culture should be altered so as to make efficient pursuit of these goals possible.

To be sure, cultural revision is debated in virtually all societies, as illustrated by Robert N. Bellah's thesis that Americans should discard their inherited Lockean individualism and Christopher Lasch's opposite call for efforts to push back such intellectual attacks against Lockean, bourgeois individualism.[20] In non-Western "latecomer" societies such as China, however, whose members largely agree with the Western view of themselves as "backward" (*lo-hou*), the overwhelming awareness of appealing foreign values greatly intensifies and complicates the debate about cultural revision. It is as though Americans perceived Japan as an exotic society vastly and dangerously superior to their own, were heatedly debating whether they should abolish their Judeo-Christian heritage in order to transform their society and make it like Japan's, and were boldly suggesting that transforming American culture need not mean entirely copying Japanese culture.

In the Chinese context, moreover, not only perceived backwardness but also a distinctive intellectual style turned the spotlight on the topic of cultural revision: the assumption that national success depends on finding a single, systematic, correct, profound theory of cultural revision (*t'i-hsi*), and that Chinese so far have disastrously failed to find it, leaning too much toward either Western or traditionally Chinese values.[21] This viewpoint includes the assumption, only occasionally challenged by Chinese, that Chinese intellectuals can use their subtle formulations to control the direction of cultural change in their huge society.[22]

A second major cluster of clichés revolves around the view, more widely established today than during the earlier Chinese discussions of cultural revision, that the goals China should pursue are distinguishable from the above cultural patterns per se. This centers on the now-familiar Chinese point that modernization is not the same as Westernization. It is widely agreed that there are (a) certain modern values China should adopt, (b) certain unmodern values it should discard, and (c) certain ills of modernization it should avoid, and there is virtually no disagreement as to the content of (a), (b), and (c). This triangular goal, for instance, is central to Yang Kuo-jung's book. Just what to "adopt and discard" in the case of Chinese and Western culture, therefore, depends on the extent to which either culture is in accord with this uncontroversial triangular goal. The controversy is only about the concrete characteristics of the traditional culture, but this controversy has raged throughout the Chinese world for most of this century.

For instance, according to the iconoclastic May Fourth

Movement, which arose at the end of World War I and is still widely revered today, Western culture was equated with (a), Confucian culture was equated with (b), and (c) was ignored. Therefore, drastic Westernization was called for. By contrast, modern Confucian humanism, a movement which also goes back to the early twentieth century, but which has become more influential only recently, argued that Confucian culture, even if contaminated by (b), still largely meshed with (a), not to mention being an antidote to (c). Thus Chinese modernization should build on Confucian culture.[23]

Yang Kuo-jung's point is that these New Confucians were on the right track but overstated their case: the "Confucian value system" indeed can serve as a powerful antidote to the ills of modernization, and it indeed includes values partly in accord with modern ones, but its undesirable nonmodern content is very great. Therefore only serious alteration of the "Confucian value system" can free it of its nonmodern side, make it accord with modern values, and allow Chinese to use it to minimize the ills of modernization. The New Confucians tried to gloss over this need for serious alteration of the traditional culture, Yang holds, while the May Fourth Movement erroneously tried to discard this culture. Only his formula of cultural revision can realize the triangular goal above, he suggests. It should be noted that basic to this Chinese discourse is the assumption that the nature of a whole civilization's "value system" can be conveniently summed up, and that, despite the complex ways that cultural diffusion often reshapes a foreign idea by blending it in with native values, the distinction between Chinese and Western values is too clear and obvious to deserve discussion.[24]

What are the uncontroversial values making up this triangular goal with which Chinese evaluate their culture and the West? Chinese on the Mainland have conceptualized desirable modern values in a way largely converging with Western modernization theory, and they have grounded this view in their picture of a global, originally Western tendency with which China must accord. Thus Kao Li-k'o notes that "all the peoples making up humankind" have formed "the great global historical tide moving toward modernization."[25] Modernization, as Alex Inkeles would agree, is especially an effort to put unprecedented emphasis on the material improvement of society, i.e. on "utilitarian" values (*kung-li*), on "instrumental reason" (*kung-chü li-hsing*), on science, technology, and industrialization.

Thus, Kao and Yang agree, individuals must have the "freedom," "autonomy," "creativity," and ability to "innovate" needed to "compete" in the effort to bring about such material improvement. Consequently, society must provide "equality," "justice," individual "rights," and a legal order free of bias and hostile to "privilege." Conversely, the non-modern attitudes that must be eliminated are those centering on "authoritarianism," the repression of "emotion," and stagnative acceptance of the status quo.

The third part of this triangular goal, avoiding the ills of modernization, also plays a central role in the modern Chinese intellectual imagination. Its importance is often overlooked by Western scholars studying modern Chinese attitudes toward modernization. Picking up on Western criticisms of the West is a Chinese habit going back at least to the thought of Liang Ch'i-ch'ao and Sun Yat-sen around World War I, and of course it was basic to Mao's rejection of Western capitalistic society.[26] Such criticism was especially plausible in the light of the sublime, utopian standards of progress which Chinese have used ever since they began to modernize a century ago, and which they indeed inherited from the Confucian tradition: a society not just realizing prosperity and freedom but without "selfishness," without any "constraints" (*shu-fu*) or patterns of "exploitation" preventing the full realization of a person's potential, and without any "conflicts or feelings of alienation coming between people" (*ko-ho*). China's "culture" was to be reconstructed as a perfect thing, combining only the "good" parts of China and the West, while discarding all the "bad" ones,[27] "a grand synthesis of all cultural tendencies in the world," as Kao Li-k'o put it (293 — all page numbers in my text refer to Kao's book).

This "grand synthesis" connoted the vision of *ta-t'ung* (the great oneness), an idea still widely embraced in China today, most prominently affirmed by the highly influential K'ang Yu-wei around 1900, and going back to one of the ancient classics (*Li-chi*). The traditional *ta-t'ung* ideal, like the equally basic Confucian ideal of *t'ien-jen ho-i* (the oneness of heaven and man), is one of those culturally rich ideas with an indefinite number of connotations. To analyze it, I have used the idea of a complete "linkage" between or synthesis of all facets of human existence: the resolution of all contradictions between all doctrines east and west, ancient and modern; the oneness of self and cosmos; the oneness of the self with all other people, whether good people throughout history or good people today throughout China and the international world; and the oneness of ideals and reality. Filled with the desire for this synthesis, the heroic person identified himself or herself with the historically immanent force moving toward this oneness, intellectually grasping the right doctrinal synthesis and then resolutely acting to effect it in the practical world.

In an article published in 1978, I argued that, although Maoism and the contemporary Confucian humanism of T'ang Chün-i (1909–1978) were usually seen as diametrically opposed to each other, they actually shared this ideal of "linkage" or "oneness." The elucidation of linkage was basic to Mao's two main philosophical texts, "On Practice" and "On Contradiction," which appeared in 1937.[28] While it was obvious that T'ang's ideal of linkage came from the Confucian tradition, scholars today such as Kao Li-k'o have come to agree that Mao's thought too was rooted in this traditional quest for oneness (see below). Indeed when the most influential post-Mao thinker in Mainland circles, Li Tse-hou, insisted in 1989 that the object of modernization was the end of "alienation" and simultaneously endorsed much of the Confucian tradition, the influence on him of the traditional oneness ideal was obvious, though he used European terminology to discuss "alienation."[29]

Given, then, this sublime ideal of "linkage" with which Chinese intellectuals discussed modernization, it was natural for them to focus on the modern problem of "dehumanization" as the most central of the ills of modernization. Today, sociologists in Hong Kong no less than philosophers in Shanghai regard as utterly authoritative Jürgen Habermas's idea that the modern pursuit of instrumental rationality causes the "dehumanization" of society.[30] For Kao Li-k'o, "dehumanization" refers to the problem of "morality," "spirit," and "values"; the undermining of "the free development of the human spirit" (293) and the "moral subject"; "spiritual crisis"; the "death of God"; the turning of people into commodities; unfeelingly impersonal legal procedures; "putting primacy on selfish interests" (283, 285); hedonism; lack of respect for ecology; and the destruction of cultural roots (282). Repeatedly, Kao summed up this point by using Max Weber's famous distinction, deploring the Western failure to join together "instrumental rationality" and "the rationality of ends" (283–285, 287–289). For Kao, to join these two together depended especially on somehow respecting the difference between the desirable competition between free individuals each seeking "reasonable" "profits" for himself or herself (*ko-t'i-chih li, ho-li-te hsien-tai kung-li ching-shen*) and the undesirable tendency to "put the pursuit of selfish interests above all else" (*i li wei pen, li-chi chu-i*) (285).[31] This can be seen either as a distinction without a difference or as an unavoidably vague but utterly central moral problem.

In a Chinese essay little known on the Mainland in the late nineties, the famous scholar Chang Hao had written, in effect, that democracy depends precisely on a pessimistic awareness that Weber's two modes of rationality cannot be fully unified, on *yu-an i-shih* (reduced moral expectations regarding social and political life).[32] Kao, however, though claiming to reject "utopianism" (285–286), actually rejected the alternative to utopianism, this pessimism identified by Chang Hao. Kao insisted that Chinese can practicably pursue their sublime goals: "We have no reason to accept a fatalistic view of history, to assume that the Western kind of modernization is the only model for the world, and that the loss of moral values is the necessary price of modernization" (285). He explained:

> Chinese intellectuals have not been satisfied with the unprecedented achievements of modern civilization with regard to the purely phenomenal realm of "wealth and power." They have ardently sought the development of moral and spiritual values and the humanistic ideal of a harmonious society based on fairness, and so they developed a tendency to try to transcend the Western model of modernization. (283)

As a sound description of how many Chinese intellectuals have thought about modernization, this passage reflects the influence on Kao of Chang Hao's 1987 *Chinese Intellectuals in Crisis*.[33] Where Chang, however, writing for a U.S. audience, just described this Chinese vision without guaranteeing its compatibility with modernization, Kao, with little fear of contradiction, endorsed it. Modernization without the ills of modernization was to him a quite practicable goal.

In Hayekian terms, then, Kao typified the continuing, widespread Chinese tendency to believe that the personalistic morals of the "ends-connected tribal society" can be synthesized with the structure of a modern, "means-connected" society, where, as Hayek put it, "the chief common purpose of all its members is the purely instrumental one of securing the formation of an abstract order which has no specific purposes but will enhance for all the prospects of achieving their respective purposes." In other words, Kao rejected the basic Millsian vision of "the three marketplaces": a society controlled not by an elite fusing together knowledge, morality, political power, and effective concern for everyone's freedom but by economic, intellectual, and political marketplaces in which individuals freely exercised their intellectually and morally ungraded preferences. What not only Maoism but the whole modern Chinese intellectual mainstream has filtered out of the Western discussion of modernization and democracy has been a two-fold pessimism: the epistemologically pessimistic view that no rational doctrine is available clearly defining the public good, and the idea that individual freedom can be secured only by letting free economic, intellectual, and political marketplaces filled with unpredictable impulses control the fate of society.[34]

While many Mainland intellectuals thus optimistically saw themselves as revising their culture fully to realize the triangular goal just described, they naturally also felt an urgent need to refute the wrong theories of cultural revision that have dominated modern China. The Chinese intellectual world is almost universally regarded by Chinese intellectuals as having been unable properly to conceptualize cultural revision because it was thrown off balance by a traumatic Western impact, which prevented it from developing a "rational, objective attitude" toward the West (267).

Paradoxically enough, however, Chinese intellectuals see themselves as not only easily thrown off balance but also quite capable of finding the one right theory of cultural revision and so guiding China toward full realization of its sublime triangular goal, thus "transcending the West," a civilization unable to realize it. This is the third "cliché" I would like to point to. This vision of China as a temporarily crippled superman has been utterly basic to Chinese thought since Chinese around 1900 started to see themselves as "backward." Repeatedly, thinkers ranging from Sun Yat-sen and Chin Yueh-lin to Mou Tsung-san have with immense confidence seen themselves as correcting the mistakes in the most advanced Western philosophies (those of Hume, Kant, and so on) and so offering China the philosophical key to a sublime future beyond the reach of the West. A basic phrase used today is *chieh-chien-te yu-shih* (the advantage enjoyed in a competition by the loser, who can learn from his adversary's mistakes) (292). Says Kao: "We believe that the great Chinese people, given the richness of their modernizing experience as latecomers able to learn from the examples of others, will offer a new, successful example of modernization to the world," "a new type of civilization" (294). In other words, a losing football team is in the happy position of being able to see the weaknesses of the Dallas Cowboys and so to "transcend" this currently dominant team in some future Superbowl. Again:

> Furnished by cultural anthropology, the principle of "cultural progress" tells us that there is a mechanism whereby the potential for progress on the one hand and a high level of specialization on the other work against each other, with the result that cultural progress cannot be linear. It occurs as various cultures rise and fall at different times. Western industrial civilization's high-level specialization has caused it to lose its potential to bring forth a new type of civilization. So there is nothing accidental or mysterious about the fact that socialist civilization arose in the non-Western world. According to the principles of cultural anthropology, to be able to achieve cultural progress transcending industrial civilization, a society must have at least three characteristics: 1. it must be a latecomer to modernization; 2. it must be a great nation with a high-level cultural tradition; and 3. it must exist on the periphery of the circle of modernized nations. China without doubt has these conditions needed to "transcend" industrial culture. (293)

This vision of China as a temporarily crippled superman who will eventually surpass all other people of course fully blends in with those powerful feelings of nationalism and patriotism common in virtually all nations today. Combined with this vision, however, Chinese nationalism has a very distinctive character. At the same time, this goal of surpassing all others is crucial to the pride of many Mainland Chinese, not just supporters of the Teng regime, because for them, as discussed below, the goal of just catching up with Taiwan would be unbearably humiliating, even if it actually is unreachable. This mix of patriotism with pride in the Mainland experience, moreover, is fueled not only by the sense of being part of a huge nation with a long, extremely remarkable history but also by the heartening scenes of prosperity and contentment that can be observed today by anyone strolling in cities like Beijing, Shanghai, Soochow, or Hangchow.

Mao's thought, therefore, is a "joke" to anyone following an abstract Hayekian or Inkelesian logic defining universally effective ways to pursue freedom and prosperity. It appears in a very different light, however, when put into the context of China's concrete historical situation as it is perceived by many Chinese intellectuals. For them, Mao's thought can be vindicated if it can be pictured as correctly addressing the central, distinctly Chinese problem of cultural revision, thus freeing up China's immense, temporarily crippled ability to startle the world by creating "a new kind of civilization" and so reversing the world's balance of prestige. From this standpoint, policies that can reverse this balance are rational, not policies that just duplicate Taiwan's success in gradually realizing material prosperity and a democratic way of life filled with the sordid interplay of interest groups and morally flawed politicians.

Besides this series of assumptions defining the Chinese as revising their culture to form a new, modern civilization wonderfully free of the ills of modernization, contemporary Mainland thought has recently undergone a major new development greatly affecting contemporary attitudes toward Mao. In the academic circles of Taiwan, the Mainland, and the West, the discontinuity between the Maoist and the Confucian intellectual traditions had long been emphasized, whether by Weberian scholars seeing Chinese modernization as antithetical to Confucian values, by Marxist scholars calling for the replacement of "feudal" with bourgeois or socialist values, or by Confucian scholars in Hong Kong and Taiwan abhorring Maoism as a rejection of Confucian humanism.[35] In recent years, however, the emphasis on continuity has become more fashionable, nowhere more so than in Mainland circles, where it has become almost a cliché to view Maoism and the Confucian tradition as a single if evolving amalgam.

This new emphasis on intellectual continuity is in accord with studies published two decades ago by one or two scholars in the West, but it was not their writings that brought about this major change in Chinese thought. It has stemmed mainly from the downfall of Mao's policies, which led, on the one hand, to a denunciation of the Maoist regime as a perpetuation of "feudal" evils, and, on the other, to a reaffirmation of the tradition as a source of pride and "identity." Curiously enough, the Communists have encouraged the rise of both these perspectives, since patriotism easily leads to support for their regime, and since their leadership decisions and Marxist principles are not the main objects of criticism when China's ills are traced back to tradition-rooted cultural patterns infecting everybody.

Thus, in some Mainland circles today, an intellectual problematique has arisen focusing on this amalgam of Confucian thought and Maoism: Is it the right cultural foundation on which to struggle toward the triangular goal above (Li Tse-hou, at least through the late eighties, leaned toward this view)? Or, is this amalgam basically a pathological force that should be uprooted and discarded, as Chin Kuan-t'ao, Liu Ch'ing-feng, and Ku Hsin hold?[36] Chinese concerned with this question discuss Chinese modernization in a way very different from the ways in which it is discussed in Hong Kong, Taipei, or the United States.

3. Kao Li-k'o's Affirmation of Mao's Vision: Modernization as Mao's "Minimal Guidelines"

Endorsing this amalgam as humankind's unique resource with which to realize a modernity free of the ills of modernity, Kao Li-k'o analyzed how Mao, from his youth onward, used "reason" (249–250, 257) and "his extraordinary gifts and power to transform Chinese history," freeing China's "modernization movement" from the "predicament" in which it had been caught (218). His thought rooted in the Confucian ideals of Mencius (ca. 300 B.C.) and the Neo-Confucianism of late imperial times, as well as the general "dynamism" of the traditional society (223, 248, 274, 276, 285), Mao built on the ideas of all the earlier Chinese modernizers, from T'an Ssu-t'ung through Sun Yat-sen, and was influenced by German philosophical idealism as well as Russian culture (263, 251–252). "Dialectically" and "creatively" synthesizing all these finest ideas from China and the West, the past and the present (271–278), Mao avoided "utopianism" while uniting "instrumental rationality" with the "rationality of ends," as previous Chinese thinkers had been unable to do (270, 284–286). He thus "transcended the West" while being fully open to its values (263, 269, 282, 271, 293).

Mao could do this because from the start he decided to deal with modernization by addressing "the root problem" (*pen-yuan*) of "thought and morality," not the merely superficial, technical details of economic or political organization (219–220), and because he understood that morality can be based only on universal principles, not just on a particular historical tradition, whether Chinese or Western. Thus, already in his youth, he saw "philosophy" as a way to grasp "the truth of the cosmos," which "governs the history of humankind," is one with "the human mind," and demands for every individual the freedom to achieve "self-realization" (220–223, 279).

This vision will strike many empiricists in Anglo-American circles as preposterously metaphysical, but it easily resonates with the Neo-Confucianism of late imperial times, shares much with modern Confucian humanism, and indeed is not too far from Hegelianism and other German and French philosophical schools which to this day have continued to fascinate intellectuals on the Mainland as well as many in the West. Mao felt that, with this philosophical message, he could mobilize other "educated persons of good will" (*jen-jen chih-shih*), and then they together with him could enlighten all other Chinese, creating a society wholly animated by "the truth" (225, 242).

Coming with this vision to Marxism by about 1920, Mao then had to face another fundamental problem: how to bring about socialism in a society that was little modernized, since it was an "oriental, agricultural empire," was "half-colonial, half-feudal," had barely begun to enter the stage of capitalism, and so lacked a sizable proletariat. Strikingly corroborating Benjamin I. Schwartz's famous 1952 study,[37] which was both celebrated and bitterly attacked, Kao, like many Mainland intellectuals, concluded that Mao faced this problem by "creatively sinifying Marxism" (261).

The saga of this creative effort during the 1920s, 1930s, and 1940s has indeed left a lasting impression on many millions of Chinese, especially in that it symbolized for them the unification of sublime ideals with practical reality, the realization of that indigenous goal of oneness or "linkage" addressed in Mao's 1937 writings, as noted above.

To achieve this, Kao explains, Mao originated a number of general principles, especially the idea of "revolution from below" (*tzu-hsia erh shang*), tapping into the social creativity of the masses (235). More particularly, he invented the idea of depending not on proletarian revolution in the cities but on rural bases from which peasant military forces could encircle the cities (239).

As important, Kao goes on, Mao gradually devised his *Hsin-min-chu chu-i lun* (Theory of New Democracy), fully articulated in a 1940 essay using this term for its title. Following an established tendency in China today to link this essay with Teng's current modernization program,[38] Kao says that

> the vigor of Mao's thought about the strategy of national development is fully reflected in the "blurredly mixed form" [*hun-ho-hsing*] (dictatorship by an alliance [of classes], the coexistence of a great variety of economic elements) of the model of society derived in the Theory of New Democracy from actual circumstances. The strategic insights implicit in the Theory of New Democracy will have great significance for a long time. They are profoundly suggestive for us today as we carry out the goal of socialist modernization. (264)

This theory divides China's revolution into two stages: (a) the "democratic revolution," which has the goal of overthrowing "feudalism" and "imperialism," which began after the Opium War in the mid-nineteenth century, which was at first led by the bourgeoisie, which came to be led by the "proletariat and other revolutionary classes" after the Russian Revolution of 1917, which thus became part of the "world revolution," and which in this way entered the stage of New Democracy; and (b) the stage of socialism.

In his 1940 essay, as Kao notes, Mao identified the first stage with "the current guidelines" (*hsien-shih kang-ling*) (Mao used *hsien-tsai-te kang-ling*) or "the minimal guidelines" (*tsui-ti kang-ling*). The stage of socialism was identified by Mao with "the highest guidelines" (*tsui-kao kang-ling*) or "the future guidelines" (*chiang-lai kang-ling*) (Mao used *chiang-lai-te kang-ling*) (258–260).[39] Mao in his 1940 essay said that "the current guidelines" were "the first step," while "the highest guidelines" were "the second step." Thus "the present still is not the time to practice socialism." Mao held that "a considerable amount of time [*hsiang-tang-te ch'ang*] will be needed to carry out the first step; this definitely cannot be done overnight. We are not dreamers out of contact with reality; we cannot ignore the actual conditions that exist today."[40] Thus Kao accurately described Mao as believing that the stage of New Democracy was "necessary to prepare for socialism" and could not be "bypassed" (260, 263).

As Kao noted, however, Mao also emphasized that these two stages were inseparable. Mao's words were: "Today, New Democracy, in the future, socialism. These are two parts of a structure based on the whole theoretical system of communism."[41] As Kao explained,

Mao meant by "structure" that these two stages were "inter-connected to form a unified process" (p. 260).

A thorough analysis of the differences between Mao's 1940 conceptualization of the New Democracy stage and Kao's 1992 interpretation of Mao's view need not be attempted here, but the main points are clear. Mao defined the New Democracy stage as overturning feudalism and imperialism while proceeding under the leadership of the Chinese Communist Party, which in turn led "the proletariat class, the peasant class, the intellectuals, and the rest of the small bourgeoisie class.... an alliance of several revolutionary classes.... excluding counter-revolutionary elements." Thus in this stage China would not become "a capitalistic society under the dictatorship of the Chinese bourgeoisie" (Mao's term for Millsian democracy).[42]

Following Sun Yat-sen's principle of "curbing capitalistic trends" (*chieh-chih tzu-pen*), Mao went on, this political alliance would nationalize all "large banking, industrial, and commercial enter-prises," and it would "sweep away feudal relations in the villages," but it "would not confiscate any other capitalistic private property," even "accepting the existence of the rich peasant economy in the villages." Thus the economy would be a "flourishing" one (*fan-jung*).[43]

Finally, Mao said that a "new culture" would be created during the New Democracy period. Summing up his transformative belief that a people can deliberately and thoroughly redesign their whole way of living and thinking, Mao said that "we want to establish a new China":

> In this new society, this new nation, there shall be not only a new government and a new economy but also a new culture. That is, what we want is not only that a China suffering from political oppression and economic exploitation should be turned into a China that is politically *free* and economically *flourishing* but also that a China controlled by the old culture and so suffering from ignorance and backwardness shall be turned into a China controlled by the new culture and so existing as a *civilized*, progressive society.[44] (Italics added)

Certainly the major difference between Mao's 1940 perspective on New Democracy and Kao's is that Mao put the emphasis on the struggle to realize "the highest guidelines," while Kao's emphasis was on "the minimal guidelines." Basic to this shift of emphasis was a point Kao respectfully avoided bringing up explicitly, the widely accepted view that Mao tragically erred in trying too soon to implement "the highest guidelines." The important thing now for Kao was better to understand "the minimal guidelines." Kao extracted from Mao's text the three adjectives in italics above and treated them as defining the "basic goals of the New Democratic revolution" (259), holding that "political freedom" refers to "a republic based on New Democracy," that "the flourishing of the economy" refers to "industrialization," and that a "civilized, progressive culture" refers to "a national, scientific, mass culture" (262–263).

More boldly, Kao equated the "minimal guidelines" with "modernization," the "highest guidelines," with the "post-modern" era. To some extent, then, modernization theory was logically integrated with the Marxist theory of history. "Marxism," he held, "can be regarded as a kind of 'post-modern' theory. Its main goal was to seek a historical solution for the problems of the modernized societies of western Europe (the original form of modernization) which were in the front ranks of historical progress" (262). In other words, "'socialism' and 'modernization' definitely do not belong to the same part of the spatiotemporal continuum.... Thus there is a clear-cut spatiotemporal gap between Marxist theory and the practical process of modernization in non-Western nations" (291).

Kao also added a certain flexibility and social inclusiveness to Mao's "minimal guidelines." There was no reference in Kao's account to keeping "counter-revolutionary elements" out of power. Although Mao's reference to nationalizing all large banking, industrial, and commercial enterprises was quoted (259), legitimizing the currently huge public sector, Kao devised a broad, generic term, missing in Mao's text, to picture a political-economic order that as a whole is eclectic, *hun-ho-hsing ... she-hui mo-shih* (a societal model blurredly mixing together different elements) (264).

It would be utterly mistaken, however, to say that Kao paid only lip service to "the highest guidelines." Kao deeply agreed with Mao that Chinese modernization has to develop in the direction of socialism: "Thus for Marx, 'socialism' is the historical outcome of 'modernization'"(291).

Kao's enthusiasm for the Theory of New Democracy turned on the point that, with it, Mao figured out how to modernize China in such a way as to lead to socialism: Mao "successfully applied a kind of 'post-modern' theory originating in western Europe to the practice of modernization in China and east Asia, causing [this post-modern, European theory] to become a new kind of Eastern 'modernization' theory" (262).

Kao's point, then, was not just that Maoism enabled east Asia to modernize. After all, much of east Asia had modernized without Mao. Kao's emphasis was on the new kind of modernization Mao made possible, one realizing the widely accepted triangular goals described above and so facilitating the establishment of socialism.

What Kao suggested — he did not fully articulate this point — is that only by modernizing while avoiding the ills of modernization and so "transcending the West" could a society successfully realize socialism. Mao therefore appeared in Kao's book as a thinker who had transcended Marx. Marx had made clear the ills of capitalism and had set forth the ideal of socialism, but he had not figured out how to realize socialism. Mao had figured out that it could be realized only by creating a "new civilization" outside and superior to the West, that is, by utilizing China's unique cultural resources to create a process of modernization free of the ills of modernization, the only kind of modernization that could lead to socialism. Given China's contemporary culture, Kao was able to assume, with little fear of contradiction in his circles, that modernization without the ills historically experienced by all other modern societies and an efficient socialistic economy were not chimera. Thus he gave expression to one of the premises most basic to Chinese culture for many centuries, a peculiarly optimistic concept of political practicability.[45]

Kao made this point in a passionate, provocative way by alluding to Arnold Toynbee's idea of "challenge" and "response" and positioning Mao's thought in relationship to the ideas of Chinese Marxism's two main ideological opponents in the 1920s, the liberal Hu Shih and the Confucian humanist Liang Shu-ming:

> Actually, the inner meaning of Hu's and Liang's debate about culture lay in this tension between the "challenge" faced by China and the "counter-challenge" China must mount. Hu's "total Westernization" referred to the need to follow the lead of Western modernization, the challenge presented by "history," while Liang's "revival of Confucian learning"

referred to transcending Westernization, mounting a counter-challenge
by fully realizing Chinese "culture." In a complementary way, they both
missed the mark. Naturally, they were unable to solve the problem of
how to develop Chinese culture and history in the right direction. Only
the path of socialist modernization can correctly address the task of both
"meeting the challenge" and "mounting the counter-challenge." What
was original about Mao Tse-tung's concept of a New Democracy was that
it included not only a response to the challenge of modernization (the
democratic revolution, the current "minimal guidelines") but also a way
of transcending the Western model and mounting a counter-challenge
(New Democracy, along with the "highest guidelines" to be realized in
the future). The goal of the "Chinese-style socialist modernization" we
currently seek is precisely to establish a kind of new civilization that will
both include and transcend modernization. (290)

Kao's understanding of Mao thus resonated with the strong
Chinese desire, simultaneously nationalistic and traditional, that
Chinese civilization be the world's most admired. As Sun Yat-sen had
said, "China should surpass Europe and America" (*chia yü Ou-Mei-chih shang*). Only China could realize the best kind of society, and
only Mao had shown how this could be done.

Moreover, in linking current mundane realities to sublime,
tradition-rooted goals that many Chinese still cherish, Kao's train of
thought was traditional not only in its affirmation of these goals but
also in its way of looking for a complex, indirect connection between
sublime moral goals and current realities, between a transformative
vision and accommodative practice. As Huang Ko-wu has shown,
much of China's "statecraft" thought (*ching-shih*) in late imperial
times, such as Wei Yuan's (1794–1856), similarly sought to unite the
sublime sage-king ideal with efforts to deal accommodatively with
currently complex bureaucratic and commercial realities perceived
as contradicting that ideal. Emphasizing both a totally practicable
ideal and the impossibility of immediately realizing it, Kao adopted
an accommodative train of thought actually contradicting Mao's
transformative approach, but both of these approaches had deep
roots in the Confucian tradition.[46]

Kao's Maoism indeed accorded with a considerable variety of
widespread Chinese views and interests. He not only fell back on a
traditionally familiar kind of accommodative reasoning to unite the
morally and economically frustrating realities of the present with a

sublime, utopian vision of Chinese progress and global centrality meaningful to many Chinese. He also offered a rationalization for the vested interests of those many millions of Chinese who today benefit from Teng's modernization program and remain proud of Mao's revolution as a whole, including, often enough, the hardships they themselves endured on account of it.

Still more, Kao's train of thought (*ssu-lu*) satisfied an extremely deep need felt by many Mainlanders, including many bitterly critical of Teng, Mao, and Marxism. This is the need to avoid seeing China today as just taking that path of modernization down which Taiwan under the Kuomintang has already gone, and down which the Communists should have started half a century ago. Avoiding this unpleasant picture is not easy if one celebrates Mao's 1940 essay on New Democracy, because in it Mao said that the "minimal guidelines" were "basically the same as the Three Principles of the People." It logically followed that, while Mao jumped the gun, the Kuomintang on Taiwan had for forty years with great success followed those "minimal guidelines" that the PRC today was just starting to apply.

This logical implication of Mao's theory is utterly unacceptable on the Mainland today. Few indeed are the Mainlanders who would agree that doing what Taiwan has already accomplished should be China's goal. Although many economists and social scientists would suggest that this goal is actually too high for the Mainland, Mainlanders need to think of it as far too low for them. Yet, paradoxically enough, such too has been the message of many Taiwan intellectuals and overseas Chinese visiting the Mainland who have repeatedly in their Mainland lectures depicted Taiwan as engulfed by "vulgarized" and "politicized" intellectual trends and the worst aspects of capitalism, democracy, and American culture, as, in a word, epitomizing those ills of modernization that China should be able to avoid if the intellectuals there with a true "critical consciousness" can come to control China's "nervous system."[47]

As I have argued elsewhere, Taiwan's spectacular economic and political achievements have been paradoxically accompanied in leading intellectual circles there by a deep "sense of predicament," a feeling that these achievements are flawed and false in some fundamental sense. Strikingly enough, this feeling has been expressed not only by the Kuomintang's many liberal enemies but also by moderates friendly to the Kuomintang. The classic example is a celebrated lecture sponsored by the Kuomintang-controlled newspaper *Chung-kuo shih-pao*, given in 1983 by the world-famous China historian Yü Ying-shih at the Sun Yat-sen Memorial in Taipei, and, after revision, published as a book by this newspaper in 1984. The book emphasized the compatibility of the Confucian tradition with modernization without including one word about the Taiwan experience or Sun Yat-sen. Far from being criticized in Taipei for this omission, it was attacked by some intellectuals there for failing to attack the Kuomintang.[48] In other words, the rejection of Taiwan as a reasonable, practical model of Chinese modernization has been a basic trend in Taiwan circles too, not just Mainland ones, and indeed in the West as well.

Maoism can be used in two ways to escape this abhorrent image of a China just following in the footsteps of the Kuomintang. One way is that taken by Mao in his 1940 essay, in which he not only said that his "minimal guidelines" were "basically the same" as the Kuomintang's Three Principles of the People but also distinguished the Kuomintang's program from his in five ways, including especially the fact that, according to his theory, the period of "the minimal guidelines" would be followed by that of "the highest guidelines."[49] Depressingly enough, however, this reasoning of Mao's still implied that, even if planning eventually to progress far more than the Kuomintang has or can, the Teng regime today is still only beginning to start down the road on which the Kuomintang has already long traveled.

Taken by Kao, the other option was just to ignore the Taiwan experience; assiduously to avoid any mention at all of Mao's identification in his 1940 essay of the "minimal guidelines" with the Three Principles of the People; and purely to view Mao's New Democracy as a unique way of both modernizing and creating a "new kind of civilization" "transcending the West." To establish this view, however, it was logically crucial for Kao to emphasize Mao's vision of "the highest guidelines," without which there was no way to "transcend the West" or even Taiwan. Mao's goal of realizing "the highest guidelines," therefore, was quite integral to Kao's legitimization of the Teng regime, as was the entire Marxist-Maoist vision on which this goal rests.

4. Conclusion

Kao's Maoism undoubtedly makes sense to many Chinese. His thought illustrates how the People's Republic of China is legitimized in the sense that its official ideological line is based on a vision of reality striking many thoughtful Chinese as moral and rational. Given the above assumptions prevalent in Mainland circles, Kao's train of thought is a way of logically reconciling the Four Modernizations with the Four Cardinal Principles. On the one hand, it accommodates a broad range of modernization policies, including much free enterprise. On the other, it stills leftist objections to these policies to the extent that its way of celebrating Mao's thought is acceptable to the fundamentalists. Certainly it illustrates considerable overlap between the official line and the intellectual world. The common Western view that, in China today after the 1989 T'ian-an-men Incident, these two starkly confront each other is misleading at best.

This overlap is illustrated also by other Chinese views, such as the well-known "neo-authoritarianism" of Xiao Gong-qin, a middle-aged, extremely astute scholar who today is associate professor of history at Shanghai Normal University. His argument supporting the current dictatorship, unlike Kao Li-k'o's, does not begin by affirming as true the principles of Mao's Marxism, which Xiao hints is a form of "romanticism." First, he criticizes as unrealistic the "romantic" view of those early Chinese modernizers who optimistically believed that, if Chinese discarded autocracy, they could realize the most advanced kind of representative government in the world. Conversely, he affirms the pessimistic views of Liang Ch'i-ch'ao and Yen Fu in the early twentieth century that China was not ready for democracy and could modernize only under the leadership of a "strong man." Second, he argues that this "romanticism" still is useful as a way of mobilizing public opinion to keep the "strong man" focused on modernization and so to prevent his lapsing back into the mire of traditional authoritarianism. Thus Xiao vindicates both the authoritarianism and the ideology of the Communist dictatorship, the Four Cardinal Principles as well as the Four Modernizations. Interestingly, when in 1988 he set forth this outlook in a Shanghai discussion with Lin Yü-sheng, a University of Wisconsin professor famous in Chinese circles as a Hayek-type liberal, Lin tended to agree with him: "Perhaps, just as you say, China needs a strong, far-sighted leader occupying a special position who, patriotically committed to the well-being of his fellow citizens, can lead them toward the establishment of democracy and the rule of law."[50]

Paradoxically enough, Mainland intellectuals may well be more persuaded by arguments such as Xiao Gong-qin's and Kao Li-k'o's legitimizing the authoritarianism of their government than intellectuals in Taiwan were by arguments supporting the much milder authoritarianism of their government before 1986, when democratization in Taiwan began. Why authoritarianism was seemingly harder to justify in Taiwan is a question worth pondering. Obviously, the conditions for democratization in Taiwan (economic modernization, urbanization, the rise of a middle class, etc.) eventually ripened, and to that extent authoritarianism came to seem inappropriate. Also, the call for democratization was increasingly identified with a nativistic desire to oust a regime allegedly imposed by outsiders. Strong Confucian elements in Taiwan's culture, inadvertently perhaps, nourished the spirit of "righteous protest" (*k'ang-i ching-shen*), while decades of harsh regimentation empty of Confucian rhetoric created a more compliant elite on the Mainland. Upholding Marxism, the Mainland regime is associated with a world-famous philosophy still respected in major Western academic circles, which have never taken seriously the Kuomintang's official doctrine, the Three Principles of the People. Unlike Chinese Marxism, furthermore, this Kuomintang doctrine has an uneasy relation with the revered May Fourth Movement of 1919, which has been widely equated by a great variety of Chinese intellectuals with China's "Enlightenment." Still more, Taiwan's regime, however brilliant its economic and political successes, ultimately lacked dignity in the context of a culture that traditionally associated rule of the Mainland with "heaven's mandate." Finally, the way respect for Mao has outlasted the shocks caused by his failures reflects how deeply so many Chinese were impressed by his personality, thought, and achievements. Indeed, for many Mainlanders, Mao's basic ideas have just become part of common sense, and Mainlanders who say they have rejected Maoism are referring not to this common sense but to some post-1949 views they indeed reject.

Thus in the Chinese competition between the two Chinese governments for legitimization and prestige, neither modernization nor democratization has served as the final yardstick, a paradoxical outcome indeed, when one thinks of the importance of these yardsticks in contemporary Western thought. Conversely, the horrors under Maoism, which set back the Mainland's modernization half a century, have led to less repudiation of Maoism than many Westerners expected. To a large extent Chinese criteria of political success and failure have not converged with those of the Western intellectual mainstream.[51]

Yet the legitimization of the Maoist regime today is of course far from complete. Inside and outside the Mainland, as already indicated, there is a complex spectrum of views, including some deeply hostile to Maoism. As ever, many Chinese oscillate between seemingly contradictory perspectives, reminding one of the great influence in China of T'ien-t'ai Buddhism, according to which blatant contradictions are quite acceptable as steps in the unfolding of a single truth.

This kind of fragmented legitimization of the political center, however, which was anticipated by some of us as likely to arise after Mao's death, has been typical of Chinese political culture for many centuries. It is integral to what has been called "the inhibited political center," a political structure that forbids the organization of any group politically challenging the ruling group but otherwise allows its citizens much freedom, being organizationally incapable of closely controlling their activities. History has shown that this kind of loosely legitimized "inhibited center" can long endure in China, so long as economic disaster does not strike.[52] "Socialist market economy" should be an oxymoron, but a complex ideological mentality has helped turn it into a reality.

That the Chinese today have committed themselves to a political-economic form diverging from the globally prominent combination of democracy and capitalism can hardly be explained by saying that people everywhere tend to pursue their interests rationally. As Hayek suggested, how a group defines what its interests and goals are and how it thinks these goals can be rationally and effectively pursued depend to some extent on the historically and culturally shaped ideas animating it.[53] Such culturally-rooted divergences limit the "convergence" of modernizing nations, as Inkeles has long pointed out.[54]

Thus the Maoism that seems fully rational to a Kao Li-k'o seems nonsensical to many Americans studying modernization. For Kao, it is in the interest of the Chinese to rely on state guidance not just to "regulate capitalism" (*chieh-chih tzu-pen*) but also to cultivate an ethos throughout society somehow distinguishing between the desirable effort of free individuals to compete for profits (*ko-t'i-chih li*) and an undesirable tendency to "put the pursuit of selfish interests above all other considerations" (*li-chi chu-i, i li wei pen*). True, Hayek himself saw the proper social order as a triangular relationship between free markets, the state, and the "ethos" pervading society. Hayek, however, insisted that, in this relationship, reason puts the emphasis on free markets.[55] For Maoists today, reason demands an emphasis on the state as the guardian of the ethos (or the state, perhaps, in dialogue with "intellectuals").

No other emphasis could be rational for a people who for more than two thousand years have believed that the social good depends more on making the individual and the government good than on leaving the individual free to choose how to define and pursue what is good for him or her. Today, just as during the centuries when Confucianism reigned, the state is looked on as currently corrupt but as corrigible and quite able, at least through dialogue with society's enlightened elite ("the intellectuals"), to serve as the indispensable agent of political and economic improvement. This vision is distinctly different from the current Western way of putting hope in "the civil society" as a conglomeration of free individual impulses largely outside an incorrigible state. The tradition-rooted, predominant Chinese view is more top-down and utopian, holding that the elites, inside and outside the state, can steer society away from the ills of modernization by following the right doctrine. These, then, are two different concepts of political rationality. Aware of this difference, Maoists like Kao think it quite rational to believe that, by making the most of this difference, the Chinese, as a uniquely talented part of humankind, will eventually displace the West as the most admired civilization in the world. For Kao as for Mao, to aim for less would be irrational.[56]

Continuing cultural divergences thus include clashing modes of political reasoning, and these differences could lead to conflict. But they need not. The revised Maoism confronted today by the United States helps legitimize and stabilize a regime the stability of which accords with not only the needs of the Chinese people but also U.S.

interests. This ideology is part of a complex, evolving spectrum of Chinese political orientations that is not necessarily incompatible with the kind of world system that the United States seeks to build. How this spectrum will evolve, moreover, partly depends on the U.S. response to it.

The Chinese people, I would not deny, suffer from a kind of cultural megalomania demanding they occupy the highest rung of the global ladder of prestige, but they are hardly unique in that respect. Moreover, this attitude traditionally has led more to the pursuit of cultural superiority than to political aggression. What is important for us Americans is to deal with the Chinese knowledgeably, respectfully, and critically, maintaining our self-respect, insisting on the principles of a just world system, and pursuing the basic ideals we share with them — in a word, following the Chinese principle of acting toward others with "neither arrogance nor excessive humility" (*pu-k'ang pu-pei*). Writing in 1955, the famous Chinese philosopher T'ang Chün-i said that, in discussing China's future, he

> based himself on three articles of faith: a person should be a person, a Chinese person should be a Chinese person, and a Chinese person part of the modern world should be just that, a Chinese person part of the modern world. Logically, these three ideas are tautological and almost simpleminded, but I never fail to feel that their meaning is inexhaustibly grave, sacred, great, and profound.[57]

When all the world's societies can thus put their nationalistic aspirations into the context of a universal humanity, it should become feasible to build a world system accommodating all these aspirations.[58]

Postscript: Kao's Thought in the Late 1990s

In 1998, six years after publishing his above study celebrating Mao's basic insights, Kao Li-k'o published *T'iao-shih-te chih-hui: Tu Ya-ch'üan ssu-hsiang yen-chiu* (The Wisdom of the Accommodative Approach: A Study of the Thought of Tu Ya-ch'üan; Hangchow: Che-chiang jen-min ch'u-pan-she, 1998) (all page references below are to this book). Comparison of this later book with his earlier one reveals an evolution in his attitude toward Maoism that probably was widespread. He no longer placed the current program of gradual reform and relative openness within the context of Mao's theory. He had lost his belief that Mao had found the one correct philosophy with which to guide China's societal development. On the contrary, he believed that it was an intellectual trend opposed to "radicalism" which had succeeded in articulating this needed philosophy. This trend was correctly founded on "universal human nature and its inherent pluralism" (201). To describe it, he borrowed the term *t'iao-shih* (accommodative) from a book published in Taiwan in 1994, Huang Ko-wu's (Max K.W. Huang's) study of Liang Ch'i-ch'ao (1873–1929),[59] but mostly used the rather different term *t'iao-ho ssu-hsiang* (an approach dialectically blending together dissimilar or opposed elements). He saw this "blending approach" as differing not only from "radicalism" but also from the "conservatism" of those seeking to base China's modernization on Confucian values. Nevertheless, in his eyes, this "blending approach" shared much ground with Maoism, and he still greatly respected the contribution made by Mao's revolution to China's modernization.

Mao's error (Kao in this book referred primarily to "radicalism," not to Mao's thought specifically) lay in his theory, Kao now argued, not just in his misapplication of his theory. Moreover, instead of basing the correct philosophy China needed on foreign wisdom (Marx's), Kao now based it on Confucian principles. Distinguishing his view from "conservatism's" excessive attachment to these indigenous principles, Kao said: "the philosophical basis of the blending approach is the philosophy of the golden mean and of harmonization. This Confucian philosophy embodies the humanistic spirit and wisdom about human life found in Chinese culture's reverence for harmonious relations" (197). Still more, instead of aiming to "transcend the West," Kao talked of resisting "Western ethnocentrism" and aiming for "the blending together of humankind's various civilizations" (201).

Yet although relieved that "during the last part of the twentieth century, China ... in the end left behind passionate radicalism and returned to reason and moderation," Kao still viewed Mao's revolution as an unavoidable part of this whole "stormy and circuitous movement to modernize China during the last hundred years" (200–201).

Agreeing with much of Huang Ko-wu's viewpoint, Kao identified the "blending approach" with the views of not only Tu Ya-ch'üan (1873–1933), who was a brilliant editor and writer famous for his grasp of mathematics and other scientific subjects and deeply influenced by Yen Fu and Liang Ch'i-ch'ao. Kao also identified it with the Marxist Li Ta-chao (1889–1927), the liberal educator Ts'ai Yuan-p'ei (1869–1940), and others, including Wang Yuan-hua, an influential editor and scholar in Shanghai today. Most significantly, Kao asserted that Tu's philosophical basis — the Confucian philosophy of the golden mean and of harmonization — "was much the same" as Sun Yat-sen's "doctrine of the Three Principles of the people," which had been adopted by the Kuomintang in Taiwan (199). Indeed, Kao even praised the Taiwan experience, noting that "the historical experience of Japan and the 'four little dragons' with regard to modernization demonstrated that the modernization of Eastern peoples definitely is not a 'Westernization' process requiring the abandonment of traditional resources" (51). Kao viewed the "blending approach" as one that had been pushed aside by the revolutionary mainstream but that today was "gradually becoming central to the consensus in intellectual circles preparing to enter a new century" (201).

While the "radical," "scientistic," "monistic" trend that Maoism was part of looked to the West for an alternative to China's allegedly discredited tradition, Tu, according to Kao, was the first Chinese intellectual to find in World War I proof that Western culture too was "in crisis" (50). In a nutshell, neither China nor the West had combined a grasp of "moral reason" with "an ability to implement ideals energetically" — the West had neglected the former, China, the latter (96, 46). With this insight, Tu developed a complex cultural analysis of global history showing that China could not just follow Western learning but must simultaneously recover the wisdom within the Chinese tradition (Tu mainly prized the Confucian classics and seldom if ever turned to Taoism and Buddhism). Thus, as Kao reports it, his "blending approach" rejected linear evolutionary theory to seek a dialectical relation between *kung-hsiang* (the aspects of life common to all of humankind) and *shu-hsiang* (the aspects characteristic of only a culturally distinct part of human history) (40–41). This dialectical relation, inherently calling for a blending of Chinese and Western learning, was then to be interwoven with four other kinds of dialectical relations: all those clustering around the distinction between "instrumental rationality" and "the rationality of ends"; the various social-political-moral distinctions, such as those between "the rights of the citizen" and "the rights of the nation" (Kao seldom referred to "democracy" in this context); the relation between "socialism" and "capitalism"; and that between "humankind and nature" (199, 201). Kao here was expressing his own convictions but effectively claiming that they coincided with Tu's.

Tu differed from the "radicals" not only in his concept of knowledge and global history but also in his admiration for the British democratic tradition, with its emphasis on "pluralism" and "tolerance." The "radicals," as Kao correctly said, were more attracted to the "French" model of the democratic republic as Rousseau pictured it (194–195). Finally, instead of seeking a "transformative" (44) revolution to realize the ideal society, Tu favored gradualistic, "accommodative" reform emphasizing education and technological, economic development.

Comparing the "radical" with the "blending" approach, Kao stated: "The view emphasizing the harmonious blending of all valuable elements alone has lasting intellectual value, because as theory it maintains a perfect balance in combining the old with the new, and, as a set of practical recommendations, it pursues progress in a gradual, orderly, solid way" (197).

How, then, could Maoism have any value at all? Basically, like his friend Gao Rui-quan at Shanghai's East China Normal University, Kao saw a "dialectical relation" between ideals and historical necessity: "What is ironic is that radicalism suited the trends of the day because it was so extreme, while the blending approach became estranged from them because it accorded with the true principles of culture" (197). Kao explained further:

> No doubt, revolution was the historical choice of the modernization movement in a China that was half colonial, half feudalistic.... Revolution was the midwife for the progress and development of Chinese society. But revolution is not a panacea.... The transformation of society requires a full, gradually progressing program of social reform. So when one looks at the process of modernization as a whole, reform and revolution are not simply opposed to each other. They are functionally complementary. Where reform falls short is where revolution is of use, and vice versa. (37)

One also has to keep in mind the vision shared by Maoism with "the blending approach" of Kao Li-k'o and Tu Ya-ch'üan. Both approaches illustrate discourse #1. Kao, like Mao and the other "radicals," was "intellectualistic," deeply believing that China cannot progress sufficiently without a systematic, intellectually formulated doctrine deriving moral-political norms from objective, universal principles (Kao's "the pluralism inherent in human nature" [201]). Kao's doctrine, like Mao's, included a teleological picture of history. And, equally important, Kao's and Tu's "pluralism" did not include the idea of three maximally free marketplaces guided primarily by the interplay of individual impulses unsupervised by an overarching moral intelligence.

They both wanted a kind of pluralism free of moral and intellectual dissonance: "I seek a society," wrote Tu, "that has the external form of a modern civilization and the inner spirit of the civilization of the future. Externally, it will consist of individuals struggling to realize their goals, while its inner spirit will be the peaceful one of socialism" (50). As Kao writes:

> For Tu, the goals should be to satisfy the legitimate needs of the masses, not to enable an upper-class minority to pursue its material desires. Tu thus dealt with the problem of science and technology by emphasizing that reason should regulate desire, thus achieving a synthesis of efficiency and justice. He thus brought out the major cultural issue of modernization, that of the ethical regulation of technology, the balance between instrumental rationality and the rationality of ends. (65)

His goal, in other words, was very close to that of the Taipei liberal Yang Kuo-shu, who sought "harmony amidst differences" (see chapter VI below). Conversely, during his debate with the May Fourth leader Ch'en Tu-hsiu (1879–1942) in 1918 and 1919, Tu criticized the way Western culture "from ancient times on had been full of a confusing variety of conflicting doctrines," and he deplored how the influx of Western ideas into China had created "contradiction and conflict between all kinds of doctrines and ideas, creating a world in which anything can be either right or wrong and indeed there is no right and wrong" (127–128; Kao's paraphrase).

All in all, then, Kao Li-k'o in the 1990s distanced his search for the correct doctrine from Mao's doctrine, but he put Mao's radicalism into a dialectical framework vindicating its historical mission, and he continued to share with Mao the ideal of a morally regulated society putting individual freedom and the three market-places within the bounds of objective, universal moral principles.

Endnotes

1. See Prybyla's piece in *The American Asian Review* 8 (spring 1990): p. 75.

2. See "Introduction: Two Diverging Societies," by Thomas A. Metzger and Ramon H. Myers, in *Two Societies in Opposition: The Republic of China and the People's Republic of China after Forty Years*, ed. Ramon H. Myers (Stanford: Hoover Institution Press, 1991), pp. xiii–xlv.

3. Ezra Vogel, *One Step Ahead in China: Guangdong under Reform* (Cambridge, Mass.: Harvard University Press, 1989).

4. See Ramon H. Myers, "The Socialist Market Economy in the People's Republic of China: Fact of Fiction?" (published as The Fifty-fifth George Ernest Morrison Lecture in Ethnology by the Australian National University in Canberra, 1994), and his *China's Economic Revolution and Its Implications for Sino-U.S. Relations, Essays in Public Policy Series* (Stanford: Hoover Institution Press, 1995).

5. See John K. Fairbank, *The Great Chinese Revolution, 1800–1985* (New York: Harper & Row, Publishers, 1987), pp. 339, 342, and his *China: A New History* (Cambridge, Mass.: The Belknap Press of Harvard University Press, 1992), pp. 406–408. For Mao's thought, I have used Mao Tse-tung, *Mao Tse-tung hsuan-chi* (Selected Writings of Mao Tse-tung), 4 vols. (Beijing: Jen-min ch'u-pan-she, all published in 1967 except for volume 3 published in 1966) and "The Little Red Book," that is, Mao Tse-tung, *Mao chu-hsi yü-lu* (Sayings of Chairman Mao; Beijing: Chung-kuo jen-min chieh-fang-chün tsung-cheng-chih-pu, 1967).

6. Fairbank, *A New History*, photograph #42.

7. See, for example, A.M. Rosenthal, "Sixteen Million Slaves," in the *New York Times*, June 19, 1992.

8. John Dunn, "The Identity of the Bourgeois Liberal Republic," in *The Invention of the Modern Republic*, ed. Biancamaria Fontana (Cambridge: Cambridge University Press, 1993). Much the same point is in Samuel P. Huntington, *The Third Wave: Democratization in the Late Twentieth Century* (Norman: University of Oklahoma Press, 1993), p. 288.

9. Chin Chung, *Feng-yun jen-wu fang-wen-lu: Chung-kuo-te yen-pien* (Interviews with People in the News: China in Transformation; Hong Kong: K'ai-fang tsa-chih-she, 1994), p. 177.

10. Li's endorsement of Maoism except for Mao's overly hasty decision to start establishing socialism was expressed in essays written about ten years after the end of the Cultural Revolution, in 1986 and 1987. In 1988, Li in an

interview referred without any reservations to these essays (or rather the book containing them) as fully setting forth his views on modern China's intellectual development. See Li Tse-hou et al., *Wu-ssu: To-yuan-te fan-ssu* (The May Fourth Movement: Reflections on Pluralism; Taipei: Feng-yun shih-tai ch'u-pan kung-ssu, 1989), pp. 252–253. In 1990, after the June 1989 massacre of students, these essays were republished in Taiwan without one word from the author advising the reader that this endorsement did not represent his current thinking. See the chapters on "The Young Mao Tse-tung" and "A Preliminary Discussion of Marxism in China" in Li Tse-hou, *Chung-kuo hsien-tai ssu-hsiang shih-lun* (The Intellectual History of China in Recent Times; Taipei: Feng-yun shih-tai ch'u-pan kung-ssu, 1990), pp. 151–259. One can better grasp the power of this endorsement of Maoism when one sees how logically it fits into Li's penetrating though flawed interpretation of Chinese intellectual history as a whole going back to ancient times. Li's 1989 essay seeking to extricate Marxist truths from the Marxist theory of revolution is in Li Tse-hou, *Wo-te che-hsueh t'i-kang* (An Outline of My Philosophy; Taipei: Feng-yun shih-tai ch'u-pan-kung-ssu, 1990), pp. 1–41. For a discussion of Li Tse-hou and Liu Tsai-fu, *Kao-pieh ko-ming — hui-wang erh-shih shih-chi Chung-kuo* (Goodbye to Revolution: Looking Back on Twentieth-century China; Hong Kong: T'ien-ti t'u-shu yu-hsien kung-ssu, 1995), and Li's whole intellectual evolution, see Huang K'o-wu (Max K.W. Huang), "Lun Li Tse-hou ssu-hsiang-te hsin tung-hsiang: Chien-t'an chin-nien-lai tui Li Tse-hou ssu-hsiang-te t'ao-lun" (On the New Direction of Li Tse-hou's Thought and the Recent Discussions of His Thought), in *Chin-tai yen-chiu-so chi-k'an* 25 (June 1996): pp. 425–460.

11. See, for example, Kuang-tung-sheng chi-nien Mao Tse-tung t'ung-chih tan-ch'en chiu-shih chou-nien hsueh-shu t'ao-lun-hui lun-wen-chi pien-hsuan hsiao-tsu, ed., *Mao Tse-tung ssu-hsiang yü hsin Chung-kuo* (Mao Tse-tung's Thought and the New China; Kuang-tung jen-min ch'u-pan-she, 1985).

12. Although he is part of the debate, Ku Hsin has written a number of books that are invaluable for those needing an overview of post-Mao intellectual trends in Mainland circles, especially his *Chung-kuo ch'i-meng-te li-shih t'u-ching* (The Historical Setting of the Chinese Enlightenment; Hong Kong: Oxford University Press, 1992). This was reviewed thoroughly by Huang Ko-wu in *Chin-tai Chung-kuo-shih yen-chiu t'ung-hsun* 17 (March 1994): pp. 44–55. Vital for understanding current Mainland trends is the historiographically major albeit deeply flawed book by Chin Kuan-t'ao and Liu Ch'ing-feng, *K'ai-fang-chung-te pien-ch'ien: Tsai lun Chung-kuo she-hui ch'ao wen-ting chieh-kou* (China's Transformation in the Course of Becoming Open to the Cosmopolitan World: Another Analysis of Chinese Society's Ultrastable Structure; Hong Kong: The Chinese University Press, 1993). Huang Ko-wu's important review of it is in *Chin-tai Chung-kuo-shih yen-chiu*

t'ung-hsun 19 (1995): pp. 130–155. For an example of the revolutionary view, see the Princeton China Initiative's *China Focus* 4 (January 1, 1996): p. 1.

13. Li Tse-hou, *Wo-te che-hsueh t'i-kang*, p. 4.

14. See note 10 above.

15. My friend pointed to the four Mao volumes cited above in note 5.

16. Published in 1992 by Kuei-chou jen-min ch'u-pan-she.

17. Ku Hsin, pp. 199–200.

18. Published in Shanghai by Shang-hai jen-min ch'u-pan-she in 1994. For a profound study emphasizing that many Chinese today continue to take pride in basic aspects of Mao's revolution and seriously to pursue his ideal of socialism, see Wang Gungwu, *The Chinese Way: China's Position in International Relations*, Norwegian Nobel Institute Lectures Series (Oslo: Scandinavian University Press, 1995).

19. Thomas A. Metzger, *Escape from Predicament: Neo-Confucianism and China's Evolving Political Culture* (New York: Columbia University Press, 1977).

20. See Robert N. Bellah et al., *The Good Society* (New York: Vintage Books, 1992), and Christopher Lasch, *The Revolt of the Elites and the Betrayal of Democracy* (New York: W.W. Norton & Company, 1995).

21. This complaint about the failure of Chinese so far to find the right formula of cultural revision is illustrated by numberless writings, such as those by Kao Li-k'o and Yang Kuo-jung. Famous examples are Tu Wei-ming, *Ju-hsueh ti-san-ch'i fa-chan-te ch'ien-ching wen-t'i* (Reflections on the Dawning of the Third Era in the Evolution of Confucian Learning; Taipei: Lien-ching ch'u-pan shih-yeh kung-ssu, 1989), and Yü Ying-shih, *Ts'ung chia-chih hsi-t'ung k'an Chung-kuo wen-hua-te hsien-tai i-i* (Modern Values and the Value System of Chinese Culture; Taipei: Shih-pao wen-hua ch'u-pan shih-yeh yu-hsien kung-ssu, 1984). On the prevalent Chinese concept of an available perfect theory of cultural revision, see Thomas A. Metzger, "A Confucian Kind of Modern Thought: Secularization and the Concept of the *T'i-hsi*" (A Deductive, Comprehensive, Correct System of Political Principles) in *Chung-kuo hsien-tai-hua lun-wen-chi* (Symposium on Modernization in China), ed. Institute of Modern History, Academia Sinica (Taipei: Institute of Modern History, Academia Sinica, 1991), pp. 277–330.

22. See Thomas A. Metzger, "Continuities between Modern and Premodern China: Some Neglected Methodological and Substantive Issues," in *Ideas Across Cultures*, ed. Paul A. Cohen and Merle Goldman (Cambridge, Mass.: Council on East Asian Studies, Harvard University, 1990), pp. 269–279.

23. The increasing prominence on the Mainland of this "New Confucian" outlook is illustrated by Lo I-chün, ed., *P'ing hsin-ju-chia* (Critiquing the New Confucians; Shanghai: Shang-hai jen-min ch'u-pan-she, 1989).

24. Two of the very few Chinese works analyzing the difference between a

Western idea and the Chinese image of that idea are Huang Ko-wu (Max K.W. Huang), "Ch'ing-mo Min-ch'u-te min-chu kuan-nien: I-i yü yuan-yuan (The Meaning and Origins of the Chinese Concept of Democracy at the End of the Ch'ing and the Beginning of the Republican Period)," in *Chung-kuo hsien-tai-hua lun-wen-chi* (see note 21 above), pp. 363–398, and his analysis of Yen Fu's concept of freedom in his book on Yen adduced in chapter I, note 138.

25. Kao Li-k'o, *Li-shih yü chia-chih-te chang-li: Chung-kuo hsien-tai-hua ssu-hsiang shih-lun* (The Tension between Historical Necessity and the Quest for Humanistic Values: An Essay on the Intellectual History of China's Modernization; Kuei-chou jen-min ch'u-pan-she, 1992), p. 287.

26. On the Chinese criticism of the West, see especially Guy S. Alitto, *The Last Confucian* (Berkeley: University of California Press, 1979).

27. For an example of this concept, see Tu Wei-ming, *Ju-hsueh*, p. 66.

28. See Thomas A. Metzger, "An Historical Perspective on Mainland China's Current Ideological Crisis," in *Proceedings of the Seventh Sino-American Conference on Mainland China (1978)* (Taipei: Institute of International Relations, 1978), pp. IV-2-1–IV-2-17. This point about Mao was also made in my *Escape*, pp. 226–31.

29. See his *Wo-te che-hsueh t'i-kang*, pp. 1–41, and chapter I, section 7.

30. The numerous Chinese references to Habermas's views on dehumaniza-tion include those in a research proposal recently prepared by leading sociologists, psychologists, and anthropologists in Hong Kong. I had the task of reviewing this proposal and noted that Habermas's view was treated in it as definitive.

31. This point is especially clear in Yang Kuo-jung, *Shan-te li-ch'eng*, pp. 371, 379.

32. Chang Hao, *Yu-an i-shih yü min-chu ch'uan-t'ung* (The Democratic Tradition and Awareness of the Dark Side of Human Life; Taipei: Lien-ching ch'u-pan shih-yeh kung-ssu, 1989), pp. 3–32. This essay is further discussed in chapter XII, section 3, note 45.

33. Chang Hao, *Chinese Intellectuals in Crisis* (Berkeley: University of California Press, 1987). My impression is that Kao translated this book into Chinese. See also Ku Hsin, pp. 199–200, for Chang's influence on Kao.

34. F.A. Hayek, *Law, Legislation and Liberty*, 3 vols. (Chicago: University of Chicago Press, 1983, 1976, 1979), vol. 2, p. 110. The mainstream modern ideological Chinese refusal to accept "the three marketplaces" is discussed in chapter I, chapter XII, note 3, and elsewhere.

35. On the problem of continuity, see chapter I, note 35.

36. See their works cited in note 12 above.

37. Benjamin I. Schwartz, *Chinese Communism and the Rise of Mao* [Tse-tung] (Cambridge, Mass.: Harvard University Press, 1952).

38. For previous treatment in the PRC of Mao Tse-tung's New Democracy

concept, see the article by Cheng Hsing-yen in the 1985 volume cited in note 11 above, pp. 167–81. Mao's essay is in Mao, vol. 2, pp. 623–670.

39. Mao, vol. 2, pp. 644–649.

40. Ibid., p. 644.

41. Ibid., p. 647.

42. Ibid., pp. 632, 637.

43. Ibid., pp. 638–639, 624.

44. Ibid., p. 624.

45. For this premise, see the thesis of "optimistic this-worldliness" in my "Continuities between Modern and Premodern China," pp. 286–89.

46. Huang Ko-wu, "'Huang-ch'ao ching-shih wen-pien' 'hsueh-shu' 'chih-t'i' pu-fen ssu-hsiang chih fen-hsi" (An Analysis of the Sections "On Learning" and "On the Foundations of Government" in "Our August Dynasty's Writings on Statecraft") (M.A. thesis, Institute of History at National Taiwan Normal University, 1985).

47. Tu Wei-ming, *Ju-hsueh*, p. 179.

48. This is the book by Yü cited in note 21 above. On the "sense of predicament" basic to intellectual circles in Taiwan, see my article in Myers, ed., *Two Societies in Opposition*, pp. 3–56. Only a few of the leading Chinese or Taiwanese intellectuals have seen the Taiwan experience as a successful mode of modernization offering an alternative to that of the Mainland. For two examples, see chapters VI and VII below. By 2001, however, a favorable view of the Taiwan experience had become more common in the Chinese world.

49. Mao, vol. 2, pp. 648–651. Mao said that, in holding that "the minimal guidelines and the political principles of the Three Principles of the People are basically the same," he was referring only to Sun Yat-sen's "true" doctrine, the one promulgated at the Kuomintang's First National Congress in 1924, when it had an alliance with the Soviet Union and welcomed into it members of the Chinese Communist Party. Mao also said that his "minimal guidelines" differed even from this "true" Sunist doctrine in four ways: (1) the Communists had a more radical program, calling for the eight-hour workday and "thorough land reform"; (2) the Communists had "highest guidelines," not only "minimal guidelines"; (3) as their "cosmology," the Communists had "the theories of dialectical materialism and historical materialism," not the Sunists' "idealism"; and (4) they, unlike the Kuomintang, had "revolutionary resoluteness" — the Kuomintang's "words are not consistent with their actions."

50. Li Tse-hou, Lin Yü-sheng, pp. 248–251.

51. This paragraph owes much to discussions with Ramon H. Myers, Huang Ko-wu, and S.N. Eisenstadt.

52. The basic view in Confucian times that the current government is

fundamentally unsound, being filled by bad personnel following wrong ways of thought and running wrongly designed institutions, has been described in various studies, such as Huang Ko-wu's M.A. thesis cited in note 46 above or my *Escape*. On the "inhibited center," see "Introduction" cited in note 2 above and chapter XII, section 1. *Escape*, pp. 233–234, considered the possibility that after Mao's death (which occurred after the book was written), "Maoist enthusiasm may give way to a more sober and traditional definition of the current order as a partial moral failure.... if the power structure and the economy are once more perceived as slipping down into the pit of moral failure ... a less politicized, more 'capitalistic,' and more particularistic kind of social order may once more appear."

53.   Hayek, vol. 3, pp. 153–155, 162, vol. 1, pp. 11, 5, 69–70, vol. 2, p. 54, vol. 1, p. 31. For his idea that culturally shaped "opinion" determines how people perceive what is in their interest, see vol. 1, pp. 69–70, 92, vol. 3, p. 33, vol. 1, p. 31.

54.   Alex Inkeles, "Convergence and Divergence in Industrial Societies," in *Directions of Change: Modernization Theory, Research, and Realities*, ed. Mustafa O. Attir, Burkart Holzner, and Zdenek Suda (Boulder: Westview Press, 1981), pp. 3–38.

55.   For Hayek on this triangular relationship, see chapter IX.

56.   My argument can be compared to the approaches of two leading scholars. In his *Confucian China and Its Modern Fate: The Problem of Intellectual Continuity* (Berkeley: University of California Press, 1958), Joseph R. Levenson saw that the modern Chinese intellectual mainstream was preoccupied with the problem of demonstrating that Chinese culture was really equal or superior in value to Western culture, even though Chinese currently had no choice but to learn from the West. My argument corroborates his insight, except for his other main point, that this preoccupation was based only on the "emotional" commitment of the Chinese to their culture, not to an intellectually viable, rational insight. His problem was that he substituted his own criteria of rationality for those of Chinese intellectual circles and presumed, in a way inconsistent with much current Western philosophy, that rationality, even with regard to cultural or normative issues, consists of a universal algorism valid for all cultures. On this latter problem, see Richard J. Bernstein, *Beyond Objectivism and Relativism, Science, Hermeneutics, and Praxis* (Philadelphia: University of Pennsylvania Press, 1983), and chapters I, VIII and XIII of this book of mine. But Levenson was brilliant in seeing so long ago how Chinese intellectual trends were deeply influenced by the fact that Chinese could not accept their being pushed out of the center of the world system into its periphery. One should not overlook, however, that, in recent years, PRC foreign policy analysts like Professor Su Hao of Beijing's Wai-chiao hsueh-

yuan have posited without qualification that the globally central role of the U.S. today is to be accepted as a feature of the current era of global history (see chapter XIV).

In Chang Hao's thought (see note 33 above), this Chinese feeling that the world is out of joint appears as the basic tendency of China's earliest advocates of modernization (around 1900) to insist on dealing not only with the practicalities of modernization but also with the "'problem of meaning'" faced, as Max Weber said, by all intellectuals (Chang Hao, *Chinese Intellectuals in Crisis*, pp. 7–8). What Chang neglected was the distinctly Chinese, tradition-rooted way that Chinese modernizers formulated their universal "problem of meaning," typically conflating it with the social-political problem of "selfishness," of "constraints wrongly limiting freedom and preventing self-realization" (*shu-fu*), and of "conflicts or feelings of alienation coming between people" (*ko-ho*), and assuming that this sociopolitical problem would be fully solved in the foreseeable future as Chinese with their unique talents found and applied the right theory of cultural revision and political organization (*t'i-hsi*) and so put the whole world into order. In determining the extent of the continuity between modern Chinese thought and the Confucian tradition, this highly distinctive Chinese concept of political practicability and way of conflating existential with political issues should not be overlooked, but this question of continuity also entails other issues that Professor Chang does not discuss.

57. T'ang Chün-i, *Jen-wen ching-shen-chih ch'ung-chien* (The Reconstruction of the Humanistic Spirit; Hong Kong: Hsin-Ya yen-chiu-so, 1955), p. 2.

58. For an attempt to spell out the guidelines that U.S. China policy today should follow, see Thomas A. Metzger and Ramon H. Myers, "Introduction: The Choice between Confrontation and Mutual Respect," in *Greater China and U.S. Foreign Policy*, ed. Thomas A. Metzger and Ramon H. Myers (Stanford: Hoover Institution Press, 1996), pp. 1–28.

59. Huang Ko-wu, *I-ko pei fang-ch'i-te hsuan-tse: Liang Ch'i-ch'ao t'iao-shih ssu-hsiang-chih yen-chiu* (The Rejected Path: A Study of Liang Ch'i-ch'ao's Accommodative Thinking; Taipei: Institute of Modern History, Academia Sinica, 1994).

CHAPTER V

The Chinese Idealization of Western Liberalism: A Critique of Li Qiang's *Tzu-yu chu-i* (Liberalism) (1998)

1. Millsian Political Theory in China: The Problems of Moral-Intellectual Dissonance and of Theoretical Inconclusiveness

Every society, it would seem, pursues the development of political theory as ideas about how to improve political life (in contrast with political science as a primarily descriptive way of analyzing political life). Political theory has long been important especially in Chinese intellectual circles deeply dissatisfied with their nation's domestic and international circumstances and often believing that the rectification of this situation depends largely on the adoption of a definitive, conclusive political theory. Even though this intellectualistic conception of historical and political causation is controversial in Western circles, Chinese and non-Chinese scholars continue to ask: What political theories have Chinese considered in modern times? Have they correctly or incorrectly understood and evaluated Western ones? Why have they discussed political theories as they have, and why did they succeed or fail in implementing one or another theory?

These questions apply especially to the Chinese discussion of liberalism. "Liberalism" refers to what can be called the Millsian wing

I am most grateful to Ramon H. Myers and Robert J. Myers for valuable advice about how to revise this piece.

of the modern, Western democratic tradition, the heart of which was classically summed up in the writings of John Stuart Mill (1806–1873). The roots of Millsianism are fairly clear. They include the Periclean idea of democracy; the Christian and especially the Lutheran idea of the dignity and total moral autonomy of the individual in the eyes of God; the Renaissance shift toward a political philosophy more focused on the "outer," material realization of values like freedom and prosperity; the rise of science as not only the key to affluence but also a new definition of knowledge; the shift to ontological individualism with Thomas Hobbes (1588–1679); Adam Smith's (1723–1790) celebration of the market economy; the trend in the nineteenth century against Jean Jacques Rousseau's (1712–1778) idea of a government directly embodying the will of the governed and toward an emphasis on governmental accountability and the right of the individual to life, liberty, and property; and what can be called the Great Modern Western Epistemological Revolution (GMWER). This latter phenomenon has often been overlooked. It was epitomized by Rene Descartes (1596–1650), David Hume (1711–1776), Immanuel Kant (1724–1804), Friedrich Nietzsche (1844–1900), and Max Weber (1864–1920). Intellectuals cumulatively influenced by them convinced many in the West that good and bad are a matter of individual judgment only, and that therefore there can be no rationally determined, objective definition of the public good.[1]

However one might outline the roots of Millsianism, many would agree that it centers on a belief in celebrating freedom by minimizing religious, political, economic, and social heteronomy; in protecting the legal rights of equal citizens with regard to life, liberty, and property; in maximally realizing democratic rule by the governed; and in combining democracy with free enterprise.

As Li Qiang writes, Millsian liberalism was put on the intellectual defensive in the first part of the twentieth century, notably by the rise of socialism. Especially after the breakdown of Soviet Communism in 1991, however, liberalism came to be increasingly regarded as the theory most in accord with the nature of the normative modern society, which can be conceived of as combining the structure of the modern national state, Millsian democracy, capitalism, and modernization with a certain state of global interconnectedness. Thus Alex Inkeles and others have strongly argued that there is a global tendency today whereby more and more nations are "converging" toward this model.[2]

Whether or not there is such a global tendency toward convergence, however, it is far from clear that Chinese intellectuals have ever accepted or even fully understood Millsianism. To be sure, even if they failed to understand it, Taiwan successfully modernized and democratized, and the Mainland may do the same.[3] If, however, there is continuing intellectual resistance in China to Millsianism, this does raise important questions: Will this resistance impede any Chinese tendency to democratize? Is China likely to pursue a type of democratization diverging from Millsian principles of social and political organization? Is such a divergence away from the Millsian model likely to succeed or fail?

Much has already been written about the Chinese intellectuals who, beginning around 1900, tried to introduce Western "liberalism" in the broadest sense to China, especially about the first influential "liberals," Yen Fu (1854–1921), T'an Ssu-t'ung (1865–1898), and Liang Ch'i-ch'ao (1873–1929); about May Fourth leaders who rose to prominence around World War I, such as Ts'ai Yuan-p'ei (1868–1940), Hu Shih (1891–1962), and Ch'en Tu-hsiu (1879–1942); about others in the 1920s, 1930s, and 1940s who worried about how to pursue liberal ideals in the face of the Communists' revolution and the Kuomintang's dictatorship, and about whether to ground these liberal ideals in science and Western culture or in humanistic learning and Chinese culture; about intellectuals like Yin Hai-kuang (1919–1969) and Hsu Fu-kuan (1903–1982), who upheld liberalism in Taiwan and Hong Kong during the 1950s and 1960s; and about figures like Yang Kuo-shu, who epitomized liberalism in Taiwan during the 1980s on the eve of democratization there. Studied less so far have been their successors discussing the relevance of liberal ideals to China in the post-Mao era, such as Chin Yao-chi (Ambrose Y.C. King), the famous Hong Kong sociologist, and Li Qiang, a prominent political scientist at Peking University whose book is the subject of this paper.[4]

Much has also been written about why, apart from Taiwan's democratization after the late 1980s, Chinese efforts to implement liberalism failed. In 1991, two years after the T'ian-an-men tragedy, three Chinese scholars, Hu Wei-xi, Gao Rui-quan, and Zhang Li-min, published a learned, moving, and perspicacious study in Shanghai trying to explain this failure, *Shih-tzu chieh-t'ou yü t'a: Chung-kuo chin-tai tzu-yu chu-i ssu-ch'ao yen-chiu* (The Ivory Tower at the Crossroads of Tyranny and Revolution: A Study of the Intellectual History of Liberalism in Modern China).[5] As discussed by them, the reasons for this failure can be put under seven categories. First, much as Seymour Martin Lipset did when he wrote about "the social requisites of democracy," they emphasized unfavorable economic and political conditions.[6] Economic development had not yet produced a "bourgeoisie" able to overcome the dominating "feudal" and "bureaucratic" elements, which resisted the establishment of a legal framework able to protect dissidents. As Yü Ying-shih put it, "intellectuals" were "marginalized." Moreover, as Li Tse-hou emphasized, the desire to establish a government respecting the rights of the individual was superseded by the need to establish a strong state able to restore order domestically and defend China against the imperialism of Japan and the West.[7] Second, influenced by Lin Yü-sheng, the three authors suggested that some traditionally inherited modes of thought impeded a proper grasp of liberalism, such as "intellectualism" (the idea that intellectual doctrines determine the course of history) and "monism" (seen by these authors as the demand that all thought conform with the ideas of those in authority). Third, popular values that were centered on familism and an authoritarian social hierarchy impeded elite efforts to pursue liberal ideals. Fourth, various situational factors impeded the rise of liberalism. In the late nineteenth century, European thought was in flux and Chinese thought mirrored this confusion. Moreover, in England liberal movements had arisen before liberal theory was developed, building up a heritage of practical experience from which liberal theory could be inferred. In China, however, this healthy sequence was disastrously reversed: theory came first, then practical efforts. At the same time, put in the humiliating position of trying to catch up with the West, Chinese intellectuals became emotional and anxious, and this inclined them toward illogical or impractical ideas, such as mixing gradualism with the radical idea of replacing Chinese with Western culture, not to mention the very notion of transplanting a whole culture from one civilization to another. Fifth, Chinese liberals were thus unable to develop a coherent philosophy resolving the basic epistemological, ontological, cultural, ethical, and political issues — for instance:

Should values be grounded in science and Western culture or in humanistic learning and Chinese culture? How should the claims of the individual and the nation be balanced? How should the traditional elitism be handed? How should one analyze the relation between objective historical forces and human will, the problem of "voluntarism" (*wei-i-chih-lun*)? Sixth, unable to devise a coherent philosophy, their "eclectic" thought increasingly incoherent, many of them more familiar with the West than with Chinese political realities, Chinese liberals were unable to act effectively. Repelled equally by the Kuomintang dictatorship and the Communist revolution, they could express only the outlook of "the young intellectuals and the cultural and educational sectors," along with the interests of a small "bourgeoisie"; they remained alienated from popular movements; and they largely retreated into the ivory tower. Especially by the 1940s, many just became narrowly centered on their own intellectual world, calling for a "rational" government that would respect the academy. There, they hoped, intellectuals enjoying freedom of thought and publication could gradually achieve a cultural transformation, which would in turn promote the rise of democracy. Seventh, aware of their predicament and moved by nationalism, many broke ranks and joined the Marxist revolution. The revolutionary moral passion in Lu Hsun's writings moved them. They had agreed with Hu Shih that the nation's five enemies were poverty, illness, ignorance, corruption, and political disorder but had also concluded that the causes of these were precisely the forces being challenged by the Communists: feudalism, imperialism, and capitalism.

Hu Wei-xi, Gao Rui-quan, and Zhang Li-min thus juxtaposed a cherished political theory with the perversities of human history. On the one hand, they depicted Chinese liberals as correctly believing that a democratic government, by applying universally valid principles to the reorganization of political life, can fashion a society in which individuals enjoy equality under the law and so can freely exercise the ability to "reason" and pursue "morality." On the other hand, while admirable historical tendencies in the West had allowed the successful implementation of this ideal there, perverse historical forces in China had impeded it — unfavorable economic-political-cultural conditions, the urgent need for a mass social revolution to overcome the most pathological of these conditions, situational problems, and the intellectual and organizational debilities of the intellectual class.

This outlook thus perpetuated the extremely influential vision of global history developed by Liang Ch'i-ch'ao around 1902: history had developed normally in the West, abnormally in China.[8] If the relation between history and liberalism can be compared to a marriage, Hu, Gao, and Zhang in 1991 viewed the failure of liberalism in China as a failed marriage in which only one party was at fault: Ms. Liberalism, a conclusive political theory, was betrayed by a bad husband, Mr. Chinese history.

This paradigm of the "bad marriage" is widely accepted today in China as an obvious fact. Another example of it comes from an intellectual milieu very different from the Shanghai setting that produced the above study. Broadly speaking, the latter exhibited the kind of philosophical approach to the history of ideas represented by the Marxist philosopher Feng Ch'i (1915–1995), who was the guiding spirit at the Department of Philosophy in East China Normal University. The other example is *Shih-tai-te ts'o-wei yü li-lun-te hsuan-tse* (Developing Political Theory during the Wrong Era), the product of M.A. students in a program led during the 1980s at Tsinghua University in Beijing by the astute historian Professor Liu Kuei-sheng, whose teaching reflected the Rankean methodology and unbending moral integrity of the great Tsinghua historian Ch'en Yin-k'o (1890–1969).

The thesis developed by Professor Liu and his graduate students also reflected the thought of Li Tse-hou (b. 1930), who, extremely influential in the 1980s, sought to combine Marxism with that affirmation of the individual as a moral subject emphasized by Kant. According to their thesis, this affirmation was basic to the European Enlightenment in the eighteenth century. Epitomized by Rousseau's idea of "natural rights," the Enlightenment was truly enlightened. (The Chinese prose here ignores the crucial distinction between "E" and "e.") By following "reason," people would honor "the autonomy of the individual based on reason," "equality and freedom," and so "liberation" from the irrational oppression inflicted on them by feudalism and particularism. These "rational" values became part of everyday life in the West, but, by the late nineteenth century, the Western bourgeoisie was no longer morally focused on the contrast between these universal values and the vested interests of irrational feudal elements and instead had itself turned into a class promoting its own vested interests, those in capitalism, national strength, and imperialism. The bourgeoisie thus distorted their enlightened heritage by combining it with a cluster of theories refuting the idea of natural rights and defining freedom and equality only as means with which to form a powerful, constitutional state able to compete in the international struggle for survival. Hence the late-nineteenth-century combination of liberalism with positivism, utilitarianism, and Darwinism.

This Western degeneration in turn aggravated China's predicament. As the Tsinghua group saw it, China before the nineteenth century had had almost no enlightened thinkers, not to mention lacking a bourgeois revolution based on enlightened ideas with which to uproot feudalism. Then China was victimized by Western and Japanese imperialism. Professor Liu's main point, however, is that when Chinese intellectuals in the late nineteenth century finally found in Western writings the enlightened ideas their ancestors had largely failed to discover independently, they encountered these ideas only in the distorted form that had crystallized in the West by that time. Therefore the leading Chinese thinkers then like Yen Fu and Liang Ch'i-ch'ao from the start put the goal of national strength above any absolute commitment to the "rational autonomy" of the individual. Consequently, instead of being replaced by the popularization of enlightened ideas, as occurred in the West, the feudal heritage in China persisted and became intertwined with the distorted, collectivistic version of these ideas prevalent in the West just when Chinese started to study Western values.

This "misplacement" of the Chinese era of initial contact with the Western Enlightenment combined with other unfortunate circumstances thus prevented China from experiencing that happy marriage of history and enlightened values which had largely occurred in the West. Moreover, this book at least implies that a bourgeois revolution is necessary to propagate enlightened values. Chinese intellectuals, however, became still less interested in developing such a revolution after the chaos and suffering produced by World War I convinced most of them that bourgeois capitalism would be as disastrous for their nation as it had proved to be in the West.[9]

This dramatic Beijing thesis, therefore, like the one above produced almost simultaneously in Shanghai, contrasted two radically different ways in which human history had evolved: a set of fortunate historical circumstances facilitating the institutionalization of the universal values dear to all human beings, and a set of unfortunate ones blocking such institutionalization. It was as though "The Fall of Man" had turned out to be the fate not of humanity as a whole but only of China. In other words, the traditional bifurcation of history had persisted, and so had the reinterpretation of this bifurcation that Liang Ch'i-ch'ao and others had introduced almost a century earlier, the shifting of history's normative epoch from the Chinese past to the Western present.

For Chinese intellectuals in the twentieth century, however, the precise way history was bifurcated remained debatable. World War I created much doubt that universal reason had been properly institutionalized in the West and stimulated the hope that China could "transcend the West." The debacle of Mao's Cultural Revolution then had an intellectual impact similar to that of World War I. It did not end the hope that China would eventually "transcend the West." It did, however, strengthen the belief that China, as a kind of temporarily crippled superman, was currently mired in a contradiction between "value and history" which the West had largely evaded.[10]

Thus contemporary Chinese discussions of Chinese political theory have usually continued to be predicated on the contrast between a troubled Chinese intellectual quest and a conclusive Western political theory, whether "liberalism" or "the Enlightenment." This approach, however, is paradoxically at odds with at least the Millsian kind of liberalism, which emphasizes two kinds of pessimism: epistemological pessimism, which precludes the idea of a conclusive political theory, and that dark Niebuhrian view of history as universally infected by the weaknesses of human nature.[11]

In other words, if these moral weaknesses and unresolved contradictions among political theories are a permanent part of all history, the idea of a political theory that can overcome them is untenable. When Chinese liberals perceived liberalism as a conclusive political theory that could eliminate moral-intellectual dissonance in China, they were brushing aside Millsianism's concept of history as well as its concept of knowledge.

This Millsian outlook resisted in China was epitomized by the complementary outlooks of two great thinkers who admired each other, Friedrich A. Hayek (1899–1992) and Karl R. Popper (1902– 1994). Like Mill, they sought "progress" in the quest for knowledge, morality, and individual freedom, but they rejected the Rousseauistic idea that this quest could be directly fused with the political power of the state by empowering elites to carry out the decisions rationally and freely made by a citizenry pursuing the public good.

Rousseau's view had been described by Joseph Schumpeter as the "classic" theory of democracy. Like Schumpeter, Hayek and Popper rejected the idea that policy decisions could be made by the citizenry as a whole. They also feared the tyranny and Jacobinism threatened by any government believing it possessed the knowledge needed fully to define the public good. Hayek in particular warned against the "fatal conceit" of a government believing it had the knowledge needed to plan the economy.

Thus they distrusted all forms of heteronomy, whether political, intellectual, or moral. In their eyes, an "open society" based on this distrust maximized the legal ability of autonomous citizens equally and freely to interact in "the three marketplaces" — the economic, the intellectual, and the political — and so minimized the parameters of freedom, thinning them down to respect for the law, for science, and for some very general moral principles (what Hayek called an "ethos"). Thus emphasizing what Isaiah Berlin called "negative freedom,"[12] they were aware that they risked moral and intellectual dissonance and entropy, since many individuals were likely to use freedom badly. They accepted this risk as preferable to that of the tyranny threatened by the Rousseauistic approach, not to mention the Marxist. Millsianism thus arose quite logically as a political theory weighing these two risks against each other and consistently regarding the risk of tyranny as the greater danger.

The four leading ideologies that developed in China during the first half of the twentieth century, however — Chinese Marxism, Sunism, modern Confucian humanism, and Chinese liberalism — held both risks could be avoided. Convinced that the corrigible state could be a vehicle of progress free of selfish interests and tyrannical tendencies, they saw no need to accept any risk of moral-intellectual dissonance. Thus they all insisted on a utopian, Rousseauistic ideal of a government fusing together knowledge, morality, political power and an effective concern with the freedom of the individual. Unconvinced by the GMWER, believing that objective knowledge of the public good could be obtained by enlightened, socially visible elites and applied by a corrigible political center, they all looked to an intellectually guided transformation of "Chinese culture" and the resulting use of the educational system to produce morally and intellectually reformed citizens. These citizens would realize what Isaiah Berlin had called "positive freedom," in other words, *min-te* (civic virtue) and *min-chih* (civic wisdom). "Negative freedom" would be enjoyed only by those who had already attained such "positive freedom." Conversely, these four ideologies rejected the idea of a society frighteningly dependent on free, morally ungraded individual impulses unpredictably interacting in the three marketplaces.

Thus, Maoism proposed simply to eliminate the three marketplaces. Sunism emphasized that those "ahead of the rest of society in terms of moral-intellectual insight" (*hsien-chih hsien-chueh*) form a political party, obtain power, and then give every individual "true freedom" and "true equality." As illustrated by the thought of T'ang Chün-i (1909–1978), modern Confucian humanism sought to end history as a process "muddling together the sacred and the demonic" (*shen-mo hun-tsa*) and to bring the cultural, economic, and political marketplaces under the "control" of those with philosophical "wisdom." To be sure, Chinese liberalism embraced "the open society" and intellectual and political "pluralism," if not capitalism. Yet it always did so with the assurance that increasing freedom would lead to a consensus based on "reason" and "morality." As Yang Kuo-shu put it, "Under the protection of the laws of a modern society," with people free to carry on a "rational competition" between "dissimilar ideas.... if a way of thinking is not good, it naturally will disappear from the social world of public discussion."[13] Huang K'o-wu's (Max K.W. Huang's) study of Yen Fu demonstrated how this founder of Chinese liberalism with all his perspicacity sought to combine Mill's liberalism with a system of government and education promoting a kind of "positive freedom" with deep roots in Confucian ethics.

There thus has then been widespread if not total Chinese resistance to the Millsian idea of a liberal society maximizing individual autonomy and so leaving the quest for prosperity, morality, and knowledge largely to unpredictable, morally dissonant interactions in the three marketplaces, instead of giving the basic responsibility for this quest to the state, or at least to a moral-intellectual elite whom the state would respect, allowing them to control society's "nervous system," as Harvard philosopher Tu Wei-ming put it.[14]

This resistance, as I have tried to argue, has deep traditional, Confucian roots. These can be described by using Ferdinand Toennies' (1855–1936) distinction between *Gemeinschaft* and *Gesellschaft*, close to Hayek's between "tribal" society and a society based on "end-independent rules." One can see here two visions of society: one is of a rural community bound together by kinship-like ties, fusing together morality, knowledge, and political power, and so meeting the true needs of all its members; the other is of a society in which individuals can pursue "life, liberty, and happiness" by plunging into an impersonal, materialistic, morally unpredictable, complex, commercialized, urbanized traffic unguided by any central, stabilizing moral force — "the three marketplaces." The longing for *Gemeinschaft* has persisted in the West, as Hayek complained. As the West secularized, however, it also legitimized the moral dissonance of *Gesellschaft*. In China, however, the longing for *Gemeinschaft* has continued to dominate the intellectual imagination (with the possible exception of the most recent trends in Taiwan). Hence the continuing intellectual resistance to the *Gesellschaft* of Millsian liberalism.

This resistance, however, has been far from blind or naive. Although it often takes the form of an inaccurate, idealized depiction of Millsianism, it can also appear as a sharply critical analysis of Western modernity. T'ang Chün-i's philosophical criticism partly parallels the criticisms of Leo Strauss and Eric Voegelin. "Hong Kong's Oswald Spengler," Henry K.H. Woo (Hu Kuo-heng), precisely described the Hayek-Popper model and its "positivistic" under-pinnings when rejecting it for producing a morally and ecologically disastrous civilization that is "out of control."[15] Ambrose Y.C. King (Chin Yao-chi), another Hong Kong scholar, has a deep knowledge of Western social science and recommends that China seek a form of democracy without Western "liberalism" and "individualism."[16]

Li Qiang's view of Western liberalism is particularly challenging. As much as Henry K.H. Woo, Li appreciates how Millsian liberalism is intertwined with the celebration of "individualism" and capitalism, the rejection of utopianism and Rousseauism, and the Great Modern Western Epistemological Revolution, including the belief that how to decide what is good and bad is a matter not of objective knowledge but of subjective preference. As clearly as Henry K.H. Woo, therefore, he analyzes the Millsian, Hayek-Popper liberal model of society as minimizing the legal and moral parameters of the three marketplaces. Unlike Woo, however, he presents this model as an admirable one China should adopt.

In doing so, Li ingeniously and provocatively argues that, rather than offering prosperity and freedom at the cost of moral-intellectual dissonance, the Millsian model combines freedom and prosperity with morality and rationality. But is this conclusion an insightful one effectively refuting the Niebuhrian pessimism integral to Millsian liberalism in the West? Or is it still another attempt to idealize the Western mix of democracy and capitalism, project onto Millsianism the traditional Chinese ideal of conclusive political teachings able to "save China and the world," and so reject or misunderstand the Millsian concept of inconclusive political theories used to pursue piecemeal progress in a morally dissonant world?

The answer is complex. On the one hand, Li paradoxically celebrates Millsian thought while stripping it of its own epistemologically pessimistic way of conceptualizing an inescapably inconclusive struggle to cope with a morally dissonant world. Thus Li follows the twentieth-century Chinese intellectual mainstream in either consciously or unconsciously rejecting the Millsian emphasis on the moral-intellectual dissonance of the three marketplaces. As a result, Li's book, despite its brilliance, is still dangerously utopian, reviving false, utopian expectations in China that there already exists a conclusive system of thought (*i-t'ao wan-cheng-te ssu-hsiang t'i-hsi*) with which to realize a world without moral-intellectual dissonance. On the other hand, Li's celebration of Millsian thought reveals a crucial Millsian premise that Western thinkers have perhaps so far failed to reflect on, Millsianism's absolutistic synthesis of two values, autonomy and equality.[17] Li's book suggests to me that at the heart of Millsian liberalism is a seemingly illogical combination of this absolutistic synthesis with the relativistic idea of the three marketplaces' moral-intellectual dissonance. Li's liberalism thus diverges less from Western Millsianism than much other modern Chinese thought.

My critique of his book begins with an outline of it and then analyzes his unsuccessful struggle logically to depict liberalism as a conclusive political theory. His thesis as I understand it is that ontological individualism and "epistemological individualism" justify liberalism's goal, namely, political and economic forms maximally facilitating the freedom and equality of individuals; that utilitarian consequentialism solves the problem of how to pursue such individual freedom while sufficiently limiting abuses of freedom; that with this way of conceptualizing goals and means, the liberal West created free, prosperous societies free of pathology except for imperialism; and that application of these ideas to China would have similarly desirable results. Thus Li leaves the impression that liberalism is "a practically useful political theory" or "doctrine for the organization of a nation" (260)[18] which successfully elucidates "the relations between the individual, society, and the state" (9), that is, the relations "between the individual and the group, between progress and order, and between universal principles and particular historical traditions" (256).

This is a seemingly persuasive thesis which, however, is either untenable or would have to be developed much more in order to be seriously considered. First, ontological individualism is simply untenable and "epistemological individualism" has been seriously challenged by scholars ranging from Leo Strauss to T'ang Chün-i. Second, utilitarianism is a hopelessly unclear doctrine. Third, the idea that Western civilization is free of serious pathology except for imperialism has been strongly attacked by Western as well as Chinese thinkers. To defend this idea, Li would have had to address a vast range of problems he ignored. Fourth, the relevance of any Western theory, successful or not, to current Chinese problems cannot be established without an analysis of these problems in China and the ways in which they are being currently addressed. Li's book, however, completely lacks such an analysis. All in all, because of all these problems, his book unfortunately evokes a utopian myth that has undermined Chinese political discussions all through the twentieth century: the idea that there is available in the world a conclusive political theory application of which to China would basically solve all the most serious problems this nation faces today. This myth, I believe, has prevented Chinese intellectuals from inductively and pragmatically addressing their nation's economic and political problems, and it continues to do so, much to the detriment of their nation. Li's book, I fear, is as much part of the problem as it is part of the solution.

I should emphasize, however, that, in criticizing Li's idealization of liberalism, I do not pretend either to favor or oppose quicker liberalization in China today. The pace of reform in China today is purely a practical issue that can be effectively addressed only by morally responsible persons with the great knowledge and wisdom needed to address it, and no foreign scholar has those qualifications, so far as I know, not to mention any of the American politicians and "experts" who today ask the Chinese people to accept their political teachings. My discussion here is restricted purely to conceptual issues. My goal is not to influence political convictions per se, only to prevent the derivation of political convictions from faulty reasoning. My own political convictions happen to be close to those in J.S. Mill's "On Liberty," but exactly what he said there and how it applies to China today are both difficult questions.

2. An Outline of Li's Book

Today a popular and influential professor of political science at Peking University, Li wrote an excellent Ph.D. dissertation at the University of London on the thought of Yen Fu, challenging Benjamin I. Schwartz's classic work on this "liberal," to use Li's term. His book on Western liberalism was published in Beijing in late 1998 by the Chinese Publication Company for Social Sciences as part of its series *Studies on Political Thought*, which also includes books respectively called *Conservatism, Communitarianism, Corporatism,* and *Nationalism* and illustrates the broad range of intellectual freedom that now exists in China. Although it can be criticized, Li's is a powerful, erudite, and well-organized analysis. With a large first printing of 10,000 copies sold out by the summer of 1999, it should be influential. Including only a few respectful references to Marx's, Lenin's, and Mao's ideas (10, 157, 165, 208, 266), it leans on classic figures like Benjamin Constant and John Stuart Mill and modern scholars like F.A. Hayek, Carl Schmitt, and Robert Dahl. Largely avoiding the question of the introduction of liberalism into China, not to mention the Taiwan experience, it focuses on the historical development of liberal thought in the West, along with criticisms of liberalism mounted in the U.S. by communitarianism and contemporary conservatism.

In the fall of 2001, I had the privilege of teaching a two-months' course at Peking University together with Li called "Modern Western Political Thought and the Evolution of Political Ideas in Modern China." Along with Dr. Huang Ko-wu (Max K.W. Huang), he and I took turns lecturing and questioning each other (the class met fourteen times, each time about two-and-a-half hours) and so in front of the class continued exploring our differences about the issues discussed in this chapter.

Li's book claims that it would be "one-sided" fully to reject or accept liberalism (4). Moreover, he greatly if briefly praises the Marxist criticism of liberalism (10). He also emphasizes that, according to liberalism, individual freedom must be limited when it threatens "social stability" (see below). Thus his message does not directly conflict with the overall policy of his government today. Nevertheless, he depicts liberalism as the dominant "ideology" of the most advanced part of the world, vindicates its basic principles, and discounts the conservative, communitarian, and "radical" criticisms of it, not to mention depicting conservative and communitarian trends, along with "post-modernism," as themselves part of an overarching liberal framework (10–12, 25). Even more, he ignores and so implicitly rejects not only the Marxist but also the Weberian criticisms of capitalism and democracy as systems serving the interests of a dominating elite (see below).

Li's generally unexceptional historical overview of liberalism, moreover, avoids Marxist categories. He is more comfortable analyzing liberalism as a mix of "theory, ideology, movements, and institutions" than as a tool of class interests (8). He periodizes history by borrowing the "traditional/modern" distinction from mainstream Western social science (109). At home with Max Weber's sense of history's complexity (146), he frequently sees historical relationships as "paradoxical" (*pei-lun*) (see e.g. table of contents, 2). By 1998, this idea of "paradox" had become a popular term among Chinese intellectuals interpreting history, supplementing or even partly replacing the Marxist idea of "contradiction" or "dialectical" relations. He uses it to highlight important historical ligatures, such as liberalism's way of insisting on the total freedom of the individual to decide what is good and bad while simultaneously relying on the authority of the Christian heritage for the production of a morally responsible citizenry (see below). This sense of history's irony, however, coexists in his mind with a picture of history as a process following some laws, such as a principle according to which the stability of governments in "modern" societies increasingly "depends on the acknowledgment of their legitimacy by the masses" (209).

With this general picture of history, Li grants that some aspects of the Chinese tradition meshed with modern liberal ideas but holds that the latter "on the whole were imports" from the West (7). In the West, he notes, they went back to Greek ideas, which he describes using Benjamin Constant's famous distinction between "ancient" and "modern liberty" (33–35). Tracing the evolution of this Greek heritage, he next emphasizes the whole problematique going back to Hobbes in the seventeenth century and increasingly revolving around the ideas of the freedom and rights of the individual, private property, the market, law, constitutional and minimal government, the civil society, and democracy, while also putting the question of freedom into the context of all the philosophical controversies arising out of the Enlightenment (rationalism, skepticism, materialism, etc.). Very aware of problems like utopianism and the tyranny of the majority (71, 122), Li analyzes this problematique by making use of the now well-established distinction between the Millsian and the Rousseauistic wings of the democratic tradition, endorsing Hayek's version of this distinction as one between "British liberalism" and "Continental liberalism." Moreover, he sees himself as inclining toward the former (8–9), even though he endorses Elie Halévi's view of a basic affinity between the two (103). Crosscutting this distinction is another one Li particularly emphasizes, that between the utilitarian justification of liberalism and the justification based on the idea of rights (82, 204–213). Li himself inclines toward British utilitarianism as the most tenable philosophical basis of liberalism.

In his eyes, this basically Millsian liberalism was challenged already in the nineteenth century by British thinkers like T.H. Green (1836–1882), who had been influenced by Hegel and resisted the liberal tendency to picture society as just a marketplace where every individual freely pursues her desires whatever their moral value (106–109). Millsianism was further defined during the Cold War years, when scholars juxtaposed it with "totalitarianism" and often linked the latter to the fallacy of "utopianism" (119–125). It was still further defined in recent years as it was increasingly interwoven with empiricism, skepticism, and rational choice theory. Li illustrates this latter development by critiquing John Rawls's synthesis of rational choice theory, ethical relativism, and social contract theory (125–129).

Discussing Rawls and his communitarian critics, Li is deeply aware of a variety of considerations in which contemporary Millsian liberalism is entangled, and which make it difficult to turn liberalism into a coherent philosophy, not to mention the kind of definitive, grand philosophical system Chinese intellectuals have often sought in modern times (*t'i-hsi*). These problems most notably revolve around the relations among liberalism's fervent commitment to the dignity and freedom of the individual, its correlated commitment to the drastically untenable theory of ontological individualism, its other faltering attempts theoretically to justify the need for a society devoted to the maximization of individual autonomy, and its messy struggles with the intractable problem of reconciling individual autonomy with the need for rationality, morality, and "progress."

Li's book is outstanding because it not only describes liberal doctrines but also probes into these problems with which liberal thinkers have struggled. Li recognizes that the theory of liberalism has not fully resolved these issues.

The questions Li's book raises, however, are to what extent did liberalism resolve them, to what extent did it facilitate the improvement of political life in the West, and to what extent does it promise to improve political life in China? Partly explicit, partly implicit, Li's answers to these questions are extremely positive. He leaves the impression that, despite certain remaining issues, liberalism is a largely conclusive political theory implementation of which has greatly improved political life in the West and would greatly improve it in China.

Admittedly, some of his insights into the success of liberalism seem to illustrate the old Chinese saying *p'ang-kuan-che ch'ing* (one can better understand a human situation when one is not part of it). Although Li, as a cosmopolitan intellectual, is very familiar with British-American culture, he does analyze it enjoying the advantage of being at a certain intellectual distance from it. Moreover, he is a very perspicacious scholar. Thus he offers an insight into liberalism that I find extraordinary and provocative — his insight into the moral implications of its synthesis of autonomy and equality (see below).

Nevertheless, in considering whether liberalism is a successful political theory, Li does not adequately analyze the problems listed above. I shall now try to explain in more detail why I think his analysis fails and again evokes the utopianism that has so long prevented Chinese intellectuals from cultivating a pragmatic approach toward the practical development of their nation.

3. Li's Description of the Millsian Ideal or Goal

Li expresses the outlook of many Mainland intellectuals today convinced by the disasters under Mao that individuals should be maximally free to follow their own wishes rather than made to conform with some centrally imposed, "utopian" vision of the ideal society. Li here is influenced by Steven Lukes' book *Individualism* (155) and some other, uncited sources. He sympathizes with the Millsian focus on freeing the individual from the pressure of unjustified group demands or knowledge claims. Thus he analyzes "the basic content of liberalism" (146) as various forms of "individualism."

He refers to "ontological" or "methodological individualism" as the view that "understanding the individual is the basis for understanding the group" (161, 163). He barely if at all connects this ontological individualism to that emphasis on privacy discussed by Lukes as arising in early modern western Europe. He does, however, link it to "religious individualism," following Max Weber to describe the Protestant idea of salvation as contingent purely on the relation between God and the free will of the individual (161). Li also emphasizes "ethical individualism" and "epistemological individualism" (160, 156–158), here referring to what I call "the Great Modern Western Epistemological Revolution" stretching from Descartes, Hume, Kant, and Nietzsche to Max Weber — the intellectual trend Alasdair MacIntyre analyzed in *After Virtue* as divorcing morality from the rational quest for objective knowledge.[19] Thus Li views as central to liberalism the doubts expressed by "empiricism" and Humean "skepticism" regarding the possibility of grasping "objective truth" (156) and the linked Nietzschean idea that "the individual is the source of moral values and principles and the creator of the standards of moral evaluation." As Li sees it, liberalism holds that "good and bad are purely a matter of what the individual evaluating something feels" (160). Li clearly agrees with Rawls that a democratic society "will necessarily accept all kinds of ideas about the good," and that, therefore, "if there were a sort of liberalism maintaining that it constitutes a teaching covering all moral, philosophical, and religious issues, it would necessarily be unable to provide stability for a truly just, well-organized society" (129).

Thus analyzing the various aspects of the liberal emphasis on the autonomy of the individual, Li repeatedly makes use of the distinction between "negative freedom" as lack of heteronomy, the condition of being free to think and act as one wishes without interference from others, and "positive freedom" as the freedom to pursue morality and rationality, to be a "creative" person exploiting his or her potential and so contributing to the well-being of humankind. Li notes that, while this distinction was prominently formulated by Isaiah Berlin, Berlin's "negative freedom" largely coincides with the notion of "modern freedom" developed by Benjamin Constant in an 1819 essay (175–178). As Li notes, from Constant through J.S. Mill, Berlin, and Hayek, liberalism's emphasis has been on "negative freedom" (179), despite T.H. Green's call for "positive" freedom (107) and J.S. Mill's similar desire to harness freedom to the purposes of morality and creativity (104). Despite this preoccupation, Mill rejected the idea of forcing an individual to act to benefit herself (183). Mill especially insisted on absolute individual freedom with regard to all aspects of the inner life, such as opinions, tastes, and styles of life (186).

Li then analyzes and clearly endorses the political and economic forms of organization recommended by liberalism as needed to pursue this multifaceted vision of individual freedom and autonomy. Government must be "limited" and "must not under any circumstances violate the freedom of the individual." Thus there must be "a clear separation between the power of government and society and the rights of the individual" (219, 259). To avoid tyranny, government must be "accountable" to the citizens. Emphasizing "accountability," Li discusses not only "the separation of powers" but also the need for the government to explain its reasons for its policies and for the citizens to evaluate and monitor these policies (210–212). Without such interaction with the citizenry, the government cannot obtain the mass support it needs to establish its "legitimacy": "with the dispersal of charisma [in modern times], authority must be based on mass agreement" with the government's basic direction (208).

Tactfully, Li avoids arguing that accountability depends on elections and party competition, but he adduces James Madison's concept of "representative government" (217) as well as J.S. Mill's idea that, as Li puts it, "the people must have the opportunity to express their own desires and interests by making use of elections or participating in the political process" (210). Again following Benjamin Constant, Li notes how, from the standpoint of liberalism, citizens holding their government accountable need be only "half-time citizens," in contrast with the "full-time citizens" of the ancient Greek city-states. Most of their time can be devoted to their "private activities," including those pertaining to their free enterprise system of economic organization (218). Li is well aware that J.S. Mill at least for a time inclined toward socialism (104), but he regards Hayek's vindication of free enterprise as the mainstream Millsian view. Again in accord with Hayek, Li notes that liberalism combines its endorsement of capitalism with recognition of the state's important role regarding not only the infrastructure but also social justice (228-229). (Hayek even suggested that the "government should ... assure to all protection against severe deprivation in the form of an assured minimum wage income, or a floor below which no one need descend.")[20]

4. The Problem of Ontological Individualism

As already indicated, Li is well aware that liberalism has consistently depended on an "ontological" or "methodological" premise in order to demonstrate that everyone should try to implement the above vision of autonomous individuals constructing a free society to benefit themselves. This is the ontological view that individuals are concrete, completely real beings with free will, while societies exist only as the accumulation of individual activities. Thus societies are not themselves concrete, completely real entities. In other words, to use Hu Shih's terms, Hu Shih as a "little self" (*hsiao-wo*) was a concrete, completely real entity, but the social-cultural whole that he saw as a "greater self" (*ta-wo*) including him was only an abstraction.

Li sees clearly how liberalism drew three crucial inferences from this ontological point. First, reality as a characteristic of one of these concrete, autonomous entities was precisely the same as the reality of any other such entity. Therefore, in the most basic sense, all individuals were equal. Second, because the enjoyment of something beneficial or of value can be experienced only by a concrete, living being, not by a concept, the goal of social organization should be conceptualized as a process benefiting individuals, not society. Third, since the goal of society is to benefit equal, autonomous individuals, and since each autonomous individual is more able than anyone else to understand how to benefit himself or herself (210), the power to decide how society should be organized should be maximally lodged in autonomous individuals. In other words, autonomy should be maximized, and heteronomy should be minimized as nothing but a kind of necessary evil. Thus the design of the polity and the economy can be deduced from this goal of maximizing every individual's ability to be the master of his or her own destiny, and this goal in turn presupposes that individuals are somehow more real than society.

So central to liberalism, however, this reasoning is barely if at all tenable, as Li is well aware. Right after the French Revolution, conservatives started pointing out that individuals do not exist apart from the fabric of society, which inevitably includes some degree of heteronomy (240–242). Beginning around 1800, Hegel and other German thinkers like Johann Gottfried Herder (1744–1803) started developing the idea that human beings are social beings shaped by their historical and cultural circumstances. Simultaneously, secularization challenged the religious idea of individual souls with direct access to truth and sacred values (again, this historicizing of human existence was part of the Great Modern Western Epistemological Revolution). Especially in the U.S. during recent decades, communitarians have challenged rational choice theorists like John Rawls by arguing that human choices about how to live are not concrete events apart from their cultural-historical contexts (127, 252).

To be sure, many of these objections to ontological or methodological individualism have been intertwined with the political if not reactionary argument that, because human beings are bad by nature, social order depends on heteronomy and hierarchy and is threatened by democratization. As innumerable social scientists and psychologists have pointed out, however, it is undeniable that socially shared patterns, transmitted especially through socialization and education, constitute what every individual is to a large extent.[21] Making this point, Li singles out Durkheim's emphasis on the nature of people as "social animals" (163). This process of socialization and education, celebrated by the Greeks as *paideia* and by the Confucian tradition as *chiao-hua*, creates what even Hayek, despite all his individualism, regarded as a shared "ethos" or system of "morals" on the proper development of which the health of society depends.[22]

Moreover, it is an obvious fact that the development of a shared "ethos" necessarily is based on the heteronomy of adults over credulous children. As even Berlin notes, "We compel children to be educated."[23] Similarly, J.S. Mill took for granted the heteronomy of adults over children, of the sane over the insane, of the "civilized" over the uncivilized, and — to some extent — of the educated over the uneducated.[24] Indeed, such kinds of heteronomy are in practice integral to virtually every society in the world, however "liberal." Unless parental love is a necessary evil, it is far from clear that one should regard heteronomy as a necessary evil rather than a universally vital part of society. Western liberals may claim to be shocked by Sun Yat-sen's "elitist" idea that society should be guided by "those who are enlightened earlier than others" (*hsien-chih hsien-chüeh*), but the structure of even Western liberal societies too puts considerable emphasis on the ability of "experts" to guide society in a top-down way. Although Chinese political thought has traditionally been more top-down than modern Western liberalism, there is a basic structural similarity between Sun's idea of an enlightened elite and the Western liberal emphasis on education and the importance of "experts." To state as an absolute that the individual always knows better than anyone else what is good for him or her is to reject principles of science and heteronomy integral to every modern society.

Individuals thus are not purely autonomous beings each depending just on his or her own cognitive ability to understand the world and decide what to do about it. Instead, they are beings produced by the partly heteronomous processes of groups with a particular historical-cultural heritage. Moreover, the very nature of their social lives precludes a clear calculus assigning more value to the individual than to the group. That is, depending on group processes to pursue whatever goals are most dear to them (freedom or prosperity, say), and often feeling bound to others by feelings of love and gratitude, individuals have historically tended to conflate their own interests with those of at least some other people.

Liberals might argue that such conflation is erroneous. Yet even they hesitate to deny that social life often entails the duty to sacrifice one's life for the sake of one's group. This duty is particularly obvious when one thinks of group life in connection with war, nationalism, and the problem of national security.

With his celebrated distinction between "ancient liberty" and "modern liberty," Constant downplayed or even ignored this duty common to both of these civic patterns. Yet just like the Greek soldiers at the battle of Marathon, modern citizens are often asked to die for their country, and they as well as the citizens benefiting from their sacrifices typically view these sacrifices as quite appropriate.

Recognizing the heroism of people dying for their country, does liberalism then not contradict its premise that value can inhere only in concrete, living individuals, not abstractions? Defenders of liberalism might reply that liberalism is free of this contradiction to the extent that it consistently views not only the heroic U.S. soldiers of World War II but also the aggregation for which they died as sets of concrete individuals. Even so, however, sets of individuals appear as corporate vehicles of value in the Kantian sense: ends for which it is worth dying. If ultimate value inheres in not only living individuals but also remembered and anticipated aggregations of individuals imaginatively depicted as transmitting a particular historical identity, the distinction between individuals and societies as vehicles of value becomes a distinction without a difference. If ontological individualism is tenable, dying for one's country makes no sense. One cannot logically say entity x has more value than entity y but should be sacrificed to preserve y.

Thus trying to develop as a political theory based on ontological individualism and unable to reconcile the latter with the moral implications of war and national security, liberal political theory has typically dealt with this embarrassing predicament by just dropping the problem of national security from its agenda. Thus, whether in this book by Li or in many other books discussing liberalism, such as John Dunn's, the question of national security is barely if at all alluded to (Li's possibly alludes to it on pp. 85, 119, 231, 247). This peculiar liberal way of conceptualizing political theory goes back to the widely shared nineteenth-century illusion that national security is no longer a salient issue, because, as the influential Auguste Comte put it, humankind has already evolved from a state of militarism to one of peace. The twentieth century, however, exploded Comte's illusion. The problem of national security is integral to that of modern political development, as illustrated most obviously by the central slogan of Chinese nationalism, "wealth and power" (*fu-ch'iang*).

Interestingly enough, had liberal theorists taken into account the need of a free nation for national security, they might have strengthened their case. In 1983, Jean-François Revel created a great stir by publishing *Why Democracies Perish*, which in effect argued that liberalism was incompatible with the effective quest for national security.[25] By 1991, however, the liberal nations had won the Cold War, just as they had earlier in the century won two world wars. A strong case can be made, therefore, that liberal societies are the ones most able not only to protect the rights of the individual but also to mobilize themselves and pursue the goal of national security. It is hard to see, however, how this train of thought can be reconciled with the premise that the individual is more real and important than the group. Rather than strengthening their case by analyzing the issue of national security, the philosophers of liberalism have clung to the mantra of ontological individualism.

As Li points out, then, many if not all such objections to liberalism's ontological individualism are sound:

> One should say that with regard to understanding the nature of society, conservatism and the communitarianism current today have obviously been far more intelligent than liberalism. Anyone with the slightest common sense will reject the idea of the individual as a kind of independent unit of existence originally unintegrated with other beings; everyone knows that there is no individual transcending society and history. Very many of the attributes of an individual are products of society and of this person's environment. (256–257)

Even more, Li astutely recognizes the paradoxical way that the rise of Western societies devoted to maximizing the autonomy of the individual depended on the moral authority of a culturally transmitted religious and indeed quite authoritarian heritage producing individuals with a deep sense of moral responsibility:

The reason that the development of liberalism in the West was so successful has much to do with the West's deep cultural and moral tradition, especially Christianity. Liberalism basically is a kind of high-level process of rationalization emphasizing progress, trying to eliminate the unreasonable constraints put by tradition on the individual, seeking to free the individual from the shackles of religion. But these religious and other traditions [including patriotism] were precisely the sources of social order and the shared moral basis on which depended this very liberalism with its focus on individualism. (258)

In Li's eyes, however, liberalism's insistence on ontological individualism is only superficially erroneous. Referring to the whole argument that there is no abstract individual transcending history, Li astutely states:

Liberalism certainly understood this. In talking so much about the individual as a kind of independent unit of existence originally unintegrated with other beings, liberalism's purpose was not to describe the actual relations between society and the individual and to deny the imprint of society on the individual but abstractly to construct the rationale of the ideal society. (257)

In other words, dealing with the no doubt irretrievably muddy problem of the relation between self and group, liberalism has succeeded not in clarifying this problem but in offering an attractive recommendation about how people should actively seek to shape that relation — by tilting it in the direction of autonomy, by thinning down the parameters of the three marketplaces. This normative model, epitomized in the thought of Popper and Hayek, is certainly a logical and practicable one, thinning the parameters of the three marketplaces down to law, respect for science, and certain highly generalized moral principles (Hayek spoke of an "ethos," Popper, of an "open society" true to the essential teachings of Socrates and Christianity).

5. The Poverty of Utilitarianism

The issue, however, is not whether the goal of a society maximizing individual autonomy is logical and practicable. It no doubt is. The problem is how to justify recommending pursuit of this goal. In the U.S., this goal is so widely accepted that it can be loosely justified by just alluding to a historically existing preference. In the more rationalistic Chinese intellectual milieu, however, it has to be theoretically derived from some universal, necessary philosophical principle. At least, Li's historical discussion interspersed with normative remarks leaves the impression he is looking for such a principle. Yet ontological individualism, mired as it is in logical and empirical difficulties, cannot serve as such a principle. Li thus also looks in the history of liberalism for other ideas that might do the job.

Li considers utilitarianism and the theory of rights, but he also adduces what might be called J.S. Mill's theory of progress. Huang Ko-wu (Max K.W. Huang) in his book on Yen Fu analyzed Mill's argument in "On Liberty" as holding that, because the human mind is drastically fallible and so can never arrive at certain truth, the "knowledge" needed to pursue "progress" can be obtained only by maximizing that free competition between "opinions" which is needed to identify and discard wrong ones. Li develops a similar account of Mill's theory of progress (157), but Li fails to note that Mill contradicted himself by describing "civilization" as the accumulation of "uncontested ... truths" and by adducing Wilhelm von Humboldt's concept of "'the eternal or immutable dictates of reason.'"[26] At the same time, Mill presupposed ontological individualism with all its problems as discussed above.

If, then, Mill's theory of progress is illogical, can one use the theory of "natural human rights" to show that the above concept of a society maximizing individual autonomy is not only a practicable goal but also a goal which people should pursue? Li identifies this theory especially with Locke and Rousseau. According to it, all persons are "born with inalienable rights," often described as the rights to be free, own property, be secure, and resist oppression (92). Li holds that "The key point that can be derived from the idea of rights to justify democracy is that democratic government is the only kind of legitimate government" (204–205). Li finds that this principle gives expression to the sociological fact that, in modern societies characterized by "the dispersal of charisma, the basis of political authority must be the agreement of the masses" with the basic direction of the government (208). Yet this principle, Li adds, also implies the people's right to replace any government they regard as illegitimate, and it has greatly influenced "modern Chinese radicalism" (209), which, in Li's eyes, was hardly an exemplary trend. For Li, moreover, the idea of natural rights is "a priori and abstract" (209), not to mention presupposing ontological individualism with all its problems (as discussed above).

Li, however, seems satisfied that utilitarianism provides a satisfactory way of showing that the above goal of a society maximizing individual autonomy is a goal people should pursue. Though paying his respects to Jeremy Bentham, Li holds that "J.S. Mill is the representative figure using utilitarianism to justify pursuit of democracy" (209, 190). Utilitarianism is based not on "a priori, abstract principles" but on the empirical proposition that human beings universally desire to obtain pleasure and avoid pain. Utilitarianism asserts that this universal desire should be the single criterion for evaluating behavior as right or wrong. In recent times, Li notes, this criterion has been interpreted as a concern with "consequences" (93).

Justifying pursuit of democracy from the standpoint of its "beneficial consequences," Mill, as Li puts it, held that democracy, more than any other system, allows individuals to pursue their interests as well as become wiser and more moral (209). In other words, the consequence of democracy is likely to be more "progress," to use Mill's term.

In discussing this approach, however, Li unfortunately ignores all the much-discussed problems raised by any such attempt to identify morality with the assessment of consequences and to derive any specific concept of consequences from Bentham's starting point, the general human or even animal desire to obtain pleasure and avoid pain.

To be sure, many, including me, welcome the idea that a government should be judged by assessing the largely material effects of its policies on the vast majority of its citizens, not by arguing about what its leaders' motives are. Yet, even apart from the problem of presupposing ontological individualism and ignoring the influence of history and culture on how concrete individuals perceive consequences, utilitarianism does not of itself constitute a clear set of norms. This is because it utterly fails to provide any way of specifying which consequences should be pursued, and which are the best means to pursue them.

For instance, should short-term or long-term consequences be pursued? Had utilitarianism reigned in England during the 1930s, could it have logically demonstrated that Great Britain must promptly resist Hitler's expansionism rather than face grave consequences in the long term? Are spiritual and aesthetic consequences important, or only material ones? How should desirable consequences be weighed against undesirable ones when the same action has both kinds?

Consequences affecting whom? Just ego, or also people other than ego? Both Bentham and Mill were great humanitarians who wanted to benefit as many people as possible, but such an altruistic, moral commitment is not a logically necessary corollary of the general proposition that people want to obtain pleasure and avoid pain. As one authority points out, there are "various species of utilitarianism," depending, among other things, on whether one is looking at consequences "in an egoistic or in a nonegoistic way."[27] It is hard to see, however, how a "nonegoistic" utilitarianism differs from the traditional ethical injunction of Confucius to *li-min* (benefit the people).

Moreover, even if "utility" is identified with "consequences" benefiting others, utilitarianism supplies no criterion for distinguishing between those within and those outside the scope of the beneficial action. Should one focus on one's family or also be concerned with the well-being of all of one's neighbors or fellow citizens? Should one also be concerned with the well-being of other nations' citizens (as a disciple of Confucius said, "within the four seas, all are brothers")? According to Li's utilitarianism, should the U.S. government be concerned with how China treats its citizens?

It is hard to see how any answer to such questions is logically implied by the pain-pleasure principle. Nor does this principle logically indicate the *extent* to which one should try to benefit others. For instance, should the U.S. government pay reparations to African-Americans for the years of slavery their ancestors endured?

The extent to which beneficial consequences should be sought entails the fundamental choice between transformative and accommodative policies: should people try to create a society without pain or moral dissonance, a *ta-t'ung* (great oneness) free of vested interests and "tricky politicians" (*cheng-k'o*), or should they have more modest goals, accepting the continuation of some pain and moral dissonance in the world, seeking "piecemeal" (Popper) improvements in the moral limbo of history?[28] The answer to this question about goals depends on how one conceptualizes the given world, especially the universal nature of human beings. Can people overcome selfishness and intellectual confusion or at least accept the guidance of an "enlightened" elite, as all the main modern Chinese ideologies have assumed, or are all persons, including elites, trapped in their unchanging sinfulness and "fallibility," as the Augustinian tradition, including Millsianism, has assumed? Li recognizes that Western liberalism is based on the assumption that "human nature is not entirely good" (232). Yet however one answers this question, the answer is not provided by utilitarianism, since this answer cannot be logically deduced from any general human desire to obtain pleasure and avoid pain. Thus the utilitarian logic itself neither supports nor opposes revolution and radicalism, just as it neither supports nor opposes egoism. As a political theory, therefore, it says little or nothing about key political choices.

Still more, the idea of consequences connotes the scientific study of cause and effect in the objective, passively observed flow of phenomena, but consequences can stem not only from such objectively given patterns of causation but also from the goals actively selected by a human agent trying morally to alter the phenomenal world.[29] Which goals should be selected and pursued cannot be inferred from any general principle that the rightness of an action depends on its consequences.

Moreover, even if utilitarianism could specify the moral consequences that people should pursue, it offers little guidance with regard to the question of means. Bentham and Mill generally believed that science answered this question. Similarly, some scholars today pursuing a version of utilitarianism, rational choice theory, believe that this theory can reveal history's causative patterns. Many historians, however, still find it difficult to explain what historical conditions caused which result, not to mention weighting the different causes responsible in combination for any one result. This is illustrated by the arguments Max Weber provoked with his theory about the causes for the rise of capitalism in the West. Often unclear about what has caused what in the past, scholars cannot easily tell what will cause what in the future. Deriving policy decisions from the analysis of history cannot be reduced to a simply scientific procedure, especially if one grants that there are few if any unifying laws governing the two kinds of causes: events determined to have caused a particular outcome in the past, and actions designed in the present to effect certain outcomes in the unpredictable future.

For instance, can science show that minimizing or expanding the role of Confucian norms would have good or bad consequences for China? The newspapers endlessly illustrate how difficult are the problems of causation that have to be addressed in order to pursue desired consequences: "Spending $300 million over 15 years to desegregate San Francisco's schools bought students computers, culturally sensitive teachers, new and remodeled schools, and the chance to sit next to kids of other races in class. It failed, however, in its first and most fundamental goal: getting black children to do well in school."[30]

All in all, then, it is hard to see how the idea that the rightness of an action depends on its consequences serves either to make clear which consequences one should pursue or to reveal history's causative patterns and so address the problem of policy choice. To deal with this mix of causative and normative issues, many assumptions are needed that cannot be logically deduced from the abstract proposition that consequences are important, and that probably can be formed only by a specific intellectual tradition, a historically specific "discourse."

There are still more problems impeding dependence on utilitarianism to demonstrate that the political order should be a liberal one seeking to maximize the autonomy of the individual. The rationalistic, "objectivistic" (Richard J. Bernstein) utilitarian thesis that the rightness of an action depends on its consequences contradicts the very "epistemological individualism" Li regards as central to liberalism, namely the skeptical view that the goodness of an action depends not on its consequences but on the subjective preferences of each individual. Seriously religious or nationalistic individuals, after all, may prefer to ignore "outer" material consequences. As one Taiwanese nationalist said, "Who cares if the Mainland attacks us? 'Give me liberty or give me death!'"

At the same time, Li runs into problems by viewing Mill as offering a utilitarian defense of liberalism. Li regards "epistemological individualism" as integral to liberalism, but Mill did not accept "epistemological individualism." Mill was only partly influenced by the GMWER. Nietzsche was outside his intellectual envelope. Despite his respect for individual preferences in many contexts, Mill also accepted the moral ideals of German humanists like Wilhelm von Humboldt as the "'eternal or immutable dictates of reason,'" and he viewed "liberty" as presupposing the "uncontested" "truths" of "civilization." Moreover, viewing the Biblical and Aristotelian virtues as self-evident, Mill sought "the highest morality," "the supreme Goodness." It is hard to see how these Christian and Aristotelian ideals of his can be deduced from the concept of "consequences."[31]

If, however, utilitarianism does not yield a completely coherent political theory, one might defend it by pointing out that no other philosophy has managed to do so either. Therefore the utilitarian justification of democracy might be defended on the grounds that what it amounts to is not a satisfactory political theory but the least unsatisfactory one.

This plausible position is indeed what Li seems to be driving at. Li reviews the criticism directed at liberalism (including its utilitarian version) by tradition-rooted conservatives (240–244), by Carl Schmitt (246–250), and by contemporary communitarian thinkers (250–253). Li grants that some of these criticisms have been justified but also says that these critics "have been more successful in criticizing liberalism than in themselves constructing a doctrine about how a nation should develop (*kuo-chia hsueh-shuo*)" (260). Moreover, Li holds that, if one avoids a mechanically literal way of studying intellectual history, one can better appreciate the success of liberalism. If one sees how liberalism actually used ontological individualism to make a normative, not an empirical point, "one will discover that a lot of the criticisms directed at liberalism by conservatism and communitarianism have actually not been on target" (257).

If, then, one defends utilitarian, Millsian liberalism as just the least unsatisfactory political theory, one can indeed begin with a widespread consensus today about the goal of political life and the nature of modern history. According to this consensus, prosperity and political freedom are the main political goals, and the modern West has impressively approximated these goals. One can then identify the utilitarian justification of democratization with the theory that the West's approximation of these goals has been the "consequence" of its pursuit of Millsian liberalism, and that this pursuit in other societies will have similar consequences.

This seems to be Li's position, which his book articulates in a resolute if somewhat indirect way. For instance, referring to the picture of the Millsian ideal outlined above, he states: "This kind of democracy not only is in accord with the necessary direction in which modern societies are developing but also is the institutional framework needed to promote social cohesion and civic morality" (218). He also repeatedly depicts the West's societal development as in accord with this "necessary direction." For instance, celebrating the need for governments to be "accountable," he enthusiastically states as a series of simple facts that:

> In the modern West, the "accountability" of the government to the people is manifested in very many ways. For instance, when the government decides on a certain policy, it must clearly explain to the people what its reasons for its policy are; the people can at various times use the mass media or other means to criticize its policy; responding to the strongly expressed views of the public, the government must publicly explain why it does or does not accept them; the government must also give the citizens full and timely reports about policy developments, accepting supervision by the people of its actions, especially the supervision effected by public opinion as the voice of the people; and, after a policy has been carried out, the government must report on the results of the policy, accept the criticism of the policy by the people, and take responsibility for its actions. This includes legal steps to replace the government should the people be dissatisfied with its actions. (212)

Painting this appealing picture of how interaction between government and "the people" occurs in "the modern West," Li's book criticizes "the Western model" only with regard to the imperialism that "the Western nations" inflicted on China (265–266).

Yet many would say that this appealing picture is Panglossian. John Dunn has vigorously denied that Western democratic governments are seriously accountable to their citizens.[32] Li's utilitarian justification of liberalism, moreover, is open to a partly different set of objections, namely, that the consequences of liberalism are undesirable even if they include a considerable degree of accountability, freedom, and prosperity. At the very least, this is a major Chinese view that has been shared by thinkers representing three of modern China's four main ideological trends — Chinese Marxism, modern Confucian humanism, and Sunism. Thus it should not be ignored by a Chinese book evaluating Western liberalism.

6. The Problem of the Social, Economic, and Political Consequences of Liberal Culture

This criticism of Western liberal society has also been expressed in the West since the nineteenth century by a range of thinkers stretching from Marx through Jürgen Habermas. As just indicated, this Western critique of the West has often merged with a dark Chinese picture of the West going back at least to World War I. The Chinese critique has included profound philosophical approaches like T'ang Chün-i's. Much of both critiques was brilliantly summed up by "Hong Kong's Oswald Spengler," Henry K.H. Woo (Hu Kuo-heng) in a book that was published in 1995 and has attracted considerable attention in China. Precisely and even sympathetically identifying it with the Hayek-Popper model of the free and prosperous society, Woo analyzed Western modernity as

> undermining pursuit of its own ideals by generating urban degradation, anomie, economic inequality, political inequality, the reduction of freedom, military inventions threatening to annihilate humankind, a mindless process of economic growth injuring the biosphere as well as exhausting the world's natural resources, contradictions between economic efficiency and political demands, global conflict, global economic inequality, and the destruction of non-Western cultures, as well as being unable intellectually to grasp the nature of these tendencies, not to mention arresting them.[33]

The West today, Woo argues, is a dynamic, hegemonic civilization that is "out of control" (*shih-k'ung*).

Woo argues that these consequences have been largely caused by the misdesign of Western culture, ancient as well as modern, as an ego-centered pattern grossly out of accord with the universal, objective standards of normative cultural development. Whether or not this ambitious causal hypothesis of his is tenable, many of the above alleged consequences have often been linked to that modern syndrome of "ontological individualism," "ethical individualism," "epistemological individualism," and "negative freedom" which Li himself views as integral to Millsian liberalism. In other words, many of these consequences have been blamed on the modern West's liberal emphasis on maximizing individual autonomy by not only minimizing the legal parameters of freedom but also putting into doubt the rational obligation of the individual to respect publicly defined, objective standards of truth and morality.

For many Western observers, the destruction of these rational, objective standards by the Great Modern Western Epistemological Revolution, which came to a climax with Nietzsche, undermined the ability of modern societies to promote the most vital moral values. Shocked by either the rise of brutally totalitarian movements or the cultural coarseness of mass democracy, such observers have been convinced that, once the existence of God could not be corroborated and the objectivity of moral norms could not be demonstrated, human beings, ever driven by their ineradicable sinfulness, would either nihilistically stop believing in any moral standards or perversely embrace evil movements as morally appealing. Thus Erich Fromm described the impulse to "escape from freedom"; Eric Voegelin spoke of the faltering human ability to stem "the disorder of the age"; Leo Strauss viewed "the true crisis of modernity" as "the inability to affirm or believe in anything or any goal or ideal"; Alasdair MacIntyre spoke of the opening of the gates of civilization to "barbarism"; Herbert Marcuse deplored the rise of "one-dimensional man"; Christopher Lasch deplored the degeneration in the U.S. of "bourgeois" civic culture and the rise of "narcissism"; and James Q. Wilson argued that "elites" in the U.S. had propagated a kind of "skepticism" that undermined "the 'civilizing' process" there.[34]

Li is well aware that in a liberal society devoted to maximizing "negative freedom," an individual can easily misuse this freedom when forming her judgments about how to act (152, 157). Paraphrasing Herbert Marcuse's point that "liberal society is a one-dimensional society" (244–245), Li is familiar with the West's internal critique. Moreover, like some other Chinese intellectuals, Li is specifically aware of the Humean skepticism which has encouraged many autonomous individuals to believe that their judgments are not subject to any objective moral standards and so cannot be justifiably denounced by anyone as objectively bad (157). Yet for Li, the lack of such objective moral standards is no cause for alarm.

Paradoxically enough, Li as a Peking University professor has an optimistic view of the West diametrically opposed to the pessimistic view of Henry K.H. Woo, an economist living amidst the splendors of modernity brought by the West to Hong Kong. While Woo has become Hong Kong's Oswald Spengler, Li's views is that, whatever the West's philosophical tribulations, these have not had undesirable societal consequences outweighing the West's successes. Indeed Li does not note any basic Western pathology except for imperialism.

Li even rejects the charge, so prominent in Western as well as Chinese circles, that capitalism creates a morally unacceptable degree of inequality in the distribution of wealth and power. Echoing views basic to the Hayek-Friedman outlook, Li states: "The market economy not only is the most efficient economic system, it also is the fairest, in the eyes of not a few liberals." Whatever inequality it creates is "possibly" less than that created by government intervention in the economy (226–227). Li thus notes the "negative effects" of welfare policies designed to reduce economic inequality (202) and emphasizes the abuses caused by state domination of the economy: "Compared with such a system, the market economy is the fairest kind of system, the one most facilitating popular participation in the economy" (226–227).

Thus depicting an economic marketplace with a minimum of moral dissonance, Li similarly depicts the political marketplace. Strikingly, despite his fervent praise of the Marxist criticism of liberalism (10), Li utterly discounts a central viewpoint developed by not only the Marxist but also the Weberian schools; furthered by Joseph Schumpeter's bluntly empirical definition of democracy as just a way of distributing power by counting votes; and embraced by Chinese critics like Henry K.H. Woo. This is the thesis that, in a democracy, policy decisions are not in practice effected by "the will of the people," which anyway is a largely metaphysical notion. Instead, elites, variously interacting to pursue their own interests, control the mass media, the interpretation of the laws, the organization and nomination processes of their political parties, decision-making by elected officials, and the private and public bureaucracies. Thus Marx regarded democratic governments as just the executive committees of the bourgeoisie, Weber regarded them as "electoral dictatorships," John Dunn has tended to agree with both of these scholars, and Henry K.H. Woo emphasized the way in which specialized knowledge determining a society's development is monopolized by a specialized minority whom the citizenry cannot hold accountable.

Scholars like Samuel P. Huntington and Seymour Martin Lipset have, cogently enough, countered these objections in a pragmatic way by arguing that "democracy is ... simply the least bad mechanism for securing some measure of responsibility of the governors to the governed within modern states."[35]

Li's viewpoint, however, is different. He not only ignores the Marxist-Weberian criticism but also sees no need to defend the liberal system as merely "the least bad" kind of government. Instead, he depicts it as a wholly benign, moral kind of governance.

He recognizes that "liberal democracy" combines "the principle of mass participation" with that of "elite rule." In his eyes, however, liberal democracy is "the product of compromise and balance between [these] two conflicting principles." Presumably, his benign view of "elite rule" connotes the tradition-rooted Chinese belief that political power should be in the hands of "those enlightened earlier than other citizens" (*hsien-chih hsien-chueh*).

Similarly, Li recognizes that liberal democracy's "political marketplace" (219) is full of "political conflict" among groups each of which feels free directly to pursue its own interests instead of the public good. In Li's eyes, however, this is a healthy frankness. Far from leading to disorder, it is the very key to "mutual tolerance and peaceful coexistence between dissimilar political interests and outlooks." As Li sees it, when pursuit of selfish interests is not legitimized, conflicting political parties can only angrily accuse each other of betraying the public good. Only if selfish interests are legitimized can compromise makes sense. Because democracies follow this rationale, "'compromise is the basis of democracy'" (220–223). Li thus ignores the possibility that compromises will be among individuals rejecting what he calls "morality."

Li discusses the role of law in democracies in a similarly Panglossian way. He just cites the general principle, emphasized since Yen Fu, that law is needed to define the "boundaries" (*chieh-hsien*) between the spheres of free action each of which belongs to a different individual (231). Li has nothing to say about how legislators and jurists defining these "boundaries" are influenced by ideology and vested interests. Li is either unaware of how the gross injustices and enormous costs of the U.S. legal system have outraged much of the public (e.g. the O.J. Simpson and Charles Ng cases) or has dismissed these problems as "minor deficiencies amidst an abundance of success" (*mei-chung pu-tsu*).

7. The Morality of Liberalism in Li's Eyes

Apart from denying that the liberal focus on maximizing individual autonomy has had "outer" (economic, political, and social) consequences that are undesirable in some basic sense, Li sees the Western focus on individual freedom and autonomy as promoting not only prosperity and equality but also "inner" values, especially morality as the attenuation of selfishness. The enormous, systematic optimism with which he makes this point is the most distinctive and challenging aspect of his perspective on Western liberalism.

His focus is precisely on the liberal belief that every individual is free to decide for herself what is good and what is bad. Noting that this belief "has had a very important role in the development of liberalism," Li describes it as combining a culturally common tendency with a distinctive Western trend epitomized by Hume's "empiricism" and "skepticism":

> Epistemological individualism is a doctrine about the ultimate nature of knowledge. Its main emphasis is on how knowledge is an individual matter, and it denies there is objective truth. Actually, every culture includes some kind of epistemological individualism. For instance the Chinese fable of "the blind men feeling the elephant" illustrates the importance of individual circumstances in the formation of knowledge about things. The same elephant appeared to one of the blind men as resembling a rope, to another, a wall.

Li notes that defenders of "epistemological individualism" recognize the relativism of such impressions but argue that "the relative truths obtained by various individuals ultimately can be combined to form an absolute truth about the thing in question." What Humean skepticism precludes is such a transformation of relative into absolute truths (156–157).

For Li, therefore, the Great Modern Western Epistemological Revolution has not radically reshaped the concept of knowledge, it has merely accentuated a viewpoint common throughout humankind. Moreover, contrary to MacIntyre, Strauss, and Voegelin, this accentuation, whether or not philosophically tenable, has had benign, not disturbing consequences. In Li's eyes, Humean relativism accords with how societies should or even do work:

> The many moral and political issues of humankind are ultimately matters of individual choice. Their resolution turns on the distinctive preferences

of people living in different societies and eras. No doubt scientific theories and precisely logical reasoning can cause people to think in better, more rational ways when making choices, but they cannot replace the preferences of different people. (131)

Moreover, "throughout history, epistemological skepticism has tended to go together with an emphasis on freedom, while epistemologies with a dogmatic approach have tended to support limits on freedom." Li here particularly has in mind J.S. Mill's way of deducing the need for freedom from human "fallibility" (193, 157) (see above).

Besides meshing with the spirit of freedom, "epistemological individualism," in Li's eyes, furthers morality. Behind his arguments in this regard, one can detect a Chinese viewpoint essentially foreign to Western thought. As noted in chapter I, many Western thinkers assume that if the *objectivity* of moral values cannot be demonstrated, people will feel free to indulge subjective impulses and alter the *content* of moral values in frighteningly unpredictable ways. In other words, if all objective moral standards are debunked, human beings with their ineradicable sinfulness will activate an unlimited ability morally to rationalize even the vilest acts. In Chinese thought, however, this causative link between the problem of objectivity and that of content is insignificant at best. Exemplifying the epistemological optimism traditionally widespread in China, Chinese thinkers like Li can agree with Humean philosophers that the objectivity of moral values has not been demonstrated and yet repeatedly take for granted that the badness of selfishness is a fully knowable, indisputable principle. For them, vile acts occur not because the content of moral principles has been left unknown but because people refuse to act on these obviously knowable principles. Li thus repeatedly refers to "moral behavior," "taking morality into account," or the "sense of moral responsibility" (e.g. 259, 170) without any doubt that the one and only meaning of "morality" is obvious to everyone.

As just mentioned, this perspective is seldom if ever challenged in the Chinese intellectual world, and Li sees no difficulty in combining the view that moral norms are not objective with the view that their content is obvious and unchanging. Even more, he celebrates the moral consequences of ethical relativism.

To be sure, in doing so he is not entirely optimistic. He recognizes that "epistemological individualism" has not dissolved all immoral tendencies, such as that hypocritical use of moral principles to pursue selfish interests illustrated by the particularism of one nation or ethnic group wanting to oppress another (263–267).

Recognizing this element of human perversity, however, Li still resists the pessimism of an American liberal like Reinhold Niebuhr, who sees this perversity as infecting all political life. Li instead tends to confine it within the international arena and implies it is not important within the political marketplace formed by a nation whose citizens have been left legally and philosophically free to decide what is good.

Li does not ask why the domestic political arena should be morally superior to the international one. Possibly he implies that the international one is worse because it has not yet been morally transformed by liberalism. At any rate, he concentrates on the transformational effects of liberalism on the domestic arena in the West. He is fascinated with what "is utterly paradoxical, namely, that just because it makes morality a matter of individual choice, individualism frequently tends to nurture the sense of public morality in an especially effective way" (170). In other words, by canceling the effort to turn morality into a public code imposed by society on the individual, society stimulates the individual's spontaneous desire to act in accord with moral standards, which anyway are obviously knowable. Put another way, Li embraces an optimistic assumption that can be inferred from Mill's "On Liberty," namely, that maximizing negative freedom is the best way to encourage the realization of positive freedom.

Still more provocatively, Li focuses on liberalism's combination of its emphasis on autonomy with its absolutization of equality. This combination, he suggests, is a peculiarly effective way of turning respect for others or even the golden rule into common social practice:

> The essence of individualism is emphasis on the rights, value, dignity, and needs of the individual, and this presupposes that in theory all individuals equally have the same rights, value, dignity, and needs. Therefore, *individualism does not support behavior centered on selfish interests* [italics added]. On the contrary, recognizing that all individuals have the same moral value, it demands that every individual respect the rights

and needs of others.... Ironically enough, just because individualism emphasizes that morality is a matter of individual choice, its effect is often still more in the direction of nurturing a sense of social morality. Thus at the same time that it makes morality a matter of individual choice, it actually instills in the individual a sense of moral responsibility.... Perhaps it is just this strong sense of individual moral responsibility which can cause an individual to internalize moral principles. Thus moral action becomes a matter of one's own self-aware behavior rather than something imposed from the outside. This perhaps is what morality really means. (169–171)

Celebrating the way "epistemological individualism" promotes moral behavior, therefore, Li astutely emphasizes the pregnant combination of an absolute, highly institutionalized commitment to equality with the indeed widespread Western idea that morality "is a matter of what the individual himself or herself chooses" (259). True, Li overlooks that both these absolutes are logically incompatible with any thoroughgoing epistemological skepticism, not to mention being logically underivable from Bentham's pain-pleasure principle. Yet he astutely captures the moral, really Lutheran preoccupation that they imply in combination, and that indeed seems to animate major institutional patterns in the West.

Given this moral core, liberalism, as Li sees it, has promoted morality in many ways. As already noted, he cites J.S. Mill's view that, with a "democratic" way of life, people are likely to become "wiser" and "more virtuous" (209). Li emphasizes that, in recognizing that people are "selfish by nature" and in holding that "Each individual has the right to pursue what he or she regards as beneficial to him or her," liberalism is not encouraging people to "ignore the public good." Using Kant as an example, he notes that liberalism has consistently emphasized that, in pursuing their own interests, people still "ought to take morality into account to some extent" (259). As already pointed out, Western individualism, in Li's eyes, "does not support behavior centered on selfish interests" (169–171).

Li especially celebrates the moral efficacy of the "epistemological skepticism" he sees as integral to liberalism. Viewing such skepticism as the opposite of "dogmatism," Li holds that "modesty" and "straightforwardness" are the "character traits" associated with it, as well as "a high degree of respect for and tolerance of others." Indeed for Li, a person with this "skeptical epistemology" is virtually free of egotism: "Her love of the truth goes far beyond her love of her own power, and her tolerance of others goes far beyond her tolerance for her own mistakes" (193–194). In effect, the citizens of Western liberal societies are viewed as models of Confucian morality! Moreover, although many liberals treat equality as a purely legal concept, many in the U.S. have viewed it in a more substantial and political way, as illustrated by the civil rights movement in the 1960s (196–199). Li also cites Tocqueville's view that democracy in the U.S. has nurtured the "civic spirit and patriotism" (212).

In Li's eyes, however, the morality of liberalism in the West stems not only from the logic of liberal thought and institutions but even more from the specifically Western cultural heritage, especially Christianity: "But these religious and other traditions were precisely the sources of social order and the shared moral basis on which depended this very liberalism with its focus of individualism" (258). (This is only one of the points that may be hard to reconcile with Li's implication that China should adopt liberalism.)

At the same time, as already indicated, Li's enthusiasm about the moral efficacy of liberalism is buttressed by his strikingly optimistic assumption that, whatever the tendencies toward misuse of freedom, the "parameters of freedom" (182) can be successfully identified and maintained. As already mentioned, Li, like many if not all Chinese intellectuals, lacks the common Western fear that, when epistemological skepticism destroys the objectivity of moral values, individuals will feel free to redefine the content of morality in frighteningly unpredictable ways. For Li, as already mentioned, the fundamental content of morality remains fully knowable, obvious, and unchanging, whatever the state of epistemological theory. Moreover, utilitarianism for Li establishes the standards with which to define the parameters of freedom in an entirely clear way (see below).

Therefore Li does not worry that governments and elites may wrongly define "the parameters of freedom" after falling under the influence of ideologies rejecting morality as he understands it, such as Nazism, nihilism, or the kind of Freudian moral permissiveness that Hayek denounced, and that has been exemplified by the advocates of legally unlimited drug use, such as the famous psychiatrist Dr. Thomas Szasz or the still more famous Dr. Timothy Leary, who began his advocacy as a member of the Harvard

University faculty in the early 1960s, became widely admired in U.S. university campuses, and had his ashes put into a satellite that today perpetually circles the earth. Today in the U.S., some of the most respected scholars advocate the basic "decriminalization" of the widespread drug culture. Approval of this culture is routinely expressed in academic organs such as the student newspaper at Stanford University (e.g. *The Stanford Daily*, April 2, 1999).

To be sure, Li is well aware of how the doctrine of freedom can be used to legitimize such views: "Any theory, if pushed to extremes, will lead to grossly exaggerated conclusions hard for people to accept. The theory of freedom also is like this" (195).

Li, however, is not worried that such "exaggerated views" will become dominant in a free intellectual marketplace. Besides his sense that the unchanging meaning of morality cannot be hidden by such exaggerations from the eyes of humankind, he clearly shares Mill's faith that free intellectual competition is likely to make moral as well as empirical "truths" more apparent. Moreover, Li argues that utilitarianism has basically solved the problem of how to define the parameters of freedom.

This argument of his begins with his high regard in general for Mill's liberalism (184, 190), which he views as based on utilitarianism. He also appreciates Mill's suggestion regarding a criterion with which to justify coercive limits on freedom: the limits are just if they prevent one person from "harming" another (183). Admitting that this idea of harm is ambiguous, Li nevertheless says that utilitarianism has "helped deal with this predicament" by using the need to preserve "social stability" as the criterion justifying limits on freedom. With this utilitarian standard, Li suggests, Western liberal governments have effectively distinguished between permissible and impermissible behavior when dealing with the problems of inflammatory or obscene language, of offensive clothing, of religious objections to the sale of certain foods, of homosexuality, and of drug abuse (188–189, 195).

Yet even if the utilitarian standard of preserving "social stability" could be unambiguously used to determine the parameters of freedom, Li's conceptualization of utilitarianism in this context contradicts his basic definition of liberalism. He suggests that, to avoid "extremist" interpretations of freedom, utilitarianism has avoided "making freedom the highest value, that is, a principle which inherently has value." Instead, utilitarianism has "made the principle of utility, which includes that of consequences, into the highest principle, higher than that of freedom, using this utility principle to evaluate the reasonableness and practicability of any particular type of freedom in the context of a particular time and place" (195).

Given Li's no doubt correct characterization of Millsian liberalism as centered on "individualism," which in turn celebrates the ultimate freedom and autonomy of the individual, how can liberalism deny that freedom is a "principle which inherently has value"? Moreover, as already discussed, the concept of consequences is far too vague to serve as a criterion resolving controversies about how to define the parameters of freedom.

What is crucial here, however, is that Li does not think so. For him, utilitarian liberalism has successfully addressed precisely the problem that many, east and west, feel it has proved incapable of handling, that of "freedom's parameters." "Liberalism," Li reassures his readers, "seeks a balance between freedom and order" (182). At least in its "utilitarian form, it absolutizes neither the value of tradition nor that of freedom. Using the idea of consequences as its standard of judgment, it holds that the expansion of individual freedom should be as great as possible so long as the stability of society is not endangered" (196). On this basis, the "law" is a "social norm" putting "minimal limits" on freedom, while the individual herself has to decide whether to limit her freedom by respecting "morality" (170). Finally, Li makes the point that, whatever the theoretical difficulties in defining the limits of freedom, China's problem today, as in the past, is not how to establish such limits but how to push back the forces of conformity and open up the sources of individual "creativity" (168).

8. Conclusion

Li Qiang's account of liberalism complements that in the book by Hu Wei-xi, Gao Rui-quan, and Zhang Li-min. As I have argued, they pictured a failed marriage between bad Mr. Chinese history and the exemplary Ms. Liberalism. While they concentrated on the shortcomings of Mr. Chinese history, Li focused on the virtues of Ms. Liberalism. None of them imagined that this unfortunate marital situation should be blamed on the woman too, not just the man.

What is striking about Li's account is the great erudition and astuteness with which he analyzed Millsian political theory, revealed many of its flaws, and yet still managed to portray it as a largely conclusive political theory. In his eyes, it brought freedom, prosperity, and morality to the West without any systemic pathologies except for imperialism, and it could similarly benefit China.[36]

Li is quite aware of the Marxist and Weberian analyses finding much alienation, inequality, and corruption intertwined with capitalism and liberal democracy. Yet he confidently maintains that the free market economy is the best way to minimize what the Chinese intellectual mainstream since Confucius has regarded as the most serious blight on any society, gross inequality. With a similarly Panglossian spirit, he simply brushes aside the Marxist-Weberian charge that democracy ends up as a kind of oligarchy, an "electoral dictatorship" serving elite interests. He also quite understands the claim that moral risks are entailed by Millsianism's celebration of moral-intellectual freedom, diversity, and tolerance as the hallmark of the free economic, intellectual, and political marketplaces. His point is not, however, that these risks are worth taking. He sees no need to seek recourse in a Niebuhrian apology for the moral limbo through which democracy stumbles; or in Churchill's witty remark that democracy is the worst type of government except for all others; or in the thesis that the unpredictability and moral dissonance of the three free marketplaces is the tragic but unavoidable price of freedom and prosperity. Instead, he sees moral success where Niebuhr saw moral dissonance. Liberalism, he holds, institutionalizes the combination of autonomy and equality in such a way as to produce citizens filled with mutual respect and virtually free of egoism.

Once again, then, Chinese praise of Western modernity has centered on the peculiar claim that Western culture has achieved the ancient Chinese goal, conquering selfishness, instead of viewing Western methods in a more modest way as merely means to achieve some "piecemeal progress" in China. The great Confucian scholar and liberal Hsu Fu-kuan in the 1950s wrote that the very nature of democracy forced U.S. presidents to act like "sages" even if they themselves were morally mediocre.[37] The distinguished Taipei psychologist and liberal Yang Kuo-shu in the 1980s said that democratization would bring about individualism without selfishness.[38] Li similarly praises a Western individualism that "does not support behavior centered on selfish interests" and pictures the liberal West as that one segment of the global community which has become systemically closer to the universal ideals of humanity than China. Confronting the debate going on still today both inside and outside the West about whether the West's liberal civilization is a model for the world or an engine of alienation and domination, Li joins the long list of scholars admiring the West. A more flattering account of Western modernity cannot be found. Such an uncritical account, however, is inaccurate and resembles a misleading advertisement exaggerating the efficacy of a particular medicine.

Besides his idealization of Western modernity and his neglect of the theoretical problems entailed by ontological individualism, "epistemological individualism," and utilitarianism, Li, like Yen Fu and the rest of the Chinese liberal tradition, resists the central premise of Millsian liberalism, the idea that the acceptance of moral and intellectual dissonance is the price that must be paid by those who want to live in a society instrumentally focused on the pursuit of freedom and prosperity. This point has been repeatedly made by standard liberal thinkers like Reinhold Niebuhr. Li argues in effect that they were wrong — in Li's eyes, freedom and skepticism in the West actually raised the moral level of humankind there. Even if this view of his is tenable, however, he should have made clear he was challenging a central premise of Western liberal thought. As it is, he left the impression that, like Yen Fu, he failed to understand it.

He also failed to identify a question underlying the global competition today between political theories: What is a useful political theory? Is it a conclusive theoretical system that can morally transform any society in the world, as many utopian supporters of Marxism and Sunism in China have assumed? Or is it just an inconclusive guide to piecemeal progress in the moral limbo of a particular society with a particular cultural-historical context?

Liberalism itself with its epistemological pessimism leans toward the latter paradigm. Thus liberals in the West might defend their theory as the best available for dealing with the political issues arising in a largely Christian culture during the modern period, though in fact many of them have actually inclined toward the former paradigm, recommending the institutionalization of liberal democracy throughout the world.

Li should, then, have not only revealed the actual inconclusiveness of Western liberal theory but also discussed the liberal methodology, which to some extent justifies this inconclusiveness. Even more, however, once political theory is recognized as a series of inconclusive suggestions applying to a particular society with a particular culture, one cannot avoid the question of Western liberalism's relevance to a Chinese cultural and historical situation so different from the Western.

Li overlooks this latter issue in his appraisal of Western liberalism. True, he might say that his book analyzes only Western liberal political theory, not its relevance to China. Given his book's provenance, however, it unavoidably if implicitly addresses this issue of the relevance of liberalism to China today. It leaves the impression, as already noted, that China should go down the path of political development indicated by Western liberalism. Li, however, does not ask three key questions in this regard.

The first is whether the goal of Millsian liberalism is entirely congruent with the political goals of those Chinese today actively shaping their nation's future. This entails the question of the relation between Millsianism and the evolving orientations scholars try to describe as constituting Chinese culture. Li asks whether "traditional Chinese thought included elements of liberalism"; grants it might have; concludes that "on the whole, [liberalism] was an import" (5–7); and refers briefly to how Chinese sometimes misunderstood or altered the liberal values they imported (159). He does not, however, ask whether orientations rooted in the traditional culture and evolving in the twentieth century have inclined Chinese toward or away from Millsian liberalism. Are certain culturally widespread orientations or modes of thought inclining China to diverge from the Western model of modernity? If they are, as Lin Yü-sheng and others have claimed, should Chinese intellectuals today try to revise these orientations and guide Chinese toward convergence? Or should they follow the advice of Ambrose Y.C. King to diverge away from Western "liberalism" and "individualism"?

Second, if China should head for convergence, how promptly should it do so? Li overlooks that the very father of modern liberalism, J.S. Mill, emphasized the crucial concept of transitional societies, societies so far lacking what Seymour Martin Lipset called "the requisites of democracy." If China today is still in a transitional stage, to what extent should it try now to implement the liberal system of government? Or should Millsianism be revised by discarding any such concept of transition and just positing that the Millsian ideal can be promptly and fully implemented anytime, anywhere?

Third, the consequence of any such implementation should be the concrete, not just the symbolic improvement of Chinese political life. Any such improvement, however, would depend on not only the efficacy of any theory of reform but also the current quality of political life in China. If the current quality is low and the theory is a coherent one promising great improvement, it is rational to begin applying the theory. If, however, the theory is inconclusive and incoherent, and the current system of governance, coping adequately with current difficulties, is bringing about continuing improvement, applying the theory to China may be imprudent. It may even put at risk the current pace of improvement. To decide what should be done now, therefore, one needs to begin with a systematic appraisal of the current pattern of governance and, most especially, the difficulties which it confronts, and with which liberalism too would have to deal.

Li, however, ignores this issue, failing even to identify the variables that should be kept in mind. More precisely, he does mention one of them, noting that "effective" "limits" on "the power of government" (as opposed to merely "formal" limits) can be based on either "law" or "custom": because of such "customs," "some aspects of the power of government are in fact limited." Illustrating this point, however, Li refers only to "the British constitution" (234). He does not note that, in China today, the power of the government to control society also has come to be limited in important ways, whether on account of customs, organizational conditions, public opinion, or new laws. Because the current system of governance, sometimes called an "inhibited center,"[39] already includes an evolving process limiting the ability of the state to control society, one has to ask whether the best chance for further improvement lies in depending on this already evolving process or in introducing the format of liberalism by promptly expanding the electoral system.

Still more broadly, if political theory is the search for the best way to discuss four logically interdependent topics (the goal of political life, the means to reach it, other aspects of the given world, and the nature of political knowledge), it seems clear that contemporary political thought today has not yet found a paradigm that coherently connects these four topics. Instead, unsuccessfully looking for such coherence, political thought east and west has exhibited a seesaw effect, and Western liberalism has not been an exception.[40]

That is, the Millsian, Hayek-Popper liberal model clarifies "outer" problems, those dealing with the avoidance of tyranny and the most efficient pursuit of prosperity, but, as T.H. Green pointed out quite clearly, it does so at the expense of failing to clarify and so leaving to chance the "inner," educational foundations of a moral citizenry, the problem of civic virtue (*min-te*) and of *paideia*. Conversely, the modern Chinese intellectual mainstream has focused on the latter "inner" problem but at the expense of developing a tenable epistemology and of dealing effectively with the "outer" problems of prosperity and the avoidance of tyranny. While modern Chinese efforts to revive Confucian theory, such as Henry K.H. Woo's, have not escaped this seesaw effect, neither has Millsian liberalism. There is today no conclusive political theory on which Chinese or Westerners can rely to improve their political lives, because there is no political theory today that, in discussing goals, means, the rest of the given world, and the nature of knowledge, deals effectively with both the "inner" and the "outer" problems, with both *tao* (the moral direction society should take) and *ch'i* (political and economic instrumentalities), with both *Wertrationalität* (the rationality of ends) and *Zweckrationalität* (instrumental rationality).

Millsianism, then, by defining the free society as three marketplaces limited only by thin parameters, effectively addresses "outer" problems but illogically and dangerously disconnects the educational cultivation of the "inner" life from any public, rational philosophy. In presenting this one-sided, logically incoherent political theory as a largely conclusive one, Li does not help the reader ponder the alternative ways of evaluating this Millsian formula relativizing all values except equality and autonomy. Believing that the content of morality is obvious anyway, and that this relativization just promotes a spirit of tolerance and humility, Li is convinced that this Millsian formula is the key to building a free, prosperous, moral society. From the standpoint of a Leo Strauss, however, this Millsian relativism encourages humankind radically to misunderstand the content of morality. And from the standpoint of a Henry K.H. Woo, reducing morality to the absolutization of autonomy and equality leads to the primacy of instrumental rationality in the service of unconstrained egotism. Instead of soberly weighing these three alternatives, Li impulsively embraces the only hopeful one.

In other words, Li believes the West has already produced a largely successful political theory from the application of which any society will benefit. He has not challenged liberal pretensions by considering the possibility that the modern study of political theory east and west is still largely incomplete, facing basic problems not yet successfully addressed. No doubt, Li's reluctance to recognize the "poverty" of political theory today (to steal from Popper's characterization of "historicism") reflects not only his epistemological optimism but also the nature of the Chinese state today, which perhaps can be effectively criticized only by an intellectual plausibly armed with a conclusively correct political theory. Thus while the world actually lacks a largely successful political theory, China's public political discussion has as usual come down to an argument about which political theory is essentially conclusive. This argument might be compared by some to an argument between two villagers about whether a ghost lives in the tree north of the village or in the tree to the south.

Participating in this unfortunate argument, Li idealizes liberalism while filtering out some of its central premises. At the same time, paradoxically enough, like the Chinese thinkers explicitly rejecting Western liberalism, such as Ambrose Y.C. King, Li exemplifies a major Chinese tendency today to resist adoption of Millsian liberalism as it is understood in the West. Whether this trend is desirable can be debated. What does seem clear, however, is that, in the discussion of political theories, one should at least begin with a clear list of the topics a political theory should deal with, and one should avoid either idealizing or demonizing the various intellectual and societal models global history has provided. As I have just tried to argue, such a critical approach is impeded by the deeply-rooted Chinese utopian tendency to assume that history has already produced a reliable canon of political guidelines, thus to idealize a particular theoretical model, and so to believe that applying this model to China can morally transform political life there. To quote a Western sage (David Hume): "All plans of government which suppose great reformation in the manners of mankind are plainly imaginary."[41]

Despite its brilliance, therefore, Li's book is useful only as a preliminary way for Chinese readers to begin understanding Western liberalism. It can also be criticized in less basic ways. It often lapses into textbook generalizations instead of probing more deeply into a particular thinker's train of thought. In other words, apart from its insight into the liberal synthesis of equality and autonomy, it is well below the level of scholarship reached, say, by the essays in Leo Strauss and Joseph Cropsey, eds., *History of Political Philosophy*, or Chang Hao's essay on "the sense of the permanently dark side of history." For instance, as I have tried to show, Li's description of Mill's liberalism as "utilitarian" is simplistic, as is his discussion of utilitarianism. Moreover, he relies far too much on the translations of Western books into Chinese; his bibliography is seriously incomplete; and his book lacks an index. A deeper understanding of Western liberalism could have been achieved by exploring the conflict between the New Left and the New Right. This conflict is outlined in an important book Li overlooked, David Held, *Models of Democracy* (Stanford: Stanford University Press, 1987), and entails the clash between Robert N. Bellah's rejection of "Lockean individualism" and Christopher Lasch's reaffirmation of it. Exploration of these issues, including the libertarianism of Robert Nozick, would have allowed Li better to analyze the great difficulties liberalism faces in defining the parameters of freedom.

Despite these shortcomings and others, however, his book should be widely read in China as a brilliant and sometimes subtle attempt to analyze the complexities of the Western liberal tradition. The Chinese encounter with this Western tradition has so far stretched from Yen Fu through Li Qiang. The goal of this encounter, a completely lucid and balanced analysis of all the issues involved, has not yet been reached. Li's book, however, has brought the Chinese intellectual world much closer to this goal than it was before. Given his perspective as an intellectual looking at Western liberalism from the standpoint of the post-Mao Chinese world, and given his impressive erudition and great perspicacity, Li has written the most interesting essay on Western liberalism that I have ever read.

I should add that Professor Li, as a scholar constantly exploring new avenues of political thought and historical research, is exceptionally inclined to consider critically not only the ideas of others but also his own. After reading the essay constituting this chapter, he had it translated into Chinese and eventually concluded that its points were not altogether inappropriate. In December of 2003, when I visited Beijing, he told me that he had come to emphasize more the political culture conditions in China today affecting the pace of democratization, and that he felt there was a growing tendency in China today toward convergence between the different ideological trends inside and outside the government.

Endnotes

1.   This outline reflects the influence of David Held, *Models of Democracy* (Stanford: Stanford University Press, 1987); the essay on "liberalism" in John Dunn, *Western Political Theory in the Face of the Future* (Cambridge: Cambridge University Press, 1990); Leo Strauss and Joseph Cropsey, eds., *History of Political Philosophy* (Chicago: The University of Chicago Press, 1987); and Li Qiang, *Tzu-yu chu-i* (Liberalism; Beijing: Chung-kuo she-hui k'o-hsueh ch'u-pan-she, 1998). On romanization, this essay of mine follows Wade-Giles with a few exceptions, such as Li Qiang's name. All page references in the text are to his book. On the GMWER, see chapter I.

2.   Alex Inkeles, *One World Emerging: Convergence and Divergence in Industrial Societies* (Boulder: Westview Press, 1998).

3.   Linda Chao and Ramon H. Myers, *The First Chinese Democracy: Political Life in the Republic of China on Taiwan* (Baltimore: The Johns Hopkins University Press, 1998). Also see issue of *Journal of Democracy* 9 (January 1998) devoted to the question "Will China Democratize?"

4.   A thorough discussion of recent liberal thought on the Mainland would deal also with other thinkers, such as Ku Chun, Wang Yuan-hua, and Hsu Chi-lin. Hsu Chi-lin's *Ling-i-chung ch'i-meng* (Another Kind of Enlightenment; Guangzhou: Hua-ch'eng ch'u-pan-she, 1999) is a fascinating, most important document for understanding the state of liberal thought in China today. Li Qiang's book is cited in note 1 above. Chapter VII is on Ambrose Y.C. King. His thesis that "political modernity" must mesh with cultural tendencies, and that China's mainstream culture, "Confucian culture," is partly incompatible with "liberalism" and "individualism" is in his *Chung-kuo cheng-chih yü wen-hua* (China's Culture and Forms of Governance; Hong Kong: Oxford University Press, 1997), p. xiii. On Yen Fu and Liang Ch'i-ch'ao, see the two books respectively on them by Huang Ko-wu (Max K.W. Huang) cited in chapter I, note 138. On T'an Ssu-t'ung, see Chang Hao, *Lieh-shih ching-shen yü p'i-p'an i-shih: T'an Ssu-t'ung ssu-hsiang-te fen-hsi* (The Spirit of Heroic Martyrdom and of Moral-Political Criticism; Taipei: Lien-ching ch'u-pan shih-yeh kung-ssu, 1988). On Yang Kuo-shu,

see chapter VI and Mo-tzu-k'o (Thomas A. Metzger), "Erh-shih shih-chi Chung-kuo chih-shih fen-tzu-te tzu-chueh wen-t'i: I-ko wai-kuo-jen te k'an-fa" (Chinese Intellectuals in the Twentieth Century and the Problem of Self-Awareness: A Foreigner's Outlook), in Yü Ying-shih et al., *Chung-kuo li-shih chuan-hsing shih-ch'i-te chih-shih fen-tzu* (Intellectuals during Periods of Transformation in Chinese History; Taipei: Lien-ching ch'u-pan shi-yeh kung-ssu, 1992), pp. 83–138. This article can also be found in *Tang-tai* 73 (May 1, 1992), pp. 56–74, and ibid. 74 (June 1, 1992), pp. 62–79, and in *Hsueh-shu ssu-hsiang p'ing-lun* 3 (1998), pp. 183–229. Much of the standard Western bibliography on modern Chinese liberals can be found in John K. Fairbank, *China: A New History* (Cambridge, Mass.: The Belknap Press of Harvard University Press, 1992).

5. Shanghai: Shang-hai jen-min ch'u-pan-she, 1991. For a partly different perspective, see Huang Ko-wu, *Tzu-yu-te so-i-jan*, pp. 36–39 (full bibliographical reference in chapter I, note 138).

6. Seymour Martin Lipset, "The Social Requisites of Democracy Revisited: 1993 Presidential Address," *American Sociological Review* 59 (February 1994): pp. 1–22.

7. For a description of Yü's overall concept regarding the way "intellectuals were always at the periphery of power ... throughout the twentieth century," see Thomas A. Metzger, "Modern Chinese Utopianism and the Western Concept of the Civil Society," in *Kuo T'ing-i hsien-sheng chiu-chih tan-ch'en chi-nien lun-wen-chi* (Papers Commemorating the Ninetieth Birthday of Professor Kuo Ting-yee), 2 vols., ed. Ch'en San-ching (Taipei: Institute of Modern History, Academia Sinica, 1995), vol. 2, p. 288. This is based on his article in *Lien-ho-pao*, December 28, 1993. This article by Yü also incorporates Li Tse-hou's famous point that "the spirit of enlightenment was overcome by the need to save the nation from destruction" (*Chiu-wang ya-tao ch'i-meng*). For this point, see Li Tse-hou, *Chung-kuo hsien-tai ssu-hsiang shih-lun* (The Intellectual History of China in Recent Times; Taipei: Feng-yun shih-tai ch'u-pan kung-ssu, 1990), pp. 1–53.

8. For this point about Liang, see book on him by Huang Ko-wu cited in note 4 above.

9. Liu Kuei-sheng, ed., *Shih-tai-te ts'o-wei yü li-lun-te hsuan-tse: Hsi-fang chin-tai ssu-ch'ao yü Chung-kuo 'wu-ssu' ch'i-meng ssu-hsiang* (Shaping Political Theory during the Wrong Era: Modern Western Intellectual Trends and the Enlightenment in China during the May Fourth Period; Beijing: Ch'ing-hua ta-hsueh ch'u-pan-she, 1989).

10. Gao Rui-quan, *T'ien-ming-te mo-lo: Chung-kuo chin-tai wei-i-chih-lun ssu-ch'ao yen-chiu* (The Collapse of Fatalism and of the Normative Cosmic Order: A Study of Modern Chinese Voluntarism; Shanghai: Shang-hai jen-min ch'u-pan-she, 1991). For the similar view that China's radical mainstream in the

twentieth century contradicted "rational thought," see Kao Li-k'o, *T'iao-shih-te chih-hui: Tu Ya-ch'üan ssu-hsiang yen-chiu* (The Wisdom of the Accommodative Approach: A Study of the Thought of Tu Ya-ch'üan; Hangzhou: Che-chiang jen-min ch'u-pan-she, 1998), p. 7.

11. On these two pessimisms, see chapter I.

12. Hayek's thesis about the necessary inefficiencies of a centrally planned economy was complemented by a bluntly scientistic political theory emphasizing not only the integrity of the economic marketplace but also many vital state functions and the need for a certain norm-defining "ethos." On the latter, see chapter IX and Friedrich A. Hayek, *Law, Legislation and Liberty*, 3 vols. (Chicago: The University of Chicago Press, 1983, 1976, 1979), vol. 3, pp. 156–166, 174–176, vol. 2, pp. 57, 74. On "negative freedom," see Isaiah Berlin, *Four Essays on Liberty* (Oxford: Oxford University Press, 1969).

13. Yang Kuo-shu, *K'ai-fang-te to-yuan she-hui* (The Open, Pluralistic Society; Taipei: Tung-ta t'u-shu ku-fen yu-hsien kung-ssu, 1985), p. 13. See chapter VI.

14. Tu Wei-ming, *Ju-hsueh ti-san-ch'i fa-chan-te ch'ien-ching wen-t'i* (Reflections on the Dawning of the Third Era in the Evolution of Confucian Learning; Taipei: Lien-ching ch'u-pan shih-yeh kung-ssu, 1989), p. 179.

15. See chapter III.

16. See note 4 above and chapter VII.

17. The David Held book mentioned above in note 1 typifies much current Millsian thought in the West in trying to derive a normative theory of democracy from two principles, "freedom" or "autonomy" and "equality." (See Held, pp. 269–270.) Li, however, uses these two ideas not to try to resolve the current tension in the U.S. between the New Right and the New Left but to describe two values strongly institutionalized in much of the West and to ponder the moral implications of this institutionalization. Reading Held, I was struck by how his Millsianism filters out one of Mill's key premises, "civilization" and all its moral connotations, an idea basic indeed to Hayek and Popper as well but too imprecise for Held's intellectual milieu. Reading Li, I was struck by the deep moral and civilizational implications of autonomy and equality as the combination of these had in historical fact been institutionalized in some Western societies.

18. All page references in my text are to Li's *Tzu-yu chu-i*.

19. See chapter I on the GMWER.

20. Hayek, vol. 2, p. 87, vol. 3, p. 55.

21. This point is central to the Parsonian tradition and the mainstream of sociological theory represented by the texts collected in Talcott Parsons et al., eds., *Theories of Society*, 2 vols. (New York: The Free Press of Glencoe, Inc., 1961).

22. Much neglected in current political theory, the broad idea of education denoted by *paideia* goes back to Greek ideals discussed in Werner Jaeger, *Paideia: The Ideals of Greek Culture*, 3 vols. (New York: Oxford University Press, 1945, 1943, 1944). On Hayek, see note 12 above.

23. Berlin, p. 169.

24. See essay on Mill in Strauss and Cropsey and my article cited in note 26 below.

25. Jean-François Revel, *How Democracies Perish* (Garden City: Doubleday & Company, Inc., 1983).

26. John Stuart Mill, "On Liberty," in *The English Philosophers From Bacon to Mill*, ed. Edwin A. Burtt (New York: The Modern Library, Random House, Inc., 1939), pp. 982, 993. For an outline of Mill's ideals and their varied epistemological basis, as well as of his conceptualization of history, see Thomas A. Metzger, "Did Sun Yat-sen Understand the Idea of Democracy? The Conceptualization of Democracy in the Three Principles of the People and in John Stuart Mill's 'On Liberty'," *The American Asian Review* 10 (spring 1992): pp. 23–29.

27. Paul Edwards, ed., *Encyclopedia of Philosophy*, 8 vols. (New York: Macmillan Publishing Co., Inc. & The Free Press, 1972), vol. 8, pp. 207.

28. Huang Ko-wu's book on Liang Ch'i-ch'ao (cited in chapter I, note 138) shows how Chinese intellectuals in the early twentieth century faced a choice between modernizing in a transformative or an accommodative way, but it is hard to see how a grasp of utilitarianism would have led them to see how they had the causal knowledge then needed to predict which actions would have which consequences.

29. This point is basic to T'ang Chün-i's epistemology. See chapter II.

30. *San Francisco Examiner*, February 21, 1999.

31. Mill, pp. 993, 1009, 988.

32. See his severe criticisms of the Western combination of democracy and capitalism in his *Western Political Theory in the Face of the Future* and chapter VIII below.

33. This quote is from my description of his thesis in chapter III, p. 305.

34. On Strauss and Voegelin, see Ted V. McAllister, *Revolt against Modernity: Leo Strauss, Eric Voegelin, and the Search for a Postliberal Order* (Lawrence: University Press of Kansas, 1995). James Q. Wilson's views are in his *On Character* (Washington, D.C.: The AEI Press, 1991), pp. 28–29, 38–39. Christopher Lasch's are in his *The Revolt of the Elites and the Betrayal of Democracy* (New York: W.W. Norton, 1995). MacIntyre's views are in his *After Virtue* (Notre Dame: University of Notre Dame Press, 1981). See pp. 31–37 above.

35. Dunn, p. 26.

36. In the spring of 2003, Li Qiang denounced the recent U.S. invasion of Iraq

as the behavior of "a nation pursuing an evil policy of imperialism" that contradicted the "traditional liberalism" of the West. He blamed this development to a large extent on the "New Conservatives," whom he saw as inspired by Leo Strauss's and Carl Schmitt's criticism of this liberal tradition. See *Erh-shih-i shih-chi ching-chi pao-tao*, April 3, 2003, and *Shu-ch'eng*, May 2003, pp. 34–38.

37. Hsu Fu-kuan, *Hsueh-shu yü cheng-chih-chih chien* (Between the Realms of Scholarship and Politics; Taipei: T'ai-wan hsueh-sheng shu-chü, 1980), p. 126.
38. Yang Kuo-shu, *K'ai-fang-te to-yuan she-hui*, p. 191. See chapter VI.
39. For the concept of "the inhibited center," see chapter XII.
40. See chapter I, section 12.
41. Quoted in Strauss and Cropsey, p. 555.

CHAPTER VI

✑

Taiwan's Utopian Liberalism on the Eve of Democratization: The Political Thought of Yang Kuo-shu in the Early 1980s

1. Chinese Liberalism and the Democratization of Taiwan

Publishing his *The Third Wave: Democratization in the Late Twentieth Century* in 1991, Samuel P. Huntington defined as a "third wave of democratization" the way that "democratic regimes replaced authoritarian ones in approximately thirty countries in Europe, Asia, and Latin America" within fifteen years, 1974–1989. He also spoke of a "second phase" of this "third wave," which, beginning in 1989, affected "countries without previous significant democratic experience, including ... Taiwan."[1] Already by 1982, however, Taiwan's impressive modernization and liberalization had convinced Ramon H. Myers and me that "within two years it will become as fashionable to praise the Guomindang's recent political development [in Taiwan] as it already has become to praise its economic policies."[2] Indeed, as Myers and Linda Chao pointed out in their 1998 study, the Republic of China on Taiwan had had a kind of "limited democracy" going back to 1949. Moreover, contrary to Huntington, its official ideology, the Three Principles of the People, incorporated an ideal of liberal democracy that strongly resonated with the moral-political logic of the inherited culture.[3] The steady

While taking responsibility for all the shortcomings of this paper, I am most grateful for help from Fu-mei C. Chen, John Dunn, Yu-ching Hu, Huang Ko-wu, Philip J. Ivanhoe, Liao Cheng-hao, Ramon H. Myers, Julia Tung, and Elsie Wu.

pace of liberalization came to a climax in 1996 with the democratic election of its president and vice president.[4]

As Huntington pointed out, and as the Chao-Myers study corroborated, any analysis of the causes for democratization in any country is bound to be "complex, dense, messy, and intellectually unsatisfying."[5] At least three points, however, can be made about the Taiwan case. First, as discussed below, the combination of circumstances encouraging democratization in Taiwan was different in important ways from the situation in the People's Republic of China today. Second, as Yang Kuo-shu has effectively argued,[6] industrialization has been a prime cause of the societal and psychological transformation in Taiwan, including democratization and increasing "individualism."

Third, Reinhard Bendix's thesis of "intellectual mobilization" goes a long way toward explaining what happened in Taiwan. Bendix had in mind political pressures stemming less from the division of labor or class interests and more from opinion trends generated by and circulating through the more educated social circles. He saw intellectual mobilization as causally crucial in the constitutional changes that occurred in England and France during the seventeenth and eighteenth centuries. He also emphasized its importance in the case of "latecomers" such as Germany, Japan, and Russia. In their cases, he said, an "educated minority" "identifies strength if not goodness with alien forces and sees weakness if not evil in the land of one's birth. In this setting, ideas are used to locate and mobilize forces which will be capable of effecting change and thus redressing this psychologically unfavorable accounting."[7]

As someone who lived in Taiwan for about two years in the early 1980s and moved to some extent in working class, not only academic circles, I was well aware that the former were largely if not totally free of any demand for democratization, content as they were with the freedoms and the vastly improved material circumstances they then enjoyed. It was some of the persons with college and graduate degrees, notably prominent intellectuals at National Taiwan University and Academia Sinica, along with their academic friends in the U.S., who beat the drums for democratization. In their eyes, the growing affluence of their society and the changing nature of Chinese Communism after the death of Mao in 1976, as well as the global trend in the 1970s and 1980s later discussed by Huntington, had removed any plausible argument against the democratization of Taiwan. Conversely, the circles resisting democratization found it impossible to support their standpoint with any arguments effective within the context of Taiwan's intellectual environment, where Burkean conservatism had never struck down any roots. The lack of such roots was a characteristic of modern Chinese political thought in general, which, like the mainstream Confucian tradition, derived political principles from some concept of universal moral truth, not from any concept of respect for the historical tradition as an organic process embodied in the status quo. A pragmatic evaluation of the status quo cannot in the intellectual climate of modern China serve as the basis for a political theory publicly affirmed by the intellectual mainstream, no matter how successful the current government in practical terms. Thus already by the 1980s, not only within the ranks of the ruling political party, the Kuomintang, but also in the columns of newspapers that this party controlled (*Lien-ho-pao*, *Chung-kuo shih-pao*), the viewpoint of the liberals in the intellectual community became increasingly accepted as political common sense.[8]

If, then, Bendix's thesis of "intellectual mobilization" accurately describes a causal process that occurred in a number of societies, not only Taiwan in the 1980s, were the liberal ideas then embraced in Taiwan simply the same democratic ideals identically affirmed in many circles around the world since the Enlightenment in eighteenth-century Europe? Or were they part of a distinctively Chinese liberal tradition continuous in important ways with premodern Chinese intellectual trends and going back to various Chinese reformers in the late nineteenth century, to Yen Fu's (1854–1921) way of interpreting Millsian liberalism, and to the May Fourth Movement?[9] Many Chinese and Western historians and social scientists still see Chinese modernizers and liberals as just using "reason" to affirm universally good political and economic forms created in the West. As chapter I documented, however, in the last twenty years, a large number of studies have appeared showing that the ideas of these Chinese modernizers and liberals exhibited a mix of continuities and discontinuities with traditional Chinese values, a tendency to diverge from as well as converge with the Western liberal tradition, and the evolution of an autonomously Chinese kind of "critical consciousness" (*p'i-p'an i-shih*).

So far no one has found a way definitively to determine whether "convergence" or "divergence" has been or will be the "more important" tendency. It is hard, however, to deny a striking historical fact indicating a crucial degree of divergence: whether in Taipei during the 1980s or in Beijing as the next century began, the ideas animating Chinese admirers of the West's Millsian democracies included premises that were common to all the major twentieth-century Chinese political ideologies (Chinese liberalism, Chinese Marxism, Sunism, and modern Confucian humanism); that were incongruent with Millsian liberalism; and that were quite congruent with basic premises of the Confucian tradition.

Most striking, comparison of the thought of Li Qiang (chapter V) with that described in this chapter shows that Taipei liberals in the 1980s and Beijing liberals in the late 1990s equally believed in democratization as a process realizing a political-social-economic life largely free of selfish interests and irrationality. Why would a Peking University professor who grew up in Communist China and received a Ph.D. in political science from the University of London share this belief with a National Taiwan University professor who grew up in Taiwan outside the Marxist milieu and received his Ph.D. in psychology from the University of Illinois? Why would Sunism, Chinese Marxism, modern Confucian humanism, and Chinese liberalism equally believe that the thorough moralization of politics is practicable? The only reasonable answer is that this belief came from what these trends all shared, traditional orientations they equally inherited.

2. Discourse #1 in Taiwan on the Eve of Democratization

This distinctively Chinese approach to cultural revision and politics has been summed up in chapter I as "discourse #1." It centers on "the two optimisms" (optimism about the scope of knowledge and about what is politically practicable). It also incorporates two other premises: a teleological view of history as a global, evolutionary, progressive process currently stalled in China but moving toward the realization of an ideal political-economic order largely free of selfish interests, and a focus on a morally and intellectually enlightened Chinese elite with the ability to overcome the obstacles to progress in China.

In combination, these four premises promote a highly

confrontational political style, because, in their light, if I disagree with you, it must be because I have exercised my moral conscience and used reason to affirm what is obviously true and you have not. This Manichaean dichotomy was applied both by political leaders in Taiwan depicting their critics as undermining progress and by the latter depicting the former as immoral and irrational.

True, this Manichaean outlook is probably part of politics everywhere, and certainly politics everywhere or in many societies also includes some tendencies toward moderation and self-doubt allowing political opponents to humor one another and find some common ground. It is well known that in contemporary Taiwan's parliament (Li-fa-yuan), representatives from opposite parties angrily denouncing each other and even coming to blows have often been old friends who went out to dinner together as soon as the TV lights went out and the parliamentary session was over.

Obviously, however, the extent to which a culture cultivates such a spirit of moderation varies and depends at least partly on the type of discourse shaping the rhetorical structure of political interaction. What was absent from this rhetorical structure in Taiwan on the eve of democratization was any emphasis on or perhaps even any recognition of the idea so central to a John Dunn that, because you and I are both morally and intellectually fallible beings dealing with all the intangibles and uncertainties of politics, both of us may be partly right and partly wrong when we disagree (see chapter VIII). In other words, what was absent was what Chang Hao has called "the consciousness of the permanent darkness of political history"; what Hu Shih in 1959 called for, a spirit of mutual forgiveness and tolerance in the relations between even an authoritarian government and its critics; the lowered moral expectations Huntington regarded as necessary for the effective working of democracy; the idea that political history is necessarily a moral limbo in which one is willing to "connect up and work with" (*chieh-kuei*) people who have political power so long as the basic direction of their policies is more beneficial than harmful.[10]

I would argue that, absent this kind of political tolerance and cooperative spirit of compromise, virtually any government appears as so outrageously irrational and immoral that the very idea of "working and connecting up with it" (*chieh-kuei*) is a preposterous act of moral betrayal. It then becomes impossible to promote energetic, imaginative cooperation between elite circles partly disagreeing with each other and thus to optimize the coordination and mobilization of the society's organizational resources. Under these circumstances, such circles can agree only to avoid provoking each other, not to "work together."

To be sure, a government can in fact be so outrageous that total denunciation of it is the only reasonable response. I would say, however, that in Chinese intellectual life, from traditional times until today, such a denunciatory attitude toward the political leadership, glorified as "righteous protest" (*k'ang-i*), remained morally appealing no matter whether the government was a grotesque dictatorship, a dictatorship promoting modernization and liberalization, or a democracy. Even though many Chinese intellectuals, perhaps the vast majority, themselves have disdained or been afraid of participating in such denunciatory activities, few have stood up for the idea of working enthusiastically to achieve piecemeal progress in the moral limbo of politics. There is still no indication today, whether in Taiwan, Hong Kong, or the Mainland, that this idea can take root in Chinese culture, totally incongruent as it is with the very premises of the Confucian heritage (see chapter XII). Thus the discourse in Taiwan on the eve of democratization, I believe, is significant not just as a part of a historical process that occurred there in the 1980s and 1990s. It also illustrates a tradition-rooted, continuing Manichaean approach to political disagreement. This approach persisted in Taiwan after democratization and is as evident today in China as it has ever been (see chapter XII).

To be sure, to what extent any denunciatory attitude toward a political leadership is justified depends on one's assessment of the latter. According to the methodology discussed in chapter I, historical figures in their discourses both respond rationally to objective realities and interpret these realities using the distinctive symbolic framework their particular group has inherited from history. Therefore, the scholar today analyzing their response must rely on her own assessment of the reality they faced in order to determine the extent to which this reality, rather than their culturally inherited framework, determined their response.

Whether readers will accept my view of Taiwan's political discourse on the eve of democratization will therefore depend on whether they can accept my assessment of the political realities then.

What readers need to assess is not only the evidence regarding the overall ideational structure of Taiwan's liberalism but also the responses of Taiwan's liberals to specific situations.

To start with the latter, one may refer to the May 1992 issue of a prominent Taiwan semi-popular periodical, *Tang-tai*, which included a conference paper delivered around September 28, 1991 by Yeh Ch'i-cheng, professor of sociology at National Taiwan University, one of the three or four most respected behavioral scientists on the island. In a brilliant, passionate way, he discussed the moral-political responsibilities of university professors in the modern world. Using the un-Humean epistemology that has continued its unperturbed reign in China, he brought together a sociological attempt to derive "ought" from "is," that is, moral norms from the "profession," "role," or "status" of the teacher or professor, as well as from the "structure" of the modern university;[11] a profound sense of the tension between a more restricted, Weberian view of the professor's moral-political responsibilities in an age of specialized learning and the "classically" Confucian, "somewhat romantic" vision of the "intellectual" as a hero resisting powerful political and economic interests by pursuing a "moral mission" to "save the world" and so playing a "prophetic" role as an agent of "enlightenment";[12] a conviction that "society" expects professors to play that heroic role;[13] another un-Humean idea, that "reason" not only is at the root of science but also is "a kind of value" implying respect for "freedom … equality … openness, pluralism";[14] a teleological view of history as a struggle to realize reason in this broad sense;[15] and an equally unquestioned, epistemologically optimistic, unapologetically scientistic assumption that an objectively identifiable elite stratum (university professors, especially those having "legitimacy" as "authorities" in the fields of law, politics, and social science) is uniquely able to implement "reason" and so to play that "romantic" role expected by "society."[16]

But how is the tension to be resolved between Max Weber's view of the more restricted moral-political responsibilities of the professor and this "rather romantic" view of the "intellectuals'" "mission"? Professor Yeh gave his opinion at a time when Taiwan had already impressed the world by largely achieving economic modernization and by entering the last phase of democratization. One might have expected him to feel that he was living in a society vigorously advancing toward his ideal of "reason" and so to define the professor's moral role in that light. After all, as Chin Heng-wei, the perspicacious, candid, and definitely "liberal" editor of *Tang-tai*, said to me in 1992: after martial law ended in 1987, "everyone" in Taiwan recognized that democratization there was genuine, and the continuing claims that it was *hsu-chia* (empty and false) were only political rhetoric used to pressure the government into progressing more.

In fact, though, whatever the successes Taiwan had enjoyed, they did not prevent a traditionally articulate part of the intellectual community from continuing to feel basically outraged by the government. There was in these circles a continuous feeling of anger, a perception of the ruling party, Kuomintang (KMT), as basically incompetent, arrogant, and eager to intimidate and dominate the intellectuals. For instance, early in the morning of May 9, 1991, police arrested four young people, including one of Ch'ing-hua University's history graduate students, charging them with "sedition." At that time, the law forbade even advocating that Taiwan become a separate nation, not to mention any conspiracy or organization in that direction. These four were accused of belonging to an "Association for an Independent Taiwan," and of having traveled to Japan to plot with a notorious revolutionary there, Shih Ming, who had once planned to assassinate Chiang K'ai-shek. The government was saying that, while it would give considerable leeway to the separatists seeking to establish Taiwan as an independent nation, it would still put some limits on this movement, which violated the most sacred principles of the ruling party and risked a disastrous confrontation with a powerful neighbor. Immediately, however, many intellectuals and others protested, variously claiming that it was outrageous for police to enter a campus and arrest a student without first notifying university authorities; that the four actually had no revolutionary intentions; that, given all the technically illegal but tolerated activity in Taiwan aiming to make Taiwan an independent nation, the government was arbitrary in deciding when to apply the law; and that, in the name of democracy, all such activity should anyway be allowed, except for terrorism.[17] After major street demonstrations, the four were released on bail, and the matter then faded from public consciousness. (The revision of the sedition law in 1992, greatly narrowing the definition of sedition, anyway eliminated any case against the four.)

Another incident occurred on the night of October 9–10, 1991, the eve of the Republic of China's holiday celebrating the beginning of the 1911 Revolution. Protestors associated with a group calling for elimination of the above sedition law had gathered on the campus of National Taiwan University. That night, meeting with the permission of the chancellor, they were protesting the military parade planned for the next day. They felt it symbolized the government's allegedly mistaken mission to unify China. By 1:00 A.M. or so, their numbers had swelled to about 800 and included many people from outside the university community. The presence of these outsiders violated the chancellor's instructions. Several hundred policemen then entered the campus without notifying university authorities and manually dispersed the protesters. The intellectual community was outraged by this blow against the "autonomy" and "dignity" of the university. On October 16, a campus rally expressed this outrage, and when the chancellor, Sun Chen, addressed it, he appeared on television momentarily choking with sobs as he told of how he had received the news that police had scattered the students. His emotional behavior sparked the second phase of this academic confrontation with the government. The premier, Hao Po-ts'un, now ridiculed the chancellor's "tears" and criticized him privately and publicly for having handled the demonstrators irresponsibly. Many intellectuals felt they had been insulted by this blunt criticism from a former military man who arrogantly treated them as his subordinates.[18]

The rage such incidents provoked in parts of the intellectual community is reflected in Professor Yeh's reaffirmation of the heroic Confucian role of the intellectual. Indeed, the outrage directed at the premier harked back to the defiant spirit of Mencius, who, around 300 B.C., proudly refused to be "summoned to court" (*chao*) by the king of Ch'i. Yet Yeh also reiterated a picture of global history that has long been basic in Taiwan — the idea of an unqualified contrast between China's moral chaos and irrationality and the happy reign of morality and rationality in the West. From this standpoint, all the progress in Taiwan had still failed even to narrow this gap between the two civilizations. When police on October 10, 1991 invaded the campus of National Taiwan University, suggested one editorial, were they not worse than even the warlords three quarters of a century earlier? Even those "barbarous" people had not dared order their troops to enter the grounds of Peking University.[19]

In the minds of many people, such outrageous events were not overshadowed by Taiwan's overall progress and, on the contrary, evidenced the persistence of moral-political chaos. Professor Yeh's main point, then, was that Weber's view of the professor's limited moral-political role presupposed the moral-rational order of the West and did not suit the moral-cognitive chaos in Taiwan. Weber's view, he said, presupposed that "the objective conditions needed for openness, freedom, fairness, and the opportunity for pluralistic discussion have already begun to emerge ..." Thus, Weber's view was appropriate for a society "like Europe and the U.S.," where these values "have for a long time been recognized and protected to a considerable extent" and where there therefore is "no need" to promote them in "an enthusiastic and dedicated way."[20] Conversely, in

> a society [like Taiwan's], where attempts are still made to restrict freedom of speech, and basic human rights are severely limited or suppressed, pursuing reason is quite impossible and is even regarded by those in power as the worst sin.... How can we expect the emergence of the opportunity to interact in terms of a rational system of discussion and interpretation based on free choice when we face a society in which the basic framework of meaning, the very symbol system has been thrown into disarray; the sense of [national] identity is unclear; values have been lost; the moral-intellectual system on which society should be based is in chaos (*hsi-t'ung wen-luan*); there is a lack of logical consistency; society itself has from the start failed to realize the preconditions of reason; and indeed the historically important concepts underlying reason — freedom, equality, man's ability to think autonomously, logic — are all equally missing.

This moral chaos in Taiwan, moreover, reflected the continuing influence of the traditional emphasis on "paternal authority": "political power overrides everything from start to finish, defining truth and justice" and "society exhibits a grave disjunction between name and reality."[21]

It is striking that Professor Yeh's view of Taiwan conditions hardly differed from the way many Peking University intellectuals viewed their society in the 1980s. Kan Yang of the San-lien Bookstore group (Wen-hua ts'ung-shu-p'ai) "held that Chinese intellectuals were stuck between two forces. On the one hand, the positive values of modern society — freedom, democracy, rule of law — were still far, far from being realized. On the other, people already were being increasingly afflicted by the negative values of modern society — the worship of money, mass culture."[22]

In such a moral-cognitive chaos, Professor Yeh said, professors cannot be "neutral" with regard to "that struggle fully to realize that justice which mankind has pursued since history began." Thus it "seems unavoidable" that professors in Taiwan carry out the "moral mission" of the "enlightened" "intellectual," even at the risk of violating their Weberian responsibility not to use their prestige to legitimize views lying outside their areas of specialization.[23]

Unfortunately, he added, many professors have resigned themselves to this Weberian view, if not just opportunistically supporting the government.[24] Indeed, this dichotomy between morally alert and inert intellectuals is fundamental for virtually all Chinese intellectuals and was even emphasized by Professor Yeh as a scientifically clear distinction basic to his sociological analysis of intellectuals.[25] In fact, as the chancellor of National Taiwan University pointed out in late 1991, of the more than 20,000 faculty and students at his university, the "vast majority" concentrated on their academic work and felt neglected by a university administration preoccupied with the problems of a protesting minority.[26] This was the majority viewed by Yeh as morally phlegmatic, but many members of this group returned the compliment, viewing themselves as morally responsible and intellectuals like Yeh as extreme. This majority was part of what Ku Ying (Min Hung-k'uei, David S. Min) had twenty years previously called "the silent majority" in Taiwan.[27]

How should a student of political thought in Taiwan regard Professor Yeh's view? Was he just "telling it like it is"? Was his merely a reasoned response to objectively clear circumstances, a fair account of the differences between Taiwan and the West? Was it an angrily irrational response? Or did it reflect a socially shared, culturally distinctive, tradition-rooted way of "defining the situation," to use W. I. Thomas's term — another example of a culturally-rooted "sense of predicament" expressed in the face of undeniable progress?[28]

I would submit that any of these three options must be based on a controversial moral-political judgment, and that, in this regard, Yeh's statement well illustrates the inherently problematic relation between culture and discourse.

Yeh himself felt he was "telling it like it is." For him, despite some reservations about the ability of a scholar to be completely objective, "reason" existed as a clearly available, universal, objective, algorismic standard for judging whether a statement had dealt accurately and morally with the facts. More politically conservative Chinese, viewing "reason" the same way, found Yeh's view to be irrational.

For both groups, however, the cultural aspects of Yeh's view were unimportant. To be sure, in Chinese eyes, "culture"(*wen-hua*) can either facilitate or hamper efforts to follow "reason"(*li-hsing*). As in many Western circles, therefore, culture can be seen as warping efforts to reason objectively. In Chinese circles, however, there usually is confidence that such cultural influences can be conveniently identified and set aside, at least in the case of ego. Thus a "culture," in just about all modern Chinese writing, becomes a discrete object that is morally evaluated by a scholar effectively adducing universal principles of morality and reason.[29] Because such scholars, whether in Taiwan or the Mainland, have seen themselves as almost effortlessly transcending cultural limitations, their quest for "self-awareness" (*tzu-chueh*) has not been a struggle to look under their conscious forms of reasoning, uncovering culturally distinctive premises previously identified with universal truths, but an effort to make use of their culturally untrammeled rationality to probe ever more deeply into the universal nature of human life. Instead of comprehensively describing their inherited ways of thinking, they have been more interested in debating which discipline or intellectual tradition most reliably grasps these universal principles: The Neo-Confucian literature? American behavioral science? The Continental study of human consciousness ranging from Nietzsche and Husserl to Sartre and Habermas? Rousseau's philosophy of democracy? Which formulation will unlock the moral energy (*li-liang*) China needs? More precisely, their methodology calls, on the one hand, for probing ever more deeply into universal existential principles, and, on the other, for selectively describing Chinese culture to determine which parts do or do not accord with these principles.

Some more examples can be adduced to show how the flood of comments and published political writings on the eve of democratization expressed the four premises above. Sublime, utopian criteria of political-economic behavior were typically used to criticize Taiwan's current situation. I remember an earnest college student who in the 1980s said to me: "How can I respect this government when it has not equalized the distribution of wealth (*chün-fu*)?" Political publications typically assumed Taiwan and the rest of China should have

> an economy free of any unfair, selfish appropriation of wealth, a [democratic] polity in which selfish interests do not affect the key leadership decisions, an international status equal to that of the two superpowers, an intellectual life free of confusing contradictions (*fen-yun*) and bringing all truths, moral and factual, into a single, unified doctrinal system (*hui-t'ung*), a civilization free of all oppression, insincerity, and selfishness, and a society in which the status of every individual is successfully and objectively based on his or her achievements.[30]

These ideals connoted a vision of "democracy" that had begun to entrance Chinese intellectuals already in the late nineteenth century. As Huang Ko-wu and others have shown, Chinese then conceptualized democracy by using Western ideas about popular sovereignty and the electoral and other procedures needed to realize it, but they conflated Western procedural notions with Confucian ideas. Huang analyzed the writings on democracy of prominent intellectuals and leaders from the late nineteenth century through the first decade of our century, especially Wei Yuan, Hsu Chi-yü, Wang T'ao, Cheng Kuan-ying, K'ang Yu-wei, Liang Ch'i-ch'ao, T'an Ssu-t'ung, and Sun Yat-sen. Huang showed that, as such people formed this idea of democracy, they combined these Western ideas with a strongly Confucian vision of rule by a successfully identified moral-intellectual elite selflessly (*ta-kung wu-ssu*) and perfectly expressing the voluntarily unified will of "the people," thus eliminating all "blockages" (*yung-o*) currently disrupting the morally harmonious flow of feelings of solidarity throughout the population, and so able to mobilize the nation, achieving "wealth and power" even to the extent of "surpassing Europe and the United States." Therefore, once full democracy was realized, the leadership would be in full communication with all citizens (*k'ai yen-lu*), and "those above and below would be one" (*shang-hsia i-t'i*), eventually forming a "great oneness" with all the world (*ta-t'ung*). This ideal, often regarded as totally practicable, was connected to the epistemological goal of bringing into one logically unified system of thought (*hui-t'ung*) all ideas — "old and new, Chinese and foreign" — that had "value" (*chia-chih*), thus ending the current intellectual stage of confusing competition between contradictory political and philosophical doctrines (*fen-yun*). Yen Fu's concept of democracy overlapped this broad trend to an important extent, especially as he analyzed democracy by comparing it to a school in which enlightened teachers give students the moral and intellectual resources needed to exercise their freedoms responsibly.[31]

The extent to which modern Chinese thought has viewed the elimination of selfishness as a practicable goal integral to "freedom" is nothing short of striking. No point is more heterological relative to at least Millsian political culture. In the twentieth century, one Chinese group after another defined itself as committed to "freedom" and dealing with political issues in a way free of selfish interest, including the Communists and the Kuomintang. The ensuing argument was always about which group was actually corrupted by selfishness, never about whether it was practically possible to base a free society on the formation of an unbiased group uncorrupted by access to power. In the 1950s and after, when liberals like Hsu Fu-kuan and Yin Hai-kuang arose denouncing the dictatorial practices of both the Kuomintang and the Chinese Communist Party, they similarly took for granted that full democratization would ensure the elimination of selfish interests in the making of political decisions. Hsu Fu-kuan, one of modern China's most astute historians and thinkers, pointed out in the 1950s that, because of the system of representative government, U.S. presidents like Harry S. Truman necessarily acted as "sages."[32] Conversely, as the ROC in Taiwan gradually democratized after 1986, politicians like Chu Kao-cheng could point to the play of selfish interests in the parliament (Li-fa-yuan) as proof, convincing to many in Taiwan, that Taiwan still lacked "healthy democratic politics" (*chien-ch'üan-te min-chu cheng-chih*).[33]

Selfishness in political life could be eliminated if only people would stop failing to recognize the actually obvious truths of human life. Highly respected contemporary thinkers like Lao Ssu-kuang have without fear of criticism compared the Chinese intellectuals' "rational" evaluation of Chinese culture to the objective way in which a doctor identifies and treats a disease. Chinese intellectuals have thus typically perceived themselves as standing on a universal platform of "reason" and morality from which to look down on and evaluate the different aspects of Chinese culture as either "good" or "bad," as "the finest aspects of Chinese culture" or "poisons inherited from the feudal era," or as "universally valid" or "closed" (*feng-pi*) (in the sense of suiting the needs of a past era only).[34] Even more, many of them have felt it quite feasible to formulate a complete philosophical system, an epistemological goal often called *t'i-hsi* (a deductive, comprehensive, correct system of political principles).

A useful way to understand this modern Chinese concept of the *t'i-hsi* is to look at Professor Chu Hung-yuan's argument in 1985 that the T'ung-meng-hui (the ancestor of the Kuomingtang) had a *t'i-hsi*, but one with "shortcomings," on the eve of the 1911 Revolution. Making this argument, he formed a definition of a *t'i-hsi* that he took for granted as self-evidently correct. A *t'i-hsi* "without defect" (*wan-cheng, wan-ch'üan*, etc.) had at least seven characteristics. First, it displayed *mo-lo* (logical, clear, unifying lines of thought). Second, it was without "omissions," in the sense that it clarified the nature of every factual and moral facet of human life, grounding morality and political programs in epistemological, ontological, cosmological, and historical theories, all forming a single logical whole. Third, the "system" was thus free of any mistakes about the ideas of the world's thinkers or about history, grasping, for instance, all the points about Rousseau, Marx, or economic development that the most sophisticated scholars have made. Fourth, such a *t'i-hsi* was also based on a full understanding of current Chinese conditions, of Chinese culture, and of Chinese history, exactly specifying the one and only correct way in which Chinese should revise or discard their culture in order to modernize. Fifth, this *t'i-hsi* must be understandable for the general public but without being "propagandistic," even as it simultaneously met the standards of the most advanced university seminar. As many Chinese intellectuals today believe, the intellectual life on which Chinese society should be based should be "profound" (*shen-ju ch'üan-mien-te fan-ssu*) and free of both "vulgarization" and "politicization," two trends afflicting Confucian thought in Taiwan, according to them. Sixth, this *t'i-hsi* must offer a practicable political program (*k'o-hsing-hsing*), one avoiding excessive optimism and thus realistically taking into account the actual capabilities present in a society — a criterion that, as Professor Chu saw it, the T'ung-meng-hui particularly failed to meet. Seventh, this *t'i-hsi* must lack all "bias," a vague idea, perhaps, but one making sense in a society optimistically believing that the public understanding of objective moral principles is a practicable goal.

To be sure, we should be careful in specifying the extent to which all of this optimistic *t'i-hsi* vision of knowledge was shared in modern China. Yet it is quite striking that an astute political scientist in the 1980s like Professor Chu at the Academia Sinica in Taiwan took for granted the validity of this kind of epistemology, seeing himself as defending his thesis only against the charge that the T'ung-meng-hui lacked any *t'i-hsi*, not against any claim that the very idea of a *t'i-hsi* constitutes an inappropriate way to form or evaluate a body of political thought.[35]

Indeed, it is hard if not impossible, despite all the immersion of Chinese intellectuals in American and British intellectual life, to find any Chinese writing that identifies the *t'i-hsi* concept in order to critique it on the basis of common if not dominant Western intellectual trends, such as historicism, ethical skepticism, and cultural relativism. Not surprisingly, therefore, when contemporary Chinese philosophers write about the epistemological problems that led to these Western trends, they often treat them as merely technical philosophical issues, confident that these technically interesting discussions in no way impede access to morality as objective, impersonal principles distinct from subjective, arbitrary preferences. Similarly, many different philosophical voices in twentieth-century China have arisen to reject what can be called the Great Modern Western Epistemological Revolution and the mix it created of logical positivism, ethical skepticism, and historicism (see chapter I, section 7).

The widespread enthusiasm about science was part of this optimistic belief that a *t'i-hsi* can be found. Western science — for example, the telescope — immediately impressed intellectuals like K'ang Yu-wei in the late nineteenth century as illuminating the moral as well as the instrumental side of life. It epitomized the new — new to Chinese — kind of highly reliable and useful ideas that so many Chinese came to regard as capable of "saving China" by facilitating realization of their high political ideals. For the modern Chinese intellectual mainstream, however, "saving China" (*chiu Chung-kuo*) required not just science in the narrower, technical sense but science as either constituting or helping to constitute a *t'i-hsi* — science as epitomizing the use of "reason" (*li-hsing*) to deal successfully with all human problems. "Scientism," as D.W.Y. Kwok discussed it, referred to the former option — the ideal of a *t'i-hsi* based purely on "science" (*k'o-hsueh*). Humanists like the late T'ang Chün-i, however, who opposed scientism, still shared with scientistic intellectuals the epistemologically optimistic faith in the human ability to devise a *t'i-hsi*. Scientism, in other words, was a controversial claim in modern China, but it was only one version of a widespread viewpoint that was taken for granted and uncontroversial: epistemological optimism. Scientism was a new trend in China, but a strong case can be made that epistemological optimism has been central to Chinese intellectual life since at least the days of Confucius and Mo-tzu.[36]

According to this epistemological optimism, the nature of history and of cultures is essentially transparent, knowable. Liang Ch'i-ch'ao's famous *Hsin-min-shuo* (On Transforming the People), first published in 1902–1903, is quite representative in confidently generalizing about the nature of one nation after another, identifying the causes for various national successes and failures, and from these causes directly deducing recommendations for how to act in the present.[37] This knowability of history should be distinguished from the concepts defining the characteristics of this transparent object of knowledge, history.

For Liang Ch'i-ch'ao, Sun Yat-sen, and perhaps even Chang Ping-lin, as well as Sunists, Marxists, humanists, and liberals during the second half of the twentieth century, history is both a naturally teleological process and one that an enlightened elite can help consummate. True, John Stuart Mill's own view of history was about as teleological as Marx's. The Millsian democratic tradition, however, became increasingly, though far from completely, divorced from such teleology during the twentieth century. When John A. Hall tried to construct even a modest theory of history, he noted he was swimming against the mainstream represented by Raymond Aron, Isaiah Berlin, and Karl Popper.[38] Nor can one underestimate the influence on Western intellectuals of Tolstoy, as he ridiculed Napoleon's belief that great leaders can control the course of history and praised General Kutuzov for seeing historical forces as powerful currents to which leaders can only adjust. Also common in the West is much skepticism about the ability fully to grasp the complexity of historical patterns, to make generalizations about the nature of a culture, or to grasp history's causal links (see chapter VIII).

In the context of this Chinese teleological view, the basic character of historical life is not uniform through time. History is currently leading, as just noted, to an era when people will be morally and intellectually quite superior to the miserable specimens running the world today. Going back to K'ang Yu-wei's (1858–1927) *san-shih-lun* (Theory of the Three Epochs) and to the Western evolutionary views brought in by Yen Fu, modern Chinese visions of history have repeatedly depicted it as a highly structured, teleological process moving as a "tide" toward the sublime goal above. Moreover, history has been repeatedly seen as inherently susceptible to Napoleonic control by enlightened Chinese, who can hasten realization of this goal. China's "new culture" is to be enacted by an enlightened elite following "a rational plan with the goal of creating a new, integrated culture," as Yang Kuo-shu put it (see below).

To be sure, not all Chinese have embraced this teleological, Napoleonic view of the historical process. Chang Ping-lin had famous doubts about it, though actually he too called for the creation of a new China.[39] Liang Ch'i-ch'ao after 1903 at the very least was sure that the grand new era was not imminent. The writers like Lu Hsun, whom Leo Ou-fan Lee has described as partly lacking revolutionary "zeal," were often pessimistic about history.[40] Professional Chinese historians such as the late L.S. Yang of Harvard have been at the forefront of international sinology and have never strayed near any simplistic teleology. Similarly, a few scholars in Hong Kong and Taiwan have expressed skepticism about the ability of any intellectual elite to control the course of Chinese culture's development.[41]

Yet the famous, erudite student of the history of Chinese philosophy, Lao Ssu-kuang, also has seen history as a highly structured, "spiral-like" series of "stages," and "Chinese culture" as a systemic pattern the evolution of which can and should be "controlled" by enlightened persons who have understood the universal principles of normative cultural change he saw himself as setting forth.[42] Tu Wei-ming has seen an imminent "third era in the evolution of the Confucian tradition," when "the intellectuals' corporate, morally critical consciousness of self will appear not only in the intellectual world but also in the worlds of business, of the mass media, of the military, and of the government." This attractive society, vastly different, in his eyes, from the "politicized" and "vulgarized" trends in Taiwan, is likely to come about, he has held, because the expansion of the service sector, especially information processing, will result in the "intellectuals' ... grasping of society's nervous system."[43]

Yet whatever the bright expectations for the future, this teleological vision also defines China's current situation as an agonizing predicament stemming from China's historical failure to evolve normally. From this standpoint, China is a kind of cultural cripple, history's "abnormally formed baby" (*kuai-t'ai*), in contrast to the normally developing West. Liang Ch'i-ch'ao's *Hsin-min-shuo* powerfully conceptualized this contrast.[44] Max Weber's ethnocentric celebration of the West's unique rationality thus meshed with this widespread modern Chinese image of China as a historical cripple. Professor Yeh's statement above is typical in this regard. Significantly, this image of China as a historical cripple (*ts'an-fei-kan*) is emphasized not only by iconoclasts, such as authors of the famous *Ho-shang* television series,[45] but also by many intellectuals who accept the New Confucians' vindication of the Confucian "spirit," such as Professor Lin An-wu, a scholar who developed the idea of the historical "abnormally formed baby" in a thoughtful essay.[46] In recent years on the Mainland too, a broad range of intellectuals have stated as a fact that, by the nineteenth century, western Europe's popular culture had already fully incorporated the Enlightenment's liberal values, for the realization of which Chinese today still need to struggle.[47]

Paradoxically enough, though, many Chinese who thus perceived China as a historical cripple did not excuse any further delay in its efforts to catch up to the West. For them, the fact that theirs was a society struggling with the difficulties of state building and economic development did not excuse such delay. As discussed below and in chapter XII, there is a difference in this regard between the intellectual situation today in China and that in Taiwan in the 1980s. In China today, there is a widespread pessimism about Chinese culture, often described as still overwhelmed by "the poisons inherited from the feudal era." Particularly but not only in the case of "The New Conservatism," this sense that Chinese culture is not a fertile soil in which to grow the tree of liberal democracy often supports the view that delaying democratization is reasonable.

In Taiwan in the 1980s, however, such pessimism about Chinese culture was far less salient. Instead, Taiwan's situation was typically regarded as a horribly exasperating, systemic predicament unnecessarily caused by perverse "vested interests" and confused intellectuals inexcusably preventing the otherwise quick realization of the wonderful new era teleologically promised by history. The anger that permeated modern politics in Taiwan was correlated to this feeling that the lack of democracy was due to outrageously inexcusable lapses, not to human frailties normal in any society, not to mention a developing one.

To be sure, as indicated above, just how to regard the flood of modern Chinese complaints about modern China's present condition is a matter of interpretive judgment, not one that can be handled in a purely positivistic way. Have these complaints been merely reasonable responses to China's actual difficulties? Or have they been a way of evaluating political life by applying to it a priori standards derived from some posited historical teleology or utopian vision of the imminent future?

This question arose only with the advent of Taiwan's recent era of economic and political success. Before this era, few suspected that this Chinese flood of complaints was anything but a reasonable response to a miserable situation. After these successes became apparent, however, this flood continued unabated.

Let me here just quickly review some examples taken mainly from Taiwan writings and conversations in the 1980s and early 1990s, instead of fully presenting all the data I have tried to pull together elsewhere. Many of the complaining statements simply deplored the fact that the current society had not met those sublime standards of success listed above. Modern Chinese history was repeatedly described as a series of failures, with no mention of the Taiwan successes. Taiwan's culture was invariably described as drastically unsatisfactory, whether the problem was "eclecticism" (Hu Ch'iu-yuan), clinging to the obsolete values of the "agricultural, traditional" era (Yang Kuo-shu), failing to understand that traditional values are compatible with modernization (Yü Ying-shih), "politicization" and "vulgarization" (Tu Wei-ming), having a "capitalistic" character (Lao Ssu-kuang), or being "colonial" (a reporter interviewing Lao Ssu-kuang in 1988). The central, widely perceived difficulty was that modern China generally and Taiwan in particular had failed to develop Chinese culture by just combining the "good" parts of Chinese and Western culture. Instead, the "good" and the "bad" from both sources had been indiscriminately mixed together. In other words, good and bad values could be objectively distinguished, and normal cultures did not mix up the two.

Immorality was pervasively focused on. The famous Mainland

critic of the Communists, Liu Pin-yen, came to Taiwan in 1989 and
without fear of contradiction stated in a Taipei seminar that Taiwan
had little to offer the Mainland with "regard to raising the quality of
the human spirit," because the "great challenge faced by the
Mainland is how to turn broken human beings into whole, perfect
ones." An internationally admired Chinese historian told me around
1991 that Taiwan was "a moral vacuum." No one disputed that
Taiwan was suffering from an epidemic of selfishness. The
innumerable examples of selfless behavior were simply brushed aside
as not enough — *hsiao-jen-ch'ing* (trivial, not necessarily sincere
expressions of moral feeling). Industrialization, all along the great
hope of Chinese modernizers, was often blamed in Taiwan for the
collapse of traditional values. A KMT member reported that she
always cast a blank ballot, because there have been no candidates
truly devoted to "the people." Democratization since 1986 aroused
little if any enthusiasm among "ordinary" people, while, as recently as
1988, the prominent liberal Ho Huai-shuo was not embarrassed to
assert in *Tang-tai*, a leading Taipei journal, that there was virtually no
difference between the government in Taiwan and that of the
Mainland. A favorite theme in Taipei by the late 1980s was that no
amount of democratization would have any serious effect on society,
because historically China's "civil society" had been so
underdeveloped.[48]

Professor Yeh Ch'i-cheng's view of the moral chaos in Taiwan has
been adduced above. Professor Ch'en Ch'i-nan was another
prominent social scientist presenting his gloomy analysis of Taiwan's
society and polity as the authoritative conclusions of an academically
validated scholar with specialized, scientific knowledge about the
subject at hand. He is a Yale University Ph.D. who in 1992 was the
chair of the Department of Anthropology, The Chinese University of
Hong Kong. A native Taiwanese intellectual who participated
vigorously in Taiwan's world of published social-political criticism, he
was far less radical than many other critics of the government.[49] In
1992, he published the following view of Taiwan's predicament,
which was typical of much current intellectual thinking in Taiwan. It
was distinctive perhaps only in the way it synthesized Liang Ch'i-
ch'ao's diagnosis (the lack of moral commitment to the nation-state)
with Rousseau's theory of the social contract.

Leaving behind a Yale anthropologist's preoccupation with

cautiously tailoring generalizations to fit factually specific observations, Ch'en indulged without apology in the fashioning of grand theory, making many forceful descriptive, causative, evaluative, and recommendatory statements applying to Chinese culture as a whole. Such indeed is the style basic to Chinese social criticism. His central point was that nothing had been done during the last century to close the huge gap between the way China is and the way "a modern nation" is.[50] True, "The Mainland cannot match Taiwan's living standard, economic institutions, or political system."[51] This difference, however, did not make much difference. Ch'en barely mentioned it and in no way suggested that such limited if major differences between one imperfect condition and another are what practicable societal progress is all about.

The important point, for him, was that Taiwan's "social order" was "in a state of grave disorder" (*she-hui chih-hsu hun-luan*) and, like the Mainland's, faced "a bottleneck" in its development.[52] In both societies, people found themselves without clear answers to basic political questions: Is this "state of disorder" the fault "mainly of the government or of the people? Should the government or the people take the lead in overcoming this disorder? Is the solution to put another political party in power? Or is the problem originally one of culture or national character?"

Many would say such questions — should another political party take charge? — are a normal part of political life anywhere, but for Ch'en, the Chinese failure to settle them once and for all was abnormal. Unending debate revolving around them, he said, went back to the 1911 Revolution, when Liang Ch'i-ch'ao and Sun Yat-sen disagreed as to whether China's main problem was the corruption of government or the inadequacy of popular values. Unable to find the answer, the Chinese had lurched from one unsuccessful movement to another: "during the last century, despite an unending series of political revolutions and reform movements, China has continuously remained trapped in the psychological fixation on revolutionary change, the predicament of a Chinese-type society lacking self-understanding and so any method to escape from the historical cycle of endless revolutions."[53]

Still stuck in this predicament today (1992), he wrote, Taiwan also suffered from "pervasive politicization," an improper way of mixing together partisan political views with not only "economic and legal issues but also all aspects of social life generally." From another standpoint, however, the individual in Taiwan unfortunately remained a "natural man," one focused only on kinship ties, instead of becoming a "social" or "political man," one devoted to "the public good" (*kung*), not just to "private" matters.[54] Criticizing the civic outlook in Taiwan, Ch'en thus seemingly fell into a contradiction, asking that citizens both avoid "political tendencies" and play a "political role."[55] Actually, like Sun Yat-sen and most other Chinese intellectuals in this century, Ch'en was merely distinguishing in a purely moral way between a desirable and an undesirable political motivation. The desirable one was based on a *kung-t'ung-t'i-te-kuan-nien* (a sense of community extending to the nation as a whole) and thus made selfish political considerations secondary. The undesirable one made them primary.[56]

Again, the key to successful political development was the moralization of politics, a distinctively Chinese problem which the West had solved. It pertained to "a way of reasoning" (*ssu-k'ao lo-chi*) exemplified by Rousseau's idea of the social contract and realizing both an ethically apolitical attitude toward professional duties and an ethical political commitment to the public good going beyond one's more private interests.[57] For Ch'en, this ethically successful "culture based on the idea of the true citizen" (*kung-min wen-hua*) had long flourished in the West, was the key to modern life, and remained absent in Taiwan as well as on the Mainland.

By 1989, martial law had been canceled and the free formation of political parties had been legalized. Even so, for most intellectuals in Taiwan, nothing had happened in Taiwan altering China's basic political predicament. Indeed, even Taiwan's economic progress was often brushed aside by intellectuals as inconsequential. To depict this progress as unrelated to any seriously promising societal change, they sometimes ascribed it to "luck," sometimes denied its existence, sometimes just changed the subject, sometimes warned that dependence on exports was dangerous, sometimes emphasized "post-modern problems," and sometimes adduced Taipei's traffic mess as proof that the people of Taiwan did not understand modern "rules of the game." A bright Taipei undergraduate's comment to me in 1984–1985 summed up this outlook: "How can you say there has been progress here? This is not an ideal society. So how could there have been progress?"

Logically integral to this great sense of disappointment and anger was the prevalent belief that the "political agency" (Dunn) needed to cause the full realization of the sublime ideals listed above was readily available. Political agency was typically conceptualized by assuming that the epistemically and morally privileged group competent to serve as the causal agents of transformation could be efficiently and publicly identified. This assumption was not only common to the self-images of the Chinese Communist Party and the Kuomintang but also basic to scholars as various as Hsu Fu-kuan, Tu Wei-ming, Yeh Ch'i-cheng, and Yang Kuo-shu. They all assumed that the public can reliably distinguish between "immorally politicized intellectuals" and "true, public-spirited intellectuals." Again, this assumption was intertwined with modern China's pervasive epistemological optimism, the belief that moral qualities can be objectively identified and made clear to the public, which in turn can be relied on to affirm them. Thus Sun Yat-sen was never criticized for being epistemologically unclear when he called for a government run by "the enlightened vanguard" (*hsien-chih hsien-chueh*), and neither was Hu Shih when he asked it be run "by good people" (*hao-jen cheng-fu*).[58] Quite the opposite is John Dunn's view: "the best moral and practical insight of the species cannot be the prerogative of reliably distinguishable or specifiable groups of persons ..."[59]

The above four premises of modern Chinese political thought — a sublime goal, epistemological optimism, a teleological view of history as about to overcome a current predicament, and faith in the ability of an objectively identified, epistemically privileged elite to intervene in history and so quickly to end this predicament — thus made up a logically unified way of reasoning and arguing about not only the goals of political life but also the instrumental means that should be used to reach them. At the same time, as chapter I discussed, such premises by their very nature remain alive only as part of an ongoing problematique: the premises remain meaningful so long as the unanswered questions they imply remain central to the concerns of the contending forces in society. In other words, these premises remain meaningful precisely to the extent that prominent public voices debate what they specifically mean, creating conflicting ideologies. For instance, Sunism, Chinese Marxism, Chinese liberalism, and modern Confucian humanism agreed that "reason" can find the correct path with which to realize a political order essentially free of selfish interests, but Chinese Marxism held that "reason" endorsed Marx's dialectical materialism, while the other three ideologies included very different ideas about what the rational interpretation of history was.

Modern Chinese had plenty to disagree about. Too many scholars, however, have looked at their disagreements without taking note of their shared premises. These premises are so pervasive that they have been basic even to the thinking of an extremely cosmopolitan and astute Taipei intellectual like Yang Kuo-shu.

Yang is not a "native Taiwanese." His family came from the Mainland after 1945, and he graduated from National Taiwan University. He described himself as "liberal."[60] In the 1980s, his political writings were widely regarded as sound rather than brilliant. His liberalism, in other words, epitomized views very common in educated circles, and he was not regarded as a highly distinctive political thinker like the philosopher Yin Hai-Kuang (1919–1969), who by the late 1990s had come to be revered by many liberals throughout the Chinese world. Yang rather was perceived as an eminently reasonable person whose professional reputation was based on his internationally known work as a behavioral scientist. He is a professor of psychology at his alma mater, National Taiwan University. When this university in 1993 looked for a new chancellor, he became a leading candidate. From 1996 to 2000, he was associate director of the Academia Sinica, Taiwan's preeminent research institution. His considerable understanding of American values evolved in two ways.

First, Yang has a Ph.D. in psychology from the University of Illinois. As an indefatigable psychologist immersed in the American psychological literature and using statistical attitudinal survey techniques to chart changing values, he has cogently argued that industrialization in Taiwan caused an increase in "individualism." Second, Yang also was obviously influenced by American values in developing his thought as a "liberal" systematically elucidating the "advantages of the open, pluralistic society."

Yet however enthusiastic about pluralism, Yang's thought fully accorded with the four premises above and was free of any conceptualization, not to mention acceptance, of the dissonance of "the three marketplaces" (see chapters I, V, and XII). Industrialization in Taiwan may indeed have been responsible for a shift to a Chinese

kind of "individualism," but what Dunn called the "radically instrumental conception of community" seemingly correlated to such a
shift was not easily found there,[61] not even in the thought of such an
America-oriented proponent of "the open, pluralistic society."

This is hardly to say that Yang himself is an authoritarian figure
with a confrontational manner. Knowing him personally, I would
describe him as a wonderfully intelligent, outgoing scholar with a
love of discussion and a strong sense of humor. When I accused him
in a Taipei coffee shop of putting a lot of faith in "reason," he was
amused: "Yes, you are right! I really do have great faith in reason!"
The point of my little essay here is that, even in the case of such a
liberal in Taiwan so genuinely and eruditely committed to the
freedom and dignity of the individual, the conceptualization of
freedom remained well within the structure of the rhetorical
situation described above, discourse #1.

Yang's extraordinary personal characteristics — his American
intellectual background, his manifest intelligence and integrity —
make his thought a particularly illuminating example of discourse
#1. We denizens of discourse #2 have to realize that persons as
sincere, intelligent, and educated as we think we are can arrive at a
definition of rationality very different from ours.

My account here relies on a collection of his essays on social,
political, and cultural matters, *K'ai-fang-te to-yuan she-hui* (The Open,
Pluralistic Society), first published in 1982 (virtually all the essays
were individually published in 1979–1981), and *Chung-kuo-jen-te shui-
pien* (The Metamorphosis of the Chinese), a collection of his more
scholarly, psychological studies published in 1988.[62] Yang also was co-
editor of a famous essay collection that was published in 1972 by the
Academia Sinica.[63]

3. Yang Kuo-shu's Thought: Universal Human Nature and World History

Yang's thought combines an empirically vigorous focus on a vast
range of human problems with the four premises above. History for
him, therefore, is based on an ontological or cosmological concept,
that is, a definition of the ultimate basis of human life. For him,
however, this does not consist of any cosmic-historical "contradiction" in the Marxist sense, or of any of those dimensions of universal

human consciousness and alienation that Continental philosophers have discussed since Kant and Nietzsche, and that continue to fascinate many Chinese intellectuals, especially on the Mainland. It consists of the universal nature of human beings as revealed by the modern, especially the American science of psychology.

Yang, in other words, was not impressed by the doubts of many Western scholars, such as Clifford Geertz, that one can accurately generalize about universal human nature.[64] Instead he joined other eminent Western scholars, such as the psychologist Abraham Maslow, who had no doubt one could. In this way, academically prestigious Western writing supported a common Chinese tendency to brush aside the Humean prohibition against deriving "ought" from "is."

Yang depicts universal human nature as a combination of "needs" (such as biological needs, the need for "bonding," the need for "self-realization") (288–289);[65] "desires," including selfishness (97); "emotions" (such as hostile feelings) (98–99); the ability to use "reason," defined as basing thought on "knowledge," "logic," and "good will" (196–197); complex "attitudes" (190) variously combining the above; and numberless activities or psychological and social processes, such as "identification" or "socialization."

These capabilities or tendencies result in behaviors following clear causal patterns. For instance, "Our work almost defines who we are" (262). Or — a more complex example — foreigners can be used as "scapegoats" on which to blame daily frustrations, a tendency politicians can exploit to whip up "overly emotional" forms of nationalism (97–98).

True, even if Western psychology allows such generalizations about universal human nature, Yang diverges from much contemporary Western thought by assuming not only that "reason" implies "good will" but also that the use of reason can specifically determine how to make a political choice. Thus in a column published on September 12, 1979 in the leading paper *Lien-ho-pao* on the eve of the Kaohsiung Incident, Yang systematically argued that "reason" demonstrated the wrongness of "emotional" attitudes on the part of both the KMT right wing and the more radical group of dissidents (155–165).

Yet the idea that reasoning is a morally illuminating activity is of course also a traditionally Western one, still presupposed by J.S. Mill, and even today there are prominent Western psychological theories that, like Yang's, ground goodness in universal human nature. For instance, Carl R. Rogers refers to how an individual's "need to be liked by others and his tendency to give affection will be as strong as his impulses to strike out or to seize for himself," while Harvard's Lawrence Kohlberg saw moral growth as a cognitive development common to people whatever their cultures.[66] Deriving morality from human nature, moreover, Yang merely needs four premises that many would find hard to deny: human needs are indeed much as Maslow described them; meeting "needs" is good; "reason," needed to meet "needs," therefore indicates what the good life is; and the needs of all people should be met, not just ego's, not only because "reason" implies "good will" but also because "every 'person' enters this world with a unique nature and set of potentialities and, so long as he or she lives, this life has value and a distinctive character" (190).

It follows, for Yang, that "reason" should govern "emotions" and "desires" (98), and that "the self-realization of an individual should be based on the principle of not interfering with the self-realization of others. Thus, in most cases, under normal circumstances, the individual on the one hand respects others, and, on the other, exerts self-control. As a result, although everyone is seeking self-realization, what is ultimately carried out is the realization of that larger self [to which every individual belongs] (*ta-wo*). Only then is a healthy 'individualism' realized" (190).

By thus picturing human nature as a struggle between "emotions" or "desires" and a morally-oriented "reason," Yang glides effortlessly back and forth between psychological and moral, humanistic discourse. For instance, describing politicians who play on nationalistic "emotions" instead of developing a "rational" kind of nationalism, he uses the moralistic phrase *chia-kung chi-ssu* (pursuing selfish ends under the pretext of promoting the public good) (98).

Yang thus feels free to make many statements about the universal nature of moral behavior. True, rejecting traditional "authoritarianism,"[67] Yang is unwilling to describe his ethics as Confucian. Yet he grants that some Confucian values remain useful (180). More important, it is hard to see any substantive difference between his ethics and the traditional Confucian emphasis on ascetically curbing bodily desires (*ch'ü-yü*), having self-respect (*t'ang t'ang tso i-ko jen, tzu-ai, tzu-ching*), practicing the golden rule (*chi yü li erh li jen*), and bringing out the best in oneself and others (*ch'eng-chi, ch'eng-wu*). His focus is on the dignity of the individual and on the giving and receiving of respect (*tsun, ching*).

According to Yang, the ideal person follows "reason"; ascetically controls desires (a young man lusting after a beautiful woman is advised to extinguish this desire by imagining how an X-ray picture of her would reveal an unappealing skeleton) (69); has self-esteem (45); respects the rights of others, dealing with them empathetically, sensitive to individual differences; is socially outgoing, maximizing fruitful communication (43); and so, "knowing propriety and accepting the limits on one's place in life" (*chih-li shou-fen*), forms harmonious relations of "interdependence with others" (191–192). (This ideal overlaps not a little with John Rawls's "the reasonable," discussed in chapter X.)

Professor Yang also explains how these general principles should influence people as they carry out different social roles — the teacher, the husband or wife, the child. The teacher, for instance, should not only ask students "deeply to respect the teacher" (*tsun-shih*) but also herself should "respect each student" (*chung-sheng*) (271). Spouses similarly need to respect each other, while special attention must be paid to the problem of the educated wife who finds her self-realization impeded by her household duties (306). Filial piety and parental caring (*tz'u*) are similarly discussed with the emphasis on mutual respect, communication, and devotion to moral principles (319–331).

While the ideal personality is thus implied by psychological facts about universal human nature, so is the nature of the ideal society that should be and is seemingly bound to be realized by history. Thus history is a teleological process publicly exhibiting the moral norms that an individual should follow. The normative society, as in virtually all Chinese thought, is defined as simply based on the highest moral ideals, not on any adjustment of these to accord with the moral infirmities of political life. The key point is raising the "quality of life" by making changes "on the material, economic, social, human rights, cognitive, and cultural levels" so as better to meet "the different kinds of human needs" (289). These are the "tangible benefits" (*shih-chih li-i*) (95) progress is all about. Such progress thus is indicated by "reason," "accords with human nature," creates a "rational environ-ment," and so gives people a "life blessed with good fortune" (*hsing-fu sheng-huo*). Individuals and society as a whole thus join in a "consciously planned quest for a kind of rational, progressive way of life," and so the Chinese, building on "the glorious great path of culture" provided by their ancestors, can "open up for themselves a broad cultural development extending far into the future" (72, 75, 159).

Given this quest, one can evaluate different social phenomena. For instance, "of all the different kinds of human groups, the family is the most important, the most basic" (303). Another crucial point is that, around the globe, the evolution of ecotypes has during recent centuries made possible the construction of societies far more "rational" than those of the past. Chinese can now create "a new Chinese culture" (46, 185):

> But from the standpoint of social evolution, the pluralistic society is more able than the monolithic one to accord with human nature, to realize human potentialities, to hasten social progress.... [and so] to create a highly civilized (*ching-chih*) way of life and culture, enabling the majority in a society to obtain the opportunity to carry out self-realization. (159, 291)

Thus passing through "three stages" — "the period of the traditional society.... the transitional period of modernization.... and the period of high-level modernization" (189) — history progresses toward the moral goal implied by universal human nature and reason. Yang has devoted much thought to this issue. The change in ecotypes is that from an "agricultural, traditional" society to an "industrial, modern" one. According to a "natural development" (3), this change effects or is accompanied by a variety of others much discussed in the modern social science literature: the change from less to more differentiation, from particularism to universalism, from reliance on custom to reliance on law, from authoritarianism and autocracy to autonomy, freedom, and democracy, from a monolithic "closed" society to a "pluralistic, open" one, from less innovation to more, from a less "civilized" or "refined" society to a more refined one, and so on.[68]

Thus seeing human history in global terms applying to all cultures, however, Yang also recognizes distinctively Chinese culture traits. To be sure, he partly sees these as the residual aspects of the agricultural stage. As China fully becomes an industrialized society, he notes, Western theories of personality and psychotherapy that currently do not apply to Chinese psychological conditions "possibly will become more or less applicable to Chinese" (248). For instance, the Chinese family today is either a "stem family" or a "large-scale household." Therefore, the psychological problems it breeds are different from those basic to the European "nuclear family" in Freud's day, and so the Oedipus and Electra complexes are rarer in China (243–245). Yang implies that as more Chinese families become nuclear ones, these complexes may become more common.

Yet Yang also recognizes culturally peculiar traits that should be carried over from the agricultural to the industrial stage. Chinese today should retain the traditionally Chinese way of "eliminating bodily desires" (*ch'ü yü*): "the person involved uses his powers of understanding to change his outlook, and, on the basis of this change, desires naturally disappear (they are not repressed) and do not continue influencing his mind." An example, already cited, is thinking of a beautiful girl as a skeleton. Yang prefers this traditional approach to the common Western therapeutic strategy, which teaches people to "try to shape the environment in order to satisfy one's lusts and desires." Thus Yang rejects the current Western attack against asceticism (Freudianism being an example) (246–247).

Connected to this view is his partial rejection of Western individualism. This point is especially important, though Yang does not clarify it.

On the one hand, he repeatedly emphasizes that industrialization leads to more individualism. On the other, he sees the degree or character of individualism as dependent on not only industrialization but also culture. When he notes that "Chinese do not focus on the individual and instead emphasize relations with others" (245), he seems to be speaking of a trait that will carry over from the agricultural to the industrial stage. Most striking, his own ideal, pluralistic society is one in which the intellectual-moral consensus is solid, all individuals are "tied together" on the basis of "relationships of interdependence" (see below), and everyone is part of the *ta-wo* (greater self). His immersion in Western psychological and sociological theories has not prevented him from inclining toward the widespread contemporary Chinese tendency to view Western individualism as inappropriate for China.

Yet, although culturally distinctive traits can thus shape history, the latter is shaped more by global principles of human nature and progress. Thus Yang, like so many Chinese intellectuals, puts less weight on disparate cultural patterns than on human reasoning about objective conditions. His approach is rational-choice, but as already noted, "reason" for him is inherently inclined toward universal morality.

At the same time, however, Yang is well aware that history progresses most inefficiently. His enormous optimism about human nature, history, and politics, diametrically opposed to John Dunn's understanding of the existential situation (see chapter VIII), in no way dulls his appreciation of the problems people must face. History's inefficiency is quite compatible with his psychological premises, which fully allow for the difficulty of using reason to control emotions. Yang is certainly not surprised to find himself surrounded by a largely unsatisfactory world. He has to reason with "emotional" extremists on both sides in Taiwan in 1979. He notes in 1988 that while "a new, modern Chinese society has already emerged in Taiwan and Hong Kong," and "a new, modern kind of Chinese also is gradually appearing, the Chinese living in these Chinese societies lack experience with regard to this new kind of Chinese society, and so totally lack understanding of the nature of this new kind of Chinese."[69] He laments the disaster of Chinese Communism. He confronts an obtuse international environment that misunderstands the nature of the Chinese Communists and fails to appreciate the merits of the "Taiwan model" (his view in 1979) (117). If one is referring to the present or the past, Yang has more than enough of that "awareness of the dark side of life" (*yu-an i-shih*) which Professor Chang Hao has emphasized. What Chang Hao said, of course, refers only to the way Yang and so many other Chinese thinkers see the imminent future as a time when historical development will abruptly stop being so inefficient.

For Yang, the inefficiencies of evolution are often connected to situational, often international complications. Thus, in his thought, the problems faced by a particular society lucidly appear as stemming from (a) issues common to nearly all societies (should high schools be co-ed?); (b) failures fully to effect the transition to the new, industrial, democratic stage of history; (c) troublesome conditions inherent in that new stage; (d) situational, often international conditions; and (e) anxieties reflecting a combination of the above.

Finally, the structure of history for Yang includes a distinction between population groups better able and less able to rise to the formidable challenges created by such problems. The former group can include some officials, and Yang sees Taiwan's "masses in general" as favoring democratization (152). His emphasis, however, is on "the intellectuals outside government" (*min-chien-te chih-shih fen-tzu*), on "us intellectuals," on people like him:

> In normal times, intellectuals are the conscience of society. In extraordinary times, they are society's Rock of Gibraltar (*ti-chu*). Because of the sensitivity of their understanding, the breadth of their knowledge, their analytical ability, and their strong sense of justice, they often can penetrate beyond the outer appearances of events, dispel the fog of illusion, and grasp the basic principles of things, choosing what is good and then, stable as a great rock, holding onto the good firmly, thus becoming that unshakable force (*ting-li*) on which society can rely. (150–151)

Similarly, Yang has found through attitude surveys that "nearly all young intellectuals" in 1979 had adopted that "rational" attitude toward cultural change he favors, one seeking to mix the "useful" aspects of both Chinese and Western cultures, instead of being "emotionally" biased against either (179–183).

Yang's thought, therefore, though essayistic in format, very consistently urges Chinese, especially those in Taiwan, to understand their world by recognizing certain ideas as rationally binding. "Reason" is the concept on which all his views depend, whether he is discussing human nature, the course of history, therapeutic methods to deal with the anxieties of young people, political conflicts, or the creation of a "new culture." The psychological facts about universal human nature imply the rational, moral goals that individuals and societies should pursue; history, though influenced by some culturally peculiar traits, is a global, teleological struggle rationally to realize these universal goals, as has been made clear especially by the transition from the agricultural to the industrial stage; societal evolution, however, is afflicted by many inefficiencies and situational complications, creating problems best understood by a superbly enlightened social stratum, "us intellectuals"; life, therefore, is an unending struggle to deal rationally and morally with problems on many different levels, though an almost perfect society is promised by the logic of human nature and history.

4. Yang's Categories as Applied to Modern Taiwan

Given this overall picture of universal human nature and the structure of global history, Yang can go on to compare specific societies to one another and to identify current problems and solutions. Taiwan exists "in the context of a worldwide tide moving toward modernization" (169), but the West has taken the lead. In about 1979, a poll of more than 15,000 post-secondary students in Taiwan revealed that most saw the U.S., West German, and British political systems as "the world's most advanced democracies," a view in accord with Yang's (152–153). As for China, revelations appearing after Mao's death in 1976 exhilarated Yang and some other Chinese by finally demonstrating that "the road taken by the Chinese Communists cannot produce results," and that "Taiwan has already become the only hope for solving the problems of China" (119, 121). Thus, Yang wrote in a 1979 article ("China Must be Unified on the Basis on 'the Taiwan Model'"): "Most overseas Chinese believe that the political, social, or economic forms established in Taiwan during the last three decades indeed are far better than those on the Chinese Mainland" (115). Unlike many Taipei liberals who then and now have discussed Chinese modernization without even mentioning what Yang here called "the Taiwan experience" (121), Yang already in 1979 — some seven years before the final phase of democratization began — repeatedly praised the modernization process in "Free China" (192), analyzing it as a major case of evolution within the context of those global principles discussed above. As a psychologist, he carried out extensive attitudinal survey studies charting changes in the values of Taiwan's college population to support his thesis that industrialization causes a shift toward "individualism."[70] He also argued there had been more progress in Taiwan than Hong Kong (101–109). His bold, consistent affirmation of "the Taiwan experience" is a distinctive aspect of his thought, not a common intellectual outlook in the 1980s (107–109, 113, 115–116, 118–119, 120–121, 126, 143, 145, 150, 153, 163, 193, 197). What was widely granted was that Taiwan was ready for democratization, not that it had made any headway towards this goal.

For Yang, Taiwan had made progress but now faced the kinds of "problems" or "contradictions" entailed by the transitional stage it was in. His writing is distinguished by vigorous, complex, specific discussions of these problems as well as by his unqualifiedly optimistic feeling that they can all be largely resolved. As already indicated, Yang, in effect, divides them up into five categories.

First, with regard to completing the transition to the stage of the modern society, Yang (like Levenson) identifies an "emotional" clinging to the past (169). Linked to it are the problem of weak "political consciousness" and the failure of many people adequately to understand the nature of democracy (135–136). To be sure, Taiwan's national development has been more "balanced" than Hong Kong's or the Mainland's, avoiding Hong Kong's one-sided emphasis on the economy and the Mainland's on the polity (107). Yet today (around 1980) Taiwan, in Yang's eyes, is failing adequately to press ahead with democratization, often as a result of the mistaken argument that "national security" should have priority over "progress" (168). The transition toward modernity is being stalled also by fruitless debates about how the inherited culture should be revised. Although most "young intellectuals" by 1979 had rejected uncritical acceptance of either Western or traditional values and adopted a "rational" way of appreciating all "useful" values from either source (179–180), Taiwan "still must increasingly face the impact of all kinds of cultures. In the process of partly accepting, partly rejecting such influences, it ought to have a rational plan with the goal of creating a new, integrated culture. It is not fitting to allow all kinds of cultures to be chaotically mixed together, without any structure, utterly unsystematically." The various cultures' "points of excellence" have to be *jung-ho* (merged together) (107).

Second, with regard to problems integral to the new kind of society, Yang discusses many problems familiar to Westerners: life lacks roots and stability, as people so frequently change their neighborhoods and friends; there is a confusing variety of ideological choices; in an era when technology is supreme, "humanistic values" lose their importance; tremendous psychological strain is caused in an achievement-oriented society by pervasive systems evaluating the individual, such as school examinations; the "consumption culture" breeds vulgarity and waste; alienation occurs between parents and children (but not to so great an extent as had been thought, Yang concluded in 1980) or between teachers and students; the problems of educated women juggling family responsibilities and careers are serious; and so on (56–57, 174, 52–53, 63–64, 175, 318).

Third, with regard to international and other situational difficulties, Yang focuses on the problem of national identity (China's disunity, the contradiction between China's desire to be at the center of world affairs and its peripheral position, the contradiction between the smallness of the Republic of China's territory and its claim to represent a large nation, and the "polarization" within Taiwan between extreme Chinese nationalists and dissidents favoring Taiwan's independence); on the threat to the ROC's security posed by Communist "totalitarianism"; on the ROC's failure to win much "respect" from other nations, not to mention diplomatic isolation; and on Taiwan's limited natural resources and overpopulation (170, 168, 174, 175, 156, 117, 193).

Fourth, with regard to difficulties reflecting all three of the above sets of problems, Yang worries about a widespread "anxiety" (*yu-hsin ch'ung-ch'ung*), a feeling that Taiwan is "like a boat being whirled about helplessly by a stormy sea," and a resulting tendency to "refuse to plough vigorously and plant deeply," just seeking "quick profits." Such feelings, according to Yang's psychological research in 1979, tend especially to afflict young people, who end up with a sense of "historical dislocation" (the Robert Lifton term Yang used) (144–145, 146–147, 173–177, 293–302). Thus, although calling for a rise in political consciousness, Yang interestingly discussed many psychological problems of the young as entailing political worries that could be reduced by using "rational" explanations. This complex anxiety, according to Yang, was also largely responsible for the fact that so many people in Taiwan were going to fortune-tellers and pursuing other superstitions (293–302).

Fifth, Yang is careful to distinguish universal problems from the four kinds just noted. For instance, young Chinese worried by Taiwan's political problems often simultaneously face that more universal "identity crisis" described by Erik H. Erikson (188).

Thus addressing one current problem after another by lucidly describing it as due to a combination of analytically separable causes, Yang is a thinker dealing with concrete, current problems on all domestic and international levels, not one conflating the study of political and economic modernization with research into either China's history and culture or the universal nature of human consciousness as explored by Continental thinkers since Kant and Nietzsche. His immersion in American psychology, his affirmation of

Sun Yat-sen's Three Principles of the People (26–27), and the pride he takes in Taiwan's political as well as economic record of development all reflect an intellect impressed by practical reality.

Even so, it is an intellect that fully shares the overriding optimism which is so typical of modern Chinese thought generally. I once wrote of the late philosopher T'ang Chün-i: "His philosophy has the cheerfulness of a kind of metaphysical YMCA. It expresses that *le* (joy) which Mencius spoke of with regard to the feeling of being one with the cosmos."[71]

Much the same applies to Yang, though his intellectual roots are in American psychology, while T'ang's were in Neo-Confucianism and Kantianism. For Yang, the problems of the society — as he himself describes them, they are formidable indeed, if not overwhelming — do not add up to some tragically inescapable predicament of modernity or of humanity in general. The key is "rational" understanding of Taiwan's historical situation, along with the need for "everyone" to "be clear" (*ming-pai*) about how satisfying ego's needs depends on ego's moral commitment to the good of the whole society (191). Thus Yang emphasizes that teachers require "a rational way of dealing with facts as they are" (*chiu-shih lun-shih*), a "correct understanding of the nature of the modernized society," and "an excellent character" (272–273). Conveying the enlightenment furnished by intellectuals, teachers can thus influence the population at large increasingly to put into practice the moral ideals and personality traits appropriate for an industrialized society. Progress will occur as the intellectual strata outside the government develop "rational" views and persuade the government to adopt them. Thus my emic analysis of Yang's liberalism reveals beliefs about historical causation close to Reinhard Bendix's etic theory of "intellectual mobilization."

As already mentioned, young men faced by the temptations of a "free," "individualistic" society can control their sexuality by imagining that their eyes are X-ray machines revealing the luscious objects of their lust to be no more than repulsive skeletons. How can a woman with the duties of a wife and mother still pursue self-development? She can, if her "husband encourages her to affirm her own being and to find activities outside the household that interest her, whether a career, acquisition of a new skill, participation in social work, or becoming an amateur artist or author" (306). How to avoid the "misery of evaluation" (*p'ing-chia che-mo*) so integral to an achievement-oriented society? There is no unavoidable predicament here either. In schools, for instance, the grading system based on percentage points could be eliminated in favor of a simple "pass or not pass," or one could even avoid all grading, just letting every student use all the time he or she might need to study a subject, though ultimately a certain "prefixed standard" must be reached (63–65). How can the problem of national identity be resolved? Writing in 1979, Yang urged more democratization, thus "allowing the future to prove that the path taken by Taiwan is right, the Mainland's, wrong"; using "reason" to end political "polarization" in Taiwan; proposing unification based on the Taiwan model; and, in the meantime, pursuing an increasingly self-confident, open, and "flexible" approach to relations with the Mainland. Reason is bound to prevail. If Taiwan and the Mainland together held a free election on how to unify China, Yang believes, "most Chinese would pick the unification method based on the Taiwan model" (118–119). Above all, the key to the solution of most problems is democratization. Indeed, one almost suspects that Yang's whole scholarly project with its complex psychological apparatus has a partly hidden agenda: scientifically proving that Taiwan must promptly pursue full democratization.

His writings and his personality both testify to the fact that democracy for Yang centers on the concrete personal freedoms of the individual, freedoms seemingly identical with those we Americans prize. Moreover, this kind of personal freedom is intensely important to virtually every literate person I have met in Taiwan. Yet even in Yang's mind — and few people have cried out in Taiwan more than he for "pluralism" and "openness" — this vision of freedom entirely omits the idea of the three marketplaces as defined in chapters I and V. Thus while Western theorists since *The Federalist* have discussed democracy by arguing about how to contain the ills of the three marketplaces, Chinese liberals like Yang have discussed it by describing an ideal society not only lacking these ills but also on the verge of being historically realized, if not already existing in a distant land. So basic to his psychological research, Yang's empiricism slips away as he discusses the nature of pluralism in a purely theoretical, unhistorical way, conflating the question of what should be with that of what will be.

Historically, the free economic marketplace as capitalism has not only proved to be indispensable to effect economic modernization but also always entailed greed and great inequality. For Yang, however, a much happier future is imminent. A "free economy" is needed (he avoids using "capitalism") (17), but there will only be "reasonable competition" (28). Among "the many obvious advantages" of the "pluralistic, open society" that Chinese "want to establish" is the fact that

> economically, it will be possible to prevent people from monopolizing sources of wealth. In such a society, the various economic and professional organizations will monitor each other in order to avoid any monopolization at the expense of their members' interests. People in such a society are extremely sensitive about their own economic rights and profits and so will always use laws to prevent monopolization or the unfair concentration of wealth.... The distribution of society's wealth will be relatively open, just, and fair.

Thus, "some equalization of wealth" (*chün-fu*) should be attained (32–33, 196):

> [To be sure, such a society will] incline toward 'individualism.' But what I here call 'individualism' definitely does not refer to selfish efforts to enrich oneself. It refers to acknowledging the value and dignity of the individual and simultaneously acknowledging the value and dignity of others as well. (44)

There will be no class exploitation (10), and "every person will be able to be vital and to realize his or her potential" (11). Thus, "everyone's social status and position will depend on your own ability, efforts, and accomplishments (in other words, the outcome of your work as an individual)" (3).

In every historical case of Millsian, pluralistic politics, there has been a political marketplace entailing interest-brokerage, that is the competition among "tricky politicians" (*cheng-k'o*), political parties, cliques, and other interest groups pursuing legal but at least partly selfish ends. As in the case of Sun Yat-sen and so many other Chinese thinkers, however, democracy for Yang completely lacks such a political marketplace. Sun explicitly called for the elimination of all "political views putting selfish interests above the public good" and of all political parties but the "good" ones (*liang cheng-tang*) devoted to the "public good."[72] Yang avoids mentioning this problem. He does say, however, that one "advantage of the pluralistic society" is that "politically, it can prevent authoritarianism." He explains that authoritarianism in politics leads to "the concentration of power," which then "can cause abuses of power" to the point that "laws based on social justice" are no longer respected. "In a pluralistic society, this kind of authoritarianism cannot easily arise" (10). Nor will "the mass media" exert any distorting influence. They "will necessarily give every group or interest an opportunity to make its views known to society" (20).

The free marketplace of ideas has historically been marked by confusing ideological contradictions and unresolved arguments weakening consensus, such as that "polarization" of opinion Yang deplored in the case of the extreme Chinese nationalists and the proponents of Taiwan independence, or the mixing of culturally disparate outlooks. This has typically been a distressing situation for many Chinese, who, like Yang, regard as obviously undesirable the "confused interplay of contradictory ideas" (*fen-yun*) (6), or a society in which "all kinds of cultures are chaotically mixed together, without any structure, utterly unsystematically ..."(107). Thus Yang is at pains to assure his Chinese audience that "pluralism" will result in a "most unified (*t'uan-chieh*) society," one of "harmony amidst diversity" (*ho erh pu-t'ung, pu-t'ung erh ho*), one in which tensions between Mainlanders and Taiwanese will be reduced to insignificance,[73] one not influenced by "bad" ideas such as "communism" or "nihilism" (6, 19, 167, 191). This position of course presupposes epistemological optimism (the belief that "bad" ideas can be objectively identified, that the public will understand and affirm this identification) and optimistically assumes that the influence of "bad" ideas can be almost entirely eliminated.

His optimism lies in his total confidence that all important human activity can be regulated by a legal system according with a complete, objective understanding of right and wrong, and that group harmony is completely compatible with any kind of morally acceptable individual freedom. There is no tragically ultimate tension between self and society. Again, "reason" can fully overcome this tension: as "each individual pursues self-realization, his or her acts in every case will be based on boundaries, standards, principles — what in China is popularly known as 'understanding moral propriety, accepting one's station in life' (*chih li shou fen*). In this way, one person's self-realization will not interfere with that of another."

The result will be a society based on "mutual respect, cooperation ... mutually beneficial relations of mutual dependence." Conversely, this happy state of affairs will preclude

> privilege, oppression, exploitation, and the control or manipulation of others for selfish ends.... The result of a [healthy] individualism, this mutually beneficial relationship of interdependence is like a circle bonding people securely together. As people are all circularly linked to one another, the whole society in a most natural way becomes harmoniously united and centripetally organized. When the nation meets with difficult times, it does not easily fall apart, because it can depend on this circle of spontaneous human relations bonding people together. Because people love a society in which they can achieve self-realization, they will be eager to protect a society of this kind. Therefore, in such a free, democratic, law-based, healthy society, the process of the individual's self-realization can be protected; the nation, relying on such individuals, also is protected; and, as a result, the needs of both the individual and the group are attended to. (191–192)

Yang sees no contradiction between this vision of a future "pluralism" "binding" all individuals together in "mutually beneficial relations of interdependence" and his central thesis that the shift from the agricultural to the industrial stage causes a shift toward "individualism" and away from the group-centered life of the Chinese tradition. As already noted, he implies that, as industrialization brings individualism to China, this individualism will be more group-centered than in the West, but he does not make this point explicitly, seemingly unaware of it and so failing to pursue it empirically (so far as go those writings of his on which I have here depended).

How can Yang's moral-political consensus be attained? His euphoria is as unqualified as K'ang Yu-wei's. "Society's customs" and "shared norms" or "shared judgments" will help set the permissible "scope" of discourse (18). These norms will include the "useful" parts of the inherited culture, since "any parts of Chinese culture still valuable today will naturally remain — they could not be lost even if we tried to lose them" (24). As a result of the "reasonable competition" of ideas, moreover, if

> some thought is not good, it will naturally fail to survive in society. If an argument makes no sense, making it is just a waste of time; one can shout it out, but no one will listen. Just let him shout. No one in society will accept his view. Isn't that a case of naturally failing to survive? Why be a

nervous Nellie (*Ch'i-jen yu-t'ien*), worrying so much [about the spread of bad ideas]? (13–14)

Moreover, Yang emphasizes repeatedly, the law in an open society, being based on "justice" (10), can be used to stop the spread of bad ideas: "Legal regulations and moral norms will naturally put obviously incorrect and bad things outside the scope of pluralistic values" (27, 18–19, 197, 159). Not to mention that in Taiwan, the "spirit" of the Three Principles of the People, already basic to the Constitution, has become part of "everyone's" outlook (27). At the same time, in a pluralistic society, "political power and means cannot be used to influence scholarship and thought, preventing them from developing normally." In other words, "all discussion and criticism must be within the bounds of scholarship, they must be based on reason and good will." Yang here suggests, again most optimistically, that in a pluralistic society, which is free of abuses of power, intellectual discourse will indeed be largely based on "reason and good will" (7).

To sum up, then, Yang's thought, which, as already argued, well illustrated the kinds of ideals and beliefs that animated democratization in Taiwan, presents a vision of individualism based much more on the search for group harmony than German, French, British, and American individualism has been since the age of industrialization began in the late eighteenth century.[74] Yet Yang's way of merging individual and group interests can be seen as different from not only this Western idea of individualism but also the more collectivistic trends in modern China.

It has been hard for Westerners to see how a Chinese thinker could avoid collectivism when he did not allow for the possibility of an ultimate tension between individual and state interests, not to mention dealing with this tension by tipping the balance in favor of the individual. Thus Liang Ch'i-ch'ao in his famous *Hsin-min shuo* (On Creating a New People) emphasized the ultimate importance of both individual liberty and national solidarity and was rewarded for his efforts by being regarded as a proponent of statism and a forerunner of Mao Tse-tung. In the case of our contemporary Yang Kuo-shu, however, whose reasoning if not terminology is about identical with Liang's, the enthusiastic commitment to pluralism and individual liberty cannot be doubted. Thus Yang's thought indubitably combines a deep commitment to individual liberty with an unqualified emphasis on a kind of morally and intellectually transparent group solidarity and unity. A Western critic might want to propose that this combination is illogical or chimerical, but she has to recognize that in Yang's mind — as indeed in Liang's — the coinciding of group harmony and individual liberty does not compromise either one, if the process is based on the totally feasible implementation of reason and morality. What Westerners encounter here, therefore, is not so much Chinese collectivism but an extraordinarily optimistic Chinese view that moral-rational principles can be fully identified, publicly promulgated, and politically implemented, complemented by a strong insistence that the people currently in authority have not done so. This is exactly the Confucian view of the world.[75] Like Liang, Yang envisioned an energetically modernizing society based on "self-propelled adults," not a centralized command structure.[76]

While Yang's liberalism thus represents an answer to the self-group problem very different from that of Chinese Marxism, it is like Chinese Marxism, Sunism, and modern Confucian humanism in seeing a future for China utterly free of "the three marketplaces." Yang's euphoric vision is that of intellectual pluralism without intellectual confusion and crisis; economic pluralism without seriously unjustified inequalities in the distribution of wealth, power, and prestige; and political pluralism without concentrations and abuses of political power — in short, a historically unknown society founded on the interactions among free individuals uninfected by either selfishness or cognitive shortcomings blocking the one rational understanding of history and politics.

5. Conclusion: Discourse #1 and the Process of Democratization in Taiwan

Fully exemplifying discourse #1, Yang's liberalism calls for a society free of selfishness, "bad" ideas, and the disorderly clash of mutually incongruent cultural orientations; is based on epistemological optimism (including the belief in vigorously building an architectonically unified system of ontological-moral-historical-political principles); includes a highly structured, teleological view of history; and defines "intellectuals" as a morally and intellectually enlightened elite able to guide the progressive evolution of society. Thus even this liberal so oriented to American culture and so admirably focused on the empirical, practical actualities of modernization addressed the problem of cultural revision by adopting a utopian, transformative approach rather than a pragmatic, accommodative one. This fact adds to the already abundant evidence that, in modern China, this utopian, transformative approach has indeed been the intellectual mainstream since the turn of the century. It is undeniable that so many concepts basic to Chinese Marxism, modern Confucian humanism, and indeed Sunism as well were also basic to Yang's liberalism.

To be sure, this Taiwan liberalism also differed in important ways from the versions of discourse #1 on the Mainland. These differences in turn were connected to basic developmental and situational contrasts. As already mentioned, one difference is that Taiwan's liberalism in the 1980s lacked a pessimistic feeling that became common in Mainland circles after the debacle of the Cultural Revolution: a strong emphasis on the difficulty of developing democracy in the context of Chinese culture. In the eyes of Taiwan's liberals in the 1980s, the only remaining obstacle to democratization was the recalcitrance of some elements in the government. Yang Kuo-shu's thought splendidly epitomized this buoyant optimism about developmental possibilities in Taiwan. On the Mainland, however, pessimism about the persisting "feudal" nature of Chinese culture still makes prompt democratization seem impracticable. So does the continuing shortage there of what Seymour Martin Lipset called "the social requisites of democracy," such as a certain level of economic development.[77] Lagging economic development in turn causes a danger somewhat peculiar to the Chinese cultural situation, an explosive coalescence of the frustration caused by persisting mass economic deprivations with the "romantic," "utopian," "radical" proclivities of those intellectuals whom Xiao Gong-qin describes as "marginal": great numbers of intellectually able, often embittered persons for whom the academic establishment, with its still limited resources, cannot find suitable positions.[78] Moreover, while many Mainland intellectuals can easily think of reasons not to democratize promptly, the authoritarian character of the political center there today is less vulnerable than was that of the Kuomintang in Taiwan during the 1980s to demands for democratization.

True, as chapter XII argues, the political center on the Mainland has already become an "inhibited" one allowing considerable development of two of "the three marketplaces," the economic and the ideological. Unlike the Kuomintang dictatorship in Taiwan, however, the Mainland's political center started out as an "uninhibited" one, leaving the citizenry accustomed to totalitarian forms of control. Moreover, its official doctrine continues to be based on a philosophy, Marxism, that still commands much respect in intellectual circles east and west; this doctrine is widely viewed in the Chinese world as a foreign theory Chinese endorsement of which stemmed from the modern Chinese episode most revered by Chinese intellectuals, the New Culture and the May Fourth Movements beginning during World War I; the historical record of the controlling political party is widely perceived on the Mainland as including not only bad mistakes but also a great, revered revolution freeing China from foreign domination and native forms of oppression, as well as a series of successful reforms after Mao's death in 1976; and, by unifying China in 1949, this party won for itself the aura of "heaven's mandate."

By contrast, the Kuomintang dictatorship in Taiwan started out as an "inhibited" center not only endorsing private property and free enterprise but also depending on an extremely eclectic official doctrine (Sunism) that implied ideological pluralism and, logically or not, incorporated the principles of liberal, Millsian democracy. One need only recall that, under this dictatorship, from 1958 through 1962, Hu Shih, who was China's most famous liberal, and who was known to be strongly critical of the official doctrine, was director of the most prestigious academic organization in Taiwan, the Academia Sinica. Even today, the head of the parallel organization in China, the Chinese Academy of Social Sciences, could not possibly be a scholar known to be strongly critical of Marxism. Thus inclined from the start to a significant degree of pluralism, the Kuomintang political center in Taiwan also was ideologically weaker than the center in China today, because Sunism could never remotely match the intellectual prestige Marxism enjoyed, and because it was to a large extent out of accord with the revered May Fourth Movement. Moreover, while for many in China today the Chinese Communist Party's failures are overshadowed by its successes, the Kuomintang's fate in Taiwan was precisely the opposite, its successes, however brilliant, forever overshadowed by its failures on the Mainland, not to mention the absence of any "mandate of heaven" aura.

Conversely, ideologically weak and systemically inclined toward considerable pluralism, the Kuomintang political center in the 1980s faced an intellectual elite largely convinced of the benefits of prompt democratization. After all, what Lipset called "the social requisites of democracy" had obviously materialized by then. Instead of a pessimistic feeling that "feudalistic poisons" (*feng-chien i-tu*) were still corroding Chinese culture, the Taiwan intellectual climate celebrated the ways in which Chinese culture meshed with the needs of modernization and democratization. Similarly, with mass economic deprivation no more than a memory, and with increasing occupational opportunities for intellectuals, the danger of an explosive coalescence between utopian intellectuals and angry masses had evaporated. "Intellectual mobilization" as Bendix conceptualized it was furthered also by two tendencies without parallel on the Mainland: the strong influence of American culture, which was conveyed especially by the many intellectual and political leaders with Ph.D.'s earned in leading U.S. universities, and the rise of Taiwanese nationalism along with its links to Japanese liberalism. Moreover, as illustrated by Yang Kuo-shu's thought, democratization was seen in Taiwan as an outstanding way to demonstrate that Taiwan was more able than the Mainland to realize modern ideals. In Mainland circles, outdoing Taiwan is not a goal that animates anyone I know of. To the extent that surpassing other societies is a goal, intellectuals on the Mainland are interested in "transcending the West," as discussed in chapter IV. This ambition has been fueled there by that emphasis on the dark side of the capitalistic West which is illustrated by H.K.H. Woo's writings (discussed in chapter III above), and which plays a far more prominent role in Hong Kong and Mainland than in Taiwan intellectual circles. Nor can one overlook the political leverage furnished to Taiwan liberals by their government's military and diplomatic dependence on the U.S., which was full of politicians, journalists, and academics despising the Kuomintang's dictatorship and clamoring for the democratization of Taiwan. There is no parallel to such leverage in China today, although many there are aware that democratization would almost certainly enhance U.S.-Chinese relations.

The relation between Chinese liberalism and democratizing tendencies in China, therefore, cannot be understood if one looks only at the conceptual structures shared by Chinese liberalism with other modern Chinese ideologies. Moreover, the extent to which these structures facilitate or impede successful modernization and democratization is a topic needing much more study. Yet the resilience of these structures in the political life of Taiwan today seems clear. To whatever extent practical people in Taiwan today see political life as fallible efforts to seek piecemeal progress in three intellectually and morally dissonant marketplaces, the utopian intellectual search continues there unabated for a political theory with which to end this dissonance, as discussed in chapter X, section 11. Conversely, disgust with this dissonance, not only economic considerations, have been involved in the recent emigration of up to one million persons from Taiwan to Shanghai and other parts of the Mainland. Many if not the vast majority of these emigrants, I would say, have not regretted losing the rights they enjoyed as citizens of a democracy in Taiwan. Citing precisely the blaring moral-intellectual dissonance of Taiwan's democracy, one such emigrant, whose cosmopolitan pattern of life included many years as a professor at a leading U.S. university, bluntly told me that Shanghai's government was better than Taipei's.

As illustrated by Yang Kuo-shu's or Li Qiang's liberalism, the idea of democracy as a way to end such dissonance has often appealed to Chinese living under an undemocratic government. What we have yet to see, however, is whether Chinese can not only build a democratic government but also live under it; be satisfied with it as the best way available to cope with and reduce, not to end such dissonance; and on this basis constructively and imaginatively cooperate to pursue progress. This outcome is unlikely so long as discourse #1 persists unrevised, because according to it, such dissonance is an abnormal aspect of political life that can and should be ended, not tolerated. This continuing Chinese desire to dispel the dissonance of clashing viewpoints in a democracy is well illustrated by the way Hsu Han, a philosopher in Taiwan, recently criticized John Rawls's theory of "reasonable pluralism" (see chapter X, section 11).

Endnotes

1. Samuel P. Huntington, *The Third Wave: Democratization in the Late Twentieth Century* (Norman: University of Oklahoma Press, 1993), pp. 21, 44.

2. Amy Auerbach Wilson, Sidney Leonard Greenblatt and Richard W. Wilson, eds., *Methodological Issues in Chinese Studies* (New York: Praeger Publishers, 1983), p. 49.

3. Thomas A. Metzger, "The Western Concept of Civil Society in the Context of Chinese History," in *Civil Society: History and Possibilities*, ed. Sudipta Kaviraj and Sunil Khilnani (Cambridge: Cambridge University Press, 2001), pp. 204–231.

4. Linda Chao and Ramon H. Myers, *The First Chinese Democracy: Political Life in the Republic of China on Taiwan* (Baltimore: The Johns Hopkins University Press, 1998), p. 14.

5. Huntington, *Third Wave*, p. xiii.

6. Yang Kuo-shu, *Chung-kuo-jen-te shui-pien* (The Metamorphosis of the Chinese People; Taipei: Kuei-kuan t'u-shu ku-fen yu-hsien kung-ssu, 1988).

7. Reinhard Bendix, *Kings or People: Power and the Mandate to Rule* (Berkeley: University of California Press, 1978), pp. 265–272. Also see Thomas A. Metzger and Ramon H. Myers, "Introduction: Two Diverging Societies," in *Two Societies in Opposition: The Republic of China and the People's Republic of China after Forty Years*, ed. Ramon H. Myers (Stanford: Hoover Institution Press, 1991), p. xxxviii. Also see latter article for basic contrasts between Taiwan's and the Mainland's political development in the late twentieth century as well as above, p. 359.

8. Thomas A. Metzger, "The Chinese Reconciliation of Moral-Sacred Values with Modern Pluralism: Political Discourse in the ROC, 1949–1989," in Myers, ed., *Two Societies in Opposition*, pp. 3–56.

9. See Huang K'o-wu (Max K.W. Huang), "Ch'ing-mo Min-ch'u-te min-chu kuan-nien: I-i yü yuan-yuan" (The Meaning and Origins of the Chinese Concept of Democracy at the End of the Ch'ing and the Beginning of the Republican Period), in *Chung-kuo hsien-tai-hua lun-wen-chi* (Symposium on Modernization in China), ed. Institute of Modern History, Academia Sinica (Taipei: Institute of Modern History, Academia Sinica, 1991), pp. 363–389; his *I-ko pei fang-ch'i-te hsuan-tse: Liang Ch'i-ch'ao t'iao-shih ssu-hsiang-chih yen-chiu* (The Rejected Path: A Study of Liang Ch'i-ch'ao's Accommodative Thinking; Taipei: Institute of Modern History, Academia Sinica, 1994); his *Tzu-yu-te so-i-jan: Yen Fu tui Yueh-han Mi-erh tzu-yu ssu-hsiang-te jen-shih yü p'i-p'an* (The Raison d'être of Freedom: Yen Fu's Understanding and Critique of John Stuart Mill's Liberalism; Taipei: Yun-ch'en wen-hua shih-yeh ku-fan yu-hsien kung-ssu, 1998), republished in 2000 by Shang-hai shu-tien ch'u-pan-she; and his "In Search of Wealth, Power, and Freedom: Yan Fu and

the Origins of Modern Chinese Liberalism" (Ph.D. diss., Stanford University, 2001).

10. See Huntington, *Third Wave*, p. 263; Chang Hao, *Yu-an i-shih yü min-chu ch'uan-t'ung* (The Democratic Tradition and the Sense of the Permanent Moral Darkness of Political History; Taipei: Lien-ching ch'u-pan shih-yeh kung-ssu, 1989); and Hu Shih's two 1959 statements on tolerance in politics. These were originally printed in *Tzu-yu Chung-kuo* and then reprinted in *Yin Hai-kuang hsuan-chi, ti-i-chüan, She-hui cheng-chih yen-lun* (Selected Writings of Yin Hai-kuang, volume 1, Writings on Society and Politics; Hong Kong: Yu-lien ch'u-pan-she yu-hsien kung-ssu, 1971), pp. 494–506.

11. Yeh Ch'i-cheng, "Ta-hsueh chiao-shou-te chiao-se ho shih-ming" (The Role and Moral Mission of University Professors), *Tang-tai* 73 (May 1992): pp. 18, 20, 23.

12. Ibid., pp. 20, 28–29, 32.

13. Ibid., pp. 17, 29, 31.

14. Ibid., pp. 17, 29, 31, 33–34.

15. Ibid., p. 35.

16. Ibid., p. 31.

17. *Hsin-hsin-wen chou-k'an* 218, May 13–19, 1991, pp. 8–38.

18. Ibid. 242, October 28–November 3, 1991, pp. 8–35.

19. Ibid., p. 8.

20. Yeh Ch'i-cheng, "Ta-hsueh chiao-shou," pp. 34–35.

21. Ibid., pp. 34–35.

22. Yang Jen, "Pei-ching wen-hua ts'ung-shu-p'ai: Cheng-chih ya-li-hsia-te wen-hua chin-lu" (The Group in Pei-ching That Published the Series *Culture: China and the World*: Working in a Politicized Environment on Cultural Issues), *Tang-tai* 73 (May 1992): p. 48.

23. Yeh Ch'i-cheng, "Ta-hsueh chiao-shou," pp. 34–35.

24. Ibid., p. 35.

25. Yeh Ch'i-cheng, *She-hui, wen-hua ho chih-shih fen-tzu* (Society, Culture, and Intellectuals; Taipei: Tung-ta t'u-shu yu-hsien kung-ssu, 1984), pp. 124–127, 148, 162. Also see Mo-tzu-k'o (Thomas A. Metzger), "Erh-shih shih-chi Chung-kuo chih-shih fen-tzu-te tzu-chueh wen-t'i: I ko wai-kuo-jen-te k'an-fa" (Chinese Intellectuals in the Twentieth Century and the Problem of Self-Awareness: A Foreigner's Outlook), *Tang-tai* 73 (May, 1992): p. 62. The second part of this article was in *Tang-tai* 74 (June, 1992): pp. 62–79. The whole article can also be found in Yü Ying-shih et al., *Chung-kuo li-shih chuan-hsing shih-ch'i-te chih-shih fen-tzu* (Intellectuals during Periods of Transformation in Chinese History; Taipei: Lien-ching ch'u-pan shih-yeh kung-ssu, 1992), pp. 83–138 and in *Hsueh-shu ssu-hsiang p'ing-lun* 3 (1998): pp. 183–229.

26. *Hsin-hsin-wen chou-k'an* 242, p. 26.

27. Metzger, "Chinese Reconciliation," p. 16.

28. Ibid., pp. 43–51.

29. Thomas A. Metzger, "Continuities between Modern and Premodern China: Some Neglected Methodological and Substantive Issues," in *Ideas Across Cultures: Essays on Chinese Thought in Honor of Benjamin I. Schwartz*, ed. Paul A. Cohen and Merle Goldman (Cambridge, Mass.: Council on East Asian Studies, Harvard University, 1990), pp. 263–292.

30. This was my generalization about political thought in Taiwan in my "Confucian Thought and the Modern Chinese Quest for Moral Autonomy," *Jen-wen chi she-hui k'o-hsueh chi-k'an* 1 (November 1988): p. 348. John K. Fairbank used it in his *China: A New History* (Cambridge, Mass.: The Belknap Press of Harvard University Press, 1992), p. 424 to characterize both Chinese political thought in general and the ideals of the Democracy Movement in the late 1980s, which culminated in the T'ien-an-men tragedy. I agree with him that these ideals, the goal of political life as defined in discourse #1, have been widely taken for granted on both sides of the Straits.

31. See Huang Ko-wu's writings cited above in note 9.

32. Hsu Fu-kuan, *Hsueh-shu yü cheng-chih chih chien* (Between the Realms of Scholarship and Politics; Taipei: T'ai-wan hsueh-sheng shu-chü, 1980), pp. 124–126.

33. *Shih-chieh jih-pao*, April 29, 1990.

34. See the articles of mine cited in notes 25 and 29 above.

35. Thomas A. Metzger, "A Confucian Kind of Modern Thought: Secularization and the Concept of the *T'i-hsi*" (A Deductive, Comprehensive, Correct System of Political Principles), in *Chung-kuo hsien-tai-hua lun-wen-chi*, pp. 277–330.

36. See chapter I, note 138.

37. Huang Ko-wu, *I-ko pei fang-ch'i-te hsuan-tse*.

38. John A. Hall, *Powers and Liberties: The Causes and Consequences of the Rise of the West* (Oxford: Basil Blackwell Ltd., 1985).

39. See my article cited in note 25 above, *Tang-tai* version, part 2, pp. 65–66.

40. Leo Ou-fan Lee, "In Search of Modernity: Some Reflections on a New Mode of Consciousness in Twentieth-century Chinese History and Literature," in Cohen and Goldman, eds., *Ideas Across Cultures*, pp. 109–135.

41. See p. 251 in Chin Yao-chi's (Ambrose Y. C. King's) 1987 volume, cited in chapter VII, note 1, and Wei Cheng-t'ung, "Liang-chung hsin-t'ai, i-ko mu-piao — hsin-ju-chia yü tzu-yu chu-i kuan-nien ch'ung-t'u-te chien-t'ao" (Two States of Mind, One Goal: A Discussion of the Conflict between the New Confucians and Liberalism), in *San-shih-nien-lai wo-kuo jen-wen chi she-*

hui k'o-hsueh-chih hui-ku yü chan-wang (Humanistic Studies and the Social Sciences in Our Nation during the Last Thirty Years: Retrospection and Prospects), ed. Lai Tse-han (Taipei: Tung-ta t'u-shu kung-ssu, 1987), pp. 58–59.

42. Thomas A. Metzger, "Chinese Reconciliation," pp. 19–21.

43. Tu Wei-ming, *Ju-hsueh ti-san-ch'i fa-chan-te ch'ien-ching wen-t'i* (Reflections on the Dawning of the Third Era in the Evolution of Confucian Learning; Taipei: Lien-ching ch'u-pan shih-yeh kung-ssu, 1989), pp. 178–179.

44. See Huang Ko-wu, *I-ko pei fang-ch'i-te hsuan-tse*.

45. Ch'en Fang-cheng and Jin Guantao, *From Youthful Manuscripts to "River Elegy": The Chinese Popular Culture Movement and Political Transformation 1979–1989* (Hong Kong: The Chinese University Press, 1997).

46. Lin An-wu, "Tao-te ts'o-chih — (i) — Hsien-Ch'in ju-chia cheng-chih ssu-hsiang-te k'un-chieh" (The Fallacy of the Misplaced Tao — Part I — The Misunderstanding at the Heart of Confucian Political Thought in the Chou Period), p. 119. A reprint put out by Tung-hai University's Wen-hsueh-yuan, Taichung. Part of the collection *Ti-i-chieh Chung-kuo ssu-hsiang-shih yen-t'ao-hui lun-wen-chi — Hsien-Ch'in ju fa tao ssu-hsiang-chih chiao-jung chi ch'i ying-hsiang*. Lin's article was apparently first published in 1989.

47. See chapter V, section 1.

48. Metzger, "Chinese Reconciliation," pp. 43–51.

49. Mo-tzu-k'o (Thomas A. Metzger), "Chung-hua min-kuo cheng-fu liang-mien p'ing-chia yü chih-shih fen-tzu-te tzu-chueh wen-t'i: Hui-ying Ch'en Ch'i-nan chiao-shou" (The Evaluation of the Positive and Negative Aspects of the Republic of China and the Intellectuals' Problem with regard to Self-awareness: Answering Professor Ch'en Ch'i-nan), *Tang-tai* 63 (July 1991): pp. 132–149.

50. Ch'en Ch'i-nan, *Kung-min kuo-chia i-shih yü T'ai-wan cheng-shih fa-chan* (The True Spirit of Citizenship and the Political Development of Taiwan; Taipei: Yun-ch'en ts'ung-k'an #34, 1992), pref., p. 7.

51. Ibid., pref., pp. 10–11.

52. Ibid., pref., pp. 3, 13.

53. Ibid., pref., pp. 3–5.

54. Ibid., pref., pp. 3, 7.

55. Ibid., pref., pp. 11–12.

56. Ibid., pref., pp. 13–15.

57. Ibid., pref., pp. 11, 13.

58. Jerome B. Grieder, *Hu Shih and the Chinese Renaissance* (Cambridge, Mass.: Harvard University Press, 1970), pp. 191–193.

59. John Dunn, *Western Political Theory in the Face of the Future* (Cambridge: Cambridge University Press, 1990), p. 113.

60. Yang Kuo-shu, *K'ai-fang-te to-yuan she-hui* (The Open, Pluralistic Society; Taipei: Tung-ta t'u-shu ku-fen yu-hsien kung-ssu, 1985), p. 14.

61. Dunn, *Western Political Theory*, pp. 20–21.

62. See notes 6 and 60 above.

63. Li I-yuan and Yang Kuo-shu, eds., *Chung-kuo-jen-te hsing-ko* (The Character of the Chinese; Taipei: Chung-yang yen-chiu-yuan, min-tsu-hsueh yen-chiu-so, 1972). Some discussion of the viewpoints in that volume can be found in Thomas A. Metzger, *Escape from Predicament: Neo-Confucianism and China's Evolving Political Culture* (New York: Columbia University Press, 1977), chap. 1.

64. See Daniel Little, "Rational Choice Models and Asian Studies," *The Journal of Asian Studies* 50 (February 1991): pp. 40, 46.

65. All page references in the text are to Yang Kuo-shu, *Kai-fang-te to-yuan she-hui.*

66. Carl R. Rogers, *On Becoming a Person* (Boston: Houghton Mifflin Co., 1961), pp. 194–195, and chapter I, note 59.

67. Yang Kuo-shu, *Chung-kuo-jen-te shui-pien*, p. 407.

68. See ibid., p. 407.

69. Ibid., pref., pp. 1–2.

70. Ibid.

71. Metzger, *Escape from Predicament*, p. 37.

72. Thomas A. Metzger, "Did Sun Yat-sen Understand the Idea of Democracy?" *The American Asian Review* 10 (Spring 1992): pp. 1–41.

73. Yang Kuo-shu, *Chung-kuo-jen-te shui-pien*, p. 228.

74. S. Lukes, *Individualism* (Oxford: Basil Blackwell, 1973).

75. Metzger, "Confucian Thought and the Modern Chinese Quest for Moral Autonomy," p. 326.

76. Metzger and Myers, "Introduction," p. xviii.

77. Seymour Martin Lipset, "The Social Requisites of Democracy Revisited: 1993 Presidential Address," *American Sociological Review* 59 (February 1994): pp. 1–22.

78. Xiao Gong-qin, *Chih-shih fen-tzu yü kuan-nien-jen* (The True Intellectual and the Person Only Immersed in Abstract Ideas; T'ien-chin: T'ien-chin jen-min ch'u-pan-she, 2001), pp. 154–161.

CHAPTER VII

The Sociological Imagination in China: Comments on the Thought of Ambrose Y.C. King (Chin Yao-chi)

1. Introduction

Ambrose Y.C. King (Chin Yao-chi) is internationally known for the knowledgeability and fluency with which he uses many of the perspectives of Western social science to discuss Chinese culture, modern Chinese history, and current developments on both sides of the Taiwan Strait. Born in 1935, growing up in Shanghai, he obtained a Ph.D. degree from the University of Pittsburgh, became professor of sociology and pro-vice-chancellor at The Chinese University of Hong Kong, and in 2002–2004 was vice-chancellor there (the chancellorship is an essentially honorary position occupied by the highest official in Hong Kong). King's life, however, has also been rooted in Taiwan, where he lived for many years after the fall of the Mainland, and where he obtained both his B.A. and M.A. degrees. Long before the promise of Taiwan's development became obvious, at least as early as 1966, he recognized it, astutely introduced Western modernization theory to analyze it, understood that pursuing it required not iconoclasm but a process of critically and creatively building on the inherited culture, and widely influenced Taiwan intellectuals as they tried to make sense out of their complicated, often distressing situation.

King, therefore, has been one of the numberless Chinese scholars since the late nineteenth century seeing themselves not just as copying the West but as trying to integrate the good points of the Chinese tradition with those of Western culture (*hui-t'ung Chung-hsi*).

His vision of this integration, however, was singular, in that he so deeply explored the West's social science literature as the key to understanding the value and "rationality" of the most recent contribution of the West to the world, the process of modernization. Understanding the latter deeply while admiring it so much, he could not support T'ang Chün-i's radical rejection of the basic direction of Western civilization after the Renaissance (see chapter II), echoed in Henry K.H. Woo's still more radical critique of the West (chapter III). Yet King was radical enough in his *Chung-kuo cheng-chih yü wen-hua* (China's Culture and Politics), published in 1977, in which he called for a kind of Chinese modernization and democratization excluding the West's "liberalism" and "individualism." Much like T'ang or Woo or even Yang Kuo-shu (see chapter VI), King viewed these as out of accord with the persisting Confucian vision of how people should feel and think about themselves and their social relations.

The Chinese tendency to reject some key aspects of Western modernity is widespread and deep-rooted indeed when one of the persons helping form it is a scholar like King who has so extensively and sympathetically explored the West's sociological efforts to understand itself. As illustrated in chapters V and VI, Chinese liberalism has tried to brush aside the emphasis of Chinese Marxism and modern Confucian humanism on the allegedly undesirable side of Western modernity. This emphasis, however, continues to be as important in modern Chinese thought as is the at least equally widespread conviction that Chinese culture has to incorporate certain invaluable orientations and institutions which the leading Western societies have already realized.

When one weighs against each other the Chinese views described in this book representing modern Confucian humanism, Chinese Marxism, Chinese liberalism, and one prominent wing of Chinese sociology, one can see that intellectually articulate circles in China have largely embraced a somewhat illogical picture of Western civilization hard if not impossible to find in modern Western writings: on the one hand, the popular society and culture of the West have fully realized in practice the highest ideals of humanity, the ideals of the Enlightenment, thus decisively reducing the flow of "selfishness" in society and so realizing the prime goal of the ancient Chinese sages; on the other hand, this stunning Western achievement has been marred or undermined by an excessive emphasis on the free use of instrumental rationality by individuals to pursue egotistic goals. As opposed to the Neo-Confucians' picture in Ming-Ch'ing times of the Chinese people in their day as dominated by *jen-yü* (selfish human desires) while trying to grasp and build on an elusive "heavenly," divine force in their souls (*t'ien-li*), the Western populations were now perceived by modern Chinese intellectuals as having achieved a kind of flawed breakthrough in global history, vigorously implementing the sublime principles that dissolved selfishness while perversely promoting the instrumental means with which to pursue selfish desires. As T'ang Chün-i put it, this was a new era "blurring together the divine and the demonic" (*shen-mo hun-tsa*) (see chapter II).

For King, the principle with which China could modernize by rectifying this flawed breakthrough was "reason." Thus he reaffirmed the epistemologically optimistic definition of "reason" basic to discourse #1 and resisted the Great Modern Western Epistemological Revolution (GMWER), which indeed was integral to not only the Western liberalism and individualism he explicitly rejected but also the Weberian sociology of which he sought to make use (see chapter I, section 6). The GMWER's evisceration of reason as a guiding moral principle could not make sense to King, not only because he, like just about all modern Chinese intellectuals, took for granted the epistemologically optimistic concept of reason basic to discourse #1 but also because there was for him no other normative concept available to do what had to be done: copying successful Western tendencies while rejecting the unsuccessful ones. All cultures undergo criticism and revision, but when revision is intertwined with the evaluation of a foreign civilization, the temptation to seek normative guidance in the idea of "reason" would seem to be irresistible.

Deeply exploring the Western sociological literature as an irreplaceable source of light on the nature of modernization, King integrated this literature with a widespread Chinese hope that, by unlocking the full meaning of "reason," Chinese could follow the path of the West while avoiding its pitfalls. Logically enough, it was within the context of this Chinese discourse that he joined in the call for the "sinification" of the social sciences.

This chapter, however, focusing on his 1992 volume, *Chung-kuo she-hui yü wen-hua* (China's Society and Culture), cannot deal with his oeuvre as a whole.[1] My emphasis is not only on how King's sociology illustrates the ambivalence of the modern Chinese response to Western modernity but also on how this ambivalence was intertwined with the epistemological optimism basic to discourse #1. One also has to note, however, that with this framework King endorsed Taiwan's "accommodative" mode of modernization already in the 1960s, when scholarly trends east and west were largely hostile to it. In the next decades, developments both in Taiwan and on the Mainland vindicated his judgment (see chapter XII). From the standpoint of the political rationality this book is trying to advertise, King's political theory is an insightful one.

2. Culture and Institutions

Like many contemporary Chinese scholars, King is unreservedly macroscopic in his study of China, discussing phenomena such as norms "prevalent throughout the society" (17) or the overall nature of Mao's regime. His ideas and data have many origins, including the flow of information available to a cosmopolitan Chinese scholar living in Hong Kong; his learning as a Chinese fully conversant with, say, the varied ways Chinese orally and in their writings have referred to "face" (*mien-tzu, lien*); the views of famous modern Chinese writers such as Fei Hsiao-t'ung, Liang Shu-ming, and Lin Yü-t'ang; the insights of the New Confucian thinkers, such as Hsu Fu-kuan and T'ang Chün-i; the findings of leading Chinese sinologists, such as Yang Lien-sheng and Yü Ying-shih; the sinological writings of some Western scholars, ranging from Etienne Balazs and Wm. Theodore de Bary to Donald R. DeGlopper; theoretical writings from the Weberian school, such as those of Max Weber, Talcott Parsons, and S.N. Eisenstadt; an impressive variety of other social science writings, such as those of Erving Goffman or Jack Douglas; and the works of some of the currently most fashionable social thinkers, such as Jürgen Habermas or Harvey Cox. Greatly relying on Western theorists like Weber and Habermas, however, he still has participated in the recent effort in Taiwan to "sinify" the social sciences, which for him means analyzing distinctly Chinese social phenomena to determine whether Western theories that claim to apply to all cultures actually do, as well as bringing a better analysis of Chinese society into the international mainstream of sociological knowledge (17–18, viii).[2]

Embracing Parsons' multi-causal approach and so insisting that sociologists can neglect neither "cultural elements" nor "institutional elements" (147), King identifies "culture" largely with "social norms" that, as "social facts," are "external to the consciousness of any one individual," and that, "consciously or unconsciously," shape "daily life" "throughout society." Chinese culture, therefore, is a way of thinking and behaving found equally on the Mainland, in Taiwan, in Hong Kong, and in overseas Chinese communities (17, vii). Culture, at least partly, can be the product of intellectual teachings, such as those of Confucius (33). "Institutions," for him, refers especially to a society's economic forms or "political tradition" (110), which, at least in the Chinese case, included certain "bureaucratic" patterns and a certain relation between "state" and "society" (114). Yet King also agrees with Dennis H. Wrong that the individual does not just play a cultural or institutional "role" but rather interacts with society in a rather indeterminate way (6).

3. Reason and Culture

Linked to his key concepts of "culture" and "institutions" are what King calls "cultural and political concepts and phenomena," by which he means various ideals, such as "nationalism" or the French Enlightenment's concept of "reason," as well as any "movements" associated with these, such as the May Fourth Movement (184, 189, 170–183). King thus refers to various "doctrines" (*chu-i*) and "ideologies" (*i-shih hsing-t'ai*), or to the "spirit" dominating a particular era (*shih-tai ching-shen*) (185, 188). Such trends can turn into a "global tide" (*shih-chieh-hsing-te ch'ao-liu*) (117).

Moreover, world history, according to King, includes the human capacity to reason critically about such trends: "What we should do is look with a critical eye at both tradition and modernity. Only in this way can we rationally build the way from tradition to modernity" (218). Thus much historical action can be evaluated by using a standard of "rationality" applying equally to different cultures and historical periods. Sun Yat-sen was a "rational nationalist" (181), while the PRC's "cultural revolution" was "irrational" (199).

In other words, for King, as much as for Yang Kuo-shu, the

analysis of social life quite centers on "reason" (*li-hsing*) as a cognitive capacity or standard that is essentially the same for all people, no matter what their cultural background (chapter VI). Yang defines "reason" as thought based on "knowledge," "logic," and "good will,"[3] while King discusses the writings of Weber and Habermas to show that "reason" includes not only the "instrumental rationality" basic to the "economic marketplace" and "bureaucracy" but also a grasp of moral or humanistic ends (216–218).

To some extent, therefore, both King and Yang Kuo-shu, centering the analysis of societies on "reason" as a transcultural category, have something in common with the Western "rational choice" school and its offshoot, the "convergence theory" approach developed by Alex Inkeles and others.[4] On the other hand, as already mentioned, the thinking of both these scholars is typical of the whole modern Chinese intellectual arena's "epistemological optimism," which gives "reason" a much broader meaning than the Western rational choice school has in mind. For King and Yang, therefore, what all people have in common is not just a utilitarian tendency to use logic when making decisions about how to pursue their interests. As people use "reason," they discuss moral principles as well as facts that somehow are pretty much the same for any person, no matter what her cultural or historical situation. From this standpoint, the global rather than the culturally disparate aspects of human life are emphasized. It is striking that even brilliant Chinese scholars like King and Yang so oriented to American social science or psychology should thus minimize the extent to which historical and cultural circumstances shape reasoning and instead emphasize the universally identical content of morality.

For instance, for King, the Chinese emphasis on "face" is just a culturally peculiar way of accentuating a "universal phenomenon" (44). Similarly, the normative principles of Confucianism are "based on the experience of everyday life and the knowledge obtained from it" (21). Still more bluntly universal, of course, are the dictates of "instrumental reason," so basic to economic and bureaucratic life (77). Most important, for King, modernization both accentuates reason as a universal faculty and develops as a global tendency relative to which cultural differences are secondary. As he puts it, "modernization is a global movement." Thus China "faces the universally significant challenges of modernization," which are the same "irrespective of any ideological boundaries." Because the "challenges of modernization" are thus global and universally significant, what Weber, Heidegger, Habermas, or even the poet Hölderlin have said about them applies to Chinese as much as to Germans:

> Modernization became the main topic of human history after the European Enlightenment, and the problem of rationalization into which Weber poured his best energies is faced not just by Westerners but by all the world's modern people, including the Chinese.... China's modernization, whether on the Mainland or in Taiwan or Hong Kong, must in its essence follow the path of reason. (213–218)

If, then, King's sociology depicts people as using or failing to use their cognitive ability to reason about facts and principles that are universally or inherently the same for anyone, what role is left for culture?

King's approach still emphasizes culturally disparate values, but only in a limited, often normative way. As already noted, he sees "everyday life" as permeated by culturally accented patterns. Moreover, completely discarding the disparate tradition that Chinese have inherited is anyway "impossible" (201–202). Any Chinese trend is affected by it at least to some extent. Thus King speaks of "the Chinese edition of the Soviet-style socialistic system" (203). After all, "the elements of political structure actually, if we look more deeply, are inseparable from culture" (140).

King follows the modern Chinese mainstream by often viewing culture in a highly normative way, distinguishing between those cultural elements that should be cultivated and those that should be eliminated. For instance, seeing China's imperial state as dominating society, King also sees this traditional trend as both contradicting the rational goal of modernization and perpetuated by the PRC (102). Similarly, the Maoist political style reflected Confucianism's tendency to merge moral ideals with the authority of the state (203, 193–194, 187–197). On the other hand, as European criticism of the Enlightenment showed, a modern society should make use of any of the "cultural resources" offered by its disparate premodern tradition (191). King implies that these are relevant to overcoming the Weberian "disenchantment" created by the modern emphasis on instrumental rationality. The Chinese tradition in particular includes values especially useful for a modern society, such as the Confucian emphasis on self-discipline and learning or even, as Yü Ying-shih suggested, the Confucian orientations enabling China to bypass any crisis of "secularization" (214, 59–60, 142–144).

In considering continuities between China's premodern and modern culture, however, King gives his detailed attention only to the norms of daily life, not to political modes and ideologies. He shows no interest in those "deeper" connections between China's disparate cultural premises and the meaning for modern Chinese of the ideas "transplanted" (*i-chih*) (203) from the West. He does not, for instance, analyze the meaning attached by Chinese since late Ch'ing times to the Western word "democracy" to see whether it differed from Western usages.[5] Instead, he assumes that, as this idea was "transplanted" from the West into China, it carried with it a rational, transcultural, universally correct interpretation.

As he sees it, his task is to determine whether Chinese correctly grasped this transcultural interpretation or not. Noting that they mostly did not — they "romanticized" the idea and "failed to understand the practical conditions of democratization" (193) — he is interested in the fact of this failure, not in dissecting any culturally disparate patterns that led to it. In other words, while he is much interested in how China's norms of everyday life differ from those of the West, he lacks such an interest with regard to modern China's political ideas and behaviors. Asking whether these have failed or succeeded in meeting a rational standard applying to all cultures, he does not question whether his own understanding of this rational standard may have been affected by his own cultural or historical background. Like Yang Kuo-shu, he sees his access to the "rational" understanding of modern world history as unclouded by any culturally disparate orientations.

To this extent, then, King's sociology, like Yang Kuo-shu's, diverges from the intellectual concerns of many Western scholars, who, brought up on anthropologists like Ruth Benedict and viewing all normative if not factual thoughts as culture-bound or historically limited, seek an empirically thorough, precise understanding of how one way of thinking and living differs from another. For them, the mind is far more able to make specific observations about human life than it is to depict global historical laws or objective moral norms all should follow. They also suspect that, without comprehensively describing the distinctive inclinations of a particular culture, revising them effectively to pursue a goal like modernization may be difficult. King actually emphasizes culture far more than most Chinese thinkers,[6] but even his thought is far from this kind of Western preoccupation with cultural differences. At the same time, as already suggested, King's bluntly teleological vision of world history as increasingly embracing "reason" is at odds with the more modest empirical goals of the rational choice school.

True, all three positions — King's rationalism, rational choice theory, and the focus on cultural differences — are wrestling with an international agenda of problems no one has so far resolved. How thinking combines rationality or reflexivity with culturally inherited premises remains a controversial question east and west, as chapter I discussed, and I believe that many Western scholars view history teleologically despite any disclaimers of theirs. Yet one cannot say that King has identified these three positions and thought through their pros and cons. At the very least, if there is some human access to transcultural standards of rationality, one needs thoroughly to describe culturally disparate orientations in order to guard against confusing the former with the latter. This is a matter of "self-awareness" (*tzu-chueh*), and this King does not do (see chapter XIII).

4. The Nature of Chinese Culture and of China's Two Paths of Modernization

It is with this teleological emphasis on "reason," which is virtually unchallenged in the Chinese intellectual arena, that King puts China into global context. His picture of China's political center before the Western impact deviates little from Weber's, though he uses post-Weberian terminology: an "'uninhibited political center'" (96) unchecked by other institutions but weaker than the modern Chinese polities and so allowing some room for the "civil society"; "it did not basically change for two thousand years" (110, 96, 104). It was part of a society permeated with Confucian values (33, 46). (Usually regarding this permeation as obvious, Chinese scholars seldom ask Patricia Ebrey's precisely descriptive questions about the extent to which elite values influenced popular patterns.) Discussing these values, King acknowledges the familiar list of familial virtues regarded today as facilitating modernization, such as self-discipline and respect for learning. Inspired by L.S. Yang's seminal article on *pao* (reciprocity), however, King mainly discusses the norms affecting life outside the family, especially "face" (*mien-tzu, lien*), "connections" (*kuan-hsi*), and *jen-ch'ing* (feelings of obligation to be kind to someone) (76). King emphasizes both the large variety of ways in which Chinese ingeniously fashioned "connections" with strangers (71) and the lack in Confucianism of any clear moral norm for dealing with those who remained strangers (12–13). (He could have deepened his analysis by referring to Yang Kuo-shu's discussion of the idea of predestination [*yuan*]).[7]

But his emphasis is on the creativity and autonomy of the individual in designing his or her "network" of relations. Here he differs (correctly, I believe) from the many scholars, including Yang Kuo-shu, who hold that Confucianism subordinated the self to the group. King has instead been influenced by Fei Hsiao-t'ung's striking views, the New Confucians' interpretation of the Confucian idea of the moral subject, and writers like Herbert Fingarette, who have argued that Confucian thought focused on the relational aspects of life rather than establishing a dichotomy between group and self (ix). Thus emphasizing the moral autonomy of the Confucian self, King refutes the idea that Confucian ethics focused only on "shame" as a reaction to criticism from others, not "guilt" as self-criticism (53). Though strangely never mentioning the central Confucian idea of a normative confrontation between the political center and the autonomous, morally inspired scholar, he does agree that Confucian ethics included a sense of "tension" between ideals and actuality, explaining how Weber misunderstood this issue (136–137, 202). At the same time, not entirely avoiding all contradictions, he also grants that the group bore heavily on the self, especially after the emergence of the *Classic of Filial Piety* "drowned the self within an ethical system regarding the family as the primary unit" (3).

Global history for King, as for nearly all Chinese thinkers since Liang Ch'i-ch'ao, is a matter of deep contrasts: the development of China's traditional society was abnormal and unsuccessful compared to Western history. While China "drowned" the self in norms devoted to group needs and suffered from the state's domination of society, the Enlightenment revealed to the world how "progress" through "modernization" could be achieved by emphasizing "reason." Reason implied not only instrumental rationality and science but also "freedom," "equality," and "democracy," values that would "liberate the individual from the constraints of the old society" (188–189). This vision was accompanied by the Industrial Revolution and the rise of nationalism, though not without a pathological twist, the Jacobinism that "fused rationalism, moralistic thinking, and absolute power" and so planted the seeds of both kinds of "totalitarianism" in the twentieth century (193).

A global drama was then created as these three elements of "progress" (nationalism, the Industrial Revolution, and the Enlightenment's concept of rational liberation), along with the menacing implications of Jacobinism, spread through the societies of the non-Western world. The latter were plunged into a desperate situation. To be sure, they suddenly were confronted by an unprecedented opportunity to "liberate" themselves from the "constraints of the old society." Hence some scholars have seen in them, or some of them, a rising sense of optimism. This is not King's point, however. As he sees it, these non-Western societies first of all had to make sense out of these Western ideas and techniques and figure out how to revise their own cultures. Enormous misunderstanding was likely at this juncture, however great the ability of the human mind to grasp "reason." These societies simultaneously suffered the impact of imperialism, finding themselves on the "periphery" of Immanuel Wallerstein's new world order (204–206). Moreover, "industrialization in its early stages usually produces the misery of social upheaval and throws values into a pathological state of confusion." Consequently, many of these non-Western societies were attracted to the Jacobinic side of modern Europe, "communism with its romantic and morally passionate" approach to modernization (211). They thus nearly all tragically failed to take advantage of a magnificent historical opportunity to progress.

China was no exception. King outlines the political disintegration that occurred: the May Fourth Movement as a properly inspired but overly "romantic" and "iconoclastic" attempt to "transplant" the values of the Enlightenment; the rise of the PRC as an "'uninhibited political center'" imposing "Soviet-style socialism" on China and leading to the "irrationality" of the Cultural Revolution; and the inadequacy of Teng's reforms, which have not basically altered the "Soviet-style" state (204) (his view in 1992). Again, King explains China's inclination to Marxism mainly in terms of imported, transcultural ideas and conditions of receptivity common to virtually all societies, de-emphasizing indigenous, culturally disparate conditions.

What is distinctive about King's account, however, is his treatment of the ROC regime after 1949 in Taiwan. In effect, he rejects the Fairbankian view of "the great Chinese revolution" as a single unfolding process climaxed by the victory of the Communists and leaving Taiwan as the "island refuge" of a defeated regime irrelevant to the problem of Chinese modernization.[8] Nor does he suggest that Taiwan's success was due mainly to situational conditions, such as American aid or the smallness of the society. For King, the ROC struggled with the same problem as the PRC, that of Chinese modernization, but devised methods that were "different in kind" (xiii, 204, 198) and far more successful: "Indeed, after 1949, the Kuomintang in Taiwan achieved a lot in the way of national development, and it set forth a practicable path of Chinese modernization.... China's true process of democratization unfolded on that beautiful island surrounded by swirling ocean waves, Taiwan" (181, 123).

What were these "differences in kind"? Like the PRC, the ROC adopted the "party-state system," which precluded any political power outside that of the ruling party (120–122). This system, King holds, somewhat as Paul A. Cohen has argued, arose as a response to the "national crisis" caused by imperialism and reflected the fact that, to deal with this crisis, "state-building was more urgent than the building of democracy" (124).[9] But while the PRC's political center was "'hard'" and "'uninhibited,'" the ROC's was "'soft'" and "'inhibited,'" not only allowing for the rise of the "free market economy" and the "civil society" but also establishing a constitution and an official doctrine (the Three Principles of People) that were committed to democratization. Thus "there appeared a new relation of mutual dependence between 'the state' and 'society'" (xiii, 121–124, 186). In other words, for King, Taiwan was more successful than the Mainland in correcting the traditional tilt toward the state at the expense of society, and democratization then emerged out of the "dialectical" interaction between the polity and the economy (124). At the same time, because the ROC avoided the excesses of iconoclasm, Confucian values, which King sees as often useful for modernization, "persisted in Taiwan as a vital cultural force" (120).

For King, therefore, the Taiwan experience represents the beginning of China's successful effort to join the global movement toward the rational liberation of human energies while rejecting the totalitarian impulses accompanying this global trend, correcting a parallel indigenous tendency toward the inflation of the state, making use of valuable traditional cultural resources, promoting Chinese political interests by resisting those emanating from the "core" nations of the new global order, and all the while coping with the cultural and economic turmoil caused by the onset of industrialization.

To be sure, for King, this beginning is a modest one, since democracy in Taiwan is still at a "crude, kindergarten" stage (deeply impressed by Hong Kong's legal system, he especially deplores the shortage of "rational respect for legal procedure" in Taiwan) (120–122, 194). Yet for King, unlike Fairbank, the Taiwan formula is a promising one with important lessons for the Mainland: modernization in the Weberian sense is China's only worthwhile path, state-building and the institutionalization of capitalism may have to precede democratization, the political center can be usefully "inhibited" without becoming democratic, the traditional culture includes invaluable resources for modernization, and the Mainland's main problem is not Chinese culture but the Marxist system (203). More broadly still, as the rise of the West presented the non-Western world with unprecedented hope as well as treacherous problems, Taiwan was one of the very few societies able to deal with this challenge in a relatively successful way. King is one of the few scholars today (1993) who is unembarrassed by this extraordinary success and willing to initiate serious discussion of it.

5. A Nonutopian Sociology in China

There are striking contrasts between King's use of behavioral science and Yang Kuo-shu's. First, as a psychologist, Yang makes virtually no use of the work of Chinese humanists and sinological experts on Chinese culture, or of that broad range of Western sociologists, historians, and thinkers basic to King's approach. Yang emphasizes the methodology of American psychology, using questionnaires to chart attitudinal changes. Second, looking at the institutional context of these personality changes, Yang is far less impressed by political development as an independent causative factor. Instead of discussing any new state-society relation devised by the Kuomintang, Yang just emphasizes the consequences of industrialization, discussing how Taiwan changed from an "agricultural, traditional" society into an "industrial, modern" one, and arguing that this change universally causes "changes from less to more social differentiation, from particularism to universalism, from reliance on custom to reliance on law, from authoritarianism and autocracy to autonomy, freedom and democracy, from a 'monolithic, closed' society to a 'pluralistic, open' one, from a less 'civilized' or 'refined' society to a more refined one, and so on."[10] Yang thus puts the increasing "individualism" his questionnaires seem to have found in Taiwan into this context of societal change based on the ecotype.

Third, although agreeing with King that the West has taken the lead in carrying out modernization, and that modernization is based on "reason," Yang grounds his emphasis on reason in a psychological theory about universal human nature rather than in a European historical development. Fourth, quite unlike King, Yang depicts the emerging democratic society in Taiwan in heavily utopian terms (see chapter VI).

In thus emphasizing a utopian goal, in adopting an "optimistic epistemology" centered on "reason" as a universal cognitive and moral capacity able to distinguish between good and bad political choices, in seeing history as a globally teleological process of "progress" based on "reason," and in identifying an epistemically and morally privileged group able to help China catch up with the global tide of progress, Yang's thought shares four premises that have been extremely widespread in twentieth-century China, as chapter VI noted.

King, by contrast, avoids the first and the fourth premises, utopianism and the celebration of "us intellectuals" as constituting a discrete vehicle of enlightenment. King is distinctive in this regard. As a thinker stationed in Hong Kong and so less caught up in the Taipei liberals' political struggle, King has developed a relatively Burkean approach to Chinese modernization, warning that demo-cratization is neither easy nor panacean and tending to support the Kuomintang's gradualism.[11] To be sure, Yang is by far not the most radical of the liberals in Taipei. Like King, he too has recognized the Kuomintang's achievements and has long endorsed "the Taiwan model" as an alternative path of modernization that the Mainland should follow. King, however, quite differs from Yang in justifying the Kuomintang's delay of democratization as needed to pursue state-building and the stable institutionalization of capitalism. Moreover, unlike Yang, King to a large extent affirms Confucian values and endorses the ROC's endorsement of them. Remembering the split, especially in Sung times, between intellectuals insisting that the political perfection of the *wang* (true kings) of antiquity could be realized again and those holding that the modest achievements of the *pa* (hegemons) were more practicable, we can see that Yang Kuo-shu has leaned toward the former approach, while King's view has something in common with "the way of the *pa*" — today as in the past outside the Chinese intellectual mainstream,

At the same time, however, King's epistemological optimism and his teleological view of the historical role of "reason" distance him, rightly or wrongly, from both of the currently more prominent American approaches to the study of Chinese society, namely, the rational choice school and the scholars trying comprehensively to describe the culturally distinctive ways in which Chinese have devised not only the norms of everyday life but also their moral-political discourse.

King has thus been original, erudite, and astute in using Weberian sociology to deal with the premises of his intellectual world and to weave together many of the key facts and ideas available to depict the relations between Chinese culture, China's modernization problems, and global history. Moreover, in depicting China as a kind of historical cripple in contrast with the normally developing West and so adopting a prevalent Chinese viewpoint first forcefully propounded by Liang Ch'i-ch'ao, King is indeed converging with an ethnocentric, teleological Western view epitomized by Weber's thesis that the West alone has been able to focus on the rationalization of life. Still widely accepted east and west, this view of the West as *the* model civilization has to a large extent withstood the winds of cultural relativism, the Saidian critique, and the criticisms coming from humanistic and Marxist circles in China (see chapters II and III). At the same time, King's appreciation of the Taiwan experience and his relatively conservative formula of Chinese modernization will win more applause today than it did a decade or so ago. Although susceptible to the kind of Marxist utopianism expressed by

Habermas, who apparently still expects that the humanistic rationality of "the public sphere" can be realized undisrupted by the clash of selfish interests (217–218), King's thought is mostly informed by what the Cambridge political theorist John Dunn regards as a key political virtue, prudence.

This is not to say that any of King's more specific insights into the nature of Chinese norms, institutions, or developments are his alone, or that he offers major new insights into sociological theory. He does not in this book raise the question of how what he calls "culture" is related to what he calls "reason," although, in his eyes, both greatly shape what he as a sociologist studies, social action. Another obvious problem is King's excessive reliance on macroscopic generalizations. For instance, the extent to which the Ch'ing political center controlled activities throughout society is a complex empirical question he deals with loosely. He ignores an important new body of research, such as the books by William T. Rowe, that has shed new light on this question precisely by avoiding the kind of macroscopic theory King favors and disaggregating the facts referred to by a broad term like "the state." Similarly, his idea that "there was no basic change" in the imperial political structure "for two thousand years" (110) is simplistic at best. Describing the imperial political center as "uninhibited" (96), and holding that "with regard to the state-society relation, there is obvious continuity between the imperial system and that of the Communists" (102), he deals in a simplistic and dubious way with a major issue.

Whether discussing Confucianism or modern Chinese ideologies, King invariably identifies a body of political thought with the doctrine explicitly emphasized by the historical actor, ignoring the work done by intellectual historians like Quentin Skinner and his sinological counterparts on unpacking the values and assumptions associated by a particular body of discourse with words like "reason," "democracy," or "morality." Thus, as already indicated, he does not study how modern China's political discourse has been affected by culturally distinctive assumptions — a task now being addressed by Ku Hsin and others.[12] Moreover, Professor King is not the most meticulous of scholars. For instance, given the complex questions raised by any comparison of the multi-state system of the Eastern Chou with that of modern Europe, King's comment that "there was no major difference" between these two patterns (110) is glib at best.

Similarly, he says "Weber's profound reflection on the meaning of Enlightenment led the way (*tao-chih*) to the twentieth century's continuous criticism of the Enlightenment" (195). What actually "led the way" was the criticism emanating from nineteenth-century figures like Schopenhauer and Nietzsche. He also is less than clear in discussing how Western scholars have reacted to Weber's thesis about Confucianism's lack of "tension."

Since at least the late 1970s, Weber's view of Confucianism has been strongly challenged in the West. Indeed, little was left standing but the usefulness of the questions he raised, as S.N. Eisenstadt noted at the 1980 Bad Homburg conference on Weber's view of China. This conference resulted in a volume edited by the leading Weber scholar Wolfgang Schluchter.[13] Writing in 1992 (148), King ignores this book and mistakenly says that "for a long time now, Weber's evaluation of Confucianism has just about become an ironclad truth tacitly respected by the intellectual world." He then presents his own article as a first attempt to challenge this "ironclad truth," but his criticisms do not go beyond those in the Schluchter book and elsewhere (129, 149 n. 5). Later in this article, moreover, King contradicts himself by noting that Weber's view has been "vigorously" criticized by some Western scholars (136–137). Then, discussing how Taiwan's economic success has cast further doubt on Weber's thesis, King makes eminent good sense but sheds no new light on this well-worn theme.[14]

One has to distinguish between such flaws and the challenge Chinese sociology presents to Western China scholars. If the understanding of history or of a society is a process of making descriptive, causal, predictive, evaluative, and recommendatory statements about it, one can say that King's sociological approach boldly tries to make all five kinds of statements at the expense of dealing more sensitively and specifically with descriptive matters. While Weber vainly tried to eschew value judgments, King unhesitatingly uses Weberian ideas to construct a highly normative view of modern world history and China's place in it. Though largely sharing Weber's lack of utopianism, King has still blended Weberian sociology with that teleological vision of Chinese backwardness going back to Liang Ch'i-ch'ao. In his case and that of other Chinese behavioral scientists, therefore, the sinification of Western social sciences has occurred, though not entirely in the ways they discussed.

His vision of "reason" and its historical role, in other words, has more in common with the modern Chinese intellectual mainstream than with Weber's thought. On the other hand, much Western interdisciplinary work on China's society and culture has tried much harder to live by Weber's injunction against value judgments, often focusing on the descriptive question of just how Chinese behavioral or intellectual modes have differed from those familiar to Western academics. Such Western work, however, typically failed to provide the causal, evaluative, and recommendatory understanding sought by those concerned as patriots with the well-being of their society.

How to overcome these two kinds of epistemic imbalances is a shared challenge faced on both sides of the Pacific. We should not prematurely assume that the Chinese epistemology is backward. Old questions may have to be asked again. For instance, what are the aspects of a society one should keep in mind as one describes it? Is moral-political discourse one of them? To what extent does adequate description of a historical pattern require analytically disaggregating the ideas or behaviors making up a particular intellectual or institutional trend? How should the description of a society be combined with the task of evaluating it and making recommendations about it? How can one justify use of those rules of successful thinking (often described as "rational") one proposes using to evaluate it? Are such rules the same the world over, essentially consisting of the principles celebrated by the French Enlightenment?

Have Western thinkers addressed these questions more successfully than King and his Chinese colleagues? In the next chapters, I argue they have not.

Endnotes

1. Unless otherwise noted, all page references in this article's text are to Chin Yao-chi, *Chung-kuo she-hui yü wen-hua* (China's Society and Culture; Hong Kong: Oxford University Press, 1992). Professor King graciously corrected mistakes in the original version of the text and made valuable suggestions but does not necessarily agree with all my conclusions. The translations are mine. His oeuvre also includes Chin Yao-chi, *Ts'ung ch'uan-t'ung tao hsien-tai* (From Tradition to Modernity; Taipei: Shih-pao ch'u-pan-she, 1979); *Chung-kuo hsien-tai-hua yü chih-shih-fen-tzu* (China's Intellectuals and the Process of Chinese Modernization; Taipei: Shih-pao wen-hua ch'u-pan ch'i-yeh yu-hsien kung-ssu, 1987); *Chung-kuo min-chu-chih k'un-chü yü fa-chan*

(Chinese Democracy as Both a Predicament and a Developmental Process; Taipei: Shih-pao wen-hua ch'u-pan ch'i-yeh yu-hsien kung-ssu, 1991); and *Chung-kuo cheng-chih yü wen-hua* (China's Culture and Forms of Governance; Hong Kong: Oxford University Press, 1997). My chapter on him is based on a good deal of his oeuvre but, concentrating on his 1992 volume, cannot be said fully to explore his thought as a whole.

2. See also his article in Yang Kuo-shu, and Wen Ch'ung-i, eds., *She-hui chi hsing-wei k'o-hsueh yen-chiu-te Chung-kuo-hua* (The Sinification of Research in the Social and Behavioral Sciences; Taipei: Chung-yang yen-chiu-yuan, Min-tsu-hsueh yen-chiu-so, 1982), pp. 91–113.

3. Yang Kuo-shu, *K'ai-fang-te to-yuan she-hui* (The Open, Pluralistic Society; Taipei: Tung-ta t'u-shu ku-fen yu-hsien kung-ssu, 1985), pp. 196–197.

4. Daniel Little, "Rational Choice Models and Asian Studies," *The Journal of Asian Studies* 50 (February 1991): pp. 35–52.

5. Huang K'o-wu, "Ch'ing-mo Min-ch'u-te min-chu kuan-nien: I-i yü yuan-yuan" (The Meaning and Origins of the Chinese Concept of Democracy at the End of the Ch'ing and the Beginning of the Republican Period), in *Chung-kuo hsien-tai-hua lun-wen-chi* (Symposium on Modernization in China), ed. Institute of Modern History, Academia Sinica (Taipei: Institute of Modern History, Academia Sinica, 1991), pp. 363–398.

6. Thomas A. Metzger, "Continuities between Modern and Premodern China: Some Neglected Methodological and Substantive Issues," in *Ideas Across Cultures: Essays on Chinese Thought in Honor of Benjamin I. Schwartz* (Cambridge, Mass.: Harvard Council on East Asian Studies, Harvard University, 1990), pp. 263–292.

7. Yang Kuo-shu, *Chung-kuo-jen-te shui-pien* (The Metamorphosis of the Chinese People; Taipei: Kuei-kuan t'u-shu ku-fen yu-hsien kung-ssu, 1998), pp. 1–30.

8. See John K. Fairbank, *The Great Chinese Revolution, 1800–1985* (New York: Harper and Row, 1987), pp. 268–269, and his *China: A New History* (Cambridge, Mass.: The Belknap Press of Harvard University Press, 1992), p. 341.

9. Paul A. Cohen, "The Post-Mao Reforms in Historical Perspective," *The Journal of Asian Studies* 47 (August 1998): pp. 518–540. This point, of course, was also emphasized by Li Tse-hou. See his *Chung-kuo hsien-tai ssu-hsiang shih-lun* (The Intellectual History of China in Recent Times; Taipei: Feng-yun shih-tai ch'u-pan kung-ssu, 1990), pp. 1–54. This famous book was originally published on the Mainland in 1987 (I rely on Huang Ko-wu's excellent article on Li in *Chin-tai-shih yen-chiu-so chi-k'an* 25 [June 1996]: pp. 425–460), but I believe Chin formed his own view of this question rather than being influenced by Li.

10. See chapter VI and Yang Kuo-shu, *Chung-kuo-jen-te shui-pien*, p. 407.

11. See Chin's 1987 and 1991 volumes adduced in note 1 above.

12. Ku Hsin, *Chung-kuo ch'i-meng-te li-shih t'u-ching* (The Historical Setting of the Chinese Enlightenment; Hong Kong: Oxford University Press, 1992). See above, chapter I, note 35.

13. Wolfgang Schluchter, *Max Webers Studie über Konfuzianismus und Taoismus* (Frankfurt am Main: Suhrkamp, 1983). For an account in English of S.N. Eisenstadt's views in this volume, see Thomas A. Metzger, "Eisenstadt's Analysis of the Relation between Modernization and Tradition in China," *The American Asian Review* 2 (summer 1984): pp. 1–87. Also in Kuo-li T'ai-wan shih-fan ta-hsueh, Li-shih yen-chiu-so's *Li-shih hsueh-pao* 12 (June 1984): pp. 1–75. For an English version of my article in the Schluchter volume, see my "Max Weber's Analysis of the Confucian Tradition: A Critique," *The American Asian Review* 2 (spring 1984): pp. 28–70. Also in Kuo-li T'ai-wan shih-fan ta-hsueh, Li-shih yen-chiu-so's *Li-shih hsueh-pao* 11 (June 1983): pp. 1–38.

14. See e.g. *Conference on Confucianism and Economic Development in East Asia* (Taipei: Chung-Hua Institution for Economic Research, Conference Series No. 13, 1989). Reprinted as Tzong-shian Yu and Joseph S. Lee, eds., *Confucianism and Economic Development* (Taipei: Chung-hua Institution for Economic Research, 1995).

CHAPTER VIII

~

History without Progress: A Critique of John Dunn's Political Thought

1. Introduction: The "Seesaw Effect" and the Problem of Political Rationality

Born in 1940, professor of political theory at the University of Cambridge, John Dunn has produced a famous oeuvre centering on the history of Western political philosophy since John Locke (1632–1704), on the state of political theory today, and on aspects of modern political development in Europe, Africa, and east Asia. This piece of mine is based on study of his *The Political Thought of John Locke* (1969), *Political Obligation in its Historical Context* (1980), *Rethinking Modern Political Theory* (1985), *Interpreting Political Responsibility* (1990), and, especially, *Western Political Theory in the Face of the Future* (1979) and *The Cunning of Unreason* (2000).

In such writings, Dunn has displayed extraordinary perspicacity, erudition, and intellectual honesty along with a deeply Christian conscience and a captivating prose style. Almost every other sentence of his makes an incisive point in a fresh, precise, subtle, elegant, and often amusing way.[1] Evoking the Socratic spirit, Dunn has said: "What matters [in analyzing political life] is not how authoritatively we can validate the answers we ourselves are tempted to give (no doubt far from authoritatively) but how clearly we can pose the questions ..." (C 196). In fact, he is immensely helpful in identifying the problems that should be addressed by those concerned with the pursuit of political theory (as opposed to practical leaders dealing with daily problems). He is unique in his ability to unveil the gap between that idea of popular sovereignty which is widely taken for granted today as denoting reality in the Western democracies and the actual lack of political potency experienced by the average citizen. Without depending on any of the conventionally polemical ways of denouncing this gap, he reveals it as a drastic dilemma colliding with the very rationale of modern politics. In restoring awareness of the need for normative political theory, his writings can be compared with Max Weber's "Politics as a Vocation." I regard him as the most interesting and capable political thinker today, one of the major figures in the history of political thought.

Yet I also think he could have done much better than he did. I have two main complaints. First, he brilliantly forces readers to confront the difficulties in holding that history has been progressive but then quite unconvincingly if not peremptorily concludes it has not been. Second, his thought is replete with one-sided ideas and contradictions and sometimes lapses into dubious reasoning.[2] In the end, he leaves the impression that, for him, political theory is almost more a matter of rhetorical success than systematic analysis.

One could adjust a remark he made about Karl Marx and Friedrich A. Hayek and apply it to his own thought. He recently observed in conversation that both of them exposed the wrongness of an economic system (Marx, that of capitalism, Hayek, that of socialism) without being able to propose a satisfactory alternative. Dunn has similarly shed light on the failings of two scientistic approaches to the analysis of Western modernity (the Marxist and that of the contemporary Weberian social science mainstream) without being able to propose a satisfactory alternative.

By "Western modernity" I refer to those societies that have arisen especially in the West combining the modern nation-state; capitalism; "the modern constitutional representative democratic republic" (W 128); modern technology; and a pattern of close interconnection with many societies around the world.[3] Not only in the West, many view Western modernity as a model the rest of the world should emulate and converge with. Dunn, however, is concerned with the incongruence between this contemporary model and the ideals basic to the Western heritage of political philosophy, "western political theory," as he terms it. Marxist scientism sought to bring Western modernity into accord with these ideals, seeing an engine of progress in the ability of people finally to grasp the laws of history. As Dunn laments, it instead created an engine of disaster, not only because there are no such laws but also because human frailties impede the ability to grasp and act on whatever truths are available. On the other hand, the Weberian mainstream succumbed to a passively empirical study of modernity and its origins, disposing of its shortcomings by not only choosing to acquiesce in them but also denying that there can be any objective moral evaluation of either the modern West or any other civilization.

Dunn actually shakes off neither the acquiescence nor the relativism but still looks for a path between the Charybdis of the impractical Marxist effort to make politics moral and the Scylla of the highly practical Weberian way of acquiescing in factual reality no matter what its moral significance. Thus he is deeply troubled by both a way of life and a way of thought closely associated with it: Western modernity and the basically Weberian social science tradition arising out of the prevalent Western mix of logical positivism and ethical skepticism. Chapter I described this mix as part of the Great Modern Western Epistemological Revolution (GMWER).

In this chapter, I try to make two main points. First, while Dunn resists Weberianism, his thought and Weberianism are still part of the same basic discourse formed by the GMWER, that is, "discourse #2." Most important, like the rest of discourse #2, Dunn's political thought fails to overcome the "seesaw effect" discussed in chapter I: if a political theory emphasizes the accurate description of the given political world and caution in defining the scope of knowledge, it will fail to conceptualize hopeful, resolute action to improve political life; conversely, if it succeeds (whether or not in an excessive way) in conceptualizing hopeful, resolute action to improve political life, it will fail to emphasize the accurate description of the given political world and caution in defining the scope of knowledge. Dunn's thought, like the rest of discourse #2, illustrates the former dilemma, while modern China's "discourse #1" illustrates the latter.

What Dunn objects to in the Weberian mainstream is especially the tendency to perceive people in third-person terms as groups each following a uniform set of culturally-determined norms. Asking for a kind of Cartesian precision in grasping the causes for societal trends and emphasizing the shortage of pertinent historical data, Dunn certainly reveals the Achilles' heel of the Weberian emphasis on shared culture. After all, few if any attempts to show how culture caused one or another trend to occur have done so by rigorously using adequate data precisely to corroborate the thesis of a specific causal sequence. Casting doubt on the causal importance of culture, Dunn has gone back to the classical, Aristotelian picture of politics as interaction between individuals expressing impulses and employing faculties grounded in the universal nature of human nature. Thus partly converging with the more individualistic interpretations of Weber,[4] Dunn has also drawn on existentialism to insist on a close empirical understanding of the historical actor in first-person terms seeking to view events as he or she viewed them. Still more, resisting Weber's fact-value dichotomy and the ethical relativism it implies, Dunn has sought to depict the historical actor as existing within a moral framework formed by the unavoidable conjoining of the purposes of the historian with her view of the historical actor's purposes. At the same time, Dunn has struggled to show that these purposes or moral standards somehow available to the student of the historical past cannot be confused with any morally limp acceptance of current trends, notably the gross inequalities in the distribution of wealth and power marring Western modernity. In sum, Dunn's assault on Weberianism draws heavily on Aristotle, Descartes, and Rousseau.

At the same time, however, Dunn accepts Weber's passive, gloomy way of facing the future. In Dunn's eyes, the study of history provides few if any grounds for hope in the future. Rejecting Marx's extravagant optimism, Dunn does not replace it with a coherent theory of progress. On the one hand, he emphasizes that the universal nature of human nature or of the human situation is more strongly inclined toward conflict than cooperation. On the other hand, according to him, the cognitive effort to understand history's causative patterns faces almost insuperable obstacles, and there is no way to define the criteria of progress in any objective or non-controversial way. Therefore, Dunn's thinking precludes the idea of any historical pattern that can cause progress to occur. Moreover the political standards with which he himself prefers to judge political life are so morally elevated that no practicable political-economic development can meet them.

Not surprisingly, therefore, looking back on history, he does not describe, much less applaud, any impressive examples of human cooperation or any cooperative creation of new epistemic, political, or economic patterns more beneficial than the ones they replaced. Therefore, his reasoning precludes any coherent theory showing that democracy is more desirable than other forms of governance, not to mention other kinds of progress. Dunn thus agrees with Weber that the prime lesson of history is the need to give up "gratuitous hope" (C 329, C 309–310), to distinguish between "what we can hope from" history and "what we must continue to fear" (C 309). Instead of seeing the nightmares of history in Hegel's or Marx's way as evidence that historical progress occurs only slowly and with terrible interruptions, he views not just the nightmares but even the Western setbacks at the end of the twentieth century as making it "hard to see History as going Reason's way" (C 32). For dealing with the future, therefore, he can recommend only efforts slightly to modify a capitalist structure he regards as "morally absurd" (W 90): "existing institutions and habits" cannot "at most times and places ... be altered greatly for better or worse by anything *we* ourselves might do, and do, not just personally, but even in active co-operation with very many of our fellows" (C 330–331).

Even more, Dunn offers no hopeful path at all to the societies outside Western modernity. The above "we," which I have italicized, refers essentially only to the citizens of "the modern republics." Although Dunn often writes about the nature of "politics" as something characteristic of history as a whole, he is aware that he is largely referring only to the modern Western experience (C 311, C 346, C 315–316). After all, for him, there is no political under-standing except that from the standpoint of the "purposes" of his particular we-group (see below). Although he is fascinated by the political world outside "the modern republics," he stands mute before it in that his beliefs allow him to recommend neither revolution to establish democracy, retention of the status quo, nor support for some sort of transitional dictatorship.

Still more basically, though rejecting "fatalism" (C 329), Dunn's thought calls for a relatively passive attitude toward political life, because it emphasizes understanding the given world rather than acting to improve it: "The goal is to grasp what is occurring, and why, and to see how it bears on the purpose of those who seek it [sic], whatever their purposes happen to be" (C 325). Dunn's thought, therefore, classically illustrates the seesaw effect as it applies to the

West's discourse #2: the combination of scrupulous attention to factual specificness and to the problem of the limits of knowledge with an inability to conceptualize hopeful, resolute action in the face of the future (or a decision not to).

This leads to the second point I shall try to make, that Dunn's thought, like all the other cases discussed in this book, illustrates the shortage in the world today, east and west, of any political theory realizing political rationality, or rather the way that the prevalent discourses are all at odds with any standard of rationality I can conceive of. Thus I dispute the prevalent idea that the Western liberal tradition has produced a rational political theory.

This second point, however, raises a variety of questions, especially the problem of the nature of political rationality. I tried to discuss these in chapter I and will here attempt to make clear how this chapter may shed some light on them. To begin with, some will say that some kind of rationally coherent theoretical or philosophical overview of political life would anyway be of little help for those many different kinds of often brilliant persons today wielding power and addressing the practical problems of public life. Rooted in our respective axial ages, however, the hope it would be of help is still widespread. It is from the standpoint of this hope that Dunn and other thinkers continue to pursue political theory, and that — so far as I can see — political theory today is in crisis.

Dunn himself agrees it is in crisis. True, he has expressed great confidence in "western political theory": "As a resource for understanding the political history of the world western political theory has great strength and no effective surviving rival" (W 130). Yet he also has said: "It cannot really be said that any extant intellectual tradition offers us reasonably explicit and plausible guidance on how to settle down" to make decisions about how to optimize "the fate of the modern republic" (C 297), not to mention that of other societies. But in trying to articulate standards of rationality with which to identify what is wrong with these "extant intellectual traditions," he and I differ.

Dunn would probably agree with my critical starting point, derived from the GMWER, that, whether or not political rationality in some metaphysical way transcends what a particular historical individual or group regards as indisputably reasonable, there is no feasible way to discuss it except as such a historical judgment.

Therefore, he would probably agree that, in trying to figure out whether one political theory is more rational than another, there is no ultimate standard beyond the variety of historical evaluations of these theories.

Whether he or the reader will accept my next steps, therefore, is precisely a matter they must judge for themselves. As stated in chapter I, I define "a correct political theory ... [as] a set of ideas that elucidate the nature of political goals, of means, of the rest of the given world, and of knowledge and elucidate them in a way according with the epistemic standards or rules of successful thinking regarded as indisputable by the we-group evaluating this theory."

The probably less controversial point here is that, as embodied in the particular judgment of a historical individual or group, political rationality is a generic label denoting all the rules of successful thinking regarded by that individual or group as both indisputable and platitudinous. Chapter I discussed this point at some length. More controversial, I think, is my claim that Dunn's thought can be best described as addressing the four questions above: how to define political goals, the means to reach them (agency), the rest of the given world, and the nature of ideas about political life (epistemology). As chapter I explains, I began some twenty-five years ago trying to build on works like Talcott Parsons' *The Structure of Social Action* to arrive at a logically comprehensive list of the "key" aspects of all human or at least all political life. If such a list was indeed logically comprehensive, these key aspects would be the topics that any political theory had to address, and every idea part of a political theory would be *nothing more* than an *idea about* one or more of these topics.

But would the inductive study of many different political writings east and west run across ideas that were not about one or more of these topics, suggesting that my list was just a parochial, Procrustean framework imposed on the ways people actually thought about politics? Always fearing it was, I tested it in one study of texts after another, ranging from classical Chinese texts centuries before Christ, the writings of Chu Hsi in the twelfth century, and twentieth-century Chinese writings to those of John Dunn and F.A. Hayek.

Use of this list, then, was my effort to probe into the vexing problem of how to describe thinking. Unlike John Dunn, but like Robert Redfield, I was and am convinced that people can in an

effectively objective way describe what people think and do, the main
obstacle being neither subjective bias nor the opacity of human life
but a kind of cousin of opacity, the danger of overlooking a crucial
detail or connection. Because of this danger, one can never more
than hope to have understood the thinking of another person.

But after more than ten years of trying, I think I have finally
understood Dunn's train of political thought and shown that it can
be best described as ideas about the four topics above, just as can the
thinking of all the other figures discussed in this book.

If, then, political rationality is a way of discussing these four
topics, it also appears as an intellectual act logically interrelating
these four topics. I made this point too in chapter I, contradicting the
rational choice school's dichotomy between culturally determined
goals and the use of a universally algorismic instrumental rationality
to weigh "evidence" about the best means to reach these goals.
My analysis of Dunn's thought, like the other studies of political
thinking in this book, should show clearly how ideas about the nature
of ideas, about goals, about the given world, and about agency are
logically or meaningfully interdependent parts of one holistic train
of thought.

For instance, one may ask: How opaque is history? How precise
does knowledge about historical causes have to be? How should
people deal with the various ideas about possible historical causes
such as universal human nature, the egotistic quest for wealth, power,
and prestige, the unpredictable impact of political leadership,
cultural orientations, and intellectual influences on culture? In
trying to assess whether history offers any hope for the future, how
should one judge whether the tendency toward conflict or that
toward cooperation is stronger? Does the Holocaust or the
performance of the R.A.F. in World War II tell more about human
possibilities? The answers to such questions determine how to
infer from history any instrumental, causal understanding pertinent
to the formation of policy in the present, but it is hard to see how
such answers can be based on any instrumental rationality
transcending cultural differences. Like the definition of goals, these
answers vary depending on the culturally shaped rules of successful
thinking a particular historical person or group regards as
indisputable.

If, then, the reader agrees with me that Dunn's political thought consists of a set of logically interdependent ideas about the four topics above, there still is the problem of what questions should be raised about these topics and what answers to these questions make the most sense. According to my rules of successful thinking, which in this case are close to Dunn's, the frontier, the battlefront in the quest for political rationality is thought about what questions should be posed. It is on this battlefront that Dunn's performance is so useful. Yet, relying on rules of successful thinking partly different from his, I disagree with many of his answers to these questions. So political rationality somehow lurks within the tension of such disagreements and the intrusion into this tension of a third party. What happens at this point can be compared to the market competition between different advertised commodities or services. The convincingness of an argument can be compared to the convincingness of a commercial advertisement. But the advertisement is not just an act of rhetoric. Constructing my advertisement about the nature of political theory and political life, I have assumed that the more I pursue a logically discursive, systematic style, the more successful my advertisement will be.

Finally, apart from the clash between Dunn's rules of successful thinking and mine, I argue that Dunn's writing contains a good number of questionable or erroneous statements, such as contradictions, exaggerations, unclear reasoning, judgments presented as statements of fact, the conflation of logically distinct issues, or neglect of a relevant issue. The criteria used to define such intellectual acts as questionable are more general than any one we-group's rules of successful thinking. They are criteria that are widely shared by intellectual circles around the world. Even if they do not amount to an algorismic standard of correct thinking, they do suggest a limited convergence of intellectual standards transcending cultural differences.

By these standards, it would seem, every thinker has lapses. But it is puzzling that someone so brilliant as Dunn should have had so many. My answer to the puzzle is that Dunn is not much troubled by them, because he regards the pursuit of political theory as partly a matter of rhetoric, not just of logically consecutive reasoning. This, however, is precisely one of the aspects of his thought at odds with my rules of successful thinking.

2. Epistemology: Should Political Theory Put Primacy on Pursuing a Logically Discursive and Systematic Train of Thought?

Dunn notes that there can be no "would-be integrative theoretical conception" revealing an "overarching order" in all the structures and processes making up what is called "the state" (C 109). He also posits a contrast between the "irretrievably confused reality" of "politics" itself and the need for "analytic" clarity in the understanding of politics. He views "political science" as committed to an empirically accurate description of politics as "confusion all the way down," and the need for clarity and some "analytic distance" as basic to "much of contemporary economics." As he sees it, the search for "political understanding" is locked into the tension between these two perspectives: "the choice, put like this, is one between an inevitably confused acceptance and embrace of confusion, and a resolutely unconfused rejection of an irretrievably confused reality: a choice between succumbing to politics and simply refusing to acknowledge its presence" (C 204–205). Dunn also says "confusion.... inheres in the very idea of what it is to have clearly good reason to act in one way rather than another" (C 287).

According to my rules of successful thinking, however, there is no such contradiction between an ontologically given condition of confusion and an intellectual search for clarity. On the one hand, I think it is important to reject Cartesian standards of precision, and I agree with Aristotle's view "that the same precision is not to be sought in the practical or political sphere as in the theoretical sciences."[5] On the other hand, I accept neither Dunn's assumption that "politics" (apart from some analytically defined, formal aspects) can be discussed as having a universal nature nor his view that this universal nature is some sort of state of confusion. Instead, I see a promising search for rather dependable if rough generalizations about empirically specified and historically limited political patterns and trends that greatly influence political events and so allow informed guesses about a partly predictable future. The more logical one can be, the more informed the guesses can be. Relaxing the search for logical consistency is not a way to improve political life.

3. Epistemology: The Relation between the Scientific Study of Political Phenomena and the Understanding of Political Praxis

How should one design the relation between the maximally scientific study of political phenomena (the making of descriptive, causal, and predictive statements about them) and evaluative and recommendatory statements about them, i.e. between the worlds of science and of moral praxis? Should one reject either approach? Subsume either one under the other? Or disaggregate these five kinds of statements and then try to make all five in some sort of satisfactory way? A closely connected question is whether the study of political life should focus on the given observed facts about politics, that is, on "what politics is and why it occurs at all" (C 346), or on political praxis, on clarifying the nature of the means currently available to improve political life, or on both. If there are no causal laws of history identically governing the past and the future and only an uncertain connection between the causes for past political events and choices in the present intended to cause desirable future outcomes, should political theory focus on one or the other of these two kinds of causes or on both kinds?

In considering the relation between the understanding of moral-political praxis and the scientific search for falsifiable descriptive, causal, and predictive propositions about political life, Dunn begins by devaluing the latter. For him, the Weberian social science tradition's attempt to view politics "dispassionately" as "just one element within the history of the universe" (C 96) has been a "bathetic failure," accomplishing no more than extending "vastly the range of matter over which it is possible for opinion to be moderately well informed" (W 105–106). Most generally, "the idea of a collective intellectual instrument of comprehensive understanding, whatever its merits in relation to natural science, is utterly misguided when applied to politics" (C 207). Thus, "over the gross question of the ultimate relations between the individual psyche and political reality no detectable headway has been made since the days of the ancient Greek philosopher Plato" (C 71).

In Dunn's eyes, the crux of the difficulty lies in the failure of Weberianism to shed light on politics as a "field of political causality" (C 325). Although there are, for instance, major studies on the causes for success and failure in national economic development, Dunn claims "few ... political scientists.... now dare.... directly and frankly" to ask "why is it that some groups of human beings groan in agony and others saunter (or cruise) the streets in relaxed well-being" (C 57).[6] Similarly, "globalization" has been much analyzed,[7] but for Dunn it has not been "transformed into a conception which really could clarify what is going on. It is the name of a cognitive challenge, not of a potential solution to a cognitive problem" (C 134). The same goes, apparently, for Samuel P. Huntington's book on the spread of democracy in recent decades.[8]

This failure to grasp causes and consequences stems especially, Dunn holds, from the failure to see that any analysis of politics is unavoidably shaped by the purposes and interests of the person carrying out the analysis, and that these purposes must be honestly recognized as integral to any search for "political understanding" (C 326). Only when they are thus recognized can the causal patterns of the past clearly appear. When Max Weber gave his famous lecture on the causes for the fall of the Roman empire, then, he was mistaken to advise his audience that this historical problem was not "a case relevant to your lives" (*de te narratur*).

Moreover, this misunderstanding of the role of the analyst has been complemented by a misunderstanding of the historical political actor being analyzed, a failure to take into account her complex existential situation by grasping "how personal, individuated and context dependent" is the reasoning with which she faced "hazards and opportunities" when combining her "beliefs" with the materialistic motives on which economists focus (C 204). This complexity of the existential situation leads to unpredictability especially in the case of political leaders: "Political judgment and choice still make the final and decisive contribution to the way in which human history goes" (W 123). At the same time, a failure to grasp the existential situation of the historical political agent in the light of the analyst's own purposes precludes "coherent grounds for regarding human beings with respect at all" (W 107).

Weberianism's failure to grasp the "field of political causality" has also been due to lack of "any conception of the difficulties posed by the inaccessibility of appropriate counterfactuals" (W 105–106). Moreover, much political science describes political phenomena "in serene incomprehension of what they are bringing about: the

Second World War, the Cold War, global warming" (C 319). Most important, this dilemma of Weberianism in Dunn's eyes also has to be connected to Dunn's mutually reinforcing emphases on the "opacity" of history and the need for extremely precise understanding (see below).

Dunn, then, does not endorse what I have loosely called Weberianism as a rich if incomplete resource for understanding political life awaiting fruitful combination with political theory. Instead, he calls for a basic methodological shift producing "human sciences.... in the tradition of Socrates and not in the tradition of Newton" (W 106–107). With this aim, he sees no hope in disaggregating descriptive, causal, predictive, evaluative, recommendatory, and epistemological propositions and just pursuing each kind as effectively as scholarly resources permit. His thought instead revolves around an emphatically synthetic, holistic cognitive act: "political understanding."

For him, "the subject matter of political understanding" is "the field of political causality." Understanding it, one understands "what politics is and why it occurs at all," and especially "what has been happening in the political history of the world as a whole over the last decades (here and elsewhere), and why it has done so" (C 325, C 346). "What has been happening" above all includes "the cumulative consequences" of what has happened relative to the "purposes" or "interests" of those engaged in the study of what has happened (C 324, C 99).

Dunn of course is well aware that "causality" refers to two kinds of causes, those observed as having had certain effects in the past, and choices made and acted on in the present with the intention of producing certain desirable effects in the unpredictable future (C 325–326, C 308). Moreover, he eschews the Marxist view that unified laws of history identically govern causes in the past and contemporary acts intended to shape the future. Nevertheless, he repeatedly refers to a single "causal field" that is the object of "political understanding," deliberately conflating my purposes as a student of history and a political agent with the causal issue in history about which I am trying to gather evidence. Dunn's elusive point is that in the very process of gathering my data and consciously organizing them in the light of my own purposes, I can discover the existential context of the historical political actors I have studied and so arrive at "an endless series of utterly exposed causal judgments" (C 314). Utterly basic to this formula of his is total rejection of a central Weberian point: not that all "value judgments" can be removed from factual description, but that an effort to minimize them is an invaluable methodological tactic by means of which a greatly deepened understanding of how people actually live and think is made possible. To accept Dunn's rejection of this Weberian point would be to reject major modern intellectual projects, such as Robert Redfield's study of "the little community" or the literature on discourses, if not Dunn's own brilliant book on Locke.

4. Epistemology: The Problems of Precision and Opacity in the Collection of Information about Political Phenomena

In Dunn's eyes, moreover, even apart from the problem of calibrating the relation between the analyst's purposes and the causal issue in history that is the object of her research, she faces two obstacles: the pertinent data are largely hidden under the opaque surface of history; and, in grasping them, only highly precise understanding will do. Thus Dunn again diverges from my view, which I think is common among historians and social scientists, that a good deal of history is transparent if one agrees with Aristotle rather than Descartes about the level of precision which political understanding requires. Moreover, pursuing his view, Dunn falls into a series of contradictions, not to mention that there is nothing "precise" about the way he conflates the two kinds of political causes discussed above.

As noted above, Dunn sees a tension between two epistemic needs: recognizing the reality of confusion in political life, and seeking precise understanding of the latter. For him, this tension cannot be alleviated by lowering the standard of precision. He cites Plato's view that "imperfect or hazy vision is simply incompatible with understanding" (C 193). Thus he seeks a "real intellectual grip" on developments like the disintegration of the Soviet Union, an understanding with some degree of "precision" (C 192). In a recent essay, he emphasized how elusive is the understanding of why democratization became a major trend in recent decades, implying that Samuel P. Huntington's book on *The Third Wave* failed adequately to "survey these endless interacting causalities synoptically, and weigh just how each bears on all the others."[9] Terms like "just how" in the latter quotation have been central to Dunn's approach in this context: "roughly how" won't do. "Quite why" and "really" are similarly used by him: "We do not at present … really understand quite why … the Germans succumbed to Adolph Hitler in 1933" (C 209). Similarly: "what we are trying to understand is what is really going on in politics today" (C 237). Speaking of the "huge shift" in economic judgment behind the "massive deregulation and liberalization of global economic relations over the last decades of the twentieth century," Dunn asks: "how exactly has it happened, and what exactly does it mean?" (C 182, C 194). Similarly: "To see why and how the British state over the eighteen years between 1979 and 1997 changed the structure of its economy and the distribution of wealth within it as it did, what we need is … to work out exactly how to combine" the view that Mrs. Thatcher's "tenure of premiership was a structure of domination with [another thesis]." Moreover, "If it was a structure of domination at all, how far was that structure in fact controlled by severely impersonal forces" rather than by Thatcher personally? "Exactly what were these forces, how did they secure their control, whatever led them to pick on *her*, and how exactly did they manage to place her *en poste* once they had done so?" (C 141–142).

Seeking an "exact" understanding of how and why political developments occurred, Dunn also faults any political program which fails to "ensure" that "human beings" will have "the opportunity to live as they please": "we cannot any longer hope, on the basis of practical understanding now at our own disposal, to pick out robust, dependable and plainly mutually supportive practices, applicable on a national or global scale, which will *ensure* that the interests of present and future human beings are secured in a steady and effective manner" (C 351, C 350; italicization is Dunn's). Dunn once asked: "But who now, except a complete imbecile, can still *expect* a *guaranteed* progress?" (W 32; his italicization). (Who indeed?)

Dunn, then, notes the collapse of the nineteenth-century hope that people would exactly grasp the laws of history and so guarantee for themselves a happy future. This hope, however, has continued to shape his way of evaluating current scholarly efforts to analyze history and politics. He is not ready to applaud the inevitably partial successes of Weberian scholars today. In his eyes, these successes are outweighed by their failure to obtain an exact understanding of history ensuring success in the future.

Simultaneously, however, he emphasizes the "formidable opacity" of "political experience" and "human history" (C 239, W ix, C 170):

> Where many individual agents or groups of agents interact with one another, struggling to aid or frustrate each other, or simply colliding inadvertently, the idea of capturing the consequences of their actions is quite unreal.... We cannot act on knowledge, or, indeed, in large measure, even on comprehension. (C 246)

Another typical comment:

> As political study moves from the behaviorally obvious towards the more grandly interpretative, it certainly gains in point, but it also loses in intellectual tractability. As it delves more deeply into what is *really* going, it strains ever more painfully the resources which human beings possess to apprehend this with any *precision*, dependability and control.... There are no strongly directive and *wholly reliable* techniques even for grasping what those who occupy a particular political milieu are *really* up to, still less for what their activities signify for anyone else. (C 303)

Again: "On present evidence, there are no *dependable* sources of insight, and no methods which, clearly grasped and accurately applied, ensure even the haziest comprehension of what is *really* going on politically" (C 170). (On this page, all italicization is mine.)

"Even the haziest" is hyperbolic indeed, but the italicized words reflect Dunn's Cartesian standards of clarity, which complement his emphasis on the opacity of history. Dunn emphasizes that people are typically unable to ascertain their own interests clearly, much less those of others (C 99, C 101); that it is hard to "pin down the consequences which flow from" political actions (C 302, C 242); and that "there is no way of thinking accurately about most aspects of the longer-term future" (C 198). Dunn thus depicts the study of politics as an epistemic dilemma: the search for an exact understanding of largely unknowable causal processes.

Yet Dunn's writing is full of statements confidently offered as knowledge about many aspects of political life. These contradict his claim that it is opaque. First, whatever his emphasis on human fallibility and the way varying historical settings affect cognitive

efforts, Dunn still presupposes the human ability to identify "false
beliefs" (C 98). Second, I would say that, far more than scholars
influenced by cultural anthropology, Dunn follows the classical and
not altogether implausible assumption that the most basic mental
and emotional conditions I find within my own mind must be typical
of the human species generally. Hence the confidence with which he
describes the universal nature of human nature and of "politics" (see
below). For instance, he thinks he knows that "All human beings wish
to live as they choose." Even more, while claiming that the causes for
the spread of democracy in recent decades are not clear, Dunn
bluntly states that this human wish is "precisely the impulse which has
given democracy its extraordinary cosmopolitan appeal today"
(C 71). Thus, as indicated also by his reference above to "the
behaviorally obvious," Dunn does not mean that political life is totally
unknowable.

Indeed, in his eyes many important developments in his own
country are knowable, such as the fact that the British state in the
period 1979–1997 "changed the structure of its economy and the
distribution of wealth and income within it" (C 141). Much else is
"clear": "it is clear that there are strong connections between the
expansion of capitalist economic organization, ecological
degradation and the limited pacification of property relations in
every community in the world today" (C 357). Also clear are some of
the views shared by large parts of the populations in foreign societies
such as Algeria, Cambodia, Burma, Ghana, China, and Tibet (C 260,
W 98, W 68, C 132). Brushing aside the Weberian emphasis on
culture, he sees no great need to study and describe a particular
culture in order to grasp how people in a particular historical and
cultural milieu define their ideals and their historical-political
situations, at least with regard to what strikes him as universally
obvious reality. Nor is the future that inscrutable. While holding that
there is no way of "thinking accurately about most aspects of the
longer-term future" (C 198), Dunn's pessimistic belief in "the
cunning of unreason" would be impossible but for three linked
beliefs of his: that the history of all of humanity has been a product
"of at least two great forces," "conflicts" between human purposes
and "endeavours to co-operate"; that politics so far has "plainly been
more a product of the conflicts than of co-operation"; and that the
"politics of the future will be a continuation of that history" (C 136).

Obviously, history in Dunn's eyes is not so opaque that he cannot know whether he should be optimistic or pessimistic about it. Most important, having himself so brilliantly discussed so much of it, Dunn could hardly hold that the world's intellectual history is not transparent to a large extent, nor would he deny that political and even philosophical ideas have been part of the causative fabric of politics (see e.g. C 356–357).

If, then, precision is so important, precisely which aspects of history are opaque, which are transparent or at least translucent? Giving examples of the kinds of phenomena that are often unknowable, Dunn asks:

> What exactly did the late Nigerian President General Abacha believe he was doing when he executed the Ogoni writer Ken Saro-Wiwa? He certainly meant to kill a man (an archaic enough political act). But, beyond that core intention, can we be sure that even he really knew? What does the Prime Minister of Britain or the President of France suppose that each has been doing even for the last six months? (C 244)

Such comments, along with Dunn's typically striking and suggestive use of the word "credulity," freshly bring out the great role of ignorance in human interactions, a point also brilliantly made by Hayek. Moreover, it is clear that the persistence of this ignorance has seriously harmful effects. Yet Dunn's focus on the urgency of the need to reduce ignorance about politics seems exaggerated. After all, he admits that the classical goal of overcoming this ignorance by solving "'the Riddle of History'" (C 235) is a chimera. Despite its harmful effects, a lot of ignorance, especially about past and future patterns of historical causation, is just a condition of human life that has to be accepted. The future, as Dunn emphasizes, is inherently unpredictable to a major extent, and, as he does not seem willing to grant, it is virtually always impossible to put the many causes for a past event into some one precise hierarchy of importance. His search for a precise understanding of the causes for a past event reminds me of my own desire, on many a Sunday afternoon in the fall, to know "just why" a favored football team lost a game. I know what happened — that it failed to complete crucial passes, that it failed to stop the other team's runners — but I never know whether it failed because it played less well than usual or because the supposedly weaker team played better than expected. I then look in the Monday newspaper for this knowledge, but all I ever find are descriptions of what happened and mere guesses as to why it did. If we cannot precisely understand the causes for the outcome of a football game, how can we precisely understand the causes for the change in British economic policy under Mrs. Thatcher?

On the other hand, it is also clear that a huge amount of what people are ignorant about does not matter. Dunn speaks of two distinct goals: "to grasp what is occurring and why," and "to see how it bears on the purposes of those seeking this knowledge." His implication is that, after everything is known about "what is occurring and why," one should consider how all this knowledge bears on one's purposes. But it is hardly necessary to know everything about a process in order to grasp how that process bears on one's purposes. Because mountains of details are irrelevant, weaknesses of the mnemonic faculty are not fatal, and people with great mnemonic skill are not necessarily those with the best political and historical judgment. How important was it for the British prime minister to know most of what the French president was doing over any period of time? After one knows that the most venerable Jewish philosopher, Moses Maimonides (1135–1204), and the most venerable Muslim philosopher, Alfarabi (ca. 870–950), both believed that killing "God's enemies" is the central task of government, how important is it to know every detail about the endless cycle of violence in and around Israel today? How much detailed information is needed to understand "exactly why" U.S. political leaders are reluctant to reform the disastrous laws governing the financing of elections? In the 1930s, a British intelligence agent, F.W. Winterbotham, penetrated Nazi leadership circles and concluded that Hitler was intending to build an airforce which could threaten Britain. That insight indeed bore on the purposes of the British government. Yet even without this piece of intelligence, Churchill well understood the threat posed by Nazism.

True, the kind of knowledge Churchill acquired about Nazism is inherently dependable only to a limited extent and often hard to present in a persuasive way. Yet it has proved to be a serviceable resource for one relatively successful society after another. Contrary to Oscar Wilde, not only the superficial look beneath the surface, but the knowable surface of political things, especially the mainstream political discourse of the society, often tells a great deal about them

that is relevant to one's purposes. Moreover, the very nature of
political-economic-social life is such that crucial aspects of it are often
revealed by a very limited sampling of the relevant data intelligently
analyzed. As a Harvard law professor once commented after spotting
an erroneous footnote, "One does not need to eat all of an egg to
know that it's rotten." Surveying the opinions of a few thousand
respondents allows social scientists to predict with considerable
accuracy how some 100 million American voters will vote. When
Stalin, right after the Nazi invasion of Russia, told Roosevelt's envoy,
Harry Hopkins, that what he needed from the U.S. was aluminum,
not already manufactured airplanes, Hopkins grasped that the
U.S.S.R. would not quickly collapse. The very broad significance of
some kinds of very limited pieces of information is a happy epistemic
circumstance that Dunn refuses to acknowledge. When a student of
a particular society astutely discovers and intelligently analyzes
many such pieces, the understanding of that society's causal trends
which she can acquire goes far beyond "moderately well informed
opinion." History, then, is not opaque. It is partly opaque and partly
transparent, and whether the opaque or the transparent parts bear
the most on "our purposes" varies from case to case. Certainly there
is little opaque about the vested interests — consumers, labor
unions, business people — preventing bold action to prevent those
consequences Dunn most fears, ecological disasters.

5. The Epistemological Basis of Political Goals: Dunn's Attempt to Anchor Goals in Human Nature

Yet even if a "purpose"-oriented organization of political data yields
causal understanding, how does such understanding include any
guidance for me in the choice of my purposes and interests? Dunn
strongly suggests it offers no guidance: "We can be relatively
confident that the problem of how to identify human interests
will never receive a conclusive solution" (C 101). We have to
"acknowledge the absence of a single plainly authoritative standard
of value" (C 102). Even if descriptive and causal statements can be
more effectively made, therefore, evaluative and recommendatory
ideas are left hanging in the vacuum of relativism implied by the
GMWER. Thus Dunn does not dispute the outcome of GMWER
logic: "not merely that there are no clear human goods or bads (or

that we can never hope to tell one dependably from the other), but even that there is nothing at all that humans are really like: no biologically or physically determinate human nature, or even no determinate nature at all, in the first place" (C 196).

Dunn is well aware that these GMWER arguments have created a predicament. As he puts it, Marx and Freud showed that "much which sounds reasonable does so because it articulates the structural requirements of social credulity or the individual subconscious" (W 32). True, Dunn effectively refutes ethical relativism (W 110) and rejects any Weberian emphasis on the importance of culturally determined values. Nevertheless, he cannot but recognize that there are culturally distinctive and causally important "beliefs and sentiments" (C 325), "belief systems which are also always the site of meaning for the lives of real living men and women. To see human history this way is perhaps the essence of the historicist experience" (W 61, C 325, C 9, C 318–319). He thus is acutely aware of the powerful historicist argument that all reasoning about how to live one's life is "personal, individuated and context-dependent" (C 204). Consequently, he sees that the plurality of these conflicting "belief systems" "brings with it a condition which may be called — if a little solemnly — a state of hermeneutic ambivalence which ... is both the central challenge facing any serious political theory today and a challenge which political theory at present is grotesquely failing to meet" (W 61). If this "central challenge" is not met, he says, it is "an open question whether our sense of these values [the goals he himself endorses] as objective and compelling is in any way epistemically justified: whether these values are in fact, as we fondly suppose, anchored to any solid bed of external reality and not merely conferred on us by an essentially arbitrary caprice of our cultural history" (W 118).

Dunn thus here seems to accept the GMWER's refutation of the discourse #3 theories trying to "anchor" these values in the idea of God, reason, natural law, the state of nature, the laws of history, the egotistic desire to obtain pleasure and avoid pain, or pragmatically justified pluralism: "there seems every reason to doubt the possibility of a comprehensive and coherent *modern* philosophy of liberalism; and perhaps more disturbingly (though perhaps also consequently) there seems little reason to believe that the more attractive values of liberalism enjoy any privileged relation to the historical process" (W 55).

Even more, Dunn of course realizes that he has not been able to solve this problem by analyzing the main epistemic mode he recommends for the study of politics, "political understanding." "Political understanding" includes no recommendation that these "more attractive values" be affirmed. In this context, whether these values are affirmed or not depends purely on the chance that individuals will freely decide to incorporate these values into their "purposes" or "interests." Dunn's concept of "political under-standing" takes these "interests" or "purposes" of people as a given "whatever their purposes happen to be" (C 325).

True, Dunn seems to introduce two normative rules regarding the definition of interests. First, he seems to say one should not seek to benefit humanity as a whole. In trying "to understand politics as it does bear on human interests" (C 99), "we" should consider how "the consequences of our actions … will affect us in particular, and those whom we hold dear, or at least minimally care about" (C 341). Yet Dunn is deeply distressed by the poverty of most of the world's population (see below). This rule, therefore, either questions the applicability of the liberal ideals Dunn adduces to reveal "the moral absurdity of capitalist society" (see below), or it turns the entire population of the world into those whose interests Dunn "minimally cares about" and so contradicts its apparent demand that one care only about the part of humanity close to one. By the same token, this rule pretends to answer the central question of political triage (what human suffering is it urgent to alleviate, what human suffering can be ignored?) while actually not answering it in any specific way. The second rule seems to be to distinguish between the appearance of interests and "what interests human beings really have." Dunn implies that the "interests human beings really have" are those which "are in fact coherent and well-conceived," and that people *should* define their interests coherently (C 104–105). Yet whether or not these two, actually overlapping rules are themselves "coherent," Dunn realizes that following them would still not make clear which purposes or interests a human being should choose to have.

First, it is very difficult to understand one's real interests:

> Only the very inattentive can suppose that anyone is a consistently sound judge of their [sic] own interests, and only the hopelessly ingenuous are likely to suppose that most human behavior dependably reveals even

what its perpetrators are up to, let alone the full range of potentially pertinent considerations which cross their minds over time. (C 99–101)

Second, according to Dunn, facing this difficulty in determining what her own interests are or should be, the political agent can find out "how far" her "purposes ... are in fact coherent and well conceived." This can be done by understanding "the causal substance of politics, as this exists at any time (the patterns of practical inter-action between human groups and their prospective consequences)." Such understanding, however, cannot show her "how far the purposes themselves are creditable or defensible.... In the end this is simply a question *to* each of us" (C 104–105). According to Dunn's concept of "political understanding," therefore, this is a question without any necessarily correct public answer.

To be sure, for Dunn himself, the "creditable" purposes or political goals are, somehow, quite clear. Much of his writing dwells on them, and, as just mentioned, they focus on the interests of humanity as a whole. For instance, he cites the "ecological critics" of Western modernity who see it as "a single great system of wrong choice." He says their view is "a natural contemporary expression of a perspective on what it is to be human which has great spiritual force and which remains all too illuminating about what it is to be human" (C 254). Assessing the politics of Western modernity, he takes for granted that the "fostering and deepening of political under-standing" is inherently desirable, and he offers a choice between an obvious good and an obvious evil: Is Western modernity "a way of living together grounded ineluctably on vanity, deception and mendacity? Or is it (can it ever be) a space of freedom and light and well-considered practical activity, a comfortable and fitting home for the industrious and rational?" (C 317).

Indeed, in attempting to set forth the goals political life should pursue, Dunn depends on the pre-GMWER concept of "reason" as not only including logic but also having a definite moral content. Thus he looks for "a morally rational order" (W 119), for "rational political conduct" (W 104), seeking "to identify how there could be at the global level (and for the first time in human history at any level) a rational political community which could be seen and acknowledged as such, without false belief, by all its members" (W 95).

A bit more specifically, Dunn, again following the tradition exemplified by Mill, seeks a "morally civilized social and political life," as opposed to "barbarism" (W 82, W 100). Morality for him entails some success in teaching people "to set the good of the community above their own individual advantages" (W 21). Economically, such a rational, moral, civilized way of life is one according to which "the human species could come to share the world and its resources with one another in security and mutual trust for a lengthy future" (W 95). This ideal refers to the avoidance of both absolute and relative suffering. The over-used "agonized" is necessary to describe how Dunn feels about the suffering of the poor, the ecological and demographic dangers of modern life, and the threat of war, especially in its technologically up-to-date forms. As already indicated, Dunn emphasizes that the capitalist global economy "poses a real threat to the future of the species" (W 73). But he is almost equally concerned with economic inequality, the international world's "devastatingly uneven economic develop-ment," the "arbitrary suffering" this causes, and the "blind hatred" directed by those who suffer against those they see as responsible for their agony (W 96, W 98).

Economic is of course intertwined with political inequality. Thus for Dunn the goal of a rational, moral, civilized world enjoying economic prosperity and justice is combined with the goal — not yet reached by any government, he holds — of "a political order in which the rulers are in practice effectively answerable to those whom they rule" (W 111). Dunn has in mind a political mode allowing an individual to control her life to the point of being able to minimize the evils afflicting her, instead of being controlled by a system "beyond political correction or restraint, and self-evidently beyond any possibility of political direction on behalf of the more durable and fundamental human interests" (W 135).

Dunn is quite aware that Rousseau's "general will" is a chimera, that "we cannot in fact *rule* our own societies," and that "the extent to which governments can in fact be rendered responsible to those over whom they rule ... is still a very obscure question" (W 111). But Dunn is inclined to believe that "democracy is the resolved mystery of all constitutions" (W 64). He is deeply impressed by the Athenian ideal of government by the governed and takes seriously Rousseau's famous point that, given their schedule of elections, the British were free only once every seven years (W 16–19). Thus Dunn seeks "to combine greater social equality with some real democratization of political authority" (W 111). He also welcomes, though with reservations, the current feminist movement as shedding light on the nature of social, economic, and political equality (W 131), though he has nothing to say about gay liberation, affirmative action, and other new ways to define equality.

Given his sense that the above political goals can somehow be promulgated as definitive even in "the absence of a single plainly authoritative standard of value" (C 102), Dunn infers from them "the moral absurdity of capitalist society" (W 90, C 332), criticizes the "facile eudaemonism" that "advanced capitalist society cultivates in its citizens" (W 118), acknowledges his own morally compromised need to continue enjoying the life made possible by this kind of society (C 254), and concludes that the Thatcher administration was morally wanting in its "purposeful redistribution from the poor to the rich," even though it partly succeeded in increasing the "operating efficiency" of the British economy (C 260–261, C 141–179).

But how can these "more attractive values of liberalism enjoy any privileged relation to the historical process" if they are not "anchored to any solid bed of external reality"? Wanting to avoid advancing these values in a merely peremptory way, Dunn has in at least one book brushed aside the GMWER and his own emphasis on the opacity of history, not to mention the Geertzian emphasis on culture, to try to anchor them in "an adequate theory of human nature" (W 102), a "coherent conception of human personality" (W 54). He has sought a way of grounding the "essentially liberal conception of human nature as free and responsible agency and a consequent entitlement to respect ... in the rational comprehension of nature as a whole"(W 107).[10]

Thus, he has criticized J.S. Mill especially for failing to develop such a "coherent conception of human personality." Because Mill was "so ambivalent in his sense of what an individual actually amounted to, he could not base his defense of a right to tolerance on any strong conception of individual personality and what aspects of this might be judged to require respect" (W 55). Similarly, Karl Popper and F.A. Hayek have impressed Dunn with their emphasis on the relation between rationality and a liberal way of organizing society, but neither "thinker offers a very robust conception of the character of the creatures (human beings) whose freedom and rationality they wish to defend" (W 51). Dunn also has hinted that such a robust conception of human nature should include the idea of "natural rights," suggesting that J.S. Mill was mistaken in failing to ground his principle of liberty in a conception of natural right (W 54).

Moreover, as discussed in chapter I, Dunn has explored the philosophical problem of finding a "middle ground" between relativism and objectivism, arguing that there is a "standard of intrinsic human value" which defines "rock-bottom duties," such as the duty "to feed the starving, when well and safely able to do so." A "theory of value" not recognizing such duties is "intrinsically discreditable" as "an unsound theory of what is of value for human beings." With this "intrinsically," he hints that such supposedly indisputable norms are grounded in universal human nature.

At the same time, criticizing John Rawls and Kant, Dunn has struggled to reconcile historicism with a concept of universal normative principle, holding that the latter has to be so phrased as to make sense to actual human beings with their historically and culturally limited social imaginations (W 46–48, W 51–52).

Whether or not such a reconciliation is plausible, Dunn has developed his theory of universal human nature by positing that "our species" acts in accord with certain relations between three variables, "natural animal affection," "natural animal antipathy," and "reason" as a cognitive tool that can be used to express either the affection or the antipathy (W 115). Human beings, moreover, are "free," but, thus freely using their reason, they function as "cognitively fallible" and "morally fallible agents" (W 113): "(We are all deplorable for some of the time and some of us are deplorable for quite large proportions of it.) ... Envy and fear are the psychic forces, the causal pressures, which we can guarantee will be in play in an interdependent world" (W 109, W 97). In other words, a major cause for the world's disastrous situation is "the distressingly myopic and irretrievably anxious capacities for social vision and prevision which human beings share and on which they depend for such secure and amicable cooperation as they can muster" (W 105). Dunn concludes that "the present human population of the world does not know what it is doing politically" (W 136).

So far as I can see, however, Dunn has failed in his effort to revive the classical belief that moral values can be grounded in knowledge about the universal nature of human nature. To be sure, relativism and its close cousins, historicism and cultural relativism, cannot logically refute the possibility of making true statements about objective reality (if they could refute it, they themselves could convey no truth). But is universal human nature the kind of determinate objective reality that can be observed and accurately characterized?

I think not. Although every discourse I know of (including my own) includes some conceptualization of universal human nature, these conceptualizations cannot be presented as knowledge about universal human nature as an observable objective reality. This is because universal human nature, like Li Tse-hou's "the history of humankind as a whole," is not an empirically observable object. Moreover, even if it were, how could the norms Dunn sets forth — a rational, moral, civilized world enjoying economic prosperity, justice, and the avoidance of gross inequality — be logically implied by Dunn's particular picture of human nature, a condition dominated by intellectual and moral failure? Dunn wants to discover an "essentially liberal conception of human nature as free and responsible agency and a consequent entitlement to respect." Yet his depressing characterization of human nature makes clear only why one should disrespect most people. How can one respect a being who has been endowed with the wonderful ability to use her "reason" to express "natural animal affection" or "natural animal antipathy" and then freely chooses to express the latter? Is not the Devil precisely such a being?

Failing, then, to "anchor" "the more attractive values of liberalism" in an "adequate theory of human nature," Dunn leaves them without any logically necessary relation to any objective reality. This is a trying situation for the political theorist, as Dunn himself emphasizes, a crisis integral to Western modernity. If values can be articulated only in an arbitrary, peremptory way, the political theorist is simply stripped of any ability to demonstrate that her goals should be preferred to those propagated by anyone else in society. At the very least, this is the victory of Protagoras over Socrates, the end of "western political theory." It also precludes any coherent theory of progress and so any coherent argument that democracy is superior to tyranny. Richard Rorty refuses to deplore this outcome of the GMWER (see chapter XIII), but Dunn perceives it as a disaster.

6. Revisiting the Ontological Context of Normative Principles: The Linguistic Symbols Embodying Them or the Realities Denoted by These Symbols?

I think, however, that this disaster can perhaps be avoided if one goes down a path Dunn resolutely rejects, the concept of cultural orientations shared by a society or social stratum, along with an offshoot of this concept, the idea of a shared "discourse." As argued in chapter I, "discourse" refers to a way of describing human communications that has been used by scholars like Kenneth Burke, Felix Gilbert, J.G.A. Pocock, and Quentin Skinner. It goes back to mostly German scholars like Weber and Husserl, who sought to depict the intersubjective world formed by human beings as "self-interpreting" beings. Increasingly concerned with "shared vocabularies," this approach has emphasized that the meanings of words depend on context, and that context is especially made up of verbal utterances regarded as clichés by all those participating in a discourse used by a limited part of humanity, such as the platitudes making up discourse #1 and discourse #2, which are set forth in chapter I.

Also crucial in the definition of "discourse" is a major category discussed in chapter I that scholars generally take for granted, the "we" or "us" illustrated by phrases such as the Chinese cliché *wo-men chih-shih fen-tzu* (we intellectuals) or by Dunn's comment "If we are most of us nationalists in some measure now, we are certainly not necessarily insensitive to claims of supra-national human solidarities and we are still more certainly most of us not at all like Nazis" (W 59). Whom does "we" denote? An answer can be given from the standpoint of the idea of discourse: "we" denotes a particular if amorphous historical group the members of which perceive themselves as together carrying on a particular, actually rational or enlightened discourse. The idea of discourse is thus highly historicist. True, this "we" is often used to denote all of humanity throughout history, as with the recent comment of a philosopher that "casuists claim that, to solve an ethical problem, we should start with the identification of uncontroversial and unambiguous cases," or the recent claim of a social scientist that "We gain knowledge about our personal and social identities through comparisons with other individuals and groups." With the idea of a discourse, however, one avoids or at least minimizes the claim that anyone is thinking on behalf of all of humanity or can know how all people throughout history have behaved and will behave. One instead maximally depends on empirically verifiable fact, pointing out that, whatever else it may be, human thought at least entails a discourse carried on by a historically specifiable we-group.

I would also see a discourse as having an irreducibly paradoxical nature in that it is made up of linguistic symbols that both give the world and human life a culturally disparate meaning and are used effectively to refer to universal issues and objective realities (as already mentioned, it would be illogical to say that thought cannot include true statements about objective realities). I would even posit a further feature of all discourses, a tension between the reflexive understanding of objective reality and the historically disparate linguistic symbols that are the medium of this understanding, and so an implicit philosophical imperative critically to assess the latter in the light of the former. That is why people with different discourses can argue with each other, and why discourses evolve as they are subjected to criticism and revised. (This problem is further discussed in chapter XIII.)

But how can this idea of discourse be used to meet "the central challenge facing any serious political theory today" by dispelling the unsettling feeling that normative principles are "merely conferred on us by an essentially arbitrary caprice of our cultural history"? After all, the idea of discourse seems to converge with that of cultural relativism.

The point blocking such convergence is that, as chapter I discussed, any discourse, whether that of historical actors described by me or my own, rests on premises which are indisputable rules of successful thinking in the eyes of the we-group carrying on this discourse, such as "our" principle that "racism is bad." In other words, ideas determining the indisputably right way to make descriptive, causal, predictive, evaluative, recommendatory, and epistemological statements are not elusive or arbitrary but unavoidable. Cultural relativism, therefore, is quite correct in holding that there is much disagreement between different historical groups about what the indisputable truths are, and that a single correct way to resolve all such disagreement has not yet been found. Yet cultural relativism is empirically inaccurate in suggesting that awareness of this fact destroys or weakens the tendency to posit indisputable rules of successful thinking. The fact that I cannot resolve my disagreement with a racist does not weaken my belief that racism is bad.

The firmness with which people adhere to the rules they believe in appears either as the obstinacy of the unenlightened or the convictions of a person with integrity. Isaiah Berlin has celebrated the latter: "'to realize the relative validity of one's convictions ... and yet stand for them unflinchingly, is what distinguishes a civilized man from a barbarian.'"[11] Either way, the empirical evidence is abundant that discourses are based psychologically on rules of successful thinking regarded as indisputable by those carrying on the discourse, and that criticism and revision of such rules itself presupposes other such rules. For instance, the persons who claim to support relativism regard intolerance as absolutely mistaken.

Relativism then is a chimera. Contrary to Leo Strauss and Alasdair MacIntyre, the problem with modern life is not lack of belief in normative absolutes but an abundance of absolutistic beliefs that strike many as wrong or barbarous. Only scholars not interested in the empirical description of thought could have viewed the horror of Nazi fanaticism and simultaneously deplored the lack of belief in binding normative principles.

The hope arises, therefore, that the binding nature of norms can be demonstrated if one seeks it not in the realities that linguistic symbols are used to denote, whether human nature, the laws of history, God, or some other aspect of the cosmos, but in the way that, in historical fact, linguistic symbols are used by human groups to form discourses. The empirical fact of these symbols also is a form of reality, but instead of serving as an "external reality" in which normative principles can be anchored, these symbols themselves inherently exist as binding principles defining the right or "rational" way to make descriptive, causal, and predictive statements, as well as normative and epistemological ones.

Edgar Allen Poe might have said that the way in which norms are binding is a kind of philosophical "purloined letter," something seemingly elusive but actually in plain sight all the time. True, the idea of "indisputables" can solve the problem of bindingness only if one gives up not only the philosophers' dream of finding a rationally transparent bindingness consisting of a complete set of irrefutable answers to all possible "why?" questions but also the assumption that all human beings are cognitively constructed so as to be able to understand these answers and act on them. The point is, however, that the full quality of bindingness is a social fact in itself and so is not contingent on either this dream or this assumption. What is binding for me is the "purloined letter" made up of all the various ideas I have always so taken for granted as indisputable that I never even supposed they were worth questioning or even noticing.

One could object that thus grounding bindingness in a complex theory of discourse is just an unnecessarily elaborate way of iterating Berlin's simple and eloquent call for "unflinching" faith in one's principles. This theory of discourse, however, offers a very different, indeed, if I may so presume, a strikingly new and hopeful answer to the question of what kind of intellectual exercise is needed maximally to justify the norms of moral-political praxis. What is needed is not a successful effort to fasten them to a reality external to the language that embodies them. What is always needed is more effort consciously to uncover them and all the other rules of successful thinking with which they are entangled in order to turn them into objects of criticism, to compare them with alternative rules of successful thinking used by other historical groups, and then through calm debate come to a judgment about whether or not to revise them. This exercise is a hopeful one because it cancels a chimerical metaphysical quest (which seduced even John Dunn) in favor of an empirical, completely feasible intellectual project. Even more, while this metaphysical quest unavoidably ended up as an evocation of a pathos encapsulated within one of humanity's culturally closed-off compartments, the empirical tactic here recommended is a way of breaking out of such ethnocentrism, of exploring "the heavens beyond the heaven that you know," as the Chinese saying has it (*t'ien-chih-wai yu t'ien*).

To sum up, the relation between normative ideas and objective reality can be explored by distinguishing between two ways of conceptualizing realities and three ways of conceptualizing ideas. The two kinds of realities are (a) *human reality as a whole*, including its historical and cosmic setting, and (b) *language* as the symbols denoting this reality. These symbols can then be viewed either as (x), *knowledge* obtained by "reason" as an ahistorical, transcultural faculty; (y), merely subjective *opinions* varying arbitrarily from one historical individual or group to another; or (z), *indisputables*, the rules of successful thinking that are indisputable in the eyes of a historical we-group, whether "ours" or any other, and that, appearing to this group as objects of *knowledge*, may or may not actually be objects of *knowledge.*

Using this framework, one can see that historically three main ways have arisen of conceptualizing the relation or lack of relation between normative ideas and reality: (a)/(x); (y); and (b)/(z). (a)/(x) refers to the belief that (x) *knowledge* includes normative ideas derived from (a) *human reality as a whole* (or some aspect of it, such as human nature). This is the pre-GMWER belief shared by the Chinese discourse #1 and the Western discourse #3, which are both epistemologically optimistic (see chapter I).

(y) refers to the GMWER's (illogical) relativism embodied in the West's epistemologically pessimistic discourse #2. It is epitomized by Popper's brilliant theory of "the three worlds." It emphasizes that normative ideas are just (y) *opinions* with no necessary relation to any objective reality, whether (a) or (b).

(b)/(z) refers to the post-Popperian belief growing out of the GMWER that normative ideas are (z) *indisputables* integral to (b) *language* as an empirical reality used by social groups to form discourses. I would associate this view with not only the literature on discourse but also Ludwig Wittgenstein's emphasis on language, which suggests that, while the ultimate nature of the objects denoted by language cannot be fully known, language itself is a reality that exists precisely as it appears in human thought. That is, not only the external world but also the inner structure of the mind do not appear simply as they actually exist, unlike the historical linguistic symbols used by a person to understand them. The only ontological or ultimate reality my mind can fully grasp is that of the linguistic symbols I use to understand myself and the world, not that of myself and the world as the objects both denoted and veiled by these culturally disparate symbols (see chapter XIII).

This argument appears as the most dependable way to derive norms from ontological considerations and thus free them from the taint of arbitrary opinion. Yet it need not be taken as absolutely precluding the (a)/(x) option. T'ang Chün-i, for instance, has raised the question of whether it is possible rationally to deny the objective value of the human ability to imagine a world better than the present, of knowledge and all the means needed to pursue it, and of cosmic creativity. Thus there may be still other ways Dunn has not discussed to deal with "the central challenge facing any serious political theory today." Dealing with it by exploring the nature of discourse, however, is an obvious way. Nothing would seem more arbitrary than mere words, but the empirical study of discourse seems to reveal the simple but momentous psychological fact that, in any discourse, mine and yours included, some verbal utterances appear as indisputable, others, as nonsense.

Dunn resists the dictum of the GMWER that only arbitrary *opinions* disconnected from any "external reality" are available with regard to praxis. He yearns to phrase the dictates of Christian conscience as *knowledge*, returning to the moral certainties epitomized by Marx's denunciation of capitalism. Yet, resisting Weberianism's emphasis on culture and its offshoot, the concept of discourse, he refuses to consider how *language*, as distinguished from *human reality as a whole*, can serve as an ontological home for moral principles to the extent that it comes in the form of *indisputables*. Hence his unsuccessful effort to ground values in the universal nature of human nature and the peremptoriness of the moral standards with which he seeks to expose the "moral absurdity" of Western modernity. In the end, then, he succumbs, however reluctantly, to the illogical relativism of the GMWER.

7. Assessing the Relation between Goals and the Practicabilities of the Given Historical World

Peremptorily or not, Dunn expresses not only an authoritative understanding of the difference between good and bad but also an equally secure understanding of how to respond to a political world that is a moral limbo. This normative question is crucial because the answer to it sets the tone of public discussion and political negotiation and so affects the extent to which a society can coordinate its energies in the pursuit of the good.

Should "morally alert" political agents (1) regard this limbo as intolerable and resolve promptly to replace it with a totally moral political system? Should they (2) give up the latter utopian ambition but still denounce this limbo as intolerable? Should they (3) resolutely pursue progress but still accept this limbo as the normal medium of progress? Should they (4) regard "the confusion and ineffectuality" of the political limbo as "hopeless but not serious: ineradicable from the state form, but readily endurable by its citizens, or at least by those among them who appear to be reasonably prosperous" (C 257)? Or should they (5) just fatalistically accept it?

Dunn rejects not only the extremes of utopianism (1) and fatalism (5) and the complacence or "eudaemonism" now widespread in the West (4) but also the prominent Western belief (3) that the moral limbo of the City of Man is still a promising medium for the resolute pursuit of incomplete but still invaluable progress. Adopting option (2), then, Dunn treats as a grave problem, a shocking condition, or a surprising outcome aspects of political and economic life that many regard as unavoidable debilities or inefficiencies inherent to the normal workings of public life.

For instance, he finds it disconcerting that there is something amorphous, unclear, and inefficient about the way a modern state defines and implements its policies (C 167); that "even the best devised of states can scarcely hope to prove impervious to human indiscretion" (C 264); that "no constitution's protection of the rights which it does effectively protect can *guarantee* that those rights are specified justly, or even clearly" (C 211) (italics added); that Montesquieu "scarcely contrived to pin down how any society can hope *dependably* to obtain the devoted and punctiliously professional adjudications on which it must ultimately rely" (C 213) (italics added); that there is bound to be some divergence between what courts decide and the standards of justice that can be developed intellectually in a society (C 84); that "to win elections it can prove helpful, perhaps even essential, to do all manner of things which might be otherwise wholly unwelcome" (C 175); that "almost any politician can happily envisage their [sic] own promotion, and often at almost anyone's expense" (C 172); that "Mrs Thatcher's image of the British state, while it was in her charge, was scarcely selfless" (C 168); that she was "overbearing" in that she had a "need, in some cases," to pursue her goals "by direct confrontation with political opponents" (C 162); that in a capitalist society many citizens will feel they are not "either effectively equal to or as free as those who plainly benefit more directly and more handsomely from the ways in which economy and society work, or those who play a conspicuously more active part in the activity of ruling" (C 35); and that "we can no longer hope, on the basis of practical understanding now at our disposal, to pick out robust, dependable and plainly mutually supportive practices, applicable on a national or global scale, which will *ensure* [Dunn's italics] that the interests of present and future human beings are secured in a steady and effective manner" (C 351, C 350). Referring to "the intense moral fastidiousness of the western tradition" (W 117), Dunn proves himself to be its worthy inheritor!

He then reinforces this listing of deplorable facts with hyperbolic, one-sided generalizations about Western modernity, such as his account of "the formidably aversive experience for most human beings of living in a largely capitalistic world.... To the members of such a species, as they live their irremediably separate lives in one another's company and prepare to die alone, it will always seem an alien, profoundly untrustworthy and potentially deeply malign reality, a world in which they can never hope to be at home" (C 336–337).

True, thus determined to expose fully the gap between the moral limbo of political life and the highest standards of altruism, personal integrity, equality, accountability to the electorate, astuteness in understanding one's own interests, effectiveness in the design of enduringly beneficent political-economic institutions, and comfortable solidarity, Dunn is aware that these standards are extremely hard to meet. Nevertheless, he is unwilling to incorporate into his political theory the frank recognition that some degree of failure in meeting them is a normal aspect of all governance, if not of the existential situation itself. He sees no need to point out that, although Thatcher and Hitler were both unable to transcend this limbo, developing a form of government led by people like Thatcher rather than Hitler was still a magnificent form of progress in the history of political life. For him, the literary need to avoid dilating on the obvious (à la Aristotle) overrides the philosophical need to analyze human life in a balanced way, not to mention his suggestion that the possibility of describing the course of history objectively is anyway a Weberian illusion.

Contrasting the City of God with the City of Man after losing Marx's faith that history will turn the latter into the former, Dunn sees no important distinction between the moral limpness of those acquiescing in the ills of the City of Man and the moral vigor of those believing in the importance and practicability of some progress within it. Thus he derides the Millsian thinkers who looked only for "the least bad mechanism for securing some measure of responsibility of the governors to the governed within modern states" (W 27–28). Underlying this viewpoint of his is his refusal explicitly to recognize that there has been a great deal of progress in history, and that the fact of this progress implies a general human capacity to effect progress. Dunn's refusal to acknowledge this capacity is basic to his characterization of universal human nature and the nature of politics (see below).

8. Dunn's Epistemology: Describing or Defining the Nature of Political Understanding?

According to Dunn's rules of successful thinking, then, political understanding is a matter of deciding how to define and pursue one's interests without enjoying access to any demonstrably binding normative principles and while trying to obtain precise information about "a field of political causation" largely hidden beneath the opaque surface of history. Thus pursuing a seemingly unattainable kind of understanding, the student of politics at best arrives at "an endless series of utterly exposed causal judgments" (C 314), but only if she remains constantly concerned about the obstacles impeding this pursuit — her own "partiality of judgment" and history's "opacity" — and is able to deal with the limited flexibility of the future by combining prudence with a kind of "recklessness" (C 314, C 312) (i.e. the willingness to act resolutely without knowing for certain what the future will bring). Even then, however, her positive contribution to public discourse will consist more of useful questions than any dependable answers to them (C 196). In other words, Dunn's "causal" understanding of Western modernity leads to the conclusion that the gap between it and the ideals that were developed by "western political theory" and that he regards as "rational" cannot be closed. Hence the "cunning of unreason."

Dunn writes: "A great deal of the understanding of modern politics consists in seeing why exactly it is that human beings today feel so effectively discouraged from even attempting bold and optimistic reorganization" of their political and economic lives (C 32). Dunn sees this popular feeling as caused by the nature of "modern politics." I would suggest, however, that a major cause for it could also be the way that scholars and educators have encouraged people to conceptualize "modern politics." Following Dunn's train of thought, one is left with the impression that resolute, collective action to improve political life is just about impossible, because knowledge about how to effect change is so elusive, and because the criteria of improvement anyway cannot be articulated in a publicly convincing way, except for the assurance that no kind of practicable change could be regarded as progress. Even more, warning that there is no fully logical way to conceptualize collective action in the inherently confused realm of politics, Dunn suggests that the public had best content itself with worrying about how to frame the questions of public debate rather than trying to devise a common program of public action.

Most basically, rather than a search for the most reasonable way to make descriptive, causal, predictive, evaluative, recommendatory, and epistemological statements, Dunn's concept of political understanding leans toward a basically passive way of interfacing with the given world — "The goal is to grasp what is occurring, and why, and to see how it bears on the purposes of those who seek it [sic]" (C 325). In T'ang Chün-i's terms, Dunn's concept of "political understanding" inadvertently ends up as a "concave" focus on phenomena (*hsien-hsiang*) rather than a "convex" focus on praxis (*shih-chien*).

9. The Given World: The Universal Nature of Human Nature and of Politics

If, then, Dunn's ideas about how to conceptualize political life undermine the confidence and hopefulness needed by people to find through calm and imaginative public discussion programs of political improvement that can be collectively and resolutely undertaken, so do the ideas he presents as knowledge about the universal or general nature of human nature, of "politics," of historical development, and of rational agency.

It is said that some years ago, after visiting Hong Kong, Liu Hsiao-po, one of the loose cannons in China's intellectual world, remarked that China would have been better off had all of it become a British colony. Whether or not this remark is apocryphal or shallow, it still strikes me as more insightful than the way so many British intellectuals have seemed ashamed of the empire their nation ruled. In my eyes at least, this unrealistically guilt-ridden British image of the British empire was at least partly responsible for the premature dismemberment of an international organization that, had it been properly and imaginatively developed, could have alleviated the terrible ills later suffered by many of the non-Western societies entering the modern age. Critics of British political culture could also point to the infuriating shortsightedness of most British politicians in the 1930s, which was directly responsible for the fifty million deaths of World War II.

Nevertheless, if one thinks of politics as a crucial and difficult art of the possible that depends on checking Manichaean passions, distinguishing between law and the subjective sense of justice, and learning to leaven political disagreement with not only respect for erudition but also a sense of humor and fellowship, it is plausible to say that few societies besides the English-speaking ones have ever mastered it. It is in mastering it, not in making foolish mistakes, that the British have differed from other nations. Therefore, it is striking that a thinker British to the core, John Dunn, instead of celebrating the distinctive British talent for politics, should have produced a picture of the general nature of politics about as dark as anyone can imagine.

From the standpoint of my rules of successful thinking, moreover, this analysis of his is seriously lacking in many ways. While it is marred by hyperbole and one-sidedness, it is also marred by his lack of awareness of the hermeneutic condition reflected by such hyperbole and one-sidedness. That is, precisely because any such general account probably cannot avoid some hyperbole and one-sidedness, a scholar has the choice of tipping his interpretation in the direction of either hope or despair. Moreover, Dunn does not suspect that maybe the dark picture of politics he propagates in a nation famous for the excellence of its political tradition is not a balanced empirical description but part of a rhetorical effort in England to cultivate that very spirit of prudence and restraint so basic to the successes of British politics. Certainly aware that political theory is at least partly a form of rhetoric, he nevertheless seems unwilling to recognize the whole causal role of political theory which his own writings exemplify, the way that the future as depicted in political theory is not so much an objective fact as a strategic challenge defined by political theory. Still more disconcerting, however, is Dunn's seeming assumption that his account of the universal nature of human nature and of politics is an empirical description. The universal nature of these two things is a metaphysical object, since it is not an empirically specifiable and observable object, such as a particular political situation or episode (e.g. World War II) or a historical discourse embodied in specifiable texts. Even though so concerned with the quest for precise understanding, Dunn suggests that a precise description of a metaphysical object is possible. In this case, I would say, he has uncritically followed the path of a heritage he reveres, "western political theory," all the heroes of which — Hobbes, Locke, and Rousseau — took the knowability of this metaphysical object for granted. In other words, rejection of Max Weber's refutation of this classical metaphysical methodology is a central component of Dunn's thought.

Moreover, Dunn seems unbothered by the contradiction between his emphasis on the opacity of history and his claim that the universal nature of human nature and of politics, along with their huge causative role in the historical past and future, are knowable. Finally, there is a major contradiction between his refusal to acknowledge that modernization and democratization reflect a creative human capacity to effect progress and his many statements recognizing their beneficial nature (see below).

Much of Dunn's writing is about "we" as a pronoun usually denoting all individual members of humanity. For instance: "the ways in which we see and feel ... will be shaped heavily by the importunities, enticements and menaces of our fellows" (C 298, C 314). True, Dunn typically speaks of "the causal substance of politics" as "the patterns of interaction between human groups" (C 104). Yet he is much less interested in how the characteristics of one group as a whole differ from those of another group than in the features shared by all or most individual human beings. Again, in his typically subtle way, Dunn wants to evade the simplistic, anthropologically controversial view that certain behavioral traits are common to all people and nudges the reader toward the existentialist idea of a shared predicament: "Insofar as human beings share a nature and a condition, they do so in the end not because of some undeniable matter of fact, but as the setting of an always common puzzle: the puzzle of how to live, of what they had better do" (C 243).

Nevertheless, Dunn sees them facing this puzzle equipped with some very determinate shared traits. He notes that "all human beings wish to live as they choose." Thus "a raw dislike for either authority or power" is "precisely the impulse which has given democracy its extraordinary cosmopolitan appeal today" (C 72). Desiring freedom, human beings also are selfish, though the latter adjective, so central to Chinese ethics, is avoided by Dunn, who speaks of their "greed" and "unreflective self-regard" (C 102, C 155). Given the latter, their primary goals are economic. Thus Marx sought to grasp "the logic of the process of global economic change which he had already long decided to be the fulcrum of the history of the modern world and which the history of the modern world ever since has increasingly confirmed to be indeed such" (W 87). Especially in the context of modern politics, the "political sentiments of the citizenry at large ... increasingly centre on the perceived requirements for agreeable and dependable consumption" (C 178–179). While people driven by self-regard resent authority, moreover, they often seek ruthlessly to dominate others, cruelly using violence. Thus "human interests patently conflict with one another," and social life is filled with "mutual hostility" (C 102).

This Hobbesian condition is then complicated by the major tendency for people to form we-groups (C 105) based on shared values and shared moral principles. As already mentioned, Dunn does not dwell on this theme of culture and social structure, but a paper he wrote on modern Japan, referring to its "enormously idiosyncratic society and culture," illustrates his awareness of the obvious importance of a shared culture.[12] Out of these we-groups in turn evolve the whole variety of often changing organizational structures and networks. Dunn discusses especially the nature of the state and what he calls "the space of modern politics," which he sees as "principally defined by two structures: the modern constitutional democratic republic and the global market economy" (C 249). With this institutional and moral frame of reference forming the symbolic context of the "mutual hostility" felt by individuals and groups with clashing interests, individuals often pursue "highly skilled and utterly morally unanchored instrumental calculations" (C 107), ranging from the grossest kinds of exploitation to the "ingenuity of free-riders" (C 290).

For Dunn, however, as already indicated, any ingenuity of

individuals is balanced by their grave cognitive and emotional weaknesses, which often block their pursuit of their own interests, especially their "partiality of judgment," their frequent inability to take the long-term into account, difficulty in cooperating with others, and lack of acumen (C 292, C 94, C 242, C 133):

> A creature (or set of creatures) of this kind is in no condition to view the causal arena within which its purposes must be effected clearly and realistically. It is already so deeply contaminated by fantasy, and so weakened by evasion, that the causal refractoriness of the external world and the bemusing logical challenges of rational co-operation are bound to prove hopelessly beyond it. (C 242–243)

To be sure, Dunn himself and his readers in fact do not see themselves as such creatures, and I certainly do not see Dunn as such a creature. Thus he implies that we are either exceptions to the rule or suffering from delusion, two possibilities that both are open to objection.

Nevertheless, for him it is the nature of the interaction between such "creatures" that determines the universal or general nature of politics. True, he is of course aware, as already noted, that much political life consists of the interaction of groups, not individuals. Nevertheless, for Dunn, the empirically clearest site of political agency as well as the only morally legitimate vehicle of political choice is the individual. Here Dunn's thought overlaps a number of trends, especially existentialism, rational choice theory, Millsianism, and the Weberian approach as it has been interpreted by sociologists like Randall Collins. Critical of Parsons' structural-functionalism, Collins writes: "The primary analytical concepts of the Weberian approach are the material and ideal interests of individuals, and the group and organizational structures developed by individuals to further these interests."[13]

These "interests," then, in Dunn's eyes, stem from the nature shared by all or most of the above "creatures." Again, as already indicated, Dunn is fully aware that "human beings differ astonishingly from one another, across time, space, culture and occupation," and that, because

> the forms which politics takes at particular times and in particular places are marked so strongly by this unimaginable range of differentiation, it will not be easy to see, underneath or within it, clear and stable structures,

> either in human agents or in their situations, which pervade it [i.e. politics] in its entirety and explain accurately why all of them have politics at all. (C 23) (Hardly a sentence worthy of Dunn's pen.)

Nevertheless, Dunn is confident he has identified the key characteristics that "pervade it," whatever the cultural differences. Thus he has steadily rejected the Weberian emphasis on the great causative impact of disparate cultural orientations on economic-political behavior. I doubt he would dispute David Landes's conclusion that cultural differences are the main reason some societies have become wealthier than others. He simply does not incorporate such findings into his analysis of political life.[14]

The characteristics that "pervade" political life in Dunn's eyes are not just what I have referred to as the "moral limbo" of political life. He goes beyond this general point about the tension between moral principles and "utterly morally unanchored instrumental calculations," because he emphatically offers as a factual statement what is actually a controversial judgment about this tension. That is, phrasing this tension as one between a "range of capacities" enabling people to "co-operate" in the pursuit of their "purposes" and the way that "human purposes have an insistent tendency to conflict with one another," Dunn posits that the former is "a weaker propensity" (C 135, C 136). For him, "mutual hostility," "the inherent difficulties of collective action" (C 133), and the "bewildering diversity" of "human purposes" and "human judgments" undermine cooperation: "This bewildering diversity is more than enough in itself to ensure that there is a clear surplus of conflict over co-operation in human interactions and that there will always continue to be so" (C 361). Moreover, cooperation is impeded by the epistemic problem in determining whether it is in one's interest to cooperate with others. For Dunn, Hamlet's predicament epitomizes the nature of individual political choice: "The more carefully and reflectively you consider the question, the less easy it is to know just what is in your own interest ... what outcomes it is reasonable even to hope to secure.... how the costs of securing this outcome are likely to be distributed, and what proportion of them, if any, it is reasonable to consider bearing oneself" (C 287).

It is fortunate for John Dunn as well as me that the pilots in the R.A.F. in World War II did not find these questions so puzzling as he does! That is, given the admittedly strong tendency to form solidarity groups bound together by the forces of cooperation and to effect cooperation between them, where is the evidence needed to show that this tendency is weaker than that leading to conflict? If the fact that "there are so many wars" (C 117) is regarded as evidence, one must first point out that a huge amount of cooperation, self-discipline, and heroic self-sacrifice is needed to wage war, as illustrated equally by the R.A.F. in the Battle of Britain and the Nazi soldiers at Stalingrad. Moreover, if all interactions among nations could be counted using some unit of social interaction common to peace and war, it is quite plausible that the units of peaceful interaction respecting international law would vastly outnumber the violent ones, just as, in the U.S. at least, grossly reckless driving violating traffic regulations is far rarer than careful driving essentially respecting them. Dunn's premise, then, not only seems counter-intuitive but also is hard to reconcile with his call for "precision" in the analysis of political facts and his emphasis on the opacity of history, not to mention the enormous differences in the extent to which groups in tension with each other lean toward violent conflict.

Adopting this premise, however, he sees political life as decisively shaped by moral and cognitive fallibility, the self-serving pursuit of short-term interests, the prevalence of political elites "dominating" others, the confusion resulting from "the logical puzzles of collective action" (C 287), and the vagaries or "wandering irresolution" of political history itself (C 137), not to mention that little is predictable about history except for the persistence of its deplorable aspects. Thus politics is largely made up of "zones of bemusement, frustration and the relentlessly cumulative weight of unintended consequences of vehemently intended actions" (C 109). In other words, the alienation of citizens from their government is a systemic condition, at least with regard to "much of the politics of the wealthier part of the world over the last decades" (C 246).

10. The Given World: The Lack of Progress in History

Depicting the general nature of politics as determined by the debilities of human nature and inclining "more" (C 136) to mutual hostility than cooperation, Dunn has made a causal as well as a descriptive statement, unambiguously implying that the nature of politics acts as a cause preventing people from cooperating to create new economic and political structures more beneficial than the old ones. In other words, his account of human nature and politics would not be tenable if people in fact had repeatedly cooperated with this progressive result. Had they done so, he would have had to depict human beings as able to attenuate their "mutual hostility" in order to cooperate in the effective pursuit of progress; to infer the possibility of future progress from the facts of past progress; and to frame current recommendations in the light of this hope.

Although not made in an entirely explicit way, Dunn's thesis that the nature of human nature and of politics has prevented such effectively progressive cooperation is central to his whole train of thought. According to my rules of successful thinking, however, he fails to set it forth in a logical, coherent way.

First, evoking Hegel's famous "the cunning of reason," Dunn's idea of the "Cunning of Unreason," which goes back at least to the first publication of his *Western Political Theory in the Face of the Future* in 1979 (W 32), certainly does not reflect any conscious belief of his that history inherently follows any law or destiny in Hegel's sense. Nevertheless, by using this phrase and then positing the perpetual causative power of a basically unchanging syndrome called "human nature" or "politics," Dunn implies that, whatever its causative basis, history is not an open, constantly unfolding Jamesean sequence of unpredetermined opportunities and challenges to the human spirit but a process which of itself is heading ineluctably toward a predetermined outcome. If it is, and if Dunn is right in predicting that the outcome is the *Götterdämmerung* of "unreason," then indeed, he is too modest in saying that "we at least, at present, have no idea whatever just what the Riddle [of History] is" (C 236). From my standpoint, however, William James's refusal to posit a determining historical force distinct from the varied efforts of human beings to deal with their unpredictably unfolding situations makes more sense. To see history as cunningly ruled by either Hegel's beneficent Spirit or Dunn's malign human nature strikes me as a return to the kind of metaphysical thinking refuted by the GMWER — in Dunn's terms, a return to "superstition."

Second, underlying Dunn's thesis is the GMWER assumption that, whatever anyone might think of various historical developments, none can be viewed as progress because there are no indisputable criteria with which to evaluate such developments. As already noted, however, Dunn himself resists this kind of relativism, and there seems to be an epistemologically coherent way to establish such criteria. (Also see chapter XI.)

Third, I have above discussed Dunn's tendency to use impracticably high standards to judge political-economic behavior. Dunn negates the possibility of progress by implying that behavior still part of political history's moral limbo cannot be regarded as progressive, but the many who believe in politics as the "art of the possible" will disagree.

Fourth, Dunn not only leaves the impression that history has lacked any great cooperative enterprises producing new social structures more beneficial than the old ones but also omits from his analysis of historical causation any kind of causative pattern that could have produced such progress. Looking at Western modernity, the failure of socialism, and history as a whole, he throws up his hands in despair. From my point of view, his problem is that, trying to set aside the Weberian idea of culture, he ignores an offshoot of this approach, the thesis that reasoning about political life is interwoven with a culturally distinctive discourse used by a population or social stratum to make sense out of human life. Consequently, he also ignores the combination of this thesis about discourse with what can be called the "trickle down" theory of intellectualistic causation, which is backed by Reinhard Bendix's thesis of "intellectual mobilization" and much scholarly opinion. This theory, it seems to me, is as logically compatible with the evidence regarding historical causation as any other. According to it, any shared pattern of social behavior, however affected by the egotistic desire for material benefits, is interwoven with a shared discourse defining for that group what is known, that is, the beliefs regarded as indisputable because they are true and justified; such discourses are formed by patterns of socialization, education, and propaganda; and these latter patterns are susceptible to the gradually spreading influence of theories originally developed in the ivory tower and then advertised in the marketplace of ideas through publications, lectures, conversations, etc.[15]

In my view, the causative importance of abstruse epistemological theorizing is best understood from the standpoint of education. Applied to credulous children, education often conveys ideas which the students shrug off as irrelevant or biased, but it also conveys knowledge, that is, ideas which, within the intellectual horizons of a particular population, are regarded as true or indisputable. These ideas then serve as the norms on which widespread social consensus and cooperation are based. As philosophers change the definition of knowledge, therefore, they can *eventually* change the norms which education conveys, and on which the coordination of social energies is based. For instance, I agree with MacIntyre's *After Virtue* that the GMWER changed Western society by conveying through education a set of epistemological beliefs which can be essentially summed up as follows: maximizing material well-being, individual freedom, and respect for a certain kind of social, political, and legal equality is the only politically relevant normative absolute. Any other values, especially those pertaining to the asceticism celebrated by Weber, are just a matter of personal preference. James Q. Wilson also emphasized the societal impact of this skepticism in the U.S.[16]

From this standpoint, contrary to Dunn, Marx failed not only because he offered no practical remedy for the ills of capitalism, but also because he deeply misunderstood historical causation. Dunn perpetuates this Marxist misunderstanding so far as go his explicit theoretical views about political causation.

Paradoxically, however, passing remarks of his seem to recognize the important causative role of ideas produced by intellectual elites, such as the intellectual trends weakening belief in God (C 356–357), or the unrivaled "intellectual power and simplicity" of "the model of pure market competition" (C 352–353). Certainly Dunn emphasizes that human interactions are motivated not by any simply economic calculations but by a "rich variety" of "political, cultural, spiritual" goals as well (C 349). Indeed his own intellectual project would make no sense if he did not believe that intellectual efforts in the ivory tower can help humankind face the future.

True, Dunn has astutely observed that "human belief is not a single sealed circuit, but an extremely porous membrane" (C 184), and that one must distinguish between a belief and "what *prompts*" changes in belief (C 173), such as changing historical circumstances making, say, Hume's skepticism more appealing in the West than Thomas Reid's "common sense" philosophy. Dunn would not deny, however, that the difference in content between Hume's and Reid's philosophies was also an important causative variable in itself. He would probably agree with Isaiah Berlin that "It is only a very vulgar historical materialism that denies the power of ideas, and says that ideals are mere material interests in disguise."[17]

Fifth, the idea that there have been no great cooperative, progressive enterprises in history is hard to reconcile with the obvious facts regarding the ancient transition from "primitive" or "primordial" societies to what many call "civilizations" exhibiting writing, commerce, urbanization, the shift to what S.N. Eisenstadt has called the "axial" stage, and so on. Dunn fails to assess the nature of human beings and politics in the light of these vast transformations.

Sixth, turning to modernization, Dunn repeatedly reveals his own belief that modern science, rising levels of prosperity, and democratization have been beneficial developments. Thus he faces the problem of reconciling this attitude of his with his refusal to recognize that there has been progress in history. He fails, however, to solve this problem.

So far as go the beneficial effects of the discovery of modern science, Dunn implicitly recognizes them, since, unlike Henry K.H. Woo, he has indicated no inclination to go down the path of Rousseau's condemnation of modern science. Similarly, Dunn has to acknowledge "the extraordinary dynamism of capitalist history" (C 337), but, struck by "the moral absurdity of capitalist society" (W 90), he does not explicitly recognize that the rising levels of mass prosperity contingent on capitalism constituted progress in the life of humanity. Nevertheless, he implicitly views them as such when he treats as a political problem the "paralysis" in Japan today that blocks the reforms needed to recapture the "widespread popular prosperity" post-war Japan enjoyed until about a decade ago, when "the boom came to its humiliating end."[18] Moreover, if he did not value "prosperity," the great sympathy he has for all those around the world suffering from poverty would make no sense.

If, then, scientific understanding and the ability to effect prosperity are beneficent in Dunn's eyes, so is democratization. Dunn is inclined to believe that "democracy is the resolved mystery of all constitutions" (W 64). Democracy is the "favored state form" of "modern political theory." It struggles with the problem of combining a "theory of institutionalized instrumental prudence and a theory of free agency" (C 265), and Dunn's writings precisely are filled with respect for "prudence" and "free agency" as ultimate normative principles. This kind of regime "pride[s] itself on the opportunity it gives its denizens to think freely for themselves and speak freely to one another" (C 316). Because "the routine politics of the modern republic.... are the most extensively and accurately recorded instances of political behavior we are likely to have available to us," Dunn suggests, it is only within this kind of political structure that there can be a good opportunity to break through some of history's opacity and foster "political understanding" (C 316–317). At the very least, he views democracy as preferable to "tyranny," the "well-ordered and economically efficacious police state," or "unbridled corruption," not to mention "the totalitarian nightmare" (C 315, C 343). Therefore it is hard to see how Dunn can logically deny that the historical transformations creating democracies exhibited a powerful human capacity to cooperate imaginatively in the pursuit of progressive change.

To avoid recognizing this capacity, Dunn employs three main methods. The first is simply avoiding the logical inference I just made. The second is to avoid celebrating or even mentioning various Western developments the value of which is hard to deny. Contrasting democracy with the "totalitarian nightmare," Dunn has not one word to say about the organizationally huge, successful, and heroic Western efforts to prevent the totalitarian regimes from destroying Western democracy. Far from suggesting that the victories over Nazism and Soviet Communism reflected any great human capacity to cooperate in the pursuit of high ideals, he describes the collapse of these totalitarian regimes as due just to their internal weaknesses (C 345). Dunn's is a view of the history of humanity without the R.A.F., without Thermopylae. Still more basically, it is an analysis of political life which, like so much liberal political theory, simply leaves out the challenge of national security, failing to see that meeting this challenge is as important a political goal as is the pursuit of equality and freedom. Dunn discusses the horror of war, the threat of thermonuclear disaster, but he is unimpressed by the way that human beings have cooperated heroically to confront these perils so as to protect a way of life he admittedly treasures (C 254).

Similarly, in contemplating the history of thought, Dunn does not acknowledge that there is anything progressive about the modern advent of concepts vital to his own quest for political understanding. He may or may not have been reasonable in saying that, since Plato, there has been "no detectable headway" made in understanding the relation between "political reality" and "the individual psyche" (C 71). After all, Whitehead said all of philosophy is but footnotes to Plato. But what about the epistemological relation between normative principles and the objective structure of the cosmos and history? Dunn is of course aware of the GMWER. Yet he comments on it only to note how the new realization that moral norms may not be divine commands has weakened social impulses trying to put clashes of interest into a moral context (C 356–357). He does not grant that his own understanding of the nature of normative principles and his refutation of Marx's deduction of them from the nature of history are indebted to the GMWER. Himself readily referring to "false beliefs" and "superstition," he does not grant that enlightenment in history has occurred and is an example of progress.

The third way Dunn avoids recognizing the progressive side of human nature is to focus his text on those aspects of science, prosperity, and democracy that are out of accord with the normative principles he and many other persons uphold. According to my rules of successful thinking, however, this cost-benefit analysis of his falls short to a large extent. Indeed, I see it more as a rhetorical effort than a systematic analysis.

Referring to modern technology and the modern engines of prosperity, Dunn suggests that "the cumulative consequences of modern economics and politics have in some ways proved astonishingly injudicious (two world wars, the thermonuclear arms race, widespread ecological degradation, global warming)" (C 241). The ecological argument, I believe, is Dunn's strong suit. No one can deny that modern technology has created terrifying possibilities, and that people have not yet found a dependable way to avoid materialization of them. But is this unhappy situation evidence that human beings lack the ability to attenuate their mutual hostility in order to cooperate in the pursuit of shared ideals or evidence that people need to develop this ability still more?

With regard to the rise of mass prosperity in much of the world during the last two centuries, Dunn does not speak of how in many societies the material well-being once confined to the mansions of privilege has come to be enjoyed in the villages, or of how islands of prosperity rose up out of the global ocean of poverty inherited from the premodern period. Instead, he emphasizes the inequality between these affluent islands and the sea of poverty remaining around them (W 96, W 98), and the way that, on one of these islands, Mrs. Thatcher weighed the imperatives of overall economic growth against those of "justly distributed personal welfare" and came down on the side of the former (C 153). He also dwells on the social, economic, and ecological dangers that globalization has brought to these islands of affluence as well as the rest of the world (C 253).

Similarly, he dwells on the ills afflicting modern democracies. Hobbes's bleak picture of politics is still valid today (C 309), he holds. Actually, the situation is worse than what Hobbes saw: "It is not hard to see why the secularizing shift within the history of Christian and post-Christian Europe should yield a distinctly bleaker vision of what politics is and what it means" (C 357), since a culture without belief in God finds it still more difficult to conceptualize any plausible commitment to the public good (C 356–357). The modern republics are mired in "confusion and ineffectuality," a problem that lies with both the voters and "the structure of decision-making" (C 256–257). The "affinity between elections and bribery is deep" (C 266), and the mix of voter confusion, media manipulation of voters, and the maneuvering of interest groups impedes the intelligent public discussion of public issues (C 148–149).

I would argue, however, that such complaints indicate only the persistence of the moral limbo of history, not necessarily any lack of progress in the organization of political life since the monarchical era.

One major complaint Dunn has voiced regarding modern democracy is that it fails to realize the accountability of the governors to the governed. Sympathizing with Rousseau's provocative comment that the British were free only when they had elections every seven years, Dunn has compared modern elections to "rituals," a "placebo" (W 16–17), worrying that elections merely ensure an "equality of impotence" (C 210). Contradicting himself, however, he also has recognized that in "democracies, what electorates consistently fail to welcome, and also mind about acutely, the state can hardly be expected to succeed in protecting" (C 334), and that within the context of "modern politics ... in the end the political sentiments of the citizenry at large dominate the purposes of political professionals" (C 178). Grappling with this issue, Dunn concedes that in a democracy "the people do indeed have some power" (C 111). His implication that they should have more, however, does not take the form of a practicable suggestion. One may ask how much political potency one voter out of a U.S. population of some 250 million should have. It would be hard to show that the power she should have is more than what she actually has. Thus the problem with democracy lies far less in the distribution of power than in the quality of intellect with which voters and leaders use this power, the question of *paideia* referred to in chapter I. Scholars like Christopher Lasch have astutely discussed this problem of moral values in the U.S.,[19] but Dunn barely comments on this crucial aspect of Western modernity. In his theory of history, the culprit is not culture but politics aggravated by capitalism and nationalism.

In one of his most hyperbolic moments, Dunn has called nationalism "the starkest political shame of the twentieth century" (W 57). Hyperbole aside, Dunn of course is well aware that one cannot simply condemn nationalism as "a bad thing" (W 78), and he realizes that people have to construct solidarity groups that are more "communities of fate" than of "choice" (W 67). Yet, looking for some "more intuitively plausible scale of community" than the nation (W 65), he seems to suggest that a global community made up of 1,000 or more smaller sovereign units would function more harmoniously than the current system based on the modern national state. This is as plausible as the Second International's dream of proletarian solidarity, which he also evokes (W 57).

Again, then, arguing that Western modernity is morally absurd, Dunn goes too far, refusing to acknowledge either the moral limbo that human progress cannot be expected to leave behind or the huge human capacity for creative and cooperative organizational and intellectual innovation within that limbo exemplified by the rise of Western modernity. All in all, I do not doubt that one can logically deny that there has been progress. For instance, a Buddhist argument could be made to that effect. Dunn's viewpoint, however, is not logically consistent and rests on judgments at odds with my rules of successful thinking.

Weberian sociology grew out of Weber's celebration of the human capacity for "rationalization," his elaborate effort to understand why the West had more successfully developed this capacity than other civilizations, and his immensely innovative and insightful conclusion that the cause for this Western success lay mostly in Western culture as a process susceptible to revision by prominent thinkers. Dunn's analysis of political and economic life can best be seen as a systematic and far from convincing assault on this Weberian outlook. But Dunn's thought is also unconvincing in the way it converges with Weber's, accepting the GMWER's conclusion that there is no knowledge about the normative principles of political life and agreeing with Weber's gloomy, epistemically passive response to the moral recalcitrance of the given world (C 309–310).

11. The Question of Agency

In all discourses, the problem of agency is logically inseparable from the way goals, the given world, and the quest for knowledge are defined. Contrary to the rational choice school, except for purely scientific or technological findings about physical processes, there is no universal algorism of instrumental reasoning uninfluenced by a historically and culturally distinctive way of defining the causative processes of the past and the future, the goals of life, and the nature of reliable beliefs. The structure of Dunn's reasoning again brings this point home. Depicting a given world of politics that is inherently inclined more toward conflict than cooperation, and that lacks any history demonstrating the ability of human beings cooperatively to create new structures better than the old ones, Dunn also emphasizes the inadequacies of the epistemic tools available for people trying to cope with this dismal situation. To be sure, he cannot deny that people have the ability to imagine an ideal world free of the problems that perturb them. Unlike T'ang Chün-i, however, he is unimpressed by the fact of this imaginative faculty, certainly not impressed enough to infer from it a kind of cosmic or historical promise that its existence cannot be in vain, that the ideals of people are ontologically susceptible to being turned by people into fact. For Dunn, as for all those viewing life through the lenses of discourse #2, there is no such ontological link between human ideals and the facts of the given world. While Chinese thinkers today still focus on the problem of specifying this link, Dunn even doubts that these ideals can be conceptualized as objective obligations everyone should respect. Moreover, he sees no way to break through the opacity of history to obtain the precise causal understanding necessary to pursue these ideals, and he sees no practicable combination of human efforts with which such causal understanding, if it could be obtained, might be used to pursue these ideals even incrementally.

Somewhat illogically, however, while Dunn pictures Western modernity as the product of a history without progress, he also sees history as having produced a kind of anomalously appealing structure: "We know of no better or more reliable mode of political organization within the modern capitalist world" than the "modern republic.... For the imaginable future, our best option is to try to learn how to make.... such republics.... go as well as they can" (C 330–331, C 310).

To do so, "it is we who must change, not the states to which we belong" (C 255). Here Dunn, again verging on contradiction, evokes a hope little supported by his analysis of human nature and history, implying that better "political understanding" resulting from the propagation of intellectual ideas can incline the citizens of the modern republics to bring their purposes and interests into closer accord with the liberal ideals he regards as obviously valid. In this way "institutions" too can be slightly changed (C 297), especially if people can check "the Platonists of the market" by reasserting the principle of wealth redistribution in the name of justice (C 200–201, C 269–273). Thus picturing the given world of Western modernity as susceptible to some slight improvements, however, Dunn does not articulate even such a minimal hope with regard to the rest of the given world.

12. Conclusion: Political Rationality and the Search for the Right Questions

What Dunn has accomplished is to offer a powerful overview of all the trends in the world at odds with the liberal ideals rooted in the Western philosophical tradition, and to make a very powerful case indeed that these trends vastly outmatch any currently detectable efforts to realize these ideals. This case, however, is certainly not what he presents it to be — an empirical account of "what is occurring, and why." It is a "definition of the situation," to use W.I. Thomas's term, an interpretation based on a particular set of "rules of successful thinking."

There is no need here to reiterate my claims that Dunn's political thought includes a good number of contradictions, hyperbolic ideas, and other kinds of lapses. These can be explained, I think, only by taking into account what I see as his inclination to view political theory as a partly rhetorical effort which cannot avoid such lapses — an inclination growing almost ineluctably out of the GMWER. At the heart of his rhetoric, however, is a triple contradiction much of which is endemic to discourse #2, and which is particularly disconcerting to me. First, not only the more "eudaemonistic" citizens of the modern Western republics but also those like Dunn highly critical of Western modernity explicitly or implicitly perceive it as a way of life and thought better than that of the rest of the world. This sense of relative superiority stems from the ethnocentrism so basic to the whole Judeo-Christian and Greek heritage, and from the perceptions of seminal thinkers like Hegel, Marx, and J.S. Mill. It is expressed today in a variety of ways, whether the passing remark of a U.S. scholar in a learned journal that the U.S. is "the greatest nation in the world," the sociology of S.N. Eisenstadt rooting in the Greeks and the Jews a unique Western inclination to pursue equality, freedom, and innovation, or John Dunn's implicit rejection of the optimistic epistemologies outside the West, his view that "As a resource for understanding the political history of the world western political theory has great strength and no effective surviving rival" (W 130), and his unhidable belief that life in a Western republic is preferable to life under any alternative form of government. I do not want here to dispute this sense of relative superiority. The problem is that it simply cannot be reconciled with the GMWER premise that "there are no clear human goods or bads," that there is no "single plainly authoritative standard of value" (C 102, C 196). The second contradiction is between this firm sense of Western modernity's relative superiority and Dunn's belief that it is a "morally absurd" civilization. The third contradiction is between this perception of relative superiority and Dunn's view of global history as an unprogressive process causally determined by the malign syndrome that is human nature.

Even if a subtle formula could be found making all these views less inconsistent with each other, a political theory embracing all of them cannot be coherent. If, then, one insists on retaining all of them, one has put the desire to express a political attitude in a rhetorically popular or elegant way above the search for political rationality and so has turned political theory into the rationalization of a particular social stratum's ethos — the victory of Protagoras over Socrates, an outcome certainly unacceptable to a John Dunn (though not to a Richard Rorty).

As already mentioned, however, the main purpose of my essay is not to look for lapses in the political thought of this major Western political philosopher. One of my main goals has been to make clearer the similarity and the contrast between the mainstream of modern Chinese political thought, discourse #1, and the leading Western political discourse, discourse #2. They both have failed to overcome "the seesaw effect," either because they have developed a concept of resolute, hopeful political action without emphasizing the accurate, specific description of the given world and caution in defining the limits of knowledge, or have emphasized such accuracy and caution without developing a concept of resolute, hopeful political action. Dunn's thought perfectly illustrates the latter dilemma, while T'ang Chün-i's is a particularly striking example of the former. Both have failed to produce a political theory that accords with my we-group's rules of successful thinking by combining emphasis on such accuracy and caution with a conceptualization of hopeful, resolute action to improve political life. By my definition of political rationality, therefore, both discourses have failed to offer the world rational guidelines with which to face the future.

My second goal has been to explore the nature of political rationality. My conclusion is twofold. First, political rationality seems to be no more than the judgment of a historical person weighing in detail competing claims about what the indisputable rules of successful thinking regarding political life are and then advertising her views in the intellectual marketplace, hoping that they will benefit the class of beings she has in mind, and that they will be widely adopted, eventually influencing governmental behaviors. Thus the pursuit of political rationality is an epistemic process inherently different from and parallel to what Popper saw as the pursuit of "objective knowledge," but it is also very different from merely expressing an opinion or a "state of mind." (It is thus outside "the three worlds.")

Second, I conclude that the key judgment to be made in the search for political rationality is the decision about what questions to raise about political life. This idea strikes me as one of those principles that may somehow enjoy the status of a universal truth or rule applying to all persons whether or not they are aware of it, along with logic or other concepts somehow appearing as inherently rational (I would include the idea of the four topics addressed by political theory, as discussed above, as well as the concept of human thought as a paradoxical mix of reflexive, critical consciousness with historically bequeathed linguistic symbols, or the idea of a universal imperative to evaluate the latter by using the former). Whether or not there are such universal truths or rules, the idea of putting primacy on the definition of questions when studying political life is an indisputable rule of successful thinking from my standpoint, and, if I am not mistaken, from Dunn's too (C 196). Therefore the doubts I have about the answers he provides for the questions he raises are not so important as the help he has given me and his other readers in identifying the questions that should be pursued.

The overarching question his writing, more than any other I am aware of, has brought to light, is whether political theory should be based on the view that there are strongly progressive forces in history on which people in the present can and should try to build. Without believing progress is possible, how can people act in a hopeful, resolute way? But can such a belief be combined with an emphasis on describing the given political world accurately and on defining the scope of knowledge cautiously instead of lapsing into excessive epistemological optimism? Can the "seesaw effect" be avoided? This strikes me as the key issue in the search today for a rational political theory.

More precisely, as discussed in chapter I, according to my we-group's rules of successful thinking, political rationality includes a belief in progress overriding the seesaw effect. In other words, if one is to construct a political theory rationally, one must avoid the seesaw effect as one conceptualizes political goals, political means, the rest of the given political world, and the nature of knowledge. To conceptualize these four more specifically, however, what are the key questions to be asked about them? Dunn greatly helped to identify these questions even as he answered them by precluding the possibility of progress. Seeking political rationality, therefore, my we-group is grateful to Dunn for helping identify them but believes they can be answered in a way very different from Dunn's and fully supporting that belief in progress integral to our definition of political rationality. Thus we see political rationality as coming down to a choice between competing advertisements for the best way to raise and answer questions about the four universal topics of political theory. In this way, then, political rationality consists of culturally disparate judgments about how ideas about goals, means, the rest of the world, and knowledge can be best made to form a coherent, morally responsible, and persuasive train of thought, not of a combination of culturally disparate goals with a globally uniform algorism of instrumental rationality.

Dunn's thought identifies eight key questions about these four topics of political theory. Each of these eight requires a bit of discussion. The first may be called spiritual, though no doubt William James, with his distinction between the "tender-minded" and the "tough-minded," would have called it a matter of temperament: how should one weigh the basic trends and possibilities history has displayed? In my view, rejecting Marx's clumsy utopianism does not necessitate rejection of Marx's magnificently optimistic determination to restructure Western modernity. Similarly, the "nightmares" of history, far from proving that the human tendency toward conflict is stronger than that toward cooperation, only prove that cooperation sometimes breaks down. A famous statement in *The Analects of Confucius* (*Lun-yü*) describes Confucius as "doing it even while thinking he knows it cannot be done." This reflected his determination not to be influenced by the apparent hopelessness of any current situation. To me, it makes sense to believe that the course of history is circuitous (Dunn speaks of the "wandering irresolution" of political history), and that this circuitousness often puts people in dangerous or seemingly hopeless situations. But it is gratuitous and without evidential basis to conclude that such hopeless situations are more typical of history than the hopeful ones, just as it is to conclude that conflict is more frequent than cooperation.

In a typically brilliant and provocative passage (C 355–357), Dunn refers to three hopeful approaches to politics that the modern West inherited from the Western philosophical tradition: "normative clarification" as the hope that people can more clearly apprehend the nature of progress, that is, can better understand the objective normative principles of moral-political praxis; "causal clarification" as the hope that people can better understand the causes of progress and then act more effectively to bring it about; and "the rectification of interests" as the hope that "the manifest disparities of interest which structure our world" can be "largely or wholly" replaced by a shared pursuit of the common good. Dunn holds that these three "strategies" made sense only so long as a strong belief in God "securely linked [them] together." He says they cannot "offer us clear and authoritative guidance through the politics of the world which capitalism has made," and which also lacks this kind of belief in God. The only strategy remaining today that makes sense, he says, is "reconfiguring interests so that we ourselves benefit directly."

In my opinion, however, this blanket judgment, reflecting the conventional epistemology of the GMWER, is doubtful. The alternative to the utopian dream of a world without clashing interests is not only trying to benefit "us ourselves," assuming this we-group can even be defined. History can easily be read as displaying the possibility of further adjusting in a large variety of hopeful ways the institutional frameworks modulating competition between interest groups. Moreover, as already discussed, I dispute Dunn's idea that no new light can be shed on the epistemic basis of norms and on the causes of progress.

To be sure, "nineteenth-century optimism" has been discredited; the epistemological problems raised by any concept of progress are serious; and Dunn justifiably worries that the demonstrated abilities of humankind are not sufficient to deal with the fearsome problems it faces (e.g. W 73). According to my rules of successful thinking, however, intellectual history has not closed off the road toward a coherent theory of progress avoiding the excesses of discourse #3 or #1.

At the same time, as one long immersed in the current Chinese discourse, I am perhaps less impressed than Dunn by what Nietzsche called "the death of God." Dunn, as just noted, sees belief in God as the architectonic concept without which people cannot rise above the anxious pursuit of egotistic interests to establish a community guided also by concern for others. Indeed, this view of Dunn's is widely shared in the West.

Once again, however, Dunn overlooks the obvious point that concern for others is actually basic to the ordinary daily life of many or all societies and jumps to the conclusion that today there is less of it than there was, say, in God-fearing medieval England, the harsh reality of which is indicated by the fact that 46 percent of the sons of English dukes born between 1330 and 1479 died violent deaths.[20] It is common for Chinese scholars to say the twentieth century was the most traumatic in Chinese history, but during it China's population more or less tripled, while during the violent change of dynasties in the seventeenth century, the population declined by many millions. Sunny interpretations of modernization (such as Alex Inkeles's) are at least as convincing as theories brushing aside the horrors of the premodern era in order to depict modernization as a process of cultural disintegration.[21] Dunn's reasoning here also collides with the problem of distinguishing between the Christian concept of God and the Jewish and Muslim. Hailing the social efficacy of the "Christian framework" (C 356), Dunn presumably would not ascribe a similar efficacy to those beliefs in God so alive today in Jewish and Muslim communities around the area of Israel. In these warring communities, after all, Nietzsche is either unknown or regarded as badly misinformed. Moreover, the claim that belief in God is no longer common in the West or in the U.S. has been challenged, notably by Robert N. Bellah.

More basically, the relation in human thought between the divine and the human cannot be grasped, I think, by taking into account only the Western belief in God. This is where Chinese thought is helpful. Especially since the publication of a brilliant book by Yü Ying-shih in 1984, students of Chinese thought have become accustomed to distinguishing between the Judeo-Christian idea of God as a divine being "external" to human beings and the idea of "heaven" as a kind of transcendently divine presence "internal to" human life.[22] Such a spatial metaphor is of course misleading, but it has been useful roughly to indicate the very important contrast between the ways in which the Chinese and Western cultural mainstreams have conceptualized the divine. How or whether to evoke the divine in order to integrate a society morally is a much bigger question than Dunn's comments indicate, and there is no evidence that the prospects for such integration are worse today than they have ever been. Again, Dunn presents a judgment of his as a statement of fact.

If, then, the spiritual decision to build on progress can be made, the second of these eight questions is whether, at least apart from this decision, the pursuit of political theory is ultimately a rhetorical act or an effort to think in as logical and systematic a way as possible. Protagoras or Socrates? If the latter, logical consistency and precision have to be guiding principles, but a variety of judgments about the degree of clarity and precision appropriate in different contexts still have to be made.

Third, what is the clearest way to conceptualize the study of political life? Determined to minimize the purely rhetorical or spiritual side of political theory because it is hard to differentiate a spiritual ideal from some culturally inherited pathos, I argue that Dunn's synthetic concept of "political understanding" precludes the needed clarity offered by disaggregating descriptive, causal, predictive, evaluative, recommendatory, and epistemological ideas. Worst of all, harking back to the nineteenth-century concept of a causal law governing both the historical past and the historical future, it blurs together two logically distinct kinds of ideas, namely ideas about what caused a past event to occur and recommendations about how to cause an intended result in the partly unpredictable future.

Fourth, can the criteria of progress be logically derived from ontological considerations or are they merely a matter of individual or group opinion? The GMWER has undermined the desire of many Western intellectuals to explore this question. Exploring it can lead to a reassessment of the Weberian sociological mainstream in the West, which emphasizes culture. Following this Weberian direction, one can see how cultures include linguistic symbols forming discourses, and how human thought is paradoxically both embedded in discourses and oriented to objective reality. This allows one to see that normative principles embedded in a discourse appear as indisputable to the people carrying on this discourse. Therefore, whether or not such norms can be "anchored" in any objective realities denoted by discourses, their indisputability is not an elusive but an unavoidable quality, and so they are available to serve as the explicit criteria of a logically formed theory of progress.

Fifth, in setting up political goals, how should people take the conditions of practicability into account? What is the nature of political progress as a practicable process? I hold that progress turns into a chimera if it is conceptualized as unadulterated by the moral limbo of political history. Hard to reconcile with his own account of human nature, however, Dunn's way of criticizing political thought and action presupposes a human ability to eliminate this limbo.

Sixth, looking for the causes of progress, one of course seeks clarity of understanding, but what is the degree of clarity to which the study of history and the future is susceptible? To what extent is history opaque? What standard of precision should be applied to the knowable facts? The Cartesian standard of exact understanding? Or the more modest degree of precision that Aristotle said was the standard suitable for the study of politics? Agreeing with Aristotle and noting that much history is knowable, I regard as unbalanced Dunn's view that the study of political causes is a chimerical quest for the utterly precise understanding of facts that are largely unknowable.

Seventh, what does history offer in the way of processes able to cause progress to occur? Unlike Dunn, I hold one cannot brush aside the evidence indicating the importance of culture and of "intellectual mobilization," of the cumulative influence of intellectual life on discourse patterns, which *eventually* shape policy, as Reinhard Bendix and others have argued. In other words, one has to take advantage of the insights of the Weberian tradition, instead of returning to the Aristotelian idea that politics just consists of the interactions between individuals exhibiting traits based on the universal nature of human nature.

Eighth, whatever the causative processes available, has progress in fact occurred? In my judgment it has, in Dunn's it has not.

My judgments about how to answer these eight questions allow me to devise a political theory including a belief in progress. With such judgments, one can not only describe political life accurately but also forthrightly evaluate the given political world and act in a resolute and hopeful way to improve it — "hopeful" in the sense of *knowing* that one's action may in fact be successful. Thus one avoids the "seesaw effect," since one has built up a theory of progress without lapsing into the excesses of epistemological optimism.

With such a theory, one can avoid a theoretical dilemma Dunn reveals in his typically candid way: the tension between his sense of moral absurdity and his personal interest in perpetuating the absurd system (C 254). I would claim Dunn here misrepresents his own character in order to make his theoretical point. No one will accept his suggestion that he is an anti-hero unable to act against his egotistic interests. What seems clear is that, wedded to his central concept of "political understanding," he lacks a coherent theory of progress distinguishing morally indisputable goals from his egotistic interests. With such a theory, he could logically distinguish between indisputable goals for society and his personal inclinations, which might or might not measure up to what indisputably should be done. In other words, if they did not measure up, that would not be a theoretically significant fact. Given his lack of a coherent theory of progress, however, the precise condition of his personal inclinations becomes the very premise of his political reasoning. Given that premise, then, how can the moral absurdity of the given world be less than an overwhelming weight crushing the hope of moral praxis? This is what T'ang Chün-i called a "concave" way of thinking about the given world.

How can I promote any intellectual mobilization if the only goal I can publicly articulate is implementation of my personal inclinations? If there can be no intellectual mobilization rearranging the questions people ask about political life, how can there be any historically concrete counterweight to the power of the given world in all its moral absurdity? If this counterweight can no longer be thought of as integral to the cosmos or to the underlying laws of history, what morally hopeful force is available besides what people do and think? If the decline of a Western religious belief cancels any sacred call for the dissolution of egotism, and if intellectual mobilization is not an option the practicability of which history has demonstrated, how can people do anything to restructure the given world? If there can be no intellectual mobilization, the search for a coherent political theory becomes no more than quibbling about trivia, and the fate of humankind is indeed as Dunn depicts it: left to be decided by the fortuitous interactions among conflicting groups each pursuing what is advantageous to them in the short run. Surrendering to this fate when there is still any possibility of overcoming it is indistinguishable from the fatalism Dunn wants to reject.

Without a coherent theory of progress, moreover, one cannot even construct a logical theory justifying democracy. Such a theory requires not only persuasive criteria of progress according to which one form of governance can be better than another, but also some way of refuting Plato's thesis that democracy is rule by the foolish. Many attempts to refute it have become controversial: that "the voice of the people is the voice of God"; that, once free, voters will accept the guidance of the most enlightened among them; that an "unseen hand" guarantees that free political competition will realize the public good; that modernization raises the intellectual and moral level of the citizenry; or that the material consequences of democracy are superior to those of other systems.[23] I would suggest, though, that democracy facilitates "intellectual mobilization," making it easier for a population to produce a discourse shedding light on the nature of political rationality.

Even this way of justifying democracy is far from invulnerable. But it has much in common with J.S. Mill's thesis that liberty facilitates finding the knowledge needed to progress. It would, moreover, be an attempt to strengthen the epistemological foundations of Mill's point, making this point by addressing the eight questions above that Dunn's thought has raised. By rejecting Weberianism, therefore, Dunn closed off a way of conceptualizing not only a progressive historical force but also democracy as a structure facilitating the realization of this force.

Mill, unlike Dunn, had an unshakable belief in progress similar to Karl Marx's. Not just rejecting Marx's extravagant utopianism, Dunn has put this very belief in progress to the test. In revealing its vulnerability, however, he has also opened the way toward a critically tenable theory of progress. The idea of progress may be hard to defend, but no more so than the idea that there has been no progress in history. If the ivory tower could produce a coherent theory of progress, moreover, the chances that it would be widely adopted east and west within a generation are not small, given the abundant historical evidence, especially from the twentieth century, that people *by nature* are often inclined to try out new ideological options, to shift to new discourses. Motivated by such a theory, people east and west could resolutely and hopefully address the fearsome global problems so central to Dunn's thought. Such a theory, however, would require a reappraisal of not just thinkers as various as Aristotle, Descartes, Rousseau, and Max Weber but also the whole epistemic tradition created in the West by the GMWER. If, then, a parallel reappraisal occurred on the other side of the Pacific, a new stage could begin in the international quest for political rationality.

Endnotes

1.   All page numbers in the text and notes preceded by "C" refer to John

Dunn, *The Cunning of Unreason* (London: HarperCollins Publishers, 2000); those preceded by "W" refer to John Dunn, *Western Political Theory in the Face of the Future* (Cambridge: Cambridge University Press [Canto edition], 1993). Dunn's prose style is usually admirable, but I am disappointed by his acceptance of certain vulgar solecisms. He writes: "You cannot comprehensively protect a free person against the readily foreseeable consequences of their own free actions" (C 266, C 172). Also showing up is "The reason is because" (C 178). Strangely, there are a few grammatically erroneous sentences, such as the second on C 204.

2.   Careless, perhaps glib reasoning is illustrated by his remark that there is something "elusive" in Max Weber's conception of the state as "that entity which 'successfully upholds the claim to the *monopoly* of the *legitimate* use of physical force' in enforcing its order within a given territory" (C 67). Dunn himself holds that "Coercion is the core of states" (C 117), precisely Weber's point, but he criticizes Weber's "successfully," because "no state has ever confronted a wholly pacified or subjugated population" (C 68). Weber, however, was referring only to a monopoly over the use of legitimated violence, not to the absence of crime. True, one could argue that "legitimate" refers also to the moral legitimization of violence, not just to legality. Admittedly, it is hard to imagine a society without some acts legally defined as crimes but viewed as moral by some of the population, such as Timothy McVeigh's recent bombing of a government building in Oklahoma City. Thus the state indeed cannot have a complete monopoly over the use of all violence regarded as moral by all of its citizens. Weber, however, was obviously aware of this and did not use "successfully" in a rigorously precise way precluding any degree of failure. He was quite clearly referring to the kind of situation illustrated by the McVeigh case: in executing him, the government in the U.S. indeed demonstrated a basically complete monopoly over the legitimate use of violence, even if, say, one percent of the U.S. population may have regarded McVeigh's act as morally justified. This is not to say Weber necessarily solved the problem of how to define the state, only that Dunn's criticism is not to the point. Like much of his writing, it presupposes a kind of Cartesian demand for precision not suited to the study of politics (see below).

3.   For the idea of the modern nation-state, see the articles by David Held and Charles R. Beitz in David Held, ed., *Political Theory Today* (Stanford: Stanford University Press, 1991). On the definition of "interconnectedness," see Alex Inkeles, *One World Emerging: Convergence and Divergence in Industrial Societies* (Boulder: Westview Press, 1998). "Globalization," an exacerbation of the "interconnectedness" long ago analyzed by Inkeles, is brilliantly discussed in a book celebrating it, Thomas L. Friedman, *The Lexus and the Olive Tree* (New York: Anchor Books, 2000), and in a book with reservations

about it, Edward Luttwak, *Turbo-capitalism* (New York: HarperCollins Publishers, 1999). Dunn's complaint (C 134) that "globalization" is just "the name of a cognitive challenge, not of a potential solution to a cognitive problem" would have been more useful had he indicated the nature of the insights into this problem which he seeks and has not found in studies like these three. The Inkeles book is also useful for defining "modernization," and a good discussion about how to define "democracy" can be also found in Larry Diamond, *Developing Democracy: Toward Consolidation* (Baltimore: The Johns Hopkins University Press, 1999).

4. See Randall Collins's introductory essay in Reinhard Bendix, ed., *State and Society: A Reader in Comparative Political Sociology* (Boston: Little, Brown and Company, 1968), p. 48.

5. Leo Strauss and Joseph Cropsey, eds., *History of Political Philosophy* (Chicago: The University of Chicago Press, 1987), p. 120. This essay is by Carnes Lord.

6. See e.g. the essays in Ramon H. Myers, ed., *The Wealth of Nations in the Twentieth Century: The Policies and Institutional Determinants of Economic Development* (Stanford: Hoover Institution Press, 1996), and the Landes book cited below in note 14.

7. See note 3 above.

8. Samuel P. Huntington, *The Third Wave: Democratization in the Late Twentieth Century* (Norman: University of Oklahoma Press, 1993). See below.

9. John Dunn, "Subject to the Sphynx: Capitalist Democracy as Solution and Enigma" (paper presented at the University of California, Berkeley, April, 2001), p. 9.

10. Recently, Dunn has suggested grounding the standards with which to evelute political behavior in Locke's concept of "the state of nature" and Locke's view that the nature of "rectitude and pravity" can be "inferred by the exercise of reason from the practical relations between human beings." See Sudipta Kaviraj and Sunil Khilnani, eds., *Civil Society: History and Possibilities* (Cambridge: Cambridge University Press, 2001), pp. 49, 57.

11. Isaiah Berlin, *Four Essays on Liberty* (Oxford: Oxford University Press, 1969), p. 172.

12. John Dunn, "Japan's Road to Political Paralysis: A Democratic Hope Mislaid" (paper presented at the University of California, Berkeley, April 2001).

13. See note 4 above.

14. David S. Landes, *The Wealth and Poverty of Nations* (New York: W. W. Norton and Company, 1999).

15. Reinhard Bendix, *Kings or People* (Berkeley: University of California Press, 1978). See chapter VI above for an application of Bendix's thesis to the history of Taiwan's democratization.

16. Alasdair MacIntyre, *After Virtue* (Notre Dame: University of Notre Dame

Press, 1981); and James Q. Wilson, *On Character* (Washington, D.C.: The AEI Press, 1991), pp. 28–29, 38.

17. Berlin, p. 119.

18. See paper cited in note 12.

19. Christopher Lasch, *The Revolt of the Elites and the Betrayal of Democracy* (New York: W.W. Norton and Company, 1995).

20. Robert L. Heilbroner, *The Making of Economic Society* (Englewood Cliffs: Prentice-Hall, Inc., 1962), p. 33.

21. See Alex Inkeles, "Two Steps Forward and One Step Back: An Assessment of Progress in the 20th Century," in *Progress and Public Policy*, ed. C. Leigh Anderson and Janet Looney (Lanham: Lexington Books, 2002), chap. 1.

22. Yü Ying-shih, *Ts'ung chia-chih hsi-t'ung k'an Chung-kuo wen-hua-te hsien-tai i-i* (Modern Values and the Value System of Chinese Culture; Taipei: Shih-pao wen-hua ch'u-pan shih-yeh yu-hsien kung-ssu, 1984).

23. John Dunn interestingly challenges that thesis in the paper cited in note 9.

CHAPTER IX

Capitalism as Progress: A Critique of F.A. Hayek's *Law, Legislation and Liberty*

1. Hayek's Thought as Political Theory[1]

In the 1950s, when this writer sat in on some of his courses, Herman Finer was a professor of political science at the University of Chicago who was a fascinating lecturer, seemingly able to make simultaneous eye contact with every student in his large class, and whose *Road to Reaction* (1945) was widely believed to have refuted Friedrich A. Hayek's (1899–1992) *Road to Serfdom* (1944).[2] Since then, to the extent that history can vindicate any idea, it has corroborated Hayek's theory that socialist economic planning cannot efficiently replace the market relations "spontaneously" formed by history, and Hayek has come to be widely and justly recognized as one of the foremost minds of the twentieth century.

As Peter J. Boettke has recently noted, from at least the 1960s on, Hayek went beyond technical economic problems to analyze "the nature of the mind and its relation to human society," carrying on a "tradition of social analysis that dates back to the Scottish Enlightenment and thinkers such as David Hume and Adam Smith."[3] This "social theory project" culminated in the three volumes on which I here presume to comment, and which were first published respectively in 1973, 1976, and 1979. To be precise, therefore, this essay does not deal with all of Hayek's political theory, only with the position he developed in these three volumes.

By "political theory" I mean that branch of learning concerned with the normative problem of how to criticize and improve political life and society more generally. In modern times, this has meant criticizing two kinds of societies. One is a new type of society that is today widely regarded as exemplary, and that combines five major traits: the structure of the sovereign nation-state; modernization (as scholars like Alex Inkeles have defined it);[4] unprecedented inter-connections with other societies, as illustrated by the global economy;[5] free enterprise; and Millsian democracy, what John Dunn calls "the modern constitutional representative democratic republic."[6] The other kind is the non-modern society, which lacks one or more of these features.

Much research has inquired in a purely descriptive or empirical way into the causes for the successful or unsuccessful institutionalization of this modern kind of society in various parts of the world, and into the consequences of its institutionalization.[7] At the same time, however, a broad variety of conflicting political theories has addressed the problem of how to criticize and improve it. As mentioned in chapter I, apart from the question of promoting prosperity,[8] political theory can be seen as seeking such improvement especially by explaining how to define the freedom of "the three marketplaces" (the economic, intellectual, and political marketplaces) and their parameters.

Few if any modern thinkers calling themselves "liberal" disagree that the free society requires three kinds of limits on freedom: respect for the findings of natural science, respect for law, and respect for morality in one sense or another. Modern political theory, as argued in chapter I, then has to meet the challenge of coherently conceptualizing the three marketplaces and their parameters by (1) avoiding "the seesaw effect" (either emphasizing hopeful, resolute political action while failing to focus on the accurate handling of empirical facts and on caution in defining the limits of knowledge, or emphasizing such accuracy and caution while failing to conceptualize hopeful, resolute political action); (2) avoiding common intellectual lapses such as contradiction, exaggeration, the conflation of logically distinct issues, and neglect of relevant issues; and (3) addressing the issues alive in non-modern societies, not only in modern societies.

My previous chapters have argued that representative contemporary Chinese thinkers as well as a contemporary Western thinker, John Dunn, all failed to meet this challenge. In this chapter,

I argue Hayek also failed. Even though Dunn, inspired by Marxism, and Hayek, the leading philosophical defender of capitalist society, hardly represent the whole spectrum of contemporary Western liberal political theory, they represent a good deal of it with an intellectual brilliance that few if any other Western thinkers have matched. Their failures, therefore, suggest that the liberal West, like contemporary China, is a civilization without a coherent political theory. (Chapter X pursues this argument with regard to John Rawls, chapter XIII, with regard to Richard Rorty.)

To be sure, this claim presupposes a definition of "coherent" and so will be unconvincing for any reader who disagrees with the way chapter I arrives at this definition. To use Richard J. Bernstein's terms, I reject "relativism," leave open the question of "objectivism," and offer a revised version of what Berstein calls the "hermeneutic" approach. To put it more simply, my claim will be convincing to the reader who agrees with the argument below about Hayek's political theory. I should also again deal with the belief, common in social science circles, that, to thrive, a civilization does not need any coherent political theory; it instead needs pragmatic, gifted political leadership, a happy conjuncture of circumstances, and organizational and cultural resources that history may or may not supply. Certainly there is no proof that a coherent political theory is a necessary condition of successful economic-political development. There is only an ancient belief, going back to Plato, that it is, as well as a lack of proof to the contrary. Many leading contemporary scholars, moreover, hold to this belief, none more strongly than Hayek.

Comparing Hayek and Dunn highlights the fact that the modern West, like contemporary China, is a culturally shaped arena of competing ideologies, not some sort of monolithic culture. Instead of contrasting two monolithic cultural systems, therefore, chapter I argued for a heuristic device fitting the empirical data without reductionism, the idea of competition among different "discourses" and among different versions of the same discourse. Chapter I, therefore, argued that in the Chinese arena, one finds competition among different versions of "discourse #1" (especially but not only Chinese Marxism, Chinese liberalism, modern Confucian humanism, and Sunism), while in the West various versions of two partly confluent discourses compete with one another: discourse #2, of which Dunn's thought is one version, and discourse #3, of which Hayek's thought, like Marx's, is one version.

Chapter I discussed these discourses. "Discourse #3" refers to the epistemologically optimistic efforts from Hobbes through Hayek to demonstrate that moral and political norms are a matter of "objective knowledge" in that they are implied by "reason" or some aspect of objective reality as it can be rationally known, such as the universal nature of human nature or the laws of history. "Discourse #2" was created by the Great Modern Western Epistemological Revolution (GMWER), the leaders of which included Descartes, Hume, Kant, Nietzsche, Weber, Popper, and Wittgenstein. The central idea distinguishing #2 from #3 is that moral or political norms are not a matter of objective knowledge in that they are largely or entirely formed by the history of a particular individual or group rather than devised by relying on reason as some universal, algorismicly correct way of thinking.

If, then, it is useful thus to highlight what I call the GMWER and to regard it as a historical development creating a new way of reasoning about political life, one still has to note considerable overlap between the older and the newer discourse. Both of them included major thinkers, such as Hayek and Dunn, viewing a nation's political goal as centered on three marketplaces — the economic, political, and intellectual — the freedom of which was to be somewhat limited by three parameters: law, respect for natural science, and certain moral norms. The divergence between the discourses concerned only the problem of how to form these parameters.

Regarding the first two of these parameters, there has been no theoretically significant disagreement between thinkers like Dunn and Hayek. Neither has questioned the need to respect the findings of natural science, and their disagreement about legal parameters stems simply from the common problem of how to assess the effects of a concrete process on humanity: should emphasis be put on the beneficial aspects of capitalism — mass prosperity — or on the problems associated with capitalism and with modernity more generally, such as ecological harm, great inequality in the distribution of wealth, the threat of war using weapons of mass destruction, and social-psychological problems? Dunn's focus is on the problems, Hayek's, on capitalism as the only effective engine of prosperity. Thus Hayek sought legal parameters maximizing the free play of market forces, while Dunn calls especially for laws mitigating ecological problems and the tendency toward inequality in the distribution of wealth and power.

The theoretically interesting difference between discourses #2 and #3 pertains to the third kind of parameter, the parameter formed by the way citizens are educated to think about the most basic normative issues. This is the problem of *paideia* discussed in chapter I, a problem revolving especially around the definition of knowledge, of the indisputable ideas it would be "unthinkable" not to follow.

Like Hayek and unlike proponents of the GMWER's "linguistic turn" such as Richard Rorty, Dunn identifies the ideas people must follow — knowledge — with propositions in accord with facts and logic. The GMWER, however, convinced Dunn that there is no knowledge about moral and political norms. With regard to norms, therefore, there can only be the preferences an individual freely or more passively adopts — "purposes" or "interests" to whatever extent, if any, mixed in with altruistic ideals — combined with what meager empirical "understanding" can be scraped together about the causal patterns with consequences affecting these interests. In other words, the empirical understanding of history is still intertwined with the moral choices made by the student of history, but there is no knowledge available with which to turn these choices into criteria of progress everyone should try to live by — no proof that what benefits me benefits you, and perhaps not even any certain understanding of what benefits me. History, moreover, includes no progress not only because there are no criteria with which to conceptualize progress but also because human nature inclines more to conflict than cooperation, and history includes no causative mechanism able to attenuate this destructive tendency. Thus Dunn is intent on refuting any outlook using the idea of science to avoid confronting and so optimally coping with this predicament. He rejects two such uses of science: the Marxist illusion that science can yield the knowledge with which to overcome this predicament; and the Weberian methodology that turns this predicament and the human beings caught in it into no more than objects of observation and analysis.

Hayek, however, brushing aside the GMWER, filled with epistemological optimism and, indeed, a degree of utopianism, is certain that scientific knowledge can include a coherent, comprehensive theory of historical progress with which clearly to define all the parameters of the three marketplaces. The reader, then, has to judge whether this attempt of his to equip the liberal West with a coherent political theory was more successful than Dunn's.

2. Hayek's Epistemological Optimism

One of Hayek's famous points is that, to be efficient, people must distinguish between what they know and what they are ignorant about, and that the scope of their inescapable ignorance, especially about the particular economic events making up an economic arena, is huge. This is Hayek's crucial insight into "incurable ignorance" and "the fragmentation of knowledge" (1.13–1.14). To that extent, Hayek was epistemologically pessimistic. Yet he actually combined this emphasis on ignorance with an epistemological optimism closer to the thought of Hegel and Marx than to the skeptical, positivistic mainstream in Anglo-American academic circles, which indeed he directly challenged. He actually sought to build a theoretical system deriving "ought" from "is" even while accepting Hume's point that this derivation is not possible (1.79). Somewhat like Leo Strauss, he attacked contemporary ethical skepticism and relativism, the "loss of belief in a justice independent of personal interest" (1.2), lamenting the "destruction of values" that are "the indispensable foundation of all our civilization." Hayek thought he might be able to revive these values by propagating an argument grounding values in principles unaffected by either personal interests or disparate cultural or historical circumstances (1.6–1.7).

With his epistemological optimism, Hayek assumed there are "rational" ideas that, either throughout the human universe or at least throughout the universe inhabited by him and all his readers, necessarily overrode false ideas, such as the "superstitions" that have dominated much modern intellectual life (3.176, 2.xii, 3.52, 1.51). Rational ideas are often evident as "common sense" (2.105) or as "fundamental truths" (3.129). A rationally justified normative idea can be readily distinguished from mere "feeling" (2.101) (*pace* C.L. Stevenson). True, for Hayek, "culture and reason developed concurrently," jointly creating "schemata of thought" regarded as "self-evident truths." Thus even "science ... rests on a system of values which cannot be scientifically proved" (1.7, 3.153–3.155, 3.162, 1.11,

1.5, 1.69–1.70, 2.54, 1.31). (With this view, Hayek straddled discourse #2.) Yet people could somehow tell which "schemata" were "fundamental truths," which were not.

In other words, though recognizing that reasoning was a culturally shaped process, Hayek, without explanation, rejected any identification of reason with the ways in which culturally formed people actually think and instead adhered to what Richard J. Bernstein called "objectivism," the belief in human access to some algorism overriding competitive ideas.[9] For Hayek, this algorism largely consisted of "science."

To be sure, it was particularly with regard to the refutation of socialist theory that Hayek insisted he was dealing with "purely intellectual issues capable of scientific resolution" and did not depend just "on different judgments of value" (1.6). In his eyes, however, this refutation was not limited to technical economic questions about the inefficiencies of planning. It included a theory about the universal nature of human beings and their normative political order. For Hayek, all these issues must be resolved scientifically, that is, by inquiring into "questions which can and must be answered on the basis of fact and logic" (1.5).

Optimistic about the range of insights that can be securely based on "fact and logic," Hayek was well aware that how to pursue "fact and logic" was a highly controversial question. Somewhat brusquely, however, he asserted that this question had been conclusively answered. With regard to the nature of scientific methodology, he held that Karl Popper's "critical rationalism" was correct, other philosophies, "erroneous" (1.5). He also posited a completely naturalistic view of human existence, rejecting Kant's idealism even while embracing much of Kant's thought about authority and freedom (1.6, 2.62). For Hayek, universal human nature and universal social principles were revealed not by any existentialist or phenomenological inquiry trying to avoid reductionism but by the empirically supported if reductionist views of biologists, anthropologists, and economists.

Yet for Hayek the pursuit of facts and logic was also exemplified by a less strictly empirical kind of process, "the efforts of judges to decide disputes," efforts "which have long provided the model which legislators have tried to emulate" (1.94). Judges used their "'trained intuition'" to infer "rules which spring from the articulation of previously existing practice" (1.85, 1.100, 1.115, 1.117). In his conceptualization of legal learning, moreover, Hayek again brushed aside controversy in an epistemologically optimistic way. Many legal philosophers, concluding that the idea of natural law is untenable, find it difficult if not impossible to show how a judge's decision can rest on more than political interests, fashionable ideology, or personal preference. Hayek, however, confidently endorsed the optimistic "belief" in "classical liberalism" that "there existed discoverable principles of just conduct of universal applicability which could be recognized as just irrespective of the effects of their application on particular groups" (1.141).[10]

Epistemological optimism was also exemplified by Hayek's fundamental point that the structure of government should be based on the distinction between "rules of just conduct of universal application" (1.55) and a government's "rules for the performance of assigned tasks" (1.49). He granted that making this distinction would "in practice ... undoubtedly raise many difficult problems" (3.121). Yet his whole concept of governmental reform depended on the epistemic ability to apply this distinction and then segregate each kind of rule, putting one kind into the hands of one representative assembly, the other kind, into those of another organ, along with identifying politicians devoted to principles instead of selfish interests and putting them and them only in charge of the "rules of just conduct" (see below).

Even more, Hayek's key argument against the unlimited right of the majority working through its elected representatives to make any laws it pleases rested precisely on this sort of elusive distinction: that between "the will of the majority" expressed through electoral machinery and "the *opinion* of a majority" or "a prevailing state of opinion," against which the elected representatives had no right to act (italics in original). This "prevailing" set of opinions was distinguished by Hayek from an empirically ascertained flow of public opinion, not to mention any voting pattern. Thus it "prevailed" without necessarily being empirically manifest. It was identified by Hayek with "the implicit terms of submission" through which the government had originally been formed. The myth of the social contract, otherwise rejected by Hayek (1.10), thus reappeared to distinguish between proper political opinions and improper ones (3.34–3.35). "Power is limited by the common beliefs which made" people "join" that particular society (3.33), and these "common beliefs" were distinguished by Hayek from current opinion trends, which may be in conflict with them. But how are these "common beliefs" to be identified? Strongly criticizing the U.S. constitutional structure as a way of identifying and implementing such common beliefs, Hayek did not answer this question, except to imply that the power of reason could identify them.

Quite similarly, Hayek's epistemological optimism was exemplified by his central assumption that people could objectively distinguish between specious political ideas masking selfish interests and disinterested political views. One can distinguish between "views about what *kind* of action is right or wrong" and views expressing "interests" (3.112). One can also distinguish between politicians who can be trusted to be "wise and fair" and those whose "thinking is shaped by their preoccupation with their prospects of re-election" (3.30), or between proper taxation and efforts to "outwit the taxpayer" (3.51). Equally clear to Hayek was the distinction between a political party "agreed on values" and an opportunistic one just "united for particular purposes" (3.29). So was the distinction between "the image that most reasonable persons would form of an assembly which has to decide on the grave and difficult questions of the improvement of the legal order" and "the reality of the concerns and practices of modern legislature [sic]" (3.27).

Hayek's epistemological optimism was evident also in his belief that historians and social scientists could analyze historical facts to distinguish clearly between those aspects of a society that had evolved "spontaneously" and "organizations" or "arrangements" that were "the product of design" (1.26–1.27). Even more, as discussed below, Hayek discussed the goals of humankind as a kind of universal pragmatic program that was self-evident ("survival," "efficiency" in "adaptation," "peace" "justice," "morals," and "freedom"); assumed that "morals" entailed a particular kind of "ethos"; and held that the historical causes for success or failure to reach this goal were knowable and indeed had been identified by him (see below).

Thus convinced that so much about human life could be objectively known, Hayek possibly wavered between the premise that science was the basis of knowledge and the broader idea that one should follow "definite principles" with "consistency," discarding excessively "vague" ideas (1.61, 3.107).

A Cloud Across the Pacific

3. Hayek's Teleological Conceptualization of History

With his epistemological optimism, Hayek confidently looked in
history for what can only be called a causative law with which one
could explain why people in the past had succeeded or failed in
pursuing the universal goals of humankind and how people in the
present could pursue them. This intellectual project, then, was quite
at odds with the epistemologically pessimistic sociological approach
of a Max Weber with his dense empiricism, his "ideal type"
methodology cautiously differentiating descriptive from causative
issues, his emphasis on cultural disparities, and his focus on the
discontinuity in world history introduced by "rationalization" in the
West. Hayek especially looked at the scientific study of social
evolution and the biological evolution of human beings, seeking to
establish universally applicable categories.

To be sure, he avoided the grossest fallacies of nineteenth-century
evolutionism, denying that there are "laws of evolution," any "necessary
sequence of particular stages or phases through which the process of
evolution must pass" (1.23). He thus avoided bluntly challenging a
Western, Popperian mainstream that tries to see history as highly
indeterminate and inherently lacking any teleological principle of
development. The Hegelian vision of history as a series of stages moving
toward an objectively moral and rational goal, such as the end of
"alienation," is, after all, seldom explicitly endorsed today except in
non-Western intellectual circles, such as the Chinese.[11] Nevertheless,
the persistence of this Hegelian vision even in the West today, albeit in
revised form, is illustrated by Hayek's thought.

Hayek began by pointing out a similarity between living things
and the rest of nature: both realms display a combination of
"regularity," whereby many different events produce "a general
pattern," with a tendency toward indefinite variability making every
concrete instance of a general pattern "unique." The nature of the
former can be predicted, not that of the latter (1.41–1.42). Hayek
then commented on continuities between humans and other animals
(1.75). He did not make the point explicitly, but such continuity is
manifest in the fact that human life entirely or largely takes the form
of group life. This idea that humans universally exhibit group life
mixing regularities with unique events may seem to be a platitude,
but it both illustrates the epistemic possibility of identifying universal

aspects of human existence and is integral to Hayek's emphasis on the universal limits of knowledge.

In this context of group life, universal human nature for Hayek had three basic aspects: "innate desires" or "instinct"; "reason," "the capacity of rational design"; and the ability cumulatively to create a "tradition," an evolving mix of "customs, habits or practices," "complex cultural structures" made up to a large extent of "non-rational customs" (3.153–3.155, 3.162, 1.11).

Hayek, moreover, held that in the interaction of these three aspects of universal human nature, certain universal characteristics or tendencies have been reliably observed. First of all, these three aspects have existed in a state of perhaps continuous and unending evolution and, in the midst of these changes, have deeply affected one another. He held that "culture and reason developed concurrently.... *It is probably no more justified to claim that thinking man has created his culture than that culture created his reason*" (3.155; italics in original). Thus the "human mind ... is the product of the same process of evolution to which the institutions of society are due" (1.5). This interdependence of reasoning and culture, in Hayek's eyes, involved a key characteristic shared by both, abstraction. The role of abstraction in reasoning is obvious, but Hayek also noted that "customs" often have "a highly general or abstract character, that is, they will be directed towards a very wide class of actions which may differ a great deal among themselves in detail." Such abstraction well precedes linguistic articulation of such customs or rules (1.75–1.76). For Hayek, then, abstract categories are universally basic to human thinking, and these categories necessarily weave together "non-rational" and "rational" ideas. It was in this sense that "culture and reason developed concurrently."

Hayek was referring to this mental tapestry when he spoke of "a prevailing opinion," "a common opinion," or "schemata of thought." He saw schemata of thought as "highly abstract and often unconsciously held ideas about what is right and proper, and not particular purposes or concrete desires." These "abstract ideas ... are treated by most people as self-evident truths which act as tacit presuppositions." This interweaving of rational with non-rational ideas in the formation of a culture was also indicated when Hayek noted that "every cultural order can be maintained only by an ideology" (1.69–1.70, 2.54, 1.31).

Moreover, in this interweaving, Hayek emphasized, conscious acts of reasoning inevitably lagged well behind the vast accumulation of spontaneously transmitted "schemata of thought" and tacitly practiced norms accepted as "self-evident truths." It was this accumulation of complex, largely tacit rules over a long period of time that Hayek called a "spontaneous order," a cultural structure largely produced by "crescive" rather than "enacted" change, to use the terminology of William Graham Sumner.

It was through this concept of "spontaneous order" or "prevailing opinion" that Hayek proposed to solve the epistemological problem of how a judge, in a legal world without natural law, can base her judgments on more than arbitrary personal preference: the judge analyzes "prevailing opinion" as a body of rules cumulatively produced over the ages and logically applies these rules to the case at hand (1.69).

Hayek also viewed "prevailing opinion" as having a great if not a decisive causative impact on history, in contrast to scholars who hold that history is determined more by economic interests, situational or accidental circumstances, leadership decisions, or patterns of multiple causation. In this regard, Hayek resembled many Western philosophers, such as Alasdair MacIntyre, as well as many modern and premodern Chinese thinkers who have been called "intellectualistic." Hayek approvingly cited Hume: "'though men be much more governed by interest yet even interest itself, and all human affairs, are entirely governed by *opinion*'" (1.69–1.70; italics in original). Iterating this point, Hayek said: "In this sense all power rests on, and is limited, by opinion, as was most clearly seen by David Hume" (1.92, 3.33). Our historical experience has "become incorporated in the schemata of thought which guide us" (1.31). Such formulations will be welcomed by historians like me who see political behavior as heavily influenced by political discourse, and the latter as shaped by culturally inherited premises, and who thus resist rational choice theory.

Similarly, Hayek repeatedly ascribed major historical developments to the power of ideas, particularly erroneous ones. For instance, referring to the "erroneous" idea that all law is the product of a deliberate action carried out by a sovereign individual or group, Hayek said that "many of the conceptions that have profoundly affected the evolution of political institutions are the product of this confusion" (1.28). (Also 3.129, 3.174.)

His emphasis on the causative power of intellectual ideas was basic also to his conceptualization of agency, the means available in the present to improve society. He held that in order to stop Western democracies from continuing down the slippery slope leading to totalitarianism, a transformation of public opinion was needed. Most important, people would have to agree that "a majority can exercise some control over the outcome of the market process only if it confines itself to the laying down of general principles and refrains from interfering with the particulars even if the concrete results are in conflict with its wishes." Propagating this view, Hayek held, required a "very difficult" act of articulation rationally making explicit the rules tacitly embedded in the spontaneous order that had been formed through social evolution, at least in the West (3.18–3.19). Hayek must have seen the publication of this three-volume study of his as part of this difficult act of rational articulation intended to change public opinion, which then would determine policy. Thus Hayek saw agency as an effort to advertise "rational" ideas by refuting "superstitions."

To distinguish "superstitions" from rational "schemata of thought," Hayek, like the classical political philosophers from Hobbes through Marx, insisted that, whatever the vast range of "schemata" that could be empirically discovered to have informed the activities of the innumerable groups in human history, certain privileged schemata denoted goals that every group necessarily affirmed or somehow should affirm, most especially "survival" in the competition with other groups and so "efficiency" in "adaptation" with regard to "the general circumstances that" surrounded it (1.11, 1.12, 1.18, 1.74). Using this Darwinian premise, Hayek was implying that the distinctly modern effort to put societal primacy on instrumental rationality and the enhancement of material well-being, what Talcott Parsons called "adaptation," somehow reflected a universal hierarchy of human goals going back to the beginning of history, if not universal human nature.

This point raised two problems. First, despite his emphasis on culture, he rejected the thesis that cultures, like individuals, freely devise goal hierarchies in disparate, incommensurable ways. Paradoxically, he thus denied there is "knowledge of a common hierarchy of the importance of the particular ends of different individuals" (2.39) even while maintaining that the particular ends of different cultures are knowable and exhibit a common hierarchy of importance. Second, Hayek viewed these universal goals in a bluntly pragmatic way, thus disconnecting his theoretical discussion of humanity from humanistic, aesthetic values that undoubtedly were central to him personally as a product of Austrian culture. His interpretation of history, therefore, was at odds with not only the methodology of a Max Weber but also the substantive analysis of an Arnold Toynbee, who held, correctly I suspect, that "the cultural element is the essence of a civilization and the economic and political elements are relatively trivial manifestations of the life that it has in it."[12]

In alluding to allegedly universal goals of group life, Hayek also referred to other values. These ambiguously appeared in his discussion as either means logically needed to pursue survival and prosperity or ultimate values in themselves, especially "peace," "justice," "morals," and "freedom" (3.129, 3.130, 3.33, 1.18). All these goals, he implied, were inseparable from "reason," which, he said, was one of the characteristics of universal nature. He may still have been wary of teleologically grounding the goals of social evolution in universal human nature, but, in a Freudian slip, he once noted that a particular behavior (gratifying human emotions) was "never an aim of evolution" (3.160).

Describing social evolution as a historical development based on three aspects of universal human nature — instinct, reason, and the ability to form non-rational customs — Hayek, as already mentioned, paid homage to the Popperian ban on any talk of "necessary stages" but still embraced really uncontested contemporary ideas about the basic stages through which humankind had in fact so far passed. He pictured a sequence of stages beginning with the "savage" period of hunting and gathering, which merged into that of the "tribal society." This was followed by the rise of "civilization" (2.110, 3.156). Hayek thus emphasized a concept — "civilization" — that was basic to Western thought at least through the nineteenth century, was rejected for decades by modern social science as suffering from imprecision and masking bias or racism, and now is making a comeback in the writings of sociologists like S.N. Eisenstadt and political scientists like James Q. Wilson.[13] Indeed, often synthesizing the act of description with that of evaluation, this term by itself is an epistemologically optimistic one implying the universal validity of certain roughly clear, traditional, humanistic ideals that Hayek through his Austrian *Gymnasium* education had come to respect as self-evident truths.

Civilizations, however, evolved in Hayek's view. True, Hayek shunned the contemporary Weberian theory of modernization in a strikingly consistent way, presumably because for him it was intertwined with the "superstition" of "constructivist rationalism" (see below). Yet he of course could not entirely avert his gaze from the appearance of "advanced Western societies" (3.41, 1.19).

In this three- or four-stage scheme, the notion of a "spontaneous order" was central, the single key to Hayek's whole system. This epistemologically optimistic idea simultaneously denoted a key factual feature of social evolution and exhibited a logically unified set of principles affirmation of which was in accord with that "reason" integral to universal human nature. Because experience had demonstrated that the groups best able to pursue natural human goals, especially survival, were those respecting the principles of the spontaneous order, respect for these principles was rational.

For Hayek, any society, except perhaps the most "savage," included a "spontaneous order," in that any society, presumably even a totalitarian one, was based on "customs, habits or practices" which had evolved crescively, without being deliberately designed, over a long period of time, and which were so complex that their workings could not be explicitly conceptualized and "known" in any Cartesian sense. A spontaneous order, therefore, existed as behavior patterns practiced in a largely unconscious way and as beliefs imbibed through long experience (1.12). Hayek equated this idea with what "Adam Smith called 'the Great Society', and Sir Karl Popper called 'the Open Society'" (1.2).

For Hayek, however, it was only with the rise of "civilization" that the universal nature of "the spontaneous order" became clearer. Indeed, Hayek largely equated these two terms (e.g. 2.146). For him, "the basic tools of civilization" were "language, morals, law and money" (3.163, 1.14–1.15). Far less carefully developed than, say, S.N. Eisenstadt's important theory of the "axial civilization," this little list was linked by him to the idea of a major if still incomplete intellectual shift. This shift was away from "primitive thinking" or "naive thinking" based on "anthropomorphism or personification" (2.32, 2.62); away from "the intuitive, and in part perhaps even instinctive, sentiments inherited from the older tribal society" (2.145); away from the kinds of "solidarity" most effective in "the small group" (2.149); away from "the interpretation of all politics as a matter of friend-enemy relations" (2.149); and away from the structure of an "ends-connected tribal society," whose members share "common concrete purposes." It was toward the structure of a "means-connected" society, where "the chief common purpose of all of its members is the purely instrumental one of securing the formation of an abstract order which has no specific purposes but will enhance for all the prospects of achieving their respective purposes" (2.110).

In conceptualizing the rise of civilized societies, therefore, Hayek echoed Ferdinand Toennies' idea of an evolutionary shift from *Gemeinschaft*, a largely rural community mostly based on kinship or kinship-like ties, to *Gesellschaft*, a large, largely urban, more impersonal society based more on legalistic relationships. Toennies' dichotomy, close to other early categorizations, such as Sir Henry Sumner Maine's idea of a shift from "status" to "contract" and Emile Durkheim's about the changing nature of solidarity, has not been overturned by recent sociological work, such as S.N. Eisenstadt's, and indeed has been used, in a reasonably effective way, I presume to say, to analyze China's societal development over the centuries.[14]

Hayek, however, made a new, seemingly undeniable point about the nature of *Gesellschaft* when he analyzed it as a "spontaneous order" systemically entailing a kind of three-fold ignorance. He showed that people are unavoidably and greatly ignorant about the innumerable, individual, particular purposes and activities needed to pursue the goals of life efficiently, and about the many complex, inherited norms governing a particular social-cultural arena. Moreover, it is epistemologically impossible to evaluate individual human purposes by putting them into an objective hierarchy of ends.

This three-fold pattern of ignorance or epistemological impossibility was for Hayek a fact as scientifically clear as was the nature of universal human nature and of human goals. He then proceeded logically to derive his concept of the normative social order from this factual picture of humanity's quest for prosperity in the context of this three-fold ignorance. In this way, he teleologically derived the rational goal of humanity from what he viewed as the facts of history.

Combined with the goal of efficiency, these threefold limits of knowledge implied the need to base society on "abstract, end-independent rules": "because we lack the knowledge of a common hierarchy of the importance of the particular ends of different individuals," and "because we lack the knowledge of particular facts ... the order of the Great Society must be brought about by the observance of abstract and end-independent rules" allowing individuals "to use their own knowledge for their own.... separate and incommensurable.... purposes" (2.39, 2.8, 2.108–2.109, 2.111). In other words, what humanity — "we" — "must" do to realize "the order of the Great Society" was largely determined by the scientifically specified boundaries of knowledge. As Hayek pictured it, however, this normative social order was a complicated one with three basic aspects: the marketplaces within which individuals could freely interact; a shared "ethos" based on the mainstream western European cultural tradition; and the large role of the state.

4. Hayek's Threefold Normative Order

Thus the key aspect of Hayek's normative order is the distinction, indeed basic to the Millsian tradition, between substantive, specific individual decisions about what to think, what to buy, and which policy to support, and "abstract, end-independent rules" or rules of the game.[15] One can thus speak of a society that not only limits *Gemeinschaft* but also avoids the Rousseauistic attempt to fuse together knowledge, morality, political power, and individual freedom, instead putting primacy on the individual's ability freely to make his or her own choices in three, maximally unregulated marketplaces: the economic, the intellectual, and the political. These abstract, end-independent rules serving as parameters of the three marketplaces were regarded by Hayek as "universal and uniform rules of just conduct," the only rules that could properly be called "laws" (3.105). (Strictly speaking, his discussion explicitly focused only on the economic marketplace. Yet the intellectual marketplace is alluded to on 2.111, his endorsement of democracy on 3.xiii and 3.5 presupposed the free political marketplace, and his endorsement of Popper's "open society" ideal also implied emphasis on the freedoms of the intellectual and political marketplaces.)

Enabling free people to administer their own affairs, the central purpose of these laws was to prevent individuals from "'collid[ing] with each other'" (quoting P. Vinogradoff on 2.31): "The aim of the rules of law is merely to prevent as much as possible, by drawing boundaries, the actions of different individuals from interfering with each other" (1.108). To minimize this interference, these laws enforced "'freedom of contract, the inviolability of property, and the duty to compensate another for damage due to his fault'" (2.40). In other words, justice especially required "a free market without deception, fraud, or violence" (1.141).

Because laws pursuing this goal logically had to meet "'standards of consistency, equivalence, [and] predictability'" (1.124), these laws had to have continuity over time. Hayek approved of the statement that "'new law is a contradiction in terms'" (1.83), in the sense that continuity and predictability could be realized only if revisions in the law had to pass the "test of consistency or compatibility with the rest of the accepted system of rules and values" (2.28). Such revision, in other words, should be based only on the "immanent criticism" of the law by judges and legislators articulating principles already integral to or implied by the body of law being revised (2.24). Only in this way could the law ensure the existence of the "protected domains" needed to realize the individual liberty indispensable for the pursuit of those universal goals rooted in universal human nature (1.106).

Moreover, while Hayek thus logically inferred the normative definition of law from the efficiency requirements inherent in the very nature of the market relations needed to pursue universal human goals, he also argued that, in point of historical fact, legal thought and practice in the West had to a large extent accorded with this theoretical definition. In other words, in contrast with Dunn's thought, history for Hayek included a progressive tendency increasing the role in human affairs of the rational part of universal human nature. Hayek cited "the tradition of the rule of law" in ancient Athens in terms of its clash there with the mistaken idea that law could be freely revised by "the people" acting as a "sovereign" group. Similarly, in ancient Rome "a body of law grew up through the gradual articulation of prevailing conceptions of justice rather than by legislation," and British common law developed the same way (1.82–1.85). Moreover, hailing thinkers like David Hume, Adam Smith, and Edmund Burke, Hayek held that a proper understanding of law had been achieved "in the liberal age" (3.34). In other words, history itself corroborated the theoretical distinction between, on the one hand, the laws of the spontaneous order as "end-independent" rules of the game devised by interpreting inherited principles of justice, and, on the other, the "rules for the performance of assigned tasks" or "rules of organization" created by a government rather than inferred from inherited practice (1.48–1.49). Hayek also cited Walter Lippmann to back up this vision of law: "'In a free society the state does not administer the affairs of men. It administers justice among men who conduct their own affairs'" (vol. 2, quote after title page).

Hayek, however, well knew that, to conceptualize "an appropriate social order," it was not enough to envisage a set of marketplaces in which the free interaction of individuals was limited only by laws designed to minimize the interference by one person in the affairs of another. Two major problem areas remained, customs and the state.

Not only law but also a certain moral "ethos" (3.164) were needed to limit individual freedom. Seeking an "end-independent" legal order that "will enhance for all the prospects of achieving their respective purposes" (2.110), Hayek believed this legal order could not be successful unless the "respective purposes" of individuals remained within certain moral parameters. In Isaiah Berlin's terms, "negative freedom" had to be combined with some degree of "positive freedom." While liberal theorists today sometimes derive all norms from only two principles, equality and freedom, Hayek's thought is typical of nineteenth-century Millsian liberalism in rejecting any libertarian ideal of the free individual as someone maximally able to follow any individual desire or impulse. The Millsian individualism Hayek followed combined the ideal of liberty with concepts morally grading individual desires and bluntly condemning a good many of them.

The "ethos" Hayek intertwined with freedom was twofold. On the one hand, the individual confidently pursued selfish interests, knowing that "we generally are doing most good by pursuing gain" (2.145) and serenely accepting the disappointments necessarily generated by the marketplace, whether her own or those of others (2.107). On the other hand, in Hayek's eyes, this legitimate selfishness had to be combined with "morals," including "the morals of the market" (2.146).

It is clear that, for Hayek, "morals" were as indispensable a part of any "appropriate social order" as any other element. Hayek, however, took this point for granted and touched on it only indirectly instead of dealing with the contradiction between it and another point of his, that "we lack the knowledge of a common hierarchy of the importance of the particular ends of different individuals" (2.39). Again, it was his epistemological optimism that allowed him to assume that his vision of legitimate rational preferences was universally valid and uncontroversial, overriding any individual preferences at odds with it.

This vision of his was an ascetic one following in the tradition of the Aristotelian and Biblical virtues, the same vision J.S. Mill equated with "reason," and so it was at odds with the more anti-ascetic, Freudian, relativistic views that today are widespread in the West, and that Hayek denounced: "The morals which maintain the open society do not serve to gratify human emotions — which never was an aim of evolution ..." (3.156–3.166, 3.174–3.176, 2.57, 2.74).

This traditional, ascetic notion of morals was already implied by Hayek's equally traditional concept of "civilization." Strikingly at odds with the current libertarian tendency to welcome almost any cultural innovation, Hayek's Burkean emphasis on continuity with a distinctive cultural heritage was partly based on his judgment that, without much continuity in customs, a society could not remain coherent and effectively pursue humankind's universal goals. His moralistic idea of an "ethos" also coincided with the idea of the civil society classically developed by Locke, Adam Smith, and Hegel.[16] Moreover, it can be viewed as one, albeit controversial way of defining the kind of normative political culture allegedly needed for the successful functioning of democratic government.[17]

This traditional view of morality, which Hayek, a bit hastily, regarded as not requiring any theoretical justification, presupposes not only epistemological optimism — the idea that right and wrong are universally obvious — but also the traditional way of avoiding the absolutization of autonomy and instead balancing autonomy with heteronomy. This notion of legitimate heteronomy as basic to freedom is illustrated by Mill's assumption that the insane should be under the control of the sane, children, under that of adults, the uncivilized, under that of the civilized, and the uneducated, under that of the educated.[18] It is also important to note Hayek's implication, which coincided with the thought of the American

Founding Fathers, that the vitality of a spontaneous order depends on the existence of citizens inculcated with virtue by their families, neighborhoods, schools, and places of worship (admittedly, Hayek, in these volumes at least, avoids any explicit mention of any need for religion). If only by implication, then, Hayek linked the thesis of the spontaneous order with that of a particular kind of educational tradition. An economist wanting to distinguish his scientific reasoning from the fuzziness of the humanistic scholar, Hayek did not present himself as a missionary for the Greek idea of *paideia*, but no one can read these volumes without sensing the atmosphere of his Austrian *Gymnasium* education.

Hayek could well have said that the problem of inculcating this "ethos," which precariously combined legitimized selfishness with traditional virtues, is "the most important problem of the social order." Indeed he implied this very point when he described human history as not only creating spontaneous orders but also repeatedly undermining them, as people failed to grasp the limits of knowledge and remained "atavis[tically]" attached to the morality of *Gemeinschaft*. After all, he deplored the continuing failure to accept "the morals of the market" (2.146) and the continuing attachment to "the older rules of conduct which have prevailed in the distant past and are still dear to men's sentiments," values that so many "prophets" had regarded as "immutable and eternal" (3.165–3.166). Hayek quite saw that, in precariously evoking a traditional morality at least indirectly rooted in the *Gemeinschaft* past and trying to graft it onto the idea of legitimate selfish interests, he was recommending a cognitive synthesis that many found "irrational and immoral" (3.165). Yet, rather than focusing on the extremely difficult problem of how to institutionalize this synthesis, he just criticized those who insisted on *Gemeinschaft* values. Moreover, although aware that it was "in the Western world" that "most men ... [had] learned to accept" this synthesis (3.164), Hayek did not address the problem of how to promulgate this far from obvious moral formula in non-Western societies, such as China, where, it is clear, the *Gemeinschaft* definition of morality has been still less challenged and altered than in the West.[19] Indeed, a basic shortcoming of his political theory is that it neglects the problems of non-modern, non-Western societies.

What Hayek viewed as "the most important problem of the social order," then, was not the inculcation of this "ethos" but "the effective limitation of power" (3.128). By "power," Hayek meant the power of the state. This problem was so central, however, because the state was so necessary. In Hayek's eyes, just as in those of nearly every student of political theory, the state was necessary in many ways, not only to administer the above system of marketplace rules. Quite paradoxically, then, despite his emphasis on individual liberty minimally limited by state intervention and his deep distrust of the state and of bureaucracy, Hayek had an extremely full and generous list of needed state functions, so generous a list, indeed, that it is not always easy to distinguish it from the principles of a liberal thinker like Robert N. Bellah.

According to Hayek, the two state functions with the highest degree of "authority" were "enforcement of the law" and "defense against external enemies," but the state also had a "wide range" of "service functions," and it needed a taxation system to finance all its functions (3.41–3.42).

In devising laws protecting property rights, for instance, the state had to take into account "neighborhood effects" of the use of private property, including ecological effects (3.43).

Hayek also approved of "removal of discriminations by law which had crept in as a result of greater influence that certain groups like landlords, employers, creditors, etc., had wielded on the formation of the law" (1.141, 1.89). Hayek's thought, therefore, is not only in accord with conservative efforts to minimize government inter-ference in the workings of the market but also not entirely at odds with New Left efforts to minimize unjustified patterns of domination and inequality arising outside the state.

He also approved of a broad range of welfare measures (of course, he religiously avoided the term "welfare") for "some unfortunate minorities, the weak or those unable to provide for themselves"(1.141–1.142). No one has called Hayek a bleeding-heart liberal. Yet he was greatly concerned with

> the fate of those who for various reasons cannot make their living in the market, such as the sick, the old, the physically or mentally defective, the widows and orphans — that is all people suffering from adverse conditions which may affect anyone and against which most individuals cannot alone make adequate provision but in which [sic] a society that has reached a certain level of wealth can afford to provide for all…. A system which aims at tempting large numbers to leave the relative security which the

membership in the small group has given would probably soon produce great discontent and violent reaction when those who have first enjoyed its benefits find themselves without help when, through no fault of their own, their capacity to earn a living ceases. (3.54–3.55)

To help such people, Hayek even proposed that "government should ... assure to all protection against severe deprivation in the form of an assured minimum wage income, or a floor below which nobody need descend" (2.87, 3.55).

Closely related to such welfare measures were government services needed for protection against epidemics and other natural disasters (3.44).

Hayek had innovative thoughts about the possible privatization of the postal and monetary systems (3.56), but he saw government services as needed to build and maintain much or most of the economic infrastructure (3.44).

Putting survival above liberty in a logically consistent way, Hayek, like J.S. Mill, allowed for a huge expansion of state power in times of grave national emergency. Even that most basic right of the individual to act with total freedom when his actions affect only "his personal domain.... may have to be suspended when those institutions are threatened which are intended to preserve [this freedom] in the long run, and when it becomes necessary to join in common action for the supreme end of defending them, or to avert some other common danger to the whole society ..." (3.111). This broad formulation gave the state great leeway. Should, for instance, the spread of the drug culture in the U.S. today be regarded as such a "common danger to the whole society"? Could non-modern societies regard their economic and military backwardness as posing such a danger? If so, did they have a right to restrict individual liberty?

To provide all these services, a system of taxation was needed, and although Hayek offered some principles with which to limit its scope, he left both "the volume" of the tax levies and "the direction of expenditure" to the discretion of the government (3.126). These three volumes lack any clear argument against the principle of progressive taxation, although one passage suggests such a view (3.52). What Hayek systematically rejected was measures designed to help "particular groups" rather than to provide "facilities to be used by unknown persons for unknown purposes," but he realized this distinction might be elusive in practice (1.140).

Given, then, the great variety and huge scope of the state's functions, huge clusters of political power would necessarily complement the realization of any spontaneous order. Therefore Hayek noted, as already mentioned, that "The effective limitation of power is the most important problem of social order" (3.128). This limitation, Hayek insisted, could be carried out much more effectively than it had been in the U.S.

All in all, then, Hayek with his epistemological optimism developed a teleological picture of history. Its foundation was an allegedly scientific account of the universal aspects of animals, of human nature, of cultural life, and of historical stages. These included the rise of "civilization" as a "spontaneous order" that people could internalize and actualize in practice but not scientifically understand due to the dispersal of information about economic conditions, ignorance about the complexities of inherited traditions, and the epistemic impossibility of grading human ends. From this picture of humanity's goals, evolution, and limitations, Hayek logically derived his threefold definition of a normative social order based on free intercourse in marketplaces, a shared ethos, and a state performing many important functions (along with a philanthropic sector).

5. Hayek's View of History as a Struggle between Correct and Incorrect Reasoning

In Hayek's teleological picture, universal goals were thus derived from the conditions of social evolution, but there were no laws of history with which to predict that pursuit of these goals would be successful. As already mentioned, in Hayek's view of historical causation, the interplay of "interests" was governed by the flow of "opinion." Opinions, however, could be "rational" or not, and the shifting tides of rational and irrational opinion were fearfully unpredictable. Having pictured universal human nature as a mix of reason, instincts, and the ability to create diverse cultural patterns, Hayek also pictured it as a frail vessel. True, it was afflicted not so much by ineradicable emotional drives as by correctable mistakes in reasoning. Yet, Hayek implied, these mistakes were so common because the right ideas were almost at odds with human nature.

Perhaps the most vulnerable part of Hayek's political theory is his pivotal concept of political rationality as simultaneously in accord with human nature and exceedingly difficult for human beings to grasp. Hayek suggested that the ethos he called for entailed "'a discipline too difficult and complex to take firm root on earth'" (2.146, quoting Ortega y Gasset). Correct reasoning for Hayek was a precariously complex process because it had to combine respect for science; the affirmation of primarily pragmatic goals (especially survival, adaptation, and prosperity); adoption of a certain traditional, ascetic ethos; understanding of the spontaneous order formed by free individuals and the limits of knowledge about it; respect for its legal structure; and so a rejection of the tribalistic, atavistic "mirage of social justice."

Incorrect reasoning was, obviously enough, the opposite of this whole fragile cognitive structure. It began with the failure to grasp the principles of modern science and naturalism and to understand the nature of the goals most basic to universal human nature. Hayek thus spoke of "primitive thinking" (2.62) and "our inveterate habit of interpreting the physical world animalistically or anthropomorphically," which in turn generated much dangerous "misuse of words" (2.32, 1.126).

Once science was grasped, moreover, there was the danger of misinterpreting the quest for logic and fact by lapsing into "Cartesian rationalism." As Hayek discussed it, this latter trend overlapped what I refer to as the GMWER. Needless to say, Hayek consciously and vigorously distinguished the GMWER from what he regarded as rational thinking.

At the heart of the Cartesian "constructivist rationalism" condemned by Hayek was Descartes' insistence on rejecting all propositions except those meeting the highest standards of clarity, precision, and specificness (1.10). Descartes had contradicted Aristotle's point that, in the quest for knowledge, the degree of precision to be sought is a function of subject matter. Made so popular by the successes of modern science, this emphasis on precision caused people to doubt that they could rely on unavoidably vague terms like "civilization" or "tradition" to form their norms, and that they were under any obligation to respect any abstract or general moral or legal norm. If such a norm could not be derived precisely from observable, specific facts, it simply appeared as nothing more than the verbal product of one human will among many. There no longer was any objective standard with which to determine that one such verbal product was better than any other.

This epistemologically pessimistic conclusion had two major, often mutually reinforcing implications, in Hayek's eyes. First, law appeared as nothing but the verbal product of a human group calling itself sovereign and acting on its own opinions or as an accumulation of such arbitrary acts of will or political interests over the centuries, and so it lost the character of "discoverable principles of universal applicability which could be recognized as just irrespective of the effects of their application on particular groups" (1.141). This view erased Hayek's key distinction between law and those "rules of organization" the state could flexibly create to carry out its many functions. Thus Hayek opposed the notion of popular sovereignty (3.123), though he accepted democracy as "the only effective method ... of making peaceful change possible"(3.xiii).

Second, once values were reduced to no more than verbal gestures or acts of will, C.L. Stevenson's "emotivism," there no longer remained any barrier of authoritative, overriding norms to hold back the flood of permissive, emotionally uninhibited, anti-ascetic behavior deplored by Hayek (see above).

Either way, the norms that had historically arisen interwoven with that spontaneous order so needed for the efficient pursuit of adaptation were intellectually stripped of any authority greater than that of any arbitrary human preferences. At the same time, however, the rise of science was accompanied by not only these lapses into epistemological pessimism but also a tendency toward epistemological optimism. Hayek, like Karl Popper and Leo Strauss, therefore, pointed to a major new problem created by science, that of refinding the proper boundary between the known and the unknown, the proper balance between epistemological pessimism and epistemological optimism.[20]

The epistemological optimists were those thinking they could fully understand the workings of their society and so fully replace the inherited spontaneous order with a superior social system designed by them in the present — the modern vision of scientism, revolution, and socialism. Once the Cartesian concept of knowledge was combined with the idea that human affairs are entirely transparent and knowable, people became unable to understand that, because of its complexity, the spontaneous order can only be carried out in practice, not intellectually mastered. This illusion of "omniscience," this "fatal conceit," was then easily combined with the erroneous idea of popular sovereignty to create a state undermining the spontaneous order by legislating into being a new, "scientifically" designed society curing all social ills.

To be sure, even if their thought was perverted by anthropomorphism, Cartesian rationalism, the illusion of omniscience, and the belief that the popular will, in the form of a sovereign body, can make or change the law, people were not incorrect in believing that society required many services which only the state or some "third, *independent sector*," a philanthropic one, could provide (3.50; original italicized). The trouble was that this correct insight was then combined with the obsolete, atavistic sentiments of *Gemeinschaft*, that personalistic vision of morality basic to "tribal society," still "dear" to many hearts in modern times, even in the West, and at odds with "the morals of the market," with that "ethos" required by a society of free people efficiently pursuing the goal of adaptation.

Thus arose "the mirage of social justice," the idea that government services should satisfy all morally-felt needs, the emergence of a "provision-state" serving "established coalitions of organized interests and their hired experts" (1.3). This expansion of the state entailed not only that of bureaucracy (3.53) but also the rise of "academic philosophers" and other kinds of people "living sheltered lives" in state and private bureaucracies and so increasingly ignorant of "the morals of the market," increasingly envisioning the "re-organization of society on totalitarian lines" (2.105, 2.134). Their "intuitive craving for a more humane and personal morals corresponding to their inherited instincts is quite likely to destroy the Open Society." Such is their "atavism," Hayek went on, describing it as "a vain attempt to impose upon the Open Society the morals of the tribal society which, if it prevails, must not only destroy the Great Society but would also greatly threaten the survival of the large numbers to which some three hundred years of a market order have enabled mankind to grow" (2.146–2.147). Hence "the great tragedy of our time" (1.6): we are "now drifting towards a system nobody wanted" (1.3); people are "losing faith in what was to them once the inspiring ideal of democracy" (3.98); as Albert Schweitzer said, "'We are living in a time when justice has vanished'" (3.128); and so the West is on a slippery slope leading to totalitarianism (1.58).

6. Hayek's Utopianism and Belief in Transformation

Hayek then went on to explain how to overcome this contemporary "tragedy." Here he really broke with Popper's accommodative, Burkean notion of "piecemeal engineering" as a way of mitigating rather than solving the problems of society.[21] Most basically, Hayek rejected Max Weber's gloomy view of democracy as an "electoral dictatorship." Hayek envisaged a democracy that would not "serve the several interests of a conglomerate of numerous groups" (3.99), that would not be dominated by "established coalitions of organized interests and their hired experts"(1.3). In other words, his teleological concept of human goals rooted in history was not only based on epistemological optimism but also combined with a utopian, ultimately Rousseauistic belief in the fusion of knowledge, morality, political power, and a full commitment to individual freedom — almost a mirror image of the utopian statism he denounced! In his eyes, thinking elites could agree on the objective nature of the public good and on the identification of the morally and intellectually enlightened persons ready to pursue it. They could then take power and transform at least the liberal democracies in the West, freeing these political systems from domination by "the several interests of a conglomerate of numerous groups." "Opinion," as already mentioned, was the prime causative force in history, as Hayek saw it, and so rational opinion could even bring into being a polity transcending bias and selfish interests. In Hayek's discourse, therefore, humanity was dramatically and precariously poised between the danger of tragedy and the hope of utopia, struggling to control its atavistic urges in order to follow the promptings of reason. Denouncing the domination of society by immoral, irrational "opinions," Hayek sought the domination of society by moral, rational "opinions." Indeed one can ask whether this definition of the human condition, not entirely dissimilar from either the Marxist or the Neo-Confucian view,[22] was reasonable or should be replaced by one avoiding both the idea of utopia and Hayek's great pessimism about current trends.

Constitutional procedures could be rationally designed, Hayek astonishingly held, to avoid the mire of selfish interests into which all historical democracies, including the U.S., had fallen. This could be done because, in the first place, "rules of just conduct" and "rules of organization" could be intellectually distinguished — a point again reflecting his epistemological optimism. They could also be operationally distinguished, even as the government carried out its vast, complex array of needed functions. Intellectually and operationally distinguished, these two sets of laws could each be dealt with by its own corresponding assembly of elected representatives. The "Legislative Assembly" would look after the law in the sense of rules of just conduct and the "Governmental Assembly" would devise rules needed to carry out governmental organizational functions. Finally, a "Constitutional Court" would resolve conflicts between these two bodies (3.120–3.123, 1.140).

The play of political interests would be restricted to the Governmental Assembly, which could not change the rules of just conduct. These could be revised only by the Legislative Assembly and only by seeing to it that any new laws met "a test of consistency or compatibility with the rest of the accepted system of rules or values" (2.28). Thus a democratic government could carry out its functions without undermining the spontaneous order's inherited rules of just conduct.

Qualificatory and other arrangements, moreover, would ensure that discussions in the Legislative Assembly and the Constitutional Court would not lapse into the political mire of rationalizations for vested interests and instead logically focus on questions of right and wrong. Said Hayek,

> Legislation proper … should not be governed by interests but by opinion, i.e. by views about what *kind* of action is right or wrong — not as an instrument for the achievement of particular ends but as a permanent rule and irrespective of the effect on particular individuals or groups. In choosing somebody most likely to look effectively after their particular interests and in choosing persons whom they can trust to uphold justice impartially, the people would probably elect very different persons....

To help voters discriminate between these two kinds of representatives, Hayek again with astonishing optimism if not naïveté proposed certain procedures. For instance, the state would

> ask each group of people of the same age once in their lives, say in the

calendar year in which they reached the age of 45, to select from their midst representatives to serve fifteen years. The result would be a legislative assembly of men and women between their 45th and 60th years.... [This assembly] would mirror that part of the population which had already gained experience and had had an opportunity to make their reputation, but who would still be in their best years.... Various additional safeguards might be employed to secure the entire independence of these *nomothetae* from the pressure of particular interests or organized parties. (3.112–3.114)

7. Conclusion

Hayek's great achievements are recognized throughout the world.[23] Particularly compelling has been his argument that, if a society seeks prosperity, its laws regarding economic life must be end-independent, because the knowledge needed efficiently to determine economic ends is dispersed throughout society and is not susceptible to centralization in one organization. In this chapter, however, I ask whether Hayek devised a political theory coherently conceptualizing the parameters of the three marketplaces, particularly the parameter made up not of laws or respect for natural science but of the normative principles used by citizens to deal with their basic moral and political issues. Do Hayek's ideas about these issues avoid "the seesaw effect," avoid common lapses in reasoning, and clarify the issues important in non-modern societies, not only in modern ones?

Unlike Dunn's political theory, Hayek's strongly conceptualizes a program of hopeful, resolute political action, including even the drastic redesign of the U.S. Constitution. In his eyes, such action can be based on a coherent theory of progress: reason, largely taking the form of science, furnishes the knowledge on which this theory is based; the criteria of progress are the universal societal goals logically implied by the universal nature of human nature; history includes a causative mechanism whereby people can act effectively to check their own irrational tendencies and pursue these natural goals (the use of intellectually devised ideas with which to alter cultures and policies); Western civilization in fact progressed as people made use of this causative mechanism; and this inspiring historical fact implies the hope that people will again make use of this causative mechanism to realize more progress.

So far as I can judge, however, Hayek did not overcome the seesaw effect, because this concept of hopeful, resolute political action was not combined with sufficient caution in defining the scope of knowledge. True, like Karl R. Popper, whom he not only admired but also was admired by, Hayek was deeply aware of this problem of epistemology. Unlike any Chinese thinker I am aware of, he, Popper and other modern Western thinkers approached it in a way I believe is useful by suggesting the need to find a route between the Charybdis of excessive "epistemological optimism" (e.g. Marxism) and the Scylla of excessive "epistemological pessimism" (e.g. relativism). Yet while both of them believed that this route had already been found, post-Popperian philosophers have suggested that it has not been, that the nature of knowledge is still an open question.

One indication it is still an open question is that Hayek and Popper actually arrived at very different conclusions about the nature of knowledge. With his theory of "the three worlds," Popper restricted "objective knowledge" to as yet unfalsified "conjectures," insisting on a "dualism" between facts and values. Thus he leaned toward epistemological pessimism (buttressing discourse #2). (Admittedly, his central concept of "the open society and its enemies" was in effect an absolute normative and teleological category utterly outside the systematic ontology of the "three worlds," just as logic and his central principle of falsification through experimentation also lay outside this ontology. Propositions subject to falsification are different from the unfalsifiable proposition that those propositions able to constitute knowledge are subject to falsification through experimentation. Only the falsifiable propositions constitute "world three." This unfalsifiable proposition, like logic, is outside "world one" and "world two" as well as "world three.") Hayek, however, leaned toward epistemological optimism. For him, "reason" not only called for respect for conjectures as yet unfalsified by scientific experiment but also revealed the important normative principles making up his theory of progress. Intentionally or not, Hayek's thought rejected that "dualism" between facts and values which Popper tried to emphasize.

That is, as noted above, Hayek weighed capitalism's ability to generate prosperity against the problems it entailed, such as ecological dangers and great inequality in the distribution of wealth and power; made the argument that the prosperity was more important than the problems, or even that the problems could be largely solved; and claimed that this argument of his was not just a matter of judgment but was founded on a scientific analysis of human nature demonstrating the "atavism" of those who emphasized the disadvantages as well as the advantages of capitalism and the need for laws remedying the various kinds of inequalities. Still more basically, Hayek in effect claimed that his scientific analysis refuted thinkers like Arnold Toynbee who had suggested that a civilization should put primacy not on the maximization of economic efficiency but on the nurturing of its most basic cultural values. Similarly, seeing the major modern conflict in the West between those favoring the ascetic ethos of the traditional Western cultural mainstream and those attacking this asceticism to promote a more permissive approach to emotional impulses, Hayek did not just make a judgment in favor of the former, he presented this judgment as based on a scientific analysis of human nature and history.

As John Dunn's thought too illustrates, however, it is hard convincingly to base norms and any hierarchy of political goals on a theory about the universal nature of human nature. True, despite Clifford Geertz's point that cultural differences preclude any but the thinnest generalizations about human nature, virtually every worldview (including mine) posits some concept of universal human nature, and some such concept has remained basic to disciplines like medicine, psychology, and economics. Nevertheless, there is no consensus on what are the most basic human traits (Hayek, for instance, but not Dunn, included the ability to create "complex cultural structures"). Moreover, whatever these traits may be, Hayek is not convincing when he says that, although the innumerable incommensurable ways in which individuals determine their goals cannot be known, the innumerable, incommensurable ways in which different cultures create different value hierarchies are all somehow governed by a single, universal, and fully knowable set of normative principles all people should follow.

To be sure, Hayek, unlike Dunn, not only embraced the idea that patterns of reasoning and of culture are interdependent but also emphasized the susceptibility of these interdependent patterns to the influence of ideas created by intellectual elites. But I would say he did not fully explore the nature of this interdependence, that is, the nature of "discourse," as discussed in chapter I. Emphasizing the primacy of economic values and of Western civilization's traditional ascetic ethos, he did not suspect that this outlook of his stemmed from culturally inherited "rules of successful thinking." Instead, he was completely confident it was logically implied by scientific truths — a classic example of the kind of scientism and epistemological optimism avoided by thinkers more influenced by the GMWER, such as Dunn. Concealed behind this optimism was the tension between Hayek's claim that his theory was in accord with human nature, and his recognition that it was difficult for human beings to grasp this theory.

Given his epistemological optimism, then, Hayek failed sufficiently to distinguish between basically uncontroversial matters of factual knowledge and inescapably controversial matters of moral judgment, legal judgment, and historical interpretation. Contrary to Hayek, it is hard to see how objective, scientific knowledge or rational insight can replace judgment and interpretation in distinguishing between politicians devoted to principles and those just pursuing selfish interests; in the making of judicial decisions; in applying Hayek's distinction between "rules of just conduct of universal application" and "rules for the performance of assigned tasks"; in distinguishing between "spontaneous" and deliberately enacted historical change; and in distinguishing between "the will of the majority" and "a prevailing state of opinion."

Even more, this epistemological optimism was directly responsible for Hayek's utopian belief that a citizenry using its reason and enlightened by a scientific theory of progress could create a governmental structure guided by leadership decisions free of partisan bias. This utopianism thus marred his conceptualization of hopeful, resolute political action. Strangely enough, his optimism is partly similar to Dunn's gloom about future possibilities: neither allowed for the idea of resolute, hopeful efforts to achieve piecemeal progress in the moral limbo of political history. In different ways, both of them retained some inclination toward the rationalistic utopianism of the Enlightenment.

Apart from failing to solve the problem of the "seesaw," Hayek ran into the problem of contradiction or implausibility not only when discussing the relation between human nature and rational thought about how the political order should be designed. He also ran into it when he defined normative legal-political evolution. In his book's discussion of normative or proper institutional change, there is only an emphasis on "spontaneous" change, on the activities of judges and legislators addressing new situations by inferring principles from the inherited order, and on philosophers like David Hume and Edmund Burke, who endorsed these activities and rejected revolutionary efforts drastically to change institutions by following visions or abstract guidelines discontinuous with inherited principles.

If such radically transformative change is precluded, however, how can one approve of many of the steps needed to establish Hayek's normative order — replacing "tribal" values with end-independent rules? replacing autocracy with democracy? abolishing slavery? or replacing socialism with capitalism? Similarly, how could one realize gender equality by just inferring rules from the inherited order? How could one establish democratic, efficiently capitalist forms in non-Western, undemocratic, economically backward societies? Many examples could be cited to show the need for quantum jumps in the development of institutions, not only reforms the possibility of which earlier institutions have implied. [24]

Hayek's failure to deal adequately with this question of transformative change is linked to the fact that, in this book at least, he largely ignored the huge discontinuity studied by the Weberian school of modernization. Yet Hayek did dwell on the change from "tribal" society to "civilization." Few historians if any could account for this change without adducing the emergence of new visions discontinuous with the inherited order, such as the intellectual and religious visions described by S.N. Eisenstadt as basic to the appearance of the "axial" civilizations.[25]

Finally, lacking a balanced approach to the problem of transformative and gradualistic change, Hayek's political theory, like Dunn's, lacks clear guidelines for the development of non-modern societies as these have been defined above. True, in contemporary China at least, Hayek's goal of a market economy based on end-independent rules has elicited more enthusiasm than the kinds of warnings Dunn has issued about the debilities of capitalism (China's New Left, however, largely shares Dunn's concerns).[26] Moreover, in my opinion, Hayek's analytical triangle, his idea of a normative society as based on the relations among markets, the state, and a guiding "ethos," is of great heuristic value. How specifically to implement this triangle in different cultural circumstances, especially non-Western ones, however, is the key question. Besides suffering from the seesaw effect and lapses in reasoning, Western political theory has not successfully addressed this question.

My conclusion is that, in not expecting the Chinese intellectual world to furnish the West with a globally valid political theory, Western intellectuals are more on target than are the many Chinese thinkers searching for one in the West, not to mention the Western intellectuals encouraging this Chinese effort. What is needed is an intelligent conversation between both sides free from the illusion that either side has already understood how to bring history to a successful conclusion.[27]

Endnotes

1. I am grateful to Ms. Elena Danielson of the Hoover Institution Archives for help in obtaining biographical data about Hayek. The work of his here reviewed is Friedrich A. Hayek, *Law, Legislation and Liberty* (3 vols., respectively titled *Rules and Order, The Mirage of Social Justice*, and *The Political Order of a Free People*, and respectively published in Chicago by The University of Chicago Press in 1983, 1976, and 1979). All page references in the text are to these three volumes.

2. See Friedrich A. Hayek, *The Road to Serfdom* (Chicago: The University of Chicago Press, 1944), and Herman Finer, *The Road to Reaction* (Chicago: Quandrangle Books, 1945).

3. See Peter J. Boettke, "The Theory of Spontaneous Order and Cultural Evolution in the Social Theory of F.A. Hayek," *Cultural Dynamics* 3 (1990): pp. 61–83, and his "Hayek's *The Road to Serfdom Revised*: Government Failure in the Argument against Socialism," *Eastern Economic Journal* 21 (winter 1995): pp. 7–26.

4. On defining the idea of the sovereign nation, see David Held, "Democracy, the Nation-State and the Global System," in *Political Theory Today*, ed. David Held (Stanford: Stanford University Press, 1991), pp. 201–202, and Charles R. Beitz, "Sovereignty and Morality in International Affairs," in ibid., pp. 236–254. As Professor Inkeles's many published discussions of modernization make clear, there is no one fixed definition of "modernization," which has been variously used to denote a goal and/or a historical trend with a somewhat indeterminate variety of characteristics. There is, however, some scholarly consensus to the effect that this term denotes a combination of trends including especially a societal emphasis on modern science and

technology and on industrialization. Inkeles distinguishes between modernization on the level of society, of organizations, and of the individual personality. My own inclination is to sum up the heart of all these trends as the determination to organize society by putting primacy or at least unprecedented emphasis on the improvement of material living standards for all classes of people and so on instrumental rationality. See Alex Inkeles, *One World Emerging: Convergence and Divergence in Industrial Societies* (Boulder: Westview Press, 1998).

5.   For interconnectedness, see Alex Inkeles, "The Emerging Social Structure of the World," in *World Politics*, 27:4 (July 1975), pp. 467–497. This also touches on another important theme Inkeles has played a major role in developing, that of the "convergence" of modernizing societies. See his "Convergence and Divergence in Industrial Societies," in *Directions of Change: Modernization Theory, Research, and Realities*, ed. Mustafo O. Attir, Burkart Holzner and Zdenek Suda (Boulder: Westview Press, 1981), pp. 3–38. Also see his *One World Emerging*.

6.   John Dunn, *Western Political Theory in the Face of the Future* (Cambridge: Cambridge University Press [Canto edition], 1993), p. 128.

7.   See e.g. Alex Inkeles, ed., *On Measuring Democracy* (New Brunswick: Transaction Publishers, 1991); Samuel P. Huntington, *The Third Wave* (Norman: University of Oklahoma Press, 1993); and Seymour Martin Lipset, "The Social Requisites of Democracy Revisited: 1993 Presidential Address," *American Sociological Review* 59 (February 1994): pp. 1–22.

8.   See Ramon H. Myers, ed., *The Wealth of Nations in the Twentieth Century: The Policies and Institutional Determinants of Economic Development* (Stanford: Hoover Institution Press, 1996).

9.   Richard J. Bernstein, *Beyond Objectivism and Relativism: Science, Hermeneutics and Praxis* (Philadelphia: University of Pennsylvania Press, 1983).

10. On this problem in contemporary legal philosophy, see Robert S. Summers, ed., *Essays in Legal Philosophy* (Berkeley: University of California Press, 1972).

11. For an influential, contemporary Mainland Chinese version of this Hegelian view, see Li Tse-hou, *Wo-te che-hsueh t'i-yao* (An Outline of My Philosophy; Taipei: Feng-yun shih-tai ch'u-pan kung-ssu, 1990), pp. 1–41.

12. Arnold Toynbee, "The Disintegration of Civilizations," in *Theories of Society*, ed. Talcott Parsons et al., 2 vols. (New York: The Free Press of Glencoe, Inc., 1961), vol. 2, p. 1360.

13. See Thomas A. Metzger, "Eisenstadt's Analysis of the Relation between Modernization and Tradition in China," *The American Asian Review* 2 (summer 1984): pp. 1–87, and James Q. Wilson, *On Character* (Washington, D.C.: The AEI Press, 1991).

14. See Thomas A. Metzger, "The Western Concept of Civil Society in the

Context of Chinese History," in *Civil Society: History and Possibilities*, ed. Sudipta Kaviraj and Sunil Khilnani (Cambridge: Cambridge University Press, 2001), pp. 204–231.

15. See J.R. Lucas, "On Processes for Resolving Disputes," in Summers, ed., *Essays in Legal Philosophy*, pp. 167–182, for a useful account of this distinction.

16. See Kaviraj and Khilnani, eds., *Civil Society.*

17. Samuel P. Huntington's assumption that the successful functioning of democracy requires a certain kind of political culture is illustrated by his comment that "Democracy does not mean that problems will be solved; it does mean that rulers can be removed; and the essence of democratic behavior is doing the latter because it is impossible to do the former. Disillusionment and the lowered expectations it produces are the foundation of democratic stability." See his *Third Wave*, pp. 262–263.

18. Regarding this aspect of Mill's "On Liberty," see Thomas A. Metzger, "Did Sun Yat-sen Understand the Idea of Democracy? The Conceptualization of Democracy in the Three Principles of the People and in John Stuart Mill's 'On Liberty,'" *The American Asian Review* 10 (spring 1992): pp. 1–41.

19. See my article cited above in note 14.

20. I am here using Popper's terms, epistemological optimism and pessimism, to describe what Hayek meant. This problem is discussed in chapter I.

21. In Hayek vol. 2, p. 157, Hayek expresses reservations about this term of Popper's but without recognizing the split I see between him and Popper in this context.

22. See Thomas A. Metzger, *Escape from Predicament: Neo-Confucianism and China's Evolving Political Culture* (New York: Columbia University Press, 1977), ch. 3.

23. Hayek's view that institutionalizing a certain order including great respect for the free workings of the marketplace causes prosperity can be seen as a causal law of history basically corroborated by research today, as the latter has been summed up in the book edited by Myers and adduced in note 8 above. Hayek's worldwide impact is illustrated by the great fame and respect his translated writings now enjoy in China. The erudite translations and studies of his works by Teng Cheng-lai are at the center of this trend.

24. Apart from any theory about how law *should* evolve, it is far from clear to me that Hayek was empirically accurate if he claimed that law in fact evolved "spontaneously" as judges and others inferred rules from the inherited order. One can leave aside the question of whether inherited principles of justice regarding property were overturned when Lincoln abolished slavery and look at other laws about property transactions. In China before the modern era, as late as the early eighteenth century A.D., it was an inherited rule of justice that, if the market value of a piece of land increased after a

sale, the person who had sold it, even thirty years after the transaction, had a right to go back to the buyer and either buy back the land or demand a further payment. The buyer of land was also burdened with other obligations preventing him from freely selling his land. If he wanted to sell it and had found an eager buyer, he could not just close the deal. He first had to see whether others wanted to buy it: his relatives, neighbors, persons holding a mortgage on it, and the first person known to have owned the land, however long ago, as well as the latter's relatives. When new laws reflecting the rise of commerce began to appear around 1700 canceling these traditional restrictions, the idea of justice embodied in these new laws was hardly "consistent" with the old ideas of justice. On the contrary, the fact that officials at that time labeled the old ideas of justice "laughable" precisely shows that the new ideas of justice were incongruent with the old ones. (See Li Wen-chih's well-known discussion of this matter in *Li-shih yen-chiu*, 1963, vol. 4, pp. 90–91.) In other words, even narrowly defined "rules of just conduct," not just social-political institutions more broadly, sometimes were the product of enacted change and quantum jumps rather than rules merely applying ancient ideas of justice to new circumstances.

25. See the article on Eisenstadt adduced in note 13 above.

26. See chapter XII below.

27. The difficulties encountered by Hayek's political theory are only compounded in the case of Ayn Rand's libertarian effort to base political theory on a concept of "reason" that is as epistemologically optimistic as Hayek's but, unlike Hayek's, is divorced from the West's "axial" virtue tradition. Her iconoclastic attitude toward this humanistic-religious tradition, which is so basic to the liberalism of J.S. Mill, Hayek, and Popper, has much in common with the iconoclasm of liberal thinkers like Robert Nozick, Rawls, and Rorty. See Ayn Rand, *For the New Intellectual* (New York: A Signet Book, 1961).

～

CHAPTER X

What Is a Rational Political Theory? A Critique of John Rawls's "Political Liberalism"

1. The Challenge Posed by Rawls's "Political Liberalism"

James Bryant Conant University Professor Emeritus at Harvard University, John Rawls (1921–2002) is widely regarded as having made the greatest contribution in the twentieth century to the philosophy of liberalism. His main aim was to make clearer how the free and equal citizens of a democracy should form a shared set of norms minimizing the conflicts resulting from the divergences between their beliefs, and how they should define the just distribution of wealth, power, prestige, and other "primary goods." His fame is due to the fact that he was so thorough, erudite, systematic, subtle, original, and intellectually honest in this effort of his to shed light on two sets of normative principles: the economic norms implied by the globally widespread endorsement of freedom and equality as the highest political ideals ("distributive justice"); and the widely institutionalized distinction between substantive beliefs or interests and what Friedrich A. Hayek called "end-independent rules." As in the case of John Dunn, whether or not one agrees with Rawls's ideas, struggling to sort out and assess them is an invaluable way to explore what in this book I have called "political theory." Basing his concept of political rationality — to use my term — on an idea of "rational," "equal," "free," and "moral citizens" (to use his terms), Rawls may or may not have provided political theory with an epistemologically sound basis. Yet many persons, including me, regard these four adjectives as accurately describing themselves. For us, therefore, Rawls's reasoning is appealing.

Rawls's originality lies in his attempt to deduce the above norms from a theory long considered defunct, the doctrine of the social contract. More basically, he was startlingly bold in insisting that, without resorting to the implausible scientism of thinkers like Hayek, one could still derive moral-political norms from rationally ascertained principles and so could resist the ethical relativism encouraged by the Great Modern Western Epistemological Revolution (GMWER). As described in chapter I, the GMWER, typified by philosophers like David Hume and Karl R. Popper, produced the belief, widely accepted in the West, that the proper use of reason is limited to logic and experimentally tested conjectures about facts and so cannot yield objective criteria with which to endorse one moral or political norm over another. Rawls won the applause of philosophers by insisting on the rational pursuit of such criteria without ignoring many of the doubts about the possibility of such a pursuit. That is, to use Richard J. Bernstein's terms, Rawls rejected not only "relativism" but also any "objectivism" as the view that some universalistic, algorismic use of reason can directly establish moral-political norms. In effect, then, Rawls, like Bernstein or Dunn, worked the "middle ground" between relativism and objectivism to find a non-arbitrary basis for moral-political norms.

What he insisted he had found in this middle ground was a concept of "the reasonable" on which the ideal of justice and pluralism in a democracy could be based. In other words, if "rationality" refers, as few disagree, to the ability of all normal people to think in a logical way about instrumental and other matters, "the reasonable" mainly refers to important normative outlooks formed as rationality is applied to social life, even though the formation of such outlooks also depends on considerable reference to a particular cultural tradition. This subtle and challenging concept is Rawls's central contribution to contemporary philosophy, not his famous notion of "the original position," which was merely derived from it. As a distinctive way of weighting the relative contributions of rationality and culture to the formation of norms, his concept of "the reasonable" seems to hold its ground as a vital hypothesis about how all human beings form political norms. The bulk of this chapter of mine tries to expose its shortcomings as a basis for political theory, but in so assiduously exploring it, Rawls did not necessarily fail to shed light on a major facet of political life.

To form this concept, Rawls drew on a variety of sources. First of all, seeing himself as pursuing "political philosophy," Rawls, like Leo Strauss, drew on the tradition of Plato's *The Republic* in that he envisaged political philosophy as centering on the question of the goal of political life, a vision of the perfect society, or at least of a perfectly just one, instead of seeing political theory as a way of improving political life by understanding all the issues relevant to such improvement — not only the goal of justice but all goals, not only goals but also the means to reach them, not only goals and means but also other relevant aspects of the given world, including the conditions impeding improvement and the nature of knowledge. Rawls's political philosophy, one can say, is more Platonic than pragmatic.

Searching for a convincing way rationally to define the goal of justice and combine it with "a reasonable empiricist framework" (285), Rawls depended on Kant's idea of reason as "self-originating and self-authenticating" (100) and on Kant's distinction between "practical reason" and "theoretical reason" (93).[1] Trying to show how "practical reason" led to the doctrine of the social contract, Rawls followed "the Kantian form of this doctrine" (258–259). To show how the conclusions reached by practical reason differed from merely arbitrary opinion, Rawls also leaned on a concept of "educated common sense" connoting the Aristotelian tradition and made use of jurisprudential reasoning, examples of which he fluently adduced (e.g. 218).

The kind of positivism represented by Karl R. Popper's epistemology and Daniel Bell's *The End of Ideology* also was basic to Rawls's concept of reason, especially to his concept of "comprehensive doctrines," one of the pillars on which his "political liberalism" rests. For Rawls, just about everyone holds to a "comprehensive doctrine," which includes beliefs about what is ultimately true and good, Paul Tillich's matters of "ultimate concern," but most or all of these beliefs cannot be objectively verified or falsified in Popper's sense. Such beliefs, therefore, are outside the family of principles that can be "reasonably" accepted by all free and equal citizens living in a pluralistic, democratic society full of clashing beliefs. Proposing that such citizens accept a concept of "public reason" distinct from these ultimate beliefs, Rawls thus asked them to demote the epistemological status of their ultimate beliefs, turning these from eternal, universal truths into beliefs the truth of which was uncertain and could be rejected by "reasonable" persons. This epistemological demotion, dictated by positivism, was epitomized by the thought of Isaiah Berlin and indeed is the hallmark of the epistemological pessimism embodied in discourse #2, as discussed in chapter I.

Unlike Berlin, however, Rawls carried out this demotion in a brusque way exemplifying a certain new American iconoclastic liberalism. Like Robert Nozick's libertarianism, Rawls's liberalism broke with the classical humanistic liberalism of J.S. Mill, that is, it broke with Mill's humanistic vision of freedom as a condition based on "civilization" and "progress." For Mill, freedom was good especially because it was needed to pursue knowledge, which was needed to pursue progress. Without free competition among "opinions," Mill argued, false opinions generated by human fallibility would preclude progress, and "progress" included the rise of a "civilization" based on the Aristotelian and Biblical virtues.

In Rawls's discussion of freedom, however, the goal of "progress" and "civilization" played no explicit role. For him, "the priority of the basic liberties" stemmed not from a need to promote civilization and progress but from what "rational, equal, free, and moral" persons agreed was a "reasonable" way to form the "basic structure" of society and so give everyone an equal opportunity to pursue his or her goals, which were not necessarily focused on "progress" and certainly not on the European values and virtues Mill treasured and identified with "reason."

Thus, although Rawls repeatedly evoked "the most deep-seated convictions and traditions of a modern democratic state" (300), he cast doubt on that humanistic vision of the liberal project in Mill's "On Liberty," a vision indeed central to this democratic cultural heritage and to the original political design of the U.S.A. That is, for Mill, the value of freedom was inseparable from the "truths" established during the great moments of European civilization — the teachings of the Greek philosophers, those of Christ, the Renaissance, the Reformation, the rise of science, and German humanism.[2] Rawls, however, depicted these "truths" as merely making up one or another of the "comprehensive doctrines" available at that supermarket of beliefs where free and equal citizens could select whatever lifestyle they might prefer.

Admittedly, Rawls vacillated between this supermarket of belief systems and Mill's vision of civilization and progress as the necessary context of freedom. Rawls almost smuggled this Millsian vision back into his theory when he defined the "interests" legally pursued in his supermarket of beliefs as those of "rational, equal, free, moral" persons who, wanting "to develop and exercise" their "two moral powers" ("a capacity for a sense of justice and a capacity for a concept of the good"), tried to realize the "higher-order interests" corresponding to these powers.

In Rawls's eyes, therefore, the persons with whose interests the makers of the social contract were concerned were not people motivated only by the egotistic desire for pleasure, wealth, power, and prestige. They all had "a determinate conception of the good, that is, a conception specified by certain definite final ends, attachments, and loyalties to particular persons and institutions, and interpreted in the light of some comprehensive religious, philosophical, or moral doctrine" (19, 74, 76). Thus they were motivated by a "natural virtue," seeking to avoid "lack of self-respect and weakness of character" (370, 77). Yet the content of the "final ends" of Rawls's citizens was far less determinate than that of Mill's humanistic vision of virtue, progress, and civilization. In the broad way Rawls defined them, these "final ends" could as easily have been the goals of the dedicated Nazi soldiers in World War II as those of their British and American enemies.

Eclectic and, if coherent, not obviously so, Rawls's thought proved appealing to many as a vindication not only of democratic ideals put into doubt by the GMWER's ethical relativism but also of the Marxist and New Left criticisms of Western capitalism and democracy (e.g. 297). Like John Dunn, Rawls saw Western modernity as deeply marred by inequalities and denied that this impression of moral failure could be dismissed as just an arbitrary value judgment. Unlike Dunn, however, Rawls sought to base this moral impression on a systematic analysis of the normative implications of reason. Moreover, this novel rationalistic analysis of his not only pleased the New Left by calling for a massive redistribution of wealth. It also pleased critics of utilitarianism and libertarianism by seemingly showing that a rationalistic commitment to freedom and equality need not end up as an affirmation of bluntly egotistic pursuits *à la* Ayn Rand.

Even more, Rawls's thought remarkably synthesized two currently widespread American viewpoints usually seen as contradicting each other. On the one hand, implicitly but vividly, Rawls's celebration of conventional American ideals incarnated the belief that the U.S. political system, however flawed by inequalities, is based on an effort much stronger than any other in world history to realize the highest political principles of the Enlightenment, equality and freedom, and so was a model for the world. Contradicting John Dunn's or Max Weber's gloomy view of human history, Rawls's philosophy with its distinctively American, indeed Harvard optimism resembled the thought of another eminent Harvard scholar, Talcott Parsons, who celebrated the structure of U.S. society as leading humanity's progressive evolutionary trend toward increasing "differentiation," or that of the eminent Alex Inkeles, also long at Harvard, who saw "one world emerging" as people from different cultures "converged" in their search for a modern way of life. On the other hand, as already indicated, by mercilessly insisting on thorough implementation of the ideal of equality, Rawls gave strong theoretical support to the leftist trends holding that evil in the world today stems mainly from the way that the U.S. social structure generates drastic inequalities between not only social strata in the U.S. but also Americans and most of the other people on this planet. Thus emphasizing inequality as the cardinal American pathology, Rawls's thought gave support to that of liberal culture critics like Robert N. Bellah and differed from that of conservative ones like Christopher Lasch, who had instead focused on the disintegration of a complex "bourgeois" pattern of civilization.[3]

More broadly still, Rawls completely accepted an originally Marxist view that has become *de rigueur* throughout much of the American academy, that a society's "economic regime" shapes its "culture," being that part of a civilization which most deeply affects the "desires and aspirations" of a population (269). Hence Rawls's emphasis on distributive justice. The opposite view, that cultural patterns are neither derived from nor less important than economic ones, was succinctly summed up by Arnold Toynbee: "... the cultural element is the essence of a civilization and the economic and political elements are relatively trivial manifestations of the life that it has in it ..."[4] Such an emphasis on culture, as illustrated by the work of Lasch or Max Weber, leads to a kind of social criticism and sociology very different from Rawls's.

Rawls has thus won much applause by trying in a most original way to resist ethical relativism, to revive the Enlightenment's faith in reason, to avoid the reduction of practical reason to egotistic utilitarianism, to put practical reason into the service of a moral quest for freedom and equality, and to evoke the vision of the United States as a nation uniquely dedicated to this quest. On the other hand, Rawls's philosophical project has also been heavily criticized. For instance, John Dunn has said Rawls's work lacks "a philosophically defensible conception of the epistemological foundations of ethical theory." Dunn also perceptively focused on the key problem of any existential or concrete linkage between Rawls's highly abstract and general conceptualization of justice and the concrete decisions of historical persons using history-bequeathed beliefs to understand and try to improve their particular political situations.[5] Dunn's point speaks to the central question raised by Rawls's Popperian concept of reason, the relation between what people think is reasonable and their cultural milieu (see below).

I do not propose here, however, to weigh all of Rawls's arguments against all the criticisms of them. For one thing, I cannot here discuss his whole oeuvre. I shall deal only with the train of thought in his major 1993 book, *Political Liberalism,* which he saw as incorporating and further developing the thesis in his most famous book, *A Theory of Justice,* first published in 1971.[6] My aim is to show how his "political liberalism" illustrates the main points made in this book of mine.

Arguing that contemporary Western political theories largely exemplify discourse #2, discourse #3, or both, I think it will be plain that Rawls's theory, like Dunn's, arose out of the GMWER, exemplifies the epistemological pessimism of discourse #2, and clashes with the epistemological optimism still reigning virtually unchallenged in the Chinese intellectual world (see below, section 11). Apart from this descriptive point, I want to show how the nature of Rawls's thought supports my approach to the evaluation of political theories: my concept of what a political theory should be; my claim that, east and west, the world still lacks a "rational" or a "reasonable" political theory; and my claim that discourse #2 theories like Dunn's and Rawls's suffer from "the seesaw effect" in failing to weave their epistemological and factual points together with a concept of resolute, trustful, hopeful, and prudent collective action to pursue progress.

From my GMWER-bred standpoint, and, I think, from Dunn's or Rawls's as well, a political theory can only be an advertisement for an allegedly reasonable way to think about political life. Dunn and Rawls might or might not accept the logical implication of this point, namely, that just as an advertisement for an automobile cannot demonstrate the objective superiority of that which it advertises, so there is no single most reasonable advertisement for how to think politically, only juxtaposed, competing advertisements subject to the judgment of someone comparing them. Thus reasonableness or (in my terms) political rationality ultimately resides in that variable judgment made by someone evaluating advertisements such as Rawls's for "political liberalism" and my criticism of it.

Dunn and Rawls both also seem to imply, though they hardly emphasize, a second point about the nature of political theory, an idea about historical causation most systematically developed by Reinhard Bendix. That is, Bendix's concept of "intellectual mobilization" can be interpreted as the thesis that, when enough people are influenced by a particular advertisement for a certain way to think about political life, this change in their political thinking will eventually have an important effect on their political behavior and so on the formation of new political institutions.[7] By thus seeing political theories as advertisements sometimes changing political behavior, one can appreciate their importance in an era when it has become difficult to dignify them as ideas conveying truths either based on a sacred canon or obtained scientifically. In this chapter, therefore, I just want to juxtapose Rawls's advertisement with mine, offering readers two contrasting advertisements for how one should define political rationality as the criterion for choosing between political theories.

2. The Problem of Rationality in the Design of Political Theories

In chapters I, VIII, and IX, I offered three criteria of rationality in the case of political theories: (1) avoidance of the "common lapses," such as contradiction and neglect of relevant topics; (2) avoidance of "the seesaw effect," that is, either emphasizing factual accuracy and respect for the limits of knowledge while failing to develop a concept of resolute, trustful, hopeful, and prudent political action, or developing the latter while failing to emphasize the former; and (3) relevance to the problems of political life in non-Western, undemocratic countries, not only to those of the liberal democracies in the West. (Actually, the third criterion can be logically subsumed under the second.)

These criteria, I argued, can be used to distinguish reasonable from unreasonable theories about the topics that political theory should address. Rawls's work, however, has made me better realize that the reasonableness of a political theory depends on not only reasonably discussing the topics it does discuss but also reasonably devising a list of the topics that should be discussed.

The problem of rationality in political theories thus begins with an observation that seems to be accurate regarding a widespread if not universal characteristic of human thinking, that unlimited regressiveness of reflexivity allowing one to ask what the reasonable starting point of political theories should be, then to ask whether it is reasonable to worry about what the reasonable starting point of political theories should be, and so on *ad infinitum.* Yet whatever might be the best way to handle this regressiveness, my starting point is that political theory has to be a way of maximizing a critical perspective on political life, as opposed to just building on conventional beliefs; that such a critical perspective depends on probing as deeply as possible into the meaning of political rationality or reasonableness; and that such probing begins by addressing what I would call "the initial questions," such as: What is the nature of political theory and what is its purpose and starting point (e.g. is it a search for scientific truth? an "advertisement"? a quest for "critical perspective"?)? What are the topics political theory should address? What are the sources of or the historical trends leading to the definition of these topics?

My answer to these initial questions consists of the post-GMWER epistemological and ontological ideas in chapter I, culminating in the idea of public political discussion as consisting of one or more discourses each of which "paradoxically" blurs together the reflexive ability to refer to objective truth with historically bequeathed, culturally formed premises. According to the premises or "rules of successful thinking" of my we-group (many of which are listed in chapter I, section 11), thinking about political life has to conceptualize the goals of political life, the means to reach them, other relevant aspects of the given world, and the nature of knowledge. These rules also include the three criteria of political rationality above — avoiding the "common lapses," avoiding "the seesaw effect," and dealing with all the conditions of progress or improvement, not only those pertaining to the Western democracies.

If, then, one seeks to define political rationality, probes into "the initial questions," and arrives at this framework, one can also begin to list the more specific questions that a political theory based on this framework of rationality has to address. The writings of Dunn and Rawls helped me to become more aware of the following nine. (This list is a revised version of the list of eight offered in chapter VIII.)

First, is the pursuit of political theory to some extent a rhetorical act, or is it a strictly discursive effort to be as logical and systematic as possible? Chapter VIII argued that Dunn leans more than a bit in the former direction. Certainly political theory is to some extent rhetorical in that it entails a spiritual act, a decision about the extent to which one should be hopeful about the future. In this regard, Rawls's strongly American optimism is in striking contrast with the darker view taken by a Dunn or a Weber. Moreover, as just indicated, political theory is a rhetorical act to the extent that it is an advertisement. I would say, though, that such an intellectual advertisement is rhetorically more effective when it makes its case as logically and systematically as possible. From this standpoint, I admire Rawls's philosophy.

Second, what is the right typology of ideas? The GMWER argued strongly that the normative ideas a political theory needs cannot be forms of objective knowledge in Popper's sense, i.e. true propositions about human realities like history or the universal nature of human nature. In the post-Popperian milieu, however, a further question arose. If they are not true propositions, are they linguistic symbols the meaningfulness of which is wholly or partly embedded within a particular historical-cultural milieu? Or are they intentionally constructed by using a reflexivity essentially uninfluenced by culture? Rawls leaned in the latter direction, as illustrated by his Kantian concept of "constructivism" (89–94), while post-Popperian approaches have leaned in the former, as illustrated by the concept of discourse discussed in chapter I, or by Richard Rorty's "pragmatism," discussed in chapter XIII.

Third, what is the clearest way to use whatever ideas are available? One answer to this question revolves around the problem of analytical disaggregation. As discussed in chapter VIII, Dunn favors a holistic concept of "political understanding." To me, however, "understanding" something means properly applying to it types of propositions that cannot be clear unless they are distinguished from each other (descriptive, causative, predictive, evaluative, recommendatory, and epistemological propositions). Indeed, the nature of clarity is a highly controversial issue, as illustrated in chapter I by the discussion of the conflicting views about how to describe ideas. When Rawls refers to "our considered convictions" without specifying the antecedent of "our," is he being clear enough? Is he clear enough when he refers to "the public political culture of a democratic society"? In describing a culture, is it important to distinguish between an etic and an emic form of description?

This issue of clarity blends into that of modes of clarification, the intellectual "exercises," so to speak, needed to make a political theory as specific as possible and to maximize one's critical perspective on political life. The nature of the exercise depends largely on one's typology of ideas. As discussed below, the exercise I recommend differs from the one Rawls designed, just as our typologies of ideas differ.

Fourth, there is the problem of the ultimate basis of political goals. As chapter I noted, "objectivistic" thinking of the discourse #3 or discourse #1 variety finds this basis in reason as a homogenous faculty possessed by all normal persons or in rationally discovered principles integral to objective human realities like history or the universal nature of human nature. In other words, if there are concepts that are largely free of cultural bias, and that accurately denote such realities, some of these realities, contrary to David Hume, carry a normative message. Significantly, even in the context of the GMWER and discourse #2, thinkers like Dunn and Rawls have repeatedly tried to depict the universal nature of human nature, an actually metaphysical object, as somehow implying moral norms. Nevertheless, given the skepticism of the GMWER, both of these scholars have also relied on the tactic of privileging a given historical body of learning and ideals (see below). As I tried to discuss in chapter VIII, there are still other possible ways of grounding normative concepts.

Fifth, whatever the ultimate basis for political goals, what should they be? Here Rawls's exclusionary focus on the goal of justice is questionable, as discussed below.

Sixth, as discussed in chapter VIII, the relation of goals to the moral limbo of history is another question the answers to which range from utopianism to piecemeal progress to passivity or fatalism. Rawls as a person certainly is comfortable with a position in the middle of this spectrum, but his theory tends logically to incline toward utopianism, in that he explicitly put forward a program of progress designed for "rational," "equal," "free," and "moral" citizens and held it was feasible (see below). A less optimistic view is that political life always consists of interactions among people who to a large extent are irrational, unequal, unfree, and immoral, and that therefore practicable political reforms are those improving such permanently deficient interactions, not those trying to turn such interactions into a community of free, equal, rational, and moral citizens. Indeed, while Rawls claimed to invoke the basic ideals of American democracy, Arthur O. Lovejoy, another distinguished American philosopher, showed that the Founding Fathers presupposed the continuing immorality of American citizens.[8] To put it another way, Max Weber agreed with Aristotle that practicable political organization cannot be based on the highest moral ideals, but Rawls held that society could practicably implement the highest principles of justice.

The problem here, however, is not only utopianism but also the broader one of conceptualizing effective action to improve political life. In this regard, I agree that both Rawls and Dunn left liberalism in that quandary of passivity to which Carl Schmitt pointed.[9] To be sure, Schmitt's analysis differs from mine. His epistemology was more optimistic than mine, since he saw political rationality as an obvious, objective standard, and he viewed political life as having a knowable, objective essence. Also, he saw liberalism's passivity in terms of a parliamentarianism turning politics into irrational discussion and the search for deals between interest groups, while my "seesaw effect" emphasizes the epistemological aspect of this passivity. While the fecklessness of the Weimar Republic brought this passivity to his attention, it was brought to mine by the contrast between China's discourse #1 and the West's discourse #2. Most important, while we both call for resolute political action, he saw the latter as meeting the need to kill enemies, while I see it as meeting the need to pursue progress and as requiring a definition of progress as a standard with which to figure out who the enemy is. Nevertheless, the resemblance between his famous argument and the point I am trying to make is not superficial.

My argument about the passivity in the political thought of Dunn, as discussed in chapter VIII, turns on his dark view of human nature, history, and politics as largely not susceptible to moral improvement. Rawls of course had an optimistic if not utopian view of these matters. In looking at the empirical nature of democracies, however, he concluded that the two needs which political theory must address are the lack of justice in the distribution of largely economic goods and the difficulty pluralistic societies have in forming consensus minimizing conflict. Thus while his concept of reasonableness, to the extent it was epistemologically tenable, logically supported his goal of social harmony and distributive justice, it was silent with regard to all the other political goals progress entails (see below). It left these to what Schmitt had called "discussion."

In other words, by distinguishing between "the reasonable" as the basis of consensus in a society and "the good" as the ultimate standard of an individual or association, Rawls tried to solve the problem of how disparate, irreconcilable definitions of "the good" can peacefully coexist in a democracy. But political progress lies in the collective pursuit of what Leo Strauss called "the good society." How can this pursuit be possible if the good as a characteristic of society is limited to distributive justice and the absence of domestic conflict?

Forming a full concept of this good, the framework of "progress," "civilization," "virtue," and "reason" into which J.S. Mill put the pursuit of freedom and equality is different from Rawls's concept of society as an arena designed only to maximize the ability of an individual freely to pursue his or her private good or end. Mill's framework suffered especially from problems of definition, but Rawls's framework left society without a shared commitment active and broad enough to deal with all the dangers threatening collective well-being. That is a major reason why the mainstream of political reflection in China has continued to resist it.

Seventh, to the extent that one does seek some progress, to what extent does one find the causative patterns of history to be knowable or opaque? How high a standard of precision should analyses of history meet? Rawls did not deal with this question, while Dunn's thought just about precluded resolute collective action by insisting on the need for an extremely precise understanding of historical causative patterns that, in his eyes, are largely unknowable.

Eighth, from what can be empirically known about history, what can one conclude about it? What are the basic structures of society? What are the means available to seek improvement? A major issue here is the tension between the economism of Marx and the culturalism of Weber, along with Bendix's issue of "intellectual mobilization." Rawls's economism is one of his theory's building blocks. Also, to what extent has history exhibited enough progress to nourish hope for future progress? This historical question is logically connected to the spiritual issue adduced above. For Rawls, history, driven by beneficent human "capacities" and "desires," has displayed much progress.

This eighth issue, however, also raises a major question generally neglected in writings on political theory, including those of Rawls and Dunn. Since a political theory, as I see it, is a theory about progress, about how to improve political life, how can it be useful without specifically indicating to whose political life it pertains — all of humanity's? the political life of a class of societies, such as Millsian democracies? that of one society in particular? Political philosophy is still in the grip of the traditional ambition to reveal the political logic of human history as a whole (*jen-lei li-shih-te tsung-t'i*), although Rawls and Dunn perhaps put this ambition to one side a bit. It is obvious to me, however, that political theory must deal with the improvement of a particular society's political life, and that it cannot do so without first analyzing current conditions in that society so as to judge which recommendations could practicably effect more improvement than is already under way. Using this criterion, one cannot easily find any successful political theory, east or west.

Ninth, to be rational, a political theory in today's world of culturally and nationalistically disparate intellectual circles must look for a framework maximally evading indigenous intellectual orientations that have not yet undergone critical scrutiny. This is the question of "epistemic smugness" discussed in chapter I. A central problem, paradoxically unmitigated by either cultural relativism or the fashionable emphasis today on "open," cross-cultural "dialogue," is the deep-rooted Western belief that non-Western conceptions of knowledge and political philosophy are significant only as cultural artifacts. Thus Leo Strauss raised no eyebrows when he identified the history of political philosophy with its history in the West. Rawls's thought implies a similar assumption that there is no urgent need for Western philosophers to become more aware of non-Western conceptualizations of knowledge and political life. If Kant saw reason as "self-originating and self-authenticating," the Western tradition of political philosophy has defined itself as a self-sufficient source of insight, a set of categories without competitors in the world today, as John Dunn put it.

On the other hand, many Chinese intellectuals today, feeling themselves intellectually subjugated by the West, have sought the "sinification" of the social sciences. Seeking it, they have argued that the value of a category can depend on its geographical origin, not only on its analytical usefulness.[10] As illustrated by Yeh Ch'i-cheng's new book (see below, section 11), scholars with this viewpoint are able to reduce the whole Weberian or Durkheimian social science tradition to an imperialistic or spiritually misbegotten impulse inflicted by the West on China. They also exaggerate the extent to which Chinese political thought has been subjugated by the West, credulously accepting simplistic Western claims that this subjugation has occurred. This approach is not based on an empirical description of China's modern intellectual evolution taking into account those persisting continuities with tradition just about impervious to Western influence.

When one uses these nine issues to critique Rawls's overall conceptualization of political rationality, one realizes that this overall conception of his was made up of not only his explicit thoughts about "the reasonable" but also many other ideas which he regarded as true or acceptable. This overall conception is best understood by looking at how he dealt with the initial questions, the typology of ideas, the problem of what is factually true about the structure of society, the problem of which normative ideas to privilege, and the problem of how to construct a clarifying exercise. As I see it, Rawls mishandled these issues, thus failed to avoid "the seesaw effect," and thus failed to produce a rational political theory.

With this approach, my focus is not on the two most famous aspects of his "political liberalism," the idea of "the original position" and that of "reasonable pluralism." As already noted, both these ideas were derivative, because they presupposed his complex concept of "the reasonable," which in turn depended entirely on his typology of ideas. Also critical were his economism, his strong optimism about history, and his main conclusion when he looked into "the initial questions," namely, that clarifying the nature of perfect political justice is the purpose of political theory.

Thus criticizing his conceptualization of political rationality, however, I have found it hard to find any of "the common lapses" in the thought of this outstandingly able philosopher. Yet no thinker can entirely avoid such lapses, as Rawls would be the first to agree.

I would note, therefore, that besides the problem of excessive redundancy, some of Rawls's distinctions seem to be elusive. When he said "society as a whole has no ends … in the way … individuals do" (276), this note of ontological individualism is not easy to reconcile with his concept of "'a social union of social unions'" (320). He wanted to contrast "the good" as an idea pursued by individuals with "the reasonable" as the basis of society (30). Yet he also said that a just democratic society "can be for each citizen a far more comprehensive good than the determinate good of individuals when left to smaller associations" (320). Indeed, if reasonableness, as Rawls defined it, could, as he hoped, become the norm respected throughout a society, how would that not be a huge good, an end with which any reasonable individual would identify herself or himself? Similarly, in trying to distinguish between a societal consensus based on moral beliefs and one based on a "freestanding" "political conception of justice," Rawls was perhaps more provocative than clear (see below).

In the rest of this chapter, I shall describe Rawls's overall concept of political rationality and explain further how it can be criticized. I start, however, with a premise of his that he inherited from the GMWER, and that I too would accept, at least heuristically.

3. The Epistemological Demotion of Normative Ideas

This demotion was the part of the GMWER that Rawls accepted, in contrast with his rejection of another GMWER insight, the post-Kantian tendency, German in origin, to emphasize the historical-cultural content of ideas originally viewed as concepts simply denoting objective reality. Rawls was certainly reasonable in avoiding the scientism used by Hayek and all the other theories holding that the principles of moral-political praxis can be derived from nothing but "logic" and "facts," as Hayek put it — all the theories making up what I have called "discourse #3." Rawls fully accepted that epistemological demotion of normative propositions demanded by the GMWER, the recognition, eloquently expressed by Isaiah Berlin, that normative beliefs cannot be ideas which one can know to be true about the objective nature of any reality, that they to some extent take the form of mere personal or group convictions which other people can reject without making untrue statements.

Rawls was fully aware of the complexity and paradoxical nature of this epistemological demotion. On the one hand, relativism was out of the question (58, 62): human beings do not just live in a chaos of conflicting opinions about what ought to be done. They or at least some of them find themselves using words such as "reason" and "reasonable" on the general meaning of which they agree, and which is that of a standard everyone should respect. So ethical discussion cannot escape this minimum level of consensus. Hence ethical discussion necessarily includes ideas put forward by a we-group, not only by one individual, by a "we," not only an "I." For instance, commenting on Kant's idea of reason as a process specifying "its own principles and canons of validity," Rawls said: "*We* cannot ground these principles and canons on something outside reason.... With these concepts explanations come to an end; one of philosophy's tasks is to quiet *our* distress at this thought" (120–121 n. 26; italics added). Language itself, as an inherently valuable (*pace* David Hume) aspect of thought, thus includes a horizon of universal meaning conceived of as something viewed by humanity as a whole, by "us." Even if ethical ideas cannot be ideas known to be true about an objective reality, they seem necessarily to involve this universalistic horizon as well as "because" propositions referring to matters of objective fact (on the latter, see chapter I). Moreover, as Rawls saw it, the "objectivity" of a judgment was a criterion contingent on the "point of view" defined as the starting point of that judgment. Therefore, he held, normative ideas could be "objective" even if not susceptible to being judged as "true" (111).

On the other hand, Rawls said: "But since we are using our

reason to describe itself and reason is not transparent to itself, we can misdescribe our reason as we can anything else" (96–97). Not surprisingly, therefore, "the idea of the reasonable especially, whether applied to persons, institutions, or doctrines, easily becomes vague and obscure" (48). Thus the GMWER note of tentativeness permeated the way Rawls set forth his central epistemological doctrine, "constructivism": "... the idea is to formulate a procedural representation in which, so far as possible, all the relevant criteria of correct reasoning — mathematical, moral, or political — are incorporated and open to view" (102). In other words, "reasonable" ideas are typically inconclusive:

> If sound, these remarks suggest that in philosophy questions at the most fundamental level are not usually settled by conclusive argument. What is obvious to some persons and accepted as a basic idea is unintelligible to others. The way to resolve the matter is to consider after due reflection which view, when fully worked out, offers the most coherent and convincing account. About this, of course, judgments may differ. (53)

For Rawls, then, statements were not reasonable or unreasonable but more or less reasonable and "appropriate" (lxii, 107). People were only able to create definitions of the criteria by which to evaluate different normative concepts in order to see which "best" met these criteria. Introducing his main normative concept, "justice as fairness," Rawls said: "I believe ... [it] to be the most reasonable conception because it best" accords with the criteria he presented: "But while I view it as the most reasonable (even though many reasonable people seem to disagree with me), I shouldn't deny that other conceptions also satisfy the definition of a liberal conception" (xlviii–xlix).

As Rawls and others (including me) thus accept the GMWER's epistemological demotion of normative ideas, giving all of them a quality of tentativeness, how then can any of us argue that one tentative normative idea is less tentative or "more reasonable" than another? This is an open-ended problem I tried to discuss when juxtaposing my "advertisement" with Dunn's in chapter VIII. Now juxtaposing mine with Rawls's, I shall look at how Rawls treated the initial questions, the typology of ideas, the question of empirically accurate analyses of the human condition, the question of the exercise needed to pursue morally critical awareness, and the linked question of which ideas to privilege.

4. Rawls and the Initial Questions

According to my "rules of successful thinking," the purpose of a reasonable political theory is to improve a concrete society's political life by understanding it as it currently is, by maximizing critical perspective on it rather than just adopting conventional beliefs, by making practicable recommendations about how to improve it, and then by advertising these recommendations with the hope of changing political behaviors and institutions. Given this purpose, a reasonable political theory cannot just discuss one political goal such as realizing a just system of cooperation between free and equal citizens, because the improvement of political life requires pursuit of a considerable number of goals. A good political life entails not only a just form of governance but also economic prosperity, national security, the promotion of a rich cultural tradition (including the whole issue of *paideia*), the solution of global problems, especially ecological ones, and no doubt other conditions. For instance, one could compare two different kinds of political life: (a) a perfectly just political structure guaranteeing freedom and equality in an economically backward society with a tropical climate, lacking any literate cultural tradition, and vulnerable to conquest by foreign enemies; and (b) an unjust political structure in a prosperous society located on the northern shores of the Mediterranean, enjoying a rich civilizational heritage, and able to defend itself against foreign enemies. If one were in Rawls's "original position" and had to choose to live in either (a) or (b) without knowing in advance what one's social status in that society would be, would one necessarily prefer (a) over (b)? Would one necessarily prefer establishing a perfectly just society in a Sahara oasis to living in undemocratic China?

Nor can one say that promoting equality and freedom is a political problem, while promoting economic prosperity, national defense, and education are non-political problems. Political life is precisely concerned with coordinating efforts to deal with all such problems. Therefore, a political theory has to explain how to prioritize all such efforts. Prioritization includes the key problem of how to define the parameters of freedom, as discussed in chapter I. That is, if the goal of just governance includes the ability of citizens equally and freely to interact in "the three marketplaces," their freedom will be bounded to the extent that other goals are judged to have priority over it. This is illustrated by Hayek's point that national emergencies may require limiting individual rights (see chapter IX).

Rawls certainly was aware that the quality of political life depends on pursuing a variety of goals besides justice, and that these goals have to be put into a hierarchy of priority which cannot be determined a priori. He knew that his political theory presupposed "the relatively favorable conditions that make a constitutional democracy possible." As he saw it, these "reasonably favorable conditions.... are determined by a society's culture, its traditions and acquired skills in running institutions, and its level of economic advance ... and no doubt by other things as well." Thus "the priority of liberty ... is not required under all conditions" (297, 155). In other words, when conditions are unfavorable, other goals may have priority over the liberties ensured by his conception of justice. Moreover, he granted that it was not yet clear how all political goals can be logically subsumed under his "political conception of justice," and that therefore he had not yet satisfied those who think that his conceptualization of justice and of "public reason.... leaves many questions without answers" (244).

Rawls's political theory, however, sheds little light on how to prioritize political goals. He did not even list the variety of goals and discuss the causal relations among them. Granting that the lack of "favorable conditions" may require rearranging priorities, he did not analyze the complex question of how such conditions affect goals, even though this lack of "favorable conditions" is typical of political life in so much of the world. He argued that, through some kind of extrapolation, the "political values" implicit in his "political conception of justice.... should admit of a balance giving a reasonable answer for all or nearly all fundamental questions" (244–245). Yet his examples of such extrapolation (243, 250) were extremely limited. He also argued that, whether or not all political goals can be subsumed under that of a just political order based on freedom and equality, the latter goal should enjoy a certain priority: "The priority of liberty implies in practice that a basic liberty can be limited or denied solely for the sake of one or more other basic liberties, and never, as I have said, for reasons of public good or of perfectionist values" (295). This "never," however, is hard to accept. As already noted, Rawls said the priority of liberty is contingent on "favorable conditions." Granting that there are "political questions" outside the "questions of basic justice," he seemed to view these as merely minor or technical questions (214). Yet how to reconcile the goal of justice with goals like prosperity and national security is a major political problem. According to Li Tse-hou, this was the central problem faced by Chinese political thought in the twentieth century, the seemingly unavoidable need to limit freedom and individual rights in order to save China from being overwhelmed by domestic and foreign sources of oppression and disruption (*chiu-wang ya-tao ch'i-meng*).

More generally still, how to prioritize goals might be a lesser problem if political life could be improved by simply enacting laws through which Rousseau's magnificently appealing concept of democracy — rule by the governed — would be realized. Laws, however, cannot by themselves realize rule by the governed, not to mention improve political life. Even apart from the threat of being subjugated by foreigners, the improvement of a society's political life, I would argue, depends on informal domestic patterns of political power and on the culture or discourse of the voting citizens, not only on the laws defining justice. This point shows again that the problem of improving the political life of a concrete society cannot be analyzed by just analyzing the nature of a perfectly just society. Political theory has to move from Platonic contemplation to pragmatism.

From my standpoint, therefore, a successful, reasonable political theory raises "the initial questions," which include definition of the purpose of political theory; concludes that this purpose is improving the political life of a concrete society; sees that improving it requires pursuit of a variety of goals; and offers guidelines for prioritizing these goals. Rawls, however, did not conceptualize the idea of initial questions about the nature of political theory and instead assumed that his purpose as a political philosopher was to make clear the nature of one goal, a just society formed by free and equal citizens.

This assumption stemmed from his somewhat simplistic perspective on the history of political philosophy. His starting point was human life in a "society" with a "basic structure," that is, "a society's main political, social, and economic institutions, and how they fit together into one unified system of cooperation from one generation to the next" (11). This "basic structure of society" was subject to changeable "principles" with which to "regulate" it (xxii).

So there was a choice between "political relations ... governed by power and coercion alone" and a "reasonably just society that subordinates power to its aims" (lxii). Simplistically assuming that this black-or-white choice constituted the options universally faced by people, Rawls viewed selection of the latter option as somehow necessary or natural. Given this commitment to the ideal of justice, the nature of justice became a major issue:

> [It] has been the focus of the liberal critique of aristocracy in the seventeenth and eighteenth centuries, of the socialist critique of liberal constitutional democracy in the nineteenth and twentieth centuries, and of the conflict between liberalism and conservatism at the present time over the claims of private property and the legitimacy (as opposed to the effectiveness) of the social policies associated with what has come to be called the "welfare state." It is this question that fixes the initial boundaries of our discussion. (22)

Thus the purpose of his two main books, *A Theory of Justice* and *Political Liberalism,* was to "try to sketch out what the more reasonable conceptions of justice for a democratic regime are" (lxii). These conceptions of justice, in turn, centered on two problems in his eyes: distributive justice and definition of the shared norms permitting the peaceful coexistence of people with irreconcilable beliefs about matters of ultimate concern ("comprehensive doctrines").

Having thus narrowed the discussion of political goals down to the issue of justice, Rawls also failed to focus on other questions that have to be grasped by people trying to improve their political life, notably, the means best suited to pursue goals, and other aspects of the given world, especially the question of historical causation. According to my "rules of successful thinking," a people cannot improve their political life unless they pursue an understanding of what actions or conditions will cause what effects, and the main if not the only way to seek this understanding of causes affecting the future is to study what caused what in the past. A rational political theory, therefore, has to deal convincingly with the kinds of historical and historiographical questions outlined in section 2 of this chapter.

Like my view of goals, my answers to these questions about the nature of history differ from Rawls's. For instance, I think that the culturally-rooted discourse of a society is central to its "basic structure," not only its "main political, social, and economic institutions." My point here, however, is not that Rawls's answers to such questions about history are to a large extent unreasonable from the standpoint of my "rules of successful thinking." At this point, my only claim is that Rawls failed adequately to raise "the initial questions."

Another of these questions is: what are the historical trends that have shaped my own way of defining and addressing the topics political theory should address? Had Rawls paid more attention to the historical background of his own epistemological outlook, he might have developed his outlook more reasonably. This historical issue especially entails the skeptical trends I have called "the GMWER." When discussing the historical trends leading to his own agenda, however, Rawls never referred to this rising skepticism. What interested him was the belief, growing since the Reformation, that all normal persons were morally autonomous and so not subject to principles and sanctions stemming from some institutional or cosmic source outside themselves (xxviii–xxix). For Rawls, the problem they then faced was how to make use of their autonomy by designing a moral order on their own. He did not fully confront the other problem they faced: whether autonomous persons unguided by any objective truths about a given moral order could produce any moral notions except arbitrary, biased opinions.

In other words, if the history of modern moral-political thought can be seen as a process liberating the ability of people to create a moral order on their own, it can also be seen as one leaving them unguided by any norms except those a particular group was accustomed to prefer. Conceptualizing only the former aspect of this history, *Political Liberalism* did not fully discuss the crucial epistemological questions raised by the latter, especially the key issue of the relation between reason or common sense and culturally-produced orientations. It was this issue, more than any other, on which Rawls's concept of "the reasonable" foundered.

5. Rawls's Popperian Typology of Ideas and the Problem of Culturally-rooted Discourses

According to the post-Popperian typology of ideas worked out in chapter I, natural science may or may not be largely embedded in the kinds of historically-bequeathed, socially formed paradigms discussed by Thomas Kuhn.[11] In the case of all ideas about moral-political praxis, however, the reflexive ability to refer to universal truths, objective realities, and "reasonable" considerations seems to be paradoxically inseparable from symbolic, linguistic forms arising out of a limited part of humanity's historical-cultural heritage and so constituting ideas meaningful or even true to people with that particular heritage but quite possibly untrue, unreasonable, or even meaningless to people without it. In other words, at least in the case of thinking about moral-political praxis, the *Lebenswelt*, there is no clean separation between Popper's "world three" of falsifiable descriptive, causal, and predictive propositions and his "world two" made up of mere "beliefs" or "states of mind."[12]

Even more, in this context, descriptive, causal, predictive, evaluative, recommendatory, and epistemological propositions are logically interdependent and make up discourses simultaneously rooted in a particular cultural tradition and reflexively open to objections in the name of universal truth and objective reality. As illustrated by discourses #1 and #2, discussed in chapter I, the tradition-rooted beliefs basic to a discourse shape not only the context of political goals and the moral evaluation of events but also the description of current domestic and international trends, of causative patterns in the historical past, of probable future trends, and of the kinds of means available to cause future outcomes, as well as the discussion of ontological reality and of epistemological criteria with which to identify "evidence" about causes. Therefore there is only a limited distinction between instrumental reasoning subject to empirical falsification and culturally-determined goals to which the criterion of truth is irrelevant.

Whether in metaphysical theories or in Rawls's Popperian typology of ideas, however, the role of such cultural traditions in the formation of ideas is strongly limited. To be sure, for Rawls, some kinds of ideas indeed are culturally-formed beliefs that can be neither verified nor falsified even if some people regard them as forms of knowledge. In his eyes, however, some very important kinds of ideas are either true or so broadly accepted that they should be deemed "reasonable." Moreover, to the extent that he mentions it, culture for Rawls is purely a third-person concept, a characteristic that can be noted when describing the lives of other people. He does not conceive of culture as influencing not only the world out there but also categories like "society" and "culture" that he himself has used to interpret what is out there (see below). Rawls's rationalism depicts him as standing on a Kantian platform high above the cultures or traditions that history has formed. His writing is empty of the suspicion that his thinking too is embedded in that tendency he observes in others to perpetuate historically-bequeathed values, and that others have shared with him both the reflexivity enabling him to transcend such values and the continuing adulteration of this reflexivity by such values.

In *Political Liberalism*, Rawls never summed up his typology of ideas, not to mention critically assessing it. Yet one can say it distinguished between six types of ideas. First, there were ideas any individual happens to have, including "claims" made by someone and regarded by her as inherently "valid" for whatever reason (32). Second, there were "comprehensive religious and philosophical doctrines — ... what we as individuals or members of associations see as the whole truth.... A doctrine is fully comprehensive when it covers all recognized values and virtues within one rather precisely articulated scheme of thought" (224–225, 175, 13). Such doctrines are typically "incompatible" with each other (xviii), and it would be "delusional" to try to give any comprehensive doctrine "a true foundation" (xx). Third, close to the latter were the ideas in the documented history of moral and political philosophy, which Rawls saw as a necessary asset for the pursuit of "political philosophy" (45). These, one could say, appeared to him as the privilegeable aspects of "comprehensive doctrines" (see below). Privileging them, he saw them as forming a "culture" or a "tradition" (see below). Fourth, Rawls depended much on a certain accumulation of human wisdom, using terms such as "plain truths now widely accepted, or available, to citizens generally" (225); "common sense" (224); "educated common sense of citizens generally" (14); "principles associated with the moral virtues recognized by common sense such as truthfulness and fidelity" (83); "considerations familiar from everyday life" (23); and "general beliefs shared by citizens as part of public knowledge" (70). Admittedly, these notions did not unambiguously refer to the wisdom accumulated by all of humankind and tended to connote Rawls's way of privileging the conventional beliefs in democratic societies (see below).

Fifth, Rawls emphasized "knowledge" obtained scientifically or otherwise, especially the knowledge of "facts." The establishment of constitutions "is guided by the general knowledge of how political and social institutions work, together with the general facts about existing social circumstances" (336–337). One can depend on "the methods and conclusions of science when these are not controversial" (224). These included the conclusions produced by "the theory of human nature" (70), including knowledge of "the laws of nature and human psychology" (xlii). Thus his political theory "tries to specify the most reasonable conception of the person that the general facts about human nature and society seem to allow" (87). Sixth, there was the type of ideas filling Rawls's books, ways of critically inquiring into, reflecting on, and reasoning about problems so as to justify one conclusion or another, producing "considered judgments on due reflection" (381) and seeking "reflective equilibrium," which he defined as a state "when judgments at all levels generally are in line on due reflection" (458, 95, 9, 381–384). Thus the "full justification of the public conception of justice.... includes everything we would say — you and I — when we set up justice as fairness and reflect on why we proceed in one way rather than another" (67).

Conceptualizing the latter four types of ideas, Rawls wanted to accent the Kantian vision of human reflection as a process that was "self-originating and self-authenticating" (100) rather than shaped by any disparate cultural heritage. For Rawls, reflection could and should be shaped not by any such inherited pattern but by "procedures" freely and deliberately thought up by an individual. True, Rawls recognized that, as meaningful objects, facts were not just given, they were products of human interpretation. For him, however, such interpretation was basically shaped not by a cultural heritage but by "a constructivist procedure yielding principles and precepts to identify which facts are to count as reasons" (122). Again, if people disagreed, Rawls was interested in how disagreement was caused not by divergences between their discourses but by the "burdens of judgment" that were faced by all reasoning humans, no matter what their culturally different discourses. These burdens included the way that "evidence — empirical and scientific — ... is ... hard to assess," and the fact that the "weight" to be put on different considerations is hard to determine (56–57).

Rawls alluded to the concept of culture when he referred to how "the way we assess evidence and weigh moral and political values is shaped by our total experience, our whole course of life up to now ..." This formulation, however, was still far from the idea of shared cultural orientations. So was his point that another "burden" consisted of the way people were "forced to select among cherished values" (54–57). A discourse or cultural pattern is to a large extent unconsciously inherited and heteronomously imposed on children, not "selected." Rawls granted that "psychology may enter in" when one asks why people have differently coped with "the burdens of judgment" (121). Again, however, he was not referring to the culturally-rooted discourses discussed in chapter I, not to mention his implication that psychology may not "enter in."

So central to his typology of ideas, Rawls's downplay of the role of culture not only accorded with naive self-consciousness (the assumption that what I think is simply what I myself think up). It also embodied the idea associated with John Dewey that, outside of what I myself think up or can creatively contribute, culture is not of great value for me.

To be sure, I do not claim that Rawls himself, an obviously cultured person, either accepted this naive self-consciousness uncritically or failed to appreciate the great civilizational riches which he could enjoy without having himself created them. According to the philosophical construction he put into *Political Liberalism*, however, a culture cumulatively created by huge numbers of gifted people over many centuries and inherited by a contemporary society was neither a priceless resource that should be critically used to improve education and political life nor a disparate set of premises shaping the philosophical tradition, common sense, factual understanding, and critical reflections of those inheriting it.

Preoccupied with the need for "fairness" in the "basic structure of a society," Rawls had an image of culture that evoked the common American ideal of "team spirit," the American pioneer spirit, the memory of frontier communities in which barn-raising was carried out by neighbors voluntarily pooling their individual skills. From this standpoint, the "basic structure" of both society and of thought depended on the freely formed intentions of individuals aiming for the fair distribution of essentially economic goods, not on the heavy hand of any cultural pattern created on many other occasions by many other people in the past and so outside the control of pioneers in the present determined freely to take charge of their own destiny.

Rawls's philosophy is infused with that famous vision of America as a fresh start in a new continent unburdened by the difficult heritage of European history.

His point was that "fair terms of cooperation" should be "determined" not by "some outside authority distinct from the persons cooperating." They should be "established by an undertaking among those persons themselves in the light of what they regard as their reciprocal advantage." Therefore he emphasized that they should not be conceptualized as based on "God's law," "an independent moral order," "natural law," or "a realm of values known by rational intuition" (22). He did not, however, even consider the possibility that in fact the "terms of social cooperation," fair or not, whether in America or in Europe, were to a large extent determined by a cultural pattern which had taken centuries to develop, and which people in the present had simply inherited, rather than assessing its value from the standpoint of "their reciprocal advantage" and then "selecting" it. A culture does not go away just because the people who inherited it change their address. Obviously, the Europeans who moved to America formed an outpost of European culture, they were not creating a culture *de novo*. Many social scientists would agree that the "terms of social cooperation" in any society are in fact to a large extent shaped by an inherited cultural pattern. Still less did Rawls consider the possibility that, to the extent that these terms are open to criticism and revision, some continuity with tradition is desirable to balance iconoclasm and further the coherence of society.

Thus seeing culture primarily not as a gift received or an organizing cultural code inherited from the past but as the outcome of "an undertaking" in the present, Rawls spoke of the need to "regard the richness and diversity of society's public culture as the result of everyone's cooperative efforts for mutual good ... something to which we can contribute and in which we can participate." Although he noted that "public culture is always in large part the work of others," "others" here referred to contemporaries with whom one cooperated in the present, not to past generations (322). His view leads to the *reductio ad absurdum* that, when I listen to a Beethoven symphony, I should be able to feel that I participated in its creation, rather than treasuring the privilege of enjoying it.

Rawls's concept of the role of culture in social life is evident not only in his embrace of Kant's vision of a self-sufficient reflexivity, which Kant set forth before Hegel and Herder put reflexivity into cultural or historical context; in his embrace of the Marxist rather than the Weberian account of the causative relation between culture and economy (269); and in his failure to take into account that culture is the cumulative product of people in the past, not only the ongoing outcome of contemporary discussions and activities (not all of them "cooperative" and few if any based on equality!). It is evident also in his handling of the major antinomy today between the fashionable ontological individualism going back to Thomas Hobbes and the equally fashionable view, exemplified by George Mead's social theory, that the ego arises out of an internalization of socially shared orientations including inherited culture. Rawls was well aware of this antinomy (286). Leaning to the former view, however, he just regarded as a fact "that society as a whole has no ends in the way that associations and individuals do" (276). Thus throughout *Political Liberalism*, his utilitarian paradigm of the human condition is that of individuals each of whom seeks "reciprocal advantage" as she pursues her "interests" ("higher-order" or not).

Yet the idea that society cannot have "interests," "ends or ordering of ends in the way that associations or individuals do" does not simply denote a "fact." On the contrary, this very idea exemplifies the way that cultural orientations influence what people perceive as "facts." Whether psychologically or normatively, the relation between individual aspirations and collective values is entirely open to interpretation. Many social scientists would agree that any culture incorporates a teleological picture of history as a series of triumphs and humiliations (*jung-ju*) experienced by "a people" (*min-tsu*) and shaping their shared sense of mission, their shared goal, in the present. The extent to which the personal goals of an individual can or should be differentiated from such a socially shared goal is not a simple matter of "facts." Hu Shih (1891–1962), China's most famous liberal, distinguished between *hsiao-wo* (the individual, flesh-and-blood self) and *ta-wo* (the larger self as humanity or one's society as a whole) and emphasized the need to identify oneself with the latter.

One is making a distinction without a difference when one insists that a nationally shared goal — preserving "the American way of life," say, or "establishing Israel as the Jewish homeland" — is not a goal or a "good" pursued by "a people" but a goal that many different individuals have thought of and separately affirmed. Even more, the idea of a long series of independent affirming decisions each made by an individual carefully considering the issues involved and then arriving at a "reflective equilibrium" misrepresents the processes whereby nationally shared goals are formed. Intent on designing a society based on "fair terms of social cooperation" arrived at by individuals voluntarily using their reason to pursue their individual ends, Rawls did not recognize that these treasured ends of theirs were in fact inseparable from a treasured cultural pattern which was the product not of their current contractual negotiations but of a long cumulative process in the past entirely out of their control. It was by brushing aside the causative importance and current value of this cumulative collective process in the past that Rawls tended to depict the factual nature of the individual and of society as a series of contemporaneous events.

To be sure, the very idea of culture, in my eyes at least, is not that of a fixed, closed system imposed by the past on the present but that of an open-ended, ongoing process "paradoxically" blurring together collective, history-bequeathed beliefs with reflexive quests for critical consciousness in the present. In Rawls's image of society, however, the latter crowds out the former.

At the heart of his typology of ideas, Rawls's complex, controversial way of defining the nature of culture, the individual, and society involved still another set of considerations. Resisting ethical relativism, Rawls claimed that "common human reason" (220) can shed light on praxis. Yet he was well aware of all the objections with which the GMWER had disputed this claim. His conclusion, I would say, resembled that of Habermas: these objections could be refuted only by showing how the very idea of reasoning was correlated to certain extremely general, universalistic values: openness, freedom, autonomy, and equality. Conversely, it was doubtful that any more determinate values could be derived from reason. Yet in fact social life seems inherently to depend on some degree of closure and heteronomy, some determination to limit freedom by distinguishing between sense and nonsense. Rawls's solution was to try to limit such boundaries of freedom to a concept of justice implied by reason (see below). Had he recognized the great role of culture in the setting of these boundaries, his effort to put praxis beyond the reach of ethical relativism would have been compromised.

Rawls's neglect of the idea of culture was evident again in his discussion of the "limits of freedom." Here he adduced "the nature of the surrounding institutional and social context" as one of the conditions putting limits on "our reason: on its development and education, its knowledge and information, and on the scope of the actions in which it can be expressed ..." (222–223 n. 9). In thus discussing "limits on freedom," however, Rawls recognized only the kinds of limits Kant was concerned with. Therefore he did not say that reasoning is inherently limited by its own embedment in a particular cultural-linguistic matrix producing disparate truth claims it cannot adjudicate.

To be sure, Rawls saw such rationally unadjudicatable truth claims as the main content of his "comprehensive doctrines," and he certainly recognized the cultural origins of the latter. According to his typology of ideas, however, three kinds of thinking — common sense, science and knowledge about facts, and critical reflection — were largely uninfluenced by disparate cultural influences. He therefore tried to base his conception of the reasonable on these three types. True, he candidly admitted that some grounding of reflection in a particular philosophical tradition was indispensable, and he privileged "the culture of a free democratic regime" (xx) (see below). His emphasis, however, was on how strongly the mental faculties largely independent of cultural influence inherently suggested the standard of "the reasonable."

Reflecting the kind of positivism illustrated by Popper's "three worlds" or Weber's distinction between "the rationality of ends" and "instrumental rationality," Rawls's typology of ideas recognized the GMWER's way of disconnecting normative ideas from the criterion of truth but rejected or evaded the historicism and culturalism developed by the GMWER after Kant. This typology was the basis for Rawls's concept of "the reasonable," and the latter was not only the basis for "the original position" but also the heart of Rawls's "political liberalism," his "reasonable pluralism" (see below). But was this typology reasonable? At the very least, to use Rawls' terms, his list of "the burdens of judgment" should have included the difficulty in weighing which typology of ideas is the more accurate and reasonable. If it is "delusional" to try to build a total philosophical system based only on objectively true propositions (xx), is it not equally delusional in today's cosmopolitan world to continue neglecting the impact of culture on how people think about how the world is and how it should be changed?

6. The Problem of the Exercise Needed to Clarify Normative Ideas

According to my typology of ideas, then, all ideas about moral-political praxis, or at least all those seriously communicated to influence public opinion, are formed through the "paradoxical" blurring together of historically bequeathed, culturally-formed premises with thinking reflexively oriented to objective reality and universal truth. These ideas cumulatively take the form of discourses each of which is based on rules of successful thinking viewed as indisputable, or virtually so, by the people engaged in that discourse, such as the premises of discourse #1, of discourse #2, and of my own we-group (see chapter I).

This is a post-Popperian view similar to the hermeneutic trends described by Richard J. Bernstein. But I would add that such an account of the universal nature of the public discussion of moral-political praxis inherently answers both the question of how to clarify ideas, maximizing one's critical perspective on political life, and that of how to privilege ideas.

As discussed in chapter I, once the character of thought as discourse is regarded as a fact or truth revealed by the GMWER, the question of how to privilege ideas disappears, since the premises of a discourse, being in fact viewed as indisputable by anyone participating in that discourse, are privileged ideas to begin with, as illustrated by our discourse's "racism is bad."

Moreover, from this standpoint, which regards discourse as an ontological given, the venue and the meaning of the privileged ideas are both clearly known. The venue is either a specific set of texts or a particular human subject, a person articulating her or his own beliefs. As chapter I showed, because their provenance is specific, these beliefs can be unpacked, revealing the specific, relatively simple notions blurred together to form broader ideas like "democracy." Thus the make-up of recommended beliefs becomes fully subject to exegesis, whether in the form of textual analysis (such as this analysis of Rawls' train of thought) or of introspection, as opposed to making only vague, general references to beliefs.

My privileging of the premises viewed as indisputable by a we-group may seem similar to Rawls's privileging of "our considered convictions" (45). The differences are crucial, however. First, the venue of the notions Rawls privileges is not clear. The antecedent of his "our" is unclear, and he also privileges "the public culture of a democratic society" (15), the ideas of an unspecified population. Second, he barely describes the content of the ideas he privileges, assuming that the nature of this "public culture" is manifest. By contrast, I am dealing with determinate empirical objects (specified texts or my own consciousness) that can be analyzed to uncover and unpack specific beliefs in much of their complexity. Third, I try lucidly to put the various privileged ideas of an individual or group into context by seeing them as basic to a discourse dealing with four seemingly universal topics (the goal of political life, means, the other aspects of the given world, and the nature of knowledge). Fourth, Rawls's "our" differs from "my we-group," because my epistemology begins not with my own convictions but with the universal, "paradoxical" nature of thought, that is, with the world's plurality of belief systems, each of which is viewed by one or another individual as "my considered convictions." After recognizing this plurality, I cannot assume that "my considered convictions" can necessarily be the basis for a political theory that will bring good fortune rather than disaster to my we-group. Instead, I have to consider seriously the question of alternative "considered convictions" and focus on the question of whether "my considered convictions" should be retained or discarded. Thus turning "my considered convictions" into objects of critical evaluation and so into opinions that can be compared to other opinions, my phraseology facilitates the opening of my mind to alien notions. Without weakening my awareness of the strength of my convictions, I open myself to the possibility other strong convictions may be preferable to mine. Fifth, recognizing this plurality, I recognize that a disparate cultural pattern has helped to form every set of notions regarded by someone as "my considered convictions." Thus my epistemology tries to avoid ethnocentrism, beginning not with conventional American ideals but with an epistemological situation common to all societies no matter what their cultural heritage. The central problem of what knowledge is is thus disentangled from the problematique of a particular civilization.

Sixth, the fact that a cultural pattern underlies "my considered convictions" dictates the nature of the philosophical exercise needed (within any culture) to pursue critical awareness (*p'i-p'an i-shih*): uncovering the culturally-bequeathed premises on which one relies and trying to assess them by comparing them to others, as illustrated by the discussion in chapter I of discourse #1, discourse #2, and the "considered convictions" of my we-group.

If, then, public political communication in fact takes the form of a discourse, this fact settles the question of what ideas to privilege and implies the nature of the philosophical exercise needed to pursue critical awareness. Positing the blurring together of culturally-bequeathed beliefs with reflexivity, the idea of a discourse inherently puts a certain primacy on the latter. It seems, in other words, to imply an imperative to uncover and assess any discourse's rules of successful thinking. To maximize critical awareness, then, one needs to describe as clearly and specifically as possible what a person, group, or text says and means about what ideas are more or less indisputable, ask whether they are indisputable, and pursue that question by comparing these indisputables with others.

For Rawls, however, critical awareness is not sought by carrying out this kind of exercise and solving the problem of privileging in the above way. According to his typology of ideas, the entanglement of culturally peculiar premises with normative ideas is not a serious problem for philosophy. It is limited to the religious, moral, or philosophical belief systems or ideologies that he can bracket as "comprehensive doctrines" and is not an important aspect of common sense, bodies of knowledge about facts, and the course of critical reflection. Normative thinking, therefore, can rely on the latter three sources of insight, borrow a few ideas from some philosophical traditions, and proceed with little fear of reiterating a culturally-formed premise that might undermine current efforts to improve political life.

My whole concept of political rationality is driven by this very fear, which was produced by the GMWER's brilliant, mostly German, post-Kantian insights into the impact of history, culture, and discourse patterns on how people characterize facts, reflect on their meaning, and consider what to do about them (see chapter I).

Among these German insights, let us not forget, were not only Hegel's and Herder's emphases on how culture affects reasoning but also Schopenhauer's argument that culture is consciously or unconsciously designed to pursue the biases and selfish interests of a group.

Lacking this fear that one may be at least partially mislead by the conventional culture one has grown up with, Rawls constructed a philosophical exercise in three parts in order to show why the pursuit of justice is the supreme goal of political life and to specify the nature of justice. First, he explicitly formed a concept of "the reasonable." Second, he used it to devise his thesis of "reasonable pluralism," a just and democratic way to set the boundaries of tolerance in a democratic, open, pluralistic society. Third, he used it to construct his idea of "the original position," from which the content of distributive justice could be inferred. When this three-part philosophical exercise, on which he explicitly focused, is combined with his less explicit way of dealing with the initial questions, the typology of ideas, his economistic theory of society, and his other premises, his concept of political rationality as a whole comes into view and can be assessed by comparing it to an alternative one.

7. Rawls's Way of Privileging Ideas

As already noted, Rawls built up his central concept of "the reasonable" especially by combining three types of ideas or thinking (simply speaking, common sense, scientific findings or other knowledge of facts, and critical reflection). He was, however, well aware that the GMWER had turned the epistemology of political theory into an effort to find a credible foundation within the "middle ground" between relativism and objectivism. Therefore political theory could no longer be exclusively derived in Kant's way from reason as an ahistorical trait of all persons. Logical trains of thought had to be filled out by privileging a set of given historical norms, trying to persuade readers to accept them as such a credible foundation. Such is the nub of political theory as an "advertisement." Thus Leo Strauss privileged the "natural" way, allegedly unbiased by culture, with which Greek philosophy had grasped the universal nature of political life. Dunn privileged the basic ideals of "western political theory." Rawls moved the privileged ground closer to the twentieth century.

He noted that philosophy cannot construct a theory of justice "apart from any tradition of political thought and practice" (45). He then picked his tradition: "In order to state what I have called political liberalism, I have started with a number of familiar and basic ideas implicit in the public political culture of a democratic society" (43). What he repeatedly called "our considered convictions" referred to this "political culture": "no political conception of justice could have weight with us unless it helped to put in order our considered convictions of justice at all levels of generality, from the most general to the most particular" (45). Throughout, Rawls's effort to pursue the goal of justice was restricted to the design of "a constitutional democracy" (126). He aimed to "work out a conception of political and social justice which is congenial to the most deep-seated convictions and traditions of a modern democratic state" (300). Thus his key doctrine of "justice as fairness" was designed to resonate with "the fundamental ideal of equality as found in the public political culture of a democratic society" (79) — "our more firm considered convictions of political justice" (28), "the public culture itself as the shared fund of implicitly recognized basic ideas and principles" (8).

True, for Rawls it was crucial that his concept of "the reasonable" be distinct from those historical traditions and belief systems he called "comprehensive doctrines." For him, "the reasonable" had to be basically independent from culture both in the sense of a tradition or ideology "out there" which one could read up on in a library, and that of history-bequeathed orientations shaping ego's ideas about all aspects of life, including the very concept of a "comprehensive doctrine." He separated his concept of the reasonable from culture in the latter sense by simply ignoring this issue. But he found himself unable to derive a politically substantive concept of justice from universally rational principles *à la* Kant transcending any particular historical-cultural value system. Forced to connect up with one of the latter, he rejected the criticisms of Jürgen Habermas and H.L.A. Hart that this connection of his to the historical liberal tradition was as substantive as that of the classical liberal thinkers (432, 370). His point was that he had only developed that "wider framework of thought in the light of which a conception of justice is to be explained" (269), not a "comprehensive doctrine." In his eyes, then, a "comprehensive doctrine" was different from the way his concept of reasonableness combined the conventional ideals of Western democracy with a Popperian typology of ideas, a naturalistic ontology, and an essentially utilitarian picture of "the basic structure of society" as a pattern of interaction among individuals each pursuing his or her own primarily economic ends. Presumably, Rawls was distinguishing between a thin and a thick connection to a historical belief system. He had to insist he had made only a thin one because he refused to see the pluralism of a desirable society as based on a historical belief system rather than on "reasonable" principles that all "reasonable" belief systems could accept.

His analysis of "the reasonable" thus both depended on privileged values and emphasized ideas allegedly based on somehow more general or ahistorical aspects of human life. He seemingly believed that in contemplating this awkward mix, one could experience what he called "reflective equilibrium." His challenge was: if you think it's awkward, come up with a better one! Indeed, once one agrees that the GMWER made just about all normative ideas tentative, coming up with a better one is far from easy.

8. Reasonableness as Justice

With this mix of privileged ideas and other, somewhat more general ideas, Rawls both showed how reasonableness implied the ideal of justice and argued that the nature of reasonableness stemmed from certain psychological "capacities" and "desires." His starting point was the distinction between "rational," which for him referred essentially to what Max Weber called "instrumental rationality" (Rawls spoke of pursuing ends "intelligently") (49–50), and "reasonable." Rawls explicitly associated "reasonable" with a "moral" "willingness" to cooperate with others by taking their interests and difficulties into account (49). He referred to "the cooperative virtues of political life: the virtue of reasonableness and a sense of fairness, a spirit of compromise and a readiness to meet others halfway, all of which are connected with the willingness to cooperate with others on political terms that everyone can publicly accept" (163). Meeting "others halfway" meant giving them some "leeway" when seeking agreement and so avoiding rigid, extreme positions (246). Thus "reasonably" could refer to being satisfied with meeting a standard only roughly rather than exactly, as in the phrase "a reasonable empiricist framework" (285), or "a reasonable combination and balance of.... political values" (241). Revolving around "the cooperative virtues of political life" (163), however, reasonableness for Rawls was inseparable from his key concepts of fairness, reciprocity, mutuality, and equality: "Fair terms of cooperation articulate an idea of reciprocity and mutuality: all who cooperate must benefit, or share in common burdens, in some appropriate fashion judged by a suitable benchmark of comparison I call 'the reasonable'" (300). Reasonableness thus implied fairness, which in Rawls's eyes was the essence of justice, given his central formula of "justice as fairness" (446).

With its emphasis on "meeting others halfway," the idea of reasonableness both intellectually and psychologically overlapped the common human inclination opportunistically to seek a modus vivendi. Rawls, however, emphasized the difference between the two. Identified with an ideal of fairness, reciprocity, mutuality, and equality as the basis of cooperation, "the reasonable" necessarily had moral and intellectual dimensions. The "cooperative virtues" certainly overlapped "the moral virtues recognized by common sense such as truthfulness and fidelity" (83). The need to give "leeway" was thus combined with respect for moral absolutes. Opposition to "grave injustices ... such as.... the great evil and curse of slavery" (398, 250) was a moral necessity. The "cooperative virtues" also entailed the "intellectual powers of judgment, thought, and inference" (81) necessary to carry out the deliberations without which compromises could not emerge. In other words, these virtues entailed both of the mental features that Kant as well as Rawls ascribed to human beings, "theoretical reason" and "practical reason" — "the fundamental concepts and principles of reason" (220). When people exercised these "intellectual powers" in accord with "the criterion of reciprocity," they "sincerely believe[d]" that the "reasons" for their political actions could "reasonably be accepted by other citizens as a justification of those actions" (xlvi).

Thus the complex norm of "the reasonable" was inseparable from the ideal of human beings as not only "free and equal moral persons" (271–272) but also rational persons. "Reasonable" ideas and actions were those arrived at by equal, rational, free, and moral persons together figuring out how best to cooperate with each other. Once this theoretical definition of "justice as reasonableness" (if I may be permitted) was in hand, all that remained was specifying the content of justice. The idea of "the original position," therefore, far from being the starting point of Rawls's analysis, was just a device he used to draw inferences from his fundamental norm, "the reasonable."

To round out this description of Rawls' conceptualization of "the reasonable," however, one must describe his elaborate effort to show that this norm somehow stemmed from the very nature of all or at least many human beings. Like Dunn, he sought to anchor political norms in the facts about universal human nature — an ancient ontological ambition unsuccessfully repressed by the GMWER.

His point, central to his whole political theory, was that natural human desires cannot be seen as primarily, not to mention exclusively, egotistic. As chapter VIII discussed, Dunn saw a natural human tendency toward conflict as well as one toward cooperation and gloomily held that the former was stronger. This gloom, as already mentioned, was at odds with Rawls's optimism. Rawls of course recognized the fearsome tendencies toward conflict, seeing a world filled with "much injustice" (285). His emphasis, however, was entirely on how nature had endowed people with a "capacity" to trust and cooperate with each other (163). "Reasonableness," as he conceived of it, would naturally be the preferred norm of creatures with this "capacity." Precisely to the extent that it would be, the logic of the "original position" was ineluctable.

Neither Dunn nor Rawls, of course, offered the slightest evidence for either an optimistic or a pessimistic way of weighting any natural human inclinations. Moreover, in describing the "capacities" or "psychology" of human beings, Rawls hovered uncertainly between the idea of universal human traits, that of traits shared by the citizens of democracies, and that of traits such citizens should try to cultivate. Unable to say he was referring only to scientifically known facts, he also did not want to admit that he was only expressing the beliefs of a particular intellectual tradition (Western liberalism). His whole discussion of natural "capacities" thus wavered between these two poles, a dilemma he was quite conscious of, although he also seemingly believed his formulation had attained "reflective equilibrium." Ultimately he was depending on the point described in section 3 above, the tentativeness typical of normative ideas. His theory did not have to be completely convincing, only more convincing than any alternative.

Yet he was confident that his idea of reasonableness, far from being contingent on a particular belief system, was supported by "the laws of nature and human psychology" (xlii), including a "moral psychology" (163). According to what he called "'a reasonable moral psychology'" (82), people who regarded themselves as "free persons" "did not think of themselves as indissolubly tied to any particular final ends" and were "always capable of appraising and revising their aims in the light of reasonable considerations" (280). These aims arose out of a variety of "desires" ranging from those that "can be described without the use of any moral concepts" to those intertwined with the articulation of principles (82–84). Such articulation stemmed from "theoretical," "moral," and "practical" "powers" (56). He especially emphasized "two moral powers ... a capacity for a sense of justice and a capacity for a conception of the good.... [as] the capacity ... rationally to pursue a conception of one's rational advantage or good" (19), that is, "a conception of what we regard for us as a worthwhile human life" (302). This typically or always included "loyalties to particular persons and institutions ... interpreted in the light of some comprehensive religious, philosophical, or moral doctrine" (74). Given these powers, he regarded "citizens as having a certain natural virtue without which the hopes for a regime of liberty may be unrealistic" (370).

Making a seemingly tenable generalization, then, Rawls was saying that people by nature not only pursue narrowly egotistic desires but also have "'higher-order' interests" in "exercising" these various "powers" (74). For Rawls, these "interests" based on a "moral psychology" determined the meaning of "reasonableness" and so of "justice": the "principles of justice" should "enable citizens ... to become full persons, that is, adequately to develop and exercise fully their moral powers and to pursue the determinate conceptions of the good they come to form" (77). He implied that the purpose of political theory was to encourage the nurturing of whatever impulses toward reasonableness could be detected in the human psyche, not worrying about proving that these impulses were stronger than the contrary ones, not to mention dilating on the latter and gratuitously minimizing the former *à la* John Dunn.

I have already noted that, with this formulation, Rawls inclined a bit toward that conception of "positive freedom" against which Isaiah Berlin warned, and toward J.S. Mill's belief that liberty is suitable only for "civilized" societies (79). At this point, however, I am only trying to show how, in Rawls's political theory, the goal of justice, his main concern, was integral to his complex concept of "the reasonable." This concept in turn was contingent on Rawls's typology of ideas and his approach to the initial questions. Given his assumption that clarifying the nature of justice is the purpose of political theory, Rawls sought this clarification by logically making use of the types of ideas he believed were available. These included not only the conventional ideals of Western democratic culture, which he privileged, but also allegedly factual knowledge supporting his hypothesis about general if not universal psychological "desires" and "capacities." As a result of these natural inclinations, "reasonable-ness" was a norm people both appreciated and were able to put into practice. Rawls also implied the affinity between this psychologically based norm and the historical ideals of Western democracy. All these considerations about the nature of justice and reasonableness were logically distinct from and presupposed by Rawls's famous theories about "the original position" and "reasonable pluralism." These theories stand or fall depending on the acceptability of all these considerations above.

Whether this concept of "the reasonable" is acceptable is a challenging question, as noted above in section 1. This concept, as just mentioned, depends on a typology of ideas according to which reflexivity with only minimum dependence on a culturally formed discourse points to norms that seem compelling to all humans facing life reflexively. Thus "reasonable" is more than a generic label denoting the rules of successful thinking that a culturally formed we-group regards as more or less indisputable (see chapter I).

I cannot refute this typology of ideas, especially since the extent to which there is knowledge about moral norms is still an open question, as noted in chapter I, section 13. In my judgment, however, this typology underestimates the role of culturally formed discourses especially with regard to the substantive options central to moral-political life. I agree with Rawls that "slavery is unjust" is a kind of "fact." Yet I believe that when I judge that "such facts [have been] coherently connected together by concepts and principles acceptable to us on due reflection" (124), I can only say that I and any others who are part of my we-group have concluded that these views accord with our we-group's rules of successful thinking, which I know are at least partly controversial. If, then, I still insist on calling these views "reasonable" in some objective sense and associate their epistemic status with Kant's concept of "practical reason," I am only indulging in the sort of fancy language and moderate exaggeration that are appropriate for advertisements. Rawls, however, resisted the degree of relativism implied by this stance of mine, having neither accepted the role of culture in the formation of rules of successful thinking nor considered the possibility of a "paradoxical" relation between culture and reflexivity. Knowing he could not call these views "true," he insisted they still could be called "objective" (119). Thus he blurred over the crucial distinction between the beliefs I regard as indisputable and the challenge of trying not only to persuade others to accept them but also to critique them in the light of different beliefs others regard as indisputable.

In other words, lack of clarity is not the only problem when one refuses to settle for "my we-group's rules of successful thinking" and instead refers to "our considered convictions" as the basis for ideas that, somehow, all "reasonable" people will accept as "reasonable." Another problem is using prestigious philosophical terms and evoking the memory of revered sages like Kant to turn what I want you to believe into something you should want to believe, to dispel my fear that I lack the power to make you want what I want, my fear that the consensus in my society will continue to veer away from the principles that are indisputable to me. Rawls used the hallowed names and categories of Western philosophy to try to persuade his readers that the ideas indisputable to him were "reasonable" in some broader sense even if not "true." I see this as philosophical legerdemain both exaggerating what political theory can accomplish and bypassing the urgent challenge it can meet — the exercise discussed above through which normative ideas can perhaps be clarified.

9. The Last Two Steps of Rawls's "Exercise": The "Original Position" and "Reasonable Pluralism"

Convincing or not, however, the reflective exercise Rawls developed using his typology of ideas formed a concept of "the reasonable" that certainly was plausible for very large numbers of readers east and west. Further developing this reflective exercise, Rawls used his concept of "the reasonable" to specify the nature of justice with regard to two problems. First, how can the above complex idea of "the reasonable" be used to conceptualize a consensus limiting the conflicts arising between free and equal citizens when the beliefs some of them have are irreconcilable with those of others? Second, how can this idea of "the reasonable" be used to realize justice in the forms through which the basic life circumstances of the citizens are arranged?

Pursuing these last two steps of his reflective exercise, Rawls in *Political Liberalism* used two overlapping tactics. One was just drawing inferences from the above concept of "the reasonable." The other was "the original position as a device of representation" (24). The following outline collapses the former into the latter.

The idea of "the original position" posits three roles summed up in this passage: "it models what we regard — here and now — as fair conditions under which the representatives of free and equal citizens are to specify the terms of social cooperation ..." (25). First, there are the philosophers — Rawls and his readers — reasonably thinking about the two problems above. Second, there are the reasonable members of an imagined meeting reasonably organized to prevent any of them from improperly influencing any others. Third, each of these imagined members represents the interests of future reasonable persons living as the free and equal citizens of a democracy. To imagine a discussion of these imagined representatives free of any biases stemming from vested interests, the philosophers assume that none of the representatives knows what will be the social status of the future citizen whose interests he or she represents. A "veil of ignorance" hangs between these citizens and their representatives. The philosophers then logically use their already-formed concept of the reasonable to describe the agreement this imagined meeting would reach. Being reasonable, the members of this meeting are committed to the ideal of equality and believe that the life chances of a citizen are determined primarily by society's "economic regime" (269). Therefore, each representative is concerned with the wealth, power, prestige and other "primary goods" (181, 308) which the future citizen he or she represents will enjoy, and the "social and economic inequalities" from which this citizen may suffer. Most important, rationally believing that most citizens will be of relatively low status, each representative logically concludes that the citizen he or she represents will probably be best off if "social and economic inequalities ... are ... to the greatest expected benefit of the least advantaged" (271). This logically implies that "the basic structure" of society must regulate not just the most salient conditions of social interaction by, say, preventing the corrupt manipulation of the stock market. It must also "secure just background conditions against which the actions of individuals and associations take place" (266), regulating "the inequalities in life prospects between citizens that arise from social starting positions, natural advantages, and historical contingencies" (271). Similarly, the need for fairness in the basic structure of societies logically implies that each citizen must have "an equal right to the most extensive scheme of equal basic liberties compatible with a similar scheme of liberties for all" (271).

How then will conflict be avoided when some citizens exercising their freedom adopt belief systems irreconcilable with those of another group? The answer again logically flows from Rawls's concept of reasonableness, which, according to his typology of ideas, is clearly distinct from such belief systems ("comprehensive doctrines"). A "well-ordered constitutional regime" will be based not on truth or ideology but on this standard of reasonableness. Belief systems that respect this standard are "reasonable comprehensive doctrines." As citizens adopt the latter, they will govern "themselves in ways that each thinks the others might reasonably be expected to accept" (218). Thus "reasonable comprehensive doctrines" will form a "reasonable overlapping consensus" amounting to a "reasonable pluralism" exhibiting the principles of "public reason" (xlvii) as a "freestanding" set of norms expounded "without reference to" any "comprehensive doctrine" (12). In this way, the standard of "the reasonable" both calls for tolerance and puts limits on the scope of tolerance.

Using his concept of reasonableness to specify the "fair terms of cooperation" between free and equal citizens in a democracy, moreover, Rawls wove into this concept a distinctively American optimism about democracy utterly missing in the thought of a John Dunn or a Carl Schmitt. Sure that this standard of reasonableness could be defined adequately, he noted:

History tells of a plurality of not unreasonable comprehensive doctrines. This makes an overlapping consensus possible, thus reducing the conflict between political and other values.... It is inevitable and often desirable that citizens have different views as to the most appropriate political conception.... An orderly contest between them over time is a reliable way to find which one, if any, is the most reasonable. (140, 227)

Holding that the concept of justice he had discussed should be "present in the public culture, reflected in its system of law and political institutions, and in the main historical traditions of their interpretation" (67), he assumed "the feasibility" of this project (70 n. 23) and outlined a "four-stage sequence" for implementing it (397–398).

10. Juxtaposing Rawls's Concept of Political Rationality with an Alternative

Rawls's conceptualization of political rationality thus entails a wide range of ideas going well beyond his concept of "the reasonable." Probing into these, the Taiwan philosopher Hsu Han noted not only the idea of "the original position" along with equality, freedom, and reasonableness as the values presupposed by the "original position" but also assumptions presupposed by these three values.[13] In this chapter, however, I have tried thoroughly to explore Rawls's whole concept of political rationality, noting the variety of concepts making up Rawls's idea of reasonableness, as well as the dependence of "reasonableness" on his positivistic typology of ideas, his economism, and his approach to the initial questions. Rawls's concept of political rationality was made up of all the ideas he either explicitly or implicitly regarded as either true or widely acceptable. They made up his "advertisement" for a successful way to conceptualize the improvement of political life.

The nub of this advertisement was that political rationality lies in making justice supreme among all the goals of political life; in specifying the meaning of this goal by appealing to the conventional concepts of freedom, equality, and fairness long familiar in Western democratic circles; in combining these ideals with a heavily economistic concept of human well-being; in viewing history in a highly optimistic way as allowing a thoroughgoing implementation of this goal; and in depending on a Popperian typology of ideas to define the standard of reasonableness with which to monitor this implementation.

To be sure, like Dunn and Hayek, Rawls put forward a political theory pertinent only to the improvement of political institutions based on the kind of democratic culture produced by the West in modern times. Rawls's theory offered no guidelines for the development of non-Western, non-democratic societies, except in the eyes of those who believe that history all over the world follows the same principles. Still more worrisome, his theory, not altogether inadvertently, left the impression that there is a mysterious affinity between some universal practical reason certified by Immanuel Kant and the conventional principles of American political culture, and that therefore the American sense of political justice should serve as the guideline for the political development of all societies. Such is the perilous outcome of a theory minimizing the impact of different cultures on political reasoning. Moreover, the nature of the radical societal transformation Rawls proposed makes sense only if one agrees that the improvement of political life is a single-, not a multi-goal affair, that such improvement should be conceptualized in a mainly economistic way, and that the radical moral transformation of a society is a practicable goal. Absent these three premises, it is hard to see how Rawls's approach to reform can withstand Burkean criticism.

To dwell on these issues, however, is to take attention away from a major problem Rawls addressed most provocatively, the problem of how to conceptualize limits on the freedom, pluralism, and tolerance so widely recognized as essential to modern life. This is the question discussed in chapter I as that of the parameters of "the three marketplaces" (the economic, political, and intellectual). More specifically, given that the parameters of law and respect for scientific knowledge are not controversial, how should the non-legal, non-scientific parameters emphasizing morality be formed?

One option is to use an official ideology to set the limits of freedom, but this solution has no normative basis except respect for political power. In the case of Taiwan before its democratization in the 1990s and that of the People's Republic of China today, this latter option overlapped a second: setting the parameters by claiming to have established what the Chinese call a *t'i-hsi* (a correct, total philosophical system). According to Rawls's typology of ideas, this *t'i-*

hsi would be not a "reasonable comprehensive doctrine" but a "comprehensive doctrine" based on truth — in his eyes, a chimera. A third option is to view the parameters as set through an inherited cultural tradition or "ethos" (to use Hayek's term) informing the *paideia* of a society. This Burkean notion violates Rawls's Kantian, Rousseauistic principles. A fourth option discussed and rejected by Rawls is basing these parameters on a modus vivendi, a "consensus founded on self- or group interests, or on the outcome of political bargaining." Rawls rejected such a modus vivendi as an insufficiently stable basis for society (147). He thus developed a fifth option: parameters based on an idea of "the reasonable," as opposed to a rational doctrine revealing the truth about the ultimate principles of human existence. The pivotal concept making this option possible was not explicitly discussed by Rawls: the GMWER demonstration that such rational doctrines are not available. What does exist in their stead are "comprehensive doctrines," bodies of thought claiming to reveal absolute truth but viewed as unable fully to verify their vision of "the true, the good, and the beautiful" (*chen shan mei*). Rawls thus tried to draw a line between such "comprehensive doctrines," any of which by its very nature one could reasonably accept or reject, and "the reasonable," a mix of ideas that no reasonable person could reject. The consensus formed by reasonable ideas, which by their very nature consisted of a narrowly "political concept of justice," would form the parameters of tolerance and freedom, a "reasonable pluralism."

This Rawlsian answer to the problem of parameters has to be seriously considered. Whether or not Rawls's reasonableness is based on a viable typology of ideas, it does point to norms of compromise that the objective reality of socially congested living seems to require. In other words, this objective reality does seem inherently to suggest both the need for a modus vivendi based on pragmatic considerations and the idea of morally principled social cooperation. Moreover, the difference between such common public norms and the inner world of deep, ultimate beliefs also is easily understood by many people. Admittedly, it may be that only some of the world's population can understand such ideas and use them to improve their political life. If so, however, why should one expect any political theory to do more than furnish such ideas?

Agreeing that such ideas are basic to modernity, however, is a far cry from agreeing with Rawls's thesis of "reasonable pluralism." The heart of the latter is that broadly shared principles defining the parameters of consensus in a pluralistic society are best conceptualized as ideas the inclination toward which is common in history and does not flow from any one or more particular intellectual or cultural tradition. These parameters, in other words, are most accurately or usefully viewed as based on a "freestanding," narrowly "political concept of justice" differentiated from any "comprehensive doctrine." Such a thesis, however, departs too far from the more holistic way mainstream Western scholarship has viewed the nature of ideas and culture. As argued above, therefore, Rawls was unconvincing in his effort to distinguish between the complex of ideas making up his "freestanding" concept and a "comprehensive doctrine."

What Rawls really proposed, I would say, was not replacing a democratic discourse based on the "comprehensive doctrine" of classical liberalism with a "free-standing" democratic discourse largely independent of any such historical belief system. He actually was engaged in an activity integral to every historical discourse, participation in a public discussion about how to revise the discourse at hand. In line with a broad variety of current U.S. intellectual trends, Rawls was proposing or rather supporting a momentous shift from a more traditionalistic to a more iconoclastic discourse. This shift indeed entails what many regard as a cultural crisis going on in the U.S. today. Much like Robert Nozick or Richard Rorty, Rawls was asking that the traditionally treasured Millsian project be epistemologically demoted from its status as an unquestionable set of ideals inseparable from reason and truth and turned into just another "comprehensive doctrine" which free and equal citizens could then select or reject as they visited a supermarket of alternative "comprehensive doctrines," none based more than any other on verifiable truth claims. He was seeking to intervene in the discussion of one of the most momentous questions of the day, that of the perspective that should be adopted on the heritage of Western civilization. Going back at least to the Enlightenment, this question in the West is entirely parallel to the problem of iconoclasm in modern China. In both cases, the problem of how to restructure *paideia* was put on the agenda of political theory.

If one grants that Rawls's philosophy thus is part of an

iconoclastic effort to revise the mainstream political discourse of his and other nations, it follows that this very effort contradicts the definition he offered of "the basic structure of society." Giving a rather economistic definition of it, he typically downplayed the role of culture, seeing the "basic structure of society" as made up of "a society's main political, social, and economic institutions" (11). He similarly viewed society's needed transformation as a change in the distribution of "primary goods." His own philosophical effort, however, presupposed that the intellectually articulated discourse of a society, its *paideia*, also is a major part of its "basic structure."

After all, according to his own train of thought, the clarification effected by the idea of "the original position" is a necessary condition for the revision of the rest of the basic structure. To put it a bit crudely, like many seemingly economistic thinkers, Rawls is a closet culturalist. His philosophy, then, calls for two major changes in the "basic structure" of his and other societies: a radical shift toward equality in the distribution of primary goods, and a radical shift toward iconoclasm in the pattern of discourse.

The objections to the former shift have been noted above. The problems with the latter shift are more complex. To be sure, there is no a priori principle determining the desirable degree of iconoclasm in a culture. A living culture is inherently a process of arguing about how to revise the culture (*ch'ü-she*), and creative revision can iconoclastically turn sacred values into objects of critical appraisal. If, however, political theory, whether in the U.S. or China, cannot avoid the problem of cultural revision, it still has to discuss the question of standards that revision of a culture should meet. Before one can applaud or criticize Rawls's support for a decisive shift toward iconoclasm, one has to ask what the standards are by which such a shift should be judged, why those standards should be preferred to others.

In other words, an iconoclastic approach to political theory is a matter of the utmost gravity. As a search for political rationality, political theory unavoidably includes recommendations about not only the legal forms of political life but also *paideia*, that is, the normative parameters of "the three marketplaces," the education of the citizens, the norms with which they distinguish between sense and nonsense, the orientations constituting the social capital they contribute to political life — in a word, the cultural underpinnings of political life. An iconoclastic approach to these underpinnings has to be weighed against the Burkean point that these underpinnings are a fragile structure consisting of historically formed traditions the persistence of which requires constant nurture. Certainly, a rational political theory can justify radically adjusting them. My argument, however, is that such a theory has to raise and persuasively address the questions discussed in section 2 above, and Rawls's theory falls short by that standard.

I would especially point to the problem of how to privilege cultural content. Influenced like Rawls by the GMWER, I agree with him that forming a political theory requires supplementing the resources of abstract reasoning or reflexivity with a decision to privilege some historically produced beliefs. I do not think, however, that one can clearly evoke indisputable premises by privileging some vaguely described part of one's historical environment "found" out there and then urging others to affirm it. That is what Rawls did when he sought to evoke "the fundamental ideal of equality as found in the public political culture of a democratic society" (79).

He was advising others to commit themselves to historical beliefs out there, so to speak, external to them as well as to him, and as such existing only as candidates for affirmation, not as specific, clear concepts refusal to affirm which was virtually inconceivable. True, in our post-GMWER milieu, the only beliefs that appear as indisputable are those indisputable to *me*, and to all those who agree with me, as the premises of "our" discourse, such as "racism is bad." The membership of this group is not only varying, except for me, but also small; "our" beliefs do not amount to any public culture; they are only one strand, perhaps a very minor one, of a society's public culture. But our group can advertise the premises we regard as indisputable and so can try to create a movement of public opinion. I see no other way to base public opinion on values that are indisputable and supremely important to "us."

The problem of indisputable premises, in other words, can be addressed in a way clearer and more practicable than Rawls's if one takes into account the nature of political thought as discourse and uses the first-person plural pronoun unambiguously. The convictions needed to effect resolute political action can be nurtured only after their venue has been precisely identified. Only then can they be clearly and comprehensively uncovered, disaggregated, debated, and advertised. If they can be evoked only as a vague conventional ideology propagated by an unspecified population, they remain swirling about in that ineffectual realm of "discussion" Carl Schmitt regarded as the hallmark of liberal democracy.

In other words, seeking to maximize a critical perspective on political life, a political theory cannot be built on the conventional slogans of any public culture, no matter how popular. Political theory is not a popularity contest or opinion survey but a Socratic attempt to find insightful and precise ideas buried beneath the ambiguous, routinized platitudes of conventional political discussion, which is likely to include unconsciously-followed premises unable to pass critical scrutiny. The intellectual exercise that critical reflection calls for, therefore, is not drawing inferences, however imaginatively, from the conventional principles of a society but uncovering the premises obscured by these conventional formulations and critically comparing them to other premises. This is the way, I suggest, to gain a critical perspective on the categories influencing the political life of one's own or a foreign society, and to bring the process of critical cultural revision to bear on any category that seems harmful. Political theory should be inferred from premises that have passed critical scrutiny, not from conventional ideals the contents of which have not been unpacked.

Moreover, as already noted, to form a successful political theory, one has not only to uncover and critically assess the premises it is based on but also to deal with the problem of goals, means, and given world in the full way outlined in section 4 above. Differing greatly from Rawls's, therefore, my advertisement for the way to conceptualize political rationality turns on the need to recognize the causal importance of culturally-formed discourses in political life; to uncover and critically assess the premises of discourses; to use the premises that pass critical scrutiny as the basis for a multi-goal program of political improvement; and to analyze the current patterns of political life in order to see whether any progress currently under way is significantly less than what one's recommendations might effect. This methodology, I believe, is applicable to non-modern as well as modern societies, Western and non-Western, and it suggests the limited relevance of Rawls's "political liberalism" to the improvement of political life whether in China or the U.S. The search for political rationality and international understanding today should be a global conversation turning all inherited cultures into objects of critical reflexivity, not an impetuous effort to turn the conventional wisdom of the liberal West into a universal paradigm upstaging the social aspirations produced in other cultural settings.

11. A Critical Response from Taiwan to Rawls's "Reasonable Pluralism": The Irrepressible Reappearance of Epistemological Optimism

The difference between my criticism of Rawls's "political liberalism" and the recent one by Hsu Han, a Taiwan scholar trained in the Anglo-American tradition of academic philosophy, is another example of the contrast between discourses #1 and #2. Hsu's erudite article addresses the question of how the tolerance, pluralism, and freedom that democracy requires can be conceptualized as compatible with the harmonious integration of society. For intellectuals in Taiwan, this question is especially sensitive, because many of them grew up resenting a Kuomintang dictatorship which used an official ideology to integrate society and long played precisely on a fear much more plausible in the Chinese than the Western world, the fear that democracy and the harmonious integration of society are incompatible with each other.

As chapter VI showed, the original answer of Taiwan liberals like Yang Kuo-shu to this problem was that, after democratization had occurred, the harmonious integration of society would naturally follow, because a consensus would form once citizens were free to discuss public issues rationally. Thus "the same viewpoint based on the same principles would be shared by everyone" (*jen t'ung tz'u hsin, hsin t'ung tz'u li*). After democratization did occur, however, few people if any perceived the rise of such a consensus in Taiwan. Throughout Taiwan and the rest of the Chinese world, many were appalled by the bitterness and uncouthness of the conflicts that now legally erupted in the political arena.

That is, as I argued in chapter I, the intellectual-moral dissonance of the "three marketplaces" was regarded as normal in the context of discourse #2, so long as it did not lead to conflicts and mass violence disrupting society. From the standpoint of discourse #1, however, it was an intolerable problem that intellectuals should analyze in order to overcome it. A typical reaction in Taiwan was that of Huang Kuang-kuo, a colleague of Professor Yang's in the Department of Psychology at National Taiwan University. In 1995 he published a widely discussed book arguing that Taiwan's democratization had led to a kind of "populism" perverting the nature of democracy.[14] Another example is a book published in 2001 by Yeh Ch'i-cheng, professor of sociology at National Taiwan University, who, as described in chapter VI, section 2, was one of the prominent, uncompromisingly liberal scholars demanding the democratization of Taiwan in the early 1990s. Arousing much discussion, his 2001 book, *Going in and out of the Predicament of the "Structure-Action" Framework*, both recognized that Taiwan had joined a global trend adopting the Western combination of capitalism and democracy and regarded this trend as morally and spiritually unacceptable.[15] As I argued in chapter I, there seems to be no intellectually serious Chinese study today holding both that modern Western liberal and capitalistic values today in fact are increasingly penetrating the Chinese world, and that this is a good thing. Yeh's criticism of this trend was based on the same ideal that informed the thought of every Chinese thinker whom I have discussed in this book, the opposition to *li-chi chu-i* (putting primacy of the pursuit of egotistic interests) as a basic societal norm, the longing for a society based on a spirit of *ch'ao kung-li* (transcending the preoccupation with the material, egotistically satisfying aspects of life). Indeed, this same longing has driven the thought of even Xiao Gong-qin, a professor of history at Shanghai Normal University, although he is famous for promoting a "neo-conservatism" that astutely recognizes the need for policies and behaviors in accord with the practical realities of modernization.[16] Expressing this longing, Yeh refused to view the capitalistic preoccupation in Taiwan with the pursuit of selfish interests as a normal historical trend that could be harnessed and regulated to pursue piecemeal progress. In a utopian way, he insisted that this prevalent preoccupation was no more than a frame of mind which had been generated by the categories of Western social science since Durkheim, and which Chinese could discard by simply seeing it for what it was and choosing to prefer Taoist and Buddhist modes of self-abnegation.

True, this recommendation of his was criticized as impracticable in a published Hong Kong seminar formed by Yeh and three critics respectively from Peking University, The Chinese Academy of Social Sciences, and Hong Kong Polytechnic University.[17] That it could be taken seriously, however, indicated the continuing vigor of the tradition-rooted optimism about political practicability and of the belief that China can improve on the Western model of modernity, that modern pluralism need not entail the kind of moral-intellectual dissonance seemingly basic to contemporary Western life.

According to this widespread, indeed tradition-rooted view, welcoming the free, pluralistic interplay of different outlooks was not obviously the same as tolerating the dissonant impact of "wrong" opinions. Yang Kuo-shu had assured his fellow citizens in Taiwan that democratization would end the prevalence of wrong opinions. In Chinese or Taiwanese eyes, however, it had not done so. This Chinese perception logically led to two possibilities: either Taiwan had not experienced the true or spiritually most desirable kind of democratization, or, in some logical but so far unclarified way, democratization required the toleration of wrong opinions. The former was Huang Kuang-kuo's and Yeh Ch'i-cheng's conclusion, the latter, Hsu Han's.

Hsu Han thus discussed Rawls's "reasonable pluralism" to see whether it furnished this needed logical justification for the toleration of false opinions. He never suspected that what Rawls really offered was a conceptualization of tolerance and a typology of ideas very different from his. With all his erudition and training in Anglo-American philosophy, Hsu did not identify Rawls's central points, not to mention addressing them.

Clearly, Hsu was not so naïve as to think that Rawls's "reasonable pluralism" might serve as a formula which, once publicly grasped, would soften political conflicts and harmonize the public life of free citizens in Taiwan. The question that intrigued him was whether the concept of freedom and democracy, revered by so many Chinese since the nineteenth century, was or was not fully coherent. That is, since freedom implied the pluralistic interplay of clashing beliefs, was it logically compatible with society's undeniable need for integration and stability, whether the latter was defined in terms of the traditional ideal of social harmony, of Rawls's "overlapping consensus," or of the idea of *ting yü i-yuan* (stabilized on the basis of a unifying principle)?[18] For Hsu as for Rawls, the consensus that even a democratic, pluralistic society needed required an intellectual demonstration of such logical compatibility. It could not just be based on a modus vivendi pragmatically arrived at by rival interest groups, on some fortuitous convergence of cultural traditions, on the epistemological skepticism allegedly part of the global process of modernization, or on some social or political tendency for people simply to be uninterested in the views of others.[19]

Thus, Hsu's focus was on showing how a "tolerant," "free," "open," "democratic," and "pluralistic" society filled with mutually irreconcilable "ways of thought" could realize "a stable social order" and "social-political unity" (*t'uan-chieh*) without logically violating its basic nature.[20] This indeed was the problem addressed by Rawls's "reasonable pluralism," but Hsu's concept of "tolerance" drastically differed from Rawls's. Hsu defined "tolerance" as a way of thinking and behaving which an individual or group more powerful than another individual or group adopts toward those behaviors or ideas of the latter which the former "regard as wrong" (*fou-ting*). Tolerating these ideas or behaviors perceived as wrong meant not purposefully using one's power to "restrict or stop" these behaviors or the overt expression if not the existence of these ideas.[21] Still more, however, as described below, such tolerant behavior even included not trying to refute ideas one regarded as "wrong." This concept of tolerance differed from Rawls's in three ways.

First, Rawls viewed "tolerance" as one of the "political virtues" (194) and as a norm adopted by all "reasonable persons" taking into account the "burdens of judgment" (59–62). He thus saw it as a norm applying to all clashes between beliefs in a pluralistic society, whatever the power differential between the clashing parties. Rawls's position, therefore, was compatible with that of Hu Shih, who in 1959 urged the politically weak liberal intellectuals in Taiwan to exercise "tolerance" in their criticism of the powerful Kuomintang dictatorship.[22] From Hsu's standpoint, however, it was "absurd" to ask people with little or no power to look tolerantly on the views of those wielding power.[23]

As I see it, Hsu's emphasis on the power differential reflected the continuing great role played in the moral imagination of many Taiwan intellectuals by their image of their earlier confrontation with the Kuomintang dictatorship, as well as the systemic inability of Chinese intellectuals, persisting even after democratization, to imagine a horizontal relationship of mutual respect between themselves and the political center as two realms equally lacking absolute political and ethical wisdom.

Second, Hsu conflated the idea of refuting ideas one regards as "wrong" with "restricting or stopping" expression of them. He thus depicted Rawls as calling for a kind of tolerance according to which one should not refute ideas one regards as wrong, and he then argued that such tolerance made no sense:

> If a person believes that what he believes is the one truth, is it not senseless to demand that that person tolerate what he regards as wrong, as perverse and evil? Every society teaches its people to pursue the true, the good, and the beautiful and to abandon mistaken, perverse, evil, and ugly things. If tolerance is regarded as a virtue and one then teaches people to tolerate what they regard as mistaken, perverse, evil, and ugly things, one does not just fall into a contradiction; even more, one undermines the coherence of moral practice[24].... can pluralism become a value demanding that an individual accept a plurality of mutually irreconcilable doctrines? If this is what pluralism requires of a person, it is fundamentally untenable. A reasonable person with a coherently unified outlook has to choose between Kantian integrity and a merely utilitarian, morally unprincipled stance. [If she rejects the latter,] she can only be a Christian, or a Muslim, or an atheist, etc. Such a person cannot believe in a plurality of mutually conflicting values.... a Christian ought not to think that the teachings of Buddhism and those of Christianity are compatible with each other. [On the contrary, a] reasonable person who has some firm beliefs *wants to argue on their behalf, to explain why those beliefs incompatible with his are wrong.* (italics added)[25]

Rawls, however, never asked people to stop arguing against ideas they regarded as mistaken. If they did stop such arguing, how could the free competition between ideas proceed? If such arguing was a form of intolerance, Rawls's own books were an obvious example of this sin. For Rawls, tolerating seemingly wrong ideas was only a matter of not acting to stop expression of them, and obvious Millsian principles justified this kind of tolerance, especially awareness of human fallibility.

Third, Hsu defined "tolerance" as a response to ideas one regarded as "wrong," but Rawls based tolerance on a typology of ideas emphasizing "comprehensive doctrines," ideas not susceptible to being judged as "true" or "false" in the eyes of "rational" persons. Only an irrational Christian would regard Islam as false. That is, for

Rawls, when rational citizens dealt tolerantly with the conflict between their "comprehensive doctrine" and another one, they did not see themselves as upholding a true idea while also agreeing that a wrong one should be allowed to exist or to be expressed. Instead, they in this context rationally regarded the distinction between truth and falsity as irrelevant. That is, they found truth not in their own "comprehensive doctrine" but in the Popperian conclusion that no set of beliefs about the ultimate nature of things can be based on verified truth claims objectively overriding contradictory claims. For Rawls, this epistemological demotion of ultimate beliefs from the status of true propositions would be taken for granted by any "rational" person, to use Rawls's definition of "rational" (see above). The pluralistic, democratic order he had in mind was for citizens who all were "rational, equal, free, and moral," and who all therefore would see that his typology of ideas accurately described the difference between "true" ideas and "comprehensive doctrines" to which the criterion of truth was not applicable.

Hsu Han to the contrary, this epistemological demotion precisely made it possible for Christians to believe "that the teachings of Buddhism and those of Christianity are compatible with each other."[26] For Rawls, what Hsu called "a reasonable person with a coherently unified outlook" (*i-ko ho-li ch'ieh yu i-chih-hsing-te jen*) would on the one hand view those teachings as compatible with each other precisely because she would not view either of them as either objectively true or objectively false. On the other hand, she could still maintain her unwavering commitment to her religious beliefs, because this commitment was not contingent on their being objectively true. This currently common Western epistemological demotion of ultimate beliefs is illustrated by Robert N. Bellah's agreement with Wallace Stevens' view that "'The final belief is to believe in a fiction, which you know to be a fiction, there being nothing else. The exquisite truth is to know that it is a fiction and that you believe in it willingly.'"[27]

For Hsu Han, had he examined it, Bellah's idea of a "'Supreme Fiction'" would have made no sense. It was incompatible with Hsu's epistemologically optimistic belief that a morally coherent life must be logically based on knowledge of the truth. Hsu was aware of skeptical or relativistic thinking, but he regarded such thinking as "a predicament that must be avoided" and/or a kind of morally-unprincipled "utilitarianism," which he and Rawls equally rejected as the basis of tolerance.[28] Hsu was not prepared to believe that this "predicament" was at the center of Rawls's proposal for how logically to reconcile the goal of pluralism with that of consensus. In Hsu's eyes, democracy had to be a coherent concept; as such it had to be logically consistent with the goal of consensus; and it could not both be coherent and incorporate this "predicament that must be avoided." Thus he did not suspect that Rawls's acclaimed philosophy on which he was pinning his hopes incorporated this very predicament. Encouraged by Rawls's own insistence that relativism should be eschewed, he did not notice that Rawls nevertheless depended on an epistemological demotion indeed rooted in that very "epistemological skepticism" which Hsu rejected.

Thus Hsu failed to see that the key to critiquing Rawls's concept of tolerance was critiquing his concept of reasonableness and his typology of ideas. On the contrary, he found nothing questionable about the latter concepts and assumed that they served as a sound basis for Rawls's idea of "the original position." Hsu's suggestion for solving the problem of tolerance, therefore, was to see whether or not the solution could be derived from the formula of "the original position," not to ask whether the latter was based on a tenable concept of political rationality.[29] Hsu's critique of Rawls's "political liberalism" is erudite indeed but by that very token neatly illustrates how Chinese liberalism, at even its most sophisticated, has habitually filtered out the epistemological pessimism basic to the Western liberalism with which it claims to converge. In this regard, the line from Yen Fu to Hu Shih, Yin Hai-kuang, Yang Kuo-shu, and Hsu Han is unbroken. Like so many other examples adduced in this book, Hsu's thought illustrates the Chinese intellectual world's prevalent epistemological optimism and its sometimes implicit, sometimes explicit rejection of the GMWER.

What Hsu effectively critiqued was Rawls's thesis that a reasonable political concept of justice could be established independent of any "comprehensive doctrine." Like a number of critics, Hsu argued that the only principles available to affirm pluralism in a principled way were the principles integral to one's understanding of truth and morality as a whole.

As already indicated, I agree with Hsu that indeed there are no "freestanding" principles outside one's belief system or discourse as a whole. As discussed above, Rawls's attempt to detach a "reasonable" conceptualization of political life from historically bequeathed, culturally shaped premises and beliefs seems dubious. In discussing the content of a principled affirmation of pluralism, however, Hsu overlooked or could not accept the possibility that a certain skepticism or epistemological demotion could be part of the belief system or discourse through which pluralism could be logically "justified" (*cheng-li*), as illustrated by the beliefs of Robert N. Bellah, Isaiah Berlin, or John Rawls.

It thus seems clear that the justification of pluralism has to be based on a historically-bequeathed belief system both insisting on a broad range of freedom and putting some limits on this freedom. This point, however, raises two different questions: Historically, what mixes of beliefs have legitimized such pluralism? Which beliefs of this kind are the most rational or philosophically tenable?

So far as the former question goes, the variety of beliefs or discourses to be considered is very great indeed. Besides Mill's classic liberal doctrine that freedom of thought is needed to pursue knowledge and progress, there is the skeptical Rawlsian formula just noted. Overlapping this skepticism of the GMWER have been all those various modern tendencies often referred to as "secularization," since they have included a belief that the pragmatic needs of modern life should be put above traditionally religious, moral, or philosophical considerations, that the "outer," institutional aspects of society are more vital to human well-being than the "inner," spiritual ones. Affirming pluralism on the basis of this belief is not the same as just opportunistically seeking a modus vivendi. As chapter II discussed, moreover, pluralism has been affirmed by Chinese using the ancient Buddhist concept of *p'an-chiao*, according to which contradictory doctrines are different versions of one truth. Indeed this concept harked back to Ssu-ma T'an's and Ssu-ma Ch'ien's thesis in the *Shih-chi* (ca. first century B.C.) that all the Chou philosophies had shed light on some facet of the truth, and to Hsun-tzu's (third century B.C.) somewhat similar points (*Hsun-tzu, Chieh-pi p'ien* and *Fei shih-erh-tzu p'ien*). At least as important has been the modern Chinese tendency to view pluralism as integral to a long transitional period of history during which the one correct philosophical system has not yet been understood and propagated. This is a profound, widespread Chinese concept that justifies considerable pluralism while consistently rejecting epistemological pessimism, as illustrated by T'ang Chün-i's philosophy, discussed in chapter II. Moreover, still widely accepted in the Chinese world, especially on the Mainland, the idea of history as a "dialectical" development could also be used to celebrate the contradictions between doctrines in a free society, but I have yet to see any explicit attempt thus to apply this principle. Nor can one overlook the influence of American culture in many parts of the world. To the extent that there is a belief, in Taiwan circles, say, that American or Western culture has been more successful than China's, this belief can legitimize the copying of Western ways including pluralism.

There is still another concept widely linked in the West to the concept of tolerance, closely connected to the epistemological demotion emphasized above, and, like the latter idea, outside the realm of values taken seriously by Hsu: that celebration of differences, discord, and conflict going back at least to J.S. Mill's "On Liberty" and the German humanism that inspired Mill. Hsu in his meticulous way has a footnote referring to Michael Walzer's idea of an "enthusiastic endorsement of difference," but he dismisses this concept as lacking "positive significance for the understanding of tolerance."[30] So far as I can see, however, Walzer's point indeed captured the heart of the Western liberal celebration of intellectual dissonance and pluralism. Moreover, Hsu's rejection of it precisely reflected a basic Chinese disinclination to embrace a disorderly diversity as the breeding ground of creativity and the essence of freedom — a major point of difference with discourse #2.

How, then, should this variety of beliefs legitimizing pluralism be philosophically evaluated? Once again, the answer lies in finding and propagating a rational political theory dealing persuasively with the questions discussed above in sections 2 and 10. I have argued that such a theory eluded Rawls's grasp in a variety of ways. At the same time, however, it also eluded the grasp of Chinese thinkers who, unlike him, rejected the GMWER's major insights: the epistemological demotion of normative concepts along with the discovery that even the most trusted conceptualizations of human reality and moral-political praxis are to a large extent made up of ideas fully intelligible or convincing only within a particular historical setting.

Endnotes

1. All page references in the text are to John Rawls, *Political Liberalism* (New York: Columbia University Press, 1996).

2. See article by Henry M. Magid on J.S. Mill in Leo Strauss and Joseph Cropsey, eds., *History of Political Philosophy* (Chicago: The University of Chicago Press, 1987), pp. 784–801; and Thomas A. Metzger, "Did Sun Yat-sen Understand the Idea of Democracy? The Conceptualization of Democracy in the Three Principles of the People and John Stuart Mill's 'On Liberty,'" *The American Asian Review* 10 (spring 1992): pp. 22–29.

3. See Christopher Lasch, *The Revolt of Elites and the Betrayal of Democracy* (New York: W.W. Norton & Company, 1996); Robert N. Bellah et al., *The Good Society* (New York: Vintage Books, 1992); Robert N. Bellah et al., *Habits of the Heart* (Berkeley: University of California Press, 1985); Alex Inkeles, *One World Emerging: Convergence and Divergence in Industrial Societies* (Boulder: Westview Press, 1998); and Talcott Parsons, *The System of Modern Societies* (Englewood Cliffs: Prentice-Hall, Inc., 1971).

4. Arnold Toynbee, "The Disintegration of Civilizations," in *Theories of Society*, 2 vols., ed. Talcott Parsons et al. (New York: The Free Press of Glencoe, Inc., 1961), vol. 2, p. 1360.

5. John Dunn, *Western Political Theory in the Face of the Future* (Cambridge: Cambridge University Press [Canto edition], 1993), pp. 51–52.

6. John Rawls, *A Theory of Justice* (Cambridge, Mass.: Harvard University Press, 1971).

7. Reinhard Bendix, *Kings or People: Power and the Mandate to Rule* (Berkeley: University of California Press, 1978), pp. 265–272.

8. Arthur O. Lovejoy, *Reflections on Human Nature* (Baltimore: The Johns Hopkins University Press, 1961), pp. 38–39.

9. See Carl Schmitt, *The Crisis of Parliamentary Democracy*, trans. Ellen Kennedy (Cambridge, Mass.: The MIT Press, 2000), and Carl Schmitt, *The Concept of the Political*, trans. George Schwab (Chicago: The University of Chicago Press, 1996). For the anticipation of Schmitt's point in the thought of Benjamin Constant and François Guizot, see Pierre Manent, *An Intellectual History of Liberalism*, trans. Rebecca Balenski (Princeton: Princeton University Press, 1994), pp. 89–91, 99–100. I am greatly indebted to Robert J. Myers for bringing this book to my attention.

10. See e.g. Yang Kuo-shu and Wen Ch'ung-i, eds., *She-hui chi hsing-wei k'o-hsueh yen-chiu-te Chung-kuo-hua* (The Sinification of Research in the Social and Behavioral Sciences; Taipei: Chung-yang yen-chiu-yuan, Min-tsu-hsueh yen-chiu-so, 1982). I certainly agree that scholarly analysis of Chinese society should discard Western categories and adopt Chinese ones whenever this is necessary to analyze Chinese behavior and societal phenomena as lucidly,

accurately, and comprehensively as possible. But such a step has nothing to do with sinification. It's merely a principle of scholarship everyone should follow. This issue is connected to the Chinese postmodernism discussed in chapter XII.

11. For a warning that Thomas Kuhn (and so Richard J. Bernstein and Richard Rorty) may have underrated the objectivity of the natural sciences, see Steven Weinberg, *Facing Up: Science and Its Cultural Adversaries* (Cambridge, Mass.: Harvard University Press, 2001), pp. 197–209.

12. See references to "world 1," "world 2," and "world 3" in the "Index of Subjects" in Karl R. Popper, *Objective Knowledge* (Oxford: Clarendon Press, 1994).

13. Hsu Han, "Tzu-yu min-chu she-hui-chung-te jung-jen wen-t'i" (The Problem of Tolerance in Free, Democratic Societies), in the Academia Sinica's *Jen-wen chi she-hui k'o-hsueh chi-k'an* 13 (September 2001): pp. 377–378.

14. Huang Kuang-kuo, *Min-ts'ui wang-T'ai-lun* (Populism and the Undermining of Democracy in Taiwan; Taipei: Shang-Chou wen-hua, 1995). Also published in Beijing by Chung-kuo yu-i ch'u-pan kung-ssu, 1997.

15. Yeh Ch'i-cheng, *Chin-ch'u "chieh-kou — hsing-tung"-te k'un-ching* (Going in and out of the Predicament of the "Structure-Action Framework"; Taipei: San-min shu-chü, 2001).

16. Xiao Gong-qin, *Chih-shih fen-tzu yü kuan-nien-jen* (The True Intellectual and the Person Only Immersed in Abstract Ideas; Tianjin: T'ien-chin jen-min ch'u-pan-she, 2001).

17. See their essays in *She-hui li-lun hsueh-pao* 5 (spring 2002): pp. 1–77.

18. Hsu Han, p. 346.

19. Ibid., p. 347.

20. Ibid., p. 345, summary.

21. Ibid., pp. 348–353.

22. See Hu Shih, "Jung-jen yü tzu-yu" (Tolerance and Freedom), originally printed in *Tzu-yu Chung-kuo* 20 (March 20, 1959): pp. 7–8, and his speech with the same title, originally printed in *Tzu-yu Chung-kuo* 21 (December 5, 1959): pp. 6–8. These are the bibliographical references given in the volume where I found these two writings, Yin Hai-kuang, *Yin Hai-kuang hsuan-chi, ti-i-chüan, She-hui cheng-chih yen-lun* (Selected Writings of Yin Hai-kuang, volume one, Writings on Society and Politics; Hong Kong: Yu-lien ch'u-pan-she yu-hsien kung-ssu, 1971), pp. 494–506.

23. Hsu Han, p. 353.

24. Ibid., p. 354.

25. Ibid., p. 364.

26. Ibid.

27. Robert N. Bellah, *Beyond Belief: Essays on Religion in a Post-Traditional World* (New York: Harper & Row, Publishers, 1970), p. 203.

28. Hsu Han, pp. 347–348, 358.
29. Ibid., pp. 377–378.
30. Ibid., p. 348 n. 7. On the German romantic celebration of differentness, diversity, creativity, change, and even discord and conflict prominent by 1800, see Arthur O. Lovejoy, *The Great Chain of Being* (Cambridge, Mass.: Harvard University Press, 1936), chap. 10.

CHAPTER XI

⇌

Western Philosophy on the Defensive?

Looking at some historical and methodological issues regarding the extent to which modern Chinese and Western philosophy can or should form a kind of international seminar discussing a shared agenda, I am writing as a student of Chinese intellectual history rather than a professionally trained philosopher. Such an international seminar has obviously already been formed, as illustrated by the ongoing discussion about the grammatical, semantic, and ontological aspects of the Chinese language, but I believe that one way to develop this seminar is to bring up some so far neglected epistemological issues.[1]

My starting point is a series of seemingly uncontroversial empirical or historical observations, combined with a bit of interpretation. First, during the last four centuries, the advent of capitalism, modern science, industrialization, modernization, and democratization in the West has been accompanied by an epistemological revolution, the Great Modern Western Epistemological Revolution (GMWER), which did not occur in China during the last century when modernization and some democratization occurred there as well. GMWER basically refers to the rising skepticism Alasdair MacIntyre described in *After Virtue*, the increasing doubt that reason can reveal the objective basis of moral norms, but I use "revolution" to avoid the common philosophical evaluation of this change as an increasing "crisis." My point is that the conceptualization of knowledge greatly changed, whether this change was good or bad (though this change did not occur throughout all of the Western intellectual world).

This change can be described by using the terms "epistemological optimism" and "epistemological pessimism." Again, Karl Popper used these terms in a philosophically evaluative way to denote two wrong ways of thinking, in contrast with the correct way, "critical rationalism." I use them just descriptively to denote two outlooks that seemingly are integral to any conceptualization of knowledge: the optimistic sense of the obvious and indisputable (I know racism is bad, I know I am mortal), and the pessimistic belief that any idea (except this one) must be cautiously and rigorously questioned before it can be given the status of knowledge (Popper denied that "all men are mortal" can be accepted as a "justified true belief").

If we use Popper's "three worlds" as an example, epistemological optimism believes there is knowledge available about all three worlds: world one, the ontological world, which Popper posited was a "physical" one; world two, the world of norms, which Popper basically regarded as made up only of "beliefs"; and world three, the world of so far unfalsified "conjectures," the only one Popper dignified with the term "objective knowledge." Epistemological pessimism, as just indicated, believes no knowledge is available about the ontological and the normative realms and sometimes even questions whether ideas tested in the Popperian way by means of experiments can count as objective knowledge.

The contrast between epistemological optimism and pessimism can be made still clearer by distinguishing between six kinds of topics which could serve as objects of knowledge. The first is Popper's world three, the realm of observable events susceptible to experimentation and the application of logic. The second consists of the introspectively observable contours of consciousness discussed by thinkers like Hume, Kant, and Husserl. The third consists of certain human characteristics which can with little risk of controversy be regarded as integral to universal human nature, such as the desire for physical health and material well-being. The fourth is the realm of more substantive and specific moral or normative questions, such as the choice between selfishness and the golden rule and specific policy choices — should China promptly democratize? should the U.S. pay reparations to the descendants of people who were slaves owned under U.S. law? The fifth is the realm of meaningful relations between all true propositions. Does knowledge include ideas demonstrating the logical unity of all true propositions, ideas forming a *t'i-hsi* (systematic, unified theory explaining the nature of all aspects of human life and its setting)? The sixth topic is that of the oneness of all aspects of existence, including knowledge, a notion described as "linkage" in my *Escape from Predicament* and summed up in Neo-Confucianism as *t'ien-jen ho-i* (the oneness of heaven and man). The focus here is on ontological knowledge.

Maximum epistemological optimism — illustrated by the thought of many modern Chinese thinkers, such as T'ang Chün-i — holds that objective knowledge is available regarding all six topics. Maximum epistemological pessimism holds that for all six there is only subjective, arbitrary opinion (if that position is logically possible).

The GMWER, epitomized by the thought of Descartes, Hume, Kant, Nietzsche, and Max Weber, arose out of causes that have been variously discussed, such as British nominalism and its religious background, the obsession with precise thinking discussed by Eric Voegelin, and a largely German talent for using ideas like history, culture, and discourse to explore the ways in which ideas subjectively shared by a we-group can constitute what they mistakenly regard as objective reality. The GMWER mostly avoided maximum epistemological pessimism and came to focus on demonstrations that knowledge about topics four, five, and six is unavailable. In twentieth-century Chinese intellectual circles, however, these demonstrations were seldom if ever accepted. For some time now, Chinese referring to some or all of them have spoken of *pu-k'o-chih-lun* (the theory that much of reality is unknowable) as a Western fallacy that Chinese thinkers must be wary of. As chapter I discussed in detail, there have been many different Chinese ways of refuting or ignoring the GMWER.

When one puts together these varied ways of refuting the GMWER with the major Chinese tendencies to ignore the GMWER as unworthy of serious discussion, one can identify a major if not complete consensus in the modern Chinese intellectual world cutting across ideological lines and rejecting the conclusions of the GMWER, reaffirming the epistemological optimism indeed inherited from the Confucian and the Neo-Confucian tradition, and so diverging from the world of modern Western analytical philosophy. It is no exaggeration to say that the agendas of these two philosophical worlds largely diverge (*ko-ko pu-ju*). Western philosophers ask how philosophy can be pursued in light of the GMWER's demonstrations that knowledge about topics four, five, and six above is unavailable (one answer being the analysis of historical languages), while the philosophical problem in much of the modern Chinese philosophical world is that of how to refute the GMWER by obtaining knowledge about these topics — how, as Feng Ch'i (1915–1995) put it, to obtain "wisdom," not only "knowledge."

If these descriptive remarks about two philosophical worlds are plausible, they indicate that, at least in the case of epistemology, traffic between these worlds has been one-way, with Chinese philosophers often addressing Western theories, while Western philosophers treat Chinese epistemological optimism much as Liang Ch'i-ch'ao (1873–1929) treated Western epistemological pessimism — by ignoring it.

Should, however, Western philosophers disregard this Chinese optimism? Even more, in the epistemological disagreements between these two worlds, are there important issues that both have so far failed to ponder? My own opinion is that the best way to look for these issues is to reopen the question of what is knowledge. It can be reopened, first of all, by using the ideas of epistemological optimism and epistemological pessimism in the purely neutral, descriptive way outlined above and asking: what is the most reasonable or desirable way to mix these two outlooks?

Second, instead of trying to answer this question in an abstract way, one can try to assess the different historical answers to it. This means first describing these answers while postponing evaluation of them, much as a jury tries to listen in an unbiased way to different witnesses before evaluating their testimonies.

Third, I suggest that, as one describes historical ideas, the attempt accurately to grasp the meaning and the context of an idea unavoidably leads to the currently fashionable concept of "discourse," which, as Richard J. Bernstein helped to show, stems from the work of a variety of scholars, such as Husserl, Weber, Wittgenstein, Isaiah Berlin, Kenneth Burke, Quentin Skinner, and Michel Foucault. What discourse suggests to me is (a) that the concept of knowledge used by a writer to address issues consists of not only any explicitly epistemological theory he or she may propound but also many assumptions, often platitudinous from the emic standpoint, scattered in his or her writings and widely shared with contemporaries; (b) that this conceptualization of knowledge does not necessarily stand alone and rather is interwoven with assumptions about the goal of life, the means to reach it, and other ideas defining the given world, including all the undesirable aspects of life, their causes, and, more generally, the nature of human nature, of history, and of the cosmos; that (c) all or many of the platitudes pertaining in a discourse to the concept of knowledge, goals, means, and the rest of the given world appear as indisputable principles or truths to the we-group pursuing the discourse (such as "our" "racism is bad"); and (d) that this concept of discourse, itself a product of the GMWER, presupposes the successful acquisition of full, absolute knowledge about the universal nature of all human knowing as a paradoxical mix of historical, cultural, and other influences shaping the subjectivity of an individual or group together with the reflexive and perceptual ability to obtain knowledge about objective reality.

If the idea of "discourse" can be thus understood, much can be said about not only the description but also the evaluation of the Chinese and the Western epistemological worlds. First, the procedures of evaluation can be reconsidered. Richard J. Bernstein explained how a hermeneutic approach could define a "middle ground" between objectivism and relativism, but this middle ground ultimately taps into the "indisputables" that are integral to any discourse. Second, according to the "indisputables" of my we-group (the platitudes that we, like Isaiah Berlin, accept as undeniable even if we cannot prove them to rest on eternal truths), the GMWER may have definitely demonstrated lack of knowledge about topics five and six, but it did not necessarily preclude all knowledge about topic four. It merely produced an attractive allegation that such knowledge is probably unavailable, making it fashionable for many Western scholars today apologetically to refer to all their premises and convictions, however adamantly defended, as mere "prejudices." Conversely, Chinese thinkers like T'ang Chün-i in effect rejected this allegation and cogently focused on the question of the limits of human fallibility. Just how cogently I am now trying to determine by studying his magnificent textbook, *Che-hsueh kai-lun* (An

Introduction to Philosophy), which was first published in 1961, and which in effect includes a systematic attempt to assess the findings of the GMWER.

True, as already indicated, the epistemological optimism of these Chinese thinkers vastly overshot the mark, since they insisted the human mind can obtain knowledge about all six of the above topics, including metaphysical understanding of the ontological basis of experience and the cosmos. So far as I can see, however, their epistemological optimism is challenging if one interprets it as referring to not only dubious metaphysical matters but also the problem of knowledge.

One can argue about what can be known and what the nature of knowledge is, but, it seems clear, one cannot logically argue that the universal, absolute, full nature of knowledge cannot be known. After all, that it can be known is a claim made by the very heroes of the GMWER, such as Hume, Kant, and Popper, not to mention epistemologically optimistic Chinese. Its knowability in turn has vast implications, especially if recognition of its knowability is combined with an idea seemingly impossible to dispute, that knowledge is good and should be pursued by people.

It follows that human thought has access to not just ideas meaningful only to a limited segment of historical humanity and to Popper's "objective knowledge" but also to a universal, absolute understanding of what knowledge is; that education should instill knowledge; that social organization should promote education (not just the principles of equality and freedom); that history is a normatively meaningful competition between those people more successfully and those less successfully pursuing knowledge; and that, as Mill and Popper said, because societies should be organized to favor the former, freedom is an objectively important value.

Such ideas are all implied even by the very epistemological pessimism of the GMWER, even while this pessimism simultaneously suggests that there is no knowledge of absolute, objective, universal norms of human action. Hence the key contradiction on which the GMWER is embarrassingly skewered: combination of the claim that there are no transhistorical norms with which to evaluate different historical societies and the unshakable belief not only that the GMWER produced a correct understanding of the limits of knowledge but also that the West, as the vehicle of the GMWER and the values it implies, is the world's model civilization. Epitomized by J.S. Mill's "On Liberty," the contradiction many of us in the West have grown up with is between the belief that, because of human "fallibility," any idea held to be true may be false and the belief that we who have this belief are more enlightened than those who lack it.

The varied Chinese epistemological arguments, I believe, are interesting for those worried by this contradiction. In my case at least, these Chinese views have suggested that, to avoid this contradiction, one must grant that there are transhistorical norms and then can view as "paradoxical" the fact that cognitive access to them is combined with historically limited subjectivity. Hence my notions about the nature of "discourse" as a phenomenon embodying this universal, indeed ontological paradox.

In other words, the objectivity of norms and values remains elusive when they are regarded as objects of knowledge but is clearer when it is inferred from the nature of knowledge itself. Whether or not this objectivity can be derived from some discursively known principle or consciousness transcending historical variations, it does seem to be implied by an idea which exists as an unavoidable part of every discourse I am aware of — the idea that people can infallibly understand the absolute, universal nature, scope, and desirability of knowledge. Even Karl Popper's discourse could not shed this idea. The GMWER shed great light on the fallibility and historicity of people trying to make absolutely true and objective statements about themselves and the world around them, and Chinese thinkers even today have still not taken its insights seriously enough. In effect, though, they have emphasized a point of which the GMWER lost sight: human fallibility has limits, and these limits have rich moral implications.

If my argument is correct, then, the contemporary Chinese and Western philosophical worlds have much work to do criticizing each other. In this way, they could arrive at a new concept of knowledge, establish the objectivity of *Wertrationalität* (the rationality of ends), and so restructure the social process that transmits knowledge, education. Such a restructuring of education would have beneficial international as well as domestic effects, because international efforts to deal with conflicting interests by peacefully discussing them are often undermined by divergent outlooks on how to make reasonable statements based on knowledge. Dangerous clashes between ideas about which data serve as "evidence" indicating the existence of which pattern of historical causation have all along been basic to the development of U.S.–Chinese relations and still are. But whether or not the renewed critical efforts of the international philosophical world can gradually improve the political life of our planet, it is not enough for one philosophical circle to criticize another. What is really difficult is redefining the most basic principles of one's own circle as ideas on the defensive. Only after such a redefinition can criticism from the outside be of any use. The point of this chapter is that such a redefinition has not yet occurred in the West. The point of the next chapter is that it also has not occurred in China.

Endnote

1.   Complementing chapters VIII, IX, and X above, the critical remarks in this chapter about the GMWER are further developed in chapter XIII below.

CHAPTER XII

China's Current Ideological Marketplace and the Problem of "Morally Critical Consciousness"

1. The Crystallization of the Inhibited, Accommodative Political Center and the Accompanying Ideological Changes[1]

Scholars sometimes describe the way that China's polity has changed in the last two decades as a transition from "totalitarianism" to "authoritarianism" and hope there will be a further transition to "democracy." This familiar typology, however, overemphasizes the legal, procedural aspects of political life at the expense of anthropological, organizational, and intellectual ones. Moreover, it often lapses into a simple contrast between "democracy" and "autocracy" (*chuan-chih*), instead of also highlighting the systemic contrasts between different types of undemocratic rule. Thus it seems more useful to see the recent change in China as one from an "uninhibited political center with transformative policies" to "an inhibited political center with accommodative policies."

"Transformative" policies are those seeking to eliminate all evil in society (*pa-pen se-yuan*), while "accommodative" policies seek piecemeal change to reduce the amount of evil.[2] The term "political center" is based on Edward Shils's distinction between a society's "center" and its "periphery." An "uninhibited political center" is organizationally as well as legally capable of tightly controlling just about all the activities under its jurisdiction and so may seek to implement transformative policies and eliminate "the three marketplaces," that is, the intellectual or ideological, economic, and political arenas in which private individuals with minimal restrictions can freely interact with each other, each person autonomously deciding which ideas to endorse, which goods to buy or sell, and which policies to back or oppose. Mao's regime after the late 1950s was an "uninhibited, transformative political center."

The "inhibited political center" on the one hand is organizationally incapable of tightly controlling the citizenry, and it allows considerable development of the ideological and the economic marketplaces. It may even allow some development of the political marketplace. On the other hand, it ruthlessly suppresses any overtly organized attempts to challenge the authority, legitimizing rationale, and dignity of the ruling group. Given its inhibited organizational capabilities, it can long endure only when the vast majority of the citizens are uninclined to act in such a politically defiant way. The Kuomintang regime on Taiwan before democratization was an "inhibited, accommodative political center."

The "subordinated political center" fully allows all three marketplaces to develop and subordinates the ruling group to them at least to the extent of using free elections to determine the officially designated leadership. Taiwan developed such a center from the late 1980s on.

As China after 1978 developed an inhibited, accommodative center, what kind of ideological marketplace arose?[3] I would try in a preliminary way to address this extremely difficult question as follows:

By the 1990s, the four main ideological trends were Chinese liberalism, modern Confucian humanism, Chinese Marxism, and neo-conservatism. These four trends, however, not only competed but also shared much common ground. This included key, tradition-rooted modes of thought, including discourse #1, as discussed in chapter I. It also included a new consensus regarding issues that had been highly controversial earlier in the twentieth century.

Earlier, the common goal was "wealth and power," some kind of "democracy," and "modernization," but there was much debate about whether socialism or capitalism was the best way to pursue "wealth." That debate has now been replaced by a consensus calling for an economy fundamentally based on the market, though still mixing in some socialistic features.

Earlier, there was much division of opinion as to whether

society's intellectual-moral elite (*hsien-chih hsien-chueh*) consisted of persons organized as a political party or just "true intellectuals." Hope has now shifted away from any political party. The emphasis is more on "true intellectuals " to whom, it is hoped, the political center will listen.

Previously, in constructing "the philosophy with which to establish the nation" (*li-kuo-chih tao*), much debate centered on whether the ontological basis of the ideology should be materialism or idealism. There also was serious disagreement as to whether the "system of thought" (*t'i-hsi*) needed by the nation had already been provided by a "great" (*wei-ta*) thinker like Marx, Mao, or Sun or was only in the process of being formed (the latter was T'ang Chün-i's position, for instance). There now is a considerable consensus that the needed *t'i-hsi* is an ongoing project still far from finished, and the debate between idealism and materialism is no longer central. Even more, there has to some extent been a shift away from the direct pursuit of a "system of thought" toward discussion of methodological problems, the clearing up of which is regarded as a preparatory stage that must precede the direct pursuit of ultimate goals. This shift partly resembles the retreat to "the tower at the crossroads," the Chou Tso-jen image used by Hu Wei-xi, Gao Rui-quan, and Zhang Li-min in a recent study of Chinese liberalism before 1949.[4] It is also reminiscent of the late Ming, early Ch'ing shift from the direct metaphysical quest for sagehood and world transformation to a focus on textual problems, on the history of "learning" (*hsueh-shu*), and on publications serving as a seminar filled with many differing outlooks (e.g. *Huang-ch'ao ching-shih wen-pien*, compiled around 1826).

Previously, there was much debate about whether the enlightened elite should pursue national goals by acting transformatively or accomodatively, violently or peacefully. There now is a broad consensus favoring peaceful, accommodative, gradualistic action.

Apart from this considerable consensus concerning national goals, the nature of the elites most able to bring the nation forward, the need to rethink methodological issues before again trying to find a "new wisdom," and the need for an accommodative political style, there also is a fundamental consensus about one part of the given world, modern Chinese history. From this standpoint, China as it is today did not evolve gradually out of the tradition blending various lines of continuity and discontinuity with the premodern past. Although the idea of such a blend is emerging in the Mainland historiography, the ideological mainstream pictures modern China as originating out of "the breakup of the traditional order" (*chieh-t'i*), which allegedly formed a coherent moral-political whole. Not yet alleviated, the "crisis" into which this alleged loss of wholeness and moral-intellectual coherence plunged China has two main, inseparable aspects: the economic backwardness and lack of democracy in China, and the marginalization of China internationally. The Mainland perception of this crisis entails a very pessimistic picture of the way China's culture turned out in modern times as a historical pattern in which liberal ideals could not and still cannot easily take root. Such pessimism was far less evident in Taiwan during the 1980s.

Such, then, is the consensus largely shared by the four outlooks above competing in the ideological marketplace. What issues are they disagreeing about? One central issue is whether or not the Western model of modernity combining capitalism and democracy is basically sound. It certainly excels in the realm of science and modernization, the whole "outer" pursuit of national and individual desires, but has it combined "instrumental rationality" with the "rationality of ends," to use the Weber distinction very familiar in China? In other words, to use the traditional terms for these two dimensions, has it successfully combined *ch'i* (instrumentalities) and *tao* (the True Way)? Illustrated in chapter V, a liberal line of argument vigorously and publicly developed in China today holds that it has.

Those who, citing the pathologies of Western modernity, deny that it has so succeeded face another major issue: to secure "inner" values and pursue "the True Way," should Chinese rely on the West's anti-capitalistic, anti-bourgeois humanistic tradition or the "spiritual resources" still to be found in the ancient roots of Chinese culture?

Including "the New Left," the Marxist train of thought, often combined with a vehement denial that such precious "spiritual resources" can be found in the Chinese tradition, is oriented to thinkers in the West who denounced the "moral absurdity" (John Dunn) of the Western combination of nationalism, capitalism, and democracy. From this standpoint, Nietzsche and Marx are central. By the same token, though fully recognizing Mao's "later mistakes," these Marxist intellectuals honor his revolution as an indispensable step taken to save China from the pathologies of both Chinese culture and the modern West. In their eyes, this revolution is the one bright spot in modern China's otherwise dismal history. In some cases, instead of turning to the Confucian "spiritual resources," they express a kind of nativist faith in a "natural" development of "Chinese culture" currently being thwarted by the intrusion of Western categories like "modernization theory" and "liberalism" with which the "world system" led by Western capitalism seeks to rationalize its efforts to dominate China.

The competing train of thought, developed by the New Confucians and other representatives of modern Chinese humanism, is that China's own "spiritual resources" are so potent that they alone can serve as the key to overcoming these Chinese and Western pathologies. These thinkers in turn have to assess the various philosophical arguments of the New Confucians claiming to synthesize these "spiritual resources" with the discursive reasoning and instrumental rationality developed in the West, as discussed in chapters II and III.

Finally, the new conservatism developed by scholars like Xiao Gong-qin emphasizes the need for gradualism and stability in a world where the pathologies of Chinese culture are complemented by the pathologies of Western modernity. Xiao attacks the "romanticism" and "utopianism" of intellectuals who, since T'an Ssu-t'ung (1865–1898), have believed that, with a single act of intellectual enlightenment, they could promptly dissolve all these pathologies and establish "the great oneness." A historian, Xiao tends to avoid the philosophical issues, seeking to promote a sober pragmatism and revering the political and humanistic approach of Yen Fu (1854–1921), who wrote before Chinese scholars started deeply exploring the Western philosophical problematique.

Some claim that Marxism and Maoism no longer are living outlooks in the Chinese intellectual world. In fact, though, they exist within the ideological marketplace both as an official doctrine openly criticized as an "ideologized" form of Marxism and as a vital scholarly current.[5] Despite the horrors of the Cultural Revolution (1966–1976), there was great interest in the 1980s in recovering Mao's basic revolutionary vision by integrating it with insights taken from the wide range of non-Marxist thought, Chinese and Western, access to which increased so much during that decade. Good examples are Li Tse-hou's influential writings, going back to the 1970s, on philosophy, intellectual history, and aesthetics;[6] the epistemological and historical studies of Feng Ch'i (1915–1995), an astute Marxist philosopher of great integrity who became the guiding spirit of the Department of Philosophy at East China Normal University in Shanghai, today led by gifted disciples of his, such as Yang Kuo-jung, Gao Rui-quan, and Yü Chen-hua;[7] Wuhan University's Kuo Ch'i-yung's subtle attempt to synthesize Marxist and Confucian humanism with the anthropological concept of culture and the whole spectrum of modern Chinese philosophy;[8] and Kao Li-k'o's interesting synthesis around 1990 of Mao's vision with the idea of modernization, discussed in chapter IV. Also noteworthy is the lucid, richly footnoted college textbook on Mao Tse-tung written by members of Tsinghua University's Department of History. It put Mao into critical perspective while expressing a deep commitment to his basic vision.[9]

Moreover, even if the brutal repression of the Democracy Movement in June 1989 weakened such commitment, a distinctly Marxist response to the post-1989 situation soon crystallized. The direct promotion of democracy was no longer feasible, and, for many intellectuals, the sober conservatism of a Xiao Gong-qin was acceptable only as a practical guideline for public behavior, not as an inspiring intellectual vision. Seeking the latter, many intellectuals preferred a focus on literature, literary criticism, and social theory reviving the hope of an eventual societal transformation.

Li Tse-hou's influential Marxism in the 1970s and 1980s had already emphasized this tradition-rooted paradigm of literature and aesthetic consciousness as central to "culture," which in turn was viewed as the key to economic-political progress.[10] Scholars from departments of literature or language thus played a dominant role in the debates over neo-Marxism during the 1990s, such as Liu K'ang (University of Pennsylvania), Chang I-wu (Peking University), Cheng Min (Beijing Normal University), Hsu Pen, a scholar in California, Chao I-heng (London University), Chang Lung-hsi (University of California, Riverside), Wang Hsiao-ming and Yang Yang, both from East China Normal University, and Wang Hui, whose book on Lu Hsun had made his reputation, and who had long been associated with the editorship of *Tu-shu*, the most influential intellectual journal in China in recent years.[11] To be sure, scholars outside literature also contributed to the new wave of neo-Marxism in the 1990s, such as Ts'ui Chih-yuan of M.I.T.'s Department of Political Science.

At the genesis of this new wave lay both a new literary trend, which had begun in the late 1980s and was later referred to as "vanguard literature" (*hsien-feng wen-hsueh*) (e.g. Yü Hua, Sun Kan-lu, Su T'ung), and a theoretical interpretation of this trend as the harbinger of a new era. This new era was conceptualized in the 1990s by Chang I-wu and others as *hou hsin-shih-ch'i* (the post-new-period period), i.e. the period after the "new period" of the 1980s, which had been focused on the Western-oriented May Fourth vision of democracy, science, and "the Enlightenment."[12] As Chang I-wu was well aware, this way of trying to break out of the conceptual box of Western modernity paradoxically relied on recent Western trends regarding "postmodernism," "postcolonialism," and various other "posts." Particularly influential in China was the Marxism of Fredric Jameson, a gifted American student of literature equipped with a deep understanding of modern French and German thought. He had lectured at Peking University in 1985. His *Postmodernism, or, the Cultural Logic of Late Capitalism* was published in 1991 in the U.S. His thought easily meshed with the kind of Marxism developed by Li Tse-hou in the 1980s, because Jameson rejected any crude theory of economic determinism and class struggle; was preoccupied with the Marxist problem of exploitation and domination; made sweeping generalizations about the stages of global history; sought the theoretical integration of all disciplinary perspectives; subsumed the epistemological skepticism of the GMWER under this dialectical integration; focused on the interaction between culture and other social spheres; and viewed aesthetic productions (from the paintings of Andy Warhol to the music of Gustav Mahler) as the key to the understanding of culture.[13] He defined modernization as "the subsumption of society under capital" and postmodernism as the capitalist phase following the completion of modernization.[14]

That Jameson's postmodernism could not begin until modernization had been completed was not a problem for Chinese intellectuals, who had long been accustomed to Lenin's and Mao's theories about how to hurry along the emergence of a new historical stage. For them, therefore, Jameson suggested a theory with which to start putting down the cultural foundations of the new era following modernization and so bypassing the ills of a modernization process dominated by the capitalistic West. Echoing the May Fourth vision of a "new culture," their quest was of course not for a Burkean process of gradual change continuous with a morally mixed historical heritage. It was for a clean historical start leaving behind all the moral dissonance of the past: "feudalism"; the excesses of Stalin and Mao; modernity as a mix of excessive individualism, the "marketiza-tion" of social relations (*shih-ch'ang-hua*), globalization, and the subjection of China to the economic and cultural interests of the capitalist West (*ya-i*); and so the whole Western intellectual "discourse" used to rationalize this intellectual-moral dissonance — the primacy of science over "critical theory," the West's moderniza-tion theory, and Western sinology as a way of distorting the true nature of what Chang I-wu simply called "China." From this standpoint, of course, the Western mix of capitalism and democracy could not be a necessary model for China. Not even the goal of democracy, revered for more than a century in China, escaped this critique, according to which liberal criticism of China's lack of democracy just expressed "the Cold War prejudice against China and communism."[15]

Its liberal critics were quick to claim that this nativistic Marxism contradicted itself by depending on a Western theory to resist Western cultural hegemony. These neo-Marxists, however, were not being illogical, because they did not reject Marx's globalism. On the contrary, they saw the dawning of a new era in China as contingent on global development.[16] Their problem was not illogicality but that utopianism which they essentially shared with their critics. What they wanted was a global "dialogue" between people east and west all of whom would be free of all the forms of "oppression" (*ya-i*) listed above. Thus all peoples would be fully able to realize their authentic identity and stop trying to crush that of others, precisely the discourse #1 goal of a domestic and international political, economic, and cultural life free of all *shu-fu* (wrongly imposed constraints). Combined with the fear of Western hegemony, of the hegemony of the marketplace, and, especially, of the erosion of the intellectuals' traditionally prestigious role as "the conscience of society,"[17] this utopian goal naturally blended in with a reaffirmation of Mao's revolutionary vision and "the cultural tradition of Marxism," the "left-wing mainstream of Chinese literature" (e.g. Lu Hsun).[18]

From this standpoint, the cause for China's crisis was not lack of democracy but the turning of China into part of a globalized marketplace dominated by Western interests. The current Chinese reform policies facilitating this oppression also were part of this cause. With this theoretical definition of the chief cause for China's crisis today, all the agonizing dysfunctions of the rising market economy today could be analyzed in a richly empirical way as effects of this cause. Thus, while deflecting criticism of their government as undemocratic, the neo-Marxists still defined it as a vehicle of oppression, albeit just a conduit of Western oppression. With this stance, they simultaneously recaptured that radically critical perspective on the current regime which has been *de rigueur* in the Chinese intellectual tradition since the days of Mencius; enjoyed the publicity (on television and elsewhere) awarded them by a government grateful to them for shifting intellectual attention away from the June Fourth martyrs; provoked the scornful criticism of liberals, who accused them of focusing on the distant or imagined threat of Western hegemony instead of on the immediate problem of dictatorship in China — *pi-shih chiu-hsu ho she-chin ch'iu-yuan* (ignoring what is real to worry about what is not, brushing aside nearby evils to address distant ones);[19] and found themselves caught up in the epistemological difficulties afflicting postmodernism and deconstructionism in the West. For instance, viewing "the West's discourse" as a tool of its political interests, they could be attacked as arguing that "truth, standards of right and wrong, everything is simply controlled by power considerations and 'discourse.'" This idea, their liberal critics were happy to point out, contradicts the assumption that this idea is true.[20]

Also involved in this debate was a quarrel over whether "the right to speak" about China should be restricted to the scholars living there or shared with those comfortably ensconced in "the top-rated American universities" (*Mei-kuo ming-p'ai ta-hsueh*) and sometimes arrogantly implying that living in a free society allowed them to speak more clearly about China than their Chinese colleagues in China.[21] Crosscutting this quarrel was some tension between Shanghai and Beijing intellectual circles. Yang Yang, a scholar at Shanghai's East China Normal University, suggested in 1995 that the flattering attentions of the mass media had corrupted both vanguard literature and vanguard literary criticism:

[The] critics celebrating vanguard literature have all been concentrated in Beijing, while most of the vanguard authors were southern authors. Gradually, however, the important activity shifted to Beijing. Beijing is a kind of symbol for the culture of our country. Absolutely, its position on the Chinese mainland is central, not peripheral. What happened was precisely that vanguard criticism and vanguard literature radiated out throughout the nation from Beijing, this central area.[22]

Another scholar from this Shanghai university also criticized the postmodernism linked to Beijing circles. Said Wang Hsiao-ming: "The 'challenge' from the West is not the only problem faced by China in the twentieth century. In many periods, disruptions coming from deep within Chinese culture and history have been far, far more serious than this challenge. A relatively recent example is the so-called 'Great Cultural Revolution.'"[23]

By the late 1990s, *hou-hsueh* (postmodernism and the other "posts") had become less fashionable. Scholars regarded as "the New Left," however, continued mining the rich Western critique of bourgeois capitalism for ideas with which to resist the powerful and often painful if not horrific development of the global marketplace in China.

Marxism and Maoism, therefore, should not be regarded as minor or fading aspects of China's intellectual and political life. True, market forces in China today are virtually irresistible. Moreover, there is evidence that the Chinese leadership today is thinking less about resisting Western hegemony and more about accepting the supreme international position of the U.S. as a permanent part of that stable international order which China needs to modernize.[24] Such acceptance of U.S. centrality goes further than the old view that China should quietly build up its strength while only temporarily accepting an inferior international position (*t'ao-kuang yang-hui*).[25] Simultaneously, despite the bold criticism of the New Left and Henry K.H. Woo's Spenglerian vision (see chapter III), the belief that China's modernization must lead to democracy is held by nearly every intellectual, including the neo-conservative Xiao Gong-qin.

Yet the New Left's sharp criticism of Western modernity has deep Chinese roots. Otherwise, such criticism would not have been basic to three of modern China's four leading ideologies (see chapters II, III, IV, VII). It makes much sense to many in China, because, as shown by the discussion of discourse #1 in chapter I, political and intellectual rhetoric there has remained focused on the ancient dream of communal harmony, a *Gemeinschaft* dissolving conflicts between self-seeking individuals, instead of fully legitimizing the moral-intellectual dissonance of "the three marketplaces." The contrast between that dream and the image of the West in China has remained basic to Chinese intellectual life. Moreover, the radical criticism of Western modernity and globalization is also prominent in the Western intellectual world and cannot be simply brushed aside.

Even more, while such criticism of Western capitalism is also alive in Taiwan intellectual circles (see chapter VI, section 5), Taiwan's society today lacks the potentially explosive social sectors with which such criticism can easily develop "elective affinity." Most important, brilliantly analyzed by Xiao Gong-qin, there is a vast sector of able intellectuals whom the academic establishment is not yet large enough to hire, and who, finding scraps of employment along its periphery, tend to welcome radical theories expressing their alienation from a market-centered modernization program producing prestigious positions from which they have been excluded. While these radical theories are prominently promulgated by intellectuals "within the establishment" (*t'i-nei*), therefore, they appeal to many "outside the establishment" (*t'i-wai*).[26] Moreover, while economic progress has not yet been enough to dissolve this *t'i-wai* sector, it also has not turned the vast majority of Chinese into economically contented citizens uninterested in the kind of radical criticism pouring out of the intellectual sector as a whole. By contrast, such intellectual radicalism is far from dead in Taiwan, but the vast majority of the citizens there long ago became an economically contented bourgeoisie or petite bourgeoisie.

China's current ideological marketplace, therefore, includes a sharp tension between those enthusiastic about Western modernity and those suspicious of it, and this tension will undoubtedly affect whatever patterns of modernization and democratization the future will bring. These two diverging outlooks, however, do not simply clash with one another. True, there is no shortage of bitter, contemptuous criticism, given the time-honored tradition whereby "men of letters have low opinions of each other" (*wen-jen hsiang-ch'ing*). "Utterly ridiculous reasoning" (*chi-k'o-hsiao-te lo-chi*) was not an unusual way to describe an opponent's view during the debate about postmodernism. As already mentioned, however, the various current ideologies share much common ground. Moreover, as illustrated by the writings of not only Li Tse-hou but also Kuo Ch'i-yung, there is a tendency to synthesize the Confucian and the Marxist criticisms of Western liberal modernity. Even more, these humanistic criticisms can be quite readily combined with enthusiastic affirmation of all the standard liberal values (representative government, freedom, tolerance, pluralism, etc.). As already noted, Kuo's thought really seeks a synthesis of Marxism, modern Confucian humanism, liberal values, and Sunism, and it does not necessarily clash with neo-conservatism. The astute Xiao Gong-qin also emphasizes the growing tendency toward consensus in the intellectual world.

Although only a few intellectuals actively try to conceptualize an ideological synthesis, there is a widespread sense that all four trains of thought above form a kind of national seminar in which people should weigh differing views. Thus prominent periodicals like *Tu shu* and *Chan-lueh yü kuan-li* in effect serve as seminars, since they print essays with different outlooks rather than seeking to develop a single coherent perspective. Many articles debating postmodernism in the 1990s appeared precisely in such periodicals, including the prominent *Erh-shih-i shih-chi* in Hong Kong. Moreover, many intellectuals waver between and blur together the competing trains of thought above rather than pursuing a single, logically coherent position clearly opposed to alternative ones.

This common tendency, allowing an individual to speak approvingly of all four trains of thought above, reflects not only the fact that Marxism and Hegelianism have made Mainland intellectuals entirely comfortable with the idea that history unfolds the truth in a circuitous, "dialectical" way. It also reflects all the traditional intellectual tendencies that Marxists like Feng Ch'i could interpret as "fledgling versions of dialectical logic." In this context, the current styles of reasoning strike me as reflecting the influence of Buddhism on Chinese culture, particularly the *p'an-chiao* tradition going back to the fifth century A.D., according to which contradictory positions could be seen as phases in the unfolding of a single truth. Thinkers like T'ang Chün-i have explicitly used the *p'an-chiao* concept to legitimize the current diversity of clashing doctrines. Similarly, in the 1990s the idea of "paradox" (*pei-lun*) became fashionable as still another way of seeking a logically coherent relation between seemingly contradictory tendencies.

It is also clear that the 1990s debate about postmodernism implied the hope that the interplay of contradictory views would eventually lead to a dialectical synthesis of them. For instance, in editing the 1998 volume representing both sides of the debate, Wang Hui implicitly identified his own thinking with the debate itself rather than one side of it, although he also was seen as leaning toward the neo-Marxist side. This ambivalence was reinforced by the ambivalence of the official ideology, which welcomed not only the liberals' approval of the globalized marketplace but also the Marxists' nativism and criticism of the liberal calls for democratization.

Most important was the widespread post-Mao perception of the current unavailability of a fully developed doctrine adequately elucidating this implied dialectical synthesis. As discussed in chapter II, T'ang Chün-i's Confucian philosophy emphasized this not uncommon idea that Chinese thinkers are currently far from having discovered that definitive philosophy China needs. In contrast with the Maoist and Sunist premise that a "great" thinker has furnished this definitive philosophy, this paradigm of an ongoing intellectual search logically implies the need for intellectual pluralism. In other words, the idea, common since about 1900, that China is in the midst of a "transitional era" was for many uncoupled from the idea that this era was proceeding under the aegis of a definitive philosophical system. Even the main Party organ, *People's Daily*, has endorsed the intellectual diversity found today on the campus of Peking University. Praising the way two professors (one a member of the Hoover Institution, hardly a bastion of Marxism) openly argued with each other during the class period, the writer of an article in this paper, a student in this class, concluded with the ancient principle that "persons of integrity will disagree while being in a state of harmony with each other, but persons without integrity will agree even while really being in a state of conflict with each other."[27] All such ideas provided an epistemological setting almost resembling J.S. Mill's concept of "fallibility" as a way to legitimize pluralism, intellectual-moral dissonance, and thus "the three marketplaces."[28] Moreover, mentioned above, the partly "romantic" retreat "into the tower at the crossroads" or into parochial, familistic concerns has also served to mute ideological zeal.[29]

692

A Cloud Across the Pacific*A Cloud Across the Pacific*

All in all, therefore, there is a striking "elective affinity" or mesh between the new inhibited, accommodative political center and much of the new thinking in the ideological marketplace that has chronologically accompanied it. Given this mesh, one cannot say this new center lacks moral legitimization, even though, as noted below, this new mix of attitudes includes the view that this new center is as morally aberrant as the old one.

If the above sketch of China's ideological marketplace is on target, one can be skeptical about a number of prominent views today. It is mistaken to believe that, outside the Party line, respect for the ideas of Marx and Mao is no longer important. It is also mistaken to regard the basic ideological bifurcation as that between state Marxism and liberal intellectual circles. At least as important, the bifurcation between acceptance of and resistance to the Western liberal model of modernity crosscuts state and intellectual circles. Moreover, it would be impossible to demonstrate that there is more of a "spiritual vacuum" or "ideological crisis" today in China than in any other modern or modernizing society. China today is full of serious, astute persons who have deep moral and intellectual convictions and are dismayed by the trends of the day. This situation is at odds with the Chinese ideal of a society in which "all agree on the same reasoning and so are of one mind" (*jen t'ung tz'u hsin, hsin t'ung tz'u li*), but it is hardly at odds with the usual condition of any modern society. Nor does the ideological marketplace in China today fundamentally resemble that of Taiwan on the eve of democratization or include a dominant tendency toward pragmatic political discussion favoring prompt democratization and convergence with the Western liberal model of modernity.

Scholars today may be more ready than they were ten years ago to recognize deep contrasts between the societal and ideological development of Taiwan and that of the Mainland.[30] One contrast stems from two ideological trends today on the Mainland without parallel in Taiwan ten years ago. True, it is striking that the tension between Chinese liberalism and modern Confucian humanism is evident in both cases. On the Mainland, however, the official doctrine is part of an intellectually respected trend and is complemented by a prominent kind of neo-conservatism.

This contrast, I would suggest, stems not only from the distinctive nature of Marxism, an internationally prestigious doctrine associated by serious thinkers like Feng Ch'i and Li Tse-hou with a sacred revolutionary movement and its charismatic leader. It stems also from an emphasis in Mainland circles stronger than in Taiwan circles on the pathologies of both Chinese culture (*feng-chien i-tu*) and the Western liberal model, combined with the still living theme of "transcending the West" and recovering China's international centrality. The Taiwan elites saw themselves as competing with the Mainland, not with the West. They wanted to show that they could pursue democracy and modernization more successfully than China, not more successfully than the West, and they did not aim to match the West's international importance, instead relying on it in their confrontation with the Mainland.

To be sure, in the Chinese ideological marketplace today, the relative importance of the various ideas above is hard to assess, and there is indeed plenty of pragmatic thinking about the practical problems of economic and political organization. Recognizing this fact, many Western political scientists, following "rational choice" theory, believe that China's political development will depend much less on the ideological debates in the ivory tower than on non-intellectual developments, such as economic trends and the policy decisions of highly pragmatic leaders, including perhaps even the recent tendency, noted above, to accept China's secondary position in the world order not as a temporarily humiliating condition but as a structural part of the world's historical development. After all, history is multicausal, and the pragmatic trend toward convergence so cogently analyzed by Alex Inkeles is extremely important.

Yet David S. Landes, Samuel P. Huntington, Thomas Sowell and others have reminded us that culturally divergent tendencies are also crucial. Apart from popular culture, the mobilization of opinion in intellectual circles can also be a major causative variable in political development, as strongly argued by Reinhard Bendix. Moreover, one cannot discount the peculiar importance with which the Confucian tradition endowed China's intellectual elite. In speaking of "the intellectual origins of the Chinese revolution," Lucien Bianco seems to have properly assessed the causative historical variables involved.[31] Chinese intellectuals today still typically see themselves as trying to develop a "morally critical consciousness" (*p'i-p'an i-shih*) on which the fate of their nation depends. They may be exaggerating the causative importance of their historical role, but it would be unwise to assume they have entirely miscalculated it. What is involved here is the ethos of a social stratum which certainly is small but on which modern Chinese life depends. The pragmatism of many business and political leaders is blunt, widespread, and easily appreciated by Western liberals and proponents of modernization theory, but there is no evidence that it can ever become the ideological foundation of the Chinese state.

2. The Problem of a Persisting Discourse

But what are the intellectual ideas most likely to affect societal development?

Opinion surveys in China can help answer this question, but this research, outside the scope of this paper, has to be complemented by the in-depth study of attitudes extensively articulated in written texts and conversations.

Such attitudes can be seen as consciously developed "doctrines" (*hsueh-shuo*) or "trains of thought" (*ssu-lu*). One could then ask which of the above four "doctrines" will turn out to be the most influential. All "doctrines," however, are controversial, and so people feel free to doubt, criticize, and reject them. After all, only two or three decades ago, the liberalism and Confucian humanism now at the center of the stage were regarded as peripheral trends that had been eclipsed by the rise of what John K. Fairbank called China's "new orthodoxy," Mao's Marxism. Given this ebb and flow of controversial doctrines, many scholars tried to set forth the basic, enduring features of "Chinese culture," but they could find no empirically sound way of dealing with such a huge topic. Thus the notion of a "discourse" became popular as a way of referring to the premises shared by a range of otherwise conflicting views expressed in a specific set of historical documents, which thus amounted to a cultural strand. The importance of this strand in the society as a whole could then be left as an open empirical question. When the strand included the most famous ideologies of the era, however, its importance could not be doubted.

As chapter I discussed, the premises of such a strand are the platitudes or clichés that a group regards as too obviously true to deserve discussion and uses to define the most basic aspects of reality. The hope motivating analysis of these clichés is that, by identifying them, one can not only identify the ideas used in many circles over a long period of time as uncontroversial principles of action but also bring to consciousness assumptions which should be subjected to critical scrutiny. Instead of just claiming to answer the questions on the agenda of the day, one can ask whether the premises leading to these questions are justified. As Isaiah Berlin wrote in 1962:

> The first step to understanding of men is the bringing to consciousness of the model or models that dominate and penetrate their thought and action. Like all attempts to make men aware of the categories in which they think, it is a difficult and sometimes painful activity.... The second task is to analyze the model itself ... accepting or modifying or rejecting it ...[32]

Chapter I, therefore, tried in some detail to identify the key categories or premises common to the competing ideologies that arose in twentieth-century China. Logically independent, four can here be singled out: the idea that the goal of Chinese political life is creation of society free from the controlling influence of selfish interests, from moral-intellectual dissonance; the vision of a morally corrigible political center (the state) as entirely capable of affirming and realizing this goal; the idea that, when the corrigible state has failed to do this, a certain moral-intellectual elite can fully commit themselves to the pursuit of this goal, rising above all selfish interests and bias and so serving as "the conscience of society";[33] and the belief that the means to reach this goal revolve around the interaction between the given teleological logic of global history moving through stages and the efforts of intellectuals theoretically to grasp this logic and thus construct the cultural basis for optimal political and economic development.

Basic to this last premise is the belief that this logic is to be found in the theoretical relations between highly generalized values the natures of which are obvious, such as "modernization," "freedom," or "democracy," and huge, objectively real, homogeneous segments of history, such as "the great power of the various forms of hegemony used by Western imperialism," "the value outlook of the West's individualism and Enlightenment," "China" (as in Chang I-wu's "concern about how to make clear the true nature of China"), "Third World Experience," "First World theory," "Third World culture," and "the Western values of modernization."[34] In other words, global history can be grasped by abstractly discussing the relations among the huge historical realities these block terms denote, as opposed to disaggregating the many ideas each of these block terms implies and then determining the usefulness of each of these narrower ideas in an empirically specific way. As emphasized in the discussion of discourse #1 (see chapter I, table 2), China's intellectual mainstream in the twentieth century has had few reservations about seeing reified concepts, such as "Chinese culture," as denoting "systems" with clear casual relations, and about assuming that these systems develop according to a teleological sequence of stages.

To be sure, this inclination toward simplistic macroscopic concepts has coexisted with a rich historiographical tradition devoted to the pursuit of significant concrete details put into the context of a cautiously crafted analysis. An outstanding example is the tradition of Ch'en Yin-k'o at Tsinghua University carried on today by Liu Kuei-sheng and his students.[35] This historiographical tradition, however, has not impaired the academic respectability of the belief that the single historical reality underlying disparate, observable, verbalized ideas can be holistically and objectively grasped without the danger of projecting subjective stereotypes into its conceptualization. There is indeed a common, uniquely Chinese term denoting this kind of holistic insight into a single essential reality that can be inferred from many facts, *tsung-chieh-ch'u-lai*, an epistemologically optimistic concept. Going beyond mere "induction"(*kuei-na-ch'u-lai*), it conflates empiricism and intuitionism. For instance, holding that Confucius's philosophy is based on the way all people in fact behave, a leading sinologist wrote: "*Lun-yü* is a book written in an utterly plain, straightforward way. In general, what Confucius said can be practiced. Moreover, his ideas were a way of bringing together what is evident from human behavior generally (*tsung-chieh-ch'u-lai-te*)."[36]

Given this kind of epistemologically optimistic belief that insight can go beyond the empiricism of propositions cautiously tailored to fit specific data, such empiricism is sometimes attacked by Chinese scholars as a "Western" inability to proceed from the sorting out of "fragmentary data" (*so-sui*) to the factual-normative conclusion they imply.[37] Thus in Beijing academic circles today, contempt for such empiricism and admiration of the more Hegelian side of modern Western thought continues to be a powerful tendency, as illustrated so vividly by the enormous impact Fredric Jameson has had on the post-Mao scene in Beijing ever since his 1985 lectures at Peking University.

Given the keen reflexivity of the energetic Chinese scholars who in the post-Mao period continuously expanded the frontiers of their knowledge, they could have identified and critically assessed these five premises. As shown by the debate in the 1990s about postmodernism, however, few if any of them chose to do this. Instead, they addressed questions arising out of these very premises, which had for so long informed China's major public debates. The only change was in some of their answers to these questions. Indeed, nothing was more continuous with the past than their belief that they were "breaking with the new era" to enter the "era following the new era" (*hou hsin-shih-ch'i*).[38]

True, the proponents of postmodernism were innovative in suggesting that, contrary to the revered May Fourth Movement and the focus in the 1980s on the West's Enlightenment, Chinese intellectuals should seek an alternative to Western liberal modernity by combining the Western critique of this Western model with a rediscovery of Mao's vision and his effort to root it in a certain collective, authentically Chinese consciousness. This innovative view, however, precisely presupposed the fourth premise above: that history moves in clearly demarcated stages according to a global, teleological logic; that history can be hurried along by intellectuals who theoretically grasp the aesthetic and cultural aspects of this logic; and that the theory of historical development can depend on block concepts denoting huge, basically homogeneous segments of history, such as "China" and "the great power of the various forms of hegemony used by Western imperialism." Indeed, if such block terms had been regarded as too loose and vague to be usable, a central category of Chinese postmodernism, the idea of the current "oppression" of "China" by "the West" (*ya-i*), would have seemed insufficiently specific.

If the proponents of postmodernism did not question this fourth premise, neither did their liberal critics, who instead accused them of dilating on the distant if not imaginary danger of Western hegemony instead of the real problem of oppression in China by the undemocratic government there. Similarly, neither of the parties to this debate doubted the third premise, namely, that intellectuals should serve as "the conscience of society," transcending all biases and self-interest to confront the forces of oppression.[39] They merely disagreed about which pattern of oppression, the foreign or the domestic, was the most immediate, and about which pattern of self-interest had corrupted the "conscience" of intellectuals: the alleged desire of some domestic intellectuals to curry favor with the government, or the alleged influence of the "First World discourse" on overseas intellectuals co-opted by "the top-rated American universities."

Nor did either party to the debate challenge the epistemological optimism basic to all four of the above premises. As discussed in chapter I, section 7, when Chinese intellectuals in the 1990s became increasingly familiar with the skeptical arguments of the GMWER, they had no trouble both accepting them and subsuming them under an absolutistic vision of history's moral and historical structure. Such a structure was basic both to postmodernism's vision of a new era bypassing the "oppression" inflicted on China by Western modernity and the liberals' vision of a democratic China free of the oppression inflicted on the Chinese people by the current Chinese government. Similarly, the persistence of the second premise, the idea of a morally corrigible political center, is implied by the intellectuals' self-image as "the conscience of society." Had the intellectuals conceptualized the political center as morally incorrigible, criticizing it for not respecting the "moral conscience of society" would not have been plausible. With their inherited ideal of a morally perfect political center (*te-chih, jen-cheng, nei-sheng wai-wang*), contemporary Chinese intellectuals continued to define political life as a dialogue between persons who, whether outside the state or leading it, are capable of fully grasping and acting on the absolute moral dictates of conscience, not as a dialogue between officials and intellectuals forgiving each other for being fallible and for unavoidably lapsing into some degree of bias and self-interest.

Most important, they continued to emphasize the belief — so vividly illustrated by the neo-Marxism beginning in the 1990s — that political progress is a matter of creating "a new culture" or initiating "a new era" leaving behind the moral and intellectual confusion of the past, not a matter of building on the foundations of an institutionally and intellectually flawed tradition. Indeed this key

Burkean point — that the histor̦ical heritage on which a nation should be built is unavoidably marred by human frailties — was not grasped when a young Chinese scholar in the 1990s tried boldly to celebrate Western conservatism as a major Western intellectual trend that Chinese scholarship had for too long ignored.[40]

What the Chinese intellectual mainstream continues to insist on is the utopian view that, necessarily and globally, history moves in stages and can be made to move from the current stage filled with troubles to one without troubles; history is not a matter of piecemeal progress in a continuing moral limbo (*shen-mo hun-tsa*). This modern preoccupation with a utopian concept of historical stages goes back to K'ang Yu-wei's (1858–1927) version of the ancient concept of "the three stages" (*san-shih-lun*), but the Confucian faith at its very core denies that the historical medium of political progress is an unending moral limbo.

3. Chinese Utopianism and the Problem of Uncovering and Critiquing It

To be sure, a realistic, pessimistic awareness of the importance of self-interest is central to many political discussions in China and indeed is the lubricant often minimizing Chinese political frictions. My point has never been that the four premises above necessarily promote a Manichaean, black-and-white outlook aggravating political frictions. As already indicated, they can also promote efforts to accommodate and minimize such frictions. Indeed, "moderate realism" was basic to bureaucratic thinking in late imperial China, as I have elsewhere discussed; Huang Ko-wu has shown how thinkers like Yen Fu and Liang Ch'i-ch'ao tried to promote an "accommodative," gradualistic approach to political development; and such an approach was institutionalized both in Taiwan under the Kuomintang during the second half of the twentieth century and on the Mainland during its last quarter.

What the four premises preclude, however, is an explicit definition of normal political life as interactions that on the one hand are necessarily influenced by bias and self-interest and, on the other, are the necessary and actually promising medium of societal progress. In other words, one of the key questions political theory has to address is how to regard those aspects of political life which virtually all persons in all cultures regard as extremely undesirable and currently pervasive — selfishness, corruption, irrationality, etc. As I argued in chapter VIII, section 7, one can (1) be determined to act decisively to end completely all this moral-intellectual dissonance; (2) give up this radical, transformative hope but still denounce the dissonance as inexcusable and intolerable; (3) regard this dissonance as the normal medium of accommodative, peaceful, piecemeal, gradualistic, progressive political efforts; (4) deplore but opportunistically accommodate this dissonance; or (5) fatalistically accept it.

Certainly all five attitudes can be found in China today or perhaps even in any major society. In China, however, the four premises above made up a coherent, widespread intellectual standpoint morally legitimizing options #1 and #2 and utterly incompatible with the moral legitimization of option #3. It is this extremely prominent and optimistic concept of political practicability for which the term "Chinese utopianism" is suitable.

Whether of the five options above Chinese utopianism is the most reasonable can be debated. Certainly it is a questionable approach from the standpoint of the current sociological literature on trust, civility, and social capital.[41] This is because it tends to define political disagreement in a Manichaean way as a conflict between people in the right and people in the wrong, instead of one between people who all are morally and intellectually fallible and flawed. The argument can be made that the latter outlook is needed to further that multilateral, trustful, imaginative coordination of organizational resources which modernization requires. Yet whether or not this argument against Chinese utopianism is reasonable, efforts in the Chinese intellectual world to identify and critique this major, tradition-rooted Chinese attitude have so far been ineffectual.

One reason no doubt is that the idea of "utopianism" is hard to define. One has to keep in mind the great difference between Chinese "utopianism" and the classical Western utopianism going back to Sir Thomas More's (1478–1535) famous book *Utopia*, which was much influenced by Plato. In this Western discussion, an ideal was put forward by thinkers doubting its practicability. This posture is absent from Chinese intellectual history, with the possible exception of T'ao Ch'ien's (A.D. 365?–427) famous poetic essay "Peach-blossom Fountain." Chinese utopianism like Western utopianism posits a huge contrast between the disastrous present and the ideals of humanity, but it goes much further than Western utopianism in generating a radical determination to implement these ideals. This is because it posits not only that these ideals are completely practicable but also that they have in fact been basically realized during one concrete segment of human history other than the present stage of Chinese history. The archetype for this unique perception of history was of course the Confucian perception of an ancient period of moral-political perfection, "the three dynasties." This archetype was inseparable from the kind of "this-worldliness" Fung Yu-lan correctly saw as the Chinese mainstream: the belief that the concrete here-and-now not only should but also could be made morally perfect. Paradoxically, then, Chinese with this optimistic concept of political practicability deny it is "utopian." When I gave a course on "modern Chinese utopianism" at the Chinese University of Hong Kong in 1994, a colleague told me the concept of utopia had never appeared in the history of Chinese thought.

Given the fact that this idea of Chinese utopianism is elusive, it is not surprising that, before the 1980s, Chinese and Western scholars seeking the intellectual roots of China's troubles seldom if ever mentioned "utopianism." The emphasis was on the "disorientation," "crisis of meaning," and "authority crisis" following "the death of the Confucian worldview" and the inability to replace this traditional worldview with another coherent moral order. In the 1970s, however, a few scholars, especially Professor Wang Erh-min, noted the rising "optimism" in the Chinese world after the Opium War — the belief that Chinese could create an ideal China if they made selective use of Western ideas. In 1981, in a Taipei talk given at the *Shih-chien-t'ang* and sponsored by *Chung-kuo shih-pao,* I tried to define the dangerous "utopianism" accompanying this "optimism," although I failed to clarify the differences between this Chinese trend and the Western utopianism classically expressed by Sir Thomas More. In 1982, Professor Chang Hao published his important article on the Western alternative to Chinese utopianism, the "sense of the permanent moral darkness of history." Still later, Mainland intellectuals started blaming the Cultural Revolution on a "utopian craze" (*wu-t'o-pang k'uang-je*). Today, the rejection of "utopianism" and the need for "gradualism" and "accommodative" policies are common Mainland themes often associated with a new appreciation of Yen Fu's rejection of radicalism.[42] Moreover, the writings of not only Chang Hao but also scholars like Cheng Chia-tung and Ch'i Liang illustrate awareness that the Confucian tradition, including the New Confucians, may have encumbered China with an overly optimistic view of human nature, political practicability, and history.[43]

Nevertheless, this awareness has hardly become the mainstream. To some extent, it has been explicitly rejected. By 2001 some scholars in China, such as Hung T'ao of Fudan University in Shanghai, vigorously confronted the argument that China's indigenous utopianism and epistemological optimism had prevented Chinese intellectuals from grasping the rationale of Millsian liberalism (which presupposed a much more pessimistic view of the scope of knowledge and of political practicability) and so had inclined them toward a Rousseauistic concept of democracy and revolutionary radicalism. The book Hung attacked, Huang Ko-wu's prize-winning study of Yen Fu (1854–1921) recently published in Taiwan and then republished in Shanghai, actually raised four distinct questions: (1) What aspects of J.S. Mill's concept of liberty did Yen not understand? (2) To what extent was his failure typical of the modern Chinese intellectual world? (3) If it was typical, to what extent was this general failure responsible for the fact that the Mainland's political development turned to radicalism and to the Rousseauistic vision of democracy rather than to the liberal, Millsian model of democracy? (4) To what extent was this turn tragic? Hung did not venture to dispute Huang's findings regarding (1) and (2). Instead, determined to refute what Huang at least implied, that China had experienced a tragic turn to Rousseauism and radicalism, he blurred the four questions together; inaccurately depicted Huang as claiming that the Chinese intellectual failure to grasp Millsiansim was *the* cause of China's turn to radicalism (according to Huang, it was *a* cause); and denounced all the "stale" criticisms of Rousseau east and west. He referred to "this great tradition stretching from Plato to Rousseau and Germany's classical philosophy" and held that Millsianism, intertwined with "conservatism," "elitism," and "authoritarianism," was part of "the politics of globalization" marginalizing "the Chinese intellectual world."

Typical of "the New Left" views discussed above, Hung's criticisms were published in a prominent academic journal in Beijing financed by the Harvard-Yenching Institute and were well received by at least some of Beijing's well-known younger intellectuals, including good friends of mine.[44] Thus in China today even outside radical intellectual circles, there is a considerable though not necessarily mainstream intellectual tendency to cling to Rousseau's optimistic belief that government should and can be the realization of absolute freedom. In 2001, one particularly astute and erudite Beijing scholar even explicitly rejected Chang Hao's seemingly impeccable thesis that "the sense of history's permanent moral darkness" (*yu-an i-shih*) has been basic to the successful practice of democratic politics in the liberal West.

There is no doubt that the contrast between this Western *yu-an i-shih* and Chinese utopianism is an issue entailing very deep and subtle cultural differences that most Chinese intellectuals have not easily grasped. Therefore they have seldom conceptualized a clear alternative to Chinese utopianism. This Western *yu-an i-shih* refers to a historical condition T'ang Chün-i called *shen-mo hun-tsa* (the blurring together of the sacred and the demonic). In the Chinese context, however, the only rational response to this condition was trying to overcome it. The Western notion so hard to grasp in China was that this condition is unalterable. Even Chang Hao, I would argue, did not fully accept it.[45]

These are two utterly irreconcilable conceptualizations of common sense. While Confucius held he could quickly reform a government if he were given the opportunity, Socrates said an honest man trying to reform government would quickly be killed. This Greek pessimism was basic to Aristotle's thesis that, while there are six kinds of political systems, the three best ones are basically beyond the ability of people to realize. With St. Augustine, this Greek pessimism merged with the Christian idea that political life was necessarily infected with original sin. This pessimistic outlook became central also in modern times. Arthur O. Lovejoy discussed its importance in the minds of the American Founding Fathers, Reinhold Niebuhr wrote about the moral pessimism basic to democracy, and Samuel P. Huntington, echoing Joseph Schumpeter, said: "Disillusionment and the lowered expectations it produces are the foundation of democratic stability."[46]

Thus perceived as a morally and intellectually dissonant process, normal political life was necessarily and permanently full of all the traits that the modern Chinese intellectual mainstream has regarded as intolerable: selfishness, insincerity, alienation, the interplay of different doctrines defining each other as irrational (*fen-yun*), "constraints" immorally inflicted on others by dominant persons (*shu-fu*), inequality, exploitation, vested interests (*chi-te-li-i-che*), and "cunning politicians" (*cheng-k'o*) representing vested interests while pretending to pursue the public good (*chia-kung chi-ssu*). Moreover, the combination of human sinfulness with the temptations of political power was especially dangerous, as Lord Acton emphasized. Thus the political center was seen as morally incorrigible.

According to this Western standpoint, then, this dissonance could be only reduced, not eliminated. It was utterly naïve to think otherwise. In history's moral limbo, there could be no transformative elimination of evil (*pa-pen se-yuan*). Politics as "the art of the possible" did not allow realization of "the way of the true king" (*wang-tao*) and instead prized the difference between Hitler and Churchill. Thus Karl R. Popper, the philosopher of the "Open Society," admired Winston Churchill, although Churchill, who was determined to preserve the British empire, was hardly a "true king." Similarly, Max Weber emphasized that the ethical vision of Jesus was too high to serve as a normative guideline for statesmen, who unavoidably used violence to pursue political goals. In thus distinguishing between political norms and the highest morality, Weber was following in the footsteps of Western thinkers going back to St. Augustine, who had distinguished between "the City of God" and the "the City of man," and to Aristotle, who had said that the principles for managing a family differ from those for running a government.

True, the Confucian tradition too included notes of appreciation for beneficial government that is not fully virtuous, but the mainstream insisted that "the way of the true king" is the only proper political norm. For the Western mainstream, however, the kind of ultimate virtue described in the Confucian *Four Books* as *ch'eng* (total sincerity) was not the norm typically used to evaluate leaders and citizens, even before that major shift toward realism brought about by Machiavelli and Hobbes and studied by Leo Strauss and Quentin Skinner.

Religion defined such ultimate virtue as needed to win salvation after death, but there was also a great emphasis on the doable virtues any decent person could practice. Such virtues cannot even be conceptualized in Chinese with concocting a preposterous term, such as *hsiang-yuan-te-tao-te* (the morality of the person who seeks to seem respectable but actually lacks a commitment to doing what is right), or *chung-jen-te tao-te* (the morality of a morally mediocre person). These doable virtues included not breaking the law, not lying, honoring contracts, cleanliness (second only to Godliness), and avoiding drunkenness, gluttony, and irascibility. To be sure, Patricia Ebrey showed that in Confucian China too, the doable virtues of the merely decent person also were emphasized. In the West, however, they were emphasized in a cultural context accepting the permanent moral dissonance of political life. Thus virtue in public life could be emphasized without implying the need to realize a society and a political life free of the pursuit of selfish interest. Indeed, "civility" as the public virtue of the merely decent person is not even a word that can be translated into Chinese.

This Western acceptance of the role of selfish interests in political interaction was then reinforced by the epistemological revolution mentioned above, which popularized the idea of unavoidable human fallibility, thus logically reinforced the willingness to be doubtful about one's own convictions, and so facilitated the willingness to compromise when cultivating "the art of the possible."

Moreover, the normative impact of the Industrial Revolution, raising mass living standards, also has to be considered in the light of this Western acceptance of moral-political dissonance. Materially improving the lives of the vast majority, finally bringing affluence out of the mansions of privilege into the villages, finally relieving the suffering of the masses, could be more easily appreciated as a precious governmental achievement when the moral dissonance still accompanying this achievement was regarded as anyway unavoidable. By contrast, many modern Chinese intellectuals, believing government has the ability and the duty to eliminate this moral dissonance, vigorously refused to recognize rising mass prosperity as an important criterion for weighing the moral legitimacy of a government.[47]

All in all, then, the utopian tendency Xiao Gong-qin criticized as "romanticism" has remained important. John K. Fairbank in 1992 thus described a major Chinese intellectual trend demanding that the leadership create

"an economy free of any unfair, selfish appropriation of wealth, a polity in which selfish interests do not affect the key leadership decisions, an intellectual life free of confusing contradictions (*fen-yun*) and bringing all truths, moral and factual, into a single, unified doctrinal system (*hui-t'ung*), a civilization free of all oppression, insincerity, and selfishness, and a society in which the status of every individual is successfully and objectively based on his or her achievements."

Accordingly, when in 2002 Hu Wei-xi, a professor of philosophy at Tsinghua University, referred to Mou Tsung-san's Confucian vision of the "great oneness" (*ta-t'ung*) as a society free of the unfair appropriation of resources by this or that "'me,'" he could without fear of contradiction remark: "This is close to what we today speak of as 'democratic government.'"[48] *Knowing* that their ideal was politically practicable, China's mainstream intellectuals continued using it to condemn the moral dissonance they saw around them and to regard as morally flawed anyone who "closely worked with" (*chieh-kuei*) rather than "resisted" (*chü-chueh*) the current structure of political power.

Well illustrated by the debate on postmodernism in the 1990s, this moralistic perspective on political life in China is a quite normal, uncontroversial one shared by radical dissidents with many intellectuals part of the institutional mainstream, including members of the Party. For instance, a publishing house in Nanchang, Kiangsi, recently brought out two prominent volumes, *Hsueh-wen Chung-kuo* (China Today in Intellectual Perspective) (1998) and *Hsueh-shuo Chung-kuo* (China Today in Scholarly Perspective) (1999). The former aimed to present to the nation the thinking of some of the most promising younger scholars in the Beijing area, the latter, of those in the Shanghai area. The latter included an essay by Chu Hsueh-ch'in, a well-known professor at the University of Shanghai, who defined the "liberalism" that had developed in England during the last two centuries as a mix of "empiricism," the rejection of "historical determinism," "gradualism," belief in "the market mechanism," belief in "representative democracy, constitutional government, and the rule of law," and belief in "protecting the value of the individual" as something that "cannot be sacrificed in the pursuit of any abstract goal." This outlook, Chu wrote, "has become the usual consensus of ordinary citizens in the civilized countries of the contemporary world." Without qualification contrasting this "consensus" with the current "system of political power" in China, Chu emphasized that "liberalism" requires translating these beliefs into morally resolute personal action:

Liberalism is not just for talking purposes, it is a matter of doing, of walking the walk. Liberalism today is not Hegel's "inner freedom." It alerts you directly to face the unfree realities outside, first of all facing up to the system of political power. This includes facing up to the academic and other systems that have connected themselves with the international world, even though they give forth the appearance of being gentle and benign. Liberalism does not demand you fight back, and it has no reason to demand you resign [from your paid position in a state institution]. It can, however, alert you to resist, to resist person by person, bit by bit. Moreover, the extent of such resistance increases quantitatively: freedom exists just to the extent that one person resists (*chü-chueh*). The number of persons obtaining freedom is precisely the number resisting the system of political power.[49]

Similarly, in Chinese intellectual circles today, one can assert without fear of contradiction that "culture criticism," which is regarded as central to any intellectual perspective on government, must eschew any "compromise with the current order, with the culture officially sponsored by one's nation."[50] Whatever the exigencies of governance in a nation with 900 million or more citizens struggling in a sea of poverty, there can be no tolerance of any politicization or vulgarization of the culture by the state.

Such, then, are the forms of Chinese utopianism persisting today. In this situation, the fashionable denunciation of "utopianism" has meant no more than rejecting the pursuit of sublime ideals in a hasty, imprudent, dogmatic, and violent way, not rejecting it as the proper political perspective of intellectuals. In other words, Chinese utopianism has persisted as the belief that the citizenry consists of not just sinners with morally mixed motivations but also a moral-intellectual elite grasping the objective truths about how political life should be, rising above selfish interests, and so serving as "the conscience of society," and the belief that the political center is morally corrigible, that is, susceptible to being directly or indirectly guided by this morally enlightened elite. This premise is directly opposed to the Western liberal vision of a morally incorrigible political center monitored not by an enlightened elite but just by ordinary, morally flawed, intellectually fallible citizens in the civil society less exposed than officials to the corrupting temptations of political power.[51]

The pervasiveness of Chinese utopianism is also illustrated by the contemporary arguments about the extent to which, if any, Confucius's humanism should be revised in order to make it compatible with contemporary China's goals of modernization and democratization. What should be "adopted" and what should be "discarded" (*ch'ü-she*)?

As is well known, going back to T'an Ssu-t'ung and the May Fourth Movement, Chinese increasingly claimed his thought should be "discarded," since all the "irrational constraints" (*shu-fu*) preventing "the liberation of the individual" stemmed from "the hierarchical ethical teachings" (*ming-chiao*) of Confucianism grounded in the thought of Confucius. On the other hand, prominent again today on the Mainland, modern Confucian humanism developed in many ways during the twentieth century emphasizing a spirit of *chi-wang k'ai-lai* (respect for the essential values of the past and openness to the new values of the modern world).

To a large extent, the argument turned on authoritarianism. Authoritarianism and sexism have been pervasive in the premodern monarchial world east and west, but the opponents of Confucianism, focusing on the *san-kang* (the three principles of hierarchy), tried to suggest that Confucianism was unusual in putting the ruler above the subject, the husband above the wife, and the father above the children. The New Confucians and others refuted this charge, documenting the pervasive Confucian emphasis on the moral and intellectual autonomy of the individual.

Both sides, however, overlooked possible problems involved in the Confucian concept of moral autonomy, including utopianism. These problems seem basic not just to the Confucian tradition but to the thought of Confucius himself. *Lun-yü* and the rest of *Four Books* hold not only that all of society can become totally good but also that the source of this "good" is an utterly pure conscience inherent in the self or the moral subject. Because this source is morally "pure" (the "not yet issued feelings implied by a person's latent sense of perfect moral balance," as the *Doctrine of the Mean* puts it), a person who sees himself or herself as having a "good" outlook views this goodness as flawless. Moreover, this self is also endowed with a reliable intellectual ability to know what is objectively good for society as a whole. Thus, in accord with the *Great Learning*'s "eight steps," a person turns into the personification of goodness after carrying out the epistemic and moral steps of self-cultivation ("investigating things," "acquiring knowledge," "purifying intentions," "rectifying the mind," and "cultivating the self"), and then everything bad and mistaken in the world is outside the self. In other words, the relation between self and other is a relation between what is good and what is not good. Embodying good intentions and an objective understanding of what is good for the world, the self then takes charge of the political center and finds that, once the ruler is good, everyone else also will be.[52]

In this train of thought one fully finds epistemological optimism, the utopian belief in the political practicability of sublime ideals, the idea of the guiding enlightened elite, and the idea of the corrigible political center. Yet most of the intellectuals today calling for a return to the wisdom of Confucius as the basis of Chinese modernization and democratization have not uncovered these premises and asked whether they are compatible with these modern goals.

As already noted, a modern critique of these premises would not necessarily show that they are incompatible with them; it would not necessarily show that these premises were dysfunctional in premodern times; and it would not necessarily cast a shadow on many aspects of Confucius's thought attracting so much admiration today. The viability of different philosophical or humanistic projects east and west is a complex question. But if "morally critical consciousness" is a matter of creatively and critically reviewing the past in the light of contemporary goals to decide what to "retain" and what to "discard" (*ch'ü-she*), it would seem desirable to uncover these premises fully, turn them from "justified true beliefs" into debatable ideas, and ask to what extent they can serve as the norms of social and political cooperation in a modern society. As already mentioned, a strong argument that these premises should be revised can be found in current sociological writings.

For the most part, however, these tradition-rooted premises still appear in the contemporary ideological marketplace as uncontroversial ideas, that is, examples of knowledge. Asking how this marketplace may affect the development of the inhibited political center, therefore, one should take these premises and all the other shared ground of this marketplace into account, not just the individual doctrines competing with each other in it. Most Chinese and Western scholars today view the basic problems of Chinese intellectual life as stemming from political or cultural constraints imposed by outside forces on the current thinking and discussions of Chinese intellectuals, whether the limits imposed by the dictatorial state on what can be published, misunderstandings inherited from the tradition, or somehow irresistible Western values and modes of thought infiltrating Chinese society. As in the West, however, the problems of intellectual life stem most fundamentally from the intellectuals' own failure to turn their own conventional discourse into an object of critical reflection.

Endnotes

1. I am grateful to the Hoover Institution and Professor Ramon H. Myers for funding that made possible preparation of this essay. It is part of a project designed by Professor Wenfang Tang and me and so complements his "Political and Social Trends in the Post-Deng Urban China: Crisis or Stability?" *The China Quarterly* 168 (December 2001): pp. 890–909. I am grateful to Professor Tang for many illuminating comments. This essay also has benefited greatly from much consultation with Professor Gao Rui-quan of East China Normal University. I am deeply grateful to him. I am also much indebted to Ms. Elsie Wu of the Hoover Institution for helping me understand a number of passages in the Chinese texts. Relatively few references will be given here, because this essay is largely based on other parts of this book. It is also based on my "Wu-t'o-pang-chu-i yü K'ung-tzu-ssu-hsiang-te ching-shen chia-chih" (Utopianism and Confucius's Humanism), *Hua-tung shih-fan ta-hsueh hsueh-pao* 148 (March 2000): pp. 18–23, and in Kuo-chi ju-hsueh lien-ho-hui, ed., *Chi-nien K'ung-tzu tan-ch'en 2550 chou-nien kuo-chi hsueh-shu t'ao-lun-hui lun-wen-chi* (Collected Essays from the International Scholarly Conference in Honor of the 2550th Birthday of Confucius), 3 vols. (Beijing: Kuo-chi wen-hua ch'u-pan-she, 2000), vol. 2, pp. 549–560.

2. The distinction between "transformative" and "accommodative" modes of political thought and action stems from the work of Ch'ien Mu and Ernst Troeltsch. My use of it goes back to my *The Internal Organization of Ch'ing Bureaucracy* (Cambridge, Mass.: Harvard University Press, 1973). It was basic to Huang Ko-wu, *I-ko pei fang-ch'i-te hsuan-tse: Liang Ch'i-ch'ao t'iao-shih ssu-hsiang-chih yen-chiu* (The Rejected Path: A Study of Liang Ch'i-ch'ao's Accommodative Thinking; Taipei: Institute of Modern History, Academia Sinica, 1994). This distinction has attracted some attention in Mainland circles. See e.g. Kao Li-k'o, *T'iao-shih-te chih-hui: Tu Ya-ch'üan ssu-hsiang yen-chiu* (The Wisdom of the Accommodative Approach: A Study of the Thought of Tu Ya-ch'üan; Hangchow: Che-chiang jen-min ch'u-pan-she, 1998).

3.   In a collection of extremely insightful essays, Xiao Gong-qin, professor of history at Shanghai Normal University and the leading proponent of "the new conservatism" in China today, describes what I call China's current "ideological marketplace" as a process of "increasing intellectual divergences" and as "debates (*lun-cheng*) between dissimilar ways of thought," which he lists as "liberalism, new conservatism, the social democracy of the new left, and fundamentalism of the old left," thus deciding not to view "modern Confucian humanism" as a distinct intellectual force. Professor Xiao's analysis, like this chapter XII, emphasizes the ground shared by the various outlooks forming this "marketplace." See Xiao Gong-qin, *Chih-shih fen-tzu yü kuan-nien-jen* (The True Intellectual and the Person Just Immersed in Abstract Ideas; Tianjin: T'ien-chin jen-min ch'u-pan-she, 2001), p. 118. This shared ground is de-emphasized by Chinese intellectuals alarmed by the irreconcilability between New Left and liberal views in recent years. See Hsu Chi-lin, *Ling-i-chung ch'i-meng* (Another Kind of Enlightenment; Guangzhou: Hua-ch'eng ch'u-pan-she, 1999). As for my typology of the three kinds of political centers, there is room for doubt that it amounts to more than a needless terminological change. Linda Chao and Ramon H. Myers used it in their *The First Chinese Democracy: Political Life in the Republic of China on Taiwan* (Baltimore: The Johns Hopkins University Press, 1998), but their use of it is open to a variety of criticisms. Unfortunately, there has been some confusion about who should be blamed for devising this dubious typology. The answer is: no one except me. Since my graduate student days, I have misused much time working on the problem of how in late imperial China inhibition of the state's organizational capabilities coexisted with the lack of legal limits on the use of state power. I gradually devised the typology in writings such as "Eisenstadt's Analysis of the Relation between Modernization and Tradition in China" in Kuo-li T'ai-wan shih-fan ta-hsueh, Li-shih yen-chiu-so, *Li-shih hsueh-pao* 12 (June 1984): pp. 1–75, also in *The American Asian Review* 2 (summer 1984): pp. 1–87, and partly translated in *Revue européenne des sciences sociales* XXV–1987–76, pp. 85–116; my "Confucian Culture and Economic Modernization: An Historical Approach," in *Conference on Confucianism and Economic Development in East Asia* (Taipei: Chung-Hua Institution for Economic Research, Conference Series, No. 13, 1989), pp. 141–195, republished in 1995 as *Confucianism and Economic Development*; and Thomas A. Metzger and Ramon H. Myers, "Introduction: Two Diverging Societies," in *Two Societies in Opposition: The Republic of China and the People's Republic after Forty Years,* ed. Ramon H. Myers (Stanford: Hoover Institution Press, 1991), pp. xiii–xlv. The latter was written by me, although it appeared under Professor Myers's name as well. As he wrote me on November 22, 1999: "I should long ago have corrected

the authorship of this introduction, written by you, in the Two Societies Book Hoover published. I was in Taiwan at the time of its editing and printing and did not insist upon giving you the authorship which you deserved to have."

Similarly, the idea of "the three marketplaces" was developed in my writings going back to the above 1989 article in order to separate out three kinds of moral or intellectual dissonance that are legitimized by the mainstream Western liberal tradition as it has been epitomized in the thought of J.S. Mill, Hayek, and Popper and yet have never been legitimized by any modern Chinese ideology: a normative free economic marketplace unavoidably including tendencies toward great inequality and strongly influenced by vested interests; a normative free political marketplace strongly influenced by vested interests and filled with the interactions of cunning, insincere politicians "serving selfish interests while claiming to act on behalf of the public good" (*chia-kung chi-ssu*); and a normative free intellectual marketplace dominated by "confusing contradictions" between seemingly erroneous doctrines (*fen-yun*). Invariably, modern Chinese writers have either pictured these three normative marketplaces as based only on "reason" and "morality" or imagined a normative society without them. To be sure, whether such moral-intellectual dissonance is an objective condition is debatable. The perception of such dissonance on the part of the public, however, seems to be an unavoidable aspect of these three marketplaces as they have historically appeared and proved themselves to be a structurally necessary aspect of the modern, free, prosperous society, as Hayek and Popper well argued. The refusal of Sunists, Chinese Marxists, modern Confucian humanists, and Chinese liberals to recognize the dissonance of the three marketplaces as an integral part of modernity has been discussed in my "Erh-shih shih-chi Chung-kuo chih-shih fen-tzu-te tzu-chueh wen-t'i: I-ko wai-kuo-jen-te k'an-fa" (Chinese Intellectuals in the Twentieth Century and the Problem of Self-Awareness: A Foreigner's Outlook), *Tang-tai* 73 (May 1992): pp. 56–74, and ibid. 74 (June 1992): pp. 62–79, as well as in *Hsueh-shu ssu-hsiang p'ing-lun* 3 (1998): pp. 183–229, and elsewhere. Also see chapters V and VI above.

4.   Hu Wei-xi, Gao Rui-quan and Zhang Li-min, *Shih-tzu chieh-t'ou yü t'a: Chung-kuo chin-tai tzu-yu-chu-i ssu-ch'ao yen-chiu* (The Ivory Tower at the Crossroads of Tyranny and Revolution: A Study of Modern Liberal Intellectual Trends in China; Shanghai: Shang-hai jen-min ch'u-pan-she, 1991).

5.   "Ideologized," for instance, was used by Hu Wei-xi, a Tsinghua University professor of philosophy, in his *Kuan-nien-te hsuan-tse: 20 shih-chi Chung-kuo che-hsueh yü ssu-hsiang t'ou-hsi* (Choosing Concepts: A Study of Chinese Philosophy and Thought in the Twentieth Century; Kunming: Yun-nan jen-

min ch'u-pan-she, 2002), p. 20. An East China Normal University associate professor of philosophy, Yü Chen-hua, who strongly affirms Mao's basic philosophic approach, similarly condemns the "textbook" Marxism that came to dominate China under Mao. See his *Hsing-shang-te chih-hui ju-ho k'o-neng?* (How Is Metaphysical Wisdom Possible?) cited in chapter I, note 35, and my review of it in *She-hui li-lun hsueh-pao* 4 (fall 2001): pp. 445–472.

6.   See chapter I, section 7.

7.   Note 4 above adduces one of Gao's books; note 5 above adduces Yü's; Yang's work is adduced in chapter I, note 35. Yang's work is also briefly discussed in chapter IV above and in my "Tao-t'ung-te shih-chieh-hua," fully cited in chapter I, note 66. On Feng Ch'i, see e.g. his *Chung-kuo chin-tai che-hsueh-te ko-ming chin-ch'eng* (The Revolutionary Development of Modern Chinese Philosophy; Shanghai: Shang-hai jen-min ch'u-pan-she, 1989), and his *Chih-hui-te t'an-so* (The Quest for Wisdom; Shanghai: Hua-tung shih-fan ta-hsueh ch'u-pan-she, 1994).

8.   Kuo Ch'i-yung, *Tzu-hsuan-chi* (A Collection of Essays Chosen by the Author; Guilin: Kuang-hsi shih-fan ta-hsueh ch'u-pan-she, 1999). These essays come from the 1990s as well as the late 1980s but still are typical of the new Marxist humanism in the 1980s.

9.   Chu Yü-ho and Ts'ai Lo-su, eds., *Mao Tse-tung yü 20 shih-chi Chung-kuo* (Mao Tse-tung and Twentieth-Century China; Beijing: Ch'ing-hua ta-hsueh ch'u-pan-she, 2000). Again, this impressive volume was developed only in the 1990s, but the perspective in it on Mao reached well back into the 1980s. Nor should one overlook the thought of Li Hon Lam (Li Han-lin) of the Chinese University of Hong Kong, although his Marxism stems from the British tradition of political philosophy, not the Maoist Marxist tradition. See his article on Michael Walzer's *Spheres of Justice* in *She-hui li-lun hsueh-pao* 4 (fall 2001): pp. 413–443, and his article in *Cheng-chih li-lun tsai Chung-kuo,* cited in chapter I, note 14.

10. See section 7 in chapter I. Some of Li's major publications are on aesthetic consciousness. For a critical overview of Li's thought, see Huang Ko-wu's (Max K.W. Huang's) essay in *Chin-tai-shih yen-chiu-so chi-k'an* 25 (June 1996): pp. 425–460.

11. See Wang Hui and Yü Kuo-liang, eds., *90 nien-tai-te "hou-hsueh" lun-cheng* (The Debate in the 1990s about "Post-ism"; Hong Kong: The Chinese University of Hong Kong, 1998). Hereafter Wang-Yü. I rely greatly on this excellent volume for my account here of neo-Marxism in the 1990s. It is one of a number of important collections of articles from the major Hong Kong journal *Erh-shih-i shih-chi,* the editing of which is under the leadership of Chin Kuan-t'ao and Liu Ch'ing-feng, themselves authors of famous books I would call neo-Marxist.

12. Wang-Yü, pp. 54–55.

13. Fredric Jameson, *Postmodernism, or the Cultural Logic of Late Capitalism* (Durham: Duke University Press, 1999). Also see Michael Hardt and Kathi Weeks, eds., *The Jameson Reader* (Oxford: Blackwell Publishers Ltd., 2000).

14. This is the interpretation given by the editors in *The Jameson Reader*, p. 16.

15. Wang-Yü, p. 37.

16. Ibid., pp. 31–32.

17. See e.g. ibid., pp. 36, 43.

18. Ibid., pp. 20, 11–15.

19. Ibid., pp. 45, 91.

20. Ibid., pp. 185–188.

21. Ibid., pp. 45–47, 188.

22. Ibid., p. 209.

23. Ibid., p. 196.

24. Conversation I had in 2002 at Hoover Institution with Su Hao, associate professor of the Foreign Affairs College in Beijing.

25. Xiao Gong-qin, p. 119.

26. Ibid., pp. 154–156.

27. This was a little essay in *Jen-min jih-pao* (February 5, 2002, p. 10) about the course given the previous fall by Professor Li Qiang and me at Peking University on modern Chinese political thought.

28. See note 3 above.

29. Leo Ou-fan Lee, "Romantic Individualism in Modern Chinese Literature," in *Individualism and Holism: Studies in Confucian and Taoist Values*, ed. Donald Munro (Ann Arbor: Center for Chinese Studies, the University of Michigan, 1985), p. 240.

30. In 1991, Paul A. Cohen and many others argued there were no systemic differences between these two cases. See Ramon H. Myers, ed., *Two Societies in Opposition*, pp. xlvii–liv. I also tried to outline distinctive aspects of the Taiwan democratization experience without parallel in China today in *Journal of Democracy* (January 1998): pp. 18–26. In contemplating the systemic differences between the ideological marketplace under the Kuomintang dictatorship and that in China currently (2001), one can remember that, under the Kuomintang, Hu Shih, whose famous writings epitomized the May Fourth call for a fundamental rejection of the traditional culture in the name of liberalism and Westernization, and who thus openly disagreed with the Kuomintang ideology developed by Sun Yat-sen and Chiang K'ai-shek, was director of Academia Sinica in Taiwan for a number of years (1958–1962). If the degree of ideological diversity were similar in China today, a scholar openly critical of Marxism could be director of the Chinese Academy of Social Sciences in Beijing. This is still inconceivable, I would say, but recently a Tsinghua University professor argued it was not in a private conversation with me.

31. Reinhard Bendix, *Kings or People: Power and the Mandate to Rule* (Berkeley: University of California Press, 1978). Lucien Bianco, *Origins of the Chinese Revolution 1915–1949*, trans. Muriel Bell (Stanford: Stanford University, 1971).

32. Cited in Richard J. Bernstein, *The Restructuring of Social and Political Theory* (Philadelphia: University of Pennsylvania Press, 1976), p. 57.

33. To give one example, the idea of intellectuals as "the conscience of society" and of the morally corrigible political center was basic to Tu Wei-ming's publications in the 1980s as reprinted in his *Ju-hsueh ti-san-ch'i fa-chan-te ch'ien-ching wen-t'i* (Reflections on the Dawning of the Third Era in the Evolution of Confucian Learning; Taipei: Lien-ching ch'u-pan shih-yeh kung-ssu, 1989). This book grew out of his lectures and the interviews with him on the Mainland during a decade or so beginning in 1978. See e.g. pp. 175, 179. Even Chinese-born or Taiwan-born scholars immersed for decades in Western academic life have seldom identified the challenge posed to these premises by the GMWER and Millsian liberalism.

34. See e.g Wang-Yü, pp. 43, 69, 70.

35. See e.g. Liu Kuei-sheng, *Hsueh-shu wen-hua sui-pi* (Notes and Essays on Scholarship and Culture; Beijing: Chung-kuo ch'ing-nien ch'u-pan-she, 2000).

36. Yü Ying-shih, *Ts'ung chia-chih hsi-t'ung k'an Chung-kuo wen-hua-te hsien-tai i-i* (Modern Values and the Value System of Chinese Culture; Taipei: Shih-pao wen-hua ch'u-pan shih-yeh yu-hsien kung-ssu, 1984), p. 16.

37. This Chinese tendency was spotted by Yuen Sun Pong (Juan Hsin-pang) in his "Chih-shih yü shih-chien: Ju-chia hsueh-shuo, che-hsueh ch'üan-shih-hsueh chi she-hui kung-tso-chih k'o-neng ch'i-ho" (Knowledge and Moral Praxis: The Possible Convergence between Confucian Doctrine, the Philosophical Hermeneutic Approach, and Social Work), *She-hui li-lun hsueh-pao* 4 (fall 2001): pp. 259–331. (The astute observation in question is on p. 295.) See also Hung T'ao's review of Huang Ko-wu's book on Yen Fu in the prominent journal *Chung-kuo hsueh-shu* 2 (spring 2001): pp. 337–341. (For full bibliographical reference to Huang's book, see chapter I, note 138.) Hung regarded Huang's complex textual analysis of what Yen meant by "freedom" as "not going beyond the organization of data, the mechanical arrangement and comparison of concepts from a superficial standpoint external to them." To avoid a merely "subjective" interpretation of history such as Huang's, Hung said, one should replace Huang's focus on describing a verbally formed train of thought with "a sense of history," "an ability to grasp the original nature of thought as part of a historical discourse."

38. Ibid., p. 43.

39. Even Xiao Gong-qin, with all of his astute analysis of the "romanticism" and

"utopianism" of modern Chinese intellectuals and his deep interest in Burkean conservatism, strongly insisted that "Intellectuals are those who with full self-awareness make it their personal responsibility to serve as the conscience of society." See Xiao Gong-qin, p. 186. The same theme is emphasized in the book by Hsu Chi-lin adduced in note 3 above.

40. Liu Chün-ning, *Pao-shou chu-i* (Conservatism; Beijing: Chung-kuo she-hui k'o-hsueh ch'u-pan-she, 1998). Without full success, I tried to make this point about the relation between tradition and human frailty in my recent discussions with the main proponent of neo-conservatism in China. See Xiao Gong-qin, pp. 41–56. A shorter version of our talk was printed in the Shanghai Academy of Social Science's *She-hui k'o-hsueh-pao*, April 18, 2002, p. 6. Already in 1983, a "battle of the pens" in Taipei's *Chung-kuo shih-pao* showed how difficult it is in the Chinese intellectual world to distinguish between conservatism as a principled political theory and mere opportunism in defending the vested interests of the status quo. In the course of this battle, I was attacked by Lin Yü-sheng, his identity concealed behind a pen name, K'ang Ch'in. Some of these essays were reprinted in Shao Yü-ming, ed., *Hai-nei-wai chih-shih fen-tzu: Kuo-shih t'ao-lun-chi* (A Collection of Essays on National Affairs by Intellectuals Here and Overseas; Taipei: Shao Yü-ming, 1983), pp. 592–639.

41. See e.g. Alex Inkeles, "Being Cooperative as a Form of Social Capital: Evidence from a National Sample of Japanese Adolescents" (paper presented at the Seminar on Social Capital organized by the Pacific Basin Research Center, Cambridge, Mass., October 8–9, 1998). On the civility and trust issues, see chapter I, notes 45, 51, and 19, the latter citing the Kaviraj-Khilnani book on the Western concept of the civil society.

42. See Huang Ko-wu's books on Yen Fu and Liang Ch'i-ch'ao and the book by Kao Li-k'o cited in note 2 above.

43. See Cheng Chia-tung, *Tang-tai hsin-ju-hsueh shih-lun* (Historical Studies on Contemporary New Confucian Thought; Nan-ning: Kuang-hsi chiao-yü ch'u-pan-she, 1997), pp. 78–85, and Ch'i Liang's article in Ku Pin et al., *Chi-tu-chiao, ju-chiao yü Chung-kuo-ko-ming ching-shen* (Christianity, Confucianism, and China's Revolutionary Spirit; Hong Kong: Han-yü chi-tu-chiao wen-hua yen-chiu-so, 1999), pp. 153–192.

44. See Hung T'ao's review, cited in note 37 above, of Huang Ko-wu's book on Yen Fu in *Chung-kuo hsueh-shu*. For a full bibliographical reference to Huang's book, see chapter I, note 138. The prizes won by this study or its version in English, a Ph.D. thesis for the Department of History at Stanford University, include the Academia Sinica's Distinguished Young Scholar Award for 2001, given to three scholars in Taiwan outside the field of economics and natural science and at the associate professor level or below (each winner was given NT 300,000 for research needs). Huang also was co-winner in 2001 of the

Elizabeth Spilman Rosenfield Prize for the Best-written Dissertation, awarded by the Department of History, Stanford University.

45. This important essay by Chang Hao was published in his *Tzu-hsuan-chi* (A Collection of Articles Selected by the Author; Shang-hai chiao-yü ch'u-pan-she, 2002), pp. 1–24. It originally was published in Taipei's *Chung-kuo shih-pao* on, I think, August 29 and September 6, 1982, and it was variously republished. One version is in Shao Yü-ming, pp. 417–436. Actually, Chang's understanding of or commitment to this Western pessimism about political life is doubtful. In the West, this mainstream political norm, going back at least to Aristotle and St. Augustine, was viewed as basic to all political life, not just life in a democracy. As can be seen from his preface to his *Tzu-hsuan-chi*, however, Chang tried to synthesize it with the May Fourth ideal of democracy, aiming to formulate a concept of "democracy with lowered expectations." He never publicly recommended that intellectuals criticizing a transitional form of government also should be satisfied with moderate progress, taking into account the universal human weaknesses emphasized by Reinhold Niebuhr, on whose thought Chang largely based his thesis. Unconsciously altering the Western norm by making its applicability contingent on democratization, Chang failed to challenge the utopian idea that no current Chinese government can be worthy of moral legitimization. When, for instance, democratization did come to Taiwan, many intellectuals agreed with Professor Huang Kuang-kuo of National Taiwan University that Taiwan still lacked true democracy.

46. Samuel P. Huntington, *The Third Wave: Democratization in the Late Twentieth Century* (Norman: University of Oklahoma Press, 1991), p. 263. It should be noted, though, that Confucian thought as found in *Lun-yü* and especially *Hsun-tzu* included appreciation for policies that were effective though not fully virtuous. This view, however, was overshadowed by Mencius's moral idealism. See Metzger, *The Internal Organization of Ch'ing Bureaucracy*, chap. I.

47. See e.g. essay by Yao Ta-li, professor of history at Fudan University, in *Hsueh-shuo Chung-kuo* (China Today in Scholarly Perspective; Nanchang: Chiang-hsi chiao-yü ch'u-pan-she, 1999), pp. 186–188. Yao here is writing about a Western opinion survey in six eastern European countries in 1993–1994 but implicitly refers to contemporary Chinese conditions. According to this research, he says, a majority of the respondents preferred economic conditions under Communism to those in the present but preferred political conditions in the present to those in the past. The moral he infers: "Economic growth in a nation does not necessarily become a basis on which to defend the legitimacy of governmental authority." Moreover, seemingly referring only to Western research on Russia but again indirectly criticizing PRC policies, Yao describes how economic reforms under a weak government lead to corruption that undermines confidence in the market

economy, and he approvingly cites the view that the ideal reform sequence begins with political reform and only ends with structural reform of the economy. His praise for a sequence opposite to that followed by his own government is unqualified and so precludes even the possibility that, in the Chinese case, the great success of the economic reforms has at least partly justified the reform sequence initiated by Deng Xiao-ping. A similarly condemnatory outlook is expressed in the essay by Professor Chu Hsueh-ch'in of Shanghai University (adduced in note 49 below). During the 1970s and 1980s in Taiwan, it was similarly common for intellectuals to brush aside material progress as a standard with which to assess the legitimacy of the government. See my article in Ramon H. Myers, ed., *Two Societies in Opposition*, pp. 43–51.

48. John. K. Fairbank, *China: A New History* (Cambridge, Mass.: The Belknap Press of Harvard University Press, 1992), p. 424. Fairbank here is describing the idealism of the 1989 Democracy Movement by quoting generalizations I had derived especially from the study of political thought in Taiwan through the 1980s. I agree with his implication that the same mind-set was present in both cases. The quote from Hu Wei-xi is from his *Kuan-nien-te hsuan-tse*, p. 40.

49. *Hsueh-shuo Chung-kuo*, pp. 204, 211–212.

50. Wang-Yü, p. 179.

51. See my article on "The Western Concept of Civil Society in the Context of Chinese History," cited in chapter I, note 19.

52. For further discussion, see Mo-tzu-k'o, "Wu-t'o-pang chu-i yü K'ung-tzu ssu-hsiang-te ching-shen chia-chih," adduced in note 1 above, and my "Continuities between Modern and Premodern China: Some Neglected Methodological and Substantive Issues," in *Ideas Across Cultures: Essays on Chinese Thought in Honor of Benjamin I. Schwartz*, ed. Paul A. Cohen and Merle Goldman (Cambridge, Mass.: Council on East Asian Studies, Harvard University, 1990), pp. 263–292, especially pp. 267–268.

CHAPTER XIII

Western Philosophy in Chinese Eyes: Do T'ang Chün-i and Richard Rorty Have Anything to Learn from Each Other?

1. T'ang's Philosophy and the Problem of Philosophic Success

One of the great philosophical minds of the twentieth century, T'ang Chün-i (1909–1978) was a member of the New Confucian school, which, on the one hand, was one of the three leading philosophical schools of twentieth-century China (the other two were Chinese Marxism and the Tsinghua school) and, on the other, being part of modern Confucian humanism, exemplified one of the four leading Chinese ideological trends of that century (the others being Chinese Marxism, Chinese liberalism, and Sunism).[1] As chapter II discussed, T'ang's main purpose was to oppose May Fourth iconoclasm by vindicating the Confucian tradition as the necessary basis for a modern, free, and humanistic way of life in China if not throughout the world. Pursuing this goal, his bluntly metaphysical philosophy deliberately contradicted the Humean, empiricist, positivistic, analytic, linguistic currents in the West; reached out for support from post-Kantian German idealism; and so epitomized what I have called "epistemological optimism."

Thus, although very concerned with many of the problems impeding the quest for knowledge, T'ang had no doubt these problems could be essentially solved. In his eyes, the scope of his own knowledge was already very great. He thought he knew that "what is immediately given in experience" (*tang-hsia*), not a sacred canon, is the starting point of knowledge; that "reason" as an ability to grasp "principles" (*i-li*) appears as part of "what is given"; that reason can reveal the nature of "existence" as a variety of *hsiang* (objects of consciousness) forming nine *ching-chieh* (realms); that these realms include "ideals," the ultimate, ontological character of the world, the data studied by science, the "circumstances" making up history, and so the differences between "cultures," such as Chinese and Western culture; that reason also reveals itself as an invaluable process of unbounded reflexivity the human agent of which can identify herself with the "highest" of these realms, thus gazing out at existence as a whole *sub specie aeternitatis*; and so on (see chapter II, section 4a).

Chapter II also discusses the criticism of T'ang's position. Much of it emerged from within the problematique of modern Chinese philosophy. Besides the famous controversies about metaphysics versus science and materialism versus idealism, as well as the claim that Confucianism was authoritarian, criticism arose from within the ranks of modern Confucian humanism, as scholars like Yü Ying-shih and Cheng Chia-tung claimed the New Confucians turned Confucian thought from norms integrated with living praxis into an ivory-tower, abstract philosophy. The Western criticism has been essentially tacit but all the more cutting for that. The dominant Western academic view has been that modern Chinese philosophy is not worthy of comment. When Charles Hartshorne chided Richard Rorty for neglecting non-Western thought, the only non-Western tradition he singled out as of possible philosophic interest was the Buddhist.[2]

Thus T'ang and the other New Confucians are usually seen today as shedding light on the historical meaning of Confucian ideas and as evoking an ethos useful in the modern revision of Chinese culture but not as contributing to the global pursuit of philosophical understanding. This pursuit, in many Chinese as well as Western eyes, is centered in Western universities.

My claim is that this geography of philosophical insight is mistaken. I would put the matter thus: it is easy to think of difficulties marring T'ang's philosophy, but it is also easy to think of difficulties marring that of Richard Rorty (b. 1931), recently hailed by Harold Bloom as "the most interesting philosopher in America today." Moreover, there is no way to show that the former difficulties are more basic than the latter. On the contrary, one can argue that each of these philosophies is unsuccessful to a large extent and succeeds where the other failed. Therefore, while Chinese have not yet adequately weighed some crucial Western insights, Chinese criticism of Western philosophy can help Western philosophers seeking a critical awareness of their own premises.

2. Defining Philosophy as an Aspect of Linguistic Practice

To be sure, if one accepts a widespread Western view that there is no algorismic standard with which to evaluate philosophical theories, it is more than obvious that, however one defines "philosophic shortcoming," T'ang's shortcomings are not provably greater than those of Rorty's. Something can be accomplished, however, if I can show that the thought of each entails difficulties which he has not addressed. Even so, how can one weigh philosophic shortcomings east and west without first defining "philosophy" as an identical activity pursued east and west?

To do so, I leave aside arguments about whether the peculiarly Western term "philosophy" should be reserved for a distinctly Western intellectual tradition. Instead, I take my premises from other aspects of that tradition, namely, empiricism, the analytic philosophy which grew out of it, and especially the "linguistic turn" taken by analytic philosophy. In this way I hope to arrive at a minimal definition of philosophy everyone can accept, whatever features they might want to add on.

Thus I agree with Suzanne K. Langer that culture is essentially a matter of symbolic behavior, and that linguistic symbols are an especially important kind of symbol. Moreover, whether or not thought, as Wittgenstein suggested, is just a matter of using words, the words used to construct a thought at the very least are an essential part of it and indeed that part which should be assiduously examined before one takes the risk of speculating about any meanings hidden beneath the verbal surface. Such indeed was my tactic when I wrote *Escape from Predicament.* Thus I am happy to derive the definition of philosophy from the empirical phenomenon Richard Rorty calls "linguistic practice" or "linguistic behavior." (Similarly, the discussion above in chapter I, section 2, trying to define "political theory" could be rephrased to describe the pursuit of "political theory" as a kind of "linguistic behavior.")

The question, however, is how to describe linguistic behavior. If

Siobhan Chapman's overview is reliable (*Philosophy for Linguists: An Introduction*), and if the writings of W.V. Quine, Donald Davidson, and Richard Rorty typify the work of philosophers taking the linguistic turn, the description of linguistic practice has so far gone largely in two directions.

On the one hand, scholars have looked for categories with which to distinguish between the aspects of any utterance (e.g. phonological, semantic, and syntactic) and between types of sentences or types of other utterances, such as "performatives," "constantives," "bound variables," "irreducible posits," and "state-descriptions."[3] On the other hand, there are many theories about the nature of language in general, especially those about the relations between meaning, words, overt behavior, physiology, the social context of utterances, and the world to which words supposedly refer. For instance, J.L. Austin "was interested in the many things which people do with language, such as asking questions, issuing orders, making requests and offering invitations."[4]

In describing linguistic practice, however, philosophers and linguists have been little if at all interested in one of the things people "do with language," namely, construct philosophical arguments about the nature of language or some other topic, challenging the views of others and so joining them to form discourses.[5] True, Chomsky pointed to this kind of linguistic practice when he referred to "the creative aspect of language use." After all, languages ultimately are products of the fecundity of the human imagination, and there is no reason to suppose the latter was more fecund in the past than the present. My emphasis, however, is on one kind of linguistic creativity: implementation of that critical reflexivity (CR) empirically found in a broad variety of oral discourses or written texts, whether Rorty's empiricist argument against the idea of the mind as a mirror of nature or T'ang's metaphysical version of this very idea. (The idea of reflexivity was first prominently put forward by S.N. Eisenstadt.)

Presumably "please pass the butter" is not an example of CR, in contrast with W.V. Quine's "we are bound to adapt any alien pattern to our own in the very process of understanding or translating the alien sentences." Just how the latter exemplifies a distinct linguistic type I shall not here try to say. I do, however, want to claim that the aspects of CR described below do not amount to categories "presupposed" by a linguistic situation or to the "functional requirements" of communication but simply to linguistic phenomena, that is, the given semantic and syntactic aspects of words.

Admittedly, I here collide with Wilfrid Sellars' acclaimed point that "the given" is a "myth." What is given, I claim, includes linguistic symbols along with their holistic interrelations. So much, I suppose, might actually be granted even by Sellars' admirers. But what is integral to these holistic interrelations, as opposed to being logically "presupposed" by them or evident as the "functional requirements" of communication?

If holism's point, as Rorty puts it, is "that words take their meanings from other words rather than by virtue of their representative character" (i.e. their correspondence with what is objectively so),[6] I assume that this verbal osmosis includes synonymy (*pace* W.V. Quine); the clustering of words around a meaning common to them even if not linguistically identical with any one of them; and meaningful relations among such clusters often revolving around the word "because." "CR" refers to one such holistic configuration, five aspects of which are described below.

First, in all cases, even that of the most anti-metaphysical texts, CR includes reference to a metaphysical object, that is, one beyond any empirical observation: one or another imagined condition of existence common to *all* human life, whether the "universal human nature" T'ang refers to, or the universal nature of language as discussed by philosophers like Quine. For instance, Quine approvingly cited the proposition that "Language is a social art which we all acquire on the evidence solely of other people's overt behavior under publicly recognized circumstances." Similarly, when Rorty claimed that "justification has always *been* behavioristic and holistic" or "that a world of pragmatic atheists ... would be a better, happier world than our present one," he was doing something basic to CR: expressing a view about the condition of his species as a whole, not just about Americans, not to mention just about his own immediately experienced world.[7] Lions, say, are interested only in the latter, preoccupied with nothing but the nearby concrete contingencies relevant to their desires and never displaying any observable concern with the fate or nature of lionkind in general. Such truly unmetaphysical behavior among people, however, is hard if not impossible to find, with the possible exception of Rorty's imagined Antipodeans.

Second, as illustrated by the way that Quine's or Rorty's arguments hang entirely on the truth of propositions about language, CR entails linguistic expressions that are presented as accurately representing objective reality, whether or not they actually do so represent it and so amount to what Chin Yueh-lin called *pen-jan ch'en-shu* (an articulated understanding of what is actually and ultimately so). True, Rorty protests that all his propositions are presented "ironically," that none is seriously meant truly to represent, correspond to, or "mirror" a specific aspect of the world as it really is. Moreover, to the extent that his words include indubitably unironic propositions about one such aspect, whether language, physiology, a historical idea (such as the Greeks' "ocular metaphor"), an academic acquaintance like Jürgen Habermas, Rorty's parents, or his existence as a man rather than a woman, Rorty is untroubled by any contradiction between that fact and his claim that all his "representational" statements are ironic. This is because he feels free to suspend the authority of logic in the name of poetry, or simply to dismiss any logical implication as pragmatically irrelevant to "'what it is better for us to believe'" (see below).[8]

I would, however, question Rorty's point here by referring to the problems of rhetoric and linguistic practicability. At the very least, Rorty's writing is a body of rhetoric with an unironic intention, namely, persuading people to stop regarding knowledge as accurate representation and instead regard it as an aspect of what Donald Davidson called "triangulation."[9] Rhetoric cannot dispense with logic. How could there be a call for irony if Rorty's propositions about the nature of language actually failed accurately to represent the objective nature of language? Does not the very recommendation to think ironically, which his rhetoric seeks to support, include a "because" concept presupposing logic and the accurate representation of some aspects of the world as it really is? How can objectivity be reduced to a language game played out in a spirit of irony, unless such a reduction implies the unironically objective reality of language games? I am tempted to hold that claiming *all* of one's ontological commitments have been made ironically is to lapse into what Rorty calls "frivolous" talk, what Akeel Bilgrami refers to as the talk of "bullshitters."[10]

With regard to linguistic practicability, Rorty is of course free to say that "I do not think that there is a Way the World Is,"[11] just as I can say "I can run a three-minute mile." But one can doubt that he can actually think this, just as one can doubt that I can actually run that fast. When Rorty says that he talks about the Way the World Is because "it pays you to talk" this way, not because he seriously thinks it is that way,[12] he is, it seems to me, admitting that his kind of radical irony cannot be clearly put into words. But can it be put into words at all?

Take the following, typical statement by him:

> For we can give better descriptions of what Plato and Kant were doing than these men were able to give of themselves. We can describe them as responding to the need to replace a human self-image which had been made obsolete by social and cultural change with a new self-image, a self-image better adapted to the results of those changes.[13]

In thus describing a causal process whereby "social and cultural change" makes "a human self-image ... obsolete," is Rorty actually making the ironical point that this description is just one among a number of alternative descriptions none of which demonstrably corresponds with reality more than the others? Such an ironical idea is simply not conveyed by his words above, not to mention the contradiction between such irony and his flat assertion that his description of what Plato was doing is "better" than Plato's. If the kind of total irony Rorty recommends is linguistically practicable, why does his own linguistic behavior fail to express it?

My answer is not that such ironical linguistic behavior is like walking a tightrope, that it takes more linguistic skill than Rorty has. He is, after all, a magnificent wordsmith. My conclusion is that such ironical behavior is both linguistically and mentally impracticable. I agree with Robert B. Brandom that Rorty actually has a "prosaic, never-questioned commitment to the existence of a world of causally interacting things that existed before there were vocabularies ..."[14] Totalistic irony, like relativism, is a chimera. One can talk about it, but one cannot do it.

Third, as a linguistic form, CR includes not only ontological commitments and other propositions depicting the given world, it also describes the goals of human life, looks in the given world to identify the means to reach them, and includes criteria with which to distinguish between sense and nonsense. Calling for descriptive, causal, and predictive ideas about the world, it also calls for evaluative, recommendatory, and epistemological ones. The characterization of the world, or at least the *Lebenswelt*, hangs on some such variety of categories, not just ontological commitments. In other words, CR seeks to offer true, reliable, or simply more "edifying" (Rorty) ideas about the epistemological-ontological basis of all human life and about moral-political praxis, depending especially on the idea of "because" to link all these ideas coherently. Thus CR addresses the whole range of questions raised by the exigencies of political life and prominently addressed today by the political theory of, say, John Dunn or John Rawls.

Fourth, whether defining the agent of CR as a "we" or an "I," CR revolves around the words "let us reflect" or (*pace* W.V. Quine) their synonyms. Thus T'ang's philosophy centers on the idea of *ch'ao-yueh-te fan-hsing* (ever-transcending reflection), by which he at the very least referred to the ability to turn any idea, including even this idea of reflection, into an object of critical reflection. Rorty similarly referred to the "potentially infinite regress of propositions-brought-forward-in-defense-of-other-propositions."[15]

This idea of reflection in turn is empirically inseparable from the following concepts: (a) a slew of words used to express CR's distinction between more and less enlightened or "edifying" thinking (in Quine's and Rorty's texts one finds e.g. "outworn," "irrelevant," "foolish," "dogma," "illusory," "vague," "rubbish," ideas "run together," "mindless defensive reflexes," "unexplained," and "pernicious," not to mention "frivolous" and "bullshitters," while on the Chinese side, inherited from Buddhism, there is the classic term *wang-chih* [foolishing clinging to a mistaken understanding of existence]); (b) a ranking of historical ideas ranging from the indisputable to the controversial and the nonsensical (as illustrated by Rorty's "better" above, CR unavoidably views all "vocabularies" as not only commensurable but also rankable according to indisputable standards); (c) an intellectual exercise recommended to pursue enlightenment (such as avoiding any "pernicious mentalism" when discussing meaning, or constructing "the original position," or making all discussion maximally "scientific," or becoming aware of *ch'ao-yueh-te kan-ch'ing* [moral feeling with a transcendent origin]); (d) a perception of history as a troubled field of competition between enlightened and unenlightened ideas (such as Rorty's vision of the history of Western culture as infected since the Greeks with an "ocular" concept of knowledge now being successfully challenged, or Popper's, of "the open society and its enemies"); and (e) the assumption that enlightenment is good or inherently desirable, addresses matters of "ultimate concern" (*an-shen li-ming*), and should serve as the "foundation" of all human life (the latter point having never been more vigorously made than by Rorty when he recommended "antifoundationalism").

Fifth, while the nature of CR as an empirical, linguistic phenomenon includes the idea of an agent of reflection usually represented by the word "I" or "we," there is an empirical difference between "I" as a word used by a "him" observed by me, and "I" as used by me. Although Rorty brushes this point aside, Bilgrami astutely notes that, once an argument is described from the first-person point of view, the search for indisputable ideas (such as "our" "racism is bad" or Rorty's "militant anti-authoritarianism"[16]) is over.[17] In other words, relativism is a chimera, because indisputable ideas are not unavailable, they are unavoidable. It is in this sense that CR, as a linguistic phenomenon, always includes reference to a spectrum of commensurable ideas ranging from the indisputable ("warranted assertibles") to the controversial and the nonsensical.

True, in the context of CR, this confrontation between indisputable and controversial ideas seems necessarily to lead to the possibility of turning the former into objects of critical reflection: is the badness of racism really indisputable? The importance of this possibility has major implications for the methodology of philosophy touched on below. Nevertheless, however the uncovering and evaluation of indisputables may proceed, I know of no empirically-examined text that fails to illustrate the distinction between ideas regarded as indisputable and those regarded as controversial. The persistence of this mix tallies with not only Wilfrid Sellars' point that "all our beliefs are up for grabs, though not all at once" but also with the Hegelian point, made by Habermas, that "language and reality interpenetrate in a manner that for us is *indissoluble*" (see below).[18]

All in all, then, the description of linguistic practice cannot just entail ideas about language in general and about types of terms or sentences, it must also look at the dynamic, indeed creative combinations of words forming arguments and discourses. Linguistic practice as it is empirically observed is a dynamic historical process constantly moving from the determinateness of forms fixed in the historical past to the indeterminateness of the future, and so study of it cannot be reduced to the search for a static typology of utterances or a static definition of its overall nature. Creative combinations of words forming arguments also are a kind of linguistic behavior, and descriptions of these combinations reveal a set of logically interdependent categories that is repeated in one text after another east and west. "CR" refers to any such set.

To be sure, when one empirically observes such a set, one associates it with one's own introspectively observable process of argument and reflection, and so one infers that CR entails a "mentalistic" impulse oriented to future events and potentially transcending any determinate, historically inherited semantic content. As Chomsky noted, however, the qualms about "mentalism" expressed by Quine and Rorty, among others, were "misconceived" (see below).[19]

Again, Quine's famous theory of "the indeterminacy of translation" seemed to split up the global flow of linguistic symbols into different languages, some "radically different." These languages, he held, are "alien" to each other, and it is not possible accurately to equate, say, any Chinese words with those English words above held to illustrate CR. This thesis ultimately rests on Quine's claim that it "is not clear even in principle that it makes sense to think of words and syntax as varying from language to language while the content stays fixed." This is because the meaning of an idea is inseparable from words and syntax (see below), and the meanings of words and syntax can be fully learned only by a child whose previous state of mind was a *tabula rasa*, not by a linguist whose previous state of mind included knowledge of a different set of words and syntax. In the position of such a linguist, "we are bound to adapt any alien pattern to our own in the very process of understanding or translating the alien sentences."[20]

Leading to fashionable talk today about the "incommensurability" of texts in different languages, this extravagant and vaguely formulated thesis of Quine's was seriously qualified even by him, ignored by him in practice (see below), based on a dubious view of meaning and "mentalism" (see below), and has since been dropped even by admirers of his like Rorty. Although Rorty believes there is no objective standard with which to evaluate one "vocabulary" as revealing more truth about the world than another, he "agree[s] with

Habermas — against Lyotard, Foucault, and others — that there are no incommensurable languages, that any language can be learned by one who is able to use any other languages ..."[21]

Indeed, even if one accepts "the indeterminacy of translation," this very idea was combined by Quine with the assumption that all languages, no matter what the cultural differences, share empirically observable characteristics. Certainly this assumption has remained central to the writings of just about all linguists and linguistic philosophers, not to mention Chomsky's concept of "universal grammar." My only point is that CR is one of these widely shared characteristics.

If this can be granted, "philosophy" can be simply defined as the discipline asking how best to use CR. That is, the five aspects of CR described above are only formal (unless one allows an implication that enlightenment is necessarily desirable and good); determination of their substantive content awaits philosophical inquiry. For instance, as linguistic individuals with CR pondering how people should live, we all distinguish between more enlightened and less enlightened ideas, but philosophical inquiry is needed to decide which substantive ideas are the more enlightened ones. Philosophy, therefore, is a most important discipline for me, because what I am anxious about in this world of ours is precisely how best to use CR, not how to emulate some admittedly valuable (if not indeed sublime) Western tradition, whether artistic or intellectual. I agree with Rorty (and disagree with Leo Strauss) that the Greek intellectual tradition or the Jewish vision of holiness, just like the Chinese, is not a *tao-t'ung* (a source of absolute wisdom discovered in ancient times and passed on down through the generations), it is just another object of critical scrutiny. After all, that would have been how Socrates himself would have regarded it.

3. Rorty's Philosophy

So is Rorty's philosophy. Does it, then, show how best to use CR? Summing it up within the space limitations I have to respect here, I can begin with Rorty's self-description as a "historicistic," "relativistic" philosopher pursuing "pragmatism," "linguistic behaviorism," "holism," "hermeneutics," and "antifoundationalism," and so seeking to go beyond analytic philosophy. Listing the contributions that have particularly influenced him, Rorty has noted a metaphysical theory (Hegel's concept of "the dialectical progress of the World-Spirit," whereby global history is a process replacing "outworn" ideas with ideas that are somehow fresh and full of life); Heidegger's claim that one such outworn idea is the Greeks' use of the "ocular metaphor" to define knowledge; and a number of overlapping ideas striking Rorty as successfully replacing the Greeks' "outworn" ocular metaphor.[22]

These latter ideas appealing to him were largely epistemological but really amounted to a quest for a new ontology centered on a Promethean autonomy, as opposed to any moral or even natural order fixed without regard to human intentions. Rejecting such an order, however, also required rejecting the corollary of that order, not just the idea of "the mind" as a "mirror" of it but also the idea that human existence includes an individual, private, mentalistic quest for enlightenment. Rorty claimed that, as an ontological given, human existence is purely a social process made up of verbal expressions, overt behaviors, and physiological processes, all susceptible to observation and analysis emulating the methodology of the natural sciences.

Basic to this notion was the idea of the sociality of human existence going back to Hegel, Herder, and the Comtean sources of social science; Dewey's view that knowledge coincides with useful action; and Wittgenstein's idea that a concept is no more than a way of using words. Fleshing out these basic points were especially Quine's linguistic behaviorism, rejection of "mentalism," and doubts about analyticity; Wilfrid Sellars' "attack on the Myth of the Given"; Donald Davidson's "triangulation" as a way of understanding the relation between language and the rest of the world; and the Kuhnian suggestion that even modern science is just another "vocabulary" or "story."

Thus the heart of Rorty's philosophy has been ideas growing out of a peculiarly Western development that has been discussed in chapter I, section 6, as the Great Modern Western Epistemological Revolution (GMWER). This was rooted in the Greek preoccupation with the distinction between opinion and knowledge, went back especially to Descartes' "era of doubt," was led by thinkers like Hume, Kant, Nietzsche, Max Weber, Popper, and Wittgenstein, and also was deeply influenced by Hegel's and Herder's ideas about the relation between reasoning and historical context, as well as the more

Comtean roots of modern anthropology and sociology. While most of the GMWER sought to shrink down the scope of knowledge as true and justified ideas about what is objectively so, Rorty has been part of a radical trend questioning whether even natural science includes any knowledge at all in this sense, not to mention philosophy and the other disciplines studying the *Lebenswelt*.

This skepticism has certainly been extravagant (Kuhnian exaggerations, for instance, have been exposed by Steven Weinberg). Yet it has also been intertwined with the major post-Kantian discovery that, to an important extent but not necessarily entirely, ideas emically viewed as rationally and truly reflecting what is objectively so reflect only paradigms or premises socially formed by one historical group, regarded as doubtful or absurd by other historical groups, and unverifiable by any objective standard. While Rorty often refers to a set of such premises as a "vocabulary," I prefer the term "verbalized rules of successful thinking" (ROST) shared by a particular "discourse."[23]

Rorty's relation to the GMWER can be described also by first noting that the GMWER was rooted in the perhaps unique Greek way of forming CR's quest for enlightenment without constructing a sacred canon and just depending on "reason." But the efficacy of "reason" was then put into question first by Pyrrhonian skepticism and then by the veil-of-ideas epistemology that arose in the seventeenth century, and that the astute modern Chinese philosopher Chin Yueh-lin called *wei-chu fang-shih* (the intellectual mode according to which a person cannot directly observe the world and can only rely on impressions, ideas, or symbols appearing in her consciousness and seeming, correctly or not, to reflect the nature of the world). When it was realized that these symbols were culturally produced, their chances of reflecting anything objective dimmed still further. Thus the GMWER turned into an effort to deal with this dilemma by retrieving some grasp of objective principles. What Rorty did, I would say, was to suggest in a strikingly daring way that the "veil of ideas" or "veil of vocabulary" was quite real but in no way constituted a dilemma. According to his pragmatism, thinking of it as a problem that philosophy should solve was a spiritually enervating exercise perpetuating the myth that the world includes objective principles with which human needs should conform.

In Rorty's philosophy, however, this rationale arising out of the

GMWER's epistemological pessimism was combined (logically or not) with at least five other currently prominent outlooks to which he was equally committed: (1) that privileged position of science emphasized notably by Quine; (2) the Enlightenment ideals of freedom, equality, and prosperity; (3) the utopian, Rousseauistic belief that democratic governance should center on the full realization of these ideals rather than aim more modestly for piecemeal, Burkean progress within the moral limbo of history; (4) a Hegelian historiographical methodology calling for a macroscopic theory of the stages of global history and so rejecting Max Weber's empiricism; and (5) an endorsement of that iconoclastic effort in the West today trying to detach Western political philosophy and culture from the Western, Socratic, Christian humanistic mainstream on which J.S. Mill's, F.A. Hayek's, Karl R. Popper's, Isaiah Berlin's, and John Dunn's liberalism were based.

Rorty's philosophy, therefore, brilliantly developed as it is, is nothing short of a complex ideological effort resonating with powerful cultural trends in the West today, including post-modernism, which he has explicitly praised, though still distancing himself from some of it. To mount this effort, Rorty — as I read him — tried to defend some twelve key propositions.

First, if there is any difference between reality and illusion, reality consists of the physical phenomena studied by modern science. (He would not make this point explicitly, but his "physicalism" implies it.)[24] Second, ideas have no meaning apart from the semantic and syntactic patterns formed by publicly observable linguistic symbols; these symbols arise out of overt behaviors; and behavior is ultimately physiological. Conversely, there are no meanings transcending and common to different linguistic forms and so no mentalistic process entailing a Kantian self or subject.

Third, his approving references to Quine's discussion of analyticity at least imply that, for him, linguistic symbols entail no analyticity in the sense of universal, necessary logical relations. Fourth, there also are no "true" a posteriori propositions that accurately represent, mirror, or correspond to a particular aspect of objective reality.

Fifth, intertwined with the social-cultural processes carried out by the physiological entities called "human beings," linguistic symbols form shared vocabularies, stories, or narratives. Sixth, there being neither analyticity nor a posteriori truths, none of these stories demonstrably reveals more truth about the world than any other. As Protagoras correctly said and Socrates incorrectly denied, there is no way to distinguish between the truth about a matter of fact and what the rhetoric of a particular group of persons claims to be the truth about this matter.

Seventh, because no vocabulary is closer to any objective truth than any other, there can be no philosophy that should be respected as providing the normative foundation of social-cultural life. Any claim to have articulated such a foundation is an authoritarian act that should be resisted. Eighth, what should be promoted is the freedom of people to pursue utility as they see it — "'what it is better for us to believe.'" Society should be organized to maximize such freedom.

Ninth, the task of philosophy, therefore, is to reveal the true pattern of subjection in human life. (Rorty does not put it so bluntly.) People are subject to the particular linguistic and institutional pattern into which history has happened to throw them, and they should not be subject to any authoritarian pattern devised by persons falsely claiming to have found the objectively valid, ahistorical principles of life everyone should follow. History, not critical reflexivity, should determine the blueprint of the world they should follow. Tenth, this pattern of subjection is not so dismal as it seems. Rorty's thought expresses a Whitmanesque celebration of the American experience that has become a major American intellectual trend (John Rawls and Talcott Parsons also exemplify it). Being enslaved to historical contingency is not a dismal fate if you are an American, because history has smiled on you by throwing you into a society that more than any other respects the ideals of the Enlightenment. As President George W. Bush recently said at a televised banquet, "Is this a great country or what?" On this point, Rorty differed with the President, if at all, only by seeking "a society even more democratic, tolerant, leisured, wealthy and diverse than our own."[25] If you are not an American, moreover, you can at least take a little comfort in Hegel's idea of that progressive World-Spirit which presumably was responsible for the American experience.

Eleventh, any logical contradictions between the above points (e.g. between his affirmation of Sellars' attack on "the myth of the given" and his view of history as inherently guided by a progressive

World-Spirit) are unimportant, because there can be no logical account of how the world is, only suggestions offered in a spirit of irony recognizing the total elusiveness of objective truth. As Susan Haack explains, "'ironists'" in Rorty's view adopt a "'final vocabulary'" but, "realizing there are no objective grounds for vocabulary choice between vocabularies," they are "'never quite able to take themselves seriously.'"[26] Even more, one finds in Rorty a kind of "trivialism," the belief that, there being no such objective grounds, one is free simply to "agree" that any idea, such as a claim of contradiction, is or is not too trivial to deserve discussion.

Twelfth, it is true, however, that philosophy today calls for a complex, easily misunderstood exercise needed to uncover and discard that outworn language game which, going back to the Greeks' "ocular metaphor," led to the idea of the mind as a mirror of nature and so to an illusion exploited by power-hungry interests: the idea that critical reflexivity rather than history should create the blueprint of human life. To carry out this complex exercise and so find out "what it is better for us to believe," one has to learn to juggle a variety of conceptual balls ranging from a grasp of the doctrine of historicity to avoiding "frivolous" reasoning; embracing the principles of science, freedom, and equality; cultivating an "openness to strangeness"[27] that can include a poetic ability to push aside the hobgoblin of logical consistency; and a kind of name-dropping implying that this mix of concepts should be affirmed because it not only inherently makes sense but also was variously endorsed by certain selected culture heroes, such as Dewey, Wittgenstein, Heidegger, and Davidson. Given his tendency to see philosophy as a kind of rhetoric, Rorty resembles a lawyer citing precedents as he supports his arguments by claiming they accord with earlier views. It is as though Kant had tried to support his theory of the a priori by arguing that it accorded with Plato's theory of ideas.

Rorty in a way that is neither ironic nor empirical depicts history as a struggle between a progressive World-Spirit and a powerful human tendency to misunderstand this Spirit and use that misunderstanding to erect oppressive structures of authority. In effect, he emphasizes the misuse of CR as a major causative force in history without conceptualizing the exercise of CR as a linguistic process able either to pursue enlightenment or to fall into misunderstanding. Thus resisting Hegel's attempt to link the successful exercise of CR with the evolution of the World Spirit, Rorty prefers the stance that has become typical of Western academic liberalism and the GMWER: combining an emphasis on the misuse of CR with the proud feeling that, in discovering this misuse, the West became more enlightened than all other civilizations.

4. Rorty in Western and Chinese Critical Perspective

a. Distinguishing between CR and ROST

In the Brandom and Saatkamp volumes, Rorty replies at length to the often sharp criticisms directed at his thought by a large number of Western philosophers, some famous, such as Charles Hartshorne, Richard J. Bernstein, Hilary Putnam, Jürgen Habermas, and Donald Davidson, some less famous but still extremely impressive, such as Jacques Bouveresse, John McDowell, Robert B. Brandom, Michael Williams, Akeel Bilgrami, James Conant, Allen Hance, Susan Haack, and Frank B. Farrell. What I want to argue here, however, though again only in a preliminary way, is that the criticisms produced by this group have been only partially insightful. When one looks at Rorty's thought after one has taken modern Chinese philosophy seriously, a far more drastic critique of it comes to mind. From this Chinese standpoint, one's object of critical reflection is not just what Rorty said but the whole tradition out of which his views and those of his Western critics grew, the GMWER. Chapter I, section 7, describes the pervasive modern Chinese philosophical tendency to reject the GMWER as a whole. Modern Chinese philosophers prominently criticized it, referring to it as "relativism," *pu-k'o-chih-lun* (the theory that the ultimate nature of reality is unknowable), etc. I disagree with a good deal of this Chinese criticism, but it has had the great advantage of turning a historical tradition from a lived experience into an object of critical reflection.

Few if any of Rorty's Western critics dispute his affirmation of what I regard as a major insight of the GMWER widely accepted in the West, the view that ROST greatly influence how an individual or group depicts the world, especially the *Lebenswelt*. A good many of them, however, criticize Rorty for dealing inadequately with the problem of truth and objective reality. In my terms, they astutely point to his failure to recognize the tension between ROST and CR.

This tension is fully identified by Conant, Habermas, Haack, McDowell, and others. As Habermas puts it, although "we cannot confront our sentences with anything that is not itself already saturated linguistically…. [the] supposition of an objective world that is independent of our descriptions fulfills a functional requirement of our processes of cooperation and communication."[28]

Language, in other words, is inherently, ontologically paradoxical. On the one hand, it is a process dependent on culturally varying syntactic and semantic structures each of which was formed in the past and exhibits much inertia (ROST). On the other, this process also is creatively and critically oriented to the goal of coping with an indeterminate future by pursuing knowledge as propositions framed in the name of universal truth and objective reality (CR).

To be sure, to claim that Rorty does not distinguish between ROST and CR is not to say that he fails to see how, in any discourse, beliefs and criticisms of them are interdependent. In his eyes, Donald Davidson's "triangulation" refers precisely to the conversational interdependence of: the world to which words refer; what someone says about it; and how others interpret and criticize her words. Thus "triangulation" allows Rorty to look for the "criteria" used by "the best, most critical, and most informed audience that I can imagine" to "justify" any proposition.[29] The question at stake, however, is three-fold, and I do not think previous criticism of Rorty has fully addressed it.

First, are there determinate parameters which are bestowed on any "conversation" by some socially formed pattern ("a language," "a vocabulary," "a society," or "a culture"), and within which the triangular interaction between "descriptions" of the world and "interpretations" of them occurs? Rorty consistently suggests there are. On the one hand, he says "the community" is the "source of epistemic authority," and he equates the latter with "what society lets us say."[30] On the other, he insists that the idea of any autonomously individual, mentalistic, private quest for a truth transcending what others say is somehow misguided. As he sees it, in appealing to such a truth when challenging the conventional wisdom of the Athenians, Socrates was positing something actually unavailable, "a permanent neutral matrix for all inquiry and all history."[31]

Yet even if such a matrix is unavailable, Socrates's challenge illustrates how the Athenian conversation, whether in the agora or the courtroom, in fact was not bounded by socially imposed parameters. Moreover, what Rorty deplores — the huge influence of Socrates's outlook on Western culture — precisely illustrates how such unbounded interaction between conventional wisdom and "thinking outside the box" constitutes the very nature of linguistic-cultural evolution. Similarly, if one looks at the intellectual discourse of, say, twentieth-century China or the U.S., one finds endless disputes about how the norms of public discussion should be defined.

The empirical description of linguistic practice — in this case, a discourse — should not be confused with either the question of how non-linguistic conditions influenced the contours of a discourse or that of how a later observer of a discourse might or might not justify any of the views making up this discourse. When one describes a particular historical discourse, the empirical evidence one can find is simply that socially shared norms (ROST) were very important and that people frequently exercised their critical reflexivity (CR) to challenge these ROST. One cannot, so far as I know, adduce empirical evidence showing that socially imposed parameters limited this interaction between ROST and CR.

My point, therefore, is that, in analyzing the triangular interaction between "descriptions" and criticisms of them, Rorty strays away from that empirical focus on linguistic practice which the "linguistic turn" brought to the fore. He puts linguistic practice into a non-linguistic, naturalistic context (as Robert B. Brandom has noted[32]) and then, arbitrarily endorsing a sociologistic concept of causation, asserts that this non-linguistic context controls this linguistic process, whether imposing the parameters of permissible discussion or "ma[king] obsolete" the "human self-image" central to what was permissible.[33]

In this reductionist analysis of Rorty's, the crudities of nineteenth-century evolutionism are fully apparent. He assumes that, despite the complex, often elusive relation between cultural continuities and discontinuities, the distinction between old and new ideas is somehow obvious. Which old ideas are "outworn," "rubbish of the past," or "obsolete" is also an obviously given reality (*pace* Wilfrid Sellars).[34] And the obsoleteness of an idea is not a function of the arguments about it but an effect of "social and cultural change."

Second, not distinguishing ROST from CR and worrying

exclusively about how to theorize about the relation between vocabularies and the rest of the world, Rorty did not notice or did not consider significant the question of whether ROST are manifest, that is, the extent to which, in being so influenced by a particular shared "vocabulary," people are aware of the beliefs they thus take for granted. Not turning his attention to this question, he did not consider whether a task of philosophy should be uncovering these beliefs and so making them available as objects of critical and comparative scrutiny. Given Schopenhauer's profound warning that thinking is often unconsciously shaped by impulses one would not consciously condone, how can Rorty continue on with his quest for "edification" while remaining insouciant about the nature of the unpacked cultural baggage he has brought to this quest? Lurking behind this insouciance is the American triumphalism noted above.

Third, not distinguishing between ROST and CR, neither Rorty nor his critics sought to describe CR as an aspect of linguistic practice, as I have tried to do above. Thus their empirical description of linguistic practice remained seriously incomplete even while they based their arguments so much on this description. At least some of Rorty's critics, however, have been well aware that, in recognizing the paradoxical tension between convention and critical awareness, they were offering a linguistic version of that dialectical relation between historicity and reason which Hegel had formulated in metaphysical terms. Thus challenging the positivistic premise that the empirically given consists only of a linear flow of events to which a logically consistent, paradox-free account should be applied, they indeed were, even if inadvertently, reopening the battle between Hegel and the positivists about the nature of "experience," participating in a recent philosophical development Charles Taylor has done so much to stimulate.

b. Meanings and Mentalism

Another point overlooked by Rorty's previous critics concerns what is not so much a "dogma of empiricism" as it is a "dogma of the linguistic turn," the idea, namely, that meanings have no existence independent of particular linguistic forms. Quine's work is a or the *locus classicus* of this dogma. He ridiculed the idea of "a realm of entities called meanings" as "Plato's heaven," "the myth of a museum in which the exhibits are meanings and the words are labels." As already noted, this outlook was the basis for his thesis that it "is not clear even in principle that it makes sense to think of words and syntax as varying from language to language while the content stays fixed."

Quine, however, overlooked that, if meanings or ideas are partly separable from linguistic forms, their ontological address need not be "Plato's heaven," it can simply be the same as that of language, namely, socially shared patterns or gestalts acquired through that process of socialization he himself emphasized. Moreover, without the slightest qualification, he viewed "Kant's intent" in distinguishing "between analytic and synthetic truths" as an idea expressed in the original German text and preserved in not only Quine's English paraphrase of this text but also the way Quine "restated" it, not to mention the "presuppositum" of "Kant's intent" (a certain "concept of meaning"), which similarly existed over the centuries (whether or not in "Plato's heaven") waiting for Quine to discover it and unaffected by differences in the linguistic forms conveying it.[35]

Indeed, unless a meaning is at least to some extent separable from the particular linguistic forms conveying it, how could the idea of the mind as the mirror of nature have remained the same as it passed from one European language to another, exercising, as Rorty tells us, its insidious influence on the development of Western culture? Similarly, if meaning were not thus separable, Arthur O. Lovejoy's study of the idea of "the great chain of being" would be utter nonsense.

All in all, when one pushes forward with a full empirical description of linguistic behavior, recognizing its mentalistic aspect, the unavoidable need to treat meaning as partly independent of linguistic form, and philosophical discourse as a linguistic phenomenon, one can suspect that "the linguistic turn" was taken in a hyperbolic way. Linguistic behavior is not "saturated" with linguistic forms; it is misleading to say "concepts are language."[36] Linguistic forms are no more than a vital part of thinking.

In other words, the huge impact of a culturally formed "conceptual scheme" or "vocabulary" on what a person believes can be fully recognized without having to claim that an idea is identical with a particular linguistic form; that thinking is done without a self doing it; that thinking cannot be used in a basically accurate way to describe specific given realities, such as texts or trees; that being a thinking self cannot possibly have any objectively moral implications; and that being a physiological entity is incompatible with realizing what J.S. Mill called "the dignity of man as a thinking being." Nor does one have to make any of these claims in order to reject Descartes' ontological dualism and embrace Darwin's theory about the animalistic origin and nature of the human species. While no one is claiming that there is a "ghost within the machine," Ryle's famous metaphor should not be used to brush aside many of the peculiar features of these ghost-less entities called human beings, especially those linguistic features clustered around the exercise of CR. As T'ang Chün-i put it, what does the nature of philosophy as an empirical fact tell us about the empirical nature of the creature capable of philosophizing? Why should one agree with Rorty when he quite gratuitously infers from Darwin's theory of biological evolution that the "moral progress" of human beings is the same sort of process that made "squirrels have more varied and interesting needs than amoebae"?[37] If Locke confused justification with causal explanation, is not Rorty here confusing normative definition with biological origin? To say that amoebae and humans are equally products of biological evolution is as useful and interesting as it is to say that a bicycle and the Hubble telescope are both machines.

c. The Question of Knowledge

Moreover, even though culturally disparate linguistic forms so greatly affect the way people conceptualize the world, it seems clear that people still can obtain some knowledge as true and justified beliefs about how the world objectively is. Although many issues can be decided only in Richard J. Bernstein's "middle ground," some "objectivism" is available. In other words, while any discourse includes ontological and other premises that the people carrying on the discourse regard as indisputable and use to evaluate any view they run across, some of these premises can indeed be a matter of knowledge in the classic sense of that term.

For instance, even though Rorty endorses Quine's attempt to discard analyticity as a source of knowledge, this attempt was hardly convincing. Quine himself backed away from challenging one "class of analytic statements, the logical truths,"[38] and, as just noted, he depended on logical inference when he wanted to "examine the concept of *meaning* which is presupposed" by Kant's distinction between analytic and synthetic truths. Of course analytic philosophy itself would be impossible if logical inference were not a reliable way to obtain knowledge. If logical inference is not a way to obtain knowledge, why pay any attention at all to Rorty's point, phrased in his typically elegant way, that "Since truth is a property of sentences, since sentences are dependent for their existence on vocabularies, and since vocabularies are made by human beings, so are truths"?[39] When Wilfrid Sellars says that the idea of the given is a "myth," this word in a logically necessary way implies a conceptualization of ideas that are not mythical, of some sort of reality. How then is analyticity precluded? Even if a necessary implication is just a matter of linguistic usage, is there not a logically correct interpretation of the linguistic convention involved?

True enough, with his famous example of the *gavagai* and his account of the "ostensive predicament," Quine argued that a posteriori propositions which seem to refer clearly to an objective reality actually vary in meaning depending on the language used and are subject to the "predicament of the indeterminacy of translation."[40] Yet, as just noted, the idea of such a predicament is dubious. Moreover, Quine himself granted this predicament "has little bearing on observation sentences."[41]

Still more, the limits of this predicament might have been clearer to him had he pondered not only the problem of words evoked by the appearance of what some call a rabbit but also that of words evoked by what T.S. Eliot called "the facts when you get down to brass tacks": "birth, copulation, and death." (A Chinese list is a bit longer: *ch'ih ho la shui p'iao tu* [eating, drinking, going to the toilet, sleeping, going with prostitutes, gambling].) To be sure, references in different historical settings to these "brass tacks" vary in "psychological associations or poetic quality," as Quine noted. In discussing the interchangeability of a word in one language with that in another, however, Quine explicitly put aside such nuances and referred only to "what may be called *cognitive* synonymy."[42] He might, therefore, have considered the problem of "cognitive synonymy" in the context of not only particular objects like the "undetached part" or the "temporal stage of a rabbit" but also death and other basic existential aspects of all human life. As Hartshorne suggests, the possibility of insight into these aspects has not been precluded.[43] Indeed, Rorty himself offers insight into them, in that he takes on the role of an optimistic "prophet" recommending an attitudinal shift with which to clear "away the rubbish of the past" and realize not just "a society even more democratic, tolerant, leisured, wealthy, and diverse than our own" but also a "better.... spiritual state."[44] Rorty thus offered a eudaemonisticly Promethean picture of the existential situation brushing aside existentialism's anxiety about historicity and finitude. So central to his whole philosophy, his point in rejecting existentialism's sense of anxiety was that the trans-lingual reality people were unable to grasp was of no value to them to begin with. If, then, it is impossible to distinguish between knowledgeable and misguided ideas about the existential situation, Rorty's own writings do not make sense (see below).

Even more, as already indicated, if it is known that CR is an aspect of linguistic behavior, is it not also known that pursuing enlighten- ment is an inherently good activity (this point is basic to T'ang's philosophy)? If it is, the basic premise of J.S. Mill's liberalism is a matter of knowledge, not just part of another historically relative "comprehensive doctrine" (to use Rawls's term).

Similarly, the ability to obtain knowledge about intellectual history is often overlooked. As I have tried to show by comparing Li Tse-hou's and W.H. Walsh's treatments of Kant's critiques, cultural and ideological differences need not affect how intellectually honest scholars describe the basic ideas found in texts.[45] Indeed, if they did necessarily affect them, one would have no reason to take seriously Rorty's historiographical thesis that Western philosophy has been influenced by the concept of the mind as a mirror of nature.

If, then, one cannot preclude the possibility of knowledge about the *Lebenswelt,* it is still clearer that any Kuhnian attempt to deny this possibility in the case of the natural world has been revealed as untenable. Quine himself resisted this attempt,[46] and Steven Weinberg seems to have put it to rest.[47]

Given, then, that the use of linguistic symbols seems to permit the pursuit of knowledge, a challenging philosophical problem arises which is obviated by Rorty's thoroughgoing skepticism: *To what extent* is it possible to bypass the biases and blind spots of one's ROST and constitute knowledge? If the given is not a myth, to what extent can an empirical approach—fraught as "empiricism" is with ambiguity and complexity — be used to apprehend the given? If linguistic practice is a given, for instance, can one know it implies that enlightenment is good? Moreover, if linguistic symbols do impede apprehension of the given, one may reopen the question of just how they are supposed to do so. The confusion here again goes back to Quine's train of thought.

If one accepts the premise that one cannot step out of one's vocabulary by comparing the nature of the world to what one has said about it, the very nature of linguistic symbols at least partly blocks the ability to acquire knowledge. This point seems plausible. Quine, however, viewed this blockage as due not to the fact that all people on the planet use language but to the fact that they do not use the same language: "Basic differences in language are bound up, as likely as not, with differences in the way in which speakers articulate the world itself into things and properties," especially in the case of "radically different languages." The result, he held, was that depictions of the world varied "from language to language," and that, given the "indeterminacy of translation," there was no way to compare one depiction to another, not to mention determining which was more correct.[48]

This Tower of Babel thesis, however, was loosely framed. Using nothing but loose terms like "our mother tongue" and "heathen speech," Quine did not make clear at what point a set of linguistic symbols became a different language and a different language became a "radically different" language. Moreover, trying to correlate linguistic differences with different depictions of the world, he could only speculate that such a correlation was "as likely as not." Claiming, then, to analyze the relation between ontological understanding and linguistic differences, Quine was unclear about what linguistic differences he had in mind; offered a weak, much disputed argument that there was no way to evaluate translations from one language to another as accurate; vaguely claimed that linguistic differences were correlated to differences in the depiction of the world; failed to confront the major empirical question of the particular ways in which differences among historical discourses did or did not alter the depiction of the world; and failed to show why the use of linguistic symbols impedes the quest for knowledge about the world more when these symbols take the form of a plurality of languages. So concerned with precision of expression and with the nature of "language," Quine to my knowledge never asked what was meant by "a language" as a somehow bounded array of linguistic symbols.

Yet if it is not the plurality of languages which precludes the apprehension of objective reality, is it really plausible to say that the very nature of linguistic symbols does so? Not necessarily. Particularly trenchant is Conant's discussion showing that truth as a person's knowledge of what actually happened in a particular case can and should be distinguished from the social-linguistic situation in which that person finds herself. Trying to rebut Conant's devastating analysis, Rorty insists that, when a person is trapped in a society denying that what she thinks is true is true, that person cannot "turn to the light of the facts" and so has "nowhere ... to turn. People in such societies are in the same position as people with real or purported psychotic delusions."[49] In other words, if I lived through the Holocaust and ended up in a society where everyone held it had not occurred, I would lack not only the psychological but even the epistemic ability to know that I know it happened. Such is the *reductio ad absurdum* to which Rorty is led by his emphasis on the sociality of the quest for truth.

Elsewhere, however, he contradicts his rebuttal of Conant's argument, averring: "Truthfulness, like freedom, is temporal, contingent, and fragile. But we can recognize both when we have them."[50] Moreover, his *reductio* implies an unexamined assumption about the nature of mental activity as apprehension and memory: they are utterly unreliable in the case of sense data but extremely serviceable in the case of socially conveyed "vocabularies." Just as there is no confusion or delusion in the perception of truthfulness and freedom, so there is none in the transmission of socially shared vocabularies. Thus Rorty's *reductio* seems to end up resting on old, largely spurious suggestions east and west about the drastic unreliability of sense experience, such as *Chuang-tzu's* truly "frivolous" idea that Richard Rorty may really be a butterfly dreaming he's Richard Rorty. According to Rorty's rebuttal of Conant, if Rorty had to live in a society thoroughly wired to insist that he really is just a butterfly, he could not apprehend the truth about his nature by turning "to the light of the facts."

d. Soliloquy and Freedom

Moreover, while denying that an individual's grasp of a truth can be to some extent independent of her social-linguistic environment, Rorty ignored the danger of contradiction by also viewing the self as an entity somehow distinct from society. He wanted people to develop a "spiritually edifying self-image" and "to think of human beings, either individually or in groups, as self-creators."[51] Indeed, in terms of the personhood abundantly revealed by his writings, self-creation for him is a matter of thinking in the first person with the integrity and the sound memory needed to insist on matters of fact and principle no matter what his critics say. The only problem is that, in terms of the theory presented by his writings, such a personhood is a chimera.

Rorty indeed is one philosopher who practices what he does not preach! The most basic point here is that, despite his immersion in analytic philosophy, he has been satisfied to treat the actual and the normative relation between socially accepted premises and the individual's exercise of critical reflexivity in an imprecise way, accepting as gospel, just as Quine did, Dewey's vague, dubious dictum that "'Soliloquy is the product and reflex of converse with others.'"[52]

On the one hand, it is hard to find empirical evidence refuting the commonsense view that soliloquy (i.e. autonomously and solitarily thinking about something) and conversation are at least partly independent of each other, and that soliloquy is often the path to the quantum jumps of creative insight. On the other hand, in trying to regard soliloquy as just an aspect of conversation, Rorty depended on a loose use of "we" or "us." Citing William James's idea that truth is "'what it is better for us to believe,'" Rorty added that, when truth is instead regarded as "'accurate representation of reality,'" "'accurate representation' is simply an automatic and empty compliment which we pay to those beliefs which are successful in helping us do what we want to do."[53] But who are "we"?

To be sure, "we" here could just refer to the metaphysical object noted above, all of humanity. Yet James's "better for us" also implies the consensus of a group, the assumption that, when a group discusses what they want or what is the truth, the ideas they share somehow supersede disagreements among individuals. Yet Rorty's disagreements with his critics are not epiphenomenal, any more than were Socrates's with his. Empirically speaking, as I have maintained throughout this book, the discourse of any group or community necessarily mixes together shared premises (ROST), the agenda of unanswered questions implied by them, and the competing, controversial answers to these questions. Thus Rorty posed an empirically false dichotomy when he contrasted individual, idiosyncratic ideas with socially shared, conventional, historically bequeathed outlooks. The former are as integral as the latter to any empirically observed discourse. I agree with Brandom: "I have been urging that the public, tradition-sustaining, and the private, tradition-transforming sorts of practices that Rorty discusses are two aspects of all discursive activity, neither intelligible apart from the other."[54]

That is, Rorty questions idiosyncratic appeals to a truth transcending any current pattern of conventional opinion as mistakenly presupposing the existence of "eternal standards." What evidence does he have, however, that a pattern of conventional opinion can be even formed without such appeals or can persist except as part of a public dialogue including them? Eternal standards may be an illusion, but cultural history free of this illusion seems to be a chimera. Linguistic practice includes discourses, which by their very nature include arguments made by individuals adducing standards of truth and reality transcending whatever the current community says. The Greek sophists Rorty so admires denied that such standards could be usefully adduced, but they simply misunderstood the nature of linguistic practice.

Insisting on the sociality of the quest for knowledge, however, Rorty not only left unclear the relation between soliloquy and dialogue as well as the extent to which knowledge can be obtained. He also found himself demanding freedom while depicting human beings as necessarily unfree.

Paradoxically enough, his insistence on the sociality of the quest for knowledge reflected his commitment to freedom, his determination to free human beings from subjection to any supposedly objective factual-normative order imposed on them whatever they might themselves autonomously wish to be and do. Yet he thus exchanged subjection to ideas based on knowledge for subjection to the ROST socially formed during the era in which people were fated to live.

Filled with a desire for "freedom" and "self-creation," he could have chosen to recognize that ROST exist in tension with CR, thus identifying the free exercise of critical reflexivity and the quest for knowledge as a hopeful if imperfect path guaranteed by the very nature of linguistic practice. Taking this option, however, would have thrust him back into that very state of subjection he most abhorred, respect for whatever objective order of truths and norms can be fully or partially known. Hence his insistence on looking for his freedom in the realm of unpredictable historical vicissitudes, daring his critics to show why such recklessness is less useful than some other approach to life.

This recklessness appears as a James Dean–like, almost nihilistic spirit of defiance in responding to the constraints of existence. In Rorty's case, however, this spirit was ultimately optimistic, not surly. As already indicated, his optimism was connected with his professed belief in Hegel's metaphysical concept of a World-Spirit guaranteeing progress in the long run. Yet given his deep-rooted empiricism and nominalism, this belief could not have been his final answer to the predicament created by his philosophy, that of a creature yearning for "self-creation" but under the control of her historical fate. Instead, the cheerfulness with which he embraced this predicament stemmed more from a certain American triumphalism, as already indicated. Although warning against the dangers of "chauvinism," Rorty rooted his choice of categories in what Susan Haack calls his "tribalism."[55] He could do so cheerfully because he felt it obvious that the World-Spirit had been kind to his tribe. Yet in leaving the fate of other tribes at the mercy of whatever conventional culture history had thrown them into, his philosophy precluded the autonomy with which any member of any tribe could conceptualize and seek freedom.

To put it more precisely, by describing linguistic practice as empty of any critical reflexivity with which an individual could autonomously criticize ROST and pursue truth and knowledge, Rorty left the idea of freedom without any basis in linguistic practice except for any ROST that happened to include this idea. While his philosophy attacked those who would use unenlightened ideas about the nature of the mind to impose their authority on others, his view that my pursuit of truth cannot transcend the consensus of my tribe precluded any way of freely discovering which ideas are enlightened.

How can the Sophist perspective on knowing, which Rorty regards as desirable, be discovered and upheld in the tribe led by Socrates? If truth is disconnected from the individual pursuit of logical inquiry and limited to the ideas forming the socially dominant rhetorical trend, the distinction between freedom and subservience is replaced by that between the illusion of intellectual autonomy and flaccid acceptance of conventional opinion.

One has to admit, however, that Rorty at least did not mince words in endorsing this option of intellectual flaccidity. True, he did recommend eagerness to embrace the "bizarre" as an alternative to it, hoping for a society in which "everybody always welcomes strange opinions on all sorts of topics." Yet he was not embarrassed to admit that, in contemplating the confrontation between Socrates's reasoning and conventional Athenian opinion, what struck him was not the moral and intellectual lethargy of the Athenians but the problem of how to justify an idiosyncratic view out of accord with their "current theory and practice."[56]

e. Seven Remaining Issues

Asking, then, whether Rorty's formidable combination of some twelve propositions offers a promising way to employ the critical reflexivity empirically integral to linguistic practice, one finds a range of Western criticisms that point to but do not fully spell out a string of difficulties: the failure to recognize critical reflexivity as a future-oriented part of linguistic practice in tension with the linguistic forms inherited from the historical past; the failure to recognize the mentalistic nature of this tension, the mentalistic process of comparing linguistic forms to intended meanings, the mentalistic ability to obtain knowledge, and the mentalistic ability to break off dialogue with others in order to reflect ("soliloquy"); and the unsuccessful effort to conceptualize the freedom of a person so locked into a socially imposed vocabulary that she is incapable of such reflection. At least seven more difficulties should be adduced, however: the problem of historiographical accuracy; the problem of dealing with lack of logical consistency; the problem of finding a surrogate for "accurate representation of reality" as a standard with which to evaluate ideas; problems in dealing with the political context of that quest for freedom seemingly integral to critical reflexivity; the problem of adequately widening the scope of self-reflection; problems in turning culture into an object of critical reflexivity; and the problem of remaining open to the possible relations between utility, virtue, and a pious attitude toward the cosmic setting of the *Lebenswelt.*

Unconcerned with any need for an objective order transcending historical contingency, Rorty was at pains to insist that the idea of such an order which the mind should "mirror" is a kind of aberration out of accord with the "natural" way to think, an unusual notion going back to the Greeks' puzzling appreciation of the gift of sight and their resulting use of the "ocular metaphor" to define knowledge.[57] True, it is hard to see how an admirer of pragmatism like Rorty would feel anything but admiration for people who valued the gift of sight and the phenomenon of light enough to refer to them metaphorically when conceptualizing the desirable way to think. What is more "useful" than light and the ability to see? Or is eyesight useful but not the use of metaphor?

More to the point, however, it is inaccurate to regard the Greeks as unusual in conceptualizing an intellectually apprehended, objective, cosmic, normative order with which ideas should correspond. This concept was as basic to Confucian philosophy as to Greek. Far from being unnatural, it probably has been basic to all the civilizations that S.N. Eisenstadt called "axial," and it obviously was basic to the Judeo-Christian tradition.

A good example in the Chinese case is the major Confucian text *Hsun-tzu* (third century B.C.), which emphasized the "principles" (*li*) inherent in the nature of "Heaven, Earth, and Man" and the need to "pile them up" (*chi*) in the "mind" (*hsin*) through "study" and "thinking" (*ssu*) in order to "know the True Way." For *Hsun-tzu*, then, objective reality itself was infused with "principles," and the ideas one sought to grasp and follow were these cosmic principles themselves, not just concepts "representing" them. Grasping them, one achieved a state of "utmost purity and clarity" (*ta-ch'ing-ming*). A logograph combining the symbol for the sun with one for the moon, *ming* (clarity, make clear, brightly clear, clearly understand, etc.) is one of *Hsun-tzu*'s most frequently used terms. So is *pien* (distinguish between), and *ming-pien* (brightly and clearly to distinguish between) came to be one of the most commonly used terms in the Confucian intellectual tradition. Thus, metaphorically using the image of light, which obviously connotes eyesight, to articulate the concept of knowledge has not been an idiosyncrasy confined to the Hellenic peninsula, not to mention the idea of a cosmic order people should completely conform to, if not even unite with. One might recall that, according to the Judeo-Christian tradition, God created light on the first day of the Creation. Rorty might want to call this an ocular perspective on cosmogony.

Rorty has been much criticized for his way of dealing with intellectual history, but the focus has been on his treatment of recent figures like Dewey and Davidson. The historiographical fallacy at the bottom of his philosophical argument has not been noted in any of the writings I have seen. It is awareness of some non-Western philosophy which allows one to notice that there was nothing "unnatural" or even impressive about the Greek attempt to exchange subjection to historical contingency for subjection to a transcendent order that the individual human mind can apprehend by "thinking" (*ssu*) in a "brightly clear" way. What was extraordinary about the Greeks was their interest in how to distinguish between knowledge and opinion, an interest Rorty ineptly regards as unremarkable.[58] He does not appreciate how this preoccupation of theirs arose out of an extraordinary circumstance. Unlike a number of peoples, including the Chinese, the Greeks lacked a sacred canon and so lacked any obvious way to make the distinction between enlightened and unenlightened ideas. To put it in another way, they were unique among the axial civilizations (so far as I know) in trying to form this distinction without creating a sacred canon. Rorty's own philosophy is just another phase in the evolution of this spectacular achievement which he regards as unremarkable.

At the same time, whether or not this idea of the mind as a mirror of nature was distinctively Western, Rorty's idea that this idea was transmitted in the West over many centuries from one language to another contradicted his central Quinian thesis that meaning is inseparable from linguistic forms, as already noted. Rorty's philosophy also exhibits the contradiction into which all relativism falls, as when he said "There are no assertions which are immune from revision."[59] Moreover, it exemplifies a kind of inconsistency seemingly endemic to analytic philosophy.

Analytic philosophy's goal, if I am not mistaken, is a verbal world in which the lighted space of precisely disaggregated meanings constantly expands and the penumbra of vagueness and meanings "run together" constantly recedes. Yet it is hard to see how the ratio of clarity to vagueness has much been altered. Picturing itself as the final answer to the problem of knowledge, analytic philosophy presents philosophers with a Sisyphean exercise leaving the basic problem of moral-political praxis unattended.

Rorty's reliance on ideas left as ambiguous as the Yalta agreement on Poland is obvious — e.g. truth should be seen as "'what it is better for us to believe.'" Even W.V. Quine, the alleged master of the "logical point of view," merely applied a kind of triage to determine which cases of imprecision were intolerable, which, tolerable.

For him, Kant's "cleavage between analytic and synthetic truths" was intolerably imprecise and suffered from dependence on metaphor. Yet it was acceptable for Quine to say that "The totality of our so-called knowledge or beliefs ... is a man-made fabric which impinges on experience only along the edges"; to hold that "Basic differences in language are bound up, as likely as not, with differences in the way in which speakers articulate the world itself into things and properties, time and space, elements, forces, spirits, and so on"; to depend on highly unspecific ideas like "primarily a property of behavior," "dispositions to overt behavior," "private language," and "radically different language" as basic categories when analyzing the nature of language; to depend on an utterly loose concept of "culture" (see below); and so on.[60]

Most important, when they took the linguistic turn, the central problem analytic philosophers encountered was that of describing the relation between language and the rest of the world. As they endlessly argued about it, however, they must have realized that their quest for the precise use of words was inherently unsuited for dealing with this problem. As Davidson's metaphor of "triangulation" implies, the boundary between language and the rest of the world seems to be inherently fuzzy.

The clash between analytic philosophy's demand for precise expression and the need to depend on vagueness was especially evident in Rorty's turn to pragmatism. What could be vaguer than being "successful in helping us to do what we want to do," the idea recommended by Rorty to replace "the accurate representation of reality" as the standard with which to evaluate ideas? As noted above, this standard turns on an ambiguous use of "we." Moreover, even apart from all the much-discussed ambiguities inseparable from any concept of utility, Rorty's use of James's "what it is better for us to believe" turned the effort to define "utility" into hopelessly vague arguments about whether the Greeks' "ocular metaphor" had been as causatively vital as, say, the Christian idea of God in the development of European civilization, and whether erecting and preserving such a civilization might be "what we want to do."

Rorty reduced the problem of "utility" to such sophomoric arguments when he suggested that the epistemological ideas arising out of this Greek metaphor "have been more trouble than they are worth, and that we should see how things go if we discard them."[61] One can easily imagine a lively debate in a college dorm about whether Europe's humanistic Great Tradition has been more trouble than it's worth. Rorty's philosophy consistently regards "openness to strangeness" and the "new" as a key aspect of the pragmatic quest for utility, but how about openness to the value of the old? More broadly still, this dorm debate could turn to the question of whether it is more "useful" to put human needs into an evolutionary spectrum going back to squirrels and amoebae, as Rorty recommends,[62] or to follow the classical principle of civilizations east and west: emphasis on the contrast between man and beast.

How then did Rorty deal with this contradiction between the need to tolerate vagueness and his driving pursuit for maximum clarity, as well as other contradictions? My suggestion is that he had a choice between (a) turning to a Hegelian notion of tension between ROST and CR, viewing logical consistency, the precise use of words, and knowledge as the goals of a necessarily imperfect intellectual struggle, and (b) somehow downgrading the importance of these goals, questioning the justifiability of the classical definition of knowledge (true and justified belief about what is objectively so). In emphasizing "irony," he picked the latter option while caricaturing the former as belief in "a permanent neutral framework for culture."[63]

Yet, as just argued, it is hard to deny that knowledge in this classical sense is unavailable. Moreover, as also already argued, it is frivolous to claim that one's discussion is irony all the way down, because there would be no call for irony unless Rorty's account about the nature of language were seriously proposed and accurate. Irony, it seems to me, cannot be used to describe a primordial standpoint, because it is inherently a derivative concept, a recommendation resting on a "because" statement. If Rorty claims that his views about "self-creation," "freedom," and the nature of language are not to be taken seriously, what is it that he proposes to contribute to that "conversation" in which, he says, he wants to participate? If even his interest in participating in it is not to be taken seriously, what are we left with but sheer nihilism?

This raises the question of Rorty's political philosophy. While John Rawls's "political liberalism" calls for a "reasonable pluralism" whereby "reasonable" citizens agree none of them possesses the objective truth about matters of ultimate concern, Rorty calls for a pluralistic democracy whose citizens agree that none of them possesses any objective truth about anything. Both formulations leave liberal democracy in the predicament Carl Schmitt so astutely wrote about, the inability to close discussion and pursue collective goals in a resolute, hopeful way. In Rorty's case, the goal of dismantling any structure of "authority,"[64] making the uncertainty of all knowledge claims the guiding principle of culture, and of absolutizing compassion not only was utopian. It also raised the question of whether any society can be formed without a set of logically connected beliefs uniting its citizens, even if, philosophically, poetry and skepticism can trump respect for logically consecutive propositions. Moreover, the problem of how to think about political ideals and political practicability can be addressed only if one's philosophic exercise includes uncovering and assessing one's assumptions about this problem, instead of just articulating ideals one feels attracted to, such as Rorty's "militant anti-authoritarianism" or T'ang's *t'ai-ho* (great harmony). Endlessly debating the right way to conceptualize ideals and their epistemological basis, philosophers often ignore the totally crucial political question of how to get from here to there (see chapters VIII and X).

This brings up the question of the scope and methodology of self-reflection, that of the exercise needed to develop one's critical reflexivity in the pursuit of freedom, "self-creation," and enlightenment. Once the tension between CR and ROST is recognized, is it not clear that the needed exercise is maximally uncovering and describing the premises of one's own discourse in order critically to reflect on and possibly revise them? This is not, however, the exercise carried out by Rorty, which is outlined above. As already noted, Rorty combined his strictly epistemological points with some five outlooks to form a complex ideological position, but he did not break down this position of his, subject it to critical reflection, and so maximize his autonomous control over his own makeup, the process he celebrated as "self-creation."

Still more basically, Rorty, like Rawls and just about all other philosophers today, regarded the content of a culture — especially "ours" — as manifest, packed and ready for convenient summarization. Lapsing into the notoriously misleading way that laymen often use stereotypes to generalize about foreign societies, Rorty once compared "the West" as "a culture of hope" to "the East" as "cultures of resignation."[65] Despite his avowed "priz[ing of] concreteness and specificity,"[66] he did not see that, in contrast with "the ROST of my we-group" or "the ROST expressed in a specific set of texts," "our culture" is a vague term including a pronominal adjective with an unspecified antecedent and projecting simple categories onto an unspecified population whose orientations are complex, diverse, evolving, and far from manifest. He thus used the concept of "culture" as a describable object without recognizing that what is actually describable is only an empirically specific set of orientations; that these ROST expressed in a text have to be laboriously and thoughtfully brought into awareness; that, as the subject-matter of the text describing them, they inherently are susceptible to critical discussion, that is, are inseparable from CR; and that this linguistic fact turns the relation between ROST and CR into a normative question: how *should* CR be pursued, given its embedment in ROST? While Rorty recommended "openness to strangeness" as the way to leave behind "outworn vocabularies,"[67] what good is such an intention to be open in the case of a strange cultural pattern unless accompanied by a serious interest in the problem of how to describe cultural patterns? If one has not discovered what the nature of something is by thoughtfully examining it, how can one be open-minded in assessing its value? Similarly, without such an examination of both native and foreign cultures, how can one figure out whether one's inherited ROST are "outworn" or just need some revision?

Like Quine, then, Rorty failed to draw a connection between his recognition that culture to a large extent determines one's views and his premise as a philosopher that one's views should be critically examined. Perhaps his American triumphalism (see above) made him confident that his basic beliefs stood in no need of critical scrutiny. His philosophy, like Quine's or Rawls's, is free of worry about how to assess his own cultural commitments, free of Robert Redfield's awareness of the complexity and unexpectedness of the way any cultural pattern or society is put together. As Hilary Putnam writes: "When, after all, has Rorty shown the slightest interest in *sociological* description of the *actual* norms and standards current in what he calls 'our' societies?"[68]

Still more, in the description of cultural orientations, Rorty's scientistic quest for precision collided with empiricism. The introspectively accessible flow of feelings and thoughts is a major part of what is empirically given. Yet this flow, whether or not characterized as a physiological activity, is not susceptible to precise description as a series of specific spatio-temporal events that can be publicly observed and measured. Therefore the quest for precision led Quine, Rorty, and others to regard reference to such an introspective flow as a "pernicious mentalism." Nevertheless, these introspective data are empirically given, and so any comprehensive description of linguistic practice has to take them into account. Moreover, as already indicated, Rorty gives the misleading impression that, in order to reject Cartesian dualism and accept Darwinism, it is necessary to reject "mentalism" and deny that linguistic symbols can represent specific aspects of objective reality. His central thesis about the mind as "the mirror of nature" conflates all these issues, even while he repeatedly invokes analytic philosophy's injunction to avoid "running together" ideas that can be disaggregated.

Finally, when one uses CR to ponder the relation between the norms of the *Lebenswelt* and what is known about the latter and about the natural world, one has to avoid dogmatically adopting a utilitarian, egoistic definition of human goals. That is, one has to remain open to the possible connection between these goals and the cosmic setting in which they are unavoidably conceptualized and pursued. The relation between virtue and a pious attitude toward this setting is central to religion and philosophy, old and new, east and west, but drops from sight when Rorty recommends pursuing "happiness" as "getting more of the things we keep developing new descriptive vocabularies in order to get." Nor is much clarified by his endorsement of "pragmatic atheis[m]."[69]

The question here is broader than whether to believe that an anthropomorphic deity rules the cosmos. Even if one does not believe this, one can still have a pious attitude toward the cosmic origin and home of humankind. When Rorty focuses on the things people want to get more of, believes "that the only reason for getting in touch with something non-human is to adapt it to our needs,"[70] and prefers "making human history the measure of all things,"[71] he supposes that human life can be enhanced by divorcing its significance from the grandeur of its cosmic setting. For someone so impressed by the holistic character of language, he is strangely uninterested in the way that human life is part of a larger whole. Just as strangely, focused as he is on the need for freedom, poetry, and the struggle to "create ever more open space for the play of the human imagination,"[72] he sees no synergy in the relation between this play of the human imagination and its cosmic setting, only creative human activity impinging on inherently meaningless materials.

This drab picture of the non-human universe, however, is abstractly deduced from the scientific analysis of natural phenomena rather than based on the empirical observation of the experienced interaction between the inner and the outer in the *Lebenswelt*. What could the human imagination possibly consist of if it were not nourished by the unlimited variety of hugely suggestive sense impressions made possible by the non-human universe? How can Rorty glorify "the play of the human imagination," emphasize the Darwinian account of the utterly non-human, cosmic, animalistic origin of this imagination, and then insist on a seemingly absolute discontinuity between the cosmic origin and the human exercise of this imagination? Does not this discontinuity between the inner and the outer push Rorty back into a dualism as severe and implausible as Descartes'? Is not his insistence on this discontinuity, contradicting virtually all of the world's philosophies and religions, an extremely iconoclastic action impetuously taken with only controversial reasons to take it?

Yet this discontinuity is not so absolute as it seems, because Rorty still regards the non-human part of the world as the object of a human attitude. As touched on above, his philosophy does express an attitude toward what T.S. Eliot called "the facts when you get down to brass tacks: birth, copulation, and death." Apart from this issue of discontinuity, therefore, one has to critique this attitude of his.

Rorty does not object to any variety of poetic or religious sentiments about birth and death. Given the utilitarianism he shares with Freud, however, he insists that "philosophy" deal only with the "things" one can not only want but also concretely get. Thus the norms recommended by his pragmatism are to be strictly differentiated from ideas about the significance of birth and death as cosmic events. As his Antipodeans at least imply, birth and death are only medical facts, and so they are irrelevant to the forming of values. Relegated to the status of a medical event, the fact of birth cannot be used in the Confucian way to link human spirituality with the cosmos as a beneficently creative process, just as the fact of death cannot be defined in the common Western way as a horizon beyond which lies either the hope of salvation or the dread of finitude and meaninglessness.

Rorty thus recommends that, in thinking about birth and death, people develop a "spiritual" state free of both this hope and this dread, replacing them with a cheerful, indeed Deweyan celebration of the pleasures people can concretely obtain. But — and this should be an important question for a pragmatist — is this recommendation practicable? Does history show that a humane society can be formed without articulating a synergistic relation between human wants and their cosmic, not only their historical context? Are human impulses, contrary to Schopenhauer, so benignly inclined to accord with human ideals that pursuit of the latter can dispense with any fear not of failing to bring more of the cosmos under one's own control but to understand and make the most of the brief opportunity to be part of the cosmos? If the free market is the proper paradigm for the economy, does it necessarily follow that maximizing what benefits one in particular is the proper paradigm for one's relation with the cosmic setting of birth and death? To the extent that Rorty's iconoclastic pragmatism overlaps a utilitarian concept of globalization and global history now animating U.S. foreign policy (see chapter XIV), does it tend to aggravate the clash between the international role now played by the U.S. and the major civilizational patterns in the world today resisting this utilitarian approach to human life?

Again, the difficult problem here is to reject not the whole of utilitarianism but a simplistic version of it. I am not suggesting return to a metaphysical derivation of virtue and rejection of the utilitarian insight that the satisfaction of egoistic, largely material needs belongs at the center of the moral-political agenda. What I question is fully identifying the norms of praxis with the satisfaction of these needs.

All in all, then, a far more drastic critique of Rorty's philosophy is possible when one puts it into the context of the GMWER and turns the latter as a whole into an object of critical reflection. On the one hand, the GMWER led to the momentous post-Kantian discovery of a major empirical fact, the great extent to which linguistic symbols purporting accurately to mirror facts and principles identical for all human beings only express beliefs shared by some human beings. This discovery stemmed from the pursuit of a straightforward empiricism that was shared by the GMWER with modern science, and that seems to be an excellent epistemological norm. On the other hand, while building on this discovery, Rorty's philosophy has been part of a highly distinctive, controversial, and indeed ideological attempt to combine this empiricism with a devotion to scientistic precisionism, Enlightenment ideals, Rousseauistic utopianism, the rejection of Weberian empiricism, a radically iconoclastic attitude toward the European humanistic mainstream, and American triumphalism.[73]

In critiquing Rorty, I picture him not as misunderstanding a progressive World-Spirit but as illustrating how the linguistically given need to utilize CR properly can never be fully met and is always entangled with the ROST with which history has equipped one's we-group. I also suspect that a historical event affecting his philosophical trajectory was his reaction as a student to the Aristotelian hegemony Richard McKeon tried to impose on the Department of Philosophy at the University of Chicago. Is there any connection between Rorty's Americanist, iconoclastic reaction to the European Great Tradition and the fact that during his formative years as a graduate student he experienced Robert Hutchins' attempt to import the study of Europe's Great Books into the most American of America's great cities, Chicago?

5. Conclusion: The Failure of Philosophy East and West

To be sure, my discussion has not definitively refuted those many Westerners and non-Westerners claiming that, overall, contemporary Western philosophy should be the model for all those around the globe looking for the best way to utilize that critical reflexivity with which biological evolution has endowed human beings.[74] I cannot deny that, having in this book made an effort to critique the thought of a good number of leading Western thinkers in recent times ranging from Leo Strauss, Karl R. Popper, F.A. Hayek, John Dunn, and John Rawls to Richard Rorty, I may still have failed to grasp the most important aspects of the Western philosophical presence in the world today. At the very least, however, I think I have shown that Rorty's historicism is not less vulnerable to criticism than T'ang's bluntly metaphysical approach.

On both sides of the Pacific, the problem is a one-sided awareness of problems: easily spotting difficulties one has become accustomed to try to shun, while overlooking problems more easily noticed by those unaccustomed to one's academic routine. Thus we in the West easily spot T'ang's vulnerabilities. He not only arbitrarily brushes aside the great influence of ROST on the exercise of CR. He also jumps to the conclusion that CR is such a powerful cognitive tool that it is able to apprehend the ultimate "rational basis" (*li-t'i*) of the cosmos and the way that all the laws of nature, history, and moral-political praxis stem from this "Logos." Moreover, positing the possibility of a kind of "ultimate wisdom" (*chih-hui*) that political leaders or at least "philosophers" can grasp, his extravagant epistemological optimism brings with it the danger of totalitarian leadership.

We in the West, however, do not easily spot important questions raised or implied by the Chinese philosophical perspective. In exploring the extent to which CR can obtain knowledge, T'ang dealt with a crucial problem that the GMWER increasingly neglected. Rorty discusses "vocabularies" without recognizing that their historical evolution includes a causative impulse that his own philosophy perfectly exemplifies, that of CR. Thus he in effect recognizes ROST without admitting that, in linguistic practice, ROST and CR are inextricably linked.

On the one hand, the GMWER snowballed into a rising accumulation of formidable arguments not just shrinking the scope of knowledge as true ideas about what is objectively so but precluding the very possibility of such ideas and so encouraging a desperate sense of the historicity, relativity, and finitude of human existence. On the other hand, Rorty in a brilliantly bold way articulated an optimistic American rejection of such despair by claiming that knowledge in this classic sense was unneeded for the pursuit of what was important for human beings. Even more, he claimed, the belief that it was needed was a perverse impulse nurturing authoritarianism. Yet the arguments precluding knowledge were more formidable than cogent. In picturing human existence as without access to objective truth, Rorty could not avoid ignoring a major empirical phenomenon, CR as an aspect of linguistic behavior, if not also projecting the capitalistic paradigm of accumulation onto the relation between human life and its cosmic context.

While T'ang's philosophy threatens dictatorship by an all-knowing elite, Rorty's threatens passive acceptance of whatever opinion trends history happens to crystallize. In T'ang's case, CR is not lost sight of, but it is inflated to create the kind of danger against which Karl R. Popper warned, an optimistic epistemology threatening dictatorship. In Rorty's case, a much more pessimistic epistemology arising out of the GMWER has effectively pointed to the importance of ROST, but, losing sight of CR, it has (like John Rawls's philosophy) created the kind of danger against which Carl Schmitt warned, a liberal polity passively exposed to whatever winds of opinion history produces.

In neither case is there the recognition that "a culture" is a set of historically bequeathed, socially shared orientations which, heavily influencing everyone, ego as well as alter, philosopher as well as non-philosopher, can be described and critically contemplated only when in the form of an empirically determinate text produced by alter or ego; that the verbalized ROST found in such a text are not manifest and so need to be brought into awareness by carefully analyzing the text; that ROST as part of linguistic practice are inextricably linked to CR; that this link produces Schopenhauer's suspicion that ROST mask egotistic urges; and that, especially because of this suspicion, the enlightenment which the polity needs has to come from a continuous intellectual and educational effort to uncover ROST and turn them into an object of CR.

On the one hand, while ROST as culture indeed constitute a "veil of ideas" or "veil of vocabulary" impeding the pursuit of knowledge as true ideas about what is objectively so, they do not necessarily preclude this pursuit. Moreover, it is far from clear that they allow knowledge only about facts, not about moral-political praxis. T'ang is right in keeping this question open. On the other hand, one can agree with Rorty's refusal to lament the limits ROST put on the pursuit of knowledge. The knowledge that cannot be pursued is not necessarily needed. Even more, I do not necessarily disagree that knowledge is a kind of constraint, and that a person is fully free only when she can make choices unconstrained by anything except her own judgments. Thus the scope of freedom grows as that of knowledge shrinks, and many would say that's a good thing.

Not lamenting the "veil of vocabulary," however, is not the end of the story. If freedom means being guided only by one's own judgments, how can one realize it unless one has maximally uncovered and critically scrutinized the vocabulary on which these judgments are based? Thus the "veil of vocabulary," that is, culture or ROST, cannot just be welcomed as the correlate of freedom. It has to be turned into an object of critical reflexivity if freedom is to be pursued.

This is the really fairly obvious point which, so far as I can see, modern philosophy east and west long failed to grasp as it struggled during the last two centuries to respond to the momentous Western discovery — really every bit as momentous as Darwinism — that the exercise of critical reflexivity is deeply affected by disparate cultural orientations and linguistic patterns. Much of the modern world's intellectual history, especially its debates about political theory, can be seen as conflicting ways of responding to this discovery: the tendency, not only in China, to ignore or minimize this discovery; Strauss's denunciation of this discovery as a relativistic attempt to deny the importance of the reflective effort to understand universal truth and objective reality; the Rortian claim that such a reflective effort not only is gratuitous but also turns reflection into a tool of authoritarianism; and the ultimately Hegelian point that the pursuit of individual freedom as control over what one is requires turning cultural-linguistic orientations into objects of critical reflexivity.

Neither T'ang nor Rorty grasped this Hegelian point. Thus neither deployed critical reflexivity to try to minimize the grip of critically unexamined cultural orientations on the way philosophers and other citizens reason about their personal and collective predicaments. In T'ang's case, this grip is rashly minimized or simply unrecognized. In Rorty's case, it is both flaccidly accepted and impulsively celebrated. Like Rawls, he turns critical reflexivity into a passive handmaiden of culture, as Frank B. Farrell brilliantly pointed out.[75] Neither this passivity nor T'ang's transformative vision encourages the education of a citizenry devoted to the pursuit of resolute collective action based on a critical understanding of their own impulses as well as their environment.

To facilitate such education, I argue, people east and west need to reexamine the philosophical foundations of education, aiming for a philosophy that somehow reconciles careful treatment of the problem of knowledge with the need for collective, resolute, hopeful, and prudent action. On the one hand, by recognizing the close connection between thinking and linguistic practice, one can deal with facts and the problem of knowledge more carefully. On the other, by recognizing that critical reflexivity and the pursuit of knowledge are basic to linguistic practice, one opens up the possibility of dealing with political problems in a collectively resolute way.

The central point is that while empiricism has long been regarded as incapable of yielding knowledge about norms, a thoroughgoing empiricism uncompromised by precisionism can yield such knowledge, because linguistic practice in fact includes critical reflexivity, which is a verbal activity positing that more enlightened are preferable to less enlightened ideas. Until one empirically finds a discourse not positing this belief, the only justification this belief requires is an awareness of what one believes when one is participating in a discourse.

To be sure, the concrete content of enlightenment will vary greatly depending on cultural and ideological trends. As the Hegelian model makes clear, in the tension between ROST and CR, ROST are always crucially important, whether they are those of Hitler's Germany or Roosevelt's America. If, however, empiricism leads people to recognize themselves as linguistic individuals seeking freedom from control by unenlightened persons rather than flaccidly accepting conventional principles, then a good deal of J.S. Mill's liberalism can be deduced from this self-knowledge, especially the importance of education in the full Greek sense of *paideia*. At that point, Mill's reliance on a vague concept of "reason" can be replaced by empiricism, and care in the study of facts and the scope of knowledge can coincide with a concept of collective, resolute, hopeful, prudent political action. Nor is this just a way of reiterating liberal platitudes. A liberal polity and a liberal education based on empiricism and organized around the Millsian quest for enlightenment will be different from one based on irony, just as it will be from one based on metaphysical dreams. From this standpoint, properly calibrating the relation between CR and ROST is a challenge carrying the hope that political life can be improved. By organizing philosophy around this challenge, one indeed explicitly returns to the foundationalism that Rorty has tried to conceptualize obliquely and so to the central point on which Confucius and Socrates converged: in a gradual but sure way, philosophical debates shape the direction of education, and the ultimate goal of philosophy has to be the improvement of political life through education.

If, then, empiricism leads to the finding that ROST and CR are linguistically interdependent, it also makes clear the linguistic interdependence of discussion about ontological-epistemological issues and about moral-political praxis. The GMWER's effort, coming to a climax with Rorty, to cut the latter discussion off from the former is as fraught with problems as is the still energetic Chinese effort to deduce the latter from the former. My claim is that a development of *paideia* based on the recognition of this interdependence will have a desirable effect on democratic political life.

Yet analyzing linguistic practice as the interaction between CR and ROST is not yet an issue on the Chinese philosophical agenda. This is because, according to the prevalent Chinese ROST today, whatever the vagaries of culture and linguistic practice, "reason" aided by "intuition" can still obtain "wisdom" about the objective, "dialectical" nature of both the natural world and the *Lebenswelt*. This pervasive standpoint immunizes Chinese thought against the influence of the GMWER. At the same time, the empirical approach to linguistic practice recommended above will not easily replace the kind of Nietzchean affirmation of a proud American ethos to which the logic of the GMWER led Rorty, and which Susan Haack has astutely described as a shift from "relativism" and "contextualism" to "tribalism."[76]

On both sides of the Pacific, then, epistemic smugness impedes the exercise of critical reflexivity and so the bridging of those civilizational differences to which Samuel P. Huntington drew attention, as well as domestic reform. Philosophers worry about whether they can devise the principles with which the crises of humanity can be overcome. Less open to doubt is that the philosophies arising in a civilization typically embody the conventional premises integral to the predicament of that civilization without uncovering and critically scrutinizing them. Neither T'ang nor Rorty can escape that criticism.

Yet one should also ask: even if such premises influence philosophical reflection and the formulation of political theories, how do they affect concrete political activity, including the ways in which governments conceptualize and carry out their relations with one another? The next chapter tries to answer this question, concern with which was presented in chapter I, section 1 as the ultimate source of this book's agenda.

Endnotes

1. In writing this essay, I benefited very greatly from an exchange of letters about it with Professor Eric M. Gander. I am most grateful to him. In March 2004 I had the great pleasure of having a conversation with Professor Rorty, and some of his comments made a deep impression on me, which, I hope, helped me refine some of my formulations. In writing this essay, I have made use especially of Richard Rorty, *Philosophy and the Mirror of Nature* (Princeton: Princeton University Press, 1980); Robert B. Brandom, ed., *Rorty and His Critics* (Oxford: Blackwell Publishers Ltd., 2000); Herman J. Saatkamp Jr., ed., *Rorty and Pragmatism* (Nashville: Vanderbilt University Press, 1995); Eric M. Gander, *The Last Conceptual Revolution: A Critique of Richard Rorty's Political Philosophy* (Albany: State University of New York Press, 1999); W.V. Quine, *Ontological Relativity and Other Essays* (New York: Columbia University Press, 1969); W.V. Quine, *From a Logical Point of View* (Cambridge, Mass.: Harvard University Press, 1953); Siobhan Chapman, *Philosophy for Linguists: An Introduction* (London: Routledge, 2000); and some books by Noam Chomsky and Charles Taylor. A preliminary version of this essay took the form of a lecture December 24, 2003 at the Department of Philosophy, Peking University, on *Ts'ung p'i-p'ing* Richard Rorty *che-hsueh-te li-ch'ang k'an T'ang Chün-i che-hsueh-te te-shih* (Evaluating the Philosophy of T'ang Chün-i from the Standpoint of a Critical Understanding of Richard Rorty's Philosophy).

2. Saatkamp, ed., p. 17. In 2003, however, the University of Michigan initiated a lecture series honoring T'ang Chün-i.

3. Quine, *From a Logical Point of View*, pp. 12–13, 23, 44.

4. Chapman, p. 116.

5. The idea of discourse is discussed in chapter I, section 8.

6. Rorty, p. 368.

7. Quine, *Ontological Relativity*, p. 26; Saatkamp, ed., p. 195; Rorty, p. 181.

8. Rorty, p. 10.

9. Brandom, ed., pp. 373–376.

10. Ibid., pp. 104–105.

11. Saatkamp, ed., p. 124.

12. Brandom, ed., p. 374.

13. Saatkamp, ed., p. 198.

14. Brandom, ed., pp. 161–162.

15. Rorty, p. 159.

16. Brandom, ed., p. 376.

17. Ibid., pp. 252, 263–264.

18. Ibid., pp. 5, 40.

19. Noam Chomsky, *Language and Problems of Knowledge: The Managua Lectures* (Cambridge, Mass.: The MIT Press, 2001), p. 9. Particularly distressing is the way *Philosophy and the Mirror of Nature* conflates the problems of mentalism, Cartesian dualism, and Darwinism. For an effective defense of mentalism using Steven Pinker's ideas, see Eric M. Gander, *On Our Minds: How Evolutionary Psychology Is Reshaping the Nature-versus-Nurture Debate* (Baltimore: The Johns Hopkins University Press, 2003), p. 163.

20. Quine, *From a Logical Point of View*, pp. 61, 20–21. Quine, *Ontological Relativity*, pp. 1, 25, 34, etc.

21. Brandom, ed., p. 18. Insisting that *all* language learning arises out of the observation of "other people's overt behavior under publicly recognized circumstances," Quine used this dubious theory to argue that "our child at home" thus learning "our mother tongue" could master "the ins and outs of our conceptual scheme," including "the trick of individuation," while the foreign linguist could not. Quine then proceeded confidently to compare how the Japanese language deals with certain problems of individuation to how English does. Quine, *Ontological Relativity*, pp. 7–9, 15, 26, 30–31, 35–36, 49.

22. On the Hegel reference, see Brandom, ed., p. 348.

23. See chapter I, section 8.

24. Brandom notes Rorty's "naturalis[m]." See Brandom, ed., p. 171.

25. Ibid., p. 7.

26. Saatkamp, ed., p. 138.

27. Rorty, p. 9.

28. Brandom., ed., pp. 40–41.

29. Ibid., p. 373. Saatkamp, ed., p. 148.

30. Rorty, pp. 174, 188.

31. Ibid., p. 179.

32. Brandom, ed., pp. 161–162, 171.
33. Saatkamp, ed., p. 198.
34. On "rubbish," see ibid., p. 201.
35. Quine, *From a Logical Point of View*, pp. 20–21, 12–13, 61, 8; and Quine, *Ontological Relativity*, p. 27.
36. Quine, *From a Logical Point of View*, p. 79.
37. Saatkamp, ed., p. 12.
38. Quine, *From a Logical Point of View*, p. 24.
39. Brandom, ed., p. 161.
40. Quine, *Ontological Relativity*, pp. 30–35, 1–6.
41. Ibid., p. 89.
42. Quine, *From a Logical Point of View*, p. 28.
43. Saatkamp, ed., p. 21. See also Arnold Metzger, *Freedom and Death*, trans. Ralph Manheim (London: Human Context Books, Chaucer Publishing, 1973).
44. Saatkamp, ed., pp. 195, 201. Brandom, ed., p. 7.
45. Chapter I, section 8.
46. Quine, *Ontological Relativity*, p. 87.
47. Steven Weinberg, *Facing Up: Science and Its Cultural Adversaries* (Cambridge, Mass.: Harvard University Press, 2001). There is also the question of knowledge as it pertains to the most ordinary aspects of human life. This goes beyond the question of "raw feels" and "observation sentences." For instance, the idea of lying implies a discrepancy between what one says one thinks to be true and what one knows one thinks to be true. There is also the very interesting issue of stupidity as a failure to meet intellectual standards that seem to be cross-cultural. For instance, Rorty writes of a Nazi who uses "arguments that nobody outside his remarkably provincial, illiterate, and stupid audience would take seriously" (Brandom, ed., p. 59). This issue of stupidity overlaps that of the "common lapses" I have mentioned elsewhere as seemingly cross-cultural concepts. In virtually any academic environment, one criticizes scholars for failing to make distinctions, ignoring relevant facts, being redundant, failing to distinguish between platitudes and new insights, failing to write in a grammatically and stylistically correct way, and so on. There is also the major question of tacit knowing raised by Michael Polanyi. See Yu Zhenhua (Yü Chen-hua), "Kant's Notion of Judgment from the Perspective of the Theory of Tacit Knowing," *Tradition and Discovery* 31:1 (2004–2005): pp. 24–35. All these questions pertain to that rediscovery of knowledge which is possible once one understands the great influence of language and other historically varying patterns on the ideas people regard as constituting knowledge.
48. Quine, *From a Logical Point of View*, pp. 61, 25, 20, 5; and Quine, *Ontological Relativity*, p. 49.

49. Brandom, ed., p. 342.
50. Saatkamp, ed., p. 205.
51. Ibid., pp. 71, 205, 195.
52. Quine, *Ontological Relativity*, p. 27.
53. Rorty, p. 10.
54. Brandom, ed., p. 179.
55. Saatkamp, ed., pp. 202–203, 137–139.
56. Brandom, ed., p. 7, Rorty, p. 179.
57. On "natural," see Rorty quote in Brandom, ed., p. 220.
58. Brandom, ed., p. 217.
59. Rorty, p. 181.
60. Quine, *From a Logical Point of View*, pp. 20–21, 42; and Quine, *Ontological Relativity*, pp. 26–27.
61. Saatkamp, ed., p. 150.
62. Ibid., p. 12.
63. Rorty, p. 269.
64. Saatkamp, ed., p. 71, Rorty, p. 315.
65. Gander, *The Last Conceptual Revolution*, pp. 115–116.
66. Brandom, ed., p. 266.
67. Rorty, pp. 9, 12.
68. Brandom, ed., p. 86.
69. Brandom, ed., p. 376, Saatkamp, ed., p. 195.
70. Brandom, ed., p. 215.
71. Saatkamp, ed., p. 35.
72. Ibid.
73. Given his admiration of the Sophists, the extent of Rorty's commitment to minimize inconsistency is open to question. Despite his objections to foundationalism, he wrote that the work of philosophers like Kant "gradually comes to have an influence on the entire culture," and he hailed the way Donald Davidson's writing would similarly "bring about ... changes in the human self-image." *Boston Globe*, October 5, 2003.
74. For an illuminating analysis of the history of evolutionary psychology, see Gander, *On Our Minds*.
75. Saatkamp, ed., p. 187.
76. Ibid., p. 137.

CHAPTER XIV

❧

Discourse #1 and the Chinese Conceptualization of U.S.-Chinese Relations

1. U.S. Foreign Policy and the Problem of Cultural Convergence and Divergence

U.S.-Chinese relations today involve not only a familiar list of frictions and shared interests but also a kind of diffuse tension. This is expressed most obviously in competing moral judgments: the U.S. complaint that China is undemocratic and the Chinese charge that U.S. foreign policy is hegemonic. It also entails the clash between the American belief that the U.S.'s leading position in the international world today does not violate any normative concept of the international world and the common Chinese belief that, in a normal world, China would have its place at the top of the global hierarchy of power and prestige.

I was surprised, therefore, in July 2002 when I talked with Professor Su Hao and his wife, Ms. Qiu Jin, at the Hoover Institution in Stanford. Both were part of what can broadly be called the Party-centered establishment in China. His wife was a lecturer at the Beijing University for Athletic Education (*Pei-ching t'i-yü ta-hsueh*), where she taught Marxism. He was an associate professor at the College of International Relations (*Wai-chiao hsueh-yuan*) in Beijing, a prestigious institution under the Ministry of Foreign Relations many of whose graduates become foreign service officers. He also was acting chair of the Department of Diplomacy at this college; chair of its Section on China's Foreign Relations; and a member of the Chinese committee participating in CSCAP (Council for Security

Cooperation in the Asia Pacific), a non-governmental organization linked to ASEAN (Association of Southeast Asian Nations). Born in 1958, he had obtained his Ph.D. from the College of International Relations in 1998 after spending two years, 1993–1995, studying at the University of London's School for Oriental and African Studies. When I saw him in the summer of 2002, he had just finished a year in the U.S. as a senior visiting scholar under the Fulbright program doing research mainly at Columbia University and the Berkeley campus of the University of California.

He said one of his interests was theorizing about the nature of the normative international order appropriate for the current stage of global history. What surprised me was his conclusion: the global community would consist of six regional systems of cooperation on economic and security matters, and the U.S. would not only head the system in the Americas but also be the leading power in the world as a whole, overseeing the other five systems. He gave me some diagrams illustrating this theory, which he had also set forth in a seminar at Columbia University.

It was hard for me to believe that a Chinese scholar, not to mention a member of the official establishment in China, would accept such U.S. global primacy except as a temporary arrangement giving China time to catch up with the U.S. A common Chinese saying recommending this stance is *t'ao-kuang yang-hui* (satisfied to remain temporarily in obscurity while quietly building up one's capabilities). Rebutting my skepticism, Professor Su insisted that, in his view, such U.S. global primacy was not a temporary situation China had to endure, it was the necessary result of the logic of historical evolution for the foreseeable future if not "forever," a word he used.

We then argued amicably about whether such a global Hegelian logic could be inferred from historical data. In my own mind, however, I put his view into the context of China's desire for smooth relations with a powerful U.S. able to guarantee that peaceful international environment which China needs to modernize. I began to wonder whether there had not been a sea change in Chinese thought about the global order of things. I saw the possibility of a dissolution of the old tension between China and the U.S. If China accepted the U.S.'s leading global role, and if the U.S. dropped what I had all along regarded as its gratuitous insistence on monitoring

China's political development, this tension would subside, leaving both sides to argue out their concrete differences in a soberly pragmatic way. When I visited Professor Su in December 2003, giving four lectures at his College of International Relations, he again assured me that his view of the U.S. as the appropriate leader of the global community was typical of thought within the Chinese foreign policy community.

He also, however, gave me a copy of his 515-page book published just a few months before, *Ts'ung ya-ling tao kan-lan: Ya-T'ai ho-tso an-ch'üan mo-shih yen-chiu* (From the Dumbbell to the Olive Model: A Study of a Security Model Applied to the Asia-Pacific Region, That of Security Based on Cooperation; Beijing: Shih-chieh chih-shih ch'u-pan-she, 2003). Well aware that viewpoints on complicated political issues can be expressed adequately only in long written texts prepared for the native audience, not conversations, I decided to find out just how this thoroughly researched, systematically organized study of his conceptualized U.S.-Chinese relations.

Although our oral dialogues, like the book, had been in Chinese, the two did not convey the same message. The main question was whether the leading global position of the U.S. is to be seen as a logical outcome of global history or as an immoral effort on the part of the U.S. to impose its "hegemony" on other nations. Su's conversations with me emphasized the former while omitting any reference to the latter. His book emphasized the latter while omitting any reference to the former.

Why this startling difference? The answer is not that Su's views changed over time, because his book had been largely written before he spoke with me at Hoover in 2002 (513).[1] Moreover, it would be ridiculous to say he was trying to fool foreigners into thinking that China accepted U.S. global supremacy when it didn't. After all, he had himself given me his book. I believe that in his mind these two Chinese attitudes toward the U.S. both exist, are both justified, and are compatible with each other. In emphasizing one idea in one context, another idea in another, Su was merely applying norms of tactful discussion common in the Chinese intellectual world.[2] Yet I suspect he also knew that fully expressing his outlook would reveal a utopian concept of international relations that U.S. political scientists could not take seriously.

Summing up his book's outlook as a whole, I would say it diverges from prevalent U.S. attitudes toward U.S.-Chinese relations in two ways: his book views as immoral and irrational the basic policies with which the U.S. is projecting its power in the Asia-Pacific region, especially its system of bilateral treaties and its support of the Taipei government, and, with regard to the nature in general of nations, history, and international relations, Su's basic beliefs, although similar to some idealistic American visions,[3] differ from the outlook of the political and academic mainstream in the U.S., which is much closer to Hans Morgenthau's realism. Moreover, as just noted, Su's norms of discourse partly differ from American academic norms.

I think there is no doubt that Su's ideas as a whole are well within the officially approved Chinese mainstream. His colleagues in the Chinese foreign policy community might or might not want to criticize some of his book's factual points or stylistic aspects, such as redundancy. I cannot imagine, however, they would feel uncomfortable with his basic approach. Therefore, analyzing his book's thesis can make clearer just how mainstream official thinking in China diverges from current American views about U.S.-Chinese relations. My point in this chapter, however, is not the pessimistic one Samuel P. Huntington made, that this divergence is likely to lead to ever more serious conflicts.[4] What I claim is that we Americans can deal more adroitly with this divergence by better understanding it.

After describing Su's train of thought, I shall offer my view about how U.S. foreign policy can best deal with the political outlook his thought expresses, taking issue with a currently prevalent American approach recently articulated by the respected columnist Charles Krauthammer,[5] basic to President George W. Bush's foreign policy as a whole, and largely accepted in liberal U.S. circles as well. To a large extent, the problem is how to relate the design of U.S. foreign policy to the profound debate today between scholars like Alex Inkeles, who see the values of all modernizing societies as "converging," and scholars like Huntington, who emphasize the persisting divergences between the values of modernizing societies.[6] How can the U.S. most effectively pursue its interests and ideals abroad if Huntington is right about the persistence of these divergences? To deal with these questions, we need above all to progress to a more precise understanding of these divergences. As a matter of fact, the Chinese need to too.

2. Su Hao's Conceptualization of U.S.-Chinese Relations

Su's book revolves around a dichotomy between searching for national security by dealing with other nations in an adversarial way and searching for it by building cooperatively on interests shared with them. Repeatedly referring to the European Union, which was established in 1992 as a result of efforts going back to the 1950s, Su laments that Asia has lagged behind Europe in seeking "national security on the basis of cooperation" (*ho-tso an-ch'üan*) (163). In his eyes, however, Asia began to move in this direction in 1967 with the establishment of ASEAN and especially in 1992 with the establishment of ARF (ASEAN Regional Forum), which includes not only the ten ASEAN nations but also nearly all the important players in the Asia-Pacific region, such as the European Union, China, Japan, the U.S., the Republic of Korea, Russia, and India. Referring much to Michael Leifer's work on ARF,[7] Su's book focuses on how ARF has dealt with international conflicts of interest in southeast Asia, especially territorial disputes; disputes about jurisdiction over certain reefs in the South China Sea; and the general jockeying for power in east Asia on the part of the leading powers (454–456, 478–479). Arguing that ARF has been successful in attenuating these conflicts of interest (475), Su also seeks to vindicate China's policies regarding ASEAN and ARF and criticizes those of the U.S.

His discussion, therefore, is both historical and normative. He bases his analytical framework without any qualification on what I have called "the two optimisms" central to modern Chinese political thought generally:[8] an optimistic, indeed utopian view of political practicability (he believes the pursuit of national security throughout the world should and can be based purely on cooperation among nations putting primacy on shared interests rather than viewing one another as adversaries); and epistemological optimism, the belief that, when nations disagree about matters of justice and national security, people can "rationally" determine which concept of national security "truly and correctly reflects the objective laws of things and events." True, Su accepts prevalent Western theories about how any nation's concept of national security is shaped by its cultural-historical context and the ways its leaders perceive their "security reality." He is well aware that, because cultural-historical contexts and perceptions of reality vary so much, different nations have different "subjective mirror images," "ways of understanding sensory data," and "conclusions" regarding the problem of national security. For Su, however, these differences are not just disagreements among people who all are unavoidably fallible and influenced by their interests and the biases of their divergent cultural-historical situations. Instead, explicitly relying on Mao Tsetung's epistemology, he holds that a "theory according with objective truth" can be determined by "testing a theory against the facts of practical action in society, seeing whether use of this theory can lead to the result originally desired" (18–24). For Su, then, the most important disagreements about how to ensure the security of one's nation occur because people with correct views are contradicted by people with incorrect ones.

Given these two optimisms, which for Su are not disputable premises but normal, correct ways to think, he sets forth what he regards as the correct way to understand the nature of global historical evolution. The central thesis of his book is that historical change requires a shift in the thought of all national leaders from the old adversarial concept of national security to a concept of "security based on cooperation." That is, new historical conditions have invalidated the old way of seeking national security by following Hans Morgenthau's realism; by viewing the quest for security as a zero-sum game based on "the security dilemma"; by thus seeking security through the strengthening of one's military and strategic position at the expense of adversaries; by using the tactics of collective defense; by aiming for either hegemony or a balance of power; and by often pursuing a policy of imperialism (7–8, 12, 28, 33, 71).

The new historical conditions invalidating this old outlook crystallized during the twentieth century. They consist of ecological problems; economic globalization and interdependence; the danger of warfare using WMD; the globalization of rebellious political forces, including terrorism; and the globalization of crime, along with the effects of urban anomie and problems in controlling epidemics (11–12). Given these new problems, Su holds, it is rationally undeniable that national security has to depend on the preservation of peace, that the importance of internationally shared interests has canceled the "security dilemma," that military power is no longer so vital to the pursuit of national security, and that national security now depends on promoting dialogue and cooperation in dealing with shared problems.

It is also rationally evident, Su holds, that dialogue leading to cooperation has to begin with the principle that all nations must be treated as "equals." This allows "mutual respect," which entails the recognition of norms he regards as self-evident, such as China's right to seek the unification of all the territory that obviously is part of it, including Taiwan. Another such self-evident norm is that by which a "great regional power" has "a decisive influence" in its part of the world, as illustrated by the "decisive influence" that China rightfully has on the handling of important security issues in the Asia-Pacific region (377). Showing respect for each other by respecting such norms, nations start to "trust" each other. This trust is needed to realize cooperation in economic, political, and military affairs and on a wide variety of governmental and non-governmental levels (492–493).

A global order pervasively based on these principles will consist of a number of "security communities" or blocs of nations, each bloc cooperating with all the others. Su, however, recognizes that in this global pattern of cooperation, there will have to be some exercise of top-down guidance. Thus he makes it clear that, within the "Asia-Pacific Security Community" (162), leadership will be exercised by China (377). But what of the leadership needed to coordinate all the different blocs of nations? As already mentioned, in his conversations with me, he said this role would be played by the U.S. In his book, he implies it belongs to the UN. (190, 150).

Having thus from new historical conditions deduced a new concept of national security, Su uses this normative principle to describe the current world situation. His discussion, like so much modern Chinese political thought, revolves around the idea of a powerful, ultimately irresistible global "tide of events" (*ch'ao-liu*) moving history from one stage to the next. Thus he sees a contradiction between the global "tide of events" moving toward this new historical era of "security based on cooperation" and the forces led by the U.S. trying to act against this tide by clinging to the obsolete principle of security based on adversarial relations.

On the one hand, even during the existence of NATO, which was based on a principle of collective security suited only to the dying era, the new era began as some Europeans in the 1950s took the preliminary steps leading to the creation of the European Union in 1992 (40–45). In Su's eyes, however, the end of the Cold War in 1989–1991 was the watershed event. This event made clear that a concept of security based on adversarial relations was bound to lead to "conflict or even war" and, based on a "Cold War mentality.... [was] not suited to the tide of events in the contemporary era moving toward peace and development" (28–29). The establishment of ARF in 1992 signified the spread of this historical tide from the West into the Asia-Pacific region (45, 185).

ARF has been criticized as long on talk and short on action (446). Su, however, holds that ASEAN and ARF have been largely successful in "lubricating" relations among the major powers interacting in the Asia-Pacific region; in containing disagreements regarding territorial boundaries and jurisdiction over the South China Sea reefs; and in developing a distinctive ASEAN style for the handling of tensions — an "Asian mode" of discussion seeking to nurture the convergence of interests rather than directly addressing divisive issues (466–467, 475, 489).

The People's Republic of China, Su holds, deserves much of the credit for ARF's success. In his view, the PRC all along had a foreign policy in accord with that new global "tide" moving toward "security based on cooperation." True, Teng Hsiao-p'ing said that "In thinking about the relations between nations, what is important is taking the strategic interests of one's own nation as one's starting point" (380). This starting point, however, was quite compatible with the moral demands of the new era. As Su put it, quoting a 2002 article in the *Asia Times*: "In adopting any policy regarding national security, China always takes into consideration the security concerns of neighboring nations" (83). Thus, Su writes,

> After the end of the Cold War, China acted as a great nation fully meeting its responsibilities. In an earnest, realistic, and prudent way, it acted positively to cooperate with other governments in the Asia-Pacific region, playing a constructive role especially in ARF, causing cooperation there on security matters — the only such official effort in the Asia-Pacific region — to move ahead in a smooth and healthy way. (377)

Again, it was certainly in China's self-interest to act this way: "The starting point of China's foreign policy strategy is its desire for a peaceful international environment, which is needed to pursue its goal of reform, increasing openness, and modernization," a strategy naturally calling for "friendly cooperation" with the nations of southeast Asia (377–379). Su also states, however, that the new era's norm of security based on mutual respect and cooperation accords not only with "China's traditional culture," given the latter's Confucian emphasis on the Golden Rule, but also with the behavior of the Chinese as a people who "over several thousand years … stayed within the geographical area needed for their own livelihood, not going beyond it to colonize neighboring peoples" (71). Su thus evokes a kind of Chinese exceptionalism: the Chinese throughout their history but especially after 1949 have been a kind of morally gifted group rising above the Hobbesian struggle in which the rest of humanity was entangled. He also evokes a paradigm of global history that has been a prominent part of modern Chinese thought: while the initiation of new global trends in modern times has always occurred in the West, Chinese have the ability to match or even surpass the West in furthering these trends.[9]

On the other hand, the new tide in world affairs moving toward security arrangements based on cooperation has met with a lot of resistance. In effect, Su analyzes this resistance under two headings: the failure of the U.S. to discard its "Cold War mentality" and leave behind the adversarial strategies of an actually dying era; and a variety of partly overlapping tendencies stirring up discord.

That is, in seeing international relations as tendencies toward conflict mixed in with tendencies toward cooperation, Su is similar to many analysts in the West. Quite unlike them, however, he sees this mix as merely characteristic of a dying era about to be succeeded by a new era during which the tendency toward cooperation should and can override that toward conflict. Besides this utopian emphasis of his on the teleological character of history, Su's view of history is decidedly intellectualistic. For him, it is mainly an intellectual failure of Americans to think rationally about history and their own true interests that retards the unfolding of the new era — the American failure to leave behind a "Cold War mentality" (*leng-chan ssu-wei*). In Su's eyes, rational understanding dissolves conflicts of interest — actually, one of the most basic premises shared throughout the whole range of modern Chinese political thought going back to the nineteenth century and inherited from the Confucian tradition.

That is, in the case of the U.S., there has been an irrational "continuation of the Cold War mentality" after "the end of the Cold War" (27). Although there have been ups and downs in U.S.-Chinese relations (154–155), the

> U.S. seeks to establish a unipolar world with itself as "leader," and so it regards as a threat those major nations the rise of which it regards as challenging its hegemony.... The U.S. in the Asia-Pacific region has continuously sought to establish its hegemony and pursue power politics, building up a series of military alliances, taking advantage of its military superiority to threaten others militarily, and using any pretext to interfere in the internal affairs of other nations.... The U.S. has used ARF to try to further its strategic intention to ensure its so-called "leading position" in the world.... To sum up, since the maintenance of military alliances after the end of the Cold War lacks any basis in objective necessity, [such a policy] can only be regarded as due to the U.S.'s persistent pursuit of hegemony, a behavior determined by a "Cold War mentality." (29, 40, 459, 489)

Moreover, the terror some Arabs inflicted on the U.S. on September 11, 2001 showed that "politics based on force and the pursuit of hegemony in the end bring disaster on oneself" (87).

Thus it is mainly the prevalence of this obsolete mentality in the U.S. that is preventing the evolution of the Asia-Pacific security structure from the stage of the "dumbbell model," whereby international trust and cooperation are adulterated by a "military alliance framework," to that of the "olive model," whereby this adulteration has ended (161–162). Su, however, also takes into account other variously overlapping conditions retarding the emergence of this new era of international cooperation, especially complicated political and economic tensions in the Asia-Pacific area and the rest of the world (14, 450–451, 477, 485, 490); crime and immigration patterns associated with globalization and undermining national solidarity in many societies; cultural-religious outlooks blocking a rational appreciation of the need for international cooperation; and the increasing economic inequality between "north and south," which entails the "increasing dependence" of the "developing nations" on Western nations almost able to "control" them (73, 14–16, 20–22).

Su, therefore, is well aware of the many conflicts of interest in the world rational resolution of which is not in the readily foreseeable future. It is precisely this dilemma which has led in the West to an intellectually prominent kind of pessimistic realism precluding any utopian hope that history is moving toward a new stage when national security can be purely based on trustful relations between nations. For Su, however, this dilemma is overridden by the global "tide" moving toward this new historical stage and based on the rationality of people everywhere.

How, then, can Su reconcile his book's picture of the conflict between China and the U.S. — the former moving in rational accord with the global tide of a new era, the latter irrationally trying to resist this tide — with his idea, conveyed to me only in conversation, that the U.S. is the appropriate leader of the global community? His answer is unspoken but obvious: when the U.S. stops resisting this historical tide, stops seeking a hegemonic position in the world, stops regarding China as a nation with interests at odds with those of the U.S., and stops using bilateral treaties to limit the exercise of Chinese power, the U.S. will be ready to play its proper role as the leader of the global community. In Su's mind, I would say, there is a bargain to be struck: if the U.S. will stop doing these things, China will recognize it as the leader of the global community. The U.S. would thus be like the ideal Confucian ruler, who presided over a harmonious world without using any of the practical tools of political power (*wu-wei erh chih*). Such indeed is the principle of international cooperation that Su summed up as "the olive model."

As I said at the outset, therefore, Su's conceptualization of U.S.-Chinese relations differs from mainstream American views not only in regarding U.S. policies in the Asia-Pacific region as immoral and irrational but also in depending on basic categories of analysis at odds with these American views.

3. Foreign Policy and Widespread, Tradition-rooted Categories Used to Interpret Political Events

Elsewhere in this book, I have presented evidence showing that these categories basic to Su's book are peculiar to neither his thought nor Chinese Marxism. Instead, they are rooted in the Confucian intellectual tradition and have been basic to just about the whole spectrum of twentieth-century Chinese political thinking, from modern Confucian humanism, Chinese liberalism, and Sunism to Chinese Marxism. I also argued that the divergence between these

Chinese categories (discourse #1) and categories basic to contemporary Western political thinking (discourse #2) impedes the smooth flow of Chinese-American communication about political differences. Previous chapters, however, were restricted to categories used in the formulation of political philosophies, and I could not directly show how the clash between these two discourses aggravated international tensions. Su's book illustrates how the Chinese categories basic to so much modern Chinese political theory are fully integral to the practical Chinese conceptualization of relations between China and the U.S.

The match between Su's categories and those of the discourse #1 model is clear. First, there is the extravagantly optimistic Chinese vision of the great extent to which trust among nations can replace adversarial relations. To be sure, such utopianism is not unknown in the West. Charles Krauthammer has recently cited Secretary of State Cordell Hull's vision in 1943 of a world in which "'there will no longer be need for spheres of influence, for alliances, for balance of power, or any other of the special arrangements by which, in the unhappy past, the nations strove to safeguard their security or protect their interests.'"[10] Easily brushed aside by Krauthammer, however, Hull's words merely expressed a hope inspiring Americans then enduring the hardships of World War II, not a view widely regarded by them as realistic. Su's utopian view, on the contrary, accords with not only the bulk of modern Chinese political thought but also the traditional intellectual mainstream, according to which it is entirely practicable to base not only international relations but also domestic politics on the same ethics and spirit of mutual trust normal in a family. Indeed, when Su warns that "conflict or even war" will be the result if each nation "competes with other nations in the pursuit of its own interests" (*cheng-li*) (29), he is echoing chapter 1 of *Mencius*. Conflicts of interest are dissolved when political leaders think rationally and activate the moral feeling they are naturally endowed with. Westerners have to understand that in articulating this moralistic idea, even Chinese like Su with the cosmopolitan learning and international experience they need to work as foreign service officers are expressing what they regard as a universal truth about political life. It is because of this prevalent outlook that the Association of Confucianism in Malaysia saw nothing naive about organizing an international conference which in August 2004 will discuss "Using the True Way of Sincerity and Empathetic Understanding of Others to Promote World Peace."[11] After all, there is no substantive difference between this Confucian ideal and Su's "olive model" of international relations.

Second, there is the belief that, in the actual world today, there are individuals or groups who have actually risen above their biases and selfish interests, are in conflict with those who have not, and so are the agents of the struggle for a world without conflict. In Su's account, the current Chinese government is such a morally dedicated group. In other Chinese cases, this same Manichaean paradigm is applied but the identity of the morally dedicated group is different. Thus Chinese liberals critical of the Chinese government and seeking the democratization of their country have often seen the U.S. government as such a morally elevated group. Given this projection of their hopes onto the U.S., they then have been shocked when U.S. policy deviated from their ideals, as when the U.S. invaded Iraq in 2003. As many of them saw it, the U.S. thus almost overnight left the road of morality to turn down that of "an evil imperialism" and so left the world without a strong force pulling it toward an era of harmony and morality. In neither such Chinese liberalism nor Su's partly Maoist thought does one find the idea that the choice in politics as "the art of the possible" is not between virtuous and evil governments but between morally mediocre governments and governments that are fundamentally repressive, brutal, exploitative, and internationally aggressive. The latter choice is the basic challenge from the standpoint of what can be called Aristotelian political realism, but Chinese often deride it by using Mencius's parable about the soldiers who cowardly retreated fifty yards and then laughed at those who had retreated one hundred yards. It is no accident that, in condemning U.S. foreign policy, Chinese writers like Su have habitually used the term "hegemonism" (*pa-ch'üan*), which connotes the absolutistic Mencian dichotomy between virtuous and evil governance.

Professor Chang Hao has described this pervasive Chinese belief in the practicability of totally virtuous government as a lack of *yu-an i-shih* (awareness of the permanent moral darkness of political life).[12] Admittedly, not a few Chinese scholars deny that Chinese lack this awareness of moral darkness. They adduce the fact that Chinese policy-makers and other citizens often display an ability flexibly to look for compromises with persons or governments they regard as morally deficient, whether officials in their own country or foreign governments. Minimal compromise, however, is not enough to build up the kind of mutual understanding with which nations can avoid conflict when serious problems arise. My argument is that the extent to which trust, fruitful compromise, and effective cooperation are possible, whether domestically or internationally, depends on how the parties involved perceive each other. It is easier, I believe, to promote trust and cooperation when all parties see themselves as morally similar, as — to use Reinhold Niebuhr's terms — sinners who to a limited extent can join together in the pursuit of some public good. It is harder to promote trust and cooperation, I argue, when each party sees itself as a moral, rational group looking down on an immoral, irrational one. As chapter XII argues, the latter self-image is integral to the orientations modern China inherited from the Confucian ethical tradition.

Again, this contrast in practice is a matter of degree. After all, if many Chinese like Su see their government as a moral group confronting a "hegemonic" U.S., do not many Americans like Krauthammer similarly see their government as committed to freedom and confronting "the butchers of Tianenmen Square"?[13] Moreover, in both these cases, the self-image is not simplistic. Su is no less aware than Krauthammer that the government he supports is far from perfect. Unlike Krauthammer, however, Su depicts his government as having consistently put the good of humanity above its selfishly nationalistic interests. To that extent, Su's conceptualization of the confrontation between good and evil is distinctly more Manichaean that Krauthammer's.

Third, in contemporary Chinese political thought there is a strongly teleological concept of history. Again, this is a difference of degree but still a crucial one. Despite Karl R. Popper's attack against teleological concepts of history, they actually have remained central to Western thought, whether modernization theory, Francis Fukuyama's idea of "the end of history," or even Popper's own vision of history as a struggle between "the open society and its enemies." In modern Chinese thought, however, moral agents fully dedicated to universal moral ideals are aided by global "tides" of events (*ch'ao-liu*) that appear as based on the rationality of people everywhere and so as ultimately dissolving the human frailties that have infected history so far. Thus for Su, the teleological tide of global history is supporting the Chinese government's struggle to realize an international order based on mutual trust. Because people east and west are all ultimately "rational," they will necessarily infer the need for such an order from the objective truth about the historical conditions that appeared during the twentieth century. In the West, many of us agree on the importance of these new conditions (globalization, etc.), on the need they imply for more international cooperation, and on the fact that such cooperation may be on the rise, as illustrated by the establishment of the EU. Few of us, however, think that in the foreseeable future such cooperation will override the need for nations to take adversarial interests into account, not to mention the idea of a harmonious world order headed by the UN.

Fourth, epistemological optimism is inseparable from this prevalent Chinese belief that modern history includes a "tide" of events pushing all nations forward into an era fundamentally free of selfishly nationalistic motivations. This epistemological optimism is illustrated by Su's belief that "reason" denotes a cognitive process which is the same in all human beings, no matter what their culture; that the "objective" nature of global history is made clear by "reason"; that every rational person east and west will eventually deduce the same normative principles from the objective nature of history; and that therefore a "systematic theory" can be devised on which policy in all societies should be based. Su shares this epistemological outlook with not only Mao's Marxism but also all the other modern Chinese ideological trends.

Again, the difference here with leading epistemological trends in the West is a matter of degree but still is crucial. In the West too it is widely believed that the key norms — "freedom" and "equality" — which all humanity should respect are clear. This moral absolutism, however, has been accompanied by the rise of influential skeptical trends going back to David Hume in the eighteenth century (the GMWER) and suggesting that knowledge about the norms all people should follow is limited at best. In China, this Western skepticism has been explicitly rejected by all leading philosophers, and it is still common there to believe that knowledge about all factual and normative questions is obtained through "science."[14]

In both China and the U.S., then, leaders and other citizens have dealt with the enormously difficult problem of how to combine two ideas: belief in the righteousness of one's own nation, and recognition that one's own nation is part of a global collection of nations which often disagree about what is right and wrong. In the West, people started to wrestle with this problem at least by the time of Hugo Grotius in the seventeenth century, but in China the sense of living in the world's only morally privileged society was not challenged until the nineteenth century. This problem, I would suggest, has not been fully solved anywhere, and the categories used by different intellectual traditions to deal with it have varied greatly.

The divergence between the Chinese and the American view of Chinese-U.S. relations, therefore, is not due only to the fact that each side perceives itself as a vehicle of morality in competition with a vehicle of immorality, and it certainly does not stem mainly from concrete conflicts of interest. It is due especially to the fact that the political reasoning of both sides entails assumptions about the nature of the conditions governing all human life east and west — the nature of knowledge, of political practicability, of human nature, and of history — and the assumptions each side makes about these conditions do not make sense to the other.

To put it in a nutshell, if the Chinese continue to believe that a powerful global tide of events is moving history from a stage of irrationally adversarial relations to an era when national security can be rationally and completely based on mutual respect and trust, they will necessarily perceive themselves as locked into a confrontation with a hostile U.S. This is because (except for some dissidents) they will never conclude that the nation doing its best to follow this historical tide is the U.S., not China. Their conclusion will necessarily be that, in continuing to emphasize its bilateral treaties with Pacific nations and its position of naval primacy in the Pacific, the U.S. is irrationally resisting the current tide of history and threatening China. Yet the Huntingtonian tension between China and the U.S. is also generated by prominent American ways of defining the relation between these two nations.

4. Avoiding International Conflict by Thinking the Unthinkable

Take for example the speech given in early 2004 by Charles Krauthammer at the annual dinner of the American Enterprise

Institute.[15] So far as I can see, many in the U.S. would disagree with much he said, since he defended President Bush's foreign policy, basically embraced Hans Morgenthau's realism, bashed "liberal internationalism" and "multilateralism," and stood up for a proactive American foreign policy putting America's enemies on the defensive. Much less controversial, however, was the heart of his speech, which consisted of two ideas equally downplaying the importance of cultural divergences in world affairs.

First, he recommended that U.S. foreign policy, while accepting "realism's insights about the centrality of power," should focus on "the advance of freedom and the peace freedom brings," seeking to "implant…. democracy" wherever feasible. He thus saw global history as having been and continuing to be "a struggle between freedom and unfreedom, and yes, good and evil." Second, he posited that the world today is "a unipolar world dominated by a single superpower unchecked by any rival and with decisive reach in every corner of the globe."

These two premises, like the four Chinese categories above, define U.S.-Chinese relations as part of a world-shaking conflict between good and evil instead of a diplomatic process pragmatically seeking to resolve certain limited conflicts of interest. Like the four Chinese categories, moreover, these two premises are controversial at best.

If consistency is the hobgoblin of little minds, hyperbole is the hobgoblin turning insights into nonsense. The world today is unipolar only if the distribution of political power in it is equated with the superiority of U.S. military forces and the major influence of the U.S. on economic and other trends. It is not unipolar if the distribution of political power also depends on how populations on the various continents largely depend on cultural and nationalistic orientations in legitimizing their patterns of governance. Similarly, it is only a dogmatically unilinear view of history which can lead anyone to believe that the cultural orientations of all major nations consist of a hierarchy of values headed by that pragmatic search for prosperity and political freedom basic to American political life. Contradicting this premise stemming from the Enlightenment are five lines of scholarship: the anthropological study of culture; sociological work on the cultural prerequisites of democratization; the Burkean insight into the importance of traditions; the emphasis of philosophers like W.V. Quine and Richard Rorty on how linguistic differences lead to different depictions of the world; and the historical study of intellectual traditions such as the Chinese.[16] All these crucial intellectual advances have demonstrated that there is no single hierarchy of values to which all of humanity in fact inclines.

True, the words "freedom" and "democracy" have wide, transcultural appeal throughout the world to the extent that they evoke the vision of a society in which "reason" and "morality" rule, every individual is free to think and do as she wishes, and government does what everybody wishes. This ideal, for instance, coincides with the tradition-rooted Chinese ideal of *ta-t'ung* (great oneness) and is often identified in China with "democracy." For many people in undemocratic, economically backward societies, it is easy to think that this ideal has been basically realized in the West and could be similarly realized in their own country, if only their own leaders were not so insincere, selfish, corrupt, and obtuse.

Many others in such non-Western countries, however, realize that the question of how to get from here to there is not so simple, especially because it entails the problem of how to weigh political freedom against other values. In China, for instance, ever since the nineteenth century, there has been a strong tendency to put "national prosperity and power" (*fu-ch'iang*) above the goal of democracy. Today, some 500,000 to one million Taiwanese have moved from their democratic society to work and live in China under a dictatorship, but I have never heard that any of them thinks of the lack of democracy there as involving any significant drawback for them. To be sure, to my knowledge all the responsible intellectuals in China today believe that China must necessarily aim to become a democracy. Many if not the vast majority of them, however, believe it cannot promptly democratize. This view is central to a consensus toward which all the leading ideological trends in China now are tending — not only Chinese Marxism but also Chinese liberalism, modern Confucian humanism, and the "new conservatism" of intellectuals like Xiao Gong-qin in Shanghai.[17] One well-known Chinese liberal recently told me he thought China could not democratize for another fifty years at least. In the last two years or so, the gap between Xiao's "conservative" support for the current regime and liberal criticism of current policies has narrowed, at least in some important cases. In the Muslim world, religious ideas complicate still further the question of where to put political freedom and democracy on the hierarchy of values, not to mention that the Muslim world has lacked anything like that powerful tendency to idealize Western modernity which has long been and still is so important in China.

There is good reason, then, to question Krauthammer's recommendation that U.S. foreign policy should leave the sober confines of Morgenthau realism by incorporating a crusade for the gradual democratization of the world. If there is no global linear dynamic producing populations around the world thirsting for political freedom American-style, Krauthammer's crusade for democracy has little political power to rely on except for the power stemming directly from U.S. military capabilities. Our current experience in Iraq suggests that military power is not enough to ensure the successful transplantation of democracy. Similarly, if this view of a linear global history dynamic is not easy to defend, what good does it do us to alienate Chinese elites by insisting that their refusal promptly to democratize goes against the tide of global history and by presenting ourselves as a nation with both the power and the wisdom to guide the political development of the whole world? Whether and how the Chinese democratize is a problem for them and the scholars interested in it, not a problem in which U.S. China policy should be entangled.

This means reexamining our tendency to demonize all societies avoiding democratization. There indeed are evil dictatorships, but we have to distinguish between undemocratic regimes which brutally regiment and repress their own populations, like Mao's, and the post-Mao regime, which many scholars today regard as having made amazing progress in trying to overcome the ills inherited from Mao's era, to raise the living standards of 1.3 billion citizens, to reduce human rights abuses, and to bring about the intellectual freedom indispensable for the vigorous development of intellectual life and of critical political discussion. Somewhat like the Kuomintang regime on Taiwan in the 1970s and 1980s, the Beijing regime today is a progressive dictatorship. Viewing its leaders in Krauthammer's way as "the butchers of Tiananmen Square" is as unrealistic as viewing the U.S. as a barbarous nation that dropped nuclear bombs on Japan because it believed the end justifies the means. The character of a regime cannot be equated with one or more acts of violence. As Max Weber said, government is always associated with some degree of violence. Assessing the moral standing of a government requires putting its use of violence and coercion into the context of its overall record and historical situation. This does not mean dealing with it in just a cynically realistic way, unconcerned with the well-being of anyone except our own citizens. U.S. foreign policy, I think, should try wherever possible to aim for the improvement of political life. The mistake is to equate such improvement with some a priori standard of increasing democratization, not to mention applying this standard inconsistently. Lapsing into this mistake, the Western sinological mainstream at least through 1980 found itself more sympathetic to Mao's disastrous totalitarianism than to the Kuomintang's progressive dictatorship on Taiwan. The intellectual confusion leading to this great mistake still infects Western thought today about China.[18]

What is needed is a U.S. foreign policy based on a more complex, empirically tenable interpretation of global history, one combining Inkeles's data on convergence with Huntington's on the persistence of divergent cultural trends. Yet if China and the U.S. are to discuss their concrete conflicts of interest in a soberly pragmatic way, the Chinese too must reexamine the categories they have habitually used to interpret their historical situation. The scope of such pragmatic discussion will remain far too narrow if Chinese continue insisting on their unilinear concept of global history, their Manichaean idea of a global struggle between nations like theirs, eager to enter a new era free of selfishly nationalistic interests, and those like the U.S., irrationally wedded to the pursuit of such immoral interests. This teleological, utopian, Manichaean outlook of the Chinese demonizes the U.S. just as surely as the American concept of a global struggle between "freedom versus unfreedom, good versus evil" demonizes the Beijing regime.

The unthinkable in the intellectual culture of the U.S. today is to consider whether a nondemocratic regime such as the Chinese state today should be respected as a progressive dictatorship trying to make the best of the horrendous mess inherited from Mao. The unthinkable in the intellectual culture of China today is to consider whether an empire based on national interests, such as the current global network of political power led by the U.S., is a normal political phenomenon, not an irrational, immoral manifestation of a dying era.[19] Unless elites in both societies start to think the unthinkable, the outlook for U.S.-Chinese relations will remain cloudy.

The unthinkable, however, consists precisely of ideas out of accord with the reigning discourse, and, as I have argued throughout this book, discourses evolve only slowly and partially, because they are tradition-rooted. Reducing the divergence between discourse #1 and discourse #2 will partly depend on intercultural intellectual exchanges, which have seldom had more than a superficial effect on the deep-rooted habits of mind dominating intellectual life, whether in China or the U.S. It is hard, however, to think of any other way to try to attenuate the Huntingtonian tension that today still endangers relations between the U.S. and China. To use Professor Su's terms, this tension cannot be attenuated by rejecting "the dumbbell model" for the utopian "olive model." Progress within the scope of "the dumbbell model" is the only practicable prospect. The key, as I see it, is to rectify paradigms, not to pursue a model that is part of a utopian paradigm.[20]

Endnotes

1. All page references in my text are to Su's book. Preparing this article, I greatly benefited from the expertise of my associate Ms. Heather Campbell in using the Internet to answer important questions. For this and much other invaluable help, I want to thank her.

2. I have in mind a Chinese tendency to deal with conflicts of opinion and seeming contradictions by seeing them as forming a "dialectical" process, by talking around them rather than directly addressing them, and by seeing them as due to the need to adjust explanations to the mind-set of a particular audience. See pp. 690–691 above.

3. A good example is the idealistic way Secretary of State Cordell Hull in 1943 conceptualized the desirable world order. This is cited in Charles Krauthammer, "Democratic Realism: An American Foreign Policy for a Unipolar World," the 2004 Irving Kristol Lecture at the AEI Annual Dinner in Washington D.C., posted February 12, 2004. See below.

4. Samuel P. Huntington, *The Clash of Civilizations and the Remaking of World Order* (New York: Simon and Schuster, 1996).

5. I refer to the Krauthammer speech adduced in note 3 above.

6. Alex Inkeles, *One World Emerging: Convergence and Divergence in Industrial Societies* (Boulder: WestviewPress, 1998).

7. Michael Leifer, *The ASEAN Regional Forum: ASEAN's Model of Regional Security* (New York: Oxford University Press for the International Institute for Strategic Studies, 1996).

8. See chapter I.
9. See chapter IV.
10. See note 3 above.
11. See the web site www.confucianism.org.my.
12. See chapter XII, note 45.
13. See note 3 above.
14. See the preface written by Hsu Chih-hung for Hu Chün, *Che-hsueh shih she-me?* (What is Philosophy? Beijing: Pei-ching ta-hsueh ch'u-pan-she, 2003). In 2003, Hsu was president of Peking University, Hu, vice chair of its Department of Philosophy. In his preface, Hsu begins by saying that the fullest development of the human personality requires two kinds of "knowledge," that about "natural science" and that about "humanistic science." On the GMWER, see chapter I.
15. See note 3 above.
16. Recently, George F. Will and Henry A. Kissinger have alluded to some or all of this scholarship to cast doubt on the idea of bringing democracy to Iraq in the near future. Kissinger, reacting to the spreading anti-Americanism in Iraq during March and April of 2004, warned that "democracy has cultural prerequisites" and pointed out that "the most successful building of democracy in the last half-century occurred when non-democratic regimes in places like Korea, Taiwan and Turkey fostered an economic growth that produced middle classes ..." See Henry A. Kissinger, "Democratic Values and U.S. Policy in Iraq," in *San Francisco Chronicle*, April 11, 2004, p. E5.
17. See chapter XII.
18. In the 1980s and 1990s, Ramon H. Myers and I were strongly criticized by the Fairbankian sinological mainstream for holding up Taiwan as a model of Chinese modernization and democratization and condemning the Beijing regime for rejecting this model. See Ramon H. Myers and Thomas A. Metzger, "Sinological Shadows: The State of Modern China Studies in the U.S.," *The Washington Quarterly: A Review of Strategic and International Issues* (spring 1980): pp. 87–114. For a sampling of the criticisms directed at this article, see the fall 1983 issue of *Republican China*. Also see Thomas A. Metzger and Ramon H. Myers, "Introduction: Two Diverging Societies," in *Two Societies in Opposition: The Republic of China and the People's Republic of China after Forty Years*, ed. Ramon H. Myers (Stanford: Hoover Institution Press, 1991), pp. xiii–xlv. This piece (p. xliv) criticized the PRC for resisting "three kinds of pluralism." By the late 1990s, it was clear that this resistance had greatly declined, and so I started arguing that the PRC had embarked on a hopeful path of development.
19. For an excellent analysis contrasting "European Colonialism — Pre–World War II" and the "American Alliance Network — Post–World War II," see Daniel I. Okimoto, *The Japanese-American Security Alliance: Prospects for the*

Twenty-First Century (Stanford: Institute for International Studies, Stanford University, 1998), pp. 8–10. Okimoto views both of these patterns as types of "institutional domination."

20. My little article "Enigma in Beijing" (*Hoover Digest*, 2005 no. 2, pp. 56–65) also is pertinent to the question of how discourse #1 affects Chinese political development and how U.S. policy should respond to that development.

Glossary and Index

In general, this section as a glossary includes logographs and page references for each mention in each chapter's text of a Chinese person's name or of a romanized Chinese word or phrase; as an index, it includes page references for all major themes in the chapters' texts, except for the topics identified in the Detailed Table of Contents; and as an index, it also references all mentions in the chapters' texts of historical figures and modern scholars. Whether as glossary or index, however, it unfortunately leaves unnoted most discussion in the endnotes and the Foreword.

Yet there is a variety of exceptions to this overall scheme. For instance, this Glossary and Index omits the logographs for a few very ordinary expressions as well as for terms denoting a famous place, a dynasty, a governmental organ, a religious sect, an academic degree, and a book, periodical, or chapter title; it omits most references to the most famous historical thinkers, such as Confucius, Mencius, Hobbes, Kant, Hegel, and Marx, when these figures are obviously relevant to an issue identified in the Detailed Table of Contents, and when the text lacks any possibly fresh remark about them; it omits the names of many Western scholars listed in the text as those whose writings Henry K.H. Woo made use of; it omits many of my references in the text to Mao Tse-tung and Maoism; and it does not include all my references to J.S. Mill, Max Weber, Karl R. Popper, F.A. Hayek, Isaiah Berlin, Leo Strauss, T'ang Chün-i, and John Dunn, because my discussion so frequently touches on some of these thinkers' most basic ideas. On the other hand, the Glossary and Index does include logographs for a few expressions in the endnotes, and it references some of the relatively important comments in the endnotes. It uses the Wade-Giles romanization system unless another romanization of the name in question has become too well-known to put aside. Crossreferencing entries, it sometimes abbreviates the referenced entry.